Magill's Survey of American Literature

Revised Edition

MAGILL'S SURVEY OF AMERICAN LITERATURE

Revised Edition

Volume 4

Leacock—O'Connor

Edited by

Steven G. Kellman
University of Texas, San Antonio

SALEM PRESS, INC.
Pasadena, California   Hackensack, New Jersey

Editor in Chief: Dawn P. Dawson

Editorial Director: Christina J. Moose   *Production Editor:* Joyce I. Buchea
Project Editor: Tracy Irons-Georges   *Acquisitions Editor:* Mark Rehn
Copy Editors: Sarah M. Hilbert   *Research Supervisor:* Jeffry Jensen
Elizabeth Ferry Slocum   *Research Assistant:* Rebecca Kuzins
Editorial Assistant: Dana Garey   *Graphics and Design:* James Hutson
Photo Editor: Cynthia Breslin Beres   *Layout:* William Zimmerman

Cover photo: Toni Morrison (Stephen Chernin/Reuters/Landov)

Library of Congress Cataloging-in-Publication Data

Magill's survey of American literature / edited by Steven G. Kellman. — [Rev. ed.].
     p. cm.
Includes bibliographical references and index.
ISBN-10: 1-58765-285-4 (set : alk. paper)
ISBN-13: 978-1-58765-285-1 (set : alk. paper)
ISBN-10: 1-58765-289-7 (vol. 4 : alk. paper)
ISBN-13: 978-1-58765-289-9 (vol. 4 : alk. paper)
  1. American literature—Dictionaries.   2. American literature—Bio-bibliography.   3. Authors, American—Biography—Dictionaries.   I. Kellman, Steven G., 1947-   II. Magill, Frank Northen, 1907-1997.   III. Title: Survey of American literature.
  PS21.M34 2006
  810.9′0003—dc22
                                                                                                    2006016503

First Printing

CONTENTS

CONTENTS

Complete List of Contents

Volume 1

Volume 2

Volume 3

Volume 4

Volume 5

Volume 6

MAGILL'S SURVEY OF AMERICAN LITERATURE
Revised Edition

STEPHEN LEACOCK

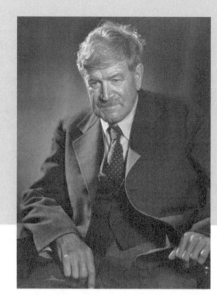

Courtesy, Stephen Leacock Museum/Archive

Born: Swanmore, Hampshire, England
December 30, 1869
Died: Toronto, Ontario, Canada
March 28, 1944

During the period between the two world wars, Stephen Leacock was one of the most widely read humorists in the English-speaking world, his sketches and comic essays revealing a gentle, kindly wit and a playful narrative voice.

BIOGRAPHY

Stephen Butler Leacock was the third child of eleven. His father, Peter, though of a respectable middle-class background, was a rootless man, a failure, moving his large family from one place to another, finally emigrating to Canada in 1876. The one-hundred-acre farm near Lake Simcoe in Ontario where the family settled and where Leacock passed his boyhood was, by his own account, an unpleasant place where he and his brothers worked long and hard, always in the face of financial difficulty. Late in 1878, Leacock's father left the family behind and went west, seeking a fortune that never came. By the time Stephen was in his late teens, his father had disappeared and was never heard from again.

Meanwhile, Leacock's mother was determined to give her children a good education. She sacrificed enough to send her sons to Upper Canada College in Toronto (the equivalent of high school), and Stephen enrolled in the institution in 1882, when he was thirteen. Here he evinced an interest in and aptitude for writing and became coeditor of the school paper.

Awarded a partial scholarship, Leacock entered the University of Toronto in 1887 and studied modern languages and literature, but financial stress at home caused him to withdraw the following year. Needing to earn money to help support his eight

brothers and sisters, Stephen took a three-month course at a teacher training institute in Ontario and in 1889 accepted a position as a language teacher back at Upper Canada College. While teaching, he continued his studies part time at the University of Toronto, receiving his bachelor's degree, with honors, in 1891.

By this time, Leacock was becoming aware of the possibility of supplementing his income by writing. He began to submit short articles to various magazines, and his first humorous sketch was published in a Toronto humor magazine in 1894. Though his major work was still fifteen years in the future, these early minor successes throughout the 1890's gave him confidence in his ability to write fluidly and easily. Meanwhile, he was spending his summers by Lake Simcoe in the village of Orillia, the "little town" that was to serve as the model for the fictional Mariposa of his masterpiece, *Sunshine Sketches of a Little Town* (1912).

During this period, he also developed an interest in economics and political science. Influenced by his reading of Thorstein Veblin's *The Theory of the Leisure Class* (1899), he enrolled in a graduate program at the University of Chicago in 1899. He married Beatrix Hamilton, an aspiring actress, in 1900 and in the same year was appointed adjunct lecturer of economics and political science at McGill University. His association with McGill was to be a crucial event in his life. After taking his Ph.D. in 1903, he was appointed to the full-time faculty and by 1908 was promoted to full professor and chair of the department of economics and political science. He was to remain at McGill for the next three decades, secure enough to begin a long career both as a professor and, in literature, as a prolific writer of humorous sketches and essays, filling more than sixty books.

By 1905, while he was honing his craft with his early humorous work, Leacock was also developing another aspect of his art that would make him equally famous. A political conservative, he began to give public lectures, mainly on the topic of the state of the British Empire. His easy manner, his knowledge of political and economic issues, and his ability to use clear, concise language prompted an offer by the Canadian government for Leacock to go on a one-year lecture tour to speak on behalf of British imperialism. The subject was treated seriously, but the experience of this first early lecture tour proved to him his ability to hold an audience and eventually to profit by it.

Throughout the first decade of the twentieth century, Leacock had been submitting comic pieces to various magazines, including the then-popular New York periodicals *Truth* and *Life*. In 1910, he gathered some of these works and privately published them under the title *Literary Lapses*. The book caught on, finally coming to the attention of a British publisher who quickly bought the rights. Containing clever sketches like "My Financial Career" and "The Awful Fate of Melpomenus Jones," about a visitor who stayed forever as a houseguest because he did not know how to take his proper leave, *Literary Lapses* was Leacock's first published humorous book and signaled the beginning of his career as one of the most popular humorists in the English-speaking world.

Over the next thirty years, Leacock published dozens of books, though critical opinion suggests that his early ones were his best. His third book, *Sunshine Sketches of a Little Town*, is regarded as the first of his two masterpieces. It was followed in 1914 by *Arcadian Adventures with the Idle Rich*, critically viewed as a kind of sequel. Together, the two works form the apex of his literary achievement.

As World War I raged in Europe, Leacock determined to do his part by delivering humorous lectures on behalf of Belgian refugees. Throughout Canada and the United States, Leacock culled from his writings his funniest and most popular material and gave public readings. Throughout the war he continued to produce sketch after sketch,

collecting them in such volumes as *Moonbeams from the Larger Lunacy* (1915), *Further Foolishness: Sketches and Satires on the Follies of the Day* (1916), and *The Hohenzollerns in America: With the Bolsheviks in Berlin, and Other Impossibilities* (1919). After the war, Leacock continued to produce almost a book a year throughout the 1920's.

His wife died of cancer in 1925, and for many years thereafter, he involved himself in speaking and fund-raising for cancer research. He was also engaged in an almost ceaseless round of lecture tours. Between 1915 and 1937, in fact, Leacock delivered his humorous talks all across the United States and Canada and throughout England and Scotland, all this while he was teaching three days a week at McGill and serving as chair of the department of economics and political science.

His busy schedule prompted him in 1927 to hire his niece as secretary and housekeeper. She eventually became his literary executor and left behind a charming sketch of her uncle, noting that in the United States, he would often make four or five trips a month to deliver lectures, sometimes three or four given on each trip.

By the 1930's, the quality of Leacock's writing began to decline, and he often turned to more serious work. His biographies of Mark Twain (1932) and Charles Dickens (1933) were workmanlike and academically sound but added little to his reputation. By 1943, Leacock began his autobiography, but it was to be left unfinished. He died of throat cancer on March 28, 1944. His autobiography, *The Boy I Left Behind Me*, was published posthumously in 1946.

ANALYSIS

Leacock's literary achievement is largely in the mastery of the comic sketch. With the exception of *Sunshine Sketches of a Little Town*, all his full-length humorous books are really compilations of short pieces that are unrelated to each other. His art is basically that of the miniaturist, the literary material honed to a fine detail. His subject matter is wide-ranging, but always there is the appeal to the middle-class sensibility. The humor is often based on some form of frustration or mild victimization: the befuddlement of the little man in confronting the large, faceless corporate structure, as in "My Financial Career" (from *Literary Lapses*) or "How to Borrow Money" (from *Short Circuits*, 1928); the arch satire of the rich man's sadness over the resignation of his butler, as in "Are the Rich Happy?" (from *Further Foolishness*); and even self-parody, as in "We Have with Us To-night" (from *My Discovery of England*, 1922), in which the narrator relates his annoyance at being misnamed or mistaken as the speaker on a lecture tour.

The typical sketch often begins with a calm, commonsense observation, as in the manner of a personal essay, but within the course of a few sentences, the piece starts to take off, unfurling into amiable nonsense.

Amiability is a key characteristic of the Leacock manner. The narrator is a genuinely kindhearted character in the piece. Never cruel or savage, the narrative voice is one of gentle bemusement, of benign recognition of life's follies, with a compassion for those who fall victim to them. As a satirist, Leacock lacks the bite of anger. His humor does not seek to point out the ills of society, least of all to redress them.

If classic satire is curative in intention, Leacock's is palliative. His narrative voice wants simply to exhibit and laugh at the silly side of human experience.

Part of Leacock's narrative technique is the use of malapropisms and other forms of wordplay. In one of his classic literary parodies, for instance, titled "The Russian Drama" (from *Over the Footlights*, 1923), the narrator describes the setting of a post station in Siberia, a cold, bleak landscape where peasants drive "one-horse tarantulas" over the vast, "endless samovars." Such parodies as this and others such "Cast Up by the Sea," a spoof of a nineteenth century melodrama, were quite popular in their time but seem rather dated to modern readers. However, the cleverly selective use of malapropisms heightens the effect of irony already implicit in the tone.

Wordplay of a different kind is evident in *Sunshine Sketches of a Little Town*. The role of the narrator is a central element in the narrative structure. The voice is at times gently sarcastic, at times naïve, so that the effect is a balanced subtlety between personal involvement and controlled objectivity—between sympathy, even admiration, for the citizenry of the little town and a gentle archness at their doings.

Another distinguishing feature of *Sunshine Sketches of a Little Town* is its unity. Unlike his other humorous books, *Sunshine Sketches of a Little Town* is not a discontinuous collection of sketches on various subjects but a cycle of interrelated short stories. The stories are clustered around a common theme or central character, and the unifying principle is enhanced both by the narrative voice and by the fictional location of Mariposa, the small Canadian town in which the characters live.

Interestingly, Leacock's technique of establishing a single setting in which characters enact their stories anticipates by several years similar devices. American poet Edgar Lee Masters, for example, produced his *Spoon River Anthology* three years later, in 1915. In this collection of poems, all the speakers are fellow townspeople, now dead, telling their verse dramas from their graves in the town cemetery. Sherwood Anderson published his influential *Winesburg, Ohio* in 1919, a collection of stories concerning tortured, frustrated men and women living in Winesburg who tell their stories to the putative narrator, the young newspaperman. *Sunshine Sketches of a Little Town* differs from its successors not only in subject matter and spirit— the stories are much more genial, as the title suggests—but also in narrative complexity, the narrator by his ambivalent position as both observer and participant playing a more active role in the book.

"My Financial Career"

First published: 1910 (collected in *Literary Lapses*, 1910)
Type of work: Comic sketch

An ordinary fellow trembles at the thought of going into a bank but gets up the nerve to open—and then close—an account.

"My Financial Career" is one of Leacock's earliest pieces, appearing in his first published humorous book, *Literary Lapses*. One of his most anthologized works, this short sketch of less than two thousand words already treats one of Leacock's favorite themes: the effect of economics on the lives of men. When one remembers that Leacock took his doctorate in economics, it is not surprising that this piece illustrates the Everyman's fear and mistrust of the bank as institution. Typical of his best work, the sketch opens quickly with the narrator's frank admission that banks and everything about them "rattle" him.

He confesses to falling into a state of near idiocy at any attempt to transact business but is determined, now that he has more than fifty dollars in his pocket, to open an account. Timidly, he asks to speak to the manager. The manager takes him into a private room, locks the door, and proceeds to assure the narrator of utmost security. Because of the narrator's air of confidentiality and distrust, the manager assumes he is a private detective or that he has a large sum to invest. Learning that the narrator has only fifty-six dollars, he "unkindly" turns him over to a clerk.

The narrator is now flustered, mistakenly walks into the safe, and is eventually led to the clerk's window, into which he thrusts the money. When assured that it had been deposited, the narrator quickly asks for a withdrawal slip. Meanwhile he feels that people in the bank are staring at him, thinking him a millionaire. Intimidated and miserable, he quickly withdraws his fifty-six dollars and rushes out. The sketch concludes with the narrator's observation that he keeps his money in his pants pocket and his life savings in a sock.

The humor of the piece is achieved not only by the exaggerated situation but also by a skillful use of short clips of dialogue. The narrator's psychological intimidation is clearly presented by an economy of detail in which the scene richly suggests more than it relates.

SUNSHINE SKETCHES OF A LITTLE TOWN

First published: 1912
Type of work: Short-story cycle

A fellow townsman of Mariposa relates the "adventures" of half a dozen characters, from the town's richest man, Mr. Smith, to Mariposa's shy little "hero," Mr. Pupkin.

In his masterpiece *Sunshine Sketches of a Little Town*, Leacock's lifelong interests in economics and political science merge, resulting in a thematic unity not found in most of his other books. After a genial

preface in which Leacock provides some autobiographical information—and in so doing prepares the reader for the narrative tone of naïveté mixed with sarcasm—the narrator, a fellow townsperson, establishes himself as the observer from whose point of view the reader is able to make a judgment about the characters.

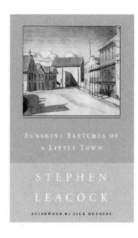

The first of these is Mr. Josh Smith. Weighing in at three hundred pounds, Smith owns the town's only hotel. Shrewd and slyly gregarious, Smith is reputed to be the richest man in Mariposa. He knows how to turn a profit and has even been fined by the License Commission for selling liquor after hours. In a financial venture intended to appease the commission while increasing business, he hires a French chef and opens a café in the hotel. The narrator'stone suggests admiration at Smith's business acumen.

Just down the street from the hotel is Jefferson Thorpe's barber shop. Thorpe is talkative and enjoys the notoriety of being a shrewd investor. The narrator admires the fact that though "Jeff" has "Cuban lands" and even gold mines, he continues shaving his customers without raising his prices. By the end of the story, Jeff has obviously lost his money on scams, but the narrator still admires the town barber's professional dedication.

In "The Marine Excursion of the Knights of Pythias," the steamboat *Mariposa Belle* sinks in Lake Wissanotti—the depth was only a few feet—and Josh Smith "rescues" the passengers—and makes a huge profit—by providing rowboats by which they get safely ashore.

The town minister, Reverend Drone, is a dull preacher, delivering sermons spiced with Greek allusions and irrelevant details. His constant worry is that he cannot make the mortgage payments on the church. The town decides to raise money by a "Whirlwind Campaign," a series of lunches at which money is pledged but never donated—a kind of pyramid scheme of promises. In the end, the church burns down, and Drone discovers that the church was insured for twice its value. The narrator is amazed at the coincidence.

Mr. Pupkin, the town banker, is in love with romance-reading Zena Pepperleigh, the judge's daughter. Shy and mousy, as his name implies, Mr. Pupkin is embarrassed by his family. His father is a millionaire who has sent his son to remote Mariposa to get the taste of luxury out of his mouth. Zena expects Mr. Pupkin to be a storybook hero, free of the trappings of wealth. The young man's problem is solved when he unexpectedly becomes a hero. He is knocked unconscious by a bank robber, and though the mystery of the Mariposa bank robbery is never solved, Mr. Pupkin's "bravery" is rewarded with Zena's hand in marriage.

The final segment ends with Mr. Smith running for mayor. He wins largely because he campaigned against a candidate who represented honesty and clean government.

The book closes with a nostalgic paeon to the little town, still as vivid to the narrator as it was thirty years earlier.

SUMMARY

Stephen Leacock's achievement lies in his ability to tell a humorous tale in a unique narrative voice. The tone of his work is one of balance, understanding, and compassion. Even his most absurd literary parodies reveal a gentle tolerance of the subject matter, a kind of live-and-let-live attitude. His best work manages to sustain a subtle tension between sarcasm and naïveté.

Edward Fiorelli

BIBLIOGRAPHY

By the Author

SHORT FICTION:
Literary Lapses, 1910
Nonsense Novels, 1911
Sunshine Sketches of a Little Town, 1912
Behind the Beyond, and Other Contributions to Human Knowledge, 1913
Arcadian Adventures with the Idle Rich, 1914
Moonbeams from the Larger Lunacy, 1915
Further Foolishness: Sketches and Satires on the Follies of the Day, 1916
Frenzied Fiction, 1918
The Hohenzollerns in America: With the Bolsheviks in Berlin, and Other Impossibilities, 1919
Winsome Winnie, and Other New Nonsense Novels, 1920
My Discovery of England, 1922
College Days, 1923
Over the Footlights, 1923
The Garden of Folly, 1924
Winnowed Wisdom, 1926
Short Circuits, 1928
The Iron Man and the Tin Woman, with Other Such Futurities, 1929
Laugh with Leacock, 1930
Wet Wit and Dry Humour: Distilled from the Pages of Stephen Leacock, 1931
The Dry Pickwick, and Other Incongruities, 1932
Afternoons in Utopia: Tales of the New Time, 1932
Funny Pieces: A Book of Random Sketches, 1936
Hellements of Hickonomics in Hiccoughs of Verse Done in Our Social Planning Mill, 1936
Here Are My Lectures and Stories, 1937

DISCUSSION TOPICS

- How do the themes of economics and political science unify Stephen Leacock's *Sunshine Sketches of a Little Town*?

- What is the role of the narrator in *Sunshine Sketches of a Little Town*?

- What are some examples of wordplay in Leacock's work?

- What is meant by a short-story cycle?

- What comic devices does Leacock use in his story "My Financial Career"?

Stephen Leacock

Model Memoirs, and Other Sketches from Simple to Serious, 1938
Laugh Parade, 1940
My Remarkable Uncle, and Other Sketches, 1942
Happy Stories Just to Laugh At, 1943
Last Leaves, 1945

DRAMA:
"Q": A Farce in One Act, pr., pb. 1915 (with Basil Macdonald)

NONFICTION:
Elements of Political Science, 1906
Baldwin, Lafontaine, Hincks: Responsible Government, 1907, enlarged 1926 (as *Mackenzie, Baldwin, Lafontaine, Hincks*)
Adventures of the Far North: A Chronicle of the Frozen Seas, 1914
The Dawn of Canadian History: A Chronicle of Aboriginal Canada and the Coming of the White Man, 1914
The Mariner of St. Malo: A Chronicle of the Voyages of Jacques Cartier, 1914
Essays and Literary Studies, 1916
The Unsolved Riddle of Social Justice, 1920
Economic Prosperity in the British Empire, 1930
Back to Prosperity: The Great Opportunity of the Empire Conference, 1932
Mark Twain, 1932
Charles Dickens: His Life and Work, 1933
Lincoln Frees the Slaves, 1934
The Pursuit of Knowledge: A Discussion of Freedom and Compulsion in Education, 1934
Humor: Its Theory and Technique, 1935
The Gathering Financial Crisis in Canada: A Survey of the Present Critical Situation, 1936
Humour and Humanity: An Introduction to the Study of Humour, 1937
My Discovery of the West: A Discussion of East and West in Canada, 1937
Too Much College: Or, Education Eating Up Life, 1939
Our British Empire: Its Structure, Its History, Its Strength, 1940
Canada: The Foundations of Its Future, 1941
Our Heritage of Liberty: Its Origin, Its Achievement, Its Crisis, a Book for War Time, 1942
Montreal: Seaport and City, 1942
How to Write, 1943
Canada and the Sea, 1944
While There Is Time: The Case Against Social Catastrophe, 1945
The Boy I Left Behind Me, 1946 (memoir)

About the Author

Davies, Robertson. *Stephen Leacock.* Toronto: McClelland and Stewart, 1970.
Doyle, James. *Stephen Leacock: The Sage of Orillia.* Toronto: ECW Press, 1992.
Lynch, Gerald. *Stephen Leacock: Humor and Humanity.* Montreal-Kingston: McGill-Queen's University Press, 1988.
_____, ed. *A Critical Edition: "Sunshine Sketches of a Little Town" by Stephen Leacock.* Ottawa: Tecumseh Press, 1996.
Staines, David, ed. *Stephen Leacock: A Reappraisal.* Ottawa: University of Ottawa Press, 1986.

DAVID LEAVITT

© Marion Ettlinger

Born: Pittsburgh, Pennsylvania
June 23, 1961

A short-story writer and novelist, Leavitt explores the intricacies of human interaction, concentrating on gay relationships and the complexities of family ties.

BIOGRAPHY

David Leavitt was born in Pittsburgh, Pennsylvania, on June 23, 1961, the son of Harold Jack Leavitt and Gloria Rosenthal Leavitt. He grew up in Palo Alto, California, where his father was a professor at the graduate school of business at Stanford University. Being the youngest of three children—his brother, John, and sister, Emily, were nine and ten years older than he—resulted in a self-described precocity, which undoubtedly contributed to his remarkably early literary success. In a 1990 interview he remarked, "I grew up being the child in the room whose presence everyone forgot about. By the time I was twenty, therefore, I had absorbed an enormous amount, but I had experienced almost nothing."

One of the pivotal events of his childhood was his mother's long, futile battle with cancer. He explains, "The enormity of that experience cannot be minimalized. It has all gone into my work. Most of what I know about living and dying I learned from my mother." The knowledge gained from his mother's illness and death is reflected particularly in the moving portrayal of Louise Cooper's twenty-year struggle against cancer in *Equal Affections* (1989) and also in the stories "Counting Months" and "Radiation," which appear in *Family Dancing* (1984).

Leavitt left the West Coast to attend Yale University, graduating in 1983. An editor for *The New Yorker* read one of his stories in a student magazine and asked to see more of his work. He obliged by sending her everything he had written to that point, all of which she rejected. She finally accepted the story "Territory," which was published in *The New Yorker* in 1982. This was reputedly the first story with substantial gay subject matter ever published in that magazine, and its appearance caused a stir.

Leavitt's first book of short stories, *Family Dancing*, was published when he was only twenty-three years old, and much was made of Leavitt's youthful success. The collection was praised by reviewers and was nominated for the PEN/Faulkner Award for Fiction and the Book Critics Circle Award. His first novel, *The Lost Language of Cranes* (1986), and *Equal Affections*, which followed, received mixed reviews. His work has met with more success in Europe than in the United States; his first three books were best sellers in Italy and Spain.

In 1989, Leavitt received a Guggenheim Fellowship, and he was appointed foreign writer-in-residence in Barcelona, Spain, at the Institute of Catalan Letters. His European experiences figure in his fourth publication, a collection of short stories entitled *A Place I've Never Been* (1990). The stories "I See London, I See France" and "Roads to Rome," in particular, are reminiscent of the work of Anglo-American novelist Henry James, who often wrote about what happens when "innocent" Americans confront the complexities of European society. In 1993, he published *While England Sleeps*, a novel focusing on the relationship between two gay men in Europe in the 1930's on the eve of World War II. Leavitt's belated acknowledgment that he had borrowed parts of the plot from events chronicled in the 1948 autobiography of Sir Stephen Spender prompted the threat of a lawsuit by the British poet. Leavitt made adjustments to the text, and the book appeared in a revised edition two years later.

The personal trauma that Leavitt experienced as a result of this public controversy resulted in a period of writer's block that the author used as the basis of *The Term Paper Artist,* one of three novellas collected in the 1997 volume entitled *Arkansas.* This collection also includes a piece set in Italy, where Leavitt and his partner Mark Mitchell, also a writer, bought a farmhouse that same year. The couple subsequently cowrote two books about their encounter with Italian culture, including *In Maremma* (2001), which recounts their often comic experience of restoring their Tuscan property, abandoned for more than twenty years. Leavitt also wrote in 2002 a guide to Florence, Italy, as part of the highly touted Writer and the City series published by Bloomsbury.

Since 2000, Leavitt has been a faculty member in the creative writing program at the University of Florida in Gainesville. In part because he divides his time between the United States and Europe, much of his work since the beginning of the twenty-first century continues to explore the international theme. Three stories in *The Marble Quilt* (2001), for example, have European settings.

In addition, as evidenced by the novel *Martin Bauman* (2000), which mirrors many aspects of Leavitt's own early career, and the nonfiction work *The Man Who Knew Too Much* (2005), which recounts the life of Alan Turing, a British mathematician who conceived the notion of the computer, Leavitt has focused increasing attention on how creative thinkers, whether gay or straight, must struggle to balance the demands of their talent and their personal desires.

ANALYSIS

Although he is regarded as one of the leading lights of gay literature, Leavitt explores universal themes, and it would do him a great disservice to portray his writing as being of interest only to a limited audience. Indeed, he confronts head-on the problems faced by homosexuals in a heterosexual world, but he also explores feelings of alienation common to all people as the result of such conditions as mental and physical illness, shame, despair,

physical unattractiveness, geographical dislocation, and career choice.

Leavitt often tackles this theme of separateness within the milieu of family life. Many of his works describe the precarious equipoise of collective harmony tentatively achieved in even the closest families while they also adroitly reveal the turmoil underlying the placid surface of everyday life. Both *The Lost Language of Cranes* and *Equal Affections,* for example, present characters shaped by apparently strong family relationships, yet those characters are ultimately defined more by what sets them apart from one another than by what binds them together.

This insight into family relations informs many of Leavitt's short stories as well, particularly in his first collection, *Family Dancing.* In "The Lost Cottage," for example, a family's attempts to re-create their annual summer vacation six months after the parents have separated fail abysmally. The family gamely behaves as if a good time were being had by all, but the charade ends when Lydia, the mother, discovers that her estranged husband has settled his new girlfriend into a nearby motel. Lydia agonizingly declares to her family, "I will always love your father. And he doesn't love me. And never will." The children, including the gay son, Mark, whose simultaneous role as family insider and observant outsider is highlighted in the narrative, come to realize the depths of their mother's despair and the fact that they are helpless to assuage her pain.

The title story, "Family Dancing," also features a broken family in which the ties, for better or worse, remain strong. Suzanne Kaplan, who has a new marriage, a new figure, and a new life since her first husband, Herb, left her for another woman, throws a large family party to celebrate her "new self" and her son's prep-school graduation. As the party guests admiringly watch a celebratory "family dance" performed by Suzanne and Herb and their son and daughter, the reader, who has been allowed a glimpse beneath the surface, knows that all is not well. Suzanne is still painfully in love with Herb, who no longer loves her; Herb's show of devotion for his ungainly daughter hides his repulsion for her unattractiveness; and their son, Seth, has yet to inform them of his homosexuality.

Leavitt often explores the effect of illness, such as cancer or acquired immunodeficiency syndrome (AIDS), on an individual's relation to family. In "Radiation," a mother named Gretl takes two of her three children to a radiation therapy center while she has her treatments. The staff and patients chat cheerfully about new lawn furniture, children play games and read children's magazines, and patients joke about the hospital gowns they must wear, belying the life-and-death purpose of the center. The mother's life begins to be defined by her illness, as she realizes that the pain, suffering, and humiliation she now accepts as normal would have been unthinkable only a few months earlier. She cries alone in her room, unreachable in her grief, unable to accept sympathy or comfort even from her family.

Sometimes, when he or she is endowed with intelligence and imagination, an outsider can derive some compensation out of alienation from others. Such separateness offers, for example, opportunities for self-reflection and self-definition. In the story "My Marriage to Vengeance" from the collection *A Place I've Never Been*, the narrator, a lesbian named Ellen, reluctantly attends the wedding of her former lover Diana, who is marrying a man so that she can have a so-called normal life and "not have to die inside trying to explain who it is [she's] with." Though the experience of seeing her former lover get married causes her considerable pain, Ellen takes some comfort in the thought that Diana will be "contemplating a whole life of mistakes spinning out from one act of compromise" while she herself, even in her present state of abandonment, has an authentic life, "harder but better."

For the literary artist, like Leavitt himself, looking at the world from the outside cultivates the essential skills of observation. In his novel *Martin Bauman*, the title character, much of whose story parallels Leavitt's own early career, is cut off from others by virtue of his sexual orientation and his interior life; his separateness is a key ingredient in his desire to write, to put into words what he sees but that others, by virtue of their active but unconscious participation in the moment, cannot. Although it can be argued that he himself shares the same raw ambition characteristic of his compatriots, the novel's narrator nonetheless hits the mark time and again in his efforts to capture the tireless machinations and shameless self-promotion of those caught up in the inbred publishing world of New York in the 1980's.

In essence, Leavitt has developed a well-deserved reputation as a prose stylist who often mines autobiographical material to validate the contention that there is something universal in the particular and that each individual situation speaks to the general human condition.

"TERRITORY"

First published: 1982 (collected in *Family Dancing*, 1984)
Type of work: Short story

A son introduces his gay lover to his mother for the first time.

"Territory," the opening story in *Family Dancing*, revolves around the first meeting between the two most important people in Neil Campbell's life: his mother, Barbara, and his lover, Wayne. Although the action revolves around Barbara and Wayne's meeting, the most richly detailed and emotionally powerful relationship in the story, as in much of Leavitt's work, is between mother and son. Barbara has been a devoted mother, PTA member, volunteer at school, and active member of the Coalition of Parents of Lesbians and Gays. Neil's father is "a distant sort," often away on business and emotionally absent even when home, so it is Barbara to whom Neil feels emotionally bound.

Neil is flooded with memories as his lover's arrival forces him to reconcile the boy his mother knew with the man whom Wayne loves. As he nervously awaits the visit, he remembers the day he "came out" to his mother and "felt himself shrunk to an embarrassed adolescent, hating her sympathy, not wanting her to touch him." He also recalls the Gay Pride parade his mother attended to show her support, succeeding only in embarrassing Neil and inflicting pain upon herself.

The story revolves around simple events: Wayne's introduction to Barbara, their first dinner together, and a trip to a theater. The meaning, however, lies not in the events themselves but rather, as is the case in the fiction of Henry James, in the small gestures. When Wayne takes Neil's hand at dinner, Barbara's almost imperceptible reaction speaks volumes about her discomfort in their presence. Later, when Neil tries to put an arm around both Wayne and his mother at the theater, she responds by stiffening and shrinking away, unwilling to give her son unqualified emotional approval of his sexual orientation.

As Barbara attempts to cope with the reality of Neil's adult life, Neil also must recognize that his mother is not the same woman he remembers. She has "grown thinner, more rigid, harder to hug," and even her dogs are not the dogs of his childhood. He no longer feels a part of her life, a condition he both desires and fears. Barbara, for her part, cannot reconcile the young man Neil has become with the child she remembers. She tells him, "I remember when you were a little boy . . . I remember, and I have to stop remembering." Neil, who "wept in regret for what he would not be for his mother, for having failed her," knows that, as he tells Wayne, "guilt goes with the territory." As Leavitt so movingly illustrates in this story, the forces that exist between parent and child are, like the power of fate, beyond the reaches of good intentions.

EQUAL AFFECTIONS

First published: 1989
Type of work: Novel

A family faces its children's homosexuality, its father's infidelity, and its mother's cancer and eventual death.

Equal Affections chronicles the history of the Cooper family: Nat and Louise, their children, Danny and April, and Danny's lover, Walter. Although the plot sounds melodramatic—Louise is fighting a twenty-year battle with cancer, Nat is having an affair with an old family friend, and both Danny and April are gay—Leavitt handles his characters and situations with such restraint and understatement that the novel never deteriorates into soap opera. Rather, it presents a subtle study of family dynamics.

The family's history unfolds through a series of flashbacks, arriving at the present as the family is brought together by Louise's final bout with illness. As they watch her die, each character struggles to define a place in the family circle as well as an identity outside it. The temptation to isolate themselves from "messy" human relationships battles with the insistent pull of family ties in each of them.

Danny, the quintessential "good son," has buried himself in a comfortable but stale upper-middle-class existence, surrounded by electronic gadgets. His lover, Walter, has become more involved with his computer sex partners than with Danny, tempted by the possibility of living "without ever having to touch, without ever having to show your face!" April, completely self-absorbed, immerses herself in her career as a lesbian folk singer, fitting her family into her life only when her busy schedule allows.

The characters also struggle between the opposite pulls of domesticity and "wildness." Walter sees parallels between his life and Louise's, noting that they have both sublimated their wild sides to domesticity and conformity. "He saw her as a woman of guileless passion who, for one reason or another, had suppressed that passion and instead fixed her gaze on the dependable horizon of the domestic sphere." Walter also has determined to "incorporate his sexual nature into a life of suburban domesticity, uproot the seed of homosexuality from its natural urban soil and replant it in the pure earth of his green garden."

Nat and April, on the other hand, rather than seeking to tame their "wildness" with domesticity, have summoned it to help them break out of the domestic rut. April, although she possesses strong domestic instincts, demonstrated by her love of baking and her desire to have a baby, escapes domestic routine through her career. Nat, a quiet and unassuming man by nature, seeks to subvert domesticity by conducting an illicit affair.

As she faces her death, Louise also comes to terms with her growing sense of "aloneness," as her illness slowly separates her from her family. She realizes that her separateness is the source of her strength as well as her pain because it allows her to control her own destiny. Conversely, Louise's death brings Walter to the realization that "like it or not, he was inextricably bound with the people who had mattered to him and who mattered to him now, the people whose loves defined him, whose deaths would devastate him. He would never, could never be. . . self-invented, untouchable, a journeyer among the keys. And for this he was glad."

THE LOST LANGUAGE OF CRANES

First published: 1986
Type of work: Novel

The lives of a quiet married couple and their son unravel as the son's revelation of his homosexuality forces his father to face and confess that he too is gay.

Leavitt's first novel, *The Lost Language of Cranes,* is the story of two men of different generations coming to terms with their sexual orientation. Like much of Leavitt's work, it is also the story of a family coming apart at the seams.

Rose Benjamin, a copy editor, and her husband, Owen, director of admissions at a private boys' school, lead a tightly structured life, devoting their days to work and their evenings to reading in their twin rocking chairs. Every Sunday, they go their separate ways; Rose reads the paper and works in the apartment, while Owen spends the day at a gay pornographic cinema. Rose has no idea how Owen spends these Sundays and would never dream of asking. When she accidentally meets Owen on the

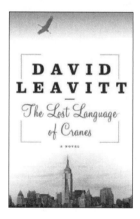

street one Sunday while taking a walk, Rose realizes that after twenty-seven years of marriage, she hardly knows him: "She had stumbled into her husband on a strange street corner, running some mysterious errand she knew nothing of, and they had spoken briefly like strangers, parted like strangers."

The first cracks appear on the surface of the Benjamin family life when Rose and Owen learn that their New York City apartment will be converted into a co-op, and they must either buy it or move out. Once their sanctuary from the outside world is threatened, the rest of

their carefully structured life begins to crumble as well. Their son, Philip, infatuated with a new lover, wants to share his happiness and reveal his homosexuality to his parents, giving little thought to the effect this announcement might have on them. Philip's "coming out" inspires his father to confess to his own long-hidden sexual orientation, and Rose is forced to confront the fact that her married life has been based on a lie.

The Lost Language of Cranes also highlights the differences between two generations of gay men. Philip, although initially hesitant to reveal his homosexuality to his parents, has come out to the rest of the world. He has a network of friends and a night life in gay bars that his father never had. Owen, aware he was "different" since childhood but believing that his homosexuality was a disease, forced himself to deny this "difference" for years. Finally, when he could no longer suppress his sexuality, he began visiting a pornographic movie house, engaging in sexual acts with nameless, faceless men but suffering severe guilt when he returned home to Rose.

This novel, like most of Leavitt's work, explores what critic Robert Jones has called "the desire to find a language that describes the isolate worlds we inhabit." The title refers to a case study of a boy abandoned by his mother in an apartment near a construction site. Lacking human contact, the child identified and "bonded" with the cranes he saw operating outside his window, devising his own language based on the noises they made, thus creating a language that had meaning and emotional resonance for him. Likewise, the members of the Benjamin family struggle to make sense of their own individual "languages" in the context of their familial relationship.

THE PAGE TURNER

First published: 1998
Type of work: Novel

A young piano student learns that both art and love have their price.

In a variation on the character triangle that Leavitt successfully explored in his groundbreaking short story "Territory," the novel *The Page Turner* features a mother and son and the effect that a third party, the son's lover, has on their familial bond.

As the novel begins, eighteen-year-old Paul Porterfield, a piano student just finishing his last year in high school and preparing to enter Juilliard in the fall, has been engaged to turn the pages of the musical score for Richard Kennington, a forty-something piano virtuoso, during a chamber music concert in San Francisco. An ardent fan of Kennington's work and ambitious to replicate the older man's success for himself, Paul relishes a chance to meet his idol. Pamela Porterfield, Paul's mother, sits in the audience in anticipation of her son's ancillary role in the musical performance, her dreams of her son's future as bright as Paul's own.

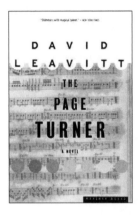

What would appear to be a relatively inconsequential event in both their lives becomes the catalyst for a life-altering relationship between Paul and Richard when the two meet again in Italy some months later. Paul and his mother are in Rome as one stop in a graduation trip for him and as a way for her temporarily to escape the pain of her husband's infidelity and desertion. Upon discovering that Kennington has just finished a concert engagement in that city, Paul tracks Richard down in his hotel room, motivated in part by his ambition and in part by his unacknowledged physical desire.

Their affair, though brief, has consequences for all three characters. Paul confirms his sexual orientation and takes his first steps toward establishing a pattern of relationships with older men. Richard, initially swept away by his passion for Paul, ultimately flees from the scene to return to the ambiva-lent comforts of his older companion and manager, the sixty-one-year-old Joseph Mansourian. Pamela, initially misinterpreting Richard's interest in Paul as an attraction to her, confronts her son's homosexuality and eventually, with the knowledge acquired through the pain of her own life, comes to be a source of wisdom to her son as he copes with the realization that ambition and love are not always requited.

The title of the novel refers to both the compromises that individuals often make regarding their initial career objectives and the secondary roles that individuals often come to play in their personal relationships. During the course of the narrative, Paul discovers that he lacks the talent to be a concert pianist; at best, he may be able to carve out a career as an accompanist. Similarly, in his connections with other men, Paul is slated to play an attendant part; he will be the companion and helpmate. In effect, his allotted role in art and love parallels that of the two principal women in his life—his teacher, Olga Novotna, who gave up her own concert career to be the mistress of the composer Kessler, and his mother, Pamela, who took on the roles of housewife and mother.

In the end, both Paul and Pamela come to share the realization that there are compensations to be found in a supporting role and that "page-turning is an art in its way."

SUMMARY

The characters populating Leavitt's fiction, whether gay or straight, strive to overcome a sense of separateness, a sense of being on the outside of life looking in, but they often succeed only briefly in making meaningful connections with the rest of the human race. At best, they come to terms with the fact that isolation is part of the human condition rather than a lonely vigil kept only by themselves.

Mary Virginia Davis; updated by S. Thomas Mack

BIBLIOGRAPHY

By the Author

SHORT FICTION:
Family Dancing, 1984
A Place I've Never Been, 1990
Arkansas: Three Novellas, 1997

The Marble Quilt: Stories, 2001
Collected Stories, 2003

LONG FICTION:
The Lost Language of Cranes, 1986
Equal Affections, 1989
While England Sleeps, 1993, revised 1995
The Page Turner, 1998
Martin Bauman: Or, A Sure Thing, 2000
The Body of Jonah Boyd, 2004

NONFICTION:
Italian Pleasures, 1996 (with Mark Mitchell)
In Maremma: Life and a House in Southern Tuscany, 2001 (with Mitchell)
Florence: A Delicate Case, 2002
The Man Who Knew Too Much: Alan Turing and the Invention of the Computer, 2005

EDITED TEXTS:
The Penguin Book of Gay Short Stories, 1994 (with Mark Mitchell)
Pages Passed from Hand to Hand: The Hidden Tradition of Homosexual Literature in England from 1748 to 1914, 1997 (with Mitchell)
Selected Stories, 2001 (of E. M. Forster; with Mitchell)

About the Author

Bleeth, Kenneth, and Julie Rankin. "The Imitation David: Plagiarism, Collaboration, and the Making of a Gay Literary Tradition in David Leavitt's 'The Term Paper Artist.'" *PMLA* 116 (October, 2001): 1349-1364.

Jones, Robert. "The Lost Language of Cranes." *Commonweal* 113 (October 24, 1986): 558-560.

Lilly, Mark. *Gay Men's Literature in the Twentieth Century.* New York: New York University Press, 1993.

McRuer, Robert. *The Queer Renaissance: Contemporary American Literature and the Reinvention of Lesbian and Gay Identities.* New York: New York University Press, 1997.

Mars-Jones, Adam. "Gays of Our Lives: *The Lost Language of Cranes.*" *The New Republic* 195 (November 17, 1986): 43-46.

Spender, Stephen. "My Life Is Mine; It Is Not David Leavitt's." *The New York Times Book Review* 143 (September 4, 1994): 10-12.

Staggs, Sam. "David Leavitt." *Publishers Weekly* 237 (August 24, 1990): 47-48.

Weir, John. "Fleeing the Fame Factory." *The Advocate,* October, 19, 1993, 51-55.

DISCUSSION TOPICS

- David Leavitt demonstrates that so much of what people assume to be true in human relationships is based on false assumptions, beliefs that they often accept and preserve because they fear peering beneath the surface to confront the reality of the situation. Can you find examples in his work?

- A major genre in gay and lesbian literature is the "coming out" story. How does Leavitt address the situation of a gay child's "coming out" to his or her parents and siblings and then reclaiming and redefining his or her place in the family unit?

- The small gestures in life, the little everyday things are fraught with meaning in Leavitt's fiction. Can you find examples in his work?

- Leavitt often explores the situation of the outsider. What are some of the ways in which a person can become an outsider? What are the handicaps and the compensations of such a condition?

- Many of the problems that one finds in heterosexual relationships are, in Leavitt's work, mirrored in the committed relationships between gay people. What are some of those problems? Do gay people seek solutions that are different from those explored by straight people?

CHANG-RAE LEE

Born: Seoul, South Korea
July 29, 1965

His first novel's superb examination of the question of contemporary Asian American identity and assimilation in mainstream American society catapulted Chang-rae Lee to literary fame. His subsequent works feature characters who hide their suffering from past events behind an attitude of emotional detachment and alienation which they must learn to overcome.

© Marion Ettlinger

BIOGRAPHY

Chang-rae Lee was born on July 29, 1965, in Seoul, Republic of Korea (South Korea), the second child to the physician Young Yong Lee and his wife, basketball player Inja (Hong) Lee. Soon after his birth, Lee's father immigrated to the United States, settling in Pittsburgh, Pennsylvania, and becoming a psychiatrist. In 1968, his father brought his wife, Lee's elder sister Eunei, and Lee from Korea to the United States, moving to Manhattan in 1969. When his father secured a position at Bellevue Hospital in New York City, the family moved to the suburbs, where Chang-rae Lee continued to grow up.

Unlike her husband, Inja Lee did not immediately learn English but required her children to do so. Korean was spoken only at home and at the Korean Presbyterian Church in Flushing, New York, which the family attended. Lee was enrolled in an English-language kindergarten, where he remained almost completely silent. Later, he won acceptance at Phillips Exeter Academy, a prestigious preparatory school, where he edited a poetry magazine. He was admitted to Yale University in 1983 and graduated with a B.A. in English in 1987, writing short stories that he did not send out to publishers.

Lee took a job as an equity analyst with the investment bank of Donaldson, Lufkin & Jenrette in 1987, a job which he soon quit in favor of writing. With a finished but unpublished novel, *Agnew Belittlehead*, written in the style of his early literary hero Thomas Pynchon, Lee received a scholarship in the creative writing department of the University of Oregon. In 1992, his mother died. In 1993, Lee earned his M.F.A. from the University of Oregon and became an assistant professor of creative writing there. On June 19, 1993, he married Michelle Branca, a graduate student in architecture. Soon, the couple had two daughters, Annika and Eva.

Lee's master's thesis was actually the text of his novel *Native Speaker*, which was published in 1995 to great critical acclaim and commercial success. *Native Speaker*, ostensibly a spy story that deeply probes the Korean American immigrant experience of Lee's and his parents' generation in New York City, won Lee numerous literary awards. Among them were the American Library Association Notable Book of the Year Award, the American Book Award of the Before Columbus Foundation, the "New Voices" Award of the Quality Paperback Club, and the Barnes and Noble Discover Great New Writers Award, all in 1995. Lee's first novel won the Hemingway Foundation/PEN Award in 1996.

For his next book, Lee wanted to turn away from examining the Asian American immigrant experience in America that had made him a famous new author. Instead, he sought to focus on the issue of Korean "comfort women," young Korean women who were forcibly reduced to sexual slavery to service Japanese soldiers during World War II. After beginning to write the novel from the point of view of one such woman and traveling to Korea to interview survivors of this era, Lee felt that his novel did not capture their true voices. He abandoned his manuscript and started afresh, this time from the point of view of one of the potential male perpetrators. This new direction would eventually become his second novel, *A Gesture Life*, published in 1999.

In 1998, Lee accepted a position as professor of writing with Hunter College of the City University of New York, and he and his family moved to New Jersey. During this period, *A Gesture Life* was published. Telling the story of a septuagenarian Japanese American of Korean ethnicity struggling to come to terms with his war memories and his rebellious adopted Korean American daughter, the book again gained critical praise and found a substantial readership.

In 2002, Lee became professor of creative writing at Princeton University, joining the elite of American academia. His third novel, *Aloft*, was published in 2004. Here, Lee took the substantial critical risk of moving further away from Asian American themes and characters: The first-person narrator of the novel is a fifty-nine-year-old Italian American man. The reader learns that many of Jerry Battle's problems originate from his troubled marriage to his Korean American wife, Daisy Han, whose suicide casts a substantial shadow over Battle's surviving family.

By 2005, at age forty, Chang-rae Lee enjoyed a substantial literary and academic career. The author further succeeded to approach ever-new themes and topics for his novels. His sustained literary output has earned Lee critical praise and a solid readership.

ANALYSIS

Language itself is a top concern of Chang-rae Lee. All of the first-person narrator protagonists of his first three novels use language very deliberately and eloquently in order to relay the results of their acute physical and mental observations to the reader. Their thoughtful and well-crafted sentences in which they convey information about themselves and their world correspond well to the emotional detachment and inner solitude felt by all of them regardless of their differences in age and ethnicity. The power that language can bestow

on the person who uses it well and the function of language to determine identity and social standing is a main subject of Lee's widely acclaimed first novel, *Native Speaker*.

Native Speaker focuses on the price paid by Asian American immigrants as they assimilate into mainstream American culture. As the novel underlines, one of the first tasks of assimilation is English-language acquisition. This issue also tends to divide the immigrant generations. While the first generation has to struggle to learn English, the second generation, such as the novel's young protagonist Henry Park, is often able to become true native speakers, although at the risk of losing part of their heritage. However, as *Native Speaker* indicates, for a non-European, second-generation immigrant—who speaks English as perfect and accent-free as Henry Park—there is still the physical difference from the Caucasian majority that makes assimilation more problematic.

Ostensibly told as a spy story, *Native Speaker* depicts the young and well-educated Park, who works for a shadowy private agency that collects incriminating information primarily on non-Caucasian persons of influence who threaten New York's establishment. Thus, Park is given the assignment to infiltrate the mayoral campaign of affluent city councilman John Kwang, who, like the narrator and the author, is a Korean American.

Lee deliberately wanted to write a first novel that was not openly autobiographical, even though there are autobiographical touches to his Korean American characters and their communities in *Native Speaker*. He felt that the profession of a spy worked well as a metaphor for the position of both the writer and the second-generation non-Caucasian immigrant who tends to blend in and observe life and power, rather than attempt to actively wield it. The latter is the choice of Kwang. Lee portrays Kwang's downfall as an ambiguous mix of personal failings and dirty politics directed against non-Caucasian challengers to the city's white establishment.

A Gesture Life and *Aloft*, Chang-rae Lee's next novels, broaden the scope of his fiction and are distanced from the theme of the Asian American immigrant in conflict with mainstream society. *A Gesture Life* features Franklin "Doc" Hata, a well-liked Asian American gentleman in his seventies living in a tranquil suburb of New York. However, Hata's own life is in turmoil, as he reveals in flashbacks that tell the story of most of his life. He is a double immigrant, revisiting Lee's earlier theme from a new angle. As a Korean child, he was adopted by Japanese parents and assimilated into Japanese culture, a forcible act juxtaposed to the American immigrant experience.

Hata is eventually drafted as a paramedic into the Japanese army in World War II. His 1944 encounter with five Korean sex slaves—the "comfort women" of the Japanese army—constitutes one of the primary themes of the novel. Originally, Lee wanted to write the novel from the point of view of one of these women, but he felt unable to capture their true voices. Thus, *A Gesture Life* examines the historic crime perpetrated against Korean women by the Japanese from the position of the ambiguous Korean Japanese protagonist who falls in love with one of these victims but fails to save her. To atone for his sins, in the United States Hata adopts a Korean orphan, Sunny, and develops a troubled relationship with her. Initially he tries to force her to lead an exemplary life that she rejects as a mere "gesture life," an inauthentic posing for society's sake.

Aloft moves even further into the direction of a mainstream American novel. The protagonist is Jerry Battle, a fifty-nine-year-old Italian American retired from his landscaping business and enjoying flights in his private plane, high above the ongoing troubles of his family. Again, Lee creates a protagonist who is visibly alienated from his own self and the people closest to him. While critics have felt that Battle's language is too eloquent for a landscaper and more similar to that of educated Henry Park and the genteel Franklin Hata, the topic of detached, alienated observation resulting from excruciating past personal pain is a main subject in all of Lee's fiction. Battle's pivotal trauma came when his Korean American wife, Daisy Han, slowly descended into mental illness, culminating in her suicide in the family's swimming pool.

The themes of alienation and emotional detachment unite all of Lee's protagonists of his novels. Indeed, each protagonist has been left by his lover at the beginning of each novel for failing to show more human warmth. All are in danger of losing love, and each novel has a strong side plot describing their ensuing actions.

With his first three novels, Chang-rae Lee has managed to move deeply into mainstream literature while keeping a strong thematic interest of alienation, either caused by immigration and assimilation or by personal loss. Lee's novels insist that in order to truly live, his protagonists have to leave their comfortable shell of detachment and reengage with life. So far, all of Lee's protagonists have done this by the end of his novels.

NATIVE SPEAKER

First published: 1995
Type of work: Novel

A young, well-educated Korean American man is hired to spy on an ambitious Korean American politician but resigns from his job and reunites with his wife while the politician self-destructs.

Native Speaker was the thesis written by Chang-rae Lee to earn his M.F.A. degree from the University of Oregon in 1993. In 1995, the novel became the first book published by Riverhead Books, a subsidiary of what became Penguin Putnam. Committed to books that open up new views and present new ideas, Riverhead fared very well with Lee's novel, which became an instant critical and commercial success and launched its author's career.

The novel begins when its first-person narrator and young protagonist, well-spoken and well-educated Henry Park, accepts a new assignment from the shadowy commercial spy agency he is working for in New York City. Because of his ethnicity and his ability to blend into a multicultural environment, he is chosen to try and collect information on the ambitious, rich Korean American businessman-turned-mayoral-candidate John Kwang. Joining Kwang's campaign undercover, Park has to make up for a previous botched assignment in which he came

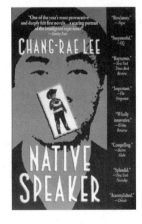

to sympathize with his target, a Filipino psychiatrist.

At the same time, Park has just been left by his Caucasian wife Lelia, who blames him for utter emotional coldness in the aftermath of the accidental suffocation of their seven-year-old son, Mitt. She has handed him a long list of all his faults, among them being too alien and detached from life.

As Park slowly makes his way into Kwang's organization, Lee enriches his narrative with Park's mental reflections and physical observations of what it means to be a first- and second-generation Korean American immigrant in contemporary New York City and the United States. Reflections on the importance of language, language acquisition, and identity are given broad play in Park's musings. The price paid for being a native speaker, the protagonist believes, is a serious risk of losing one's cultural heritage and identity and of becoming deeply alienated from one's parents. At the same time, there is a lingering suspicion that mainstream America does not really accept Asian Americans as fully American.

Rather than living as a detached observer of American life, Kwang wants to obtain actual power, which causes hostility from the Caucasian establishment. When Kwang learns that one of his closest friends, a colleague of Park, has been hired to spy on him, he reacts violently to this betrayal in his own ranks. He secretly orders the bombing of his own campaign headquarters, and his life spins out of control, leading to his eventual departure for Korea. Disgusted with his job, Park quits the agency and reunites with his wife, and they jointly run a speech clinic for immigrant children.

Native Speaker stresses the author's point that mainstream politics are jealously guarded by the establishment that is unwilling to accept democratic competition from recent immigrants. His portrayal of Kwang is that of an ambitious but ultimately flawed man, one who is partially responsible for his own downfall that is cheered on by his rivals. Park manages to pull back from the brink and reconnect to a meaningful existence with his loving wife.

A GESTURE LIFE

First published: 1999
Type of work: Novel

In his seventies, a Japanese American gentleman of Korean birth must come to terms with his wartime experience and his rebellious adopted young daughter.

Originally meant to tell the story of a Korean "comfort woman" during World War II from her point of view, *A Gesture Life* was eventually changed by Chang-rae Lee to focus on a potential tormentor of the comfort women. The novel begins as the first-person narrator, Franklin "Doc" Hata, is apparently at ease with his life in his seventies. Well-accepted, integrated, and esteemed in his fictional suburban New York community of Bedley Run, he owns a large home with pool and appears to be an immigrant success story. After selling the medical supply shop he has run for more than thirty years to a young family, he looks set to enjoy tranquil retirement.

It is after a minor fire accident sends him to a hospital that Hata's exemplary life begins to unravel as he reviews his existence in a series of sustained flashbacks. Born in Korea, as a young child he was adopted by a Japanese family and raised in Japan, assimilated into Japanese culture and language. Having lost his Korean birth name, he was called Ziro Kurohata. Introducing the historical fact of the assimilation of Koreans into imperial Japan serves Lee an interesting counterpoint to the assimilation of Asian Americans in the United States and makes his protagonist twice removed from the place where he lives now.

Drafted into the Japanese army as a paramedic in World War II, he finds himself in 1944 in a remote outpost in Burma. Suddenly, five Korean "comfort women" are brought to camp. Historically, the Japanese army forced or tricked women from conquered Asian territories, particularly Korea, to submit to sexual slavery for Japanese soldiers. The protagonist bonds with the most attractive of the five, elegant Kkutaeh, who was raised like him in Japan and reserved for the commanding officer. Their common Korean heritage and language reinforce their bond, but the protagonist fails to save her from death.

After the war, the protagonist immigrates to the United States, shortening his name to Hata and adopting Franklin as first name, thereby substituting one assumed identity for another. He attempts to live an exemplary, cultivated life but refuses to emotionally attach himself to anyone. A lifelong bachelor, his American girlfriend, the kindly widow Mary Burns, eventually leaves him because of this emotional coldness; she dies while he is recovering in the hospital.

Hata's adoption of a young orphan girl of partial Korean heritage, Sunny, serves as his gesture of atonement for his wartime failure to save his lover. However, his decision to raise his daughter with the highest standards fails as she rebels against what she calls his empty "gesture life," a life designed only as a gesture to impress society. In a telling scene, Sunny asks her father to let her help him with home improvement, only to be told not to bother and to continue practicing the piano.

Hata's refusal to let Sunny bond with him leads her to become wild. By the time the novel opens, the reader learns later, Sunny has run away with a drug dealer and is pregnant.

Shocked after his accident, the death of Mary Burns, and his mental assessment of his life, Hata decides to change. He finds Sunny and promises to support her with the baby. Thus, *A Gesture Life* ends on a hopeful note of redemption, as Hata is seen to cast off his armor of emotional detachment that has alienated him from his loved one.

ALOFT

First published: 2004
Type of work: Novel

Fifty-nine-year-old Italian American Jerry Battle learns that he has to reconnect with his family if he wants to live a meaningful life.

In his third novel, *Aloft*, Chang-rae Lee moved even further away from his reflection on contemporary Asian American immigrant life in New York City that established his literary fame. *Aloft* begins similarly to Lee's second work, *A Gesture Life*, with an older male character apparently in full control of his life.

Flying in sunny weather above the suburban landscape around New York City, Jerry Battle congratulates himself on his decision to turn over his family landscaping business to his son Jack and retire, freeing up his time to fly or work as a part-time travel agent. At first there is only a hint at his immigrant experience when he confesses to having Americanized his Italian last name of Battaglia to Battle.

With his own cranky father in a nursing home, his son and his materialistic wife and two spoiled children the heirs to his business, and his daughter Theresa engaged to a Korean American writer in Oregon, Battle does appear to enjoy retirement; his children treat him amicably. The only trouble is the fact that Rita, his Puerto Rican girlfriend of twenty years, has recently left him because of his emotional detachment.

Battle's tranquil life is shaken up by his attempts to win back Rita, Theresa's pregnancy and simultaneous diagnosis with cancer, Jack's failure in business, and his own recollections of the death of his wife when he was in his thirties. The reader suddenly learns that Battle met his wife, Korean American Daisy Han, when she squirted him with the cologne that she was hired to promote in a department store. Fascinated by her personality and exuberance of life, Battle married Daisy when such marriages where still rare in America.

It is in Battle's recollections of Daisy's slow slide into mental illness that Lee gives *Aloft* its darkest atmosphere. When she finally commits suicide by drowning herself naked in the family pool while Battle is away, Lee successfully raises the question of the extremely tentative nature of all human bonds, including that of marital love. *Aloft* reveals through Daisy's fate the difficulty to ever fully connect, engage, and understand another human being.

While Battle remains relatively stable and succeeds to raise his children with Rita's help, his growing emotional detachment makes him lose his connections to them. Confronted with Theresa's refusal to allow cancer therapy that would kill the child she is carrying, however, draws Battle out of his emotional reserve. In a stunning, albeit not realistic, climax, Battle, who has never flown in anything but good weather, flies Theresa in an instrument flight through severe weather and lands with almost zero visibility in time for her to get to the hospital. There, her child is born as she herself dies.

Aloft successfully realized Lee's desire to create an American novel that only touches on ethnic issues. The plight of Battle to reconnect with his growing children and to win back Rita's love is told compellingly, even though the plot is not always realistic.

SUMMARY

Chang-rae Lee entered the American literary scene with a stunning debut novel examining questions of Asian American immigrant identity, ethnic politics, urban alienation, betrayal, and espionage. He moved on to create a haunting novel examining personal guilt related to wartime atrocities and a father's imminent failure to raise his daughter successfully, while keeping his protagonist Asian American. In his third novel, the characters are deliberately multiethnic and deeply steeped in contemporary American culture, as a father tries again to reconnect with his surviving family.

Characteristic of Lee's fiction, many of his characters, regardless of their age or ethnicity, share a sense of initial emotional detachment from their most intimate partners and family members. This alienation is rooted in their perceived necessity to reinvent themselves in order to cope with a new life circumstance, whether as immigrant, father, or retiree. It is this need for reinvention, critics have suggested, that unites and ties Lee's characters to the quintessential immigrant experience of starting afresh in a new land.

R. C. Lutz

BIBLIOGRAPHY

By the Author

LONG FICTION:
Native Speaker, 1995
A Gesture Life, 1999
Aloft, 2004

About the Author

Case, Kristen. "Turbulence in Suburbia." *The New Leader* 87, no. 2 (March/April, 2004): 26-28.

Chen, Tina. "Impersonation and Other Disappearing Acts in *Native Speaker* by Chang-rae Lee." *MFS: Modern Fiction Studies* 48, no. 3 (Fall, 2002): 637-667.

Corley, Liam. "'Just Another Ethnic Pol': Literary Citizenship in Chang-rae Lee's *Native Speaker*." *Studies in the Literary Imagination* 37, no. 1 (Spring, 2004): 61-82.

Engles, Tim. "'Visions of Me in the Whitest Raw Light': Assimilation and Doxic Whiteness in Chang-rae Lee's *Native Speaker.*" *Hitting Critical Mass* 4, no. 2 (1997): 27-48.

Lee, Rachel. "Reading Contests and Contesting Reading: Chang-rae Lee's *Native Speaker* and Ethnic New York." *MELUS* 29, nos. 3/4 (Fall/Winter, 2004): 341-353.

Magarian, Baret. "Guilty Secret." *New Statesman* 129, no. 4478 (March 20, 2000): 56.

Park, You-Me, and Gayle Wald. "Native Daughters in the Promised Land: Gender, Race, and the Question of Separate Spheres." In *No More Separate Spheres!,* edited by Cathy N. Davidson and Jessaym Hatcher. Durham, N.C.: Duke University Press, 2002.

Reese, Jennifer. "A Flight for Glory: A Father Tries to Connect with His Scattered Family in Chang-rae Lee's Sparkling *Aloft.*" *Entertainment Weekly* no. 755 (March 12, 2004): 117.

Sayers, Valerie. "Little Comfort Given." *Commonweal* 126, no. 22 (December 17, 1999): 19.

HARPER LEE

Born: Monroeville, Alabama
April 28, 1926

Lee's reputation rests on her novel To Kill a Mockingbird, *a moving account of a Southern lawyer's battle against prejudice and injustice.*

BIOGRAPHY

Nelle Harper Lee was born in Monroeville, Alabama, on April 28, 1926. Her father, Amasa Coleman Lee, was the son of a Confederate veteran and a Florida legislator. A. C. Lee himself was a prominent citizen of Monroeville, a practicing lawyer who served in the Alabama legislature for twelve years. He was also involved in the management of the local newspaper. Harper Lee's mother was Frances Finch Lee, whose family had moved from Virginia to Alabama, where they founded Finchburg.

With her sisters, Alice and Louise, and her brother, Edwin, Harper grew up in the quiet little town of Monroeville. In her childhood, like Jean Louise (Scout) Finch in *To Kill a Mockingbird* (1960), Harper used to go up to the courthouse balcony to watch her father appear in court. Like Scout, Harper and Edwin had a friend from the city, Truman Capote, who spent much of his childhood with elderly relatives in Monroeville and who was later to become a distinguished writer. Harper herself had begun writing by the time she was seven.

After attending the public schools in Monroeville, Lee went to Huntington College in Montgomery, Alabama, for one year, then in 1945 transferred to the University of Alabama, where she remained from 1945 to 1950, except for one year

spent as an exchange student at the University of Oxford. At the University of Alabama, Lee continued her writing, contributing to various campus publications. Then she made her decision. She must be a writer. Much to her father's disappointment, Lee left the University of Alabama six months short of a law degree. She moved to New York, where she supported herself by working as an airline reservations clerk for Eastern Airlines and British Overseas Airways. Eventually, she took some of her work to a literary agent. He was particularly interested in one of the short stories, and he suggested that she expand it to a novel.

Quitting her job, Lee began working full time on what was to be *To Kill a Mockingbird*. In 1957, she had a manuscript completed; however, the editors at the publishing committee to which she submitted it asked her to rework it, tightening the structure. She did, and the book was published in 1960.

To Kill a Mockingbird was a best seller. It was a Literary Guild Selection, a Book-of-the-Month Club alternate, and a *Reader's Digest* condensed book. The novel also gained critical acclaim; in 1961, it won the Pulitzer Prize. The following year, it was made into a motion picture, which won an Academy Award. At that time, Harper Lee announced that she was working on a second novel. During the next three decades, several essays and articles appeared, but Lee published no more fiction. Lee still lives in her native Monroeville.

ANALYSIS

To Kill a Mockingbird is a novel of childhood, but it is not told by a child. The narrator, Jean Louise (Scout) Finch, is an adult, recalling events that occurred in the mid-1930's, when her older brother

Jem Finch was nearing his teens and she was four years younger. This narrative stance has several advantages. By using the first person, Lee gains immediacy and dramatic effect; by placing the events in the past, she can evaluate incidents that have become much clearer over the years.

The novel concerns innocence and experience, and its theme is more complicated than it might appear. Scout, Jem, and their friend from Meridian, Mississippi, Dill Harris, are not naturally cruel; however, they have not yet learned to empathize with others. To them, outsiders have no feelings. Therefore, it is all right to run up to the porch of a recluse, as a game; it is all right to rub a poor boy's nose in the schoolyard dirt; it is all right to make a snowman in the image of a neighbor; and it is all right to make fun of crabby old ladies. Although Atticus Finch, the father of the motherless Scout and Jem, is not particularly concerned with proper clothes for them, he is concerned about teaching them to imagine themselves in the position of others, even of people who are not particularly friendly or appealing. In this sense, then, the children's innocence, which dictates instinctive aversion, must be modified. On the other hand, Atticus hopes that his children will preserve another form of innocence—that they will not learn the prejudices that society is so willing to teach them.

Structurally, then, the novel is organized to show the development, or the moral education, of Atticus's children. In episode after episode, the pattern is repeated. The children (or one child) will assess someone by superficial standards; then, either on their own or, more often, in a conversation with Atticus, the children discover the truth—that the person whom they condemned has hidden sorrows and, often, hidden strengths.

Since the first-person narrator is the adult who, as a child, experienced all of these revelations, Harper Lee could have had her introduce the characters in these episodes with a full description and analysis. Instead, she chooses to let the readers follow the children to their discovery of the truth. This technique not only increases suspense, it also dramatizes the process through which the children themselves are going on their way to understanding.

One of those brief but significant episodes occurs at the end of part 1 of the novel, which is divided into two parts. It begins with the narrator's explaining the antipathy that both she and her brother feel toward Mrs. Henry Lafayette Dubose, a woman who lives alone and whose chief pleasure seems to be sitting on her front porch and shouting criticisms and insults at passing children, especially at Jem and Scout. They cannot understand why their father behaves in so courtly a manner toward Mrs. Dubose. As far as they are concerned, she deserves their hatred.

Finally, Mrs. Dubose hurls one insult too many at the children, this time one equating their father with the black people and poor white people for whom she says Atticus works. When the children pass her house again a short time after this diatribe, Jem notices that Mrs. Dubose has retreated from the porch: In a fury, he destroys every one of her camellias.

As soon as he has done it, Jem begins to anticipate his father's rebuke. What he does not expect is the punishment that he receives: Atticus not only makes Jem apologize, he also has him offer amends. What Mrs. Dubose decides that she needs of Jem is to have him read to her every day but Sunday for a month. Atticus finds that penalty appropriate and makes sure that Jem lives up to the contract. Even when Jem reports Mrs. Dubose's continuing insults about Atticus helping black people, Atticus will not relent. Finally, the month is up, and Jem thinks that he is free of Mrs. Dubose.

Some time later, however, Mrs. Dubose dies; Atticus then feels free to explain to Jem why, despite her prejudice and her crankiness, he considers Mrs. Dubose one of the bravest people he has ever known. Mrs. Dubose was addicted to morphine; however, when she knew that she was dying, she was determined to break that habit, even though by doing so she would ensure herself an agonizing death. Atticus does not have to explain further to his son; Jem now knows that he will never be free of Mrs. Dubose, will never forget the lesson he has learned.

In brief episodes such as this, Lee chronicles the children's moral development. The fact that generally she has her adult narrator move through events like the child she was when they occurred is one reason that *To Kill a Mockingbird* so effectively dramatizes the journey from innocence to experience, from amorality to morality.

TO KILL A MOCKINGBIRD

First published: 1960
Type of work: Novel

Three children learn about goodness and courage from the small-town Alabama lawyer who defends an innocent black man in court despite community disapproval.

To Kill a Mockingbird has been discussed by many critics simply in terms of racial prejudice; however, it is clear that in both the novel and the film the theme is more universal than a portrayal of the evil of racial prejudice. That evil is shown as an example of humankind's intolerance. In all of its forms, people's inhumanity to others is the real antagonist of the enlightened. In the novel, there are many minor instances of prejudice, including the encounter between Jem and Mrs. Dubose, with which part 1 of the book ends. These incidents prepare for the concentration on the two major plot lines in part 2. Neither of the plot lines dominates the novel. Structurally, they are brilliantly interwoven. Thematically, they complement each other.

The first of these plots is introduced in the first few sentences of the novel, when the narrator says that the story to be told really began when Dill Harris got the idea of getting Arthur (Boo) Radley to come out. The setting is the small town of Maycomb, Alabama; the time is the mid-1930's. Boo Radley is the neighbor of the Finches. When he was a teenager, he got into minor trouble, and since that time, he has been imprisoned in his home by his father, who is a religious fanatic. Because no one in the community ever sees Boo, much less gets to know him, everyone has come to fear him.

At first, the children share this fear. They dare each other to run up to the house where Boo is incarcerated, as if he were a supernatural monster. Gradually, however, they become aware that Boo is observing them and that he wishes them no harm. Indeed, in his loneliness, he reaches out to the children. He keeps Jem from getting in trouble by returning his torn pants, mended; he leaves the children little presents in a hollow tree; he even gets near enough to put a blanket around Scout when she is standing outside to watch a neighbor's house burn. Once the children begin to share secrets with Boo, they have admitted him to their world. He is

no longer a stranger; he is a friend. The children have surmounted the prejudice of their community.

There are many parallels between this plot line and the second plot line, which involves a black man, Tom Robinson. Like Boo, Robinson is imprisoned within his community, but unlike Boo, Robinson has never committed any action that might produce punishment. His only crime is to have been born black in a society that has certain assumptions about black people—among them, the assumption that black men always desire white women. That assumption is based on another assumption: that white people are always superior to black people.

Like Boo Radley, Tom Robinson is a kind person, drawn toward those he perceives as helpless. Certainly the white girl Mayella Ewell is pitiable. The entire community, black and white, looks down upon the Ewell tribe, which is headed by the despicable Bob Ewell, Mayella's father. Bob Ewell is the only character in *To Kill a Mockingbird* who has no virtues. He is mean, abusive, filthy, and shiftless. When he is drunk or simply in a bad mood, he beats his children. Given this family situation, it would be natural for anyone to respond to a plea from one of those children. From time to time, when Tom is passing by the Ewell place, Mayella asks him to help her with some heavy task that her 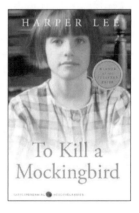 father has assigned her to do, and innocently, Tom does what she asks. Unfortunately, like Boo Radley, Mayella is desperately lonely, and she does the unthinkable: She makes a sexual advance to Tom. Shocked and terrified, he leaves; shocked at her own conduct, she connives with her father to accuse Tom of rape. Thus it is Tom's compassionate attempt to transcend community prejudice, to treat an outcast white girl as a friend, which puts him in peril and which finally, despite the impassioned legal defense by Atticus Finch, costs Tom his life.

There is no question that both Boo Radley and Tom Robinson are acting correctly when they reach out to others. By example, Atticus Finch is attempting to teach this kind of behavior to both his children and his community. Yet Atticus would be the first to admit that there is danger in defying prejudice, in breaking down barriers that have been erected over the years and throughout the generations. Tom's moral action is misinterpreted; to believe him would be to admit that a white girl could desire a black man, and thus to upset the entire social hierarchy. Therefore the community must doom Tom, even though many people secretly do believe him. Boo Radley, too, runs a risk by befriending the children, not only from his tyrannical father but also from the law. When Bob Ewell ambushes Jem and Scout, planning to maim or kill them as a revenge upon Atticus, Boo goes to their defense and in the scuffle kills Bob Ewell. Atticus Finch—the man of honor, no matter what the consequences—believes that he must turn Radley over to the sheriff; however, the sheriff refuses to prosecute Radley and persuades Atticus on this occasion to put justice ahead of the letter of the law and to let Radley go free. If the timid recluse had been sent to prison, he would have died as surely as Tom Robinson dies when he attempts to flee.

If compassion in the midst of prejudice costs Tom Robinson his life and puts Boo Radley in peril, it can nevertheless sometimes win a victory. During Tom's arrest and trial, the community tension mounts, and with it, hostility toward Atticus. Finally, a mob gathers at the jail where Tom is being held; outside the jail, Atticus is on guard. Undoubtedly, he would have been attacked, even killed, if a past kindness had not been remembered. Scout had befriended the child of one of the members of the mob. Innocently unaware of the danger, Scout runs to her father and singles out that other father with inquiries about his son. Shamefacedly, he answers, the anger is dispelled, and Atticus is safe. Although she is a realist, Harper Lee refuses to be a cynic. If there is evil in humanity, there is also good, and sometimes the good is recognized and even defended.

SUMMARY

In *To Kill a Mockingbird*, Harper Lee not only captured the essence of what it was like to grow up in a small Southern town in the 1930's, but she also showed what it was to grow up in such a society with a father who was a man of principle, who would risk his reputation and his life to defend a black man accused of a crime that violated the most sacred taboos of his society.

By making Tom Robinson's story only one of a number of episodes in the novel, all with a similar pattern, Lee broadened the subject of her work and expanded its theme. What Atticus is endeavoring to give to his children and to his community is the power to empathize with others and the courage to defend them against injustice.

Rosemary M. Canfield Reisman

BIBLIOGRAPHY

By the Author

LONG FICTION:
To Kill a Mockingbird, 1960

About the Author

Betts, Doris. Introduction to *Southern Women Writers: The New Generation*, edited by Tonette Bond Inge. Tuscaloosa: University of Alabama Press, 1990.

Bruell, Edwin. "Keen Scalpel on Racial Ills." *English Journal* 53 (December, 1964): 658-661.

Cook, Martha. "Old Ways and New Ways." In *The History of Southern Literature*, edited by Louis D. Rubin, Jr., et al. Baton Rouge: Louisiana State University Press, 1985.

Going, William T. *Essays on Alabama Literature*. Tuscaloosa: University of Alabama Press, 1975.

Schuster, Edgar H. "Discovering Theme and Structure in the Novel." *English Journal* 52 (October, 1963): 506-511.

DISCUSSION TOPICS

- What does *To Kill a Mockingbird* gain from being narrated retrospectively? What qualities are lost in this type of narration?

- How does Harper Lee develop the character of Boo Radley?

- What principles of plot construction does Lee master most thoroughly in her novel?

- Does the film version of *To Kill a Mockingbird* magnify the character of Atticus Finch beyond his status in the novel?

URSULA K. LE GUIN

Born: Berkeley, California
October 21, 1929

*Le Guin has been a central force in making science fiction and
fantasy into serious genres for adult and younger readers.*

Courtesy, Allen and Unwin

BIOGRAPHY

Ursula Kroeber Le Guin was born in Berkeley, California, on October 21, 1929. Her mother, Theodora Kroeber, had a graduate degree in psychology, and Le Guin's father, Alfred Kroeber, was a well-known anthropologist. Le Guin and her three older brothers, Karl, Theodore, and Clifford, grew up in a household that placed strong emphasis on reading.

Le Guin's father taught at the University of California at Berkeley, where the family spent the academic year. With the arrival of summer, they would move to Kishamish, their forty-acre estate in the Napa Valley. Le Guin spent much time exploring this area with her brothers, which is perhaps why so many of her novels include journeys by foot. Summer guests at Kishamish included intellectual celebrities such as Robert Oppenheimer as well as anthropology scholars. Le Guin's exposure to anthropology dates from before she could read, as her father often told his children stories about the local Native Americans.

Le Guin's reading was not confined to anthropology, however, for she read all genres available to her, ranging from the romantic works of Lord Dunsany to the Taoist writings of the legendary seventh century Chinese figure Laozi, whom she read while still in her teens. In 1951, she completed a B.A., Phi Beta Kappa, in French and Italian, with an emphasis on Renaissance literature, at Harvard

University's Radcliffe College. She completed her M.A. at Columbia University in 1952, and then began a doctoral program at Columbia. In Paris, in December, 1953, she ended doctoral study and married Charles Le Guin, a history professor whom she had met on shipboard, while traveling to France for a year of Fulbright-supported study.

The end of Le Guin's doctoral aspirations proved to be the beginning of her career as a writer. Her mother had begun a writing career in middle-age; her *Ishi in Two Worlds* (1961) appeared a year after the death of Le Guin's father. Le Guin began writing much younger, producing her first fantasy story at age nine. Her first science-fiction story was rejected by a magazine when she was eleven, and she waited ten years before submitting another. With her marriage, she began writing poetry, later collected in *Wild Angels* (1975), and novels, all of which were rejected by publishers because they did not fit neatly into a commercial genre.

Le Guin began to achieve serious recognition for her fiction with what is now called the Hainish trilogy: *Rocannon's World* (1966), *Planet of Exile* (1966), and *City of Illusions* (1967). These science-fiction novels were followed with a series of award-winning novels and story collections in both fantasy and science fiction. *A Wizard of Earthsea* (1968) won the *Boston Globe*-Horn Book Award. *The Left Hand of Darkness* (1969) won both the Hugo and Nebula awards. When *The Dispossessed: An Ambiguous Utopia* (1974) accomplished this feat as well, Le Guin became the first writer to win both awards twice for novels. Since the 1970's, Le Guin has won many awards, including several more Hugos and Nebulas, Pen/USA, Locus Readers Awards, and a Pushcart Prize. Her works have been on "short lists" for the National Book Award and the Pulitzer

Prize. She also has received several honorary degrees, including degrees from Bucknell University, Lawrence University, the University of Oregon, and Kenyon College.

A Wizard of Earthsea was the first novel of the Earthsea trilogy, followed by *The Tombs of Atuan* (1971) and *The Farthest Shore* (1972). This trilogy eventually expanded into a fantasy series that includes *Tehanu: The Last Book of Earthsea* (1990), *Tales from Earthsea* (2001), and *The Other Wind* (2001). *The Left Hand of Darkness* and *The Dispossessed* continued the series of science-fiction novels and stories set in the Hainish universe; this series comprises short stories that appear in most of the collections, notably *A Fisherman of the Inland Sea* (1994) and *The Birthday of the World, and Other Stories* (2002) and several other novels, including *The Word for World Is Forest* (1972), *Four Ways to Forgiveness* (1995), and *The Telling* (2000).

Occasionally, Le Guin has combined her writing career with teaching. She has taught French as well as writing and has served as a writer-in-residence at the University of Washington. In 1976, Le Guin was a visiting fellow in creative writing at the University of Reading, in England. She has also taught in writing workshops in Melbourne, Australia, and in Oregon, Washington, and Indiana.

Though probably better known for her contributions to the genres of adult science fiction and fantasy, Le Guin also has written children's literature, including the Catwings series beginning in 1988. In 2004, she began a new series of young adult fantasies with the award-winning *Gifts*, followed by *Voices* (2006). Her later work has been excerpted in magazines such as *Harper's Magazine* and *The New Yorker.*

As she became well known, Le Guin expanded her work significantly outside the popular genres in which she began her career. Her collections of essays indicate the range of her thought: *The Language of the Night: Essays on Fantasy and Science Fiction* (1979), *Dancing at the Edge of the World: Thoughts on Words, Women, and Places* (1988), *Steering the Craft: Exercises and Discussions on Story Writing for the Lone Navigator or the Mutinous Crew* (1998), and *The Wave in the Mind: Talks and Essays on the Writer, the Reader, and the Imagination* (2004). In these lively and engaging essays, reviews, and speeches, she discusses feminism, science fiction, literary theory, politics, and many other topics of enduring interest.

ANALYSIS

Jungian psychoanalysis and Daoism are central to Le Guin's worldview, though she has been influenced by many other thinkers and writers and by her lifelong interest in anthropology. Many of her novels and stories explore oppositions between, on one hand, an aggressive, technological, male-dominated culture that depends upon coercive controls to produce and maintain social order and, on the other hand, a more peace-loving, egalitarian, female dominated culture that depends on consensus and nature-based "magic" and ritual for social cohesion and cooperation. Though a reader might easily conclude that Le Guin would simply affirm the egalitarian in place of the authoritarian mode, Le Guin's Daoism and Jungian ideas lead her to recognize that both sides of this opposition are necessary to human existence. The tension between them produces change and the possibility of progress, keeping society lively and interesting. The key to a culture's success in Le Guin's works is achieving a balance between these human tendencies that is creative and life-affirming. A culture that allows either tendency to stifle the other becomes stagnant, oppressive, and finally deadly.

Though this opposition is central to her work, Le Guin does not believe that the basis of writing is conflict. In her essay, "Conflict," from *Dancing at the Edge of the World*, she writes that to base one's writing on conflict is "to use an aspect of existence, conflict, to subsume all other aspects, many of which it does not include and does not comprehend."

Philosophically, Le Guin recognizes a need for balance between traditional masculine and feminine modes, but she also makes clear that for much of history, little attention has been paid to articulating and understanding the "feminine" side of humanity. For example, in her short story "Crosswords" (first published in *The New Yorker* on July 30, 1990), her main character describes the easiest way of dealing with most men:

> It was easier to smile. It's like there's a kind of oil that makes their wheels go round, and smiling is part of it, women smiling. They expect it, and when they don't get it they may not know what's missing but they tend to seize up and get mean, like a motor you don't oil.

Part of her point is that while women are required to understand how men operate in order to function in society, men seem not to be under a similar requirement with regard to women. Le Guin saw part of her mission as pushing readers to remedy this basic injustice. She said in a 1990 interview with *Publishers Weekly* that neither she nor "literature was ready for a female point of view in the early 1970's."

Until she wrote *Tehanu,* she believed herself unable to write fiction from the viewpoint of a mature woman. The absence of females as main characters in her early fiction had been noted by some feminist critics, though Le Guin had been incisively exploring gender issues throughout her career. Le Guin has said that she does not make up ideas; rather, images present themselves, and she writes about these images. Therefore, her choice of a male over a female protagonist is not an antifeminist statement; it is merely based on the image that appears, an arbitrary happening, not a choice. Le Guin does not view feminism as a side in a perpetual gender war, but as an assertion that in gender relations, balance and cooperation and justice and the affirmations of life and creativity are the essential elements. Many of her works, notably *The Left Hand of Darkness* and *Always Coming Home* (1985), represent sexual difference as creative on multiple levels.

With *Tehanu,* Le Guin took an important step toward exploring mature feminine consciousness, and she continued in this direction from that point onward. She has described her works as "thought experiments about the meaning of sexuality and gender." She does not blindly assume that female qualities are innately good and male qualities are naturally bad. Her female characters are not perfect; the problems they face are not solved any more easily because they are applying "female intelligence" to them.

During her career, Le Guin has achieved ever wider recognition and appreciation. Her work has helped to expand the audience for science fiction and fantasy, and she has broadened readers' ideas about the potential and the values of these genres.

THE LEFT HAND OF DARKNESS

First published: 1969
Type of work: Novel

An alien envoy tries to convince the inhabitants of the planet Gethen to join a loose federation of other planets.

In *The Left Hand of Darkness,* Genly Ai is an envoy from the Ekumen, an ambassador sent to recruit the planet Gethen to join this assemblage of planets in peaceful intergalactic exchange. The Ekumen offers communication with many distant worlds throughout the known universe.

Gethen's inhabitants are different from most human inhabitants of the known planets in that they do not have two separate sexes; each person is a hermaphrodite. The Gethenians regard Ai as the freak, a person perpetually male and perpetually ready to reproduce, while they have monthly reproductive cycles and hormonal systems that arbitrarily determine which sexual role each member of a pair will assume during the reproductive period.

Ai's mission is complicated mainly by the fact that Gethen's two main cultures are differentiating. Ai first negotiates with the king of Karhide, a culture that is feudal and tribal in its organization. Failing there, he travels to Orgoreyn, which is shifting into a nationalistic and authoritarian, bureaucratic state.

Ai's success depends finally upon his relationship with Estraven, the prime minister of Karhide, who is persuaded of the value of Ai's mission and risks "his" life and reputation to help Ai. Ai finds the process of understanding and dealing with a person who is both sexes at once disconcerting and complicated. Political intrigue and physical hardships bring the two into a deep friendship that eventually allows Ai to think "outside the box" and, with Estraven's help, to develop a risky strategy that will allow the planet to accept the offered contact with the Ekumen.

The novel takes the form of an official report. Ai's narrative chapters are interspersed with folktales of Gethen and selections from Estraven's journal. These three voices help the reader to appreciate different points of view and the difficulty Ai faces in attempting to understand an alien culture. Ai is like an anthropologist who undertakes the study of a new and previously unknown culture. This is a form that Le Guin uses often in her works. In addition to the gender themes, such stories also raise themes of tolerance, cooperation among people with deep differences, and the values and difficulties of dealing with cultural diversity.

One critic has noted, "the goals and concerns of Le Guin's characters are closely related to her own." Ai's acceptance of Estraven as a being beyond sexual labeling speaks for Le Guin's hope that one day society will accept all of its members without regard to their sex or sexual orientation.

THE DISPOSSESSED: AN AMBIGUOUS UTOPIA

First published: 1974
Type of work: Novel

A physicist from a socialist world attempts to reestablish a broken relationship with its capitalist, materialist sister world.

In *The Dispossessed: An Ambiguous Utopia,* Urras and Annares are twin planets. To deal with Odo, a troublesome revolutionary anarchist, and her followers on Urras, they were allowed to colonize Annares, with the understanding that they would mine the planet and supply the exhausted resources of Urras. Though the Odonian principles of consensus politics and cooperation are utopian, the actual culture on Annares, after more than a century of development, is bureaucratic and anti-individualistic. As a result the culture is stagnating. A great physicist, such as Shevek, the protagonist, finds his work thwarted repeatedly and his talents often wasted because his culture has come to use "the collective" to devalue the individual.

Shevek is a key character in the novels of the Hainish series, because he is the inventor of the ansible. He develops a temporal theory that makes it possible to build a device for instantaneous communication across light years of space. Whereas radio signals travel at light speed through ordinary space, the ansible "signals" can appear in two places simultaneously. The ansible makes the Ekumen

possible, the Ekumen being a federation of planets connected primarily by the ability to exchange information quickly but the inability to exchange persons, materials, or ships with such speed. One result is that they can communicate more easily than they can fight wars. The ansible has become one of the key inventions of recent science fiction and has been used by other authors, notably Orson Scott Card in the series of science-fiction novels that begins with *Ender's Game* (1985).

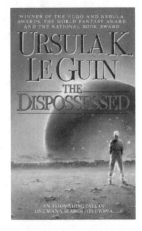

Shevek goes to Urras in the hope of having his "temporal theory" accepted by the scientific establishment there. Urras resembles Earth during the Cold War, with powerful but opposing materialistic societies, complicated political intrigue, and multiple factions in conflict within the warring cultures. Shevek finds this culture fascinating but finally destructive, as he inevitably becomes a pawn in games that are difficult to fathom. He comes to see that on Annares the collective makes for stability, while Urras teaches him that the individual makes for change. In order for freedom to persist in a way that guarantees survival, there must be a balanced opposition of these forces. Without the binding promise of social cooperation, nothing can be done and survival becomes impossible. Without freedom of the individual to oppose the majority and bring about change, there will be no renewal, only another kind of stagnation in which survival is at least difficult.

A main theme of the novel is breaking down walls. A literal wall between the two planets stands at the Annares space port. Shevek's invention of the ansible promises to penetrate and, perhaps someday, remove the walls that separate individuals and cultures, by freeing communication between everyone.

THE TELLING

First published: 2000
Type of work: Novel

Sutty Dass, an envoy from the Ekumen, comes to terms with her painful personal history while trying to understand the conflicted culture of another planet.

Like several other novels of the Hainish series, *The Telling* brings a representative of the Ekumen, a benevolent interplanetary organization, into a cultural conflict on an alien planet. Sutty Dass is insecure in her first assignment, mainly because of scars that she carries from growing up on Earth. She spent her childhood in India and Canada, fleeing the Unists, Christian fundamentalists bent upon world domination, on destroying all knowledge except the one true book, the Bible. She was a lesbian at a time when the Unists were attempting to erase all sexual "deviance." Perhaps the most traumatic event of her life was the Unist-inspired terrorist bombing of her university, in which her partner of several years was killed.

On the planet Aka, she finds an opposite tyranny, a secular materialist, corporation state that is bent upon destroying "The Telling," the ancient culture of the planet that is preserved in a highly inclusive canon of stories, images, myths, parables, and legends, a fragmentary and gigantic collection of cultural memory. She expected to find a planet where her sexual orientation would not matter, but she finds a culture of rigidly enforced heterosexuality.

Both the Unists and the dominant culture of Aka are animated by a desire to impose a rational order on a world that to them seems threatening because it evades intellectual control. Both are reactionary, in that what they care most about are the hardest to control features of the cultural values they oppose—religious belief, sexual behavior, language usage, and so on.

Aka has been transformed from its traditional culture toward this new authoritarian state in less than a century, since the planet was first contacted by the Ekumen. Furthermore it seems that unauthorized missionaries from Earth have actually triggered this change and that it has taken place during the time that Sutty was traveling to the planet to study its ancient culture and add that information to the Ekumen's accumulation of such knowledge. When she arrives, her task has become impossible because the culture that she came to study is forbidden, and she finds herself living in another version of the nightmare of her childhood.

In a plot that echoes *The Left Hand of Darkness*, Sutty journeys to cold and distant places, gradually entering forbidden territory, where she arrives at an understanding of a religious culture that emphasizes balance, mutuality, and egalitarian values. At the same time, she comes to believe that she can contribute in several ways to restoring balance to life on Aka and preserving the deep cultural wisdom of its ancient culture.

ALWAYS COMING HOME

First published: 1985
Type of work: Novel

Living a future that may not exist, a woman recounts events from her past.

Always Coming Home is a multimedia novel, including with the text a tape of songs and poetry from the novel's world. Set in Northern California, this novel recounts the history of several peoples in the distant future. In *Buffalo Gals and Other Animal Presences* (1987), Le Guin explains how writing "May's Lion," a story in that collection, helped her to find a way from the Napa Valley of her childhood to the imaginary future of the Na Valley in *Always Coming Home*.

Le Guin writes in her introduction to the novel that these peoples may not exist and that their future might not take place. The people are, however, present in the book, if not in the real world. She discusses the difficulty of translating this story from the language of the Kesh, comparing her novel to Laozi's *Dao De Jing*—a book translated into Chinese "at every cycle of Cathay, though it is not available in the original and was written by someone who may not have existed."

The Kesh have a peaceful, matrilineal society. Their opposites are the aggressive, patrilineal Condors. The history of these peoples is told by Stone

Telling, a Kesh woman whose mother was a Kesh but whose father was a Condor. Stone Telling has different names, depending on her stage in life: North Owl, Ayatyu, and Woman Coming Home.

Le Guin's message is that Western civilization's paternalistic aggressiveness needs to be tamed by taking a more maternalistic approach to social structure. Without peace, there may be no future. Her title, *Always Coming Home*, reflects one of her Taoist themes—to go is to return. All Stone Telling's journeys lead to her return home.

Always Coming Home was viewed by feminist reviewers as a statement that Le Guin had moved toward more woman-centered writing. Here and in *Tehanu* and most of her work after 1985, Le Guin emphasizes a feminine point of view, but she shows little interest in excluding men or masculine viewpoints from her fiction. As always, she emphasizes balance, cooperation, and mutuality as key values for cultural health and individual happiness.

TEHANU

First published: 1990
Type of work: Novel

A widow's quiet life changes as she cares for two deeply wounded people and discovers a new feminine power in her male-dominated world.

Tehanu: The Last Book of Earthsea, the fourth book of Le Guin's Earthsea series, takes up the story of the Earthsea characters after Ged/Sparrowhawk, the protagonist in two of the first three books, has nearly died, struggling with an evil wizard, who attempted to achieve immortality by breaking down the barrier between the worlds of the living and the dead. *Tehanu* deals with dark themes of child molestation and abuse and death. The book can be seen as a feminist coming-of-age novel, as the main female characters both discover more fully who they are.

Tenar, the main character, first appeared as the protagonist of *The Tombs of Atuan*, where she was rescued from a destructive religious cult and brought to the island of Gont by Ged, who has become the most accomplished wizard in the world of Earthsea. There she has lived a rich and mainly

happy life as a farmer's wife. Now widowed and using her Gontish name, Goha, she is called to assist in the treatment of a badly burned and sexually abused young girl, whom she adopts and names Therru. Later called to see the dying Ogion, Ged's first teacher and their mutual friend, she learns that there is a powerful and dangerous presence in Therru. Another emergency then takes up her attention, the dramatic return of Ged. The dragon, Kalessin, brings him home to Gont, broken in body and having lost his vast magical powers. She and Therru undertake his care, nursing him back to health.

As Tenar gradually adjusts to the idea of Ged having lost his magical power, she begins to learn about a kind of magic that has been suppressed in Earthsea, the kind of magic that belongs to the feminine side of humanity. This leads to a startling discovery of great power in Therru, and the beginning of a restoration of balance and order in their world.

SUMMARY

Ursula K. Le Guin's best writings, notably *The Left Hand of Darkness*, *The Dispossessed*, and the Earthsea books, have become widely accepted modern classics, and Le Guin's work is known by readers who, otherwise, read little fantasy or science fiction. Widely studied in high schools as well colleges and universities, her books are regularly the subject of doctoral dissertations. *The Lathe of Heaven* (1971) has been adapted to film twice, in 1979 and 2001. The first three books of the Earthsea series were adapted to film in 2005. Literary critic Harold Bloom says that her work is among the best by modern writers: "Le Guin is the overwhelming contemporary instance of a superbly imaginative creator and major stylist who chose . . . 'fantasy and science fiction.'"

Jo-Ellen Lipman Boon; updated by Terry Heller

BIBLIOGRAPHY

By the Author

LONG FICTION:
Rocannon's World, 1966
Planet of Exile, 1966
City of Illusions, 1967
A Wizard of Earthsea, 1968
The Left Hand of Darkness, 1969
The Tombs of Atuan, 1971
The Lathe of Heaven, 1971
The Farthest Shore, 1972
The Word for World Is Forest, 1972
The Dispossessed: An Ambiguous Utopia, 1974
Very Far Away from Anywhere Else, 1976
The Eye of the Heron, 1978
Malafrena, 1979
The Beginning Place, 1980
Always Coming Home, 1985
Tehanu: The Last Book of Earthsea, 1990
Searoad: Chronicles of Klatsand, 1991
Four Ways to Forgiveness, 1995 (four linked novellas)
The Telling, 2000
The Other Wind, 2001
Gifts, 2004
Voices, 2006

SHORT FICTION:
The Wind's Twelve Quarters, 1975
Orsinian Tales, 1976
The Water Is Wide, 1976
Gwilan's Harp, 1981
The Compass Rose, 1982
The Visionary: The Life Story of Flicker of the Serpentine, with Wonders Hidden, 1984
Buffalo Gals and Other Animal Presences, 1987
Fish Soup, 1992
A Fisherman of the Inland Sea: Science Fiction Stories, 1994
Unlocking the Air, and Other Stories, 1996
Tales from Earthsea, 2001
The Birthday of the World, and Other Stories, 2002
Changing Planes, 2003

POETRY:
Wild Angels, 1975
Hard Words, and Other Poems, 1981

DISCUSSION TOPICS

• In what ways would your life change if everyone became like the Gethenians in *The Left Hand of Darkness*, both sexes at the same time?

• In several of her novels, Ursula K. Le Guin opposes a forward-looking, ambitious, and progressive culture against a quieter, present-centered, and slow-changing culture. If this opposition appears in the story you are studying, which group or groups come closest to representing each side? What are the advantages and disadvantages offered by each side? In which would you prefer to live? Which do you think that Le Guin herself prefers?

• Often in Le Guin's works, the main characters have to change in important ways in order to solve a central problem or overcome a key obstacle. Does this happen in the text you are studying? What is the main change that the character has to make? What makes this change hard to achieve?

• The first three of the Earthsea books tell stories of quests in which the protagonist seeks knowledge and power. What does the protagonist want in the story that you are studying? Explain how this quest ends.

• In the later Earthsea stories, protagonists seem mainly to search for self-knowledge. What does a main character in the story that you are studying learn about himself or herself during the story? Why is this self-knowledge important to this character and to the outcome of the story?

Ursula K. Le Guin

In the Red Zone, 1983
Wild Oats and Fireweed: New Poems, 1988
Blue Moon over Thurman Street, 1993
Going Out with Peacocks, and Other Poems, 1994
Sixty Odd: New Poems, 1999
Incredible Good Fortune: New Poems, 2006

NONFICTION:
From Elfland to Poughkeepsie, 1973
The Language of the Night: Essays on Fantasy and Science Fiction, 1979 (Susan Wood, editor)
Dancing at the Edge of the World: Thoughts on Words, Women, and Places, 1988
Napa: The Roots and Springs of the Valley, 1989
The Way of the Water's Going: Images of the Northern California Coastal Range, 1989 (text by Ursula K. Le Guin; photographs by Ernest Waugh and Alan Nicholson)
Steering the Craft: Exercises and Discussions on Story Writing for the Lone Navigator or the Mutinous Crew, 1998
The Wave in the Mind: Talks and Essays on the Writer, the Reader, and the Imagination, 2004

CHILDREN'S LITERATURE:
Leese Webster, 1979
The Adventure of Cobbler's Rune, 1982
The Visionary, 1984
Solomon Leviathan's 931st Trip Around the World, 1988
A Visit from Dr. Katz, 1988
Catwings, 1988
Catwings Return, 1989
Fire and Stone, 1989
A Ride on the Red Mare's Back, 1992
More Tales of the Catwings, 1994
Wonderful Alexander and the Catwings, 1994
Tales of the Catwings, 1996
Tom Mouse, 1998
Tom Mouse and Ms. Howe, 1998
Jane on Her Own: A Catwings Tale, 1999

TRANSLATIONS:
Tao Te Ching: A Book About the Way and the Power of the Way, 1997 (by Laozi)
The Twins, the Dream/Las Gemelas, el sueño, 1996 (with Diana Bellessi)
Selected Poems of Gabriela Mistral, 2003
Kalpa Imperial: The Greatest Empire That Never Was, 2003 (by Angélica Gorodischer)

EDITED TEXT:
Norton Book of Science Fiction: North American Science Fiction, 1960-1990, 1993
Selected Stories of H. G. Wells, 2005

About the Author

Bittner, James W. *Approaches to the Fiction of Ursula K. Le Guin.* Ann Arbor: University of Michigan Research Press, 1984.
Bloom, Harold, ed. *Modern Critical Views: Ursula K. Le Guin.* New York: Chelsea House, 1986.
Cadden, Michael. *Ursula K. Le Guin Beyond Genre: Fiction for Children and Adults.* New York: Routledge, 2005.

Davis, Laurence, and Peter G. Stillman. *The New Utopian Politics of Ursula K. Le Guin's "The Dispossessed."* Lanham, Md.: Lexington Books, 2005.

Reid, Suzanne Elizabeth. *Presenting Ursula K. Le Guin.* New York: Twayne, 1997.

Rochelle, Warren. *Communities of the Heart: The Rhetoric of Myth in the Fiction of Ursula K. Le Guin.* Liverpool, England: Liverpool University Press, 2001.

Spivack, Charlotte. *Ursula K. Le Guin.* Boston: Twayne, 1984.

Ursula K. Le Guin's Web Site. www.ursulakleguin.com/UKL_info.html

Wayne, Kathryn Ross. *Redefining Moral Education: Life, Le Guin, and Language.* San Francisco: Austin & Winfield, 1996.

White, Donna R. *Dancing with Dragons: Ursula K. Le Guin and the Critics.* Columbia, S.C.: Camden House, 1999.

Madeleine L'Engle

Born: New York, New York
November 29, 1918

L'Engle has written in various genres but is best known for her Time Fantasy series of children's books, particularly A Wrinkle in Time *(1962).*

BIOGRAPHY

Madeleine L'Engle Camp was born in New York City on November 29, 1918. Her mother, Madeleine Barnett Camp, was a pianist who, although talented, chose not to become a concert pianist and to stay at home with her family. L'Engle's father, Charles Wadsworth Camp, was a foreign correspondent whose lungs were damaged by exposure to poison mustard gas during World War I. L'Engle had a younger brother who died as an infant. Her subsequent childhood was somewhat secluded from other children, as she spent much of her time writing short stories, poems, and journals rather than concentrating on her schoolwork.

As her father's condition worsened, her family decided to move to Europe, where the air would be easier on her father's lungs and he would be less susceptible to diseases such as pneumonia. In 1930, at twelve years of age, L'Engle relocated across the Atlantic Ocean to Switzerland, where her family rented a chateau and she entered a Swiss boarding school.

However, at age fourteen, because of her parents' declining health, L'Engle was sent back to the United States to attend high school in Florida and live with her grandmother. She did not adapt to life in Florida schools and was sent to a girls' boarding school in Charleston, South Carolina, to finish her high school diploma. Once at the boarding school she acted in plays and worked for the school's liter-

ary magazine as a writer and editor. As she was finishing her final year at school, her father passed away.

In 1941, L'Engle graduated from Smith College in Northampton, Massachusetts, where she received her B.A. in English and continued her own creative writing. After graduation, instead of returning to the South, where her family lived, she moved to New York City and shared an apartment in Greenwich Village with two aspiring actresses. She attended the New School for Social Research in New York City from 1941 to 1942. Through luck and perseverance she acquired a job working in theater in 1941 and spent the subsequent seven years living on her union pay and writing in her spare time. Her first novel, *The Small Rain*, was published in 1945.

While working in the theater she met her husband-to-be, actor Hugh Franklin, in a performance of Anton Chekhov's *The Cherry Orchard*. She later married him in 1946 and became Madeleine L'Engle Franklin; however, she retained the pen name Madeleine L'Engle throughout her writing career. In 1952, her husband retired from theater, and the family took their small daughter Josephine and moved to a farmhouse, which they named Crosswicks, in the rural town of Goshen, Connecticut. In order to survive they acquired an old general store and brought it back to life. The family lived here for about ten years with their daughter Josephine, son Bion, and adopted daughter Maria.

The family moved back to New York City in the early 1960's, as Hugh Franklin decided to revitalize his acting career and L'Engle took on a six-year teaching period at two Anglican private schools in the city. Crosswicks in Goshen remained the family's summer home and is still in family ownership.

After twenty rejections by publishers, *A Wrinkle in Time*, L'Engle's most renowned science-fiction and fantasy novel for young readers, was published by Farrar, Straus and Giroux in 1962. It won the Newbery Medal and was runner-up for the Hans Christian Andersen Award. This long-awaited success began a string of well-received novels for young adults and became the first in her popular Time Trilogy, which also includes *A Wind in the Door* (1973) and *A Swiftly Tilting Planet* (1978). L'Engle revisited the Time Trilogy with a fourth book titled *Many Waters* in 1986, thus creating the Time Quartet. Together with *A House Like a Lotus* (1984) and *An Acceptable Time* (1989), they are called the Time Fantasy series. She won subsequent awards for her science fiction and fantasy, including the American Book Award for Best Children's Paperback in 1980 and the Newbery Honor Award in 1981 for *A Swiftly Tilting Planet*.

L'Engle has written in various genres, including adult fiction and nonfiction, drama, poetry, and theology, and she continued this style of crossover writing in later works. *A Wrinkle in Time* is by far her most famous book and the Time Quartet her most widely read series; however, she has won substantial awards for her other novels. Her poetry volume *The Weather of the Heart* (1978) won the National Religious Book Award in 1979, and her picture book *Ladder of Angels* (1979) won this same award in 1980. L'Engle has also written semiautobiographical works inspired by life experience, such as her book *Two Part Invention: The Story of a Marriage* (1988), which recounts her forty-year marriage to Franklin and his battle with the cancer that killed him in 1987.

L'Engle's recent works include the collection of poetry *The Ordering of Love: The New and Collected Poems of Madeleine L'Engle*, which was published in 2005, and a compilation of her tour speeches, writings, and thoughts, compiled by Carole Chase and titled *Madeleine L'Engle Herself: Reflections on a Writing Life* (2001). Despite her age, L'Engle continues to live in her West End Avenue apartment in New York City and continues to write and work as a librarian with the Cathedral Church of St. John the Divine.

ANALYSIS

While L'Engle's works have been defined as Christian science fiction and fantasy, she resists this label. The books of the Time Quartet do lend themselves to a religious aspect, in that L'Engle presents an incarnation of evil and sets it in opposition with the powers of good represented in the power of love and selflessness. She considers herself religious and close to God, and a fair amount of her recognition and interviews appear in Christian publications. She attends an Episcopal church in New York and is affiliated with the Cathedral of St. John the Divine, where she serves as writer-in-residence.

L'Engle feels herself very connected to a God of love and was greatly influenced as a child by her reading of George Macdonald's books in which he tells the story of being excommunicated from his church because he refused to believe that two-thirds of the world's peoples (those who are not practicing Christians) were not worthy of a heavenly afterlife. She commented in an interview that she was very inspired by Macdonald's theology of love. The manifestation of religious belief in her Time Quartet lies in the fact that what triumphs in these novels over the incarnation of evil is the power of love, which each character discovers.

The series trilogy of time travel-centered novels for young adults has been criticized, however, by fundamental Christian groups as defying the text of the Bible in its portrayals. For example, *A Wrinkle in Time* is often criticized for portraying the three female guides as witches and the brain which stands for the evil that takes over Charles Wallace as Satan. Each of the trilogy's novels uses some element of the supernatural, such as a unicorn or unconventional cherubim, to aid the child characters in their quest against the forces of evil. L'Engle allows her imagination to wander and create a world of possibilities which she does not consider contradictory to a belief in God, because she asserts that belief in God does not require facts.

What these unconventional novels did was take two ideas, science fiction and religion, and link them as they had never been linked before. L'Engle says that science fiction takes a scientific idea and poses the question, "What if . . . ?" It is this type of speculation that stirs the imagination of the young reader. Also, by setting up a dichotomy between good as embodied in the child characters and their guides and evil as embodied in those who aim to destroy and thwart the children, L'Engle enters the realm of religion because the power these children possess is the power of belief and love, which L'Engle posits as essential to Christianity and true knowledge of God.

This dichotomy of good, the children and their quest, versus evil, the force which destroys all things, gives way to two major themes which dominate this series. The first is the search for identity, or self-discovery (the eternal questions of "Who am I?" and "Why am I here?"), and the second is the power of love, communication, and selflessness over hate, division, and greed.

The discovery of self which each character undergoes and develops in the series is aided and supported by the characters who serve as guides and partners to the children in their quests. This discovery leads the children to the mastery and recognition of the second theme, the power of love and faith or belief. When the children are impatient, prideful, and controlled by fear, they begin to lose to evil, but when they let go and follow their guides and their compulsions, opening themselves up to each other and acting out of love, they are victorious and able to conquer the evil that threatens them and their loved ones.

The science-fiction devices which L'Engle uses to create the foundation of the novels' plots include the presence of supernatural beings with superhuman powers, the ability to kythe (communicate with a being through thoughts only), and the ability to tesser (travel back and forth in time and place). These devices recur in each of the quartet's novels. The characters' abilities to use and accept them correspond to their success and their discovery of their true valuable and loving self.

A WRINKLE IN TIME

First published: 1962
Type of work: Novel

Meg, Charles Wallace, and Calvin travel (tesser) through time, with the help of three guides, to find their father, who got lost experimenting with time travel.

A Wrinkle in Time was L'Engle's third novel to be published. The novel opens with Meg Murray, a

girl just entering high school, the middle child and only daughter, going downstairs in a storm to find her little brother, Charles Wallace, waiting for her. The reference is made to the ability of Charles Wallace to know her thoughts, which readers later discover is the ability to kythe, or communicate thought from mind to mind without speaking. This is the first indication of the special abilities Charles Wallace possesses and develops throughout the trilogy.

During this storm, the children's first guide appears at the Murrays' door dressed as an old homeless woman might and calling herself Mrs. Whatsit. She informs the family that the tesseract is real. The tesseract is the physics formula explaining time travel which Mr. Murray was exploring at the time of his disappearance.

When Meg and Charles Wallace later go to visit Mrs. Whatsit, they encounter Calvin, a fellow student with Meg, who tells them he also followed a compulsion that led him to come to Mrs. Whatsit's house at the same time. They enter the house, where they meet for the first time their other guide, Mrs. Who. She tells the kids to leave and that she and her cohorts will fetch them when the time comes.

Meg spends the next few chapters attempting to come to grips with herself and her unhappy situation at school, in which her teachers think she is not intelligent and she is not doing well. She also struggles with her own security because she compares her plainness to the beauty of her mother and other peers. She encompasses the common insecurities of the adolescent girl. However, she is aware that Charles Wallace is special and that she has a special connection to him.

Then, on a walk in the garden, they encounter the two guides and a new one, who appears only as an ephemeral shape of a person, Mrs. Which. The guides proceed to attempt to explain tessering (or time travel), and they take the children to a pleasing planet from which they come and teach them about the evil forces they refer to as the Black Thing, which is a sort of cloud covering many planets. At this point in the novel the dichotomy sets the evil as a cloud that surrounds a planet and thus infiltrates the minds of its people, dictating their actions. The planet they see, they are informed, is the planet on which their father is located. Thus the quest is developed.

The three guides give each child a gift and send them tessering to the planet. The discovery begins for the three children as they attempt to understand the odd planet, where everyone acts, speaks, and dresses alike. Guided by the impulse of Charles Wallace, they children enter the CENTRAL Central Intelligence Agency.

Charles Wallace believes that he can gain the information from the being by agreeing to go into his thoughts, which results in Charles Wallace becoming controlled because of his pride in his kything abilities. Thus, they have failed their first test, and Charles Wallace's overconfidence in his own power of intelligence causes him to be lost to the evil. He then leads the other two children to the controlling being and their father. The being controlling Charles Wallace shows them the chamber where their father is kept, and Meg, after much struggle and thinking, realizes that she has her gift from the three guides, a pair of glasses that, when she puts them on, allows her to enter the chamber with her father. Then her father puts on the glasses and carries her in his arms through the wall of the chamber.

At this point, Charles Wallace leads the three of them to It, the supreme controlling evil embodied in the live brain. They fight with It, communicating through Charles Wallace with their thoughts and words. At this point in the novel, Meg loses faith in herself and their ability to save Charles Wallace from the control of It: She had put all of her faith in her father saving them, but he was as powerless as she felt. As they converse with It, the powerful rhythmic brain begins to take over their thoughts and overpower them. Then Calvin yells to Meg's father to tesser (time travel) as he had before, and they narrowly escape It to a planet nearby, outside the Black Thing's cloud.

Meg is nearly killed by the force of evil that almost took her, and she must be nursed back to health by creatures of this planet. Despite her fear, the three guides and the beings of this foreign

planet help her to realize that she is the only one who can save Charles Wallace: She knows him better than anyone, and they have a special kything connection. As she leaves with Mrs. Which to tesser back to the planet, for the first time she recognizes her love for a foreign being that saved her. Thus begins her discovery of the power of love, because she felt without analyzing her gratitude or qualifying it. Also, she is communicated love by Calvin, who kisses her for the first time before she leaves, Mrs. Whatsit tells Meg that she loves her and to remember that fact, and Mrs. Who leaves her a biblical quote to aid her. Meg is strengthened by this love as she returns to the planet.

Meg she meets up with It again in the same chamber. She tries to discover what she has that It does not, and, as she pieces her thoughts together, she realizes what she has is love—everyone's love behind her and her ability to love. She thinks about her love for Charles Wallace and then begins to shout that she loves him. A moment later, he comes running toward her and is in her arms, and she is back at home.

Meg is forced to discover that the true power she possesses is intangible and greater than intellect. The power of love evident in her allows her to conquer the evil that wanted to control her with hate. Her belief in Charles Wallace's love and her selfless behavior and courage saved both her father and Charles Wallace.

A WIND IN THE DOOR

First published: 1973
Type of work: Novel

With the help of their teacher Blajeny and their partners, a cherubim and a farandola, Meg and Calvin must pass three tests and save her brother Charles Wallace from dying.

A Wind in the Door takes the children of the Time Quartet even further into the science-fiction and fantasy world of the tesseract as they eventually travel time and space to enter the mitochondria of Charles Wallace's cells, as tiny as the farandola that they are accompanying.

The novel opens with the discovery that Charles

Wallace is ill and weakening. This illness, readers discover later in the novel, is caused by evil forces of the Echthroi, who are eliminating stars in the universe and creating a rip in the galaxy. The forces of the Echthroi are also affecting Charles Wallace's mitochondria by encouraging his fanadolae not to follow their course and take root and grow strong. Therefore, he is weakening and dying from lack of oxygen.

He leads Meg to make the discovery of the cherubim, Progo, a supernatural creature with many wings and many eyes who looks nothing like the human idea of a cherubim. He will be part of her class, and the teacher Blajeny will instruct them in their three tests. Calvin is also part of this class and will be alongside Meg again to communicate his love and confidence to empower her. With the cherubim, she must pass the first test: identify the real principal Mr. Jenkins, whom she dislikes, out of three other imposters. She struggles and eventually is able to choose the real Mr. Jenkins by thinking of something lovable about him and using that against the others.

The reoccurrence of the guide, as seen in Progo, follows the theme of the series, which presents the children with a quest and supernatural obstacles to overcome. However, it differs a bit in *A Wind in the Door* as Progo is also learning and must pass these tests with the children, or he will cease to exist. The group must tesser not only in time but also in space, as they shrink in size to that of a farandola and enter Charles Wallace's body. Once they learn to breathe and kythe as the farandolae do, their second test requires them to convince the farandole Sporos to deepen and grow roots in the mitochondria and become a fara in order to save Charles Wallace by fixing his mitochondria. The group, including the real Mr. Jenkins, Progo, Calvin, and Meg, attempt to kythe to Sporos, without luck. Meg is saved by Mr. Jenkins when she is pulled into the Echthroi. Their final test is to save Mr. Jenkins, as he is pulled into the Echthroi for Meg's sake. She must then kythe to him and fill the emptiness created by the evil with her love for him, for Calvin, and for Charles Wallace.

She succeeds by forcing all of her power of love into the Echthroi and naming it herself, giving it a meaning. As she does this, she is returned to Charles Wallace, along with Mr. Jenkins and Calvin.

Her power of love again allows her to place herself between the powers of evil and those whom she must save. L'Engle gives readers another dichotomy of supernatural ability paired with the ultimate power that is love and the discovery that she can love strongly and deeply even those whom she believed she could not love.

A Swiftly Tilting Planet

First published: 1978
Type of work: Novel

Charles Wallace is give a run by Mrs. O'Keefe and a calling to find a way to save the world from nuclear war.

A Swiftly Tilting Planet presents Charles Wallace with a quest to save the world from Maddog Branzillo, who would start nuclear war. He is given only an ancient rune as clue by a mysterious Mrs. O'Keefe. Charles Wallace goes out to the star-watching rock to contemplate and, after saying the rune, is greeted by Gaudior, a unicorn who takes him back and forth through time on the wind as he attempts to discover what in history caused the nuclear threat to appear in the present.

L'Engle explores the idea of the butterfly effect—the idea that one decision or flap of a butterfly's wing can affect the present or the future—in this final novel of the original trilogy. She gives Charles Wallace the ability to go within people as he travels and to live through their eyes, hopefully changing for the better the outcome of his present. Charles Wallace's mission is to find the might-have-been whom he can change, therefore preventing the present threat from ever having happened.

Meg is married and pregnant with Calvin's baby, and her function in this novel is to support Charles Wallace and kythe with him her love and the information that she finds out about the history he is experiencing. The plot moves between her experiences of what he sees and his conversations with Gaudior.

This novel allows Charles Wallace to develop his talents and to learn patience and love for all the characters from history whom he inhabits. By letting go and being them, he is taken to the right place and is able to change the course of history, with Meg's support and love to back him. The power of love is present here in two aspects: the love that Meg gives Charles Wallace, which sustains him, and the love that Charles Wallace develops for the people he embodies. This selfless love is what allows him to make the right decision at the right time when he is in the body of the correct person. This supernatural out-of-body experience is the most extreme form of science fiction and fantasy in the series, yet it allows Charles Wallace to understand and love Mrs. O'Keefe, the bitter old mother-in-law of Meg who renounced love years ago and rediscovers it through Charles Wallace.

SUMMARY

In the series of books referred to as the Time Quartet, L'Engle skillfully blends themes of adolescent discovery of self with religious questions of the incarnation and battle of good versus evil to create a fiction with which young readers can identify and through which they are forced to stretch their imaginations.

John L. Grigsby

DISCUSSION TOPICS

- In what ways does Madeleine L'Engle's Time Trilogy support or challenge traditional Christianity?

- How does this trilogy allow Charles Wallace and Meg to realize their weaknesses and to develop their strengths?

- How does L'Engle's trilogy illustrate her vivid imagination and her religious beliefs on good verses evil?

- How are the guides in this trilogy (unicorn, cherubim, three women) like and unlike the traditional idea of guardian angels?

- How is the butterfly effect demonstrated in *A Swiftly Tilting Planet?*

- What is the most powerful force for good in L'Engle's trilogy?

BIBLIOGRAPHY

By the Author

CHILDREN'S LITERATURE:
And Both Were Young, 1949
Meet the Austins, 1960 (part of the Austin Family series)
A Wrinkle in Time, 1962 (part of the Time Fantasy series)
The Moon by Night, 1963 (part of the Austin Family series)
The Twenty-four Days Before Christmas: An Austin Family Story, 1964 (part of the Austin Family series)
Camilla, 1965
The Arm of the Starfish, 1965 (part of the Cannon Tallis Mystery series)
Prelude, 1968 (adaptation of her novel *The Small Rain*)
The Young Unicorns, 1968 (part of the Cannon Tallis Mystery series)
Intergalactic P.S.3, 1970
A Wind in the Door, 1973 (part of the Time Fantasy series)
Dragons in the Waters, 1976 (part of the Cannon Tallis Mystery series)
A Swiftly Tilting Planet, 1978 (part of the Time Fantasy series)
Ladder of Angels, 1979 (picture book)
A Ring of Endless Light, 1980 (part of the Austin Family series)
The Anti-Muffins, 1981 (part of the Austin Family series)
The Sphynx at Dawn, 1982
A House Like a Lotus, 1984 (part of the Time Fantasy series)
Many Waters, 1986 (part of the Time Fantasy series)

An Acceptable Time, 1989 (part of the Time Fantasy series)
Troubling a Star, 1994 (part of the Austin Family series)
Wintersong: Christmas Readings, 1996 (with Luci Shaw)
Miracle on Tenth Street, and Other Christmas Writings, 1998
A Full House: An Austin Family Christmas, 1999 (short story)
The Other Dog, 2001

LONG FICTION:
The Small Rain, 1945
Ilsa, 1946
Camilla Dickinson, 1951
A Winter's Love, 1957
The Love Letters, 1966
The Other Side of the Sun, 1971
A Severed Wasp, 1982 (sequel to *The Small Rain*)
Certain Women, 1992
A Live Coal in the Sea, 1996

POETRY:
The Weather of the Heart, 1978
The Ordering of Love: The New and Collected Poems of Madeleine L'Engle, 2005

NONFICTION:
A Circle of Quiet, 1972 (autobiography; part of *Crosswicks Journals*)
The Summer of the Great-Grandmother, 1974 (autobiography; part of *Crosswicks Journals*)
The Irrational Season, 1977 (autobiography; part of *Crosswicks Journals*)
And It Was Good: Reflections on Beginnings, 1983
Dare to Be Creative, 1984
Trailing Clouds of Glory: Spiritual Values in Children's Books, 1985 (with Avery Brooke)
A Stone for a Pillow: Journeys with Jacob, 1986
Two Part Invention: The Story of a Marriage, 1988 (autobiography; part of *Crosswicks Journals*)
Sold into Egypt: Joseph's Journey into Human Being, 1989
The Rock That Is Higher: Story as Truth, 1993
Glimpses of Grace: Daily Thoughts and Reflections, 1996
Penguins and Golden Calves: Icons and Idols, 1996
Bright Evening Star: Mystery of the Incarnation, 1997
Friends for the Journey: Two Extraordinary Women Celebrate Friendship Made and Sustained Through the Seasons of Life, 1997 (with Luci Shaw)
A Prayerbook for Spiritual Friends: Partners in Prayer, 1999 (with Shaw)
Madeleine L'Engle Herself: Reflections on a Writing Life, 2001 (with Carole Chase)

EDITED TEXT:
Spirit and Light: Essays in Historical Theology, 1976 (with William B. Green)

About the Author

Bloom, Harold, ed. *Women Writers of Children's Literature*. Philadelphia: Chelsea House, 1998.

Chase, Carole F. *Suncatcher: A Study of Madeleine L'Engle and Her Writing*. Philadelphia: Innisfree Press, 1998.

Hein, Rolland. *Christian Mythmakers: C. S. Lewis, Madeleine L'Engle, J. R. Tolkien, George MacDonald, G. K. Chesterton, Charles Williams, Dante Alighieri, John Bunyan, Walter Wangerin, Robert Siegel, and Hannah Hurnard*. Chicago: Cornerstone Press, 2002.

Hettinga, Donald R. *Presenting Madeleine L'Engle*. New York: Twayne, 1993.

Shaw, Luci, ed. *The Swiftly Tilting Worlds of Madeleine L'Engle*. Wheaton, Ill.: Harold Shaw, 1998.

© Linda Solomon

ELMORE LEONARD

Born: New Orleans, Louisiana
October 11, 1925

Generally acknowledged to be the most accomplished writer working in the genre of the realistic crime novel, Leonard has also earned recognition as an important literary artist.

BIOGRAPHY

Elmore John Leonard, Jr., was born in New Orleans on October 11, 1925, to Elmore John and Flora Rivé Leonard. His father traveled widely for his job, and the family moved several times before finally settling in Detroit in 1934. Leonard attended the University of Detroit High School, where he earned the nickname "Dutch" as a baseball player (after the Washington Senators pitcher Dutch Leonard). After being rejected by the Marines for his poor vision, he was drafted by the Navy in 1943 and served with the Seabees in New Guinea and the Admiralty Islands. After World War II, he enrolled at the University of Michigan, where he majored in English and philosophy. He married Beverly Cline in 1949, graduated in 1950, and took a job with an advertising agency that same year, first as an office boy and then as an advertising copywriter, specializing in advertisements for Chevrolet trucks.

Leonard had always loved literature, and he began to train himself to be a writer, deciding to begin with Westerns because he enjoyed reading them and believed there was a ready popular market for the genre. He studied Western films, travel maga-

zines, and histories and also the novels of Ernest Hemingway, upon whom he began to model his writing style. He published his first story, "Trail of the Apache," for which he was paid a thousand dollars, in the December, 1951, issue of *Argosy*. Within little more than a year, he had published nine more stories and his first novel, *The Bounty Hunters* (1953). He kept his full-time job during these early years, doing his writing from 5:00 to 7:00 A.M. every morning before work.

By 1961, Leonard had published more than two dozen short stories and four more novels, all Westerns—*The Law at Randado* (1954), *Escape from Five Shadows* (1956), *Last Stand at Saber River* (1959), and *Hombre* (1961)—and decided to quit his job and become a full-time writer, although he and his wife by then had four children. Ironically, the market for Western writing seemed to have dried up at just that moment; Leonard failed to publish another novel in the following eight years, and he was forced to earn a living as a freelance writer of advertisements and educational films. In 1965, he sold the film rights to *Hombre* for ten thousand dollars and was again able to devote himself to writing fiction full time.

The resulting novel was completed in 1966 and was rejected by eighty-four publishers within three months. After revision, Leonard finally published his first non-Western novel, *The Big Bounce*, in 1969. It was made into a film that same year, and most of his novels since have been sold to Hollywood. Leonard then began writing screenplays himself, selling a screenplay of his next novel, *The Moonshine War* (1969). He also produced two more Westerns, *Valdez Is Coming* (1970) and *Forty Lashes Less One* (1972).

A turning point in his career came with *Fifty-two Pickup* (1974), the novel that firmly established his direction as a writer of contemporary crime fiction. His personal life took a turn as well; his marriage broke up after twenty-five years, and he joined Alcoholics Anonymous. In 1977, he managed to quit drinking, and in 1979 he married his second wife, Joan Shepard. As his personal life recovered, so did his literary fortunes improve, and in the mid-1970's he rapidly produced a series of novels in which he began to define his own distinctive approach to crime fiction: *Mr. Majestyk* (1974), a novel based on one of his own screenplays; *Swag* (1976); *The Hunted* (1977); and *Unknown Man No. 89* (1977). All of these works appear regularly on lists of Leonard's best books and constitute a distinct middle period of high-quality output. *The Switch* (1978); his eighth Western, *Gunsights* (1979); and *Gold Coast* (1980), the first of his novels set in Florida, are generally considered to represent a brief decline in his writing during a period of transition that was to lead to his best work.

Leonard's novels had always been notable for their realism, and in 1978 he spent two-and-a-half months observing Detroit police at work in order to research a magazine article. He also hired two research assistants (college friend and private investigator Bill Marshall, who began researching Leonard's Florida novels in 1977, and then Gregg Sutter, beginning in 1981), helping him to produce the more fully developed and detailed worlds that characterize the work of Leonard's latest—and strongest—period, beginning with *City Primeval: High Noon in Detroit* (1980) and continuing through *Split Images* (1981), *Cat Chaser* (1982), *LaBrava* (1983), and *Stick* (1983). Critical recognition finally came with these novels, and *LaBrava* earned the Edgar Allan Poe Award from the Mystery Writers of America as the best novel of the year. Leonard's next novel, *Glitz* (1985), was his first to reach *The New York Times* best-seller list, and similar national success followed for all of his subsequent books.

Despite its mixed critical reviews, *Get Shorty* (1990) turned out to be the breakthrough commercial success that had long eluded Leonard, thanks to a 1995 film adaptation starring John Travolta that opened at number one in U.S. box office its first week. High-profile directors quickly became interested in Leonard's work: Quentin Tarantino directed *Rum Punch* (1992), retitled *Jackie Brown*, in 1997, and Steven Soderbergh directed a film version of *Out of Sight* (1996) in 1998; the latter was only a moderate commercial success but won the Best Film award from the National Society of Film Critics. *Get Shorty* was so popular as both book and film that Leonard followed it with a sequel, *Be Cool* (1999), with the same protagonist; it was made into a film version in 2004 with Travolta reprising his role as Chili Palmer. *Maximum Bob* (1991) even had a short-lived run as a television comedy series in 1998.

Leonard's high visibility in Hollywood was accompanied by increasing academic recognition, with the awarding of an honorary doctorate of humane letters from the University of Detroit in 1997 and a volume of the well-respected Twayne United States Authors Series devoted to him in 1999. In addition to writing contemporary crime thrillers, Leonard has occasionally returned to the interest in historical fiction that produced his early Westerns: *Cuba Libre* (1998) is set during the Spanish-American War, and *The Hot Kid* (2005) is set in Oklahoma during the 1930's. Leonard lives in Detroit with his third wife, Christine Kent, and continues to produce roughly a book a year.

ANALYSIS

The oddity of Leonard's finally being "discovered" by critics and a wide reading public with *Glitz*, his twenty-third novel, has attracted puzzled comments from most reviewers and from Leonard himself and probably has no simple explanation. The novel immediately before *Glitz*, *LaBrava*, had sold only twenty thousand copies by the time that *Glitz* had sold two hundred thousand and spent sixteen weeks on the *New York Times* best-seller list, yet there seems to be no clear difference in the style, tone, or quality of the two books.

While careful students of Leonard's work have noted a greater degree of fine detail and texture in his work since the 1980's, the broad similarities between his later books and the best work of the 1970's, beginning with *Fifty-two Pickup*, are far more striking than any minor differences. As the critic Peter Prescott put it, "the margin of difference between Leonard's better and lesser works would admit, with difficulty, a butterfly's wing." Leonard attributes his change of style at the time of *Fifty-two Pickup* to his reading of George V. Higgins's *The Friends of Eddie Coyle* (1972), from which he learned valuable lessons about the use of point of view and dialogue, the handling of which were to become his stylistic trademark.

Part of the explanation for his sudden success with *Glitz* was the publisher's decision to promote the novel more aggressively by spending more money and, perhaps oddly, by saying as little as possible about it in the advertising. Earlier advertising campaigns had made the mistake of comparing Leonard to earlier crime writers who had elevated the genre to the level of serious literature, including Dashiell Hammett, Raymond Chandler, and Ross Macdonald. Readers who expected similar work must have been frequently disappointed, because, apart from the high quality of his work, Leonard has almost nothing in common with these predecessors. In particular, he scrupulously avoided using the sort of colorful metaphors and similes that are typically thought to characterize good writing; as Leonard himself says, "If it sounds like writing, I rewrite it."

The great difference between Leonard's style and that of his forebears may be the best explanation for his long wait for success: Readers needed a long time to get used to his unique approach to crime fiction and to accept it on its own terms. Earlier writers of "hard-boiled" detective fiction had almost universally relied on first-person narratives, related from the point of view of a continuing character who is the protagonist for all the novels in a series. While Hammett, the originator of the hard-boiled genre, switched characters from book to book and sometimes relied on an objective, "camera-eye" point of view, Chandler's Philip Marlowe and Macdonald's Lew Archer always told their own stories through a series of books, establishing a formula followed by innumerable later writers. Leonard, on the other hand, seldom uses a character in more than one or two books.

The reader's expectations about crime novels are further compounded by Leonard's characteristic practice of relying on multiple points of view, perhaps his most distinctive and original stylistic contribution to the field. Rather than having the protagonist tell the reader the story as a consistent first-person narrative, Leonard typically shifts point of view from one character to another. In many of the novels, the reader is not sure until well into the book who the main character will eventually be, because so many characters' viewpoints are

rendered. In *Maximum Bob*, Leonard goes so far as to include a scene written from the point of view of an alligator. Leonard never speaks in his own voice in his later books, delegating all the narrating to one or another of his usually numerous cast of characters. One critic has remarked that "Leonard is a skilled ventriloquist whose own lips never move."

The technique of rapidly shifting points of view seems at first to have more in common with the difficult experimental literature of William Faulkner and Virginia Woolf than with traditional popular fiction, and such an approach could certainly become confusing in the hands of another writer. Leonard, however, always manages to get the reader just the information needed to follow the story. He accomplishes this, in part, through a heavy reliance on dialogue, always couched in each character's individualized mannerisms of speech and presented in short, dramatic scenes. Usually, he ends each scene with a punch line or unexpected twist for closure. He eschews entirely the typical novelist's use of blocks of narrative exposition.

Another interesting effect of the use of multiple points of view is that the reader is privy to the thoughts of virtually every character, hero and villain alike, and therefore quickly knows much more about the story than any one of the characters in the book ever could. The result is that Leonard's novels are not, in fact, mysteries in the traditional sense: the reader knows exactly who has committed every crime, and in fact usually witnesses them from the criminals' viewpoints. Leonard's practice of giving the criminal's point of view equal time creates yet another problem for some readers, who can be disturbed by his ability to render the thoughts and feelings of the most depraved characters accurately and even sympathetically. That this intimate association with evil characters never becomes oppressive for the reader results from Leonard's gift of making a sort of deadpan satire come through the realistic dialogue; few of his characters intend to be funny, but the reader finds humor in unexpected places.

CITY PRIMEVAL: HIGH NOON IN DETROIT

First published: 1980
Type of work: Novel

Homicide detective Raymond Cruz relies on both conventional and unorthodox methods to bring psychotic killer Clement Mansell to justice.

City Primeval is widely regarded as the first book of Leonard's strongest period. As the allusion to the classic 1952 Western film *High Noon* in the subtitle suggests, the novel marks a conscious adaptation of the characters and themes of Leonard's earlier Westerns to the modern urban settings of his later crime novels. The book's protagonist, Detroit homicide detective Raymond Cruz, is a Texan of Mexican descent who thus has the background appropriate to a Western hero. Leonard describes Cruz's relationship with Clement Mansell, the book's villain, in terms of classic Westerns: "No—more like High Noon. Gunfight at the O.K. Corral. You have to go back a hundred years and out west to find an analogy. But there it is." References to Westerns are scattered throughout the book, which opens with a dinner conversation between Cruz and a reporter who accuses him of trying to emulate Wyatt Earp, Clint Eastwood, and John Wayne. It closes, appropriately, with an old-fashioned showdown between Cruz and Mansell.

This frontier imagery is integrated into a thoroughly realistic context that reveals Leonard's recent in-depth study of the daily operations of the Detroit police department. Particularly well-handled are a series of interrogation scenes in which the detectives use subtle techniques of misdirection to gain information from uncooperative suspects, who never realize how much they have given away. As in most of Leonard's novels, the difference between the good and bad characters is not strictly a matter of following or breaking the law; the players on both sides operate very near the border between right and wrong, with their ends differing much more than the means used to achieve them.

Mansell has, in fact, found the legal system to be in some ways his best ally; he has been freed from earlier murder charges on legal technicalities.

Cruz, on the other hand, is forced to work outside the law, tampering with evidence and eventually forcing a confrontation in which he kills Mansell under circumstances that are ethically, and perhaps legally, suspect. As Mansell says to Cruz in the final scene, "Me and you are on different sides, but we're alike in a lot of ways," an observation that typifies the similarity, and even sympathy, that usually exists between antagonist and protagonist in Leonard's work. Mansell's point of view is relied on just as much as that of Cruz or of Sandy Stanton, Mansell's girlfriend, and the reader consequently acquires a degree of familiarity with and understanding of a totally amoral character that is unusual in popular fiction.

GLITZ

First published: 1985
Type of work: Novel

Miami police detective Vincent Mora pursues—and is pursued by—psychopathic killer Teddy Magyk from Puerto Rico to Atlantic City and back.

Glitz was Leonard's first best seller. The book represents an artistic success as well, epitomizing the author's mature style with a complex plot, memorable characters, and crisp dialogue. While most of his earlier crime novels had been set in Detroit, the later novels range more freely, and the action in *Glitz* shifts from Miami to Puerto Rico to Atlantic City, all depicted with his usual meticulous accuracy. Before visiting Atlantic City, Leonard had his research assistant, Gregg Sutter, collect a series of interviews with casino employees and police and take 180 photographs in a sequence that would give Leonard views of the entire town.

Miami police detective Vincent Mora is a typical Leonard protagonist, as Atlantic City casino operator Jackie Garbo describes him: "I said to myself, this guy's got nice easy moves, never pushes, he listens and he learns things." While Leonard's "heroes" are all capable of violent behavior and are as likely to be criminals as lawmen, they prefer a subtle approach to a problem rather than direct confrontation, and they view violence as a last resort. His amoral antagonists, however, invariably consider violent solutions first. The antagonist in *Glitz* is Teddy Magyk, who had been arrested by Mora for first-degree sexual battery several years earlier and now, after seven and a half years in prison, is intent on revenge. He lures Mora to Atlantic City by killing a friend of his there, and Mora, on leave recovering from an injury, works unofficially with the local police to capture Magyk. This unofficial capacity enables him to work outside the rules, as do all Leonard's main characters. The relatively simple main plot is filled out with a number of subplots involving local mobsters and drug dealers who are loosely affiliated with the city's casino industry.

As in all of Leonard's novels, however, the interest of the book lies not in the plot but in the brilliantly drawn characters and tightly crafted individual scenes. Leonard has remarked that "I'm not a good narrative writer. I put all my energies into my characters and let my characters carry it." Typical of his style is a scene in which Nancy Donovan unexpectedly turns the tables on her husband, Tommy, who owns a casino, and his manager, Jackie Garbo, establishing that she is the one in control of them and their business. Leonard first wrote the scene primarily from Nancy's point of view, found that it did not work, and then rewrote it from the viewpoint of Garbo, who can observe, after a careless remark by Tommy, "Mistake. Jackie knew it immediately; he saw Nancy's expression tighten just a little, a hairline crack in the facade." Such an observation would be dramatically impossible for Nancy or Tommy to make, and another writer might have merely included it in third-person authorial narration. Leonard's meticulous attention to such supporting characters and his care to make every detail, every word, fit their personalities makes even his minor characters memorable and fully developed.

KILLSHOT

First published: 1989
Type of work: Novel

A working-class couple become witnesses to an extortion scheme and find themselves the targets of the two killers, against whom they are expected to testify.

Leonard continues to work new variations on his own formula in *Killshot*, this time by focusing on a typical working-class married couple, Wayne and Carmen Colson, rather than on his more typical characters who live near the fringes of law enforcement and crime. The book begins with chapters from the points of view of Armand Degas, a professional killer, and then Richie Nix, an armed robber and ex-convict. The reader is thus able to learn about these characters from the inside as they meet and develop a plan to extort money from the Detroit real-estate agency where Carmen works. Wayne drives the men away by force, temporarily disrupting their plan but also turning himself and his wife into eyewitnesses and, therefore, targets to be eliminated by the two criminals.

The genesis of the book, which Leonard had originally planned to revolve around Wayne, exemplifies the way in which his books are driven by the development of his characters rather than by any preconceived ideas about plot or structure. He begins not with a plot but with a set of characters. He decides first on the right names for characters, then works out the details of their background and, especially, the way they talk. Once he has created a set of interesting characters, he improvises a situation that puts them into conflict and lets them dictate the action to him as it goes along, seldom knowing himself what will happen more than a scene or two ahead or how the book will end. This improvisational approach also accounts for the fact that so many of his best characters are minor ones who develop unexpectedly as he writes. As Leonard explained in an interview about *Killshot*, "I started with a husband and wife who get involved in the Federal Witness Protection program. He's an ironworker, and he was going to be the main character—he's a very macho kind of guy. . . . She takes over; she becomes the main character and I was very glad to see it happen."

The Colsons are eventually put in a witness protection program and relocated to Cape Girardeau, Missouri, a location carefully researched and depicted in Leonard's usual manner. Carmen finds herself in nearly as much danger there from Ferris Britton, the deputy marshal in charge of their case, as she had been from Degas and Nix. The couple eventually discover, as do most of Leonard's characters, that the legal system is an inadequate defense against the evil that surrounds them, and they are forced to take matters into their own hands. The book ends in typical fashion with a dramatic armed confrontation among Carmen, Degas, and Nix back in Detroit.

GET SHORTY

First published: 1990
Type of work: Novel

Chili Palmer, a loan collector for the Miami mob, follows a runaway debtor to Las Vegas and Los Angeles and works his way into the film business.

Leonard drew upon his personal experiences with the film industry for *Get Shorty,* including modeling Michael Weir, the actor whose short height and large talent and ego provide the title, on Dustin Hoffman, who had been in line to play the lead in a film version of Leonard's *LaBrava* (1983). The novel transplants one of his typical self-reliant tough guys, loan shark Chili Palmer, from the Miami criminal underworld to Hollywood. The plot begins, after a series of deftly handled flashbacks, with Palmer's assignment to collect a debt from Leo Devoe, a dry cleaner who supposedly died in a plane crash but turns out to have not only avoided the crash but also collected insurance money for his own death. As usual in Leonard's novels, the plot is simply a mechanism for putting colorful characters into dramatic confrontations with each other, and the dry cleaner and his money belong to a subplot that fades away, without being fully resolved, well before the end of the novel.

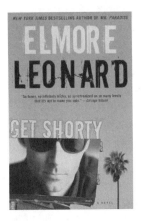

While all of his novels incorporate humor, albeit often bleak and ironic, *Get Shorty* emphasizes comic elements to an unusual degree as Leonard highlights the contrasts, and similarities, between the dishonesty and callousness of criminals and those of actors and producers. By the end of the book, Palmer has successfully made the transition from mob enforcer to film producer, with the implication that the differences are not profound. Among the running jokes are the characters' discussions of writing and film adaptations as they try to develop a screenplay based upon the ongoing events of the novel itself. Their comments range from insights of which the author himself would approve—as when loan shark-turned-screenwriter Palmer explains, "I don't think of a plot and then put characters in it. I start with different characters and see where they take me"—to satire of Hollywood's dismissive attitudes toward writers, exemplified by Bo Catlett, another criminal who is convinced that anyone can do it. "You asking me," Catlett said, "do I know how to write down words on a piece of paper? That's what you do, man, you put down one word after the other as it comes in your head. It isn't like having to learn how to play the piano, like you have to learn notes."

Leonard's novels seldom fuss over neat closure and the tidying up of loose ends, often leaving plot lines and the fates of significant characters unresolved, another of his practices slyly mocked by the closing sentence of *Get Shorty:* "endings, man, they weren't as easy as they looked." In this instance, the open-ended structure clears the way for a sequel, this time satirizing the music industry, with many of the same characters, including protagonist Palmer, in *Be Cool.*

OUT OF SIGHT

First published: 1996
Type of work: Novel

Career bank robber Jack Foley's chance encounter with U.S. Marshal Karen Sisco during his prison escape leads to romantic complications.

In *Out of Sight,* the trademark gritty realism of Elmore Leonard's oeuvre is blended with a romance between criminal Jack Foley and U.S. Marshal Karen Sisco. The novel's opening is widely acknowledged to rank among Leonard's best, as he takes the reader through a daring prison break, modeled on a real escape from that same prison in 1995. As is his practice, the point of view shifts among three different characters in the first three chapters, as the same scene is viewed from three different angles.

The opening sentence of the novel, "Foley had never seen a prison where you could walk right up to the fence without getting shot," immediately locates the reader both psychologically—within Foley's consciousness, attitudes, and experience—and physically—just inside the fence of a medium-security Florida prison. The second chapter begins as Sisco pulls up to the parking area just outside that same fence, looking at the same point from the other side, both literally—outside the prison versus inside—and figuratively—cop versus criminal. As she sits in her car, the headlights from a car pulling

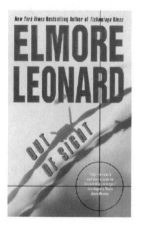

into the row behind her hit her rearview mirror. The opening of chapter 3, "Buddy saw the mirror flash and blond hair in his headlights, a woman in the blue Chevy Caprice parked right in front of him," takes the reader inside that second car as it introduces a third major character, Orren "Buddy" Bragg, a former partner of Foley who has arrived to help him escape. The escape itself is thus rendered in great visual depth, as the reader sees Buddy see Sisco see Foley as he emerges from a tunnel by the fence. Such detailed multiple visualizations are especially common in Leonard's later novels, which can resemble screenplays in their rapid cuts from character to character and their close specification of the precise angles and fields of vision from which characters view scenes.

After the successful prison break, the plot takes all these characters to Detroit, where the suspense intensifies as the relatively gentle and sympathetic Foley and Buddy are thrown into an uneasy alliance with a set of violent sociopaths seeking to rob a wealthy financier. Critic James Devlin notes the symbolism of the settings in the novel, as the sunny Florida setting of the opening scenes gives way to the dark and cold of the Detroit scenes. Brutal scenes of rape and murder alternate uneasily with scenes sketching the developing love story between the criminal and the cop pursuing him. For some critics, the conventional story of love at first sight, complete with a film-friendly "meet cute" when Foley and Sisco are locked in the trunk of a getaway car, is a rare misstep by Leonard that ultimately breaks the book into two incompatible halves, one a screwball romantic comedy and the other an usually violent portrait of depravity and urban violence. Although not a hit at the box office, the motion picture adaptation starring George Clooney and Jennifer Lopez earned high praise from film critics such as Roger Ebert for its success in translating "the texture of the pacing and dialogue" and the large cast of colorful characters to the screen.

SUMMARY

Leonard has been called a "Dickens from Detroit" because of his remarkable ability to invent a fresh cast of memorable characters for each new book and to depict with realistic detail every nuance of each character's distinctive voice. Critics have increasingly come to recognize that the apparent ease and naturalness of his style is deceptive and that the authenticity and precision of his depictions of contemporary people and places make him an accomplished and important American novelist.

William Nelles

BIBLIOGRAPHY

By the Author

LONG FICTION:
The Bounty Hunters, 1953
The Law at Randado, 1954
Escape from Five Shadows, 1956
Last Stand at Saber River, 1959 (also known as *Lawless River* and *Stand on the Saber*)

Elmore Leonard

Hombre, 1961
The Big Bounce, 1969
The Moonshine War, 1969
Valdez Is Coming, 1970
Forty Lashes Less One, 1972
Mr. Majestyk, 1974
Fifty-two Pickup, 1974
Swag, 1976 (also known as *Ryan's Rules*)
The Hunted, 1977
Unknown Man No. 89, 1977
The Switch, 1978
Gunsights, 1979
City Primeval: High Noon in Detroit, 1980
Gold Coast, 1980
Split Images, 1981
Cat Chaser, 1982
Stick, 1983
LaBrava, 1983
Glitz, 1985
Elmore Leonard's Double Dutch Treat: Three Novels, 1986
Bandits, 1987
Touch, 1987
Freaky Deaky, 1988
Killshot, 1989
Get Shorty, 1990
Maximum Bob, 1991
Rum Punch, 1992 (also known as *Jackie Brown*)
Pronto, 1993
Riding the Rap, 1995
Out of Sight, 1996
Naked Came the Manatee, 1996 (with twelve other Florida writers)
Cuba Libre, 1998
Be Cool, 1999
Pagan Babies, 2000
Tishomingo Blues, 2002
Mr. Paradise, 2004
The Hot Kid, 2005

SHORT FICTION:
The Tonto Woman, and Other Western Stories, 1998
When the Women Come Out to Dance, 2002
The Complete Western Stories of Elmore Leonard, 2004

CHILDREN'S LITERATURE:
A Coyote's in the House, 2004

SCREENPLAYS:
The Moonshine War, 1970
Joe Kidd, 1972

DISCUSSION TOPICS

- Analyze Elmore Leonard's distinctive handling of point of view, in which the author seldom comments upon the action and narration is almost entirely filtered through the multiple viewpoints of several characters.

- Discuss the moral implications of Leonard's frequent use of criminals as the protagonists of his novels. What codes or principles do they follow instead of the law?

- Most of Leonard's novels are set in Detroit or Florida; all include detailed descriptions of real places. How do these highly realistic settings function in his novels?

- One of Leonard's great strengths as a writer is his use of dialogue. Analyze a scene in one of his novels that is handled almost entirely in dialogue. Show how his characters are developed through their manner of speaking.

- Almost all of Leonard's novels have been bought by film studios, and many have been made into motion pictures. What aspects of his writing lend themselves particularly well to film adaptation? What aspects might cause problems for adaptation?

Mr. Majestyk, 1974
Stick, 1985 (with Joseph C. Stinson)
Fifty-two Pickup, 1986 (with John Steppling)
The Rosary Murders, 1987 (with Fred Walton)

TELEPLAYS:
High Noon Part 2: The Return of Will Kane, 1980
Desperado, 1987

About the Author

Devlin, James E. *Elmore Leonard.* New York: Twayne, 1999.

Geherin, David. *Elmore Leonard.* New York: Continuum, 1989.

Gorman, Edward. "Elmore Leonard." In *Mystery and Suspense Writers: The Literature of Crime, Detection, and Suspense,* edited by Robin W. Winks and Maureen Corrigan. New York: Scribner's, 1998.

Grella, George. "Film in Fiction: The Real and the Reel in Elmore Leonard." In *The Detective in American Fiction, Film, and Television,* edited by Jerome H. Delamater and Ruth Prigozy. Westport, Conn.: Greenwood Press, 1998.

Haut, Woody. "Maximum Elmore." *Sight and Sound* 15, no. 4 (April, 2005): 26-27.

Hynes, Joseph. "'High Noon in Detroit': Elmore Leonard's Career." *Journal of Popular Culture* 25 (Winter, 1991): 181-187.

Lupica, Mike. "St. Elmore's Fire." *Esquire* 107 (April, 1987): 169-174.

Pelecanos, George. "The Best of Elmore Leonard." *Sight and Sound* 15, no. 4 (April, 2005): 28-30.

Sutter, Gregg. "Getting It Right: Researching Elmore Leonard's Novels, Part 1." *The Armchair Detective* 19, no. 1 (Winter, 1986): 4-19.

_____. "Advance Man: Researching Elmore Leonard's Novels, Part 2." *The Armchair Detective* 19, no. 2 (Spring, 1986): 160-172.

DENISE LEVERTOV

Born: Ilford, Essex, England
October 24, 1923
Died: Seattle, Washington
December 20, 1997

One of the leading American poets of the second half of the twentieth century, Levertov has had her work widely anthologized, and her poetry and theories are widely studied to this day.

L. Schwartzwald/Courtesy,
New Directions Publishing

BIOGRAPHY

Denise Levertov was born October 24, 1923, in Ilford, Essex, England, the daughter of Paul Philip Levertoff, a Russian Jew who converted to Christianity and became a minister, and Beatrice Spooner-Jones, a Welsh preacher's daughter. Until she was thirteen years old, Denise and her sister were educated by their parents at home. The environment was rich in books and cultural discussion; her mother read the great works of nineteenth century literature aloud to the family, and her father was literate in four languages. She did receive some formal education in the form of ballet study from age twelve through seventeen and, in addition, took French lessons, learned piano, and painted, all of which would later aid the development of her rhythm and style. Her parents had been prisoners of war at Leipzig during World War I, so many refugees came to their home. The resultant religious, social, and ethical discussions that took place there profoundly influenced her life and works.

This background provided a natural environment for learning to write, and at age five, Levertov decided to become a poet. When she was twelve, she sent some of her work to T. S. Eliot, himself a venerable poet of great esteem and, at the time, someone dealing with conflicting concerns about poetics, religion and social issues, who responded with an encouraging letter of advice. At sixteen, she corresponded with the poet and critic Herbert Read and also became acquainted with editor Charles Wrey and author Kenneth Rexroth.

During World War II, she underwent nurse's training and worked for three years at St. Luke's Hospital, where she helped to rehabilitate returning soldiers. During the evenings, she continued to write poetry. As noted, her family was actively engaged at this time in the relocation of Jewish refugees, so the war figured prominently in her life. Yet the political climate of the war did not directly figure in her first book, *The Double Image* (1946). The poems, here, dealt more from a personal vantage point of the loss of childhood, death, and separation, and Levertov composed them in more standard and regular stanzas than the free verse which she became synonymous with in her later work. She would continue to develop these themes, alongside her social and political ideas, but in a very different style.

In 1947, Levertov married an American soldier, novelist Mitchell Goodman. The next year, they moved to New York City, where their son, Nikolai, was born the following year. This move engaged Levertov in a new life and culture and radically changed her poetics. Her American settlement built upon her mother's instruction on the nineteenth century and introduced her to the Transcendentalism of Ralph Waldo Emerson and Henry David Thoreau, not to mention the more recent poetics of Ezra Pound and his Imagism. Her second book, *Here and Now* (1957), though somewhat reminiscent of her early style, showed promise of what was to come with her newly developed line which bore the vestiges of travel, marriage, and intellectual maturation.

In the United States, Levertov met her mentor, the poet and novelist William Carlos Williams, who taught her to focus though his famous credo "no ideas but in things," with the concrete things, themselves, being carriers of powerful emotion and ideas. She also became involved in the social scene of New York City, its streets and people as well as its artistic movements. She became friends with poets Robert Creeley and Robert Duncan, both of whom taught at Black Mountain College and were early publishers of her work in the *Black Mountain Review.* By the time she became associated with New Directions Press in 1959, her voice had reached its maturity. *With Eyes at the Back of Our Heads* (1959) illustrates her full involvement with the American literary movements of the times.

In *The Jacob's Ladder* (1961) and in *O Taste and See* (1964), Levertov's poetry begins to shift into a discussion of poetic theory and the imagination. In both of these books, she continued to use the natural world as her subject. More and more, however, she focused on social issues. When the United States became involved in the Vietnam War in the 1960's, Levertov's personal and poetic life began to reflect more of her social consciousness. With several other poets, she founded Writers and Artists Protest Against the War in Vietnam. She participated in antiwar protest marches and was jailed at least once for her involvement.

Relearning the Alphabet (1970) contains many such poems protesting the war, but it also contains poems dealing with other social concerns, such as the Detroit riots and the famine in the African country of Biafra. Levertov's antiwar poetry was collected in the 1971 volume *To Stay Alive;* though well crafted, these social and political poems did not receive as much critical acclaim as did her other work. Levertov continued to produce collections of poetry throughout the 1970's that demonstrated her technical, social, and spiritual development. She divorced Goodman in 1972, and *The Freeing of the Dust* (1975) illustrates her journey toward a balance and integration in her life and verse.

In addition to her poetry, Levertov also wrote many essays and short articles. She worked as an editor and translator, and she taught at Stanford University, the Massachusetts Institute of Technology (MIT), the City College of New York, and many other colleges. She received numerous awards for her writing, including a Guggenheim Foundation Fellowship in 1962, a Lenore Marshall Poetry Prize in 1975, and an Elmer Holmes Bobst Award in 1983. Levertov's final years were spent in Seattle, Washington, where she converted to Catholicism; she died on December 20, 1997, from complications of lymphoma.

ANALYSIS

In her collection of essays *The Poet in the World* (1973), Levertov explains the close connection between the poetic and the political: "A sense of history must involve a sense of the present, a vivid awareness of change, a response to crisis, a realization that what was appropriate in this or that situation in the past is inadequate to the demands of the present, that we are living our whole lives in a state of emergency which is unparalleled in all history." It is her contention that, as a poet, she cannot stand aside and ignore these events happening around her, but rather she must address these threats to humanity. Poetry is the appropriate medium to do this because the poet can personalize these concerns.

In the same book, Levertov discusses her craft and its process. For her, to write poetry is not simply to manipulate words. Perhaps conflating both Pound and the nineteenth century Transcendentalists, Levertov contends that creating poetry requires the writer to transform personal experience into words by intuiting an order into the experience. To those ends, not to mention or note her further conflation of meditation, spirituality, nature, and (eventually) Judeo-Christianity would be to miss a large element of her later career. How exactly Levertov constructs or understands religion and spirituality is difficult to discern and often seems to modulate with the passage of time. It is fair to say, however, that in her poetry the words result from intense perception and immersion into the experience itself, in a sort of deep trance.

This meditative state brings about her words and invigorates them with life through the spoken word. This action of saying something leads to further deep perception, and the cycle of poetry reiterated becomes almost unending. As complex as that epistemology sounds, aside from her first volume of poetry, Levertov's poems use concrete, everyday language in a free verse form that is organic, growing from within the experience that gave rise to the words. The idea is that, while the thoughts behind the words are complex and manifold, the words themselves are easily accessible.

Levertov uses her political experiences as sources for many of her poems. She shies away from very little in the political arena, having written on topics such as pollution, the destruction of the rain forests, the acquired immunodeficiency syndrome (AIDS) crisis, animal rights, and many others. In all these poems, Levertov juxtaposes images of life and nature with images of death so that the reader will personalize these events and, as she did, make the political become personal.

Because Levertov is so intensely immersed in these events, she can turn them into poetry successfully. In each poem, language and vision are equally dependent upon each other. Each experience has a form that the poet intuits, an order that perhaps she alone can see. In "Some Notes on Organic Form" (1965), she writes of a poetic process in which a cross-section of several experiences comes together in a moment. The poet is the person who can capture the experiences in words. The form that the resulting poem takes is self-reflexive and becomes determined by the experience.

For example, in "Carapace," from *Oblique Prayers* (1984), she writes of the desire to retreat into a shell that will protect her from the horrors of people's inhumanity. The poem's stanzas are arranged so that longer lines enclose shorter ones, creating a visual carapace, or shell, in the text itself. In "Snail," from *Relearning the Alphabet*, the form the poem takes imitates a snail's slow movement. In "A Marigold from North Vietnam," from the same book, the lines are disjointed, with large spaces between the images. The form imitates what was done not only to the country of Vietnam but also to the American spirit by the war. Levertov writes in free verse, but the form is internal—there is definitely a form, but it is liberated from conventional verse forms.

"THE STRICKEN CHILDREN"

First published: 1987 (collected in *Breathing the Water*, 1987)
Type of work: Poem

Returning to the scene of her happy childhood, the poet contemplates children who have lost their childhoods.

In "The Stricken Children," the persona governing the poem—many attribute it as Levertov herself—recalls her return to a wishing well of her childhood. During that time, the well was a clear bubbling spring less than three feet across, with a bank of rocks protecting it from falling leaves. It was a tiny personal place which the speaking persona recalls as likely holding within it the wishes of many others from the past. People who came here did not throw money but, rather, searched themselves for the right small wish to throw into the well in the form of a pebble or rock. The immediate juxtaposition here is that visitors did not throw money, as wishes are not meant to be bought but rather hoped for with deepest interest and concern. This well was the place where, year after year, she returned to launch her journeys into the imagination. Like the spring, her childhood imagination could roam uncluttered, and the experiences she encountered nourished her.

When she returns as an adult, however, the wishing well has changed. She had hoped it would be familiar, merely older. Instead, it was marred, unfamiliar and sickly. The naïve beauty and appreciation she had for it in the past has been tarnished by a modern society who had filled it with its consumer excess, which she views, quite literally, as pollution. She wonders if the spring, so clogged, still flows, and if it was children who deposited the trash. If so, she muses, how damaged are these children by such consumerism? From the persona's perspective, could children who would exact such violence on Nature actually dream; would they understand real desire? Were they raised by people who could instill virtue and imagination within them?

She leaves quickly, for the urgency of her own dreams pushes her onward. She continues to wonder, however, about the children of today, these stricken children who cannot find a source of nourishment for their dreams anywhere in a disposable culture of throwaways. The past, the generative wellspring that gave her the stability to dream and to act on dreams, has been, like the well, choked up. From the persona's perspective, modern culture has strangled the imagination of these children at exactly the time of life when they most need to develop it.

It is possible that the personal awareness of what her own childhood offered in nourishing her life leads Levertov to reexamine the concept of childhood itself, here in the light of the cultural and political climate that could produce stricken children. In the poem's view, the world is violent, and this violence enters every life soon after birth. The child does not have time to develop an imagination or a sense of wonder. Levertov's poem re-creates that wonder at the same time that it warns against the political and social consequences of careless actions.

"CADEMON"

First published: 1987 (collected in *Breathing the Water,* 1987)

Type of work: Poem

Utilizing the British tale of the first Christian poet, Levertov asserts a method for finding a poetic voice.

Denise Levertov's own footnote for this poem tells the reader that the plot of "Cademon" comes from the *History of the English Church and People* (731), by Saint Bede the Venerable, the first known British Christian poet. That information tells readers that the historical analog of "Cademon" is the story of an illiterate stable hand who received a divine call to sing in praise of God.

Even armed with that knowledge, readers may find that the tight line and verse structure of "Cademon" obviates simple readings of the poem. It is reminiscent, perhaps, of the laconic verse of Levertov's Imagist mentors: Ezra Pound, William Carlos Williams, and H. D. The message appears to be simple enough: Any beings who come into contact with the spirit can be transformed into some-

thing magnificent. Here, the clumsy, inarticulate persona informs the reader of his inability with words by comparing the situation to being trapped in a dance without any knowledge of steps or grace.

Yet when he is touched by the divine hand of an angel while attending to his duties as a cowhand, he finds his mouth and lips touched, burned even, by the fiery hand of God, and he discovers his poetic voice.

Whether the poem is meant to be didactic, with Levertov asserting the ways of finding one's own poetic voice utilizing the tale of Cademon as an example, or whether it is an autobiographical analog to both her own poetic ascension and her Christian conversion, is debatable. There is little biographical evidence to assert the latter reading, but given the persona's self-effacing attitude toward himself, there is some credibility to consider the discussion. Regardless of how one interprets the intention of the piece, "Cademon" illustrates Levertov's transformative reliance upon her reconceptualization of the divine as a source material separating herself from her more Transcendental roots to ones assuredly more Christian.

"CARAPACE"

First published: 1984 (collected in *Oblique Prayers,* 1984)

Type of work: Poem

Levertov asserts that a person needs a protective shell to avoid the tragedies of life but, at the same time, needs to reach out for the experiences that life offers.

In "Carapace," Levertov writes about her response to the world's political tragedies. A carapace is the hard shell of an animal, such as a turtle or crab, that protects the soft inner part from harm. The poem's persona announces that she herself is growing a shell, even though she regrets the shell-like exteriors of other people that render them insensitive to the world's problems. In the poem, she contemplates children. She begins as though the poet and a child were talking about a situation. The child has seen her own father shot by police; the poet asks the child if she knows what the word "subversive" means. The child's somewhat attentive somewhat sardonic reply indicates that despite her youth, this child is already an adult, a product of modern inhumanity.

The poet then goes back to contemplating how well her shell is growing and how superior it is to mere skin. Speaking as though she could control the growing of a body part, she remarks that there will be chinks in the armor where the sections in the carapace do not completely meet. Whether or not the insinuation here demands that these are welcome points of entry where someone could still reach the soft underbelly is debatable, as one could read that act as one of violation or one of nurture. Yet, the poem's ending is telling, depending upon how one invokes the tone.

Another child enters, this boy only nine years old. When asked how he feels about his missing father, who has "disappeared," he replies with a shrug and says only that he is sad. The repeated violence that the boy has seen in his short life has rendered him unemotional about even his own father.

The poem ends with an urging to the shell to grow faster. At the same time, the world's problems still intrude. Levertov seems to write of two minds here: She wants to hide from the evil that destroys the wonder of the world; at the same time, she realizes that it is impossible to so do. If the shell encased her like a suit of armor, then she would entirely lose the sensitivity to life and the will to try to change things.

The probable political message here is one of a poet responding not only to the explicit situations of missing persons in Central America but also to all inhumanity. The concrete situations and the dialogue, written in everyday language, paint clear images. A man is shot as he is escaping over a wall, and a young person responds to deep grief with only a shrug. The visual structure of the text itself resembles the subject, a shell. The two scenes with the children are inset, while the comments on the growth of the shell surround them, in the same way that the growing shell covers the vulnerable animal inside. The form and the subject mesh, as the poet arranges these scenes to force the reader to contemplate such inhumanity.

"DEATH IN MEXICO"

First published: 1978 (collected in *Life in the Forest*, 1978)
Type of work: Poem

A parable of a Mexican gardener, the poem finds Levertov contemplating the responsibilities and complexities of harvesting the power of nature.

Somewhat autobiographically connected to Levertov's mother, "Death in Mexico" tells the story of the old woman's attempts to cultivate a British-styled garden in a considerably more arid climate. The narrative's central plot is simple enough: Levertov muses upon the deterioration of her mother's well-kept garden over the course of three weeks when the old woman is taken from her home as the result of what will eventually be a fatal illness. The poem's persona indicates that she did attempt to keep the garden up for the old woman, and encouraged others to as well, but, in lieu of the gardener's personal care, the garden deteriorates and quickly becomes overwhelmed.

Behind the poem's narrative lie further examples of Levertov's Transcendental roots. Death and deterioration are inextricably tied together in the ultimate fate of the old woman and that of her garden. Likewise, death and the transition to it are met not with remorse or even anger but merely with an acceptance that it is a natural state in the cycle of life. The persona, like the gardener, offers up no sentimentality for the garden that took twenty years to assemble, but rather she spends the length and breadth of the poem musing and observing upon the garden as it decays.

What is questioned, though, is whether humanity has the right to attempt such cultivation in the first place. In many ways, Levertov constructs the old gardener as a stubborn and obdurate surrogate for God in her cultivation of a garden in a place where no earthly garden should be (drawing a parallel to God's creation of a Garden of Eden in what is now an arid desert climate). The old woman's gaze, shown by Levertov as she is taken away, is one of God's determined fixity looking upon his creation in disrepair. The gaze fixes upon a single blossom and understands with acceptance that it was only meant to live, as such, for a single day. As the poem closes, the persona notes that the garden, likewise fixed in its place for twenty years, now too will pass away as part of the natural process.

"WHAT WERE THEY LIKE?"

First published: 1971 (collected in *To Stay Alive*)
Type of work: Poem

A commentary on what Levertov perceived to be the American policy toward Vietnam, this poem vilifies the idea of the loss of an entire culture because of war.

"What Were They Like?" illustrates Levertov's political concerns; here, her interests lie in questioning, quite literally, the U.S. involvement in Vietnam. The poem itself is little more than a list of six questions and answers. The questions come forth from a voice almost childlike in design and naïveté, while the answers solicited are dismissive and irritated in their tone and content.

The questions show concern for the loss of knowledge about the Vietnamese people, but they are by no means of an outwardly political or journalistic nature. Rather, the persona, which seems youthful but is not, asks questions germane to a deeper understanding of the culture of Vietnam: What were their religious mores? What made them laugh? Can the person answering the questions tell the persona anything of their literature? The persona seems aware that the idea of Vietnam might already be lost or be in the process of being expurgated rather than studied or illuminated.

The responses, while not terse, are stultifying and try to obviate the discussion. They are also sarcastic in tone, as the responsorial voice twists the wording of the questions to mock the person asking them. For example, when the questioner asks whether the Vietnamese used stone lanterns, the responsorial voice declares that the Vietnamese people held light hearts that had turned to stone.

In this dismissal, the respondent echoes and amplifies the idea that, even if any of these questions had once been germane, most of this otherwise arcane knowledge has long since been forgotten.

American military policy is illuminated here as destructive and unconcerned with the collateral damage of the war brought about by its tactics. Frequently mentioned are allusions to fire, burning, bombing, and the charred remains of a people and their civilization. Given Levertov's political stances, it is almost self-evident that the respondent's voice is to be vilified as destructive and genocidal, as it is more concerned with reporting the decimation of the Vietnamese people than with knowing anything about them. The ultimate answer of the respondent is that it is impossible to know these people now, as they are largely silent and forgotten.

"A NEW YEAR'S GARLAND FOR MY STUDENTS/MIT: 1969-1970"

First published: 1970 (collected in *Footprints*, 1972)
Type of work: Poem

Thirteen vignettes of students in a poetry seminar create precise portraits of young people developing into adults.

The thirteen sections of "A New Year's Garland for My Students/MIT: 1969-1970" were inspired by the students in a poetry seminar during Levertov's year as a visiting professor and poet-in-residence at the Massachusetts Institute of Technology. Each section is dedicated to one student, and each varies in length and line arrangement. Levertov captures the essence of the students by observing telling details and making frequent comparisons with nature.

For example, in "Arthur," Levertov sees a person at a stage in life when nothing seems to be happening. She compares him to the buds of trees and bushes that in winter go unnoticed. Yet the buds are there and are as complex and beautiful as are the "eventual silky leaves in spring." Using the word "silky" indicates her positive attitude toward his development. Silk is a fabric highly valued as well as smooth to the touch; the comparison calls to mind the lowly silkworm that produces the luxurious strands.

In "Bill," Levertov sees a questioner who can disturb the pleasant atmosphere by posing important but dark thoughts. She pictures a garden with a fence around it, but the fence has an open gate. Perhaps she is comparing this garden to the classroom, an enclosure that has an open atmosphere in its encouragement of creativity. The garden is pretty and stable, predictable. Yet in a dark corner lurk threatening eyes that interject an element of uncertainty into the otherwise pleasant surroundings. Like a sharp question that hits a sensitive topic in a discussion, this presence in the garden is disturbing yet necessary.

Levertov sees herself in another student, "Judy." Because Judy is petite, Levertov imagines her to be as light and airy as Greek goddesses or characters in the plays of William Shakespeare. The real Judy, as she sets off bundled up on a winter's evening, reminds the poet of herself at a young age, trudging to and from the library overloaded with books, as reading was nurtured in her home. As a child, the poet's active imagination turned the commonplace objects on city streets into things of beauty; she imagines Judy to have this same inner quality.

In "Ted," Levertov sees several different people, two clearly. Both are by the sea, but they perceive things differently. A young girl dances with joy and speaks brightly in the sunlight, but a ruminative and apparently despondent old man sees the sea as a horror of unseen terrors, and he is quiet. There are also other voices in Ted, but they must be quiet until the old man issues a decree, as he appears to want to. These other voices will wait until this stage in life is over before they rise to be heard.

In nature, a closer look reveals an intricacy unnoticed by the ordinary person and perhaps unrealized itself. In the case of her students, Levertov takes a close look beneath the surface to find their potential for imaginative development. As in her other poetry, Levertov uses experiences as springboards for description that reaches the essence of what is important in humanity. She obviously cares for these people and wants them to develop to their fullest.

"SEPTEMBER 1961"

First published: 1964 (collected in *O Taste and See*, 1964)
Type of work: Poem

Lamenting the loss of her poetic mentors, Levertov devotes a poem to the inspiration that they provided her while announcing her own poetic intentions.

Bordering upon a threnody, or song of mourning, "September 1961" finds Levertov's poetic persona crying out in lament for many of her high modernist mentors: Ezra Pound, William Carlos Williams, and H. D. Indeed, when the poem was published in 1964, only Pound was still living, and, as noted in the poem, he was operating within his "quiet years," having spent copious time in an Italian prison and American sanatorium.

The poem's voice finds itself, presumably the voice of Levertov (though among others), alone on a road bereft of her poetic masters, anticipating their loss. Strangely though, this road leads to a sea, often the symbol of fecundity and generative power. In her pockets are words and themes, the building materials of her poetry, Williams's "no ideas but in things," but her advisers no longer light a candle for her to follow. They have withdrawn into private conditions, silent like Pound or hobbled by medical ailments like Williams.

Whether this loss is problematic or emancipating to the poem's voice is debatable. Of particular note is the construction of the third-person collective "we" that the persona uses. Levertov creates a subject position that many may occupy—the inheritors of the high modernist tradition—but, assuredly, the high modernists whom she invokes are those poets who touched her life personally and specifically.

The persona is unsure how she will be affected by the loss of these great voices, but she continues along the path, realizing that she has some distance to go. However, the voice is somewhat assured that she is going in the right direction, as she can smell the sea air wafting upon a breeze approaching her. She invokes her own Transcendental predecessors and places her trust in nature. Armed with the tools given to her by her mentors, she is confident that she will find the generative sea, alone, eventually.

"THE JACOB'S LADDER"

First published: 1961 (collected in *The Jacob's Ladder*, 1961)
Type of work: Poem

Invoking a passage from Genesis, Levertov issues a possibly ambiguous manifesto on poetic construction.

Invoking the story of Jacob's dream from Genesis 28:10-17, "The Jacob's Ladder" utilizes the dream as metaphor for poetic construction. The plot from Genesis maintains that when Jacob came to rest his head at the end of the day, he dreamed that he saw God's angels ascending and descending a great ladder reaching from Earth to the heavens. God announced to Jacob that all the land that he surveys should belong to him and his descendants, and his descendants should be so many that they would be as the dust is to the Earth. Jacob awakened and acknowledged that this place upon which he had slept was holy and touched by God.

Levertov picks up the story and utilizes it as a leitmotif (with subtle emendation) for her thoughts on a poetic construction that, she asserts, can approach the divine. In the poem, her narrator observes that the ladder is, in fact, a stairway (possibly referring to one of many actual geographical locations, such as the cut-in steps of Cheddar Gorge in the United Kingdom) of a cut, rosy stone meant as much, if not more, for human steps as for those of angels, who would not need to tread upon the tangible. However, the stairway itself is sharp, jagged, and a difficult climb that scrapes the knees of the climber who would dare ascend it and approach God in Heaven. Yet this pain, in some way, consoles the climber.

The last line suggests an interesting ambiguity in the poem, as it seems to imply that the ascendant of the stairs is not a mortal but rather the poem itself ascending into the heavens. This ambiguity is hardly minor, however, as the possible difference in meanings allows for a shift in the agency of the written word: Does poetry come from a person, or is it inspired by something incorporeal, living and breathing with its own life? That Levertov constructs the stairway not as a mystical, gleaming thing made of evanescent materials but rather as one made of rock lends to a particular reading, but even this thought becomes complicated as the staircase sits in front of a doubting, gray skyline. The tenor of the piece suggests that the biblical Jacob's remarks are indeed true, but whether poetry is the stuff of the divine or the corporeal is left for the reader to ponder.

SUMMARY

In her book of essays *Light Up the Cave* (1981), Levertov states that politics are a poetic concern because they are a human concern, an integral part of daily life. A poet who is committed to affirming life is also bound to defend it against political threats of destruction. The best of Levertov's poems in her more than forty books do just that. She writes in direct language, using organic forms appropriate to the contents of the poems. Throughout her career, Levertov's changing styles and explorations brought her readers many moments of pleasure and enlightenment.

Louise M. Stone; updated by Joseph Michael Sommers

BIBLIOGRAPHY

By the Author

POETRY:
The Double Image, 1946
Here and Now, 1957
Overland to the Islands, 1958
Five Poems, 1958
With Eyes at the Back of Our Heads, 1959
The Jacob's Ladder, 1961

O Taste and See: New Poems, 1964
City Psalm, 1964
Psalm Concerning the Castle, 1966
The Sorrow Dance, 1966
A Tree Telling of Orpheus, 1968
A Marigold from North Vietnam, 1968
Three Poems, 1968
The Cold Spring, and Other Poems, 1969
Embroideries, 1969
Summer Poems, 1969, 1970
Relearning the Alphabet, 1970
*A New Year's Garland for My Students: MIT, 1969-
    1970,* 1970
To Stay Alive, 1971
Footprints, 1972
The Freeing of the Dust, 1975
Chekhov on the West Heath, 1977
Modulations for Solo Voice, 1977
Life in the Forest, 1978
Collected Earlier Poems, 1940-1960, 1979
Pig Dreams: Scenes from the Life of Sylvia, 1981
Wanderer's Daysong, 1981
Candles in Babylon, 1982
Poems, 1960-1967, 1983
*Oblique Prayers: New Poems with Fourteen Translations
    from Jean Joubert,* 1984
The Menaced World, 1984
Selected Poems, 1986
Breathing the Water, 1987
Poems, 1968-1972, 1987
A Door in the Hive, 1989
Evening Train, 1993
Sands of the Well, 1996
The Great Unknowing: Last Poems, 1999

LONG FICTION:
In the Night: A Story, 1968

DRAMA:
El Salvador: Requiem and Invocation, pr. 1983 (libretto; music by W. Newell Hendricks)

NONFICTION:
The Poet in the World, 1973
Light Up the Cave, 1981
New and Selected Essays, 1992
Tesserae, 1995
The Letters of Robert Duncan and Denise Levertov, 2004 (Robert J. Bertholf and Albert Gelpi, editors)

TRANSLATIONS:
In Praise of Krishna: Songs from the Bengali, 1967 (with Edward C. Dimock, Jr.)
Selected Poems, 1969 (of Eugene Guillevic)
Black Iris, 1988 (of Jean Joubert)

DISCUSSION TOPICS

• Tracing Denise Levertov's religious dispositions throughout her life, how does religious, mystical, or Transcendental discourse operate in her poetry?

• How do the high modernists, Imagists, and postmodernists affect Levertov's line, meter, and imagery? From whom does she borrow, and how does she implement her acquired tools and materials?

• Where and how does Levertov insert herself and her own life into her work?

• Considering a piece such as "Carapace," does Levertov try to teach with her poetry? If so, who would be her audience?

• How does the interplay between domestic and global policy play into works such as "What Were They Like?" and "A New Year's Garland for My Students/MIT: 1969-1970"?

• How does nature operate in Levertov's poetry? Is it generative? Destructive? Containable?

EDITED TEXTS:
Penguin Modern Poets Nine, 1967 (with Kenneth Rexroth and William Carlos Williams)
The Collected Poems of Beatrice Hawley, 1989

About the Author

Block, Edward, ed. *Renascence: Essays on Values in Literature* 50, no. 1 (Fall, 1997). Special Levertov issue.

Gwynne, R. S., ed. *American Poets Since World War II.* Vol. 5 in *Dictionary of Literary Biography,* edited by Matthew J. Bruccoli. Detroit: Gale Research, 1980.

Hollenberg, Donna. "'History as I Desired It': Ekphrasis as Postmodern Witness in Denise Levertov's Late Poetry." *Modernism/Modernity* 10, no. 3 (September, 2003): 519-537.

Janssen, Ronald, ed. *Twentieth Century Literature* 38, no. 3 (Fall, 1992). Special Levertov issue.

Little, Anne Colclough, and Susie Paul, eds. *Denise Levertov: New Perspectives.* West Cornwall, Conn.: Locust Hill Press, 2000.

Long, Mark. "Affinities of Faith and Place in the Poetry of Denise Levertov." *ISLE* 6, no. 2 (Summer, 1999): 31-40.

Rodgers, Audrey. *Denise Levertov: The Poetry of Engagement.* Cranbury, N.J.: Associated University Presses, 1993.

Wagner, Linda W. *Denise Levertov.* New York: Twayne, 1967.

_____, ed. *Denise Levertov: In Her Own Province.* New York: New Directions, 1979.

Wagner-Martin, Linda, ed. *Critical Essays on Denise Levertov.* Boston: G. K. Hall, 1991.

Library of Congress

SINCLAIR LEWIS

Born: Sauk Centre, Minnesota
February 7, 1885
Died: Rome, Italy
January 10, 1951

The first American novelist to win the Nobel Prize in Literature, Lewis gave the American public its first literary view of the emerging middle class during the 1920's.

BIOGRAPHY

Harry Sinclair Lewis was born in Sauk Centre, Minnesota, on February 7, 1885, the youngest of three sons of a country doctor, Edwin J. Lewis. One year after the death of Harry's tubercular mother, Emma, in 1891, his father married Isabel Warner, whom Lewis felt was psychically his own mother. Unlike his older brother, Claude, Harry cared nothing for sports, was not popular in school, and received little praise from his father. So, like so many lonely children, he found solace in books, read voraciously, and began writing regularly in diaries which he kept throughout his life.

Fred, the eldest son, dropped out of school and worked as a miller all of his life. Claude, however, was a constant success and an example held up to Harry, so that Claude's decision to become a doctor undoubtedly had some influence on Harry's educational plans. After six months of preparation at Oberlin Academy, Harry enrolled in Yale University, but there again he was friendless, an outsider. He did gain a place on the editorial staff of the *Yale Literary Magazine*, but by the beginning of his senior year he left New Haven to become a janitor at Halicon Hall, the experiment in communal living established by writer and social reformer Upton Sinclair.

After about a month the restless young man went to New York and tried to live by writing; he soon took off for Panama to work on the canal. Lewis then decided to return to Yale, and graduated in June, 1908. In 1914, when his first novel, *Our Mr. Wrenn: The Romantic Adventures of a Gentle Man*, was published, he married Grace Livingston Hegger and settled down to a life of commuting to Manhattan for his daily stint at Doran Publishing and writing furiously at home.

After *The Saturday Evening Post* had accepted several of his short stories at a thousand dollars each, Lewis felt that he could devote his entire time to writing. It was not until 1920, however, with the publication of *Main Street: The Story of Carol Kennicott*, that Sinclair Lewis became famous. It is significant that Lewis had planned originally to call the novel "Village Virus." It was unremitting in its criticism of provincial America and of what H. L. Mencken later called "boobus Americanus," and it evoked what Mark Schorer (in his biography of Lewis) calls "a storm of vilification and applause."

Even though his first son, Wells, had been born in 1917, Lewis insisted that the family keep moving about the United States, indicating a restlessness that he would never lose. Actually, what he called his "research" made it necessary that he live like a field sociologist, filling many notebooks with intricate maps, accurate descriptions of houses (complete with furniture placement), and verbatim conversations before writing each novel.

As biographer Schorer explains, the next novel, *Babbitt* (1922), caused even more consternation than *Main Street*, and Lewis was denounced as a "villain and a traitor." All over the United States, however, thousands of people bought the book. Lewis next planned to write a labor novel, but while in Chicago, he met a young medical researcher, Paul de Kruif, and the two men began discussions of a book dealing with corruption in the medical profession. They went together to the Caribbean, an important locale of the proposed novel, and then to England, where Lewis began work on *Arrowsmith* (1925).

Although still sharply critical of certain segments of American society, this novel had an idealistic hero and a wife who was almost saintly, so that *Arrowsmith* was a huge success, both critically and financially. It was no surprise, then, when the Pulitzer Prize was awarded to Lewis; it was something of a shock, however, when he refused it. He declared publicly that the prize was awarded only to novels which showed the "wholesome atmosphere of American life," and in his open letter to the Pulitzer Prize Committee insisted that acceptance would indicate that their approval equaled authority to make final literary judgments. There is some suspicion that Lewis would have accepted the prize for *Main Street* or *Babbitt* and that he was "thumbing his nose" at those who had deprived him of the award earlier.

The next major novel, *Elmer Gantry* (1927), dealt with the most negative aspects of evangelical religion, and in typical fashion Lewis carefully cultivated many members of the clergy in Kansas City before beginning to write. The result is possibly the most savage satire in the Lewis canon, with hardly one admirable character surrounding the villainous protagonist. In addition, Lewis featured sex quite prominently, so that it caused the greatest furor of all of his books. The bans that followed, from Boston to Glasgow, had the effect of making the book an immediate best seller, but Lewis was widely denounced from many pulpits and was even invited to a lynching party in Virginia. By now, his marriage had begun to disintegrate, attributable particularly to quarrels over his addiction to alcohol.

Lewis went to Europe alone, looking for subject matter for his next novel, following his familiar pattern of wandering almost aimlessly. He stopped in Germany, however, when he met Dorothy Thompson, the best-known newspaperwoman in Europe. After Lewis was granted a divorce from Grace in 1928, the two were married.

Although he continued to write for the rest of his life, the last important novel, *Dodsworth*, appeared in 1929. As the decade ended, newer, shriller voices were being heard, and from this point on Lewis would be considered somewhat old-fashioned.

Nevertheless, in 1930, he was awarded the Nobel Prize in Literature, and his acceptance speech was a benchmark in the history of American literature. In it, he announced: "Our American professors like their literature clear and cold and pure and very dead."

At age forty-six, Lewis was the author of twelve published novels and would write ten more in the final twenty years of his life. In 1937, his second marriage dissolved, with his second son, Michael, remaining with Thompson as Lewis continued his peregrinations throughout the world. For a time he became enamored of the stage and even tried acting during the late 1930's and 1940's.

Unfortunately, his problem with alcoholism grew worse as he continued his lifelong pursuit of what Schorer calls "some vague and undefined glimmer of a happier place, a richer life." There may be some doubt about whether Sinclair Lewis had ever really left Sauk Centre, as he admitted that the heroine of *Main Street*, Carol Kennicott, was really himself, and it is significant that by the novel's end Carol has returned to Gopher Prairie and her dull but steady husband, Dr. Will. Lewis died among strangers in an Italian hospital on the outskirts of Rome on a rainy January 10, 1951.

ANALYSIS

The principal themes of Lewis's major novels are concern with the effects of small-town life and narrow-minded people on those who do not conform to established patterns, and a castigation of American middle-class materialism. His first two successful novels, *Main Street* and *Babbitt*, clearly illustrate these ideas even by their titles. In the first, his main character, Carol Kennicott, tries to raise the level of life in Gopher Prairie, the small town to which she has come after her marriage. She finally "settles" for the dullness of Main Street, which typifies such places.

In *Babbitt*, Lewis creates a protagonist so symbolic of the emptiness inherent in the middle-class pursuit of material things that his name can now be found in the dictionary, defined as "a self-satisfied person who conforms readily to middle-class attitudes and ideals." In *Arrowsmith*, Lewis continues his castigation of small-minded individuals, this time showing how their lack of vision and their emphasis on "the practicality of profit" hamper the work of scientific research and negatively affect those in the medical profession. Finally, in *Elmer Gantry*, Lewis draws his most loathsome character, a man who manipulates unthinking people in order to advance his career in the ministry. By the novel's end, Elmer Gantry has achieved his materialistic goals, but he is shown to be an empty shell of a man, so evil that he is almost unaware of his own hypocrisy.

Lewis's work relies but little on plot. The author acts as a photographer of the locales in which his novels are set, creating them and the characters who inhabit them with exactness. He relied heavily on careful research before writing each book, and his ability to re-create so exactly the places, speech, and manners he writes about has made a number of critics call him a consummate mimic. His work is somewhat regional in the sense that his four most outstanding novels are set in the American Midwest, his own bailiwick.

He is a satirist, somewhat sarcastic in tone even when he is drawing the portrait of a character to be admired by the reader. What his work lacks, however, is sufficient probing below the surface of characters to give the reader a genuine sense of each one's motivations. Like a professional photographer, Lewis carefully sets his camera angles to give a particular slant to each picture, a slant usually planned to call attention to the most negative aspects of both the setting and the people pictured.

The era in which Lewis produced his four best novels is an important factor to consider in evaluating them. *Main Street* appeared just after World War I, when small-town America had passed its original frontier days but had not yet truly begun its emancipation from the set patterns and values so much a part of the earlier rural society.

With *Babbitt*, set two years later, Lewis shows the following stage in American development. In midsized cities, the emphasis on "not being a hick" has led to an emphasis on the possession of the most up-to-date models of all material objects as being equal to success. It is notable that this novel does not deal with social criticism of genuine business tycoons or "robber barons," as some earlier muckrakers had, but rather with the almost pitiful

strivings of those who are the very antithesis of those earlier individualists. To George Babbitt and the other characters in the novel, the most important factor is conformity—being well-liked, being part of the herd.

One of the usual criteria in literary analysis is the manner in which the writer develops characterization. Do the people in the novel exhibit more than a single side, or are they so inhumanly consistent that they become stereotypes? With a few exceptions, it is in this area of his work that Lewis may be faulted. Granted, this is the pitfall of the genre—satire—and Lewis based his characters on models he observed in his society. Nevertheless, taking only the photographer's view of his subjects detracts in some cases from the verisimilitude. As critic Geoffrey Moore put it, "Lewis's method was to choose an institution or a class of people, decide on a point of view, and then flatten his characters into the mould he desired. . . . [t]here is no 'innerness.'" When Lewis does go beyond this tendency toward a journalistic style, however, as he does with Carol Kennicott in *Main Street*, Max Gottlieb and Martin Arrowsmith in *Arrowsmith*, and a few other of his creations, he avoids completely the charge of creating caricatures.

Lewis can certainly be seen as a critic of the era in which he wrote his best novels, but he was no reformer; he does not suggest solutions. In the manner of some European novelists, such as Émile Zola, he merely points out, through satire, what he sees.

MAIN STREET

First published: 1920
Type of work: Novel

A young, idealistic bride tries unsuccessfully to alter life in a small midwestern town circa 1920.

Carol Milford, an attractive, eager librarian, marries Dr. Will Kennicott and comes to Gopher Prairie with every expectation of seeing the town through her husband's eyes. Will, a character based to a great extent on the novelist's father and brother Claude, both country doctors, is proud of Gopher Prairie and does not see clearly the faults which become so apparent to Carol almost at once. Carol Kennicott would like to change everything, from the dull buildings that line Main Street to the people who inhabit the houses, people whose interests in life are very narrow indeed. Will's friends assume that Carol will "settle in" and embrace their values, and when she does not do so, they are quite disturbed.

Lewis constantly emphasizes the freedom of the countryside surrounding the town, so that nature, even in the midst of stormy winter, is preferable to the stultifying atmosphere of Gopher Prairie. Some of Carol's happiest times are spent with her husband, tramping through the area, appreciating nature.

She tries various plans to "raise the cultural level" of the town. She gives well-planned parties, instead of the usual dull ones that seem to her to be funereal. She offers to use her skills as a librarian to upgrade The Thanatopsis, a ladies' literary discussion group which specializes in brief summaries of the lives of great literary figures; she organizes a drama club to produce plays of more lasting merit than *The Girl from Kankakee*. She consistently fails.

Furthermore, she finds that even in Gopher Prairie, a village of about four thousand souls, there are strict notions of "social class," prejudice against the Swedish and German immigrants, rigid notions about morals, anti-union feeling, an avid love of gossiping, and, above all, a sense of unremitting dullness.

Carol does find a few friends. There is Guy Pollock, a lawyer who at first seems to share her views of Gopher Prairie. There is her hired girl, Bea Sorenson, a young Swedish farm girl who (by contrasting it with Scandia Crossing, population sixty-seven) looks at Gopher Prairie as a big city. There is the town outcast, Miles Bjornstain, an independent "Red Swede" who marries Bea. There is Erik Valborg, a would-be artist/designer who works as a presser in a local tailor shop, and there is Fern Mullins, a young schoolteacher.

Yet each friendship comes to naught. Guy confesses that "village virus" has infected him even unto death; Miles loses his beloved Bea and their little son, Olaf, to death and leaves his farm to travel west; Erik becomes a small-time film actor; and Fern Mullins is forced to resign from school and is run out of town on a trumped-up morals charge based entirely on malicious gossip.

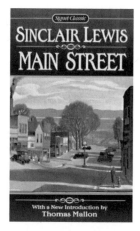

The Kennicotts have a son, Hugh, and for a while the child fills Carol's life; however, even after she and Will have had an extended vacation in California, she finds that life in Gopher Prairie is intolerable. In addition to the faults Carol has found from the beginning, the town has succumbed to the new "booster" mentality, which has raised the price of land but has not raised the level of everyday life one iota.

With her husband's reluctant approval, Carol and Hugh go to live in Washington, D.C., where she gets a job in the Bureau of War Risk Insurance. It is a first step toward her independence, but she finds a "thick streak of Main Street" even there. After a year, her husband comes to Washington; they take a short trip south, which Will calls a "second wooing," and five months later, Carol decides to return to Gopher Prairie, pregnant with her daughter and determined to continue "the good fight."

Lewis leaves little doubt about his opinion of Gopher Prairie and its faults, but the reader also sees that although Carol has good intentions from the beginning, she is not really focused on what changes she wants to make. She is somewhat immature. Perhaps her character represents the American woman of the postwar period searching for her role in a radically changed society. It is only after she has lived in Washington and had contact with the suffragists that she begins to define herself as an individual. Her speech to Will at the end of the book is quite prophetic. She takes him to look at their sleeping baby daughter and says:

> Do you see that object on the pillow? Do you know what it is? It's a bomb to blow up smugness. If you Tories were wise, you wouldn't arrest anarchists; you'd arrest all these children while they're asleep in their cribs. Think what that baby will see and meddle with before she dies in the year 2000! She may see an industrial union of the whole world, she may see aeroplanes going to Mars.

Dr. Will Kennicott seems sometimes to be a father figure to Carol. He loves her deeply and is more than patient with her peccadilloes. He is a good doctor, but he sees no romance in his profession; he has accepted some of the less attractive qualities of Gopher Prairie, such as the notion of social classes, as shown in his disapproval of having Carol take Hugh to visit Bea and Miles to play with their son, Olaf. He is somewhat interested in making money to secure their future; he is also completely honest, basically kind, and thoroughly loyal. Most of the other inhabitants of Gopher Prairie are not particularly memorable. They are, for the most part, types rather than distinctly drawn individuals.

The fact that Lewis has put Jim Blausser, the publicity person hired for the booster campaign, so near the end of the novel is significant. This huckster exaggerates everything from the genuine natural beauty to be found in the local countryside to the new "White Way" which is now to be found on Main Street. He assures the citizens that their town can easily expect to become a city of 200,000 and a manufacturing center very soon. As Carol Kennicott wryly comments, "There's where I want to go; to that model town Gopher Prairie." Lewis is foreshadowing next stage in the development of Main Street as he takes it to the city of Zenith, the locale of his next novel.

BABBITT

First published: 1922
Type of work: Novel

George F. Babbitt, representing the new middle class, depends on material possessions and conformity to validate his existence.

Rebecca West, in her 1922 essay "Babbitt," makes a statement that encapsulates Lewis's attitude toward the world of his novel *Babbitt*: "To write satire . . . one must hate the world so much that one's hatred strikes sparks, but one must hate it only because it disappoints one's invincible love of it."

This statement also illustrates strikingly the novelist's disappointment in its protagonist, Babbitt. Here is a man with a dim perception that what he has accepted as the "good life" is not entirely satisfying; yet he lacks the power to do more than dream of the "fairy child" who beckons him to a better

way. For Lewis, George F. Babbitt is the Everyman of his time.

In the real estate business with his father-in-law, Babbitt has convinced himself that he is indispensable as a facilitator. He does not think himself dishonest when he "puts over a deal" whereby a client receives information about a piece of property before the seller is aware of its increased value. He loves his wife, Myra, and their three children, but it is only in times of crisis that he gives them an honest thought. Supposedly a graduate of the state university, Babbitt is really quite ignorant, and in the "poetry" created by one of his fellow Boosters Lewis has created a hilarious put-down of popular taste in the arts through the verses of T. Cholmondeley Frink, who also writes "Ads, that Add."

George Babbitt thinks that he has many friends, whereas in reality he has but one, Paul Reisling, and it is with Paul on a few days vacation in the Maine woods th Babbitt finds his only true happiness. It is the closeness of a friendship that temporarily frees Babbitt from his boring life in Zenith, but this scene serves also as the author's insistence that nature has a salutary effect on all human beings, even the silliest. Paul's wife, Zilla, is a vindictive shrew who finally frustrates her husband to the point of shooting her in the shoulder. In all sincerity, Babbitt goes to Paul's lawyer in an offer to concoct a story to make the crime seem less deliberate, but his suggestion is refused, and Paul goes to state prison for three years. George misses him sorely.

At this time George's wife, Myra Babbitt, and her youngest child, Tinka, go East to visit relatives, leaving only George, his daughter Verona, and his son, Ted. Busy with their own lives, the young people are unconcerned and do little to assuage George's loneliness. His group at the Athletic Club is no help, and he begins to think of female companionship as a viable option. After Babbitt has been further depressed by a visit to Paul in prison, he makes several timorous attempts at flirting with his neighbor's wife and with a young manicurist. Both these women rebuff him, but an attractive widow, Tanis Judique, accepts his attentions after he has found her "just the right apartment."

He feels guilty about his affair and anxious about his activities, which include drinking and partying with "the Bunch," a group of Tanis's friends who consider themselves urbane bohemians. He does not stop being "Old Georgie," however, until his wife requires surgery. Meanwhile, Zenith is torn by a strike which divides the city into factions and finds Babbitt confused. He wants to believe that Seneca Doane and the other liberals supporting the strikers have their rights, but he is afraid that those who characterize them as "dirty socialists" will censure him, and he gives in to his fear.

His former friends, the respectable members of the Athletic Club, have formed a Good Citizens League—with all the characteristics of the Ku Klux Klan, minus the white hoods—and George is urged (even mildly threatened) to join. He resists briefly; then agrees with Vergil Grunch that he is being foolish, and within two weeks he is bellicose regarding the wickedness of Seneca Doane, the crimes of labor unions, and the perils of immigration. Babbitt also returns to the Boosters' Club, the church, and the Elks, and his father-in-law announces that their business is back to where it was before George's brief rebellion.

Lewis does, however, allow him one saving act. His son, Ted, has married the girl next door, much to the consternation of her parents. Furthermore, the boy has decided to skip college and work as a mechanic, and it is George Babbitt who tells him, "[d]on't be scared of the family. No, nor all of Zenith. Nor of yourself, the way I've been. Go ahead, old man! The world is yours!"

ARROWSMITH

First published: 1925
Type of work: Novel

An idealistic doctor finds his life's work in research.

In this novel, Lewis's protagonist, Martin Arrowsmith, is much more fully developed—more of a three-dimensional person—than are the characters in his earlier books. From the first, when he is shown as an adolescent, Martin makes mistakes; he is not always the perfect hero. He is, in fact, recognizably human.

The locale (Elk Mills, in the state of Winnemac) represents Lewis's midwestern roots. There is the inevitable Main Street and the feeling of transition from rural life to that of a small town; there is also the alcoholic Doc Vickerson, who encourages the fourteen-year-old Martin to "study medicine, go to Zenith, and make money."

Martin goes to the state university as a medical student and has a professor, Dr. Max Gottlieb, who is to influence significantly the rest of his life. He also meets a number of other students who continue as characters throughout the novel. There is Ira Hinkley, the future medical missionary, Angus Duer, the future surgeon, and Clif Clawson, the practical joker, whose dismissal from medical school and subsequent appearance as an automobile salesman give Lewis a fine chance to satirize hucksterism. At this point Martin also meets the love of his life, Leora Tozer, a young nursing student.

As Dr. Gottlieb's assistant, Martin is becoming very interested in the research area of medicine, but he makes a mistake, argues with Gottlieb, and after a night drinking, tells Dean Silva that he will not apologize, so he is suspended from the university. With little sense of direction, and a lot of drinking, Martin actually becomes a hobo, but he finally heads west to Leora, who has returned to her hometown at her parents' insistence. Her family opposes their marriage, but they elope, and the Tozers must accept it.

In the flush of graduation and a decision to set up practice in Wheatsylvania (Leora's hometown), Martin's devotion to research (and to Max Gottlieb) is temporarily forgotten. Gottlieb has been discharged from the hospital; his wife is ill, and the doctor is nearly at his wit's end when he is offered a position at a pharmaceutical firm, formerly a target of his scorn. From this time on, *Arrowsmith* deals largely with the commercial exploitation of scientific findings versus the need for pure research.

When Gottlieb refuses to turn his incomplete research into a salable product, he is fired from Hunziker Pharmaceutical, but he finds a place at the McGurk Institute almost immediately. Lewis criticizes the politics common at such institutions, based on Paul de Kruif's actual experience at the Rockefeller Institute.

Bored with his small-town practice, Martin obtains a position as second-in-command to the director of public health, Dr. Almus Pickerbaugh, in Nautilus, Iowa, and becomes director himself after Pickerbaugh is elected to Congress, but his role there is short-lived. Next, he obtains a position at Rouncefield Clinic in Chicago, through Angus Duer, and changes his goal of becoming a researcher to becoming a material success. He does qualify this new ambition by thinking that after he has made enough money, he will be able to have his own laboratory. Nevertheless, Lewis makes him very believable in his desire to be a monetary success rather than a man dedicated to pure science who is frustrated at every turn by those holding the purse strings.

A paper published by Martin reaches Gottlieb, who then invites him to McGurk, and the two are reconciled. All goes well despite the factions at the institute. Then the bombshell hits: Martin has been working tirelessly and has made a significant discovery. Those in power, eager to enhance the reputation of the institute, want to make the research public at once. Finally, with Sondelius and Terry Wickett, Martin is able to work on an antidote for bubonic plague just when such a plague is breaking out in the West Indies. Sondelius, Martin, and Leora, who insists on going along, will represent the McGurk Institute, while Gottlieb has been made the director in New York.

Dr. Ira Hinkley, now a medical missionary in the West Indies, returns to the cast of the novel as he tries to thwart Martin's work by lying about Martin's days at Winnemac and by referring to the plague as "the wrath of God." Martin, however, continues his mission and succeeds, although both Sondelius and Leora die. Martin is devastated and returns to New York, little comforted by the success of his research. Max is no longer director of McGurk, and once more there is a conflict between Martin and the new director, who wants immediate publication to glorify the reputation of the institute.

In due time Martin decides to remarry, this time to a wealthy socialite, Joyce Lanyon, whom he had met briefly in the Islands. The marriage does not work out, however, despite the couple's having a son. Joyce is not unsympathetic to his work, but she is not the ever-patient Leora, who truly understood that science was Martin's first love, his true passion.

Finally Martin decides to refuse the directorship at McGurk, to get a divorce from Joyce, and to defect to Terry Wickett and a simple life in the woods, dedicated to pure scientific research. It is the most romanticized ending of the four Lewis novels discussed, representing Lewis's rather naïve notion regarding a person in a natural setting, in the tradition of Huck Finn. In this same sense, it shows Martin as an eager adolescent akin to George Babbitt when he takes his vacation in the Maine woods with Paul, his one true friend.

ELMER GANTRY

First published: 1927
Type of work: Novel

A completely evil man uses evangelical religion as his road to undeserved success.

In this novel, Lewis's satire is unrelieved, beginning with his first description of Terwillinger College on the outskirts of Gritzmacher Springs, Kansas, where Elmer (nicknamed Hell-cat) Gantry is wasting his time and his mother's money pretending to get an education.

Elmer meets Judson Roberts, a preacher, and is beginning to consider a career as an evangelical minister when he is pushed into the position of leading a crowd to exhort God. Because his original plan to become a lawyer would have required study, it is easy for him to change his vocational goal, but he needs to "get a Call." This he fakes, with the help of some whiskey, and he is on his way.

At Mizpah Theological Seminary, near Zenith,

he meets Frank Shallard (one of the few decent characters in the novel), with whom Elmer shares a part-time assignment at a small country church. Always extremely interested in sex, Elmer cannot resist seducing Lulu Bains, virginal daughter of the deacon, but when the girl begins to talk of marriage, Elmer devises a scheme to marry her off to Floyd Naylor, claiming her infidelity. For this, he is rewarded with a larger church in Monarch.

Unable to reach the deacon when he arrives,

Elmer falls in with some salesmen, gets drunk, and forgets the Easter service completely. Summarily dismissed, and no longer a reverend, he becomes a salesman himself for the next two years. Although he is quite successful and enjoys the freedom to drink and womanize, Elmer misses the adulation he had as a preacher, so he becomes the assistant of an evangelist, Sharon Falconer, hoping to share the profits of her well-organized group.

Although Sharon remains "in charge," Elmer does well until Sharon is killed in the fire which destroys the new tabernacle they have built. Elmer becomes a Methodist, marries Cleo Benham with an eye to promotion, and becomes a minister in Zenith, where he meets Frank Shallard again. An influential parishioner, T. J. Riggs, helps Elmer mount a phony anti-vice crusade. The publicity results in standing-room-only crowds, but Elmer's greed is not satisfied. He wants a very rich parishioner to leave Frank's church for his; as a result of his plotting, Frank is branded an infidel, loses his pulpit, and eventually is taken for a 1920's-style "ride" when he gives a lecture titled "Are Fundamentalists Witch Hunters?" at the Zenith Charity Organization.

Elmer now has his new church and is accorded a doctorate of divinity; his services are being broadcast by radio. All should be well, but once more his lust gets him into trouble. He needs a new secretary, and the sexy Hettie Dowler seems an answer to his prayer. He gets rid of Lulu and begins an affair with Hettie. One evening, however, the two are interrupted by Hettie's husband, Oscar, who produces a gun and threatens suit for alienation of affections. He wants fifty thousand dollars but will settle for ten thousand in cash. As Elmer turns back to Hettie, he realizes that she is in on the scam—for once, the great pretender seems to be the loser.

T. J. Riggs, however, comes through with a private detective who checks out the Dowlers; as a result of what he finds, they are glad to leave town with two hundred dollars, but not before they have signed a sworn statement describing Elmer as a Christian saint. He receives telegrams giving him a large church in New York and appointing him head of Napap, an organization formed to protect American morals. His congregation reassures him with a loud hallelujah, as he prays aloud: "Dear Lord, thy work is but begun! We shall yet make these United States a moral nation," as he eyes with appreciation the new member of the choir, "a girl with charming ankles and lively eyes." It is quite clear why *Elmer Gantry* infuriated clergy of every denomination and their parishioners as well.

SUMMARY

Although since Lewis's works were first published there have been some marked changes in the style of popular novels, his books retain their place in American literature. Not only do they present a picture of an era, the 1920's, but they also make it uncomfortably obvious that, in some unpleasant ways, American society has not changed very much. Materialism and hucksterism still reign supreme. Prejudice has not been eliminated. Outward show is accepted in place of inward substance. Lewis's satirical style points up some serious faults, and the passage of time has done little to correct them.

Edythe M. McGovern

BIBLIOGRAPHY

By the Author

LONG FICTION:
Our Mr. Wrenn: The Romantic Adventures of a Gentle Man, 1914
The Trail of the Hawk: A Comedy of the Seriousness of Life, 1915
The Innocents: A Story for Lovers, 1917
The Job: An American Novel, 1917
Free Air, 1919
Main Street: The Story of Carol Kennicott, 1920
Babbitt, 1922
Arrowsmith, 1925

Mantrap, 1926
Elmer Gantry, 1927
The Man Who Knew Coolidge: Being the Soul of Lowell Schmaltz, Constructive and Nordic Citizen, 1928
Dodsworth, 1929
Ann Vickers, 1933
Work of Art, 1934
It Can't Happen Here, 1935
The Prodigal Parents, 1938
Bethel Merriday, 1940
Gideon Planish, 1943
Cass Timberlane: A Novel of Husbands and Wives, 1945
Kingsblood Royal, 1947
The God-Seeker, 1949
World So Wide, 1951

SHORT FICTION:
Selected Short Stories of Sinclair Lewis, 1935

DRAMA:
Jayhawker: A Play in Three Acts, pr. 1934 (with Lloyd Lewis)

NONFICTION:
From Main Street to Stockholm: Letters of Sinclair Lewis, 1919-1930, 1952 (Harrison Smith, editor)
The Man from Main Street: Selected Essays and Other Writings, 1904-1950, 1953 (Harry E. Maule and Melville H. Crane, editors)
Minnesota Diary, 1942-1946, 2000 (George Killough, editor)

DISCUSSION TOPICS

- Is *Main Street* primarily a novel about Carol Kennicott or about Gopher Prairie?

- Is Sinclair Lewis's characterization of George Babbitt thoroughly satirical, or does Babbitt have dimensions that encourage the reader to view him sympathetically?

- Is Martin Arrowsmith as convincing a character as George Babbitt or Carol Kennicott?

- What descriptive techniques contribute to the success of Lewis's depiction of village and small-town settings?

- The title of one book about Lewis refers to his "quixotic vision." What does this phrase mean, and what in Lewis's novels justifies its application to him?

- Lewis was the first American writer to be awarded the Nobel Prize in Literature. Did he deserve it?

About the Author

Bucco, Martin, ed. *Critical Essays on Sinclair Lewis*. Boston: G. K. Hall, 1986.

_____. *"Main Street": The Revolt of Carol Kennicott*. New York: Twayne, 1993.

_____. *Sinclair Lewis as Reader and Critic*. Lewiston, N.Y.: Edwin Mellen Press, 2004.

DiRenzo, Anthony. *If I Were Boss: The Early Business Stories of Sinclair Lewis*. Carbondale: Southern Illinois University Press, 1997.

Fleming, Robert E., and Esther Fleming. *Sinclair Lewis: A Reference Guide*. Boston: G. K. Hall, 1980.

Hutchisson, James M. *The Rise of Sinclair Lewis, 1920-1930*. University Park: Pennsylvania State University Press, 1996.

Koblas, John J. *Sinclair Lewis: Home at Last*. Bloomington, Minn.: Voyageur Press, 1981.

Light, Martin. *The Quixotic Vision of Sinclair Lewis*. West Lafayette, Ind.: Purdue University Press, 1975.

Lingeman, Richard R. *Sinclair Lewis: Rebel from Main Street*. New York: Random House, 2002.

Love, Glen A. *Babbitt: An American Life*. New York: Twayne, 1993.

Parrington, Vernon Louis. *Sinclair Lewis: Our Own Diogenes*. Seattle: University of Washington Press, 1927. Reprint. New York: Haskell House, 1973.

Schorer, Mark. *Sinclair Lewis: An American Life*. New York: McGraw-Hill, 1961.

_____, ed. *Sinclair Lewis: A Collection of Critical Essays*. Englewood Cliffs, N.J.: Prentice-Hall, 1962.

Library of Congress

JACK LONDON

Born: San Francisco, California
January 12, 1876
Died: Glen Ellen, California
November 22, 1916

Drawing on his own life, London wrote fiction filled with high adventure that posed thoughtful, provocative reflections on the contemporary questions of philosophy.

BIOGRAPHY

Jack London was born on January 12, 1876, in San Francisco, the son of Flora Wellman and William Henry Chaney. Chaney, an astrologer and confidence man, had deserted his common-law wife when he learned she was pregnant, which led Wellman to attempt suicide. In September of 1876, she married a widower with two daughters, John London, who gave her son his name. The family was poor, made poorer by Flora's imprudent investments in get-rich-quick schemes, and was constantly moving between apartments and small ranches. Unable to put down roots, Jack was lonely as a child. He worked hard and spent every spare moment reading dime novels and romances.

After completing grammar school in Oakland, California, in 1891, he borrowed money and bought a sloop on which he engaged in oyster piracy. At fifteen he was a petty criminal, by night raiding the beds where food companies kept their stocks and by day drinking in waterfront saloons. After a rival burned his boat, he decided to join the other side, the Fish Patrol, which had been established to guard the beds.

Soon his adventuring took a wider circuit; he sailed the North Pacific on a seal-hunting ship and then became a hobo, trekking across the United States with Coxey's army, a group of unemployed workers who were marching on Washington to demand jobs. This experience with the underprivi-leged converted London to socialism. Returning to Oakland in 1896, he completed high school and attended the University of California at Berkeley for two semesters. The following year he was off again, this time joining the Yukon gold rush. Although unsuccessful in his search for riches, he had collected a wealth of material by the time of his return to California in 1898, which would bring him his first literary success.

Failing as a prospector, he was determined to make his living with words, and he began a ferocious regimen of pouring out essays, poetry, and stories with which he deluged every conceivable literary outlet. Soon he was making enough money to live on, writing mainly juvenile fiction, horror stories, and jokes—that is, "hack work." In 1900, however, he achieved his first recognition and financial stability with the publication of a book of his Alaskan stories, *The Son of the Wolf.* In the following three years, he published three fictional works, culminating in *The Call of the Wild* (1903), the story of an Alaskan sled dog that brought London fortune and international acclaim.

It could be said that once he entered the public eye, he gave it an eyeful. For one, there was his extravagant lifestyle, hardly becoming for a man who lectured for the Socialist Party. The first object of his conspicuous consumption was the grand yacht the *Snark,* which he constructed for a round-the-world cruise. This tour was dropped abruptly because of London's ill health, but he immediately began sinking his burgeoning income into another monstrosity, the Beauty Ranch in Sonoma Valley, California.

Another factor that caught the public's attention was the author's flamboyance. He reported the Russo-Japanese War with great derring-do, scandalized the country by marrying his second wife shortly after divorcing his first, and aroused the public by his flaming speeches on class war. At the same time, he followed up his first best seller with equally popular works. These included such novels of rousing adventure as *The Sea-Wolf* (1904) and *White Fang* (1906).

The wide range of interests he displayed in his earliest hack writing did not desert him, and in the sixteen years after his first success he was to compose in many genres, including futuristic political fiction (*The Iron Heel* in 1907), reportage (*The People of the Abyss* in 1903), and polemics (*John Barleycorn* in 1913).

By 1914, London's health was failing. His mammoth expenses kept him writing at a furious pace; while during his South Sea voyages and war reporting he had contracted malaria, dysentery, pleurisy, yaws, and other diseases. His health worsened over the next few years, and matters were not helped by his refusal to slow down or by his eccentric enjoyment of the taste of raw meat. As the end of his life neared, he was often in intense pain, which he alleviated by drugs. On the night of November 21, 1916, in an action that may or may not have been intentional, he injected himself with an overdose of morphine and was found near death in the morning. He died that day.

ANALYSIS

American fiction writers in the second half of the nineteenth century turned to Europe, and France in particular, for inspiration. Authors such as William Dean Howells, Hamlin Garland, and Frank Norris with one hand wrote essays on the validity of European writing practices and with the other composed their own stories and novels in the European realist or naturalist manner. Works such as Garland's *Main-Travelled Roads* (1891) or Norris's *McTeague* (1899) matched the European writers in their ability to capture sordid surroundings and present controversial themes. What the Europeans had that the Americans did not, however, was a serious, adult reading public of significant proportions.

There was no place in the United States for the like of Émile Zola, the savage French writer who raked his society over the coals in novel after novel.

It was possible for Garland and Norris to turn out occasional hard-hitting works, but in order to earn a living they also had to lower their standards and turn to writing pot-boilers and sentimental stories.

London, who came nearly a generation after such men, solved the problem of how to treat serious themes while making money by coming up with the realistic, philosophically oriented adventure tale. His life gave him an edge over those other authors in writing of adventure. Norris, for example, wrote a weak novel about Arctic exploration, but he had never been to the Far North. When London, on the other hand, wrote in *The Call of the Wild* about prospectors and sharpers in gold-rush Alaska, he was drawing on his own very real experiences. He was also well read in the philosophy of the day, and this aided him in conceiving his stories as parables that tested and commented on contemporary thought.

The leading discussions of late nineteenth century social science were at the center of London's fiction. He was not intent on embodying these ideas uncritically but rather on probing them for weaknesses. Questions about the effect of the environment on individual development and about the ability of the environment to screen out the best individuals for special positions were among the issues being debated. The biologist Charles Darwin's theory of evolution had been interpreted as implying that because an organism had to adapt to the ecological system in which it resided, human free will was drastically limited.

Naturalist writers such as Zola and his American followers wrote books in which vicious and villainous characters were shown to be products of unhealthy living conditions and heredity. The sociologist Herbert Spencer added a new twist to this interpretation. Coining the term "survival of the fittest," he noted that every society had top places and that to reach those positions demanded willpower and perseverance. Though the conquerors of society's heights may have had to adapt themselves to the law of the jungle, they were magnificent successes when compared to the miserable failures that populate the lower ranks.

Such a Spencerian interpretation of Darwin dovetailed with American puritanism, which held that achievement in life corresponds with God's approval of one's righteousness, or, to put it in secularized terms, that success is testimony to one's virtue and abilities. This concept might certainly serve as a guiding star over London's life: He had risen from being a street brawler to being one of the most celebrated writers of his time—certainly this proved that one could rise and triumph over one's natal circumstances.

Rather than wholeheartedly endorsing this idea, London repeatedly questioned its optimistic slant. In *The Sea-Wolf* the ship's captain is a man of indomitable will, a leader, a physically strong man, and an avid reader of profound books (particularly Spencer's). His superiority has raised him over others, but it has had the fatal consequence of making him arrogant and friendless. In a novel that brings this theme even closer to home, *Martin Eden* (1908), a writer who has risen from obscurity to fame finds that his working-class viewpoint makes it impossible to associate with his new middle-class literary peers. Moreover, his new learning isolates him from the type of people he grew up with and once could love. The fittest, in London's presentations, are so superior as to be unnatural.

A related sociological theme, developed particularly at the end of the nineteenth century by American writers such as Brooks Adams, was the doctrine of racial hierarchy. This doctrine, particularly appropriate as a justification when the United States was beginning to acquire colonies, held that just as superior individuals rose to the top of a society, so superior races, such as the Anglo-Saxons, would naturally become the leaders and teachers of inferior races, such as the Eskimos.

Again, London accepted the theory but highlighted its tragic implications. In "In the Forests of the North" (1902), a lone white man survives an Arctic expedition and finds himself in a remote Indian village. He decides to throw in his lot with the tribe that has nurtured him, and, because of his natural superiority, which London explicitly attributes to his race, he can lead the tribe to victory over all the surrounding Eskimo tribes. Yet his superiority makes it impossible for him to communicate intimately with the people of the village, and he lives with a tortured longing for his own kind.

A final important theme in London is the place of love in the world. London clearly sympathized with his superheroes, yet he seemed to see no hope for their integration into society unless it be through heart-humbling love. Again his thought chimed with contemporary speculation. Spencer argued that, although among savages strength and cunning set a person apart, in modern civilization it is a person's ability to sympathize widely that would take him or her to the top.

Although in his major texts London did not show his strong men bowing to romance, it was an important secondary theme, becoming uppermost in minor novels such as *White Fang*. In this book a savage dog, who has been leading a wolf pack and who is subsequently caught and mistreated by a succession of masters, is obtained by a gentle Weedon Scott, "The Love-Master." Through all-enduring patience and caring, Scott converts the Arctic beast into a top-notch dog. In this case, a being has passed from barbarism to civilization without losing its superior ranking.

In every work discussed thus far except the last, London was setting forth a viewpoint that would not recommend him to a large audience. He was pronouncing negatively on the American credo of success at any price, for example, by showing that success leads to isolation and unhappiness. In compensation for this sobering message, London spun a whopping good yarn for his readers. One especially remarkable aspect of his narrative skills was the fashion in which he could transform metaphysical questions into dramatic tableaux. In *The Sea-Wolf*, for example, the captain, Wolf Larsen, maintains that people crave life above anything. The anemic intellectual Van Weyden, who has accidentally landed on Larsen's ship, continues to hold an idealistic position. Suddenly Larsen springs from his chair, grabs the intellectual by the throat, and nearly chokes him to death. After letting him up, Larsen asks him if he now gets the point. Through such maneuvers, London gave philosophical discussions the excitement of an adventure tale.

THE CALL OF THE WILD

First published: 1903
Type of work: Novel

A domesticated California farm dog is stolen and transported to Alaska, where his wild instincts gradually surface.

The Call of the Wild was London's first success, and it represented an imaginative recasting of strands of thought from Darwinism and literary naturalism. The general concept of the book is a clever play on themes generated by attacks on the theory of evolution. Religious writers ridiculed the evolutionists' idea that humans were the descendants of prehistoric apes and poured scorn on the concept that a being with a godlike soul shared traits with other members of the animal kingdom. Thinkers of this ilk lambasted writers such as Frank Norris, who in *McTeague* showed animal traits appearing in his characters when they were under stress.

London found a creative way to sidestep such objections, while maintaining central evolutionary tenets. Rather than showing a person descending to animalistic behavior, he describes a dog making

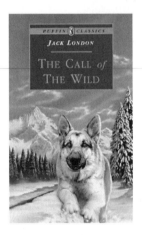

such a descent. Certainly a dog is already an animal, but in *The Call of the Wild*, through a series of misadventures, a pampered domestic dog is transformed into an Arctic wolf.

A central motor of this transformation is the influence of the environment. The dog protagonist, Buck, has adapted to life as a doted-on member of the family, but his life is imperiled by the Alaskan gold rush. Sled dogs are at a premium, and dognappers are scouring the country for hardy brutes. Buck is stolen and sold north to a government courier, Perrault, and learns to adapt to the hard life of pulling a dogsled through the snowy wastes.

Buck's adaptation is eased by the revival of ancestral traits. As London notes, "not only did he learn by experience, but instincts long dead became alive. . . . [h]e remembered back to . . . the time the wild-dogs ranged in packs through the primeval forest." Such a note was often struck in Darwinian novels that described human behavior. In the already noted *McTeague*, the hero's wife, Trina, becomes increasingly miserly as characteristics of her German peasant forebears come to life. More startlingly, the hero, McTeague, when pursued by the police, resurrects lost animal behaviors, such as wonderfully keen hearing. The ethnic note is also sounded. Where writers describing humans noted

the part that racial qualities played in the individual personality, London sees the same type of qualities accounting for Buck's growing superiority over the other dogs in the team: "His cunning was wolf cunning . . . his intelligence, shepherd intelligence and St. Bernard intelligence."

The novel is more than a vigorous endorsement of such biological themes; it is also a *Bildungsroman*, that is, a novel concerned with the education of the protagonist to the ways of the world. Bought by Perrault, Buck's main teachers are the seasoned sled dogs. He learns from them, for example, that he must not only "wolf" down his food ration to avoid having it stolen by other canines but must try to rob others' portions to increase his prestige. Buck caps this stage of his education by killing the top dog and assuming his post.

These examples may suggest that a dog's life is all violence and competition, but, in fact, primitivism has two faces. London's unusual subject allows him to see virtues in a return to an aboriginal state that could not be found if humans were his subjects. To continue using Norris's novel as a counterpoint, when McTeague becomes as wily as a hunted animal, there is little but degradation in his reversion to earlier animal patterns. When Buck recalls his ancestors' activities, however, there is the feeling that he is returning to a truer world. Life is hard there but authentic. The pampered house dog could never experience the joy of the hunt. Buck is "ranging at the head of the pack . . . [in] an ecstasy that marks the summit of life."

The shift in perspective allows London to stand the typical ending of the Darwinian novel on its head. In Zola's *Le Bête humaine* (1890; *The Human Beast*, 1891), for example, the complete emergence of the protagonist's hereditary tendency to alcoholism leads to villainous actions. In London's novel, in sharp contrast, when Buck is at his most savage he is also most completely fulfilling his potential—utilizing his brain, muscles, and heart to the utmost.

After running a gamut of human masters, Buck is obtained by the kindly John Thornton, who allows him to wander in the woods, where he learns to hunt. One day Buck returns from an expedition to find Thornton killed by Indians; his last ties to humanity have been cut, so he gives in to the call of the wild. He ends the novel at the head of a wolf pack, a legend to the Indians.

Such an upbeat ending was out of keeping with the general tenor of fiction that dealt with such themes, but it was appropriate for a work that had shifted the terrain of such writing from human to canine society. The optimistic but logically consistent presentation of how the law of the jungle could turn the protagonist from a civilized pet into a legend of the wilderness won readers who could not stomach the representation of similar themes in a human milieu.

THE SEA-WOLF

First published: 1904
Type of work: Novel

A literary dilettante undergoes a rough education at the hands of a seagoing superman.

The plot of *The Sea-Wolf* was a popular one in the late nineteenth century; Rudyard Kipling, for example, had used something similar in *Captains Courageous* (1896). A snobbish, upper-class weakling is forced to obey the commands of a harsh, lower-class dictator and ends up greatly profiting by the experience. In London's novel, a literary gentleman, Humphrey Van Weyden, is washed off a San Francisco ferryboat and taken up by an outgoing seal hunter. The imperious captain, Wolf Larsen, has just lost a hand and decides to press the protesting Weyden into service as cabin boy for the long voyage.

An apter parallel for London's book than Kipling's novel may be found in Herman Melville's *Moby Dick* (1851). In both London's and Melville's novels, the center of attention is not the slowly maturing, sensitive narrator but the superhuman ship's captain. In *Moby Dick*, Captain Ahab is a monomanical, charismatic zealot, and the critical light thrown on him is also used to criticize basic premises of a then-current theoretical posture, Byronic Romanticism. In something of the same way, in *The Sea-Wolf* the judgment passed on Wolf Larsen, the dynamic, intelligent, yet brutal captain also undercuts the materialism he espouses.

Larsen is contradictory. At first Van Weyden sees the ship's master as nothing more than an unfeeling hulk. He witnesses Larsen tossing a dead body overboard without a proper burial ceremony and forcing his men to obey him through fear of his fists. As the trip progresses, however, Van Weyden finds in the captain's cabin a well-stocked library of current literature: science, history, even grammar. At this discovery he says to himself about Larsen, "At once he became an enigma."

As it turns out, the captain's violence is rooted in a materialist metaphysics—and violent he is. When a crewman complains of an arrangement, Larsen and the first mate beat him senseless. When the cook does not keep the mess clean, he is dangled over the ship's side until a shark lops off his foot. Larsen's study of Darwin, Spencer, and other evolutionists has taught him that life, in his preferred phrase, "is like yeast." It is a battle that goes to the strong, and, according to Larsen, every noble sentiment that Van Weyden defends is so much "bosh."

Furthermore, as if to corroborate the captain's doctrine, the ship is run on the law of the strong. The captain fights with the crew, terrorizing them—they futilely attempt a mutiny at one point—and almost every sailor plots vengeance against another for a real or imagined slight. Van Weyden himself is pushed around by the cook until, as if to confirm the captain's ideas, Van Weyden employs threats to subdue his enemy, calmly sharpening the blade of a dirk until the cook is scared witless.

Although the captain's philosophy accounts rather well for the dog-eat-dog atmosphere onboard ship, there are a number of fatal chinks in it. For one, it is a philosophy reserved for winners. It is small consolation for the sailors that the one beating them is their natural superior. Moreover, it is a philosophy of hopelessness. When the captain's debilitating headaches weaken him, his metaphysics offers him no solace, leaving him to a titanic despair. Larsen's superb fitness isolates him, and he is particularly unsuited for mixing with women. When the sealer picks up a young shipwrecked woman, Maud Brewster, Larsen treats her as roughly as he does his men and ends by trying to rape her.

As in most adventure tales, the actions and characters are exaggerated. The ship seems to undergo every catastrophe: losing its seal boats in a storm, a mutiny, pitched battle with a poaching sealer, and multiple desertions. Wolf Larsen is a larger-than-life but memorable creation, and it is to London's credit that he never softens the portrait. Though he is betrayed by his body, blind and half paralyzed, Larsen remains a staunch atheistic materialist. Even blind, he tries to kill the narrator, Van Weyden. It begins to appear that materialism begets violence as the only way for the unbelieving soul to make a mark on a world that holds neither immortality nor lasting value.

London locates his final criticism of materialism in his depiction of Larsen's bodily dissolution. The captain's powerful will, trapped in a frame struck down in its prime, seems to be crying out for a way to continue. Although the arguments for immortality offered by Van Weyden are less than convincing, the book does leave a powerful impression that there must be something to life beyond the physical world. Nevertheless, it is Wolf Larsen, a man so sincerely and devastatingly criticized, that fascinates the reader. Van Weyden, who gradually comes to accept a part of the captain's philosophy and learns how to be a good sailor, becoming a man in the process, is a much less interesting character.

Near the end of the novel, Van Weyden and Maud Brewster escape the ship and land on a desert island. A plodding Robinson Crusoe-type episode follows, which, without the presence of the captain, has little life in it. Happily, this section is brief: By a rather implausible coincidence, Larsen, abandoned in his blindness by the crew, lands on the same island. The story gathers excitement again as a cat-and-mouse game ensues between Van Weyden and the dying Larsen. In *The Sea-Wolf* London finds that the savagery which he believes is relatively laudable in the canine world of Buck is much less palatable in human society.

MARTIN EDEN

First published: 1908
Type of work: Novel

A poor sailor sets out to turn himself into an intellectual and successful author to win a middle-class woman.

In *Martin Eden*, London turned away from writing science fiction and adventure tales to write a realistic study of a working-class writer's struggle to survive while educating himself. Many critics have called this book London's masterpiece.

For all their verve and philosophical pungency, London's adventure novels lack the breadth and sympathetic observation found in serious realistic fiction. In *The Sea-Wolf*, to take one example, although there is a wealth of incident, the actions revolve around the three central characters. No broad social canvas is painted. The complexity of the plot of *Martin Eden*, on the other hand, makes it necessary for the author to portray all of San Francisco society.

Martin Eden is an out-of-work sailor who is invited to the Morse home because he has helped one of the sons, who had been set upon by ruffians. In the home, he is enthralled by the college-age daughter, Ruth Morse, having never encountered such a vision of feminine purity before. Spurred by his growing affection, Martin determines to live by his brain rather than his back: He will be an author.

While keeping contact with Ruth, he is forced to take handouts from his sister or work at casual labor when his money runs low and the rejection slips pile up. He moves through many sectors of society, from the upper-middle-class world of the Morses to the petit bourgeois world of his sister to the lower-class environs of his sailor friends to the sub-proletarian bowels where he seeks employment. A reader completes the book with an awareness of life as a whole in early twentieth century California.

One drawback to London's more popular adventure yarns is that they seem to lack subtlety of observation, or, to put it another way, the scenes of dogsled travel or seal hunting described in this fiction are so out of the ordinary that their novelty overrides any question of their freshness. In *Martin*

Eden, by contrast, London depicts typical everyday events with a brilliant eye for detail along with a fine sense of structure. The long opening scene, for example, in which the hero comes to his first Morse dinner party, moves back and forth narratively between the sailor's self-conscious gaucheries and Ruth Morse's alternating attraction and repulsion toward the stranger.

Another beautifully rendered and observed scene occurs when Martin, after months of study and composition, attempts to rejoin his old mates for an evening of dancing and flirting. The failure of the attempt is poignantly pictured. As London concludes, "He was too far removed. Too many thousands of opened books yawned between them and him." Scenes such as these hit home with the sensitive reader in a way the scenes in London's more fabulous stories cannot.

The core of the book concerns the struggles of a writer in the United States, struggles which can be divided into two phases. In the first, before the writer is recognized, everyone disregards him. Martin does not know the ropes, so the magazines reject or fleece him. What work he does sell is underpaid. His girlfriend, who started him on this course, tells him to get a regular job.

The second phase starts when the writer becomes well known. Now everyone ignorantly lionizes him. Magazines beg for pieces they had previously rejected as obscene. His brother-in-law, who had despised him, now sheepishly comes to borrow money. Ruth, who had broken off their engagement because she believed a vituperative, false newspaper report about him, now comes back. His embittered conclusion is that genuine talent is never recognized for what it is. Although he has met a few discerning critics along the way, the vast majority merely follow the prevailing winds of fashion. This realization leads to Martin's suicide.

The fact that Martin has met some truly selfless critics and writers during phases of his life makes his chosen ending somewhat puzzling and unconvincing, as it is more pessimistic than the evidence warrants. The suicide, though, as is all of the book, is described with London's trademark vivacity.

London's adventure writing, whatever its limitations, did have positive value. This discipline taught him to write sentences that crackled with a crisp authority. He puts his finger on that trait in his own writing when he mentions the critics' growing appreciation of Martin's prose. "It had been discovered that he was a stylist, with meat under his style." To take one example from *Martin Eden*, this description of Martin's early failures: "Even his earliest efforts were not marked with the clumsiness of mediocrity. What characterized them was the clumsiness of too great strength." Stephen Crane or Ernest Hemingway, to whom London can be compared, could not produce such pithy, telling phrases.

Arguably, London's most interesting innovation, following the lead of Kipling and Robert Louis Stevenson (though London introduced a more philosophical bent), was to use adventure tales to delve into the troubling questions of evolution and the environment's effect on human will. Yet to create his greatest novel, he had to step away from this type of fiction; in *Martin Eden*, he used a broader canvas to depict the adventure that is writing.

"TO BUILD A FIRE"

First published: 1908 (collected in *Lost Face*, 1910)
Type of work: Short story

A prospector in the Yukon makes the mistake of setting out on a day's trek alone when the temperature is 75 degrees below zero.

London was not one to gloss over unpleasantness, and in "To Build a Fire" he described just how harsh the world can be to someone who disregards its laws. As the story opens, life seems benign enough. It is a still, clear day, and the unnamed protagonist has plenty of time to make the one-day walk to the camp where his friends wait. He is in fine fettle, alert and careful of his footing on the frozen riverbed. He has his dog for company. The only troubles are that it is fearfully cold—75 degrees below zero—and he is "without imagination." From this seemingly slight situation, London crafts a tale of a universe where any step can be fatal, looking backward to the metaphysical despair of Stephen Crane and forward to the stoic code of Ernest Hemingway.

In Crane's short story "The Open Boat" (1897), a number of survivors of a sunken ship ride on a lifeboat in heavy seas. The fact that they may drown in sight of the shore underlines to them the indifference of the cosmos to human undertakings. In London's tale, the omnipresent cold, though ready to sweep away human life, is simply part of the universe's thermodynamics. When the protagonist has gotten into a desperate plight, having fallen through the ice and wet his legs, the author emphasizes the larger picture: "The cold of space smote the unprotected tip of the planet, and he, being on that tip, received the full force of the blow." The largeness of the forces involved reduce his plight to insignificance.

In the works of Hemingway, such as *A Farewell to Arms* (1929) and *The Sun Also Rises* (1926), the author prescribes that the acknowledged indifference of the larger forces of reality be met by a stoic code of honor on the part of his characters. Though London's protagonist, foolhardy in attempting the trip alone, lacks the judgment of Hemingway's ideal heroes, he does display admirable coolness in trying to build a fire to thaw out his legs, taking each difficulty in stride. When he finds, for example, that he can no longer work his numb fingers, he picks up wood with his two palms. Also, after an initial panic when he loses his fire, he resigns himself to death and musters whatever dignity he can, sitting down for the last time quietly.

The story is a short one (fifteen pages), and the compression works to magnify some of London's strengths while helping to diminish some of his weaknesses. His writing was often marred by obtrusive passages, especially when discussing such charged topics as women or Anglo-Saxon superiority. In this piece, where the concentration is so tightly focused, his prose is always spare and telling. Each stroke of his pen underlines the tenuousness of life in the North or grimly describes the doomed man's survival strategies.

London had another weakness—for all his experience in the Yukon, he often overstretched his imagination and presented scenes that rang false. This was particularly true in his rendering of In-dian life, a favorite subject of his and yet one he had never penetrated with any clarity, preferring clichés to anthropological understanding. The limited matter of this story, a man walking with his dog, meant that London never strayed from what he knew, and the tale has a raw authenticity.

Finally, one of London's strengths was the ability to draw a landscape vividly. This skill was often downplayed, perhaps because long descriptions would have slowed the pace of his eventful narratives. In this piece, however, such descriptions come to the fore and serve as pointers to the theme of the piece: The seeming quiescence of the landscape he describes is undermined with pitfalls for the inexperienced.

As in *The Call of the Wild*, London draws attention to the importance of primitive instincts. In a surprising but appropriate manner, he contrasts the dog's intelligent intuitions to the man's wrongheaded reasoning. The dog "knew that it was no time for travelling. Its instinct told it a truer tale than was told to the man by the man's judgment." The dog's instinctive reactions, developed over generations in the Arctic, far outmatched the brainpower of man, a recent visitor. As in other places, London finds a novel way to plump for primitivism.

Summary

London developed what might be called the "thinking man's adventure story." Drawing on his own experiences as a sailor and gold prospector, he wrote rip-roaring sagas that went beyond being simple entertainments to broach speculative issues concerning evolution, free will, and the survival of primitive instincts in the civilized. His training as an action writer led him to rely on a pungent, direct prose that was a major asset in his non-genre novel, *Martin Eden*. In this triumphant work, he added the new strengths of breadth and keen observation to the skills he had already displayed in adventure stories.

James Feast

BIBLIOGRAPHY

By the Author

LONG FICTION:
A Daughter of the Snows, 1902
The Call of the Wild, 1903
The Sea-Wolf, 1904
The Game, 1905
White Fang, 1906
Before Adam, 1906
The Iron Heel, 1907
Martin Eden, 1908
Burning Daylight, 1910
Adventure, 1911
The Abysmal Brute, 1913
The Valley of the Moon, 1913
The Mutiny of the Elsinore, 1914
The Scarlet Plague, 1915
The Star Rover, 1915
The Little Lady of the Big House, 1916
Jerry of the Islands, 1917
Michael, Brother of Jerry, 1917
Hearts of Three, 1920
The Assassination Bureau, Ltd., 1963 (completed by
    Robert L. Fish)

SHORT FICTION:
The Son of the Wolf, 1900
The God of His Fathers, and Other Stories, 1901
Children of the Frost, 1902
The Faith of Men, and Other Stories, 1904
Moon-Face, and Other Stories, 1906
Love of Life, and Other Stories, 1906
Lost Face, 1910
When God Laughs, and Other Stories, 1911
South Sea Tales, 1911
The House of Pride, and Other Tales of Hawaii, 1912
Smoke Bellew, 1912
A Son of the Sun, 1912
The Night-Born, 1913
The Strength of the Strong, 1914
The Turtles of Tasman, 1916
The Human Drift, 1917
The Red One, 1918
On the Makaloa Mat, 1919
Dutch Courage, and Other Stories, 1922

DRAMA:
Scorn of Women, pb. 1906
Theft, pb. 1910

DISCUSSION TOPICS

- *The Call of the Wild* is a title that has given a common phrase to the English language, and the book itself became a model for many later writers. What are the ingredients of the novel's originality?

- Jack London accepted the notion, popular in his time, of the superiority of gifted individuals and of some racial and ethnic groups but felt that such superiority imposed certain limitations. What were they?

- Contrast London's view of nature in "To Build a Fire" with Stephen Crane's in "The Open Boat."

- What elevates London's fiction generally above routine adventure stories?

- To what extent do Martin Eden's circumstances and response to them parallel Stephen Crane's?

The Acorn-Planter, pb. 1916
The Plays of Jack London, pb. 2001

NONFICTION:
The Kempton-Wace Letters, 1903 (with Anna Strunsky)
The People of the Abyss, 1903
The War of the Classes, 1905
The Road, 1907
Revolution, and Other Essays, 1910
The Cruise of the Snark, 1911
John Barleycorn, 1913
Letters from Jack London, 1965 (King Hendricks and Irving Shepard, editors)
No Mentor but Myself: Jack London on Writers and Writing, 1979, revised and expanded 1999 (Dale L. Walker and Jeanne Campbell Reesman, editors)

CHILDREN'S LITERATURE:
The Cruise of the Dazzler, 1902
Tales of the Fish Patrol, 1905

About the Author

Auerbach, Jonathan. *Male Call: Becoming Jack London.* Durham, N.C.: Duke University Press, 1996.

Cassuto, Leonard, and Jeanne Campbell Reesman, eds. *Rereading Jack London.* Stanford, Calif.: Stanford University Press, 1996.

Hedrick, Joan D. *Solitary Comrade: Jack London and His Work.* Chapel Hill: University of North Carolina Press, 1982.

Kershaw, Alex. *Jack London: A Life.* New York: St. Martin's Press, 1997.

Labor, Earle, and Jeanne Campbell Reesman. *Jack London.* Rev. ed. New York: Twayne, 1994.

Reesman, Jeanne Campbell. *Jack London: A Study of the Short Fiction.* New York: Twayne, 1999.

Sinclair, Andrew. *Jack: A Biography of Jack London.* New York: Washington Square Press, 1979.

Stefoff, Rebecca. *Jack London: An American Original.* New York: Oxford University Press, 2002.

Watson, Charles N. *The Novels of Jack London: A Reappraisal.* Madison: University of Wisconsin Press, 1982.

HENRY WADSWORTH LONGFELLOW

Born: Portland, Maine
February 27, 1807
Died: Cambridge, Massachusetts
March 24, 1882

Longfellow was one of the first to see the value of distinctly American myths as proper subjects for poetry; he also refined American poetry by his metrical skill and pure language.

Library of Congress

BIOGRAPHY

Henry Wadsworth Longfellow was born into a well-to-do family in Portland, Maine, in 1807, a mere thirty years after the American Revolutionary War began. He entered Bowdoin College in Maine at the age of fourteen, and he studied the usual classical curriculum taken from British universities. He graduated from Bowdoin in 1825, having made such an impression upon the faculty there that he was given a fellowship to go to Europe to study the modern languages to prepare himself for an appointment as a professor at Bowdoin. In 1829, he was appointed a professor of modern languages at Bowdoin and remained there for seven years. He was a successful and industrious teacher; he provided materials for his classes because there were no texts in the modern languages at the time. In 1831, Longfellow married Mary Potter, a fellow native of Portland. His success was marred by Mary's death in 1835. The sunny poems of Longfellow, in fact, often mask private tragedies.

Longfellow's success at Bowdoin led to an appointment as professor of modern languages at Harvard College, which he began in 1835. Longfellow was writing poems at the same time. There was an obvious conflict between his duties as a professor and the demands of a career as a poet. He published *Ballads, and Other Poems* in 1841; the first important poem by Longfellow was *Evangeline*, published in 1847. Suddenly, Longfellow made Ameri-

cans see that their experience was as fit a subject for serious poetry as Greek myth or British history. *Evangeline* is a narrative poem that tells the story of the expulsion of a group of settlers from Acadie (now Acadia) in Nova Scotia; it was popular with critics and readers alike and retained a place as a school text for American students until the 1960's.

Longfellow married Fanny Appleton in 1843 and received the Craigie House in Cambridge as a wedding gift. The beautiful Victorian house is now a tourist attraction on Cambridge's historic Brattle Street.

In 1854, Longfellow resigned his professorship at Harvard to devote more time to poetry. In 1855, he published *The Song of Hiawatha*, another long narrative poem based on American legends. *The Song of Hiawatha* surveys the career of an American Indian hero, Hiawatha. Using as a structural model the Finnish epic *The Kalevala*, Longfellow brought together a number of Indian tales into one unified book. His view of the American Indian, however, seems to have been constructed to please the taste of his audience. It has little of the violence or nobility others found in that people. The poem was immensely successful and was translated into many languages; Longfellow was becoming the model of the poet to most Americans.

The Courtship of Miles Standish (1858) is another long narrative poem on an American subject, the Pilgrims of Massachusetts. Personal relationships and marriage are the subject; it is a domestic poem, not a heroic one. It did re-create and make accessible another period of American history. Longfellow's great success as a poet was tarnished by the death of his wife Fanny in a fire at Craigie House in 1861. His last years, however, were serene. He received honorary degrees from the universities of Oxford and Cambridge in 1869. Between 1867 and 1869, he translated Dante's *La Divina Commedia* (c. 1320, *The Divine Comedy*, 1802), although he did not write many new or important poems. He died in Cambridge in 1882 and was honored as America's greatest poet.

ANALYSIS

The major problem in analyzing Longfellow as a poet in the early twenty-first century is disinterring what was once a great reputation. The values of Longfellow's audience and time—metrical skill, the long narrative poem, and an abundance of sentiment—are not those of modern poets. By the moderns Longfellow was judged, perhaps, too harshly and too unhistorically. One can still recover some of Longfellow's poetry, although what one sees in it today may not be what the nineteenth century valued.

Longfellow's use of American myths and legends—and the way he altered them—remains important. There had been tales and novels in which American Indians appeared before those of Longfellow. Most prominently, there are the novels of James Fenimore Cooper; however, in those novels, the Indian is never the hero and never has a central position in the narrative. There is always a white man to lead or defeat the Indians, and the rites and ways of the Indian are seen as barbarous or passed over. Longfellow attempted to make the American Indian an epic hero on the scale of Achilles or Odysseus.

He is, perhaps, less successful in his attempt to make Evangeline into an epic heroine; she does not approach the heroes of Homer or Vergil. She is all too accepting of the fate that overcomes her. Finally, in *The Courtship of Miles Standish*, Longfellow attempted to make the Puritan past of New England into a charming world where repression and the inculcation of dogma become a marriage triangle in which (in the classical comic mode) an old man is forced to relinquish a young woman to one who is more fitting.

Longfellow's social goals seem very similar to those of the British Victorian poets. Longfellow's

"Psalm of Life" proclaims: "Life is real! Life is earnest! / And the grave is not its goal." This earnest striving to improve oneself and society is at the heart of many of his poems. Even Evangeline's tragedy is blotted out by a submission to a beneficent God who is working to make things better. There is a firm belief in progress. In addition, Longfellow portrays women in a very Victorian manner. They are pure and virginal, and their primary goal is to follow their male leader.

Longfellow's vision, in fact, was primarily domestic. The scenes between Evangeline and her father, Hiawatha and his mother, and Pilgrims Priscilla and John Alden all evoke the world of the parlor. Longfellow is not really interested in the wildness of the Indian or even the tyranny of the British in driving out the Acadians. One hears nothing of the dark worlds of Nathaniel Hawthorne and Herman Melville—or even Henry David Thoreau.

In its place is the Angel of the House, the woman who is at the center of nearly all Longfellow's works, who offers solace to all. One reason for his (once) nearly universal acceptance is his ability to present the sometimes violent American past as easily accessible and comforting. Rather than make the American past dark and mysterious, as other writers had, he attempted to make it familiar. His own sunny boyhood, very early success, and European sojourns may have led him to portray America in such a genteel manner.

EVANGELINE

First published: 1847
Type of work: Poem

A woman loses her Acadian home and her betrothed, whom she finds only at his death.

Evangeline had its origin in an anecdote. A South Boston man named Connolly urged Nathaniel Hawthorne to write the tale of a young woman who was exiled from Nova Scotia and searched for her lost love, only to find him a moment before his death. Hawthorne never picked up the subject, but Longfellow did. He believed that it was a wonderful tale of a woman's fidelity; it was a perfect subject for his gentle sensibility. He also used historical sources, so the basic tale and the historical frame were given to the poet.

Evangeline begins with a brief introduction in which Longfellow evokes the "forest primeval" that remains while the hearts "beneath it" have vanished. His poem has a "woman's devotion" as its epic theme and an Eden, "Acadie, home of the happy," as its beginning scene. The village of Grand Pre in the land of Acadie is a "fruitful valley" filled with happy peasants from Normandy, France. Evangeline, "the pride of the village," is a maiden of seventeen living with her aged farmer father, Benedict. Her life is a pastoral one; she helps the workers in the field and directs the household of her father.

The first scene in the poem is the visit of Basil the blacksmith and his son, Gabriel, to Benedict. Their purpose is to sign a contract of betrothal between Evangeline and Gabriel. The joyous occasion is threatened, however, by news of a British warship in the bay. Father LeBlanc believes that they are safe because they are "at peace." Basil, however, objects, saying that in this world "might is the right of the strongest!" The old notary reconciles these positions with a tale about a maid unjustly accused of stealing a necklace of pearls; as she is on the scaffold about to be hanged, a bolt of thunder reveals the "necklace of pearls interwoven" in a magpie's nest. The tale obviously mirrors that of *Evangeline.* An innocent girl is freed from an her unjust oppression, although only at the end of a long trial.

The next day is one of feasting, especially in the house of Benedict, but this is broken by the arrival of British troops. The language changes from the soft descriptions of nature to legal language: "By his Majesty's orders . . . all your lands, and dwellings, and cattle of all kinds/ Forfeited be to the Crown." The settlers are to be "transported to other lands." In the rush to depart, Gabriel is separated from Evangeline. Evangeline has other problems, however; her father cannot bear the thought of being separated from his land and dies of age and sorrow.

The second part of the poem deals with Evangeline's search for Gabriel. She descends the established settlements of early America to the Mississippi River and the bayous of Louisiana. She hears news of Gabriel, but she always seems to miss him.

She has a guide, Father Felician, who attempts to assuage her sorrow and lead her to her beloved. Longfellow effectively conveys the mysteriousness of America at this time in the resonant names of places, rivers, and Indian tribes. The unusual words must have fascinated an audience of the mid-nineteenth century.

Evangeline finds Basil the blacksmith in Louisiana, but Gabriel "is only this day" departed. Basil is happy in Louisiana, as it is a more fertile land than Acadie and there is no winter; however, Evangeline yearns for Gabriel. Basil leads her into Indian country to search for Gabriel; they come upon a Shawnee maiden who leads them to the Mission of the Black Robe. The Shawnee maiden, after hearing the tale of Evangeline, tells her of Indian myths that mirror her tale. Longfellow uses the Indian tales as parallels and contrasts to Evangeline's tale. However, the fatalism of the Indian myths is very different from the Christian providence that dominates the main tale.

The priest at the mission tells Evangeline that Gabriel had been there six days before. He had departed, saying he would return to the mission. Evangeline decides to wait. When the seasons pass and he does not return, however, she goes in search of him in the "Michigan forests." Evangeline finds another refuge in a Moravian community and finally settles in Philadelphia, where the gentle Quakers are dominant. She becomes a Sister of Mercy, nursing the sick and comforting the dying. In the hospital, she notices a man dying of fever. Suddenly, the decrepit man assumes "once more the forms of [his] earlier manhood." She cries "Gabriel! O my beloved!" and he calls to his mind:

> Green Acadian meadows, with sylvan rivers among
> them,
> Village, and mountain, and woodlands; and
> walking under their shadow,
> As in the days of her youth, Evangeline rose in his
> vision.

While Evangeline has the power to convey Gabriel back to his earlier and happy life, she does not have the power to save him. He dies in her arms. Evangeline does not complain about this cruel trick of fate, but "meekly" accepts it: "Father, I thank thee!" Evangeline does find her beloved, even if it is at the moment of his death. Longfellow's world is one of affirmation, not doubt.

One reason that *Evangeline* is no longer popular is the passivity of the main character. She undergoes terrible trials but never seems to lose her optimism. The reader does not see any internal conflict, only a chain of accidents that separate the pair. Her affirmation at the seeming irony of discovering Gabriel on his deathbed rings hollow in the twenty-first century.

"THE JEWISH CEMETERY AT NEWPORT"

First published: 1854 (collected in *The Courtship of Miles Standish, and Other Poems,* 1858)
Type of work: Poem

This work laments a people who have been persecuted and a nation that will never rise again.

"The Jewish Cemetery at Newport" is structured by a series of contrasts. The silent "Hebrews" in their graves are contrasted with the motion of the waves. Death, declare the mourners, "giveth Life that nevermore shall cease." The central contrast is the one between the living and the dead. The synagogue is closed, and the living have gone, "but the dead remain,/ And not neglected; for a hand unseen,/ Scattering its bounty, like a summer rain,/ Still keeps their graves and their remembrance green." The dead seem to be especially blessed by that "unseen hand" of nature or God. Longfellow then traces the historical situation of the Jews, however, showing that no "unseen hand" has protected them from persecution.

Longfellow is very direct in assigning "Christian hate" as the cause of the persecution and dislocation of the Jews. He imaginatively captures the persecution in significant detail. He imagines their exile over the sea, "that desert desolate," and their lives in "narrow streets" and "mirk and mire." In another set of contrasts, the Jews "fed" upon the "bitter herbs of exile" and "slaked [their] thirst" with tears. In addition, they are "Taught in the school of patience to endure/ The life of anguish and the death of fire." The contrasts of the poem are re-

solved by reversing the positions of past and future: "And all the great traditions of the Past/ They saw reflected in the coming time." Longfellow then uses an appropriate and powerful metaphor reversing past and present, the living and the dead.

> And thus forever with reverted look
> The mystic volume of the world they read,
> Spelling it backward, like a Hebrew book,
> Till life became a Legend of the Dead.

All the negative elements of the poem are contrasted with or overcome by their opposites. Death leads to life, and exile to knowledge.

The last stanza of the poem, however, reverses the patterns that have been established: "But ah! What once has been shall be no more!" The people of Israel may find life in death and endurance in exile, but the nation of Israel cannot. Its creation is described in a metaphor of birth. "The groaning earth in travail and in pain/ Brings forth its races, but does not restore,/ And the dead nations never rise again." A nation, in Longfellow's view, is bound by natural laws, while a people are free of such restraints. (It is ironic that the nation of Israel was indeed to "rise again" in 1949.)

Longfellow overcame the prejudices of his time in imaginatively and sympathetically portraying the Jews, but in the last stanza, he becomes a man bound by his time and place by being unable to overcome ideas of the life cycle of a nation. Nevertheless, "The Jewish Cemetery at Newport" is a beautifully constructed and powerful poem.

THE SONG OF HIAWATHA

First published: 1855
Type of work: Poem

An Indian hero and teacher leaves a land that is soon to be transformed by white people.

Longfellow gathered the material for *The Song of Hiawatha* from many sources, and his aim was to codify the various tales he read into a coherent mythology. He sought to introduce a white audience to Indian mythology. It begins, as most mythologies do, with people and their god. Gitche Manito, "the mighty/ He the Master of Life," brings the various tribes together to smoke the peace pipe. Gitche Manito will also send a prophet to the people "Who shall guide you and shall teach you,/ Who shall toil and suffer with you." This prophet, who sounds very much like Jesus, will bring prosperity if the people listen. The prophet is Hiawatha.

Section 2 of the poem shows the taming of nature, of the four winds—especially the West-Wind, which is to be Hiawatha's father. Hiawatha, after his mysterious conception (an element common to nearly all mythologies), lives with his grandmother, Nokomis, who teaches him about nature. In the fourth section of the poem, Hiawatha goes to see his father, the West-Wind. The West-Wind praises him and defines Hiawatha's mission in life:

> Go back to your home and people,
> Live among them, toil among them,
> Cleanse the earth from all that harms it,
> Clear the fishing grounds and rivers,
> Slay all monsters and magicians.

One of the most important contributions Hiawatha makes to his people comes after a long fast. Hiawatha is challenged by Mondamin, "a friend of man," to wrestle. The wrestling takes three days, and on the third day Hiawatha defeats, strips, and buries Mondamin. Soon after, plant shoots appear, then maize, the staple food of the people. Hiawatha does not go in search of great deeds so that he might win praise or honor; rather, he struggles to bring benefits to his people. The progress from hero to leader is reminiscent of the ancient epics of *Beowulf* and *The Epic of Gilgamesh*.

Hiawatha has, as an epic hero should, friends who embody lesser skills: Chibiabos is a musician, and Kwasind is "the strongest of all mortals." Hiawatha goes wooing, but once more it is not for his own pleasure but for the people. He will woo and marry Minnehaha, a Dacotah maiden. Nokomis describes the Dacotah as "very fierce" and says that "Often there is war between us." The wooing, therefore, has political and social benefits; a marriage will unite the warring Dacotah and Objibway tribes. Minnehaha is the only character in the poem invented by Longfellow, and she is another of his long-suffering and passive women. Her answer to Hiawatha's proposal is, "I will follow you, my husband!"

There are some disturbing events in this saga:

Hiawatha loses his two friends, Chibiabos and Kwasind, and his wife, Minnehaha. His friends die in action, but Minnehaha dies in a famine. Significantly, Hiawatha has no power to overcome this natural event. Her death, however, is seen as something of a blessing, as she will be carried to the "Islands of the Blessed," where there is no labor or suffering. Hiawatha had discovered the existence of these islands earlier in the poem, bringing consolation to the people—and to himself for the loss of his bride.

The next-to-last section of the poem deals with the coming of the white people. A canoe "Bigger than the Big-Sea Water,! Broader than the Gitche-Gumee" appears. Hiawatha counsels peace: "Let us welcome, then, the strangers,/ Hail them as our friends and brothers,/ And the heart's right hand of friendship/ Give them when they come to see us." This vision of peace and brotherhood is, however, immediately obliterated by another vision. Hiawatha sees "our nation scattered" and the "remnants of the people" swept away "Like the withered leaves of Autumn." It is a poignant passage that reveals the historic fate of the American Indian and destroys the optimistic dream. Longfellow does not assign any blame to white people for the destruction of the Indian way of life.

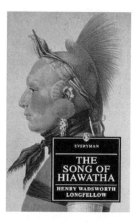

The last section of the poem describes Hiawatha's departure. He will not be there for the uprooting of the people he has served. Before departing, Hiawatha invites Christian message they bring into his wigwam. The Christian message is then received and welcomed by the chiefs. (There is no hint of the historic martyrdom that was to come to so many Jesuits or of the lack of interest in the Christian message by the Indians.) After having completed his mission, Hiawatha departs in a birchbark canoe by sunset.

The Song of Hiawatha is one of Longfellow's most successful poems. It portrays the Indians with sympathy and some understanding. The meter of the poem is very noticeable. Longfellow rejected the long dactylic hexameters of *Evangeline* for a short unrhymed trochaic tetrameter. It has the effect of a chant and often fits the material perfectly. The hero of the poem may be a little too noble, good, and unselfish. He has none of the human faults that make Beowulf and Gilgamesh, for example, so interesting. At times, Hiawatha is more a Victorian gentleman bringing progress to "lesser breeds without the law" than an American Indian warrior.

THE COURTSHIP OF MILES STANDISH

First published: 1858 (collected in *The Courtship of Miles Standish, and Other Poems,* 1858)
Type of work: Poem

In this Puritan idyll, an old warrior surrenders his claim to the hand of a young woman to a more appropriate young scholar.

The Courtship of Miles Standish is another historical narrative poem; this time Longfellow turns to the Pilgrims of Plymouth Plantation for his material, and he once more softens the harshness of his subject and makes it accessible to his audience. The meter he chose for the poem is dactylic hexameter, but it has none of the monotony of *Evangeline*; it is very loosely structured and at times seems on the edge of prose. It also has none of the heroic treatment of *Evangeline* or *The Song of Hiawatha*. It is really a romantic drama, not an imitation of Greek or Finnish epic.

The poem begins with a description of Miles Standish as "strongly built and athletic,/ Broad in the shoulders, deep-chested, with muscles and sinews of iron." John Alden is not described in the same detail, but it is clear that he is the opposite of Miles Standish. Alden is no soldier but is called a scholar. Standish is a man of few words, while Alden is a closet poet hymning the name of Priscilla. The conflict of the tale is quickly brought out. Miles Standish has lost his wife and uses biblical authority rather than personal passion to justify his search for a new bride. She is to be Priscilla Mullins.

Standish does not have the words to woo a maiden, however, so he turns to Alden. Alden's conflict is quickly resolved: "The name of friend-ship is sacred;/ What you demand in that name, I have not the power to deny you!" His divided feelings emerge, however, love contends with friendship, and he wonders if he must "relinquish" the joys of love. He resolves the dilemma by seeing his love as vanity; "I have worshipped too much the heart's desire and devices." Religious authority prevails.

Alden's delivery of Standish's proposal to Priscilla is surprisingly blunt. There is no poetic prologue or honeyed words, merely the facts of the case. "So I have come to you now, with an offer and proffer of marriage! Made by a good man and true, Miles Standish the Captain of Plymouth." Priscilla replies directly: "Why does he not come himself, and take the trouble to woo me?" She is not the submissive Minnehaha or the dutiful Evangeline but an independent and witty woman. She takes the failure of Standish to woo her as a reason to reject him. She sees him as "old and rough" and one lacking in the basic elements of courtship: He will never win her.

Alden tries to make a case for Standish, but Priscilla is not interested in his virtues. Instead she give Alden hope and increases his conflict by uttering the famous words, "Why don't you speak for yourself, John?" Alden is filled with joy, yet downcast at his betrayal. He vows to depart from Plymouth and return to England on the *Mayflower.*

Standish is shocked and angered when he hears of Priscilla's rejection of his proposal and her encouragement of Alden's suit. More weighty matters demand his attention, however: How shall the Pilgrim settlers answer the Indians who have sent the "skin of a rattlesnake" as a challenge to war? The Elder of Plymouth counsels peace; Standish is adamant for war. "Truly the only tongue that is understood by a savage/ Must be the tongue of fire that speaks from the mouth of the cannon!" Standish consistently rejects language and translates words into military action. The next day, Alden's conflict over whether to sail for England or stay and woo Priscilla continues. He decides to stay but not to woo. The pair's relationship is redefined; he will be her friend. Priscilla defines the relationship with precision and candor. "Let us, then, be what we are, and speak what we think, and in all things/ Keep ourselves loyal to truth, and the sacred professions of friendship."

Standish goes to war and answers the words of

the Indian chief, Pecksuot, with action: He snatches Pecksuot's knife from him and kills him. Priscilla is not pleased by this valor but repelled by it. The poem's conflict is partially resolved when news comes that Standish has died in battle. Alden and Priscilla are free to marry, but the shadow of Standish still hovers over their relationship.

The denouement of the poem comes on the wedding day of Alden and Priscilla. After the service, the ghost of Standish appears to bless the marriage. "Mine is the same hot blood that leaped in the veins of Hugh Standish/ Sensitive, swift to resent, but as swift in atoning for error./ Never so much as now was Miles Standish the friend of John Alden!" Standish remains his old self, telling the people that he "had rather by far break into an Indian encampment,/ Than come again to a wedding to which he had not been invited." With his presence removed, the familiar landscape of Plymouth is transfigured into the "Garden of Eden."

The Courtship of Miles Standish is one of Longfellow's most successful poems. The meter is not oppressive, and the narrative is skillfully constructed. The biblical language elevates the romance without overwhelming it. The characters are also well conceived. Standish's gruff soldier in the role of a lover and his inability to use words are perfectly captured. Priscilla Mullins is a clever and imaginative creation, very different from the submissive female Longfellow usually portrays. Longfellow also removes some of the excessive solemnity of the Pilgrims and makes their world delightful and human.

SUMMARY

Longfellow contributed much to American poetry. He showed that Americans had a marvelous and important history. He makes early America into a mythic land: The Indians, the Pilgrims, and the exiles from Nova Scotia are all given a treatment that had previously been reserved for Greek or Roman myth. Longfellow also opened American poetry to a variety of poetic meters and structures. Certain themes recur; Longfellow generally portrays women as submissive and passive. He also suggests that there is progress in the world; the disaster of Evangeline or the dislocation of the Indians cannot drive out the optimism that things are getting better and humankind is becoming more civilized.

James Sullivan

BIBLIOGRAPHY

By the Author

POETRY:
Voices of the Night, 1839
Ballads, and Other Poems, 1841
Poems on Slavery, 1842
The Belfry of Bruges, and Other Poems, 1845
Evangeline, 1847
The Seaside and the Fireside, 1850
The Golden Legend, 1851
The Song of Hiawatha, 1855
The Courtship of Miles Standish, and Other Poems, 1858
Tales of a Wayside Inn, 1863
Flower-de-Luce, 1867
The New England Tragedies, 1868
The Divine Tragedy, 1871
Three Books of Song, 1872
Christus: A Mystery, 1872
Aftermath, 1873
The Hanging of the Crane, 1874

The Masque of Pandora, and Other Poems, 1875
Kéramos, and Other Poems, 1878
Ultima Thule, 1880
In the Harbor, 1882
Michael Angelo, 1883
Longfellow's Boyhood Poems, 1925

LONG FICTION:
Kavanagh: A Tale, 1849

DRAMA:
The Spanish Student, pb. 1843

NONFICTION:
Elements of French Grammar, 1830 (translation)
Manuel de Proverbes Dramatiques, 1830
Outre-Mer: A Pilgrimage Beyond the Sea, 1833-1834
Hyperion, 1839
Drift-Wood, 1857
The Letters of Henry Wadsworth Longfellow, 1966-1974
   (5 volumes; Andrew Hilen, editor)

EDITED TEXTS:
The Poets and Poetry of Europe, 1845
The Waif: A Collection of Poems, 1845
The Estray: A Collection of Poems, 1847
Poems of Places, 1876-1879

TRANSLATION:
The Divine Comedy of Dante Alighieri, 1867-1869

DISCUSSION TOPICS

- What features of the traditional epic are found in *Evangeline*?

- What innovative and unusual metrical schemes does Henry Wadsworth Longfellow employ in his poetry?

- What would you judge to be Longfellow's greatest virtues as a lyric poet?

- How is the twentieth and early twenty-first century reassessment of Longfellow's poetry reflected in the republication and anthologizing of his work?

- Longfellow wrote a large amount of poetry and wrote rather quickly. Are such composition habits more likely to mar the quality of a poet's work or increase the chances of scoring successes?

- Longfellow's poetry was long considered accessible to, and appropriate for, elementary school children. To what extent is this judgment true today?

About the Author

Calhoun, Charles C. *Longfellow: A Rediscovered Life.* Boston: Beacon Press, 2004.

Gale, Robert L. *A Henry Wadsworth Longfellow Companion.* Westport, Conn.: Greenwood Press, 2003.

Gartner, Matthew. "Longfellow's Place: The Poet and Poetry of Craigie House." *The New England Quarterly* 73, no. 1 (March, 2000): 32-57.

Pearce, Roy Harvey. *The Continuity of American Poetry.* Middletown, Conn.: Wesleyan University Press, 1987.

Suchard, Allen. "The Nineteenth Century: Romanticism in American Poetry." In *American Poetry.* Amherst: University of Massachusetts Press, 1988.

Trachtenberg, Alan. *Shades of Hiawatha: Staging Indians, Making Americans, 1880-1930.* New York: Hill and Wang, 2004.

Tucker, Edward L. "The Meeting of Hawthorne and Longfellow in 1838." *ANQ* 13, no. 4 (Fall, 2000): 18-21.

Turco, Lewis P. *Visions and Revisions of American Poetry.* Fayetteville: University of Alabama Press, 1986.

Wagenknecht, Edward. *Henry Wadsworth Longfellow, His Poetry and Prose.* New York: Ungar, 1986.

Waggoner, Hyatt H. "Five New England Poets." In *American Poets: From the Puritans to the Present.* Baton Rouge: Louisiana State University Press, 1984.

AUDRE LORDE

Born: Harlem, New York
February 18, 1934
Died: Christiansted, St. Croix, Virgin Islands
November 17, 1992

Ingmar Schullz

Describing herself as a "black lesbian feminist warrior poet," Lorde used her powerful writing to battle for the rights of all people and helped to legitimize the use of poetry as ethical, moral, and political commentary.

BIOGRAPHY

Audrey Geraldine Lorde was born on February 18, 1934, in New York City, the third child of Linda Gertrude Belmar Lorde and Frederick Byron Lorde. Her parents had immigrated to the United States from Grenada ten years previously. After the births of his three daughters, Lorde's father attended real estate school and began to manage small rooming houses in Harlem. Lorde later remembered how consistently her parents shared responsibility for the family.

Lorde was an inarticulate child who did not begin to speak until she was approximately five years old. At that time, she was charmed out of a tantrum in a library by a librarian who read several storybooks to her. The young Audrey then began to interact with the world, learning to read, then to speak, and then to write. As she was growing up, Lorde communicated through poetry, responding to questions or comments with poems she had memorized. When she was twelve or thirteen, she began to write her own poetry to express feelings that were not reflected in what she had been reading. Initially, Lorde did not write down her poems; rather, she preferred to memorize them.

Even as a child, Lorde exhibited independence in her approach to life. For example, as she recounts in *Zami: A New Spelling of My Name* (1982),

when she was first learning to print her name, Lorde disliked the tail of the "y" in "Audrey." Instead, she liked the evenness of "Audre Lorde," a lifelong preference. Part of her unique view of the world may stem from the fact that Lorde was vision-impaired. When she was three years old, she recalled that "the dazzling world of strange lights and fascinating shapes which I inhabited resolved itself in mundane definitions, and I learned another nature of things as seen through eyeglasses."

Lorde progressed through grade school in New York, finally spending four years at Hunter High School, where her poetry became an accepted effort rather than a "rebellious vice" and where she was elected literary editor of the school arts magazine. This period in her life was tumultuous and was marked by a strained relationship with her parents, her mother especially. However, her first published poem was accepted during her high school years by *Seventeen* magazine. About her first love affair with a boy, the poem was judged by her English teachers to be "too romantic" to be included in the school paper.

Two weeks after her high school graduation, Lorde moved out of her parents' home and became self-supporting. After a few years of working as a nurse's aide and at various other jobs, she had saved enough to take her to Mexico, where she attended the National University of Mexico in 1954.

After her return from Mexico, Lorde worked as a librarian while continuing to write poetry and essays. She completed her bachelor of arts degree at Hunter College in 1959 and her master of library science degree at the Columbia University School of Library Science in 1960. In 1962, Lorde married Edwon Ashley Rollins and subsequently gave birth to a daughter and a son. She and Rollins divorced in 1970. In 1968, shortly after the publication of her first book of poems, Lorde was offered a position as poet-in-residence at Tougaloo College, an experience she called pivotal. Her first trip into the South, it was also her first time away from her children and the first time that she had to deal with young black students in a workshop setting. During this time, she realized that writing and teaching were inseparable and that she had found her calling.

Lorde had continued to teach, write, and travel when, in 1978, she discovered a lump in her breast which turned out to be malignant. Though battling breast cancer, Lorde kept writing and, later, collated some of her writings into *The Cancer Journals* (1980), a remarkable story of despair, hope, support, and courage. *A Burst of Light: Essays* (1988) similarly documents her illness. Such candidness was typical of Lorde, whose life experiences and work are inextricably woven together.

Among other honors, Lorde was the recipient of two National Endowment for the Arts grants (1968 and 1981), and she received the Walt Whitman Citation of Merit, which conferred the name of poet laureate of New York in 1991. The following year, she succumbed to cancer, though recognizing that "What I leave behind has a life of its own. I've said this about poetry, I've said it about children. Well, in a sense I'm saying it about the very artifact of who I have been."

ANALYSIS

As a young girl, Lorde expressed nearly all of her daily conversation by quoting poetry she had memorized. As she began to grow up, however, she realized that there were no poems that addressed many of her feelings and experiences as a black feminist lesbian. She felt "totally alienated, disoriented, crazy." Thus, Lorde began writing to fill her own needs. She said that she wrote for herself, for her children, and for those women who do not speak because they have been silenced or because they have been taught to respect fear more than they respect themselves. Lorde wrote, often militantly, always expressively, of racism, sexism, homophobia, love, and pain as well as on political, social, and en-

vironmental issues. Critic Jerome Brooks has discerned three central themes in Lorde's work: the issue of power, her quest for love, and her commitment to intellectual and moral clarity about so-called familiar things.

Lorde's discussion of the existence and use of power is not limited to an examination of the power of words, a theme she uses frequently; it also includes explorations of black versus white, female versus male, child versus mother, the disadvantaged versus bureaucratic institutions, patients versus the medical establishment, and smaller nations versus the United States.

Lorde's poem "Coal" (1976) is, on the surface, a study of the power of a word, of "how sound comes into a word, colored/ by who pays what for speaking." A closer examination indicates the poet's own power, which, one critic has noted, helps her to "transform rage at racism into triumphant self-assertion." Another example of the theme of power appears in "From the House of Yemanja" (1978), in which Lorde's troubled childhood relationship with her strong mother is painted.

Lorde's love poetry deals not only with romantic love but also with the many different faces of human love: love between parent and child, love between friends, love for one's family, and love for one's art. While she does occasionally use the theme of heterosexual love, it is clear from her work that she is "woman-oriented." As the scholar and poet Joan Martin has commented, however, "anyone who has ever been in love can respond to the straightforward passion and pain, sometimes one and the same, in Lorde's poems."

The poem "From the House of Yemanja" also witnesses Lorde recalling a childhood that made her feel imperfect and unloved. She cries, "Mother I need/ mother I need/ . . ./ I am/ the sun and moon and forever hungry" and is left craving the mother-love that she missed. In contrast, "Now That I Am Forever with Child" (1976) is a rapturous song to her new parent-child relationship, which bears no resemblance to her earlier troubled childhood.

While these poems display beauty, and roughness, strength, and emotion, Lorde's writings dealing with mature love include some of the most beautiful poems in her work. For Lorde, there is no such thing as universal love in literature; there is only immediate, particular love, which results in art. The prose work *Zami: A New Spelling of My Name* is a blend of autobiography and fiction that provides accounts of Lorde's childhood years and of her coming of age as a lesbian; the book is a celebration of all the women whom she loved and from whom she learned.

Many of these formative experiences are referred to or form a base for some of Lorde's poems. For example, in "Fog Report," she writes, "In this misty place where hunger finds us/ seeking direction/ I am too close to you to be useful," a comment about a relationship that is decaying. Another of Lorde's best poems is "Walking Our Boundaries," which was written after a battle with cancer and which honors the wonder of life and love. Lorde's experience with cancer was, like most of her experiences, incorporated into her work. One result was Lorde's first major prose piece, the extraordinarily honest and descriptive *The Cancer Journals*, which describes the course of her battle from the first discovery of a lump in her breast to her post-mastectomy experiences (which include such telling moments as a nurse's informing her that not wearing a prosthesis is bad for the morale of the office and a physician's claiming that no truly happy person gets cancer).

Such experiences evoked the "warrior" in Lorde, which had previously been roused in poems such as "The American Cancer Society: Or, There Is More than One Way to Skin a Coon," in which Lorde vehemently attacks racism in the United States. Lorde saw social protest as a means of encouraging people to realize the inconsistencies and horror in modern life; for her, the issues of social protest and art were inseparable.

Another example of her artistry, her social commentary, and her talent for making her readers squirm is the poem "The Brown Menace: Or, Poem to the Survival of Roaches," in which the pests symbolically represent black Americans, whose destruction will extend to their destroyers. While Lorde's skillful poetry reflects the intensity of her life and feeling, her work's most outstanding characteristics are her complete honesty and her sincere love for the world and the people in it.

"POWER"

First published: 1974 (collected in *The Collected Poems of Audre Lorde,* 1997)
Type of work: Poem

"Power" is Lorde's enraged response to the acquittal of a white policeman who shot and killed a ten-year-old black boy.

"Power" is based on an actual event and Lorde's personal reaction, which she recorded in her journal. While driving, Lorde heard a radio broadcast announcing the acquittal of a white policeman who had shot and killed a black ten-year-old. She was so furious and sickened that she felt that the sky turned red, that she had to park the car before she drove it into a wall. Then and there, she inscribed her feelings of outrage over the decision of the jury of eleven white men and one black woman.

In the unforgettable imagery employed in "Power," the streets of New York become "a desert of raw gunshot wounds," a white desert where the only liquid for miles is the blood of a dead black child. Through this poem, Lorde tries to "make power out of hatred and destruction," to heal her "dying son with kisses." Yet she cannot help expressing her rage at the policeman's comment, offered in his own defense, that "I didn't notice the size or nothing else/ only the color."

While expressing her rage over this story, "Power" also illuminates Lorde's ability to provide what one critic has called a "relentlessly clinical analysis" that "often leads to a perception of human character that is, perhaps, the ultimate justification for art." For example, Lorde writes that the black jurywoman said that she had been convinced, "meaning/ they had dragged her 4'10" black woman's frame over the hot coals of four centuries of white male approval/ until she let go the first real power she ever had." Lorde's own powerful imagery returns in the following lines, as she compares this surrender to the jurywoman's lining "her own womb with cement/ to make a graveyard for our children."

The final stanza of "Power" begins with the poet unable to deal with the destruction and the rage she feels. As the stanza continues, what she fears and what her audience fears become one: Unless

1539

she (representing black youth) can learn from her experience, her rage will corrupt her. She will seem inert—until, one day, she will explode into frenzied violence against an elderly white woman "who is somebody's mother." In this version, Lorde hears "a greek chorus . . . singing in 3/4 time/ 'Poor thing. She never hurt a soul. What beasts they are.'"

The haunting imagery serves to highlight the themes of rage and power that are woven through Lorde's writings. She directs rage not only at the glaring injustice of racism, as characterized in "Power," but also toward sexual oppression and, to a lesser extent, political issues and the slight cruelties of everyday life. Lorde is particularly sympathetic to the anguish of all outsiders, especially the young black population of New York. Despite the intense physical and emotional pain she and all outsiders experience, Lorde manages to transform that rage into a force for change.

"WALKING OUR BOUNDARIES"

First published: 1978 (collected in *The Collected Poems of Audre Lorde*, 1997)
Type of work: Poem

In this quiet, spiritual poem written after her confrontation with cancer, Lorde and her partner walk together through their garden.

One of Lorde's best poems, "Walking Our Boundaries" was written after she was forced to confront her own mortality in a battle with breast cancer. About a walk she shared in the small garden surrounding the house that she and her partner owned, this poem is beautifully narrated and quietly blends symbolism together with deep feeling. The poem begins, "This first bright day has broken/ the back of winter./ We rise from war/ . . . / both stunned that sun can shine so brightly/ after all our pain."

As the pair cautiously inspects their "joint holding," they talk of "ordinary articles/ with relief." A sense of delicacy and unexpected peace is conveyed, which implies just how severe was the "last winter's storm." In the midst of the symbolism Lorde employs, she does not lose her sense of perspective, saying that "it does not pay to cherish sym-

bols/ when the substance/ lies so close at hand/ waiting to be held." This thought blends into the next, as her lover's hand "falls off the apple bark/ like casual fire/ along my back," the light, affectionate touch breaking the back of her emotional winter as the sun has broken the back of the physical winter.

The calm delicacy of tone and technique in this poem is in startling contrast to the passions and turmoil Lorde expressed in *The Cancer Journals*, reflecting the peace that comes after "war"; the battle is, at least for the time being, over. In *The Cancer Journals*, Lorde wrote that it was very important for her to develop and regain her own sense of power, to be able to view herself as a warrior rather than a victim.

Her anger that the medical establishment encourages its patients to behave as victims is expressed in an extremely biting manner, and her writing drips with scorn as she details the ways in which she was encouraged to pretend, during treatment and after her mastectomy, that everything was back to normal. Another theme in *The Cancer Journals*, however, is the strength that Lorde gained through the love and support of her network of friends as well as her partner, who is compared to a sunflower. It is this love that she cherishes so deeply and for which she expresses her gratitude in "Walking Our Boundaries."

The final stanza of "Walking Our Boundaries" continues the moods of delicacy, fragility, and wonder. The voices of the two women "seem too loud for this small yard/ too tentative for women/ so in love." Despite the physical decay that has occurred ("the siding has come loose in spots"), the human spirit is triumphant ("our footsteps hold this place/ together/ as our place"), and the life surrounding and filling the house and garden is made possible by the joint decision of and the love between the partners. The poem ends on a beautiful note of hope: Although Lorde does not know when they will laugh freely again, they are planning to dig up another plot for the spring's seeding.

"COAL"

First published: 1976 (collected in *The Collected Poems of Audre Lorde*, 1997)
Type of work: Poem

"Coal" is a study of the power and the form of words that represents a declaration of the poet's self-awareness and self-confidence.

In her essay "Poetry Is Not a Luxury," Lorde argues that poetry, as a revelatory distillation of experience, provides the illumination by which people scrutinize their lives and give substance to their unformed ideas. She also believes that each woman's being holds a dark place where her true spirit  grows hidden, forming a reservoir of creativity, power, and unexamined and unrecorded feeling. She has written that "the woman's place of power within each of us is neither white nor surface; it is dark, it is ancient, and it is deep." It is not surprising, then, that one of Lorde's most frequently anthologized poems is "Coal," with its final two lines independently declaring "I am Black because I come from the earth's inside/ now take my word for jewel in the open light." This self-assertion and her awareness of the power of words are not merely themes but a necessity and a way of living for Lorde.

In form, "Coal" is a discussion of the many different forms that Lorde's words can take, "colored/ by who pays what for speaking." Lorde's imagery is as skillful as ever, as in such phrases as "singing out within the passing crash of sun," an "ill-pulled tooth with a ragged edge," or "seeking like gypsies over my tongue/ to explode through my lips/ like young sparrows bursting from shell." The words that she analyzes, however, are both servant and served. The phrasing she employs seems to imply that Lorde herself is trapped by her words: "Some words live in my throat/ breeding like adders . . ./ Some words/ bedevil me."

One of Lorde's principal themes concerns her reaction to racist attitudes and acts; her response to racism is, in a word, anger. Lorde lived with that anger for her entire life; and she once remarked that it "has eaten clefts into my living only when it remained unspoken, useless to anyone." For Lorde, the expression and use of anger was not destructive. Rather, as one critic has explained "the poem 'Coal' suggests the strength through which she can transform rage at racism into triumphant self-assertion."

SUMMARY

Lorde is noted for her poems and essays expressing rage at the injustices of modern American society. Her work is distinctly political and her subjects topical. Lorde sought to encourage awareness of and to provide an example for other "outsiders." Nevertheless, she remained a caring individual whose love poems are moving and poignant. In the words of teacher and writer Jerome Brooks, the world is reflected in Lorde's poetry "mainly through the conflicts and confrontation of her coming to terms with herself or with very private pain."

Katherine Socha

BIBLIOGRAPHY

By the Author

POETRY:
The First Cities, 1968
Cables to Rage, 1970
From a Land Where Other People Live, 1973
New York Head Shop and Museum, 1974
Between Our Selves, 1976

Coal, 1976

The Black Unicorn, 1978

Chosen Poems, Old and New, 1982 (revised as *Undersong: Chosen Poems, Old and New,* 1992)

A Comrade Is as Precious as a Rice Seedling, 1984

Our Dead Behind Us, 1986

Need: A Chorale for Black Woman Voices, 1990

The Marvelous Arithmetics of Distance: Poems, 1987-1992, 1993

The Collected Poems of Audre Lorde, 1997

NONFICTION:

Uses of the Erotic: The Erotic as Power, 1978

The Cancer Journals, 1980

Zami: A New Spelling of My Name: A Biomythography, 1982

Sister Outsider: Essays and Speeches, 1984

I Am Your Sister: Black Women Organizing Across Sexualities, 1985

Apartheid U.S.A., 1986

A Burst of Light: Essays, 1988

The Audre Lorde Compendium: Essays, Speeches, and Journals, 1996

Conversations with Audre Lorde, 2004 (Joan Wylie Hall, editor)

DISCUSSION TOPICS

- By what techniques does Audre Lorde convert outrage to poetry?

- What is the symbolic force of boundaries in "Walking Our Boundaries"?

- How does the imagery of "Coal" express Lorde's "dark place"?

- Consider *The Cancer Journals* as a response to the insensitivity and tactlessness that Lorde encountered among medical professionals.

- What array of personal traits and experiences combined to facilitate Lorde's uniqueness as a poet?

About the Author

Avi-Ram, Amitai F. "*Apo Koinou* in Lorde and the Moderns: Defining the Differences." *Callaloo* 9 (Winter, 1986): 193-208.

Hull, Gloria T. "Living on the Line: Audre Lorde and *Our Dead Behind Us.*" In *Changing Our Own Words: Essays on Criticism, Theory, and Writing by Black Women,* edited by Cheryl A. Wall. New Brunswick, N.J.: Rutgers University Press, 1989.

Olson, Lester C. "Liabilities of Language: Audre Lorde Reclaiming Difference." *Quarterly Journal of Speech* 84, no. 4 (November, 1998): 448-470.

Opitz, May, Katharine Oguntoye, and Dagmar Schultz, eds. *Showing Our Colors: Afro-German Women Speak Out.* Translated by Anne V. Adams. Amherst: University of Massachusetts Press, 1992.

Parker, Pat. *Movement in Black: The Collected Poetry of Pat Parker.* Oakland, Calif.: Diana Press, 1978.

Perreault, Jeanne. *Writing Selves: Contemporary Feminist Autography.* Minneapolis: University of Minnesota Press, 1995.

ROBERT LOWELL

Born: Boston, Massachusetts
March 1, 1917
Died: New York, New York
September 12, 1977

Lowell revolutionized American poetry in the years after World War II with his confessional and political subject matter and the intensity of his language.

Courtesy, Allen & Unwin

BIOGRAPHY

Robert Trail Spence Lowell, Jr., was born into the well-known Lowell family of Boston. His father, however, was not a distinguished member of that family, being a commander in the United States Navy and later an unsuccessful businessman. At the time of Robert's birth, his mother's family, the Winslows, had more money and more prestige, and his mother smothered her son with affection, while denigrating her husband's incompetence. Lowell's memoir "91 Revere Street" in *Life Studies* (1959) shows a sensitive child caught in the perpetual conflict of his parents.

Lowell attended a fashionable prep school, St. Mark's, from 1930 to 1935 and Harvard University until 1937. He rebelled against his respectable parents in 1937 and left Harvard to pursue a possible career as a poet by going to live with the established poet Allen Tate in Clarksville, Tennessee. In 1937, Lowell entered Kenyon College to study with the poet John Crowe Ransom; he graduated summa cum laude in 1940. Lowell also met such lifelong friends at Kenyon as Randall Jarrell and Peter Taylor; he would often write about them in his later poetry.

Lowell was attempting to become a modern American poet by absorbing the ideas and techniques of Tate and Ransom; both poets exemplified and supported the New Criticism. The New Criticism focused on the poem rather than the

poet, and it used as models such seventeenth century poets as John Donne. A proper poem, in the New Critics' view, was complex, with rich imagery, and filled with recondite allusions.

In 1940, Lowell married his first wife, the fiction writer Jean Stafford. The marriage was stormy. Each writer was producing significant work at the time, although Stafford was more financially successful than was Lowell. Lowell's political beliefs added to the complexities of his life. He became a conscientious objector in the early 1940's when he learned about the bombing of the civilian population in Germany. In 1943, he was sentenced to a year in prison for refusing to be inducted into the military. He wrote a letter to President Franklin Roosevelt stating his position, his "manic statement/ telling off the state and president." During this period, Lowell converted to Catholicism; this provided the subject matter for many of his early poems. He was later to reject Catholicism as the answer to his quest for a higher authority.

In 1944, Lowell's first book of poetry, *Land of Unlikeness*, was published. It was in the complex and allusive style that the New Critics favored, and the reviews, while not extensive, were favorable. The true breakthrough volume for Lowell was his next book of poetry, *Lord Weary's Castle*, published in 1946. It was an advance in style and technique, and, while it was still complex, it was much more forceful than the earlier book, especially such poems as "The Quaker Graveyard in Nantucket" and "After the Surprising Conversions." In 1947, *Lord Weary's Castle* was awarded the Pulitzer Prize in poetry.

Although Lowell was recognized as an impor-

1543

tant American poet at this time, his life was troubled. He was subject to manic-depressive episodes and regularly spent brief periods in mental hospitals. The manic periods were especially disturbing because Lowell would claim that he was an all-powerful ruler and refuse the reasoned appeals of those closest to him. These episodes were usually accompanied by Lowell's acquiring a new girlfriend while he announced to whoever would listen that he meant to leave his wife. During one of these episodes he wrecked a car and seriously injured Stafford. He divorced her in 1948 and married another writer, Elizabeth Hardwick, in 1949. In 1951, Lowell's third book of poetry was published; *The Mills of the Kavanaughs* is a series of dramatic monologues and is perhaps the least representative book he ever published. Critically, it was also one of the least successful.

The Beat poets of the 1950's and Lowell's turning to William Carlos Williams as a model (rather than T. S. Eliot) led to a significant change in Lowell's style. In 1959, he published *Life Studies*, his most important book. *Life Studies* was nothing less than a revolution in American poetry. It included poems about his troubled relationship with his parents (who had died in the 1950's), his imprisonment for refusing induction into the military, and his confinement in mental institutions. It dealt with personal subjects—indeed, some believed that it was too personal. The style was no longer the complex style recommended by the New Critics but a simpler, much more direct and striking one. *Life Studies* won the National Book Award for 1959.

In 1964, Lowell published *For the Union Dead*: most of the poems in the book were in the "confessional" mode of *Life Studies*, but there was one exception—the title poem. "For the Union Dead" is a political poem, not a confessional one. It contrasts the integrity and dedication of the nineteenth century Bostonians who fought for the liberation of black people with the decadent and materialistic twentieth century. Appropriately, Lowell read the poem on the Boston Common at the Boston Arts Festival. Lowell's interest in politics is also reflected in the publication, also in 1965, of *The Old Glory*; this is not a book of poems but dramatizations of Herman Melville's "Benito Cereno" (1856) and Nathaniel Hawthorne's "My Kinsman, Major Molineaux" (1832). It later had a successful run on the New York stage.

In 1967, Lowell published *Near the Ocean*, which, with the exception of "Waking Early Sunday Morning," is a forgettable book. In some passages Lowell attacks President Lyndon Johnson for his continuation of the Vietnam War; this clearly shows Lowell's continuing interest in power and American politics. In 1968, he campaigned for and became very friendly with Eugene McCarthy in an attempt to defeat Johnson and end the Vietnam War. He was becoming a public figure. In 1969, Lowell published *Notebook 1967-1968*, later revised as *Notebook* (1970) and later still revised as *History* (1973) by excerpting the political poems. Some of the poems are about the private life of the poet, sometimes expressed in a very intimate manner, but the book also contains a number of poems on leaders and political subjects. Another innovation is that the poems are all written in a loose sonnet form.

In 1972, Lowell divorced Elizabeth Hardwick and married Caroline Blackwood. That divorce and the troubled and loving relationship between Lowell and Hardwick became the main subjects of *The Dolphin* (1973) and *For Lizzie and Harriet* (1973). Lowell even included letters from Hardwick in a nearly complete form in some poems. His last book of poems was *Day by Day* (1977); it dealt with the difficult marriage between Lowell and Caroline and their residence in England. He was visiting Elizabeth Hardwick and his daughter Harriet in 1977 when he had a heart attack; he died on September 12.

ANALYSIS

Nearly all Lowell's poems have a richness of imagery, a wide range of references and allusions, and a density of syntax. His first two books stress religious themes and subjects. Such poems as "The Drunken Fisherman" and "Between the Porch and the Altar" clearly demonstrate his abiding religious concerns. They are difficult to unravel and do not easily yield themselves to the reader. Lowell was, as he often mentioned, trying to write poems in the manner of Hart Crane while under the critical influence of the New Critics. The last stanza of "The Drunken Fisherman" shows the richness and the difficulties of such poems.

> Is there no way to cast my hook
> Out of this dynamited brook?
> This Fisher's sons must cast about

When shallow waters peter out.
I will catch Christ with a greased worm,
And when the Prince of Darkness stalks
My bloodstream to its Stygian term . . .
On water the Man-Fisher walks.

The poem is undoubtedly powerful, but it is not the best or most typical type of Lowell poem. Here he is trying to be another T. S. Eliot—writing learned and academic poetry with religious and mythic themes. He was not the equal of the Eliot of the *Four Quartets* (1943), however, and his natural bent lay elsewhere.

Life Studies led to the coinage of the term "confessional poet." The subjects of its poetry were Lowell's parents and grandparents, his bouts of madness, and his friends. The style is also freer and looser; in place of learned allusions there are ironic references to the misspelling of "Lowell" on his mother's coffin. In "Waking in the Blue," Lowell describes the inmates in McLeans Hospital for the "mentally ill." Lowell does not stand aloof but includes himself within the group of "thoroughbred mental cases." The last two lines convey Lowell's recognition of his state and make the reader a participant, not merely an observer: "We are all old-timers,/ each of us holds a locked razor." It is a direct and immensely moving poetry.

Lowell never ceased to write "confessional" poetry, but he expanded the range of his poetry by turning to political subjects. "For the Union Dead" is an indictment of modern life and leaders: There are no more Colonel Shaws to lead Negro infantry but only politicians who refuse to allow Negro children to attend school with whites. Lowell makes clear that twentieth century materialistic society has perverted once-noble values. A few years later, his politics became much more direct. In "Near the Ocean," for example, he portrays Lyndon Johnson "swimming nude, unbuttoned, sick/ of his ghostwritten rhetoric!" Later, Lowell was a part of the march on Washington to stop the Vietnam War and wrote about his experience in a number of poems in *Notebook*. There are also studies of such leaders and power figures as Alexander the Great, Abraham Lincoln, and Adolf Hitler.

One aspect of Lowell's poetry that is often ignored by critics is the many elegies on and tributes to his friends and fellow poets. In *Life Studies*, there are poems on Ford Madox Ford, Delmore Schwartz, and Hart Crane. The finest ones, however, come from *Notebook*, especially the poem on Robert Frost. Lowell portrays Frost not as a genial New England sage but as a tortured man with "the great act laid on the shelf in mothballs." Lowell's Frost says at the end of the poem, "When I am too full of joy, I think/ how little good my health did anyone near me." There are poems on T. S. Eliot and Ezra Pound and a moving elegy to his friend Randall Jarrell. Lowell was the greatest elegiac poet of his time, whether the subject was his family, his friends, fellow poets, or great men. "The Quaker Graveyard in Nantucket" and "My Last Afternoon with Uncle Devereux Winslow" are among the finest elegies in American literature.

The later books of Lowell show one surprising change; where before he had written in loose verse paragraphs and occasionally in stanzas, he now takes up the sonnet form. All the poems in *Notebook* and most of the other later books are written in a very idiosyncratic sonnet form. Lowell usually keeps to the sonnet's fourteen-line pattern but does not use rhyme or observe the usual Italian or English sonnet divisions. "Dolphin," for example, begins with a traditional quatrain but then does not continue the quatrain pattern; it breaks the meaning at the seventh line. The last section does, however, provide a counter-statement to those first seven lines which speak of being guided by a muse in the way that Jean Racine was:

I have sat and listened to too many
words of the collaborating muse,
and plotted perhaps too freely with my life,
not avoiding injury to others,
not avoiding injury to myself—
to ask compassion . . . this book, half fiction,
an eelnet made by man for the eel fighting.

Then a very unconventional fifteenth line is added to complete the poem: "[M]y eyes have seen what my hand did." Some of Lowell's experiments with sonnet form seem casual and erratic, but "Dolphin" breathes a new life into the most fixed form in literature. Lowell was nevertheless worried that he had not successfully escaped the trap of that form. In an "Afterthought" to *Notebook* he said, "Even with this license, I fear I have failed to avoid the themes and gigantism of the sonnet."

"MY LAST AFTERNOON WITH UNCLE DEVEREUX WINSLOW"

First published: 1959 (collected in *Collected Poems*, 2003)
Type of work: Poem

A moving elegy on the poet's uncle analyzes the divisions in the Lowell and Winslow families.

"My Last Afternoon with Uncle Devereux Winslow" does not begin like an elegy, focusing instead on Lowell's childhood affection for his grandfather Winslow and his distance from his own parents. It begins, "'I won't go with you. I want to stay with Grandpa!'" Grandfather Winslow's world was one of adventure and freedom. "the decor/ was manly, comfortable,/ overbearing, disproportioned." At his farm are photographs of silver mines and "pitchers of ice-tea,/ oranges, lemons, mints, and peppermints,/ and the jug of shandygaff." Most significant is the fact that "[n]o one had died there in my lifetime." The boy (young Lowell) is busy playing with a "pile of black earth" and one of "lime," an image of play and death that runs through the poem.

The pastoral innocence of the first part of the poem is swiftly challenged. The boy is now inappropriately dressed and is described as a "stuffed toucan/ with a bibulous, multicolored beak." There is a recognition of failure; Great Aunt Sara had once slaved away at perfecting her ability on the piano, only to fail to appear at the recital. She now plays on a "dummy" and "noiseless" piano. Uncle Devereux, however, is still as young as the posters and photographs that fill the cottage he is closing "for the winter." Suddenly, reality intrudes upon the stasis of old photographs: "My Uncle was dying at twenty-nine." Devereux resists the fact of death by sailing with his wife "for Europe on a last honeymoon" in a joyous affirmation of life. His parents are shocked at his seeming frivolity. The child has altered as well; he becomes an observer of bizarre and unfamilial behavior, an accomplice rather than an innocent child.

The last part of the poem contrasts Devereux's appearance with his fate. He appears to be "as brushed as Bayard, our riding horse," but he is "dying of the incurable Hodgkin's disease." The last image of the poem is of the boy mixing "earth and lime,/ a black pile and a white pile." He becomes a mythic figure sifting the sands of life and death; the innocent play of the earlier image of mixing earth and lime has become ominous. The last two lines have a child's simplicity and all the weight of fact: "Come winter,/ Uncle Devereux would blend to the one color."

"My Last Afternoon with Uncle Devereux Winslow" is an unusual elegy. It mourns the loss not only of a person but also of a hitherto unchanging and innocent world. Another change from the traditional elegy is that the main focus is the boy, not Uncle Devereux. His loss of innocence, his being cast out of an Edenic refuge, seems to be stressed much more than the actual death of Devereux Winslow. Lowell has expanded the usual range of the elegy to include the observer and a whole society.

"SKUNK HOUR"

First published: 1959 (collected in *Life Studies*, 1959)
Type of work: Poem

Lowell provides a devastating analysis of the material and spiritual decay in modern life that contrasts to instinctual nature.

"Skunk Hour" is the last poem in *Life Studies*, and as such it was meant to sum up the themes and tone of the collection and suggest some sort of resolution. The first four stanzas portray a decayed Maine coastal town. The "hermit heiress" who should be a leader in the society isolates herself; her main activity is buying up houses near her to ensure her privacy and isolation: "[S]he buys up all/ the eyesores facing her shore,/ and lets them fall." She contributes to the decay rather than overcoming it by her wealth and position. In the third stanza, "our summer millionaire" has departed, and "[t]he season's ill." The change is also suggested by an image: "A red fox stain covers Blue Hill." The last stanza in this sequence portrays a "fairy decorator" whose trendy and unsuccessful shop is filled with the tools (fishnets and orange cork) that were once used by fishermen. Since "there is no money in his work,/

he'd rather marry." Love and marriage have become commodities in a once fruitful and organic society that is now sunk in decay.

The next two stanzas shift from an analysis of the society to one person. He is the Lowell speaker, mad and in search of sexual experience. The setting is ominous: "One dark night," which is not merely the time of day but also an allusion to Saint John of the Cross's *Dark Night of the Soul.* The speaker's car climbs "the hill's skull" (a reference to Golgotha) to look for "love-cars." The cars lie "hull to hull" where "the graveyard shelves on the town." It is a wonderful image of mechanical sexuality amid the grotesque graveyard that overlooks the town. All that the speaker can do is declare, "My mind's not right." This section culminates with another declaration: "I myself am hell;/ nobody's here." The first line echoes John Milton's Satan in *Paradise Lost*, while the last line repeats the isolation and decay that began the poem.

Both society and the individual are sick and perverted; there seems to be no hope anywhere. The last two stanzas, however, turn the poem around. Suddenly a group of skunks appears marching down Main Street, strutting by the no longer life-giving "chalk-dray and spar spire/ of the Trinitarian Church." In the last stanza, the mad speaker of the second section of the poem watches as "a mother skunk with her column of kittens swills the garbage pail./ She jabs her wedge-head in a cup/ of sour cream, drops her ostrich tail,/ and will not scare." The skunks are a remarkable and very appropriate modern symbol. They do not redeem the society of the speaker, but they do provide an alternative. They live off the decay that was so noteworthy in the first section of the poem. In addition, they will not "scare" or give in to an overly morbid consciousness as the speaker so obviously does. The scene also shows a mother nurturing her "kittens," something that cannot be found in the decayed and isolated society.

"Skunk Hour" became one of Lowell's most popular poems. It perfectly captures the troubles of society and the individual while also offering a powerful and natural symbol that opposes both. Modern poetry can no longer draw on the traditional natural symbolism of centuries before. Lowell could not instantly evoke eagles or hawks in his poetry, and he had the genius to discover a modern symbolism.

"FOR THE UNION DEAD"

First published: 1960 (collected in *For the Union Dead*, 1964)
Type of work: Poem

This work contrasts the aristocratic code of the nineteenth century and modern materialism.

"For the Union Dead" is an unusually public poem; Lowell wrote it to deliver on the Boston Common before a large audience. It is also one of his finest poems. It begins with a childhood memory of the South Boston Aquarium, where his hand had "tingled/ to burst the bubbles/ drifting from the noses of the cowed, compliant fish." Now, however, the aquarium "stands in a Sahara of snow." The "broken windows are boarded," and the "airy tanks are dry." Lowell has found perfect images of emptiness and desolation in what was once a place of life-giving joy. Next he notices "the new barbed and galvanized/ fence on the Boston Common." Once a symbol of openness and community, the common is now enclosed.

The only thriving elements are the parking spaces that "luxuriate like civic/ sand-piles in the heart of Boston." The construction of an "underworld garage" is shaking the famous seventeenth century Massachusetts Statehouse. The images are no longer of fish but have become "yellow dinosaur steamshovels." A mechanical and destructive world is replacing the traditional Puritan one. The only reminders of that heritage are the ironic "Puritan-pumpkin colored girders" that brace the "tingling Statehouse."

Lowell then shifts to imagery based on a statue and bas-relief of a Civil War hero, Colonel Shaw, a New Englander who led a regiment of free black soldiers in an attack on the fort at Charleston. The famous bas-relief of Colonel Shaw and his regiment has also been assaulted by the modern instruments of destruction and needs to be "propped by a plank splint." What the statue represents has also changed; no longer does Boston support the abolitionist cause or lead Negro infantry in a noble cause. Now, "[t]heir monument sticks like a fishbone/ in the city's throat." Colonel Shaw still possesses some of those older virtues: "He has an angry wrenlike vigilance,/ a greyhound's gentle tautness."

Shaw's father had thought an appropriate monument would be "the ditch,/ where his son's body was thrown/ and lost with his 'niggers.'" Lowell then makes another contrast between the past and the present. The "ditch is nearer," and the only monument from the recent war is an advertisement that "shows Hiroshima boiling/ over a Mosler Safe." War is no longer noble but has become mechanized and more destructive; advertisements replace the statues of Civil War heros.

Colonel Shaw awaits the "blessed break" that will complete his cause, but instead "the drained faces of Negro school-children rise like balloons" as they attempt to enter an all-white school. The image of the "bubble" encloses the fish in the aquarium, Colonel Shaw, and the black children, but there is no "blessed break." There is only a final and devastating symbol:

> Everywhere,
> giant finned cars nose forward like fish;
> a savage servility
> slides by on grease.

Once more, Lowell uses a mechanical symbol and opposes it to a natural one. No longer do aristocrats serve the republic; everyone is now mired in "servility" and a corrupt selfishness.

"For the Union Dead" is one of Lowell's finest poems; it brings together a number of image patterns and themes. The "fish" in the childhood reminiscence become "dinosaurs," then a "fishbone" that sticks in the city's throat, and finally "giant finned cars." The "bubbles" from those fish enclose (or imprison) the fish, Colonel Shaw, and the "Negro school-children"; all wait for the "blessed break," but it has receded rather than come closer in twentieth century Boston. The poem also successfully blends the public with the private interests, something that Lowell did not always achieve.

"WAKING EARLY SUNDAY MORNING"

First published: 1967 (collected in *Near the Ocean*, 1967)
Type of work: Poem

The poem portrays the universal desire for freedom and a natural life and how obstacles such as religion, politics, and human nature prevent it.

"Waking Early Sunday Morning" is the first section in the long poem called "Near the Ocean"; it attempts to find some relief or escape from humanity's disturbed, anxious, and apparently unnatural condition. It begins with that desire for an instinctual escape: "O to break loose, like the chinook/ salmon jumping and falling back." This leads to a childhood memory of freedom, "the unpolluted joy/ and criminal leisure of a boy." Such escapes are quickly closed, however, and the imagery shifts to the "sure of foot" and natural "vermin" in the walls of his house. In addition, dawn brings no renewal in this fallen world but only "business as usual in eclipse." Everything is stained or tarnished, so the speaker turns to religion, to the congregation at Sunday worship; however, that is no solution. Each day God recedes and "shines through a darker glass."

Having rejected the impossible instinctual life and the evasive spiritual one, he turns to another possibility: "O to break loose. All life's grandeur/ is something with a girl in summer." Love (or sex), however, has lost its power in a politically dominated world in which "earth licks its open sores" and man is "thinning out his kind." The last stanza reduces the escape to a plea for mercy.

> Pity the planet, all joy gone
> from this sweet volcanic cone;
> peace to our children when they fall
> in small war on the heels of small
> war—until the end of time
> to police the earth, a ghost
> orbiting forever lost
> in our monotonous sublime.

The Vietnam War and American foreign policy in general do not bring peace, only war upon war.

Noble aims have become illusory, ghostlike, and all joy is gone from the planet. The image of humankind "orbiting forever lost" is frightening and unrelieved. The universal desire to be free is frustrated not only by human nature but even more so by an environment of war and hostility.

"THE NIHILIST AS HERO"

First published: 1967 (collected in *Notebook, 1967-1968,* 1969)
Type of work: Poem

This paradoxical analysis of the claims of stasis and change is one which Lowell refuses to resolve.

"The Nihilist as Hero" is a sonnet from *Notebook* and a poem that reveals much about Lowell as a poet and a man. The poem begins with a quote from poet Paul Valery about sustaining a work of art beyond a single line. It is a vision of poetry as formal perfection. Lowell then announces a very different view of the nature of art: "I want words meat-hooked from the living steer." Such direct (confessional?) poetry is blocked, however, by the "metal log,/ beautiful unchanging fire of childhood/ betraying a monotony of vision." Life, too, is not based on stasis but "by definition breeds on

change"; however, change means only that "each season we scrap new cars and wars and women." It is an endless round of activity without hope or joy. The last lines of the sonnet bring the contrasts together. First, he states that when he is "ill or delicate,/ the pinched flame of my match turns unchanging green." The image of an illusionary stasis echoes the "tinfoil" flame of childhood. The last two lines complete the poem by balancing the two sides: "A nihilist wants to live in the world as is,/ and yet gaze the everlasting hills to rubble."

There is no easy solution; one desires both reality and destruction, an unchanging art and a live one, stasis and continual activity. This does not mean that Lowell is a nihilist; he recognizes the claims of both sides and cannot find a way to synthesize them. Humans are doomed to live with a dream of perfection in an imperfect world. It is a haunting conclusion to one of Lowell's most revealing poems.

SUMMARY

Lowell is perhaps the most important American poet of the last half of the twentieth century. He expanded the range and possibilities of poetry's subject matter with his confessional and political poems; no longer would poets have to write in the prescribed New Critical fashion. He also altered the way in which readers look at such traditional forms as the elegy and the sonnet.

Lowell's style was also innovative. Those "words meat-hooked from the living steer" in his later poems showed that letters, diaries, and advertisements could become forceful entities in poetry. Above all, Lowell's voice added an intensity and power to American poetry that had been lacking.

James Sullivan

BIBLIOGRAPHY

By the Author

POETRY:
Land of Unlikeness, 1944
Lord Weary's Castle, 1946
Poems, 1938-1949, 1950
The Mills of the Kavanaughs, 1951
Life Studies, 1959

Imitations, 1961
For the Union Dead, 1964
Near the Ocean, 1967
Notebook, 1967-1968, 1969
Notebook, 1970
The Dolphin, 1973
History, 1973
For Lizzie and Harriet, 1973
Selected Poems, 1976, revised 1977
Day by Day, 1977
Collected Poems, 2003 (Frank Bidart and David Gewanter, editors)

DRAMA:

The Old Glory, pb. 1965 (includes *Endecott and the Red Cross, My Kinsman, Major Molineux,* and *Benito Cereno*)
Prometheus Bound, pr. 1967, pb. 1969

TRANSLATIONS:

Phaedra, 1961 (of Jean Baptiste Racine)
The Oresteia of Aeschylus, 1979

NONFICTION:

Collected Prose, 1987
The Letters of Robert Lowell, 2005

Discussion Topics

- With reference to the traditional ballad of Lord Weary, what makes *Lord Weary's Castle* an appropriate title for Robert Lowell's book?

- What aspects of the New England past provided Lowell with material for his poems and plays?

- What is the theme or cluster of themes in the poem "For the Union Dead"?

- How does Lowell unite the diverse images of "For the Union Dead"?

- How do the formal aspects of Lowell's poetry change over the course of his writing career?

- What is confessional poetry? What are Lowell's principal achievements in this mode?

- What insights into other creative spirits of Lowell's time do you find in *Life Studies*?

About the Author

Axelrod, Steven Gould, ed. *The Critical Response to Robert Lowell.* Westport, Conn.: Greenwood Press, 1999.

Cosgrave, Patrick. *The Public Poetry of Robert Lowell.* New York: Taplinger, 1970.

Hamilton, Ian. *Robert Lowell: A Biography.* New York: Random House, 1982.

Mariani, Paul L. *Lost Puritan: A Life of Robert Lowell.* New York: W. W. Norton, 1994.

Perloff, Marjorie G. *The Poetic Art of Robert Lowell.* Ithaca, N.Y.: Cornell University Press, 1973.

Wallingford, Katherine. *Robert Lowell's Language of the Self.* Chapel Hill: University of North Carolina Press, 1988.

Williamson, Alan. *Pity the Monsters: The Political Vision of Robert Lowell.* New Haven, Conn.: Yale University Press, 1974.

ALISON LURIE

Jimm Roberts/Orlando

Born: Chicago, Illinois
September 3, 1926

Winner of the Pulitzer Prize in fiction in 1985, Lurie writes satirical novels of manners and academic behavior that have brought her recognition as one of America's finest comic writers.

BIOGRAPHY

Alison Lurie was born in Chicago on September 3, 1926. She attended Radcliffe College, where she received an A.B. degree in 1947. The following year she married Jonathan Peale Bishop, Jr., who went on to become a professor of English at Cornell University. Before their divorce in 1985, the Bishops had three sons, John, Jeremy, and Joshua.

Lurie's first book was a privately printed memoir of a close friend, poet and playwright Violet Lang, but her first significant work of fiction was *Love and Friendship* (1962), a novel that contains the themes of domestic dissatisfaction and adultery that Lurie would continue to explore in later work. Its principal character, Emily Stockwell Turner, is the prototype of Katherine Cattleman, Erica Tate, and the other unfulfilled, frustrated, middle-class American women who populate Lurie's narratives.

In addition to being a housewife and mother and working occasionally as a ghostwriter and librarian, Lurie continued to publish her novels, gaining more critical acclaim and a wider readership with each one: *The Nowhere City* (1965), *Imaginary Friends* (1967), and *Real People* (1969). Moreover, she began to garner fellowships and grants that helped further her career as a writer: Yaddo fellowships in 1963, 1964, and 1966 (Yaddo, an artist's colony, gave Lurie material for *Real People*); a

Guggenheim grant in 1965-1966; and a Rockefeller Foundation grant in 1967-1968. Finally, in 1968 she joined the faculty of Cornell, where she eventually became, like her husband, a professor of English, teaching fiction writing and children's literature. Cornell became the fictional Corinth University of her later novels, and its faculty served as models for the well-educated, crisis-ridden academics that she places there.

It was her fifth novel, *The War Between the Tates* (1974), that earned Lurie an international reputation. Her most ambitious novel, the book captures the flavor of the early 1970's—its radical chic, comic conservatism, mindless rebellion, generation gaps, confused feminism, political marches, and private battles between the sexes. Nothing escapes Lurie's sharp tongue and witty intelligence, and the result is a mercilessly satiric attack on American middle-class values. It remains her best-known novel, and it was adapted as a television movie.

Her reputation secure, Lurie published four novels after *The War Between the Tates. Only Children* (1979) appeared to mixed reviews, but *Foreign Affairs* (1984) earned for Lurie the Pulitzer Prize in fiction, as well as an American Book Award nomination and a National Book Critics Circle Award nomination for best work of fiction. *The Truth About Lorin Jones* appeared in 1988, and *The Last Resort* was published in 1998. In addition, she began publishing children's fiction: *The Heavenly Zoo* (1980), *Clever Gretchen, and Other Forgotten Folktales* (1980), *Fabulous Beasts* (1981), and *The Black Geese: A Baba Yaga Story from Russia* (1999, with Jessica Souhami), stories that often privilege women in ways that traditional folk tales do not.

In 1981, Lurie published a comprehensive history of clothing, *The Language of Clothes*, which argues for clothing as a communication system, a "language" that presents nonverbal information about people's occupations, interests, personalities, opinions, and tastes. The author employs photographs and illustrations, insights from literature, psychology, and sociology, and examples from her own experiences to inform this highly original work.

Lurie became a member of the prestigious American Academy of Arts and Letters in 1989. In addition to teaching at Cornell in Ithaca, New York, she lives in London and Key West, Florida.

ANALYSIS

Lurie has been compared to Jane Austen, Henry James, and Mary McCarthy (another satiric novelist who finds comic material in the American university), and to contemporaries such as Kurt Vonnegut, John Updike, Norman Mailer, and Philip Roth. Like Austen, she can be viewed as a novelist of "manners," a writer concerned primarily with the follies of highly sophisticated people who are often emotionally self-indulgent and insecure, caught between sense and sensibility, pride and prejudice. In fact, one of Austen's juvenile works is titled *Love and Freindship* (sic; wr. 1790), almost the same title that Lurie used for her own first novel, *Love and Friendship*.

Like James, Lurie is concerned not only with the manners and customs of Americans but also with their moral and psychological problems, with the "felt life" of the imagination as well as the realistic terrain of the social world. James was concerned with American character and often placed his Americans in European settings (or Europeans in American settings) to show them in stark contrast. In *Foreign Affairs*, Lurie employs James's "international theme" by sending her two principal Americans, Vinnie Miner and Fred Turner, to London, where American naïveté encounters European sophistication. Lurie's similarities to her contemporaries are more obvious. Like McCarthy in novels such as *The Groves of Academe*, Lurie finds comedy in academe; like Vonnegut, Roth, and others, her basic mode is satire.

Like many satirists throughout the history of literature, Lurie chooses sex, class, and religion as her targets. Adultery and sexual intrigues are common in her novels, and while such behavior always creates human complication, it is not at all clear that Lurie condemns it. In fact, she refuses to judge sexual behavior at all. In *The Nowhere City*, Katherine Cattleman's affair with Dr. Isidore Einsam strengthens her, making her more self-assured as a woman, while in *The War Between the Tates*, Danielle Zimmern's affair with Dr. Bernard Kotelchuk weakens her, making her more dependent and turning her from an independent, intelligent woman into a frumpy housewife. Wendy Gahaghan and Cecile O'Connor, two of Lurie's younger women, both emerge from their sexual affairs with little emotional damage.

On the other hand, few of Lurie's men fare well from their sexual escapades. Paul Cattleman, after flings with a youthful hippie and an aging Hollywood starlet, slinks back East to a safe teaching job, a defeated man. Brian Tate, publicly humiliated by a group of radical feminists, is a victim of self-deceit, hypocrisy, and vanity. Einsam and Kotelchuk are little better than rapists, both forcing themselves on the women they want, but each ends up condemned to a lifetime of timid devotion to their women. Roger Zimmern, the narrator of *Imaginary Friends*, longs for Verena Roberts but flees from her when she becomes sexually aggressive; even worse, Sandy Finkelstein, the pathetic mystic who has worshiped Erica Tate for years, is unable to get an erection when she offers herself to him. In sum, Lurie's view of sex (and its concomitants, marriage and adultery) is essentially that of a social scientist. She is more concerned with its effects on individual lives than on its moral significance.

Lurie's characters are usually well-educated, upper-middle-class adults who are respectable, responsible, and conservative—just those Americans that one would expect to uphold virtues of family, marriage, and society. The power of sexual passion, ennui, or simply contradictory human nature proves too much for them, however, propelling them headlong into strange alliances and complicated sexual games. At their best, sexual encounters change the individuals involved by giving them self-knowledge they otherwise would not have gained.

Complicating matters further is Lurie's distinctly feminist view of marriage, children, and men. Her suburban, intelligent, middle-aged housewives have been left for younger women, have fallen victim to graying hair and sagging breasts, have been uprooted from friends and comfortable surroundings to follow their husbands' careers, or have witnessed their children grow from cherubic babyhood to monstrous adolescence. They have made their choices, chosen their men and their lives long ago (when they were inexperienced), and now that they have knowledge of themselves and their world, they have no choices to make. Their husbands are sexually bored, professionally frustrated, and emotionally restless. Such marriages as these stay together for the sake of what Lurie calls The Children.

Typical of such children are the Tates' two teenagers, Jeffrey and Matilda, once known as "Jeffo" and "Muffy." Now growing into adulthood, they have become rude, abusive, profane, lazy, and selfish. They fight constantly, and both Erica and Brian Tate have come to despise them; to Erica, they are aliens who have taken over the bodies of the children she once loved. Lurie continually undermines the romantic notions of marriage and family that keep women from becoming fully developed, independent human beings. Women who spend their lives raising children, she insists, might find those children growing into hateful monsters. Wives who devote their lives to the careers of their husbands might be left with no lives of their own if the husband leaves them for another woman, and women without men are subjected to the mindless stereotypes of society. Divorced women who take lovers, such as Danielle Zimmern of *The War Between the Tates*, are categorized as sluts by society, while professional women who do not marry, such as Vinnie Miner of *Foreign Affairs*, are thought to be sexless spinsters.

Vinnie, in fact, is a good example of the realistic way that Lurie portrays women. A woman in her fifties who is not pretty by traditional American standards, Vinnie is juxtaposed to her English department colleague Fred Turner, a Hollywood-handsome young man. In London to do academic research, both have "foreign affairs," Vinnie with a somewhat loutish American tourist, Chuck Mumpson, and Turner with a famous British beauty and television actress, Lady Rosemary Radley. That Vinnie should have any affair whatsoever may seem surprising, for, as Lurie points out, society does not seem to expect physically unattractive women over fifty to have any sex life at all. Vinnie, however, though far from promiscuous, has been sexually active all her life, usually with male friends she has known for a long time. Sex, as she ponders at one point, has never been hard to attain, though love has been. (Sex, in fact, is not hard for any woman to attain, she concludes, if she sets her sights low enough.) Ironically, oafish Chuck Mumpson turns out to be a tender and sensitive lover, while the dazzlingly beautiful Rosemary is revealed as shallow, vain, incapable of love, and inwardly ugly. The beautiful and the handsome, like Fred and Rosemary, have just as much difficulty finding genuine love and affection as, by society's standards, the unattractive and no longer youthful.

Another favorite target of Lurie's satire is class, not only in the United States but, in *Foreign Affairs*, in England as well. Her upper-middle-class American academics range from uptight, conservative boors such as Don Dibble, who gets trapped in his office by a group of radical feminists in *The War Between the Tates*, to aspiring young professors such as Fred Turner, whose theatrical good looks make him suspect to his more conventional-looking male colleagues. Lurie's academics are pigeonholed in their sequestered world not only by whom they are sleeping with but also by how well they keep it hidden, by meaningless books and articles (and how well they are received by reviewers), and by the whimsical regard or disregard of their more powerful colleagues.

Lurie has a wonderful eye for details of clothing, material possessions, and surroundings that typify middle-class American life. Her biting satire of Southern California, *The Nowhere City*, ridicules the tacky architecture, labyrinthine freeways, twenty-four-hour "Joy Superdupermarkets," littered and smelly beaches, and voracious realty development that only a confirmed easterner such as Lurie could describe with such gleeful malice. To Lurie, Los Angeles is a "nowhere" city: a stratified geographical area with a central valley thick with smog and poverty, topped by the private pools and hillside palaces of the tastelessly rich.

Finally, there is the subclass of hippies, gurus, student groupies, and dropouts that appears frequently in Lurie's novels, not so much representing a class as a counterculture of the young and disenfranchised. Like Wendy Gahaghan and Ceci O'Connor, they live in "the now"—with no emotional commitment, no sense of responsibility, no ambition, and no hope. Small wonder that Wendy, at the end of *The War Between the Tates,* plans to go off with her latest casual lover to California, Lurie's favorite nowhere.

In *Imaginary Friends,* Lurie satirizes American religion, another favorite subject of traditional satirists. Reminiscent of both Sinclair Lewis's *Elmer Gantry* (1927) and Henry James's *The Bostonians* (1886, a satire not on religion but on the feminist movement of his day), the novel explores a spiritualist group called the Truth Seekers, a group of lower-middle-class losers who are convinced they are in touch with a spiritual space traveler named Ro of Varna, who sends messages (via automatic writing) through a young woman in the group named Verena Roberts.

The Seekers could be one of any number of similar groups throughout the United States, trying to find spiritual uplift for their pathetic and uneventful lives. The group is infiltrated by two sociologists from Corinth University who are out to prove a hypothesis about belief systems and find in the Seekers a perfect control group. As it turns out, the senior sociologist, Thomas McMann, is more lunatic than any of the Seekers (the novel also lampoons social scientists) and winds up in an asylum, believing that he himself is Ro of Varna. Both seekers and sociologists, Lurie tells us, get caught up in their own delusionary systems, irrational wishes, and distorted perceptions of reality—perhaps everyone does at one time or another—and who is to say that one form of delusion is better or worse than another?

Aside from the intelligence, social commentary, and sheer fun of Lurie's novels, many admire them simply for their artistry. Her carefully constructed novels often employ several voices and points of view, effortless shifts from present to past time, believable dialogue, and arresting images. Her prose is admirably lucid, concise, and direct, always perfectly suited to the narrative and subject. Her wit and use of irony are those of a highly sophisticated social novelist, and her illumination of the self-deceptions and disappointments of adult life reveal a novelist of serious intent for mature readers.

THE NOWHERE CITY

First published: 1965
Type of work: Novel

A young history professor and his wife encounter culture shock in Southern California.

The Nowhere City, Lurie's second published novel, is a somewhat malicious satire on California manners and customs, written from the point of view of someone who believes in the superiority of life in the eastern United States. In this early work, some of Lurie's dominant themes become evident: marital disharmony, the transformational effect of adultery, and the shabbiness of American middle-class culture.

The central characters are Paul and Katherine Cattleman, a young historian and his wife who have come to California from Harvard University, where Paul was completing work on his doctorate. Paul has taken a job with The Nutting Research Development Corporation, a large electronic firm in Los Angeles; his assignment is to write a history and description of the company's operations. To Paul, it is an ideal position: He will have time to write his dissertation and will be making twice the salary he would make as a young college instructor. Besides, he thinks of Los Angeles as an exciting and vital American frontier—the city of the future.

To his wife, Katherine, however, Los Angeles is a nightmare. The smog irritates her sinuses, the people look weird and freakish, the weather is hot and uncomfortable, and the city seems plastic and unreal. She is even attacked by a buffalo while visiting a zoo. Katherine's Los Angeles is a cheap, shoddy city of commercial exploitation, with desperate people seeking success, love, some hero to worship, or some beauty to ogle.

A subplot involves Hollywood starlet Glory Green and her husband, Dr. Isadore Einsam, a successful Beverly Hills psychiatrist. Lurie often casts dissimilar characters into her novels, comparing and contrasting their lives and bringing them into unexpected relations with each other. In this novel, Katherine takes a job as a research assistant at UCLA, working for Einsam, and later, through Einsam, she becomes secretary to Glory Green. Paul, who has been having an affair with Ceci

O'Connor, a coffee-shop waitress and California hippie, meets Glory when he goes to her Beverly Hills mansion to pick up his wife.

Typical of Lurie's novels, too, the couples become sexually involved with each other. Katherine has an affair with "Iz" Einsam, while Paul has one with Glory. These brief encounters go nowhere and each partner goes back to the original spouse. Intellectual Iz goes back to Glory, the stereotypical dumb blonde, while neurotic Katherine returns to Paul, whose desire to be a California swinger is tempered by eastern common sense and propriety. At the end of the novel, he accepts a teaching job at Convers College, north of Boston, and flies off to what presumably will be a more responsible and satisfactory life.

Lurie's main thrust in this novel is to lampoon Southern California manners, morals, and lifestyles. Paul, when he takes up with Ceci, becomes a ridiculous figure—a mature, well-educated man who dresses in paint-splattered chino pants, sweatshirt, and sandals, grows a beard, and hangs around espresso bars with Ceci. He even prides himself on getting busted by the police during a coffeehouse sweep for drug violators. Katherine, who hates Californians for their indifference and irresponsibility, goes Californian herself at the end of the novel, transforming from a neurotic, self-conscious, and somewhat plain young woman into a tanned, sexually flirtatious, and flashily dressed "Los Angeles type" who is indifferent to any responsibilities she might have as a wife. When Paul returns East, she remains behind.

Lurie has further fun with California freeways, buildings (homes shaped like pagodas, grocery stores like Turkish baths, and restaurants like boats), art (vulgarly sensual nudes), self-indulgence (a billboard advertising coffee proclaims in huge red letters "Indulge Yourself"), and the state's seeming obsession with speed and the present, its apparent rejection of reason and the past. Children have names like Psyche, Astarte, and Freya, and Hollywood beauties such as Glory Green are beautiful only at a distance, for up close, as Paul notices, she is vulgar, freckled, and commonplace. Nothing in the Nowhere City is what it seems: Dashing Hollywood he-man Rory Gunn is gay, the Nutting Corporation (the name is suggestive) cares nothing for history and is even afraid that Paul Cattleman will find out some of the unsavory truth about its past.

To Lurie, Californians seem subject to what she calls Watson's Law (named after a Boston mathematician), which states that the purpose of the economy is to expend as much time, money, and energy as possible without creating anything useful. That, in fact, seems precisely what has taken place in *The Nowhere City*. The activity of the characters has produced exactly nothing, and at the conclusion of the novel, they are right back where they started.

IMAGINARY FRIENDS

First published: 1967
Type of work: Novel

Two sociologists join a religious-spiritualist group called the Truth Seekers in order to write a sociological study of belief systems.

Imaginary Friends is unlike Lurie's other novels in that marriage, adultery, and the continuing war between the sexes, Lurie's most common themes, give way to other concerns. She does, however, continue to explore academic lives—in this case, an older sociology professor, Thomas McMann, and his younger colleague, Roger Zimmern—and she once again juxtaposes two kinds of culture; the simple, lower-middle-class Truth Seekers with the intellectual, well-bred, and sophisticated sociologists who come to study them. Lurie demonstrates that the rational beliefs and pretensions of intellectuals are often more monstrous than the seemingly lunatic beliefs of the uneducated and that the most revered institutions of American life—colleges and churches, for example—are no more preferable to mystical cults and religious fringe groups, and often have fewer answers.

Lurie's interest in such things as spiritualism and automatic writing may have come from her friendship with poet James Merrill, whose long narrative poem *The Book of Ephraim* (1977) recounts twenty years of experience with seances and Ouija boards. The novel is, in fact, dedicated to Merrill and another Ouija board enthusiast, David Jackson. Like them, Lurie takes the supernatural seriously. Verena Roberts, a young Seeker through whom higher beings speak by way of automatic writing, often gives messages that are difficult to explain rationally, although McMann, the senior sociologist, is always ready with a glib explanation.

At one point, for example, Zimmem (through Verena) receives a message from MAKES FAVOUR, SEE RIGHT ILLS, and O MAKE A VEIL HIGH, obvious puns on classic sociologists Max Weber, C. Wright Mills, and Nicolo Machiavelli, about whom Zimmern was thinking at the time. Moreover, Verena seems to have extrasensory perception when it comes to such things as finding lost car keys: Zimmern's, she tells him correctly, had slipped down behind some furniture and were lying next to the wall. To Lurie, there are more things in heaven and earth than are dreamt of in sociology.

A more literary influence on *Imaginary Friends* is Henry James's novel *The Bostonians*. In James's novel, principally concerned with the American women's movement of the late nineteenth century, Verena Tarrant is a young, charismatic public speaker who is an inspirational apostle of the feminist cause. In Lurie's novel, Verena Roberts is a similar inspirational apostle for the Truth Seekers. Both are objects of adoration by young men who wish them to renounce their passionate beliefs: Verena Tarrant is pursued by Basil Ransom, who, by muscular force, carries her off with him at the end; Verena Roberts, having been pursued by a tall, gawky boy named Ken (and worshiped from afar by narrator Roger Zimmern), finally gives up her beliefs, marries Ken, and goes off to Albuquerque, New Mexico.

Both novels are about contemporary social movements (feminism in James's time, religious fundamentalism in Lurie's), and both novels contain conflicts between the natural, instinctive, naïve gifts of an idealistic young woman and the educated, neurotic, and insensitive demands of others who want her for personal gratification.

As Lurie's novel progresses, the story's narrator, Roger Zimmern, becomes aware of the increasing duplicity, neurotic behavior, and peculiarity of his senior colleague, Thomas McMann. Having gone to the home of the Seekers in Sophis (another suggestive name) to prove an academic theory that opposition and doubt unite rather than weaken a group such as the Seekers, McMann manipulates data to make the hypothesis come true. The Seekers have been in contact, by way of Verena's automatic writing, with a spiritual alien named Ro of Varna, and when Ro promises to appear physically at a certain date, McMann and Zimmern have an ideal test situation. What will happen to the group when Ro fails to materialize, as will surely be the outcome?

On the evening of his promised appearance (which, of course, does fail to happen), Ro sends a final message: "I am in Man on earth." This is interpreted by some of the Seekers to mean that Ro has become incarnate within McMann here on earth—an interpretation that McMann does not try to deny or dispel. Further, McMann assumes deific powers within the group when he takes it upon himself to "protect" Verena against the attempts of Ken to contact her, and, finally, when he chases Ken off the premises with a gun. The result is that Zimmern comes to realize that his colleague is mad, and McMann ends up in a mental asylum, believing he is Ro of Varna.

Lurie's novel ultimately asks the reader to consider some very serious questions. Who is more self-deluded, those who believe in flying saucer saviors from the planet Varna or those who spend fruitless lifetimes studying them? Which of them live in the "real" world, those who believe that Varnians will deliver them the truth or those who believe the same from the high-level abstractions of the social sciences? Who do more harm, the Seekers with their weekly meetings of hymn singing, automatic writing, and nonsense about astral projection or McMann and Zimmern with their biased conclusions, their egomaniacal self-importance, their willingness to use others, and their questionable perception of reality? Lurie clearly comes down on the side of the Seekers. Ultimately, she forces one to question the ideals and attributes considered sacrosanct in American life—education, religion, science, society, and truth.

THE WAR BETWEEN THE TATES

First published: 1974
Type of work: Novel

The marriage of Erica and Brian Tate is a war between the sexes, not unlike actual battle with its victories, defeats, and victims.

The War Between the Tates, Lurie's best-known novel, is a wickedly humorous satire on marriage, infidelity, and American society. Lurie sets her narrative during the time of the Vietnam War, and early in the novel she develops an extended comparison between that disastrous American conflict and the typically American Tate marriage.

Brian and Erica Tate, like the South Vietnamese, find that their territory (an upper-middle-class house on Jones Creek Road, near Corinth University) is being taken over. The Tates liken their teenage children, Jeffrey and Matilda, to North Vietnamese invaders. Like America's involvement in Vietnam, the conflict between the Tates and their children began in a way analogous to a police action and has steadily escalated into all-out deadly warfare. From the children's point of view, their parents are the American invaders—superior in experience and resources but deeply hypocritical. While the children want only independence and self-government, the parents refuse to negotiate, so the children retreat into the jungles of their upstairs rooms, coming out only briefly for guerrilla skirmishes.

Brian and Erica, on the other hand, regard themselves as democratic and freedom-loving people; never having officially declared themselves at war, they see their mission as a peace-keeping and advisory effort. Although they have won most of the brief, pitched battles, however, the parents know that in the long run they will never win the war. The separation of powers by which they have operated their marriage—Erica as the executive branch and Brian as the legislative and judicial—has utterly failed to suppress colonial revolt. The Tates' victories are now all negative ones; the best they can hope for is to contain the enemy within the existing combat zone.

Lurie's witty metaphor is carried throughout the novel (perhaps too much so, as some have criticized). Brian and Erica's separation is like the division in America itself. Erica, tired of her selfish, rude, and rebellious children, has given up the fight, while Brian finds her desertion disheartening and disloyal. Just as there was student unrest in the colleges during the early 1970's, so is there unrest at Corinth, where Brian teaches political science. Radical feminists, taking Brian's advice, protest the sexist remarks of Brian's department antagonist Don Dibble, and when things get out of hand, they invade Dibble's office. Attempting to help, Brian himself is taken hostage, becoming a prisoner of war.

The novel concludes with a protest march on the Corinth campus, attended by most of the characters as well as an assortment of Maoists, gay activists, feminists, students, and local citizens. While the reader does not witness it, Lurie states that the group will eventually encounter violence at a bar called the Old Bavaria. This war has its victims, daily combats, withdrawals and retreats, and in the long run no one really wins.

The war that this novel is primarily about, however, is the war between the sexes. Brian, bored with Erica and suburban life, drifts into an affair with Wendy Gahaghan, a young graduate student in social psychology, while Erica, hurt by her husband's affair, attempts an affair of her own with Sandy Finkelstein, an old school friend who now goes by the name of Zed and manages a local metaphysical bookstore. Brian finds himself a victim of the generation gap; he disapproves of Wendy's use of marijuana, while she disapproves of his drinking alcohol. Her friends seem immature and shallow; Brian seems hopelessly uptight and square. When Wendy becomes pregnant with (possibly) Brian's baby, Brian urges abortion, while Wendy wants a love child.

Erica, on the other hand, with a newly found freedom, finds herself a prisoner of sex. Finkelstein-Zed seems an intelligent, gentle, sensitive man (although an incredibly unattractive one), and she decides to give herself to him. Zed, however, proves impotent, and the affair is fruitless. Erica's friend Danielle Zimmern (who is divorced from Leonard Zimmern, brother of the Roger Zimmern who narrates *Imaginary Friends*) is an example of what Erica would have to look forward to after divorce. Having slept unhappily with various men, Danielle passively winds up with Dr. Bernie Kotelchuk, a loutish veterinarian who, after raping her, convinces her to marry him. In the war between the sexes, both Brian and Erica are defeated, and at the end of the novel they march together against the Vietnam War, imagining reconciliation. Yet, just as the Southeast Asia conflict divided the United States long after the war's end, so does the Tates' truce suggest that unity will be a long time coming.

The War Between the Tates is Lurie's writing at its best. The novel is carefully crafted, with the controlling metaphor of the war keeping the material well focused. Her main characters are sympathetic and genuine, and the details of the narrative capture with great accuracy the rebellious period of the early 1970's, a period of midlife crisis for the nation as well as for the Tates. The conflict between generations, between radical passions and conventional morality, between those who experimented with sex, drugs, and Eastern philosophy and those who believed in all the traditional American ideals and institutions—these are captured with irony and wit and with an admirable detachment that avoids moralizing and sermons.

FOREIGN AFFAIRS

First published: 1984
Type of work: Novel

Two Corinth University professors travel to London, where they are confronted by experiences that alter their perceptions and values.

Foreign Affairs won the 1984 Pulitzer Prize in fiction and was nominated for both the American Book Award and National Book Critics Circle Award. Lurie juxtaposes American characters with British ones in order to explore national traits of both. "It's a complex fate to be an American," Henry James once said, and the complex fates of Lurie's two American academics in this novel are a good example.

In the opening chapter, Virginia "Vinnie" Miner, a small, plain, unmarried, fifty-four-year-old Corinth professor of children's literature, is traveling by plane to London, where she intends to do re-

search on folk rhymes of schoolchildren. Feeling alone and having just read a bad review of her latest book, she visualizes herself traveling with an invisible dog named Fido, an imaginary manifestation of her self-pity. The worse she feels, the more Fido whines for attention, until he finally scrambles into her lap and goes to sleep. Seated next to her is American tourist Charles (Chuck) Mumpson, an engineer from Tulsa specializing in waste-disposal systems. Vinnie suffers his amiable conversation during the trip.

In the second chapter, the reader meets Vinnie's colleague Fred Turner, a strikingly handsome young man who is in London to do research on the eighteenth century poet and playwright John Gay, author of *The Beggar's Opera* (1728). Turner, too, is lonely, having just separated from his wife, Ruth, and knowing no one in London except some graduate school friends and Vinnie, with whom he has had little contact at Corinth. Ripe for female companionship, if not an affair, Turner takes up with Lady Rosemary Radley, a beautiful British television actress whom he meets at a party. Equally lonely, Vinnie goes out with Mumpson, the waste-disposal specialist.

For the remainder of the novel, Lurie alternates chapters involving Vinnie and Turner, juxtaposing each one's British "affair" with the other's. Neither turns out happily. Mumpson, who seems to Vinnie's British friends like a comic American stereotype of the blustering tourist, dies of a heart attack while scouring the English countryside for traces of Mumpson family roots. Vinnie comes to realize, however, that he truly loved her and was an admirable human being. It was her blind Anglophilia, her tendency to become more snobbish and timid than the worst of the British, that prevented her from loving him completely. Vinnie, who has often had sex but never love, goes back home to Corinth knowing that at least once in her life, someone has loved her.

Turner is less fortunate. Gay, vivacious Rosemary turns out to be lecherous, ugly Mrs. Harris, a drunken, filthy cockney charwoman she dresses up as and pretends to be when she wants to keep Fred and others at a distance. An actress who has specialized in the role of an upper-class beauty, Rosemary plays that role in her public daily life, though her real self, the Mrs. Harris side, comes out when she is alone. More accurately, Rosemary does not seem to know who she is, Lady Radley or Mrs. Harris, and she consequently has lost touch with reality. Like many things in London, the Americans conclude, she is sophisticated and alluring on the surface but ugly and commonplace beneath.

In some ways, *Foreign Affairs* is like the fairy tales that Vinnie Miner (and Lurie) teach and love. Vinnie, the ugly princess, is turned into a beloved beauty by Prince Charming Mumpson, while Fred Turner, the handsome prince, falls in love with Rosemary, whose outward beauty hides the wicked witch within. Like those tales, fact and fancy intermingle (Vinnie's invisible dog, Fido, for example), to raise troubling questions about illusion and reality. Contrary to the way things seem, the novel insists, true love, true goodness, and true beauty and ugliness exist, almost magically, beneath the surface of things.

SUMMARY

Author Gore Vidal has called Alison Lurie the "Queen Herod of modern fiction," a reference to her capacity for slaying what seems most sacred to many people—marriage and the family, higher learning and intellect, and American lifestyles and values. While Lurie has an undeniable wit and savage irony in her novels, she also has a passion for truth, a generosity of spirit, and a reluctance to judge human conduct by any one set of restrictive standards.

Taken together, her novels constitute a major achievement of comic writing and detached observation of American life, and the artistry of her prose and carefully crafted narratives place her in the tradition of America's finest novelists.

Kenneth Seib

BIBLIOGRAPHY

By the Author

LONG FICTION:
Love and Friendship, 1962
The Nowhere City, 1965
Imaginary Friends, 1967
Real People, 1969
The War Between the Tates, 1974
Only Children, 1979
Foreign Affairs, 1984
The Truth About Lorin Jones, 1988
The Last Resort, 1998

SHORT FICTION:
Women and Ghosts, 1994

NONFICTION:
The Language of Clothes, 1981
Don't Tell the Grown-Ups: Subversive Children's Literature, 1990
Familiar Spirits: A Memoir of James Merrill and David Jackson, 2001
Boys and Girls Forever: Children's Classics from Cinderella to Harry Potter, 2003

DISCUSSION TOPICS

- In what ways does Alison Lurie make the university campus a microcosm for American society?

- Compare the treatment of feminism in two Lurie novels.

- How does Lurie's children's fiction reflect the themes of her adult novels?

- How are Lurie's novels comedies of manners in the style of Jane Austen?

- Compare the views of marriage in two Lurie novels.

- In *The Nowhere City*, how does Lurie's vision of California differ from her view of the eastern United States in her other novels?

- How are *Imaginary Friends* and Henry James's *The Bostonians* similar and different?

- How is *The War Between the Tates* a portrait of the American political turmoil of the 1960's and 1970's?

Alison Lurie

CHILDREN'S LITERATURE:
The Heavenly Zoo: Legends and Tales of the Stars, 1979
Clever Gretchen, and Other Foreign Folktales, 1980
Fabulous Beasts, 1981
The Black Geese: A Baba Yaga Story from Russia, 1999 (with Jessica Souhami)

EDITED TEXTS:
The Oxford Book of Modern Fairy Tales, 1993

About the Author

Costa, Richard Hauer. *Alison Lurie*. New York: Twayne, 1992.

Helfland, Michael S. "The Dialectic of Self and Community in Alison Lurie's *The War Between the Tates*." *Perspectives on Contemporary Literature* 3, no. 2 (1977): 65-70.

Kruse, Horst. "Museums and Manners: The Novels of Alison Lurie." *Anglia: Zeitschrift fur Englische Philologie* 111 (1993): 410-438.

Lurie, Alison. "Alison Lurie: An Interview." Interview by Liz Lear. *Key West Review* I (Spring, 1988): 42-52.

———. "An Interview with Alison Lurie." Interview by David Jackson. *Shenandoah* 31, no. 4 (1980): 15-27.

Newman, Judie. *Alison Lurie: A Critical Study*. Amsterdam: Rodopi, 2000.

Pearlman, Mickey, and Katherine Usher Henderson, eds. "Alison Lurie." In *Inter/View: Talks with America's Writing Women*. Lexington: University Press of Kentucky, 1990.

Stark, John. "Alison Lurie's Career." In *Twayne Companion to Contemporary Literature in English*. Vol. 1. New York: Twayne-Thomson Gale, 2002.

Watkins, Susan. "'Women and Wives Mustn't Go Near It': Academia, Language, and Gender in the Novels of Alison Lurie." *Revista Canaria de Estudios Ingleses* 48 (2004): 129-146.

David Styles

CORMAC MCCARTHY

Born: Providence, Rhode Island
July 20, 1933

McCarthy, one of the most significant contemporary American writers, has consistently extended the boundaries of what can be done with the English language and the novel.

BIOGRAPHY

Cormac McCarthy, like many of the characters in his novels, has kept moving from place to place, responding keenly to the pulse of his new settings. McCarthy was born in Providence, Rhode Island, and at the age of four moved to Knoxville, Tennessee, with his parents, Charles Joseph and Gladys McGrail McCarthy. After graduating from a Catholic high school in Knoxville, McCarthy attended the University of Tennessee in 1951-1952. The next year he spent wandering around the United States, doing odd jobs. He finally returned to the university in 1957 after four years' service in the Air Force. In 1960, the English department recognized his talent by granting him an Ingram-Merrill Award for creative writing. This may have encouraged him to leave school and devote his attention completely to his writing, which he did the same year, without receiving a degree. Since then McCarthy has eschewed academic patronage, though he has been the beneficiary of a number of generous institutional grants.

McCarthy's first novel, *The Orchard Keeper* (1965), like his subsequent fiction up to *Blood Meridian: Or, The Evening Redness in the West* (1985), draws upon his intimate knowledge of eastern Tennessee, the area where he spent his childhood and early adulthood. The novel, written in Sevier County, Tennessee; Asheville, North Carolina; and Chicago, won the William Faulkner Foundation Award for best first novel by an American writer. By the time the novel was published, McCarthy had been granted a fellowship by the American Academy of Arts and Letters for travel abroad. His European travels, supported further by a Rockefeller Foundation grant (1966-1968), took him to London, Paris, and the Spanish island of Ibiza, while he worked on his second novel, *Outer Dark* (1968).

McCarthy returned to the United States in 1967, now married and with a completed novel. He and his wife, Anne de Lisle, a singer from Hamble, England, whom he had met on his travels, settled on a small farm in Rockford, Tennessee. Yet another grant, a Guggenheim Fellowship for writing fiction, came his way in 1969.

During his career, McCarthy has, on the average, produced a novel every five or six years. *Child of God* came out in 1973, followed by *Suttree* in 1979, a novel on which he had worked throughout the late 1960's and the 1970's. Between the publication of those two novels, McCarthy, collaborating with film director Richard Pearce, wrote the script for *The Gardener's Son*, included in the Public Broadcasting Service's series *Visions*. The drama, based on an actual 1876 murder in Graniteville, South Carolina, embodies themes to which McCarthy has typically been drawn. Rob McEvoy, a crippled son of a laboring family, kills the son of a mill-owning family. The event, as portrayed by McCarthy, is fraught with moral ambiguity. Of McEvoy, the murderer, McCarthy has said, "The kid was a natural rebel, probably just a troublemaker in real life. But in our film he has a certain nobility. He stands up and says, 'No, this is intolerable and I want to do something about it.'"

McCarthy's move to West Texas in the early

1980's marked a significant shift for the writer. Supported by grants from the Lyndhurst Foundation and the John D. and Catherine T. MacArthur Foundation, he worked on his fifth novel, *Blood Meridian*, deemed by many critics his most masterful novel to date. The narrative movement in *Blood Meridian* and in his subsequent works called *The Border Trilogy*—consisting of *All the Pretty Horses* (1992), *The Crossing* (1994), and *Cities of the Plain* (1998)—occurs against a precisely drawn backdrop of the border regions of Texas, New Mexico, and Mexico. These four novels offer a stunning, vivid sense of the Southwest and northern Mexico, just as his first four novels capture and inscribe areas of Appalachia.

McCarthy's five-act play *The Stonemason* was published in 1994, though it had been written some years before. The play, set in Kentucky, features a young black man, Ben Telfairs, who, like the protagonists of *The Border Trilogy*, determines to adhere to traditional values and follow the family trade as a stonemason. In the late 1990's, McCarthy married for the third time. He now lives in Santa Fe, New Mexico.

The value and significance of McCarthy's fiction was quickly acknowledged by early reviewers and writers such as Robert Penn Warren, Saul Bellow, Ralph Ellison, and Guy Davenport, but only since the 1990's, with his move from Random House to Knopf and the publication of *All the Pretty Horses*, has his work gained a wider public audience and recognition. Though not going to the lengths of his contemporary Thomas Pynchon, McCarthy has chosen to live a secluded life, preserving his privacy and avoiding publicity, having granted permission for just one interview (published in *The New York Times Magazine*) during his career.

ANALYSIS

An overview of McCarthy's work shows the sure and steady development of the writer's craft, a deepening of metaphysical content, and expansion of thematic interests. His first four novels are rooted in the geography and experience of East Tennessee, the region where McCarthy grew up, while his next four novels, beginning with *Blood Meridian*, are set in the American Southwest and Mexico.

Early in his career, following the publication of *The Orchard Keeper*, comparisons were drawn between the Tennessee writer and William Faulkner, his Mississippi predecessor. There is certainly ample ground for comparisons to be made. The fictional worlds of both writers are grounded in their southern experiences. Like Faulkner, McCarthy has been an innovator in language, capturing regional idioms and imbuing his prose with a luminous verbal quality. The narrative designs, not to mention the naturalistic burdens, of *Outer Dark* and *Child of God* often remind one of Faulkner, especially novels such as *As I Lay Dying* (1930) and *Sanctuary* (1931).

McCarthy's work, however, is not derivative, and any comparison must emphasize his uniqueness. The social fabric of Faulkner's world is generally much richer and more interlocking than that of McCarthy, with the possible exception of *Suttree*. Faulkner's modernistic narrative technique allows for the expression of more of his characters' thoughts and subjective reactions than do McCarthy's tightly controlled, omniscient storylines. With *Blood Meridian*, McCarthy's style and concerns become unquestionably his own, not only as a result of shifting the locus of dramatic action from the South but also by concentrating more intently on the problematic nature of human violence and evil. The more recent novels have often been situated within the context of the traditions of the Western, both in film and literature. No contemporary American writer has devoted this kind of attention to the cultural interactions between the United States and Mexico.

McCarthy's narratives are shaped by the journeys they inscribe. The condition of homelessness and wandering are themes that run through the writer's oeuvre. In *The Orchard Keeper*, John Wesley Rattner's search seems, in part, to be for his father who, unbeknown to him, has been murdered. At the end of the novel, he is paying homage to his mother's grave. The movement of Culla and Rinthy Holme, in *Outer Dark*, as they look for each other and the offspring of their incestuous union, is a relentless groping for familial bonds and for an elusive home. Lester Ballard, the central character in *Child of God*, is left an orphan after his mother deserts him and his father hangs himself. Ever the outcast, fleeing the law, Lester turns to necrophilia in what seems a grotesque parody of love, a doomed attempt to reconstitute the family he never had. In *Blood Meridian*, "the kid" loses his mother at birth and runs away from his father when he is fourteen, initiating a story chronicling his vagrant travels in an amoral universe. Both John Grady Cole and Billy Parham leave their families at a young age and embark on journeys that expose them to a radically different cultural landscape, as they move from adolescence to adulthood.

McCarthy forces one to see and contemplate things one would normally find repulsive and would rather turn away from. In writing on *Child of God*, critic Doris Grumbach asserts that McCarthy "has allowed us direct communion with his special kind of chaos; every sentence he writes illuminates, if only for a moment, the great dark of madness and violence and inevitable death that surrounds us all." Lester Ballard's necrophilia, Culla and Rinthy Holme's incestuous relationship in *Outer Dark*, and the gross violence in *Blood Meridian* are all rendered beautifully, with subdued values of a sympathetic human vision, producing for the reader that odd union of disgust and thrill often associated with the gothic. Energies in *The Border Trilogy* often refuse to be contained, propelling characters into realms of tragedy and death.

McCarthy's project is an exploration of what humanity is, and his investigations take him to the fringes, aberrations where something has gone slightly afoul. His naturalistic inclinations lead him unflinchingly to follow the course of deformed lives, suggesting what delicate social and biological machines humans are and in what close proximity humankind is to perversion and violence. Lester Ballard, the reader is told, is "a child of God much like yourself perhaps." A haunting ambivalence lurks in the positioning of that "perhaps."

Subterranean worlds exist concurrently with the world on the surface, a thin membrane separating the two. The cavern figures frequently throughout McCarthy's early work as a metaphor for the submerged and primordial. In *The Orchard Keeper*, young boys explore caves and find "the inscriptions etched in the soft and curdcolored stone, hearts and names, archaic dates, crudely erotic hieroglyphs—the bulbed phallus and strange centipedal vulva of small boys' imaginations." In *Child of God*, Lester Ballard finally takes refuge in a cave, moving his collection of dead companions. In *Suttree*, one of Gene Harrogate's hare-brained plots is to cause the city's bank to collapse into the cavernous reaches beneath Knoxville. With Suttree he talks over his scheme:

> I reckon once a feller got in under there he could go anywheres he took a notion right in under the ground there couldnt he?
> I dont know, Gene. There's lots of cave under there. Suttree was pulling a wire minnowbucket from the bottom of the river by a long cord. He swung it dripping to the rail and opened the top and lifted out two beers and . . . handed one to Harrogate and leaned back against the houseboat wall.
> That goddamned truck like to of fell plumb out of sight.
> I saw it.
> What if the whole goddamned building was to just up and sink?
> What about two or three buildings?
> What about a whole block? Harrogate was waving his bottle about, Goddamn, he said. What if the whole . . . city was to cave in?
> That's the spirit, said Suttree.

Billy Parham and John Grady, in *The Border Trilogy*, become self-imposed exiles. Though the borders that they cross are geographic rather than moral, the motivation and effect is similar. They wish to come to know a world profoundly "other"; their choices and course of their narratives result in a sense of separation from their fellow men, a sense of separation from humanity itself.

A salient feature of McCarthy's fiction is the rich linguistic texture of the prose itself. Opaque, concrete, deceptively realistic, the words turn in on themselves, creating a world of their own, cut from their referential moorings. Detailed descriptions of the physical landscape are juxtaposed with sparse dialogue. The end result is that humans are given a place in the universe no more elevated or sacred than the natural world which surrounds theirs. McCarthy's characters are not loquacious. They say what they need to in order to get what they want, in a thoroughly natural diction. Rarely is access given to the consciousness of characters. One sees what they do and what they say, but seldom are motives explicitly displayed, leaving readers to form their own interpretations and moral judgments. Characters themselves, in fact, seem to lack any self-consciousness of their own actions. Detached from their egos, they perceive things "unshaped by the construction of a mind obsessed with form."

Underlying McCarthy's work lies the profound mystery of what incomprehensible, implacable force moves humankind. What keeps these characters going? This sense of mystery and limitless possibility might even be thought to be the very grounding of writing, of the construction of stories. "Where all is known no narrative is possible," asserts a character near the end of *Cities of the Plain*. McCarthy's vision may often seem to be nihilistic and cruelly gothic, with a relentless rapacity, yet it is not without a slim possibility of grace and redemption.

THE ORCHARD KEEPER

First published: 1965
Type of work: Novel

The lives of three men, outlaws of different kinds and ages, and various animals crisscross in the hills of eastern Tennessee.

Upon the publication of *The Orchard Keeper,* granted the William Faulkner Foundation Award for the best first novel by an American writer, McCarthy's promising literary talents were recognized. The young writer was singled out as a force to be watched and to be reckoned with.

Like a number of McCarthy's early novels, *The Orchard Keeper* is set in eastern Tennessee. Its topography is related intimately in stunning prose, creating a remarkable, richly textured linguistic surface to the novel. Setting, for McCarthy, is of paramount importance. In fact, geographic contours seem to precede and form the characters that act within their folds. This stands as a kind of philosophical principle for McCarthy, who places the human dimension of life in perspective, always vigilantly invoking the presence of larger, more powerful, mystical forces that drive and control people's lives. The hilly region east of Knoxville is perfect for supporting the thematic thrust of the novel. During the time the novel is set, in the 1930's and early 1940's, the area was yet outside the jurisdiction of law and beyond the reach of modern civilization. The land itself, and the connection of its tenants to

it, represents a cultural value akin to that espoused by southern Agrarian writers such as John Crowe Ransom, Robert Penn Warren, Allen Tate, and others.

Threatened is humankind's ability to live independent of society's conventions and inflexible legal dictates. The novel serves as an elegy to a heroic past in which people lived in harmony with nature and made, individually, their own moral determinations. As McCarthy writes in the last lines of the novel, its characters are among the last of their kind: "They are gone now. Fled, banished in death or exile, lost, undone. Over the land sun and wind still move to burn and sway the trees, the grasses. No avatar, no scion, no vestige of that people remains. On the lips of the strange race that now dwells there their names are myth, legend, dust."

Only gradually does the reader come to know about the three main characters whose lives the novel intertwines: Marion Sylder, a bootlegger; John Wesley Rattner, a young boy who traps game illegally; and Arthur Ownsby, an old, single man who is the orchard keeper. Though these characters have no discernible relation to one another when the reader meets them, they are drawn to one another as the narrative unfolds. Sylder has killed John Wesley's father, partly in self-defense, without even knowing who the man was. Sylder dumps the body of the dead man into an insecticide spray tank on the old decaying orchard kept by Ownsby. Ownsby finds the body but keeps it a secret, making periodic ritualistic visits to the makeshift grave, watching the body decay. Ownsby knows Sylder only by the car he used to run whiskey past the orchard, and he has no inkling he is responsible for the murder. John Wesley, however, knows both of them. He develops a friendship with the old man and comes to know Sylder after rescuing him from a creek where Sylder lands after driving his car off the road.

All of this is gathered in bits and pieces throughout the novel, for the narrative of *The Orchard Keeper* is the most disjunctive of any of McCarthy's novels. The characters themselves are thrifty with their speech; they keep things to themselves. Scenes are short and episodic, with periodic flashbacks triggered by characters' memories. Because the focus continually shifts, abruptly, without any signs as to with whom and where one is, the reader must continually adjust to new orientations. Plots are arrogant impositions on disconnected events. What McCarthy seems intent on uplifting in this novel is the remarkable random rhythm of human experience.

A sense of defeat lies heavily over the novel's end. The law, standing in conflict with a harmony of natural and human values, prevails. The old orchard keeper is hunted down, finally arrested for shooting an "X" in a metal tank, which he takes as a gross intrusion in his life, and committed to an asylum. Sylder is picked up by the law, too, for transportation of illegal substances. The boy, John Wesley, leaves the area, returning some years later, in the last episode of the novel, to find his mother's grave.

OUTER DARK

First published: 1968
Type of work: Novel

A brother and sister search for each other and the child born of their incestuous union, abandoned by its father and found by a tinker.

McCarthy's second novel pursues thematic issues raised in *The Orchard Keeper,* though its narrative is channeled more rigorously. The novel is about union, its sundering, and the perpetual questing which ensues.

The narrative is set in motion by the birth of a son to Rinthy Holme, the product of a union with her brother, Culla, with whom she lives alone in an unspecified place (bearing resemblances to eastern Tennessee). No genealogical or social references guide or orient their lives. Living alone, cut off from any social contact with anyone, theirs is an order primordial, prior to civilizing influences. Despite the absence of underpinnings for a socially determined morality, their acts have consequences, and the brother and sister are condemned to wander across the countryside, by foot, helplessly and ceaselessly.

After the baby's birth, Culla, feeling the guilt associated with the unnatural union, takes the child into the woods to die. An old tinker, however, comes across the child and picks it up to carry along with his other illegitimate wares—dirty books and moon-

shine. Instinctively Rinthy knows that the tinker has taken her child and commences her search for him. Culla, in turn, leaves to find his sister when he realizes that she is gone. The story then follows the respective journeys of the brother and sister, parallel yet separate and unique. The worlds of the brother and sister are kept distinctly apart in the metaphysical realm and in the narrative. Neither sees the other; neither path intersects the other, as close as they might get to each other. One knows little of what they think, or if they think at all.

The two seem to move through the landscape almost like apparitions, guided by some omnipotent force unknown to either. Rinthy is driven by her maternal instinct to find and care for her child. Her milk never dries up, a sign that the forces that move her are deep, impersonal, and universal. Though distinctly vulnerable, she seems only vaguely aware of possible dangers along the way. She is taken care of by those whose paths she crosses, as if they intuitively recognize her natural purity and innocence of the world's ways.

Culla, responsible for the child's conception and the abandonment that sent Rinthy off in its search, is driven by guilt. Indifferent to his fate, perhaps thinking his ill luck a fitting retribution for his acts, he takes what comes to him, moving "in a void, claustral to sound." His wandering itself, let alone his cowed attitude, marks him. As he passes through places of permanence, he is suspect, taken one time for a fleeing felon, another time for a grave robber. Another time he is accused of causing a horde of hogs to march off a cliff to their death. Finally, after a dramatic scene in which he barely survives the overturning of a makeshift river ferry, Culla is driven into the company of three malevolent marauders who abuse him, take his shoes, and bend his will by threats. The unprincipled nihilism of the gang's leader, who follows a law of brute force, stealing and torturing as he pleases, foretells the lawlessness of Glanton, the judge, and the wandering band of Americans in *Blood Meridian.*

The journeys come to tragic ends. Rinthy finds the tinker, but he refuses to relinquish his hold on the child, saying that she is poor and has nothing to give him in return for his provisional care. His own relationship with the child is a thin bulkhead holding back the huge lurking darkness of his own loneliness. The child, meanwhile, passes from the hands of the tinker to the three night riders, who taunt Culla, trying unsuccessfully to get him to admit to his paternity. They finally cut the throat of the baby and leave the remains, which Rinthy discovers shortly thereafter in a glade, with the tinker hanging from a nearby tree, vultures pecking at his carcass.

Outer Dark provides some basis for the comparisons often made between Faulkner and McCarthy. The handling of narrative in the novel and the almost absurd journeys of its characters call to mind *As I Lay Dying*. The poor, wandering Rinthy seems cut from the same pattern as Lena Grove's in Faulkner's *Light in August* (1932). A gothic atmosphere hangs heavily over the novel. Dead corpses hang from trees, characters trudge through the night followed by ominous sounds and small unidentified lights, cannibalism lurks on the edges, and darkness surrounds things.

With all its journeying and strident tone, the novel, like John Bunyan's *The Pilgrim's Progress* (1678) or John Milton's *Paradise Lost* (1667), invites allegorical interpretations. What purpose do these roads and these wanderings have? If some meaning is to be distilled, it might be simply that lives, by their very nature, must take some path which, in the end, will add up to no more or no less than those lines that have been traced. The human condition itself is a condemnation to homelessness. "They's lots of people on the roads these days," Culla says to a blind man he meets toward the end of the novel. The blind man agrees: "I pass em ever day. People goin up and down in the world like dogs. As if they wasn't a home nowheres."

In *Outer Dark*, McCarthy explores what a human being is when stripped of all encumbrances, material and spiritual. Like the best of his other novels, it is a testimony to man's amazing endurance and survival in spite of himself At one point the tinker says to Rinthy, "I've seen the meanness of humans till I don't know why God ain't put out the sun and gone away."

SUTTREE

First published: 1979
Type of work: Novel

Stalking death, Cornelius "Bud" Suttree comes and goes from his houseboat on the Tennessee River, associating with the wretched of the earth.

Much distinguishes *Suttree*, McCarthy's fourth novel, from his previous fiction. More expansive and ambitious than his earlier work, *Suttree* traces the life of one single central character, Cornelius Suttree, from October, 1950, to the spring of 1955. The world the novel displays is primarily urban, with most of the action taking place in McAnally Flats, a down-and-out district of Knoxville, Tennessee, whose grim landscape McCarthy describes with startling precision and beauty. The comic elements of the novel offset the continual presence of death and despair.

At the heart of the novel are Suttree and the river on which he lives on a houseboat at various intervals in the story. Rejecting the sober, comfortable middle-class values of his father, he chooses instead to explore the more essential, unseemly side of life on the edge in the underground world of McAnally Flats—home of drunks, derelicts, gamblers, whores, homosexuals, murderers, evangelists, and thieves. Suttree continuously returns to the river, where he sets up his fishing lines, until the end of the novel, when the Flats are threatened by demolition for the construction of a freeway. His is a search for living authentically, reconciling himself to the world around him.

Much of the heavily populated novel chronicles Suttree's intermittent interactions with a constellation of colorful characters: the ragpicker, J-Bone, Oceanfrog, an old former railway worker, a family of musselhunters, hulking black Ab Jones, an Indian fisherman, Blind Richard, a black sorceress, the gay Trippin Through the Dew, a whore he shacks up with for a spell, and, most memorable of all, Gene Harrogate, the infamous watermelon humper whom he first meets in the workhouse where both are serving time for their dubious wrongdoings. Anytime Harrogate appears, the reader is assured of some comic mishap. Suttree himself, a solitary creature whose main difficulties in life seem to be associated with living with himself, proves to be immensely tolerant and compassionate. He stands by his fellow outcasts, regardless of their race, creed, or felony, and lends a hand when they are in need—fleeing from the law, trying to get rid of a dead body, or engineering an illegitimate plot.

The omniscient narrative, centered on Suttree, moves fluidly from experience to experience. He is an American Ulysses; when Suttree bumps into people and forms attachments, things happen. Seldom does he take his fate into his own hands. Trouble tracks him down, and he does not run from it. As in life, characters leave the scene, die, are abandoned or forgotten, and sometimes reappear unexpectedly, unpredictably, and inopportunely. Until the end, Suttree and the river remain. McCarthy rarely admits his reader to the workings of his characters' minds. From actions and speech one must form impressions about what motivates Suttree.

The world Suttree inhabits and internalizes is filled with loneliness and death. It is never clear whether death stalks him or he stalks death. Death hovers over his very birth, snatching the twin brother with whom he has shared his mother's womb. At one point in the novel he learns of his son's death and, in a rare assertion of will, leaves Knoxville to attend the funeral. Even there he watches from the side, cast out by his in-laws, who blame him for his treatment of their daughter, his estranged wife. Suttree also lives through the deaths of several friends, and toward the end of the novel, in a feverish bout with typhoid, he nearly crosses the threshold himself. As he is recovering, he shares his message from the other side with the nurse: "I have a thing to tell you. I know all souls are one and all souls lonely."

Suttree becomes attached to two women during the course of the novel, each of whom, for a time, lifts him out of his solitude. The nature of his problematic relationships with women, including his mother and his first wife, is a pressing theme throughout. With Wanda, the daughter of the man with whom he had become partners in a mussel shell-gathering operation, Suttree experiences a wholly innocent, idyllic sexual relationship, broken off first by his fear and eventually by her death in a rock slide. Not long afterward, Suttree takes up with Joyce, whose work as a prostitute brings in enough money for them to move into an apart-

ment together and buy a roadster. This connection, too, must end, though not in death.

Suttree finds a kind of redemption that is rare in McCarthy's work. He confronts and transcends his own death, both in his battle with typhoid and in the form of a corpse he finds in his own bed on his houseboat when he gets out of the hospital. In another assertion of his own will, Suttree finally decides to leave McAnally Flats. The last time the reader sees him, he has gotten into a car that has stopped for him, and he is heading for some destination unknown.

An outstanding feature of the writing in *Suttree* is the fine balance achieved between dialogue and lyric descriptions of landscapes. McCarthy's rendering of the unique, natural dialect of the region is unprecedented and unsurpassed. As in *The Orchard Keeper* and *Blood Meridian*, the geographical terrain is tangible and vibrant. The relation between description and dialogue is analogous to the dialectic between the natural and the human world in the novel. Each plays a part, as they interact with and shape each other.

BLOOD MERIDIAN

First published: 1985
Type of work: Novel

A band of American renegades indiscriminately murders, plunders, tortures, and scalps Indians, Mexicans, and others on their expedition through the Southwest and Mexico in the 1840's.

With *Blood Meridian: Or, The Evening Redness in the West*, a novel of epic proportions and startling originality, McCarthy shifts his eye from Tennessee to the American Southwest and northern Mexico. The novel, set in the 1840's, when the border between the United States and Mexico was under dispute, is an orgy of violence, vain striving, and desperate marauding. It gives form to the frontier theory, the idea of manifest destiny, which inspired Americans to seek dominion over the land and to expel, murder, or subjugate those peoples who stood in the way of their dominion over the mission. As the subtitle of the novel suggests, the book has elements of the Western, though McCarthy rigorously subverts the convention and its values. There are indeed cowboys, Indians, and Mexicans, but the shoot-outs, massacres, and raids (all depicted in graphic detail) take place in a vacuum of values where there is no such thing as a "good guy" or a "bad guy." Alan Cheuse is on track in calling *Blood Meridian* "a Western that evokes the styles of both [film director] Sam Peckinpah and [artist] Hieronymus Bosch."

The narrative loosely follows a young protagonist whom the reader knows only as "the kid" (born a hundred years before his creator, in 1833) as he leaves his Tennessee home at the age of fourteen, winds his way west to Texas, and is enlisted in a vigilante army of Americans who, under the command of Captain Glanton, march through the inhospitable plains, deserts, and mountains of Texas, Chihuahua, Sonora, Arizona, and southern California, terrorizing Indians, Mexicans, and one another along their wrathful path. Hosts of colorful characters appear and vanish through the journey's course. Most important among them is Judge Holden, who first meets and observes the kid early in the novel and then picks up his trail later, following him until their ultimate showdown near the novel's end.

Early in the novel, the kid meets a hermit who propounds his belief in evil and its mysterious, self-generating nature. This is one of the first instances of the novel's preoccupation with evil, and it serves as a reference for one's acquaintance with the judge, an embodiment of evil as formidable as any found in American fiction, Herman Melville's Ahab included. Judge Holden propounds and elaborately defends his Nietzschean worldview in a long speech to his companions:

> Moral law is an invention of mankind for the disenfranchisement of the powerful in favor of the weak. Historical law subverts it at every turn. A moral view can never be proven right or wrong by any ultimate test. . . . Man's vanity may well approach the infinite in capacity but his knowledge remains imperfect and however much he comes to value his judgements ultimately he must submit them before a higher court. Here there can be no special pleading. Here are considerations of equity and rectitude and moral right rendered void

and without warrant and here are the views of the litigants despised. Decisions of life and death, of what shall be and what shall not, beggar all questions of right.

Knowledge, for the judge, is a weapon. To know things is to control them. His imperialistic view of knowledge is an extension of eighteenth century European Enlightenment attitudes. "Whatever in creation exists without my knowledge exists without my consent," he proclaims at one point. In this spirit, he carries with him a journal in which he scrupulously records the minute details of flora and fauna, preserving specimens of birds, catching and drawing butterflies. To what end? In order to gain mastery over things, people, and new territory.

If this novel is about the nature of tyranny and the violence it looses on everything around it, it is also about the unconquerable mystery of the world and its laws, omnipresent and omnipotent. The force of the natural world challenges an anthropomorphic view of the universe. The novel itself is a veritable catalog of plant and animal life, a verbal map of the territory. The landscape is described with the same scrupulous attention to detail that has characterized McCarthy's writing since his first novel, *The Orchard Keeper.*

What is amazing in this picture of things is that humans survive at all. Characters in this novel live far longer than either logic or luck would have it. That, too, is part of the mystery and awe. Figures trudge through the landscape, often freezing in snow or parched and hungry, dressed in tatters, covered in dust, and caked with blood from their last battle. The novel miraculously transforms such grotesque ghouls and hideous happenings into objects of aesthetic beauty.

In the end, in an unavoidable face-off, the judge—now in the garb of the authority that society has bestowed on him—overpowers the kid, annihilating the witness, the potential promulgator of stories of his malicious deeds. Once again McCarthy prompts a critique of the moral underpinnings of society, opens to question the goodness of the man in the white hat, and ominously entertains the possibility of evil's triumph.

ALL THE PRETTY HORSES

First published: 1992
Type of work: Novel

The novel traces the journeys of three young Americans who cross into Mexico from the United States on horseback and experience love, death, and hardship.

This novel, the first of Cormac McCarthy's *The Border Trilogy*, is likely also his most famous novel, in large measure as a result of the 2000 film version directed by Billy Bob Thornton and starring Matt Damon and Penélope Cruz. There is no way, however, that the medium of film can capture the rich linguistic texture of the novel that is a hallmark of McCarthy's writing.

The opening scenes of the novel, set in the late 1940's, show the sixteen-year-old protagonist, John Grady Cole, at his grandfather's funeral. The grandfather's death precipitates the sale of the San Angelo Ranch that had been in the family for generations. In the wake of this news, John Grady heads out West, and then south into Mexico, on horseback, with his friend Lacey Rawlins. As the young Americans cross the border, they experience a kind of exhilaration and freedom not unlike that felt by Ernest Hemingway's American characters in *The Sun Also Rises* (1926). Much of the narrative's interest and drama stem from the characters' negotiation of differences in language, customs, food, and national character, as innocence gives way to experience. Mexico, an unknown region, represents adventure: "There were roads and rivers and towns on the American side of the map as far south as the Rio Grande and beyond that all was white." Once across the border, they find that Mexicans, likewise, often have a vague impression of the country to their north. A group of *vaqueros* asks them about the United States: "Some had friends or relatives who had been there but to most the country to the north was little more than a rumor. A thing for which there seemed no accounting."

Along the way, a third character calling himself Jimmy Blevins attaches himself to Cole and Rawlins. Stubborn, with a "loose wing nut," as Rawlins describes him, Blevins is one of McCarthy's most memorable comic characters. The boy, who claims

he is thirteen, lies habitually. As is the case with Eugene Harrogate in *Suttree*, the reader quickly learns to anticipate trouble anytime Blevins comes on stage. At one point, the kid gets so drunk that he falls off his horse. Another time, he loses his horse during a flood. The young American's foolishness and bravado finally get him killed, and cause a good deal of trouble for his two compatriots.

Cole and Rawlins, leaving Blevins to his own devices, get jobs on a Mexican ranch, proving their abilities through a marathon breaking in of a corral full of horses, then hunting down groups of wild horses in the surrounding mountains. So descriptive are the pages on horse-breaking that they could serve as an instruction manual. John Grady wins over those around him (and the reader) with his skill as a horseman and chessplayer, his proficiency in Spanish, his genuine decency, and his impressive knowledge, especially given his youth. He and the *hacendado*, or ranch owner, agree upon two things "wholly and that were never spoken and that was that God had put horses on earth to work cattle and that other than cattle there was no wealth proper to a man."

A romance develops in the middle of the novel between the young protagonist and Alejandra, the slightly older, attractive daughter of the Mexican *hacendado*. Readers sense that the romance is doomed from the start, however, because of the great obstacles imposed by differences in cultural conventions, nationality, and economic class. The Americans' stay on the ranch ends abruptly when they are apprehended by Mexican authorities, put in jail, and interrogated regarding their association with Blevins, who had killed three men.

The novel comes full circle in the end, with John Grady's return to Texas. In his dogged quest to find the rightful owner of Blevins's horse, John Grady comes across a radio evangelist bearing the name Jimmy Blevins, leaving readers with the distinct impression that among the things Blevins lied about was his own name. Rawlins gets his horse back, John Grady's father is dead, and the ranch is gone. Funerals frame the novel's action. In the final scenes, John Grady looks on as the Mexican woman "who had worked for his family fifty years" is buried in the Mexican cemetery. The protagonist then turns his back on a disintegrated legacy and heads off toward parts farther west.

THE CROSSING

First published: 1994
Type of work: Novel

The protagonist, Billy Parham, makes three separate trips to Mexico—one to return a captured wolf, another to find stolen horses, and a third to retrieve his brother.

Set in the years leading up to World War II, the second novel in *The Border Trilogy* focuses on the lives of two brothers, Billy and Boyd Parham, who are, respectively, sixteen and fourteen at the beginning of the novel and living with their parents in Hidalgo Country, on the border between New Mexico and Mexico. Billy initiates three distinct expeditions across the border, each with its own mission, and each mission is executed, though not in intended ways. As in the other two volumes of the trilogy, the dialogue (portions of which are in Spanish, untranslated) is crisp and lean; descriptions are precise and finely chiseled.

Billy makes the first trip alone, to return a pregnant she-wolf that he has trapped around his family's home. Crossing into Sonora, Mexico, he finds the place "undifferentiated in its terrain from the

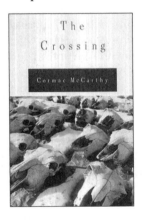

country they quit and yet wholly alien and wholly strange." Though his motivations for making the trip are not made explicit, Billy seems to feel a sense of kinship with the wolf because of its wild, untamed spirit. The wolf, readers are told, "knew nothing of boundaries." He engineers elaborate devices for subduing and feeding the animal and does his best to defend it from those who would do the animal harm or exploit it for their own selfish purposes. The wolf is finally taken from him by Mexican authorities and subsequently handed over to display in a fair, then to use as sport. Billy, fearful of what would happen, tracks the wolf down and follows it. Seeing the wolf forced to fight one dog after another in a cruel and futile battle, Billy

ends the wolf's suffering, shooting the animal he loves and swapping his rifle for the creature's carcass, which he takes off to bury.

On the way home, Billy comes upon a Mormon in an abandoned church, one of those spectral figures haunting McCarthy's fiction, who feeds him and provides hospitality. The Mormon's stories have a metafictional, allegorical, even prophetic quality to them, offering something like a theory of narrative. "Things separate from their stories have no meaning," he tells Billy. "The story . . . can never be lost from its place in the world for it is that place" and "Acts have their being in the witness."

> The task of the narrator is not an easy one, he said. He appears to be required to choose his tale from among the many that are possible. But of course that is not the case. The case is rather to make many of the one. Always the teller must be at pains to devise against his listener's claim—perhaps spoken, perhaps not—that he has heard the tale before. He sets forth the categories into which the listener will wish to fit the narrative as he hears it. But he understands that the narrative is itself in fact no category but is rather the category of all categories for there is nothing which falls outside its purview. All is telling. Do not doubt it.

One of the stories that the Mormon tells is of a boy who loses his parents. At the time he hears the story, Billy does not realize that the story will become his own. When he returns home, however, he finds himself an orphan. His home is empty, his parents massacred and his brother Boyd living with neighbors. (Others along the way seem almost mystically to have received the news earlier, addressing Billy as "orphan.")

The two brothers set off on another trip to Mexico, this time to retrieve horses stolen from their family at the time of their parents' massacre. The two travel a good deal in silence, their grief and guilt unspoken. Along the way, Boyd develops affection for a young Mexican woman whom they rescue from men apparently intent on raping her. They locate the horses but have trouble keeping them in their possession. Boyd is wounded while protecting the retrieved horses. Without saying anything to his brother, Boyd leaves with the Mexican girl.

Billy returns from this second trip to Mexico without his brother to find the country at war. He tries to enlist several times in several places and is rejected each time because of a heart murmur. After several years, he sets out on his third trip south of the border, this time to find his brother and bring him home. Boyd is dead, and legends of his valor seem to have worked their way into popular songs, indistinguishable from other popular heroes. Billy locates his brother's grave, digs him up, and loads up his remains to take back home. A group of robbers set upon him, rip apart the coverings of the corpse, and stab his horse Niño. Billy wraps the corpse back up, continues on his journey, and buries his brother upon arriving home.

CITIES OF THE PLAIN

First published: 1998
Type of work: Novel

John Grady Cole's passionate pursuit of an epileptic Mexican prostitute results in the tragic deaths of both.

Cities of the Plain, set in the early 1950's around El Paso, Texas, and across the border in Juarez, Mexico, brings together the protagonists of the first two novels of *The Border Trilogy*. Billy Parham, now in his thirties, and John Grady Cole, now nineteen, both find themselves working on a ranch in the Tularosa Basin, an area threatened by U.S. government appropriation for military purposes. "Anyway this country aint the same," Billy tells John Grady. "The war changed everthing. I don't think people even know it yet."

The central action revolves around John Grady's single-minded obsession with a young Mexican epileptic prostitute, Magdalena, an obsession that readers understand better in the light of his experiences in *All the Pretty Horses*. The extent to which John Grady is devoted to this woman and willing to sacrifice for her shows how difficult it can be to distinguish between foolishness and heroism. Grady's powerful emotions propel him along the path of romance, despite cautions and counsel offered by older men such as Billy, Mac the ranch owner, and the maestro, a blind Mexican musician who subscribes to a kind of fatalist philosophy: "Men imagine that the choices before them are

theirs to make. But we are free to act only upon what is given. Choice is lost in the maze of generations and each act in that maze is itself an enslavement for it voids every alternative and binds one ever more tightly into the constraints that make a life."

There are plenty of signs that the relationship will not work; the narrative bears the usual markings of tragedy. The most stubborn, insurmountable obstacle turns out to be Eduardo, the girl's pimp who is also in love with her. Despite her mortal fear of Eduardo, Magdalena finally arranges to escape with John Grady. The price of her defiance is death: She is caught and killed in her attempt to flee. When John Grady finds out what happened, he seeks revenge, going after Eduardo. An extremely graphic knife fight between the two men ends with a critically wounded Grady killing his rival. Despite Billy's attempt to save him, Grady dies from his wounds. Neither energies nor the beings housing them stay within prescribed boundaries. Grady's obsession, the woman's epilepsy, Eduardo's capacity for jealousy and desire for triumph over his rival—all are displays of excess, and, while this excess leads to tragedy, it at least is vivid proof of life's intensity, perhaps preferable to a dull, lifeless, modern existence, void of tragic potential.

As do the first two novels in the trilogy, *Cities of the Plains* discloses the complex dynamics between the United States and Mexico, fraught with tensions, mutual suspicions and fascinations. Both Billy and John Grady, fully aware of cultural differences, register a real appreciation of their neighbors south of the border. Billy recounts the extraordinary generosity and hospitality of ordinary Mexicans:

> I was just a kid. I rode all over northern Mexico.... I liked it. I liked the country and I liked the people in it. I rode all over Chihuahua and a good part of Coahuila and some of Sonora. I'd be gone weeks at a time and not have hardly so much as a peso in my pocket but it didn't make no difference. Those

people would take you in and put you up and feed you and feed your horse and cry when you left. You could of stayed forever. They didn't have nothin. Never had and never would. But you could stop at some little estancia in the absolute dead center of nowhere and they'd take you in like you was kin. You could see that the revolution hadn't done them no good. A lot of em had lost boys out of the family. Fathers or sons or both. Nearly all of em, I expect. They didn't have no reason to be hospitable to anybody. Least of all a gringo kid. That plateful of beans they set in front of you was hard come by. But I was never turned away. Not a time.

For Grady, Mexico has retained a certain vitality lost in the United States. "Don't you think if there's anything left of this life it's down there?" he asks Billy at one point. His obsession with the Mexican woman might be seen as a way to come to terms with, even to embrace, the "other." The presence of Americans south of the border is not welcome by all, as shown in Eduardo's remarks to John Grady during their knife fight: "They drift down out of your leprous paradise seeking a thing now extinct among them. A thing for which perhaps they no longer even have a name." The story's outcome underscores how difficult it is to surmount a history of hostility, distrust, and misunderstanding.

The novel's epilogue, transcending the tragic story, features a seventy-eight-year-old Billy, at "the second year of the new millennium" and his encounter with a Mexican fellow-traveler. In their exchange, in the mutual listening and telling of dreams and stories, readers are urged to consider the metaphysical import of dreams, stories, death, the relationship between life and representations of it, and the contingent forces that conspire to make a particular life what it is, and not something else. "Every man's death is a standing in for every other," the Mexican pronounces toward the end, as a kind of moral. "And since death comes to all there is no way to abate the fear of it except to live that man who stands for us."

SUMMARY

Any reckoning of those voices in contemporary American literature that have been most innovative and have spoken most powerfully about the human condition would surely grant a place to Cormac McCarthy, who has provided such vivid and poignant depictions of the cultural and geographic landscapes of Appalachia and the U.S.-Mexico border region. The issues arising so naturally from McCarthy's fiction are those that have always been at the center of American literature—an uneasy truce with the land, the conflict between the individual and society, the relation between technology and nature, the struggle to come to terms with genealogical and historical precedents, and the eruption of violent potential. All of this is made the more remarkable by McCarthy's distinctive literary style—his vibrant images, rugged language, and precise diction.

Allen Hibbard

BIBLIOGRAPHY

By the Author

LONG FICTION:
The Orchard Keeper, 1965
Outer Dark, 1968
Child of God, 1973
Suttree, 1979
Blood Meridian: Or, The Evening Redness in the West, 1985
All the Pretty Horses, 1992
The Crossing, 1994
Cities of the Plain, 1998
The Border Trilogy, 1999 (includes *All the Pretty Horses, The Crossing,* and *Cities of the Plain*)

DRAMA:
The Stonemason, pb. 1994

SCREENPLAY:
The Gardener's Son, 1996

TELEPLAY:
The Gardener's Son, 1977

About the Author

Arnold, Edwin T., and Dianne C. Luce, eds. *Perspectives on Cormac McCarthy*. Jackson: University Press of Mississippi, 1993.

Bell, Vereen M. *The Achievement of Cormac McCarthy*. Baton Rouge: Louisiana State University Press, 1988.

Jarrett, Robert L. *Cormac McCarthy*. New York: Twayne, 1997.

Lilley, James D., ed. *Cormac McCarthy: New Directions*. Albuquerque: University of New Mexico Press, 2002.

Owens, Barley. *McCarthy's Western Novels*. Tucson: University of Arizona Press, 2000.

Wallach, Rick, ed. *Myth, Legend, Dust: Critical Responses to Cormac McCarthy*. New York: Manchester University Press, 2000.

Woodward, Richard B. "Cormac McCarthy's Venomous Fiction." *New York Times Magazine* 19 (April, 1992): 28-31.

Young, Thomas Daniel. *Tennessee Writers*. Knoxville: University of Tennessee Press, 1981.

DISCUSSION TOPICS

- One of the key features of Cormac McCarthy's fiction is his vivid and precise description of specific geographic locales. How do particular places affect the action in the story and shape the fictional characters involved in the action?

- McCarthy's work is often described as "naturalistic." What, if any, philosophical views can be extracted from his work, particularly with respect to free will and destiny, the nature of evil, and the forces responsible for creation, destruction, and the course of events?

- Journeys are an important component, and even an organizing principle, in McCarthy's fiction. What specific journeys take place, and how do those journeys affect those who take them?

- At the heart of much of McCarthy's fiction is a transgressive act, or some kind of border crossing. What function do these crossings serve? How do readers respond to those crossings and transgressions?

- "Each man is the bard of his own existence," a character pronounces in *Cities of the Plain*. McCarthy's fiction displays a keen interest in the act of storytelling, the role of the witness, and the process by which tellers and listeners construct meaning from stories. How does this work in specific novels?

MARY MCCARTHY

Born: Seattle, Washington
June 21, 1912
Died: New York, New York
October 25, 1989

Known predominantly for her adversarial literary stance,
McCarthy enlarged the tradition of autobiographical fiction
through her satirical analyses of societal weaknesses.

Courtesy, Vassar College, Special Collections

BIOGRAPHY

Novelist, short-story writer, essayist, drama critic, and poet, Mary Therese McCarthy was born the first of four children to Therese Preston and Roy Winfield McCarthy on June 21, 1912, in Seattle, Washington. Although the first six years of her childhood were nurtured within her close-knit family, McCarthy's life changed abruptly when her parents died in the 1918 flu epidemic.

For the next five years, McCarthy and her brothers were forced as orphans to live in a deceit-filled, irrational, abusive Minneapolis house. This atmosphere, as well as the never-mentioned death of her parents, conditioned McCarthy to detach from her emotions, to distrust others, to see herself as an outsider, and to avoid intimacy. She also learned to depend upon her Roman Catholic religion and her mind in order to survive. At eight years old, she began writing poetry. Satire became her weapon against despair.

The children were rescued in 1923 by their grandfather Preston; the boys were separated from their sister, who joined the Protestant Preston household before attending a Catholic boarding school, Forest Ridge Convent. Again, McCarthy was isolated. This isolation continued throughout her college preparatory education as she struggled to discover the means to acceptance. Exploring options that ranged from joining a convent to committing suicide, the adolescent repeatedly reinforced her self-antagonism by trying to conform. During McCarthy's one year in a public high school, the academically gifted student's grades verged on failure, so her grandparents sent her to an Episcopal boarding school.

At Vassar College, she majored in Elizabethan literature, acted onstage, and founded an alternative literary magazine with three other students. Discovering that a literary career was more appealing to her than one onstage, McCarthy moved to New York City following graduation as a Phi Beta Kappa and successively became a book reviewer, an editor, and a theater critic. She also spent three years (through 1948) as a college instructor. The Horizon award for *The Oasis* (1949) and a Guggenheim Fellowship (1949-1950) enabled her to devote more energy to literary writing. Consequently, a collection of short stories, *Cast a Cold Eye* (1950), and the novel *The Groves of Academe* (1952) were published.

In 1957, McCarthy received a National Institute of Arts and Letters grant. *A Charmed Life* (1955), lauded for its caustic, provocative characterization, and the nonfictional *Venice Observed* (1956) and *The Stones of Florence* (1959), praised for humanistic style, brilliant literary precision, and historical accuracy, were the three books that immediately preceded her second Guggenheim Fellowship (1959-1960). After having been intentionally delayed for almost two decades, *The Group*, a best seller, was published in 1963. *Vietnam* (1967) and *Hanoi*

(1968) are the results of her tour in Asia during the Vietnam War. In 1979, the author published *Cannibals and Missionaries*, a novel she described as her last. Collections of McCarthy's essay and reviews have also been published.

In 1984, McCarthy was awarded the National Medal of Literature and the Edward MacDowell Medal for her extraordinary contributions to the field of literature. She was accorded membership in two prestigious organizations, the National Institute of Arts and Letters and the American Academy of Arts and Letters.

McCarthy became infamous for transferring recognizable physical, emotional, and behavioral characteristics of acquaintances to the fictional page. Her husbands have been no exception; McCarthy fictionalized the players in each of her four marriages and three divorces. After twenty-eight years of marriage to James West, McCarthy died in 1989 from cancer.

ANALYSIS

McCarthy's primary literary technique, direct and indirect satire, is uniquely suited to her personality and writing style. McCarthy mercilessly focuses upon issues of self-deception, ignorance of history, and lack of human emotional ties. Her dominant societal target, and the one with which she is most familiar, is the "privileged" class. Nevertheless, this familiarity, as some have suggested, does not prevent her from achieving the distance to maintain a compelling satirical stance. What is at times problematic is her lack of internal character development, which, in turn, dilutes the satirical impact of her writing. Greet in *Cannibals and Missionaries*, Libby in *The Group*, and Alma in *The Groves of Academe* are three characters whose more fully realized presentation could have maximized McCarthy's point of view.

As a social critic, McCarthy is least likely to tolerate that form of self-deception in which the individual opts to negate his or her own knowledge in favor of external conformity. Kay, *The Group's* protagonist, who dies at twenty-nine, seeks out and adapts to external expectations rather than developing her own sense of self-worth. On the other hand, in *Cannibals and Missionaries*, the most conspicuous quarry by normal expectations for satirical focus is Jeroen, a character whom McCarthy instead respects for his integrity and commitment.

Characteristically, McCarthy writes about a human behavior that intrigues or baffles her, seeking the underlying causes for a sociocultural pattern she perceives as destructive. As a result, the author inundates her writing with intricate detail. Such details, both personal and environmental, help to define the incongruity with humor and give her work the precision for which it is justifiably renowned. McCarthy's intellectual humor, in the form of purposefully inept literary allusions voiced by a pretentious character (Harald in *The Group*), serves admirably as a device by which the character undermines himself or herself.

The author also uses historical allusion to emphasize the critical condition she has targeted. *The Groves of Academe*, centered upon the adaptive and deviant behaviors of a college administration and faculty, is rife with both forms of allusion.

Four other forms of humor are employed by the author as reinforcing stylistic devices: antithesis, exaggeration, irony, and parody. In *The Group*, a classic example of antithesis is Pris and Norine's conversational skirmish regarding child-rearing practices. Pris, whose child is raised according to the discipline of a strict schedule, battles Norine, whose child is brought up with complete freedom for experimentation. Exchanging verbal blow for verbal blow, Pris (who can be intimidated by any obstreperous voice of authority) predictably yields the victory to Norine.

Foreshadowing (most often in McCarthy's first chapters) and dramatic irony underscore the author's themes. Two examples of foreshadowing are the discomfort at Kay's wedding in *The Group* as a predictor of her untimely death and, in *Cannibals and Missionaries*, the cat's first escape from its cage on the Boeing 747 airplane, precipitating thoughts among the passengers of hijacking so that the actual hijacking is discounted as the cat's having again escaped. After the explosive conclusion to the hostage situation, McCarthy provides an epilogue chapter heavily underscored with dramatic irony. As the two relatively unscathed survivors board a plane to take them home and review the journalist's diary written during their captivity, they note a passage in which she states that she would sacrifice an arm for Jeroen to achieve his end in style; she has.

Mary McCarthy

THE GROVES OF ACADEME

First published: 1952
Type of work: Novel

> *Professor Henry Mulcahy of Jocelyn College deceives his colleagues into pressuring the administration for a renewal of his teaching contract.*

The Groves of Academe is McCarthy's satiric foray against the administrations and the faculties of liberal higher education. The title is derived from a Horatian quote concerning the search for "truth" within the "groves" of academia. Clearly, from the opening of the first chapter, Henry Mulcahy and the other erudites who scheme to manipulate people and situations to their own ends do not have the search for truth first on their agenda. Even the most nobly portrayed professor, Domna Rejnev, places her own self-interest above truth and the safety of a colleague.

The plot of this scathing comedy of manners advances through the psychological machinations of Mulcahy, a pale, bulbous, tense, incompetent but intelligent instructor with a one-year contract, who fights for reinstatement on the basis of having previously been a member of the Communist Party and of his wife's devastatingly poor health. The ingenuity of his first claim is that no progressive college such as Jocelyn College, in the age of Joseph McCarthy's anticommunist witch-hunts, would risk a public accusation of terminating a contract on the basis of political beliefs. Underlying his second claim is the idea that the news of his termination would seriously endanger the life of his wife, Cathy, because of the dangerous illness of which she has no knowledge. Neither basis is true; however, Mulcahy has a facility for convincing himself that a lie is truth and then for rallying others to believe. His perceptive reading of what motivates others to act, as well as of their subsequent predictable actions, illustrates his perverted brilliance.

He is also capable of manipulating the truth in his favor. At the end of the novel, when the president and involved faculty members in desperation conduct a covert interview with a visiting poet, who confirms that Mulcahy has never joined the Communist Party, Mulcahy uses the president's actions as blackmail to retain his position. In addition, he admits to the defeated college president that self-serving justice, not truth, is his preeminent issue. As such, Mulcahy functions as the entrenched antithesis of the utopian standards set by the progressive college.

In direct counterpoint, Domna Rejnev is the altruistic, nobly bred, well-intentioned, intelligent young professor of Russian and French who has dedicated her life to her students. She is both responsible and competent. She is also the "friend" whom Mulcahy beguiles into his most determined advocate. In concert with Alma Fortune, a more politically experienced but equally sincere faculty member, Rejnev and committee successfully present a case for the renewal of Mulcahy's contract.

Once Rejnev discovers the truth, her only recourse is to withdraw from contact with Mulcahy and to begin quietly documenting Mulcahy's reckless and incompetent behaviors. Nevertheless, when he later confronts her with the question of who was responsible for the departmental meeting in which he was forced to justify the guest list for his poetry conference, Rejnev tarnishes her idealistic passion for justice by misleading the villainous professor to blame Fortune, when Rejnev herself had reported her concerns. Thus, the contamination spreads.

McCarthy presents Jocelyn College as a progressive educational institution that, based upon a student's aptitudes, interests, and psychological profiles, ideally functions to maximize the student's self-actualization. The inevitable problem is the human equation. Individualized instruction, a tutorial course of study in the student's major field, suffers from both faculty and student abuse or neglect. In another program, the February field-period, consisting of one month of off-campus work in the student's chosen field, any number of complications sabotage the founder's intent. Nevertheless, every fall term the faculty, cognizant of the abuses, manage to retain their four free weeks by voting to maintain the field-period.

McCarthy's satiric thrust in this novel is against those colleges with utopian goals who lack concrete objectives and who do not take into account the human factor. In other words, blind trust in people's hunger to expand their minds and to share their knowledge freely is destructive without direction. The search for truth is withering on the vines of academe.

THE GROUP

First published: 1963
Type of work: Novel

The lives of nine Vassar College women, eight of whom make up "the group," are depicted in the seven years following graduation.

Popular acclaim for *The Group*, McCarthy's only best seller, has not been reflected by critical reaction. The novel has been lambasted as being written on the level of pulp romance fiction and as containing stock, barely distinguishable characterizations and a strategic lack of focus. On the other hand, many Vassar graduates have been incensed at the apparently realistic characters portrayed without empathy. Both groups have overlooked the penetrating satire through which McCarthy so often expresses her themes.

Three interrelated themes are presented through each chapter's focus on one character at a time. The women, well educated and not devastatingly affected by the Depression, are ill prepared to cope with life in the real world. One crucial detriment, manifested repeatedly by the different characters, is that these aware women are incapable of putting their progressive philosophies into action. Instead, they become caught up in their own immediate needs or in surrounding circumstances.

Another recurrent McCarthy theme revolves around the inadequacies of living entirely for the present moment without a sense of history. Even as the women delight in Kay's nontraditional wedding celebration, they are also discomfited by the absence of any member of Kay's family and are superstitious about Kay's behaviors that are traditionally considered unlucky. Without the emotional and the spiritual foundations of a family heritage, a stable self-identity is difficult to realize.

Although McCarthy extensively employs in this novel a technique she has termed ventriloquism (allowing the actions, the words, and the intonations of each character to evolve as unique to that character without the controlling intervention of the novelist's voice), expression of her belief system was important enough to her that she set aside her writing of *The Group* for eighteen years to find the appropriate internal voice. In the early 1960's, her development of Kay as a dynamic, rather than a static, character became the voice she had long sought.

Kay Leiland Strong Petersen, whose marriage opens the novel and whose death concludes the novel, is the unifying thread among the other characters' stories. A shy, slightly overweight westerner upon her arrival at Vassar, Kay outwardly transforms herself into the stereotypical ambitious, iconoclastic disbeliever in all but the material real. Inwardly, however, she remains the shy outsider, lacking self-awareness, seeking to identify herself by association with her friends and her husband. What her friends think of as snooping and confrontive behaviors are actually Kay's means of discovering an acceptable identity. Kay's marriage to Harald is another form of this destructive dependency. While she looks to him for love (in which she has externally professed not to believe), guidance, support, and identification, he is indolent, uncaring, self-involved, adulterous, deceitful, and abusive. Reputed to be modeled after McCarthy's first husband, Harald is, in fact, one of the most villainous male characters in the author's entire body of fiction.

Nevertheless, Kay maintains the facade of their marriage for her friends and her family in Salt Lake City because she does not believe that she has the ability to accomplish her dreams on her own. Only after her husband has hit her, locked her in their dressing room, and committed her to a mental institution is she able to acknowledge her hatred of him. Within the year, she divorces Harald and dies in a mysterious fall out the window of her Vassar Club room.

In the first chapter, McCarthy caustically discloses a "modern" philosophy of relationships: "If you were going to use a person, then you had to make the best of them." In her succeeding chapters, the consequences of each character's life choices indicate that the opposite may instead be true. Three of the six married women have marital relationships about which no serious defects are revealed. Actually, little is known about Pokey's marriage other than that she has continued in the role of New Jersey wife. Libby has been married to a famous author-client for about a year. Empathetic Polly, a hospital technician, has married a good-hearted former psychiatrist now turned medical researcher.

The intelligent, aloof rationalist, Helena, appears comfortable with the persona she has achieved. Competent and single, she and her mother, Mrs. Davison, are largely responsible for Kay's funeral arrangements. Having returned from Europe three months earlier, the forthright Lakey brings her opening actions in the first chapter full circle by buying Kay the off-white designer dress she had always wanted. Unmarried, Lakey is fulfilled in a lesbian relationship.

Shy, stammering Pris has adjusted, with some reservations, to motherhood and marriage with a pediatrician who uses his family as guinea pigs for his child-rearing theories. Dottie, the only group member absent from Kay's funeral, has compromised her affectionate, sensual nature by settling for a pragmatic marriage to an Arizona widower rather than seeking a relationship with the man she says she loves. Norine, the morally corrupt outsider of the group, first marries an impotent man and engages in several adulterous affairs, including one with Kay's husband, then marries a Jewish banker even though she admits to still loving Harald.

One of the problems in *The Group* is the unevenness of its characterization. Although the novel is saturated with detail, some characters (Pokey, Helena, and Libby in particular) are not given as full a treatment as they deserve. Another difficulty may be that the author's ventriloquistic distance fosters ambiguity. Nevertheless, McCarthy's writing is most vital when she describes the attitudes and the interactions of a society trapped by its own conditioning. For example, each episode of Dottie's love affair, including her pre-wedding talk with her mother, scintillates with humor and pathos, and Helena's reactions to Norine and Norine's home are exquisitely drawn in an unexpectedly dramatic confrontation. *The Group* is considerably more than a venture into the pulp romance genre.

CANNIBALS AND MISSIONARIES

First published: 1979
Type of work: Novel

A handpicked group of liberals investigating rumors of the shah of Iran's torture of prisoners and tourists of millionaires' art collections are hijacked by a multinational terrorist group.

Cannibals and Missionaries, McCarthy's least autobiographical novel, is more a character study of human response to fear, deprivation, and imprisonment than a classic espionage tale. The title is derived from a classic riddle asking how, using a two-passenger boat, three cannibals and three missionaries can cross a river without ever having the missionaries outnumbered. Even though the solution is supplied by the "friendliest" captor, Ahmed, the answer to the question of which group (terrorists, millionaires, or liberals) is the cannibals and which is the missionaries is left to the reader.

The investigative committee led by Senator Jim Carey and Dutch Parliamentary Deputy Henk van Vliet de Jonge is the terrorists' primary target; the first-class tour group with Charles Tennant as self-appointed liaison is a secondary target. Jeroen, a surprisingly sympathetic figure, leads an international terrorist force that has secured a farmhouse stronghold in Flevoland on the polders of Holland by posing as a television crew filming a documentary.

The terrorists' demands are fivefold. For the helicopter that transported them to the polders and its crew, the ransom is more than one million dollars, half to the terrorists and half to the Surinam poor. For the liberation of the committee members (including a college president, two religious figures, an international journalist, a Middle East specialist who is an undercover agent, and a history professor), the stipulations are more complex: the withdrawal of the North Atlantic Treaty Organization (NATO) from Holland, cessation of Dutch-Israeli relations, and the release of "class-war prisoners." For their wealthy captives, the terrorists have demanded a one-person helicopter to carry taped ransom demands to families of the prisoners.

Jeroen believes that murder should be the last

avenue of action. Formerly an artist, he has conceived a plan by which his wealthy prisoners can ransom themselves and pay for their capitalistic crimes by relinquishing to his group specific art masterpieces from their collections. In this way, he lowers his captive count and holds instead as hostage paintings that the world might be even more reluctant to count as casualties. The first-class prisoners are eventually exchanged for their artworks; however, the investigative committee remains hostage because the Dutch government cannot accede to the demand of NATO withdrawal. Consequently, Jeroen, who understands action as his only remaining art form and who sees a primary aim of terrorism as retributory, taking from a corrupt society that which is irreplaceable, acts.

After ordering all prisoners and guards out of the house for an extended exercise period, he detonates the farmhouse, the paintings, and himself. Unfortunately, Greet, one of the terrorists, senses impending disaster and returns early. As a result, only the Episcopalian priest, Frank Barber, and the college president, Aileen Simmons, escape death or serious injury. Jeroen dies in the explosion, knowing that his precautions to avoid senseless slaughter have been futile.

Expected and unexpected character bonding, as well as the materialization of idiosyncratic behaviors, create a spell-binding effect. The most sympathetic terrorist characters are self-sacrificing Jeroen, dedicated to his cause; Ahmed, the young poet; and Greet, once a KLM hostess and now (out of love) committed to Jeroen. The most sympathetic among the captives include de Jonge, the flawless poet-politician who understands Jeroen's commitment; Senator Carey, an alcoholic widower poet-politician past his time of effectiveness; Sophie Well, a brilliant and beautiful journalist uncomfortable with the spoken word; and Tennant, the wealthy raconteur who cannot bear to be separated from the action. The author's characterization of these, as well as many of the other less sympathetic characters (such as the alcoholic, cat-carrying undercover agent Victor Lenz), is witty, perceptive, and provocative.

Nevertheless, certain deficiencies detract from the potency of this novel. McCarthy stated that *Cannibals and Missionaries* was her last novel because as one ages one's awareness is blunted. Although she had conducted detailed factual research for the book, her nonrealistic, soft-edged portrayal of the terrorist force is disappointing. Furthermore, her customary philosophical editorializing is conspicuously absent except for discussions of art. Finally, whether intentionally or unintentionally, the author's pace distractingly falters.

MEMORIES OF A CATHOLIC GIRLHOOD

First published: 1957
Type of work: Autobiography

McCarthy subjectively relates her childhood experiences and her family memories, with editorial comments on their verifiability.

Memories of a Catholic Girlhood, the most deeply passionate of McCarthy's published writings, is a moving chronicle of her early years, through her adolescence. Beginning her account with a careful, italicized address to the reader, the author sets the tone for the following eight chapters by philosophizing that "to care for the quarrels of the past . . . is to experience a kind of straining against reality, a rebellious nonconformity that, again, is rare in America." Although this was written within the context of discussing the merits of Catholic education, it is also a skillful summary of *Memories of a Catholic Girlhood*, her other writings, and her life.

Discriminating between what she remembers but cannot be corroborated, what has been corroborated, and what is in conflict with her memories, McCarthy painstakingly pieces together the fragments of her early history. Following each chapter except the last, she acknowledges, again in italicized print, the substantiations and the contradictions to her story. This technique imbues *Memories of a Catholic Girlhood* with an almost indisputable credibility.

Although McCarthy's presentation is essentially chronological, as with all memories, there occurs an associational movement back and forth in time. Gradually the full picture emerges. Recollections of a favored beginning reveal a period of delightful surprises and unconditional love. Her father, at home because of a chronic heart problem, was an irrepressibly joyful companion. Both parents, deeply in love and married against their families' wishes, willingly shared that love with their children.

The flu epidemic in 1918 raged through her family when her father's parents withheld his monthly stipend and insisted that the family return from Seattle to their hometown of Minneapolis. Only dimly aware of her surroundings by the time the train reached its destination, McCarthy awoke some days later in a bleak, institutionalized sewing room of her wealthy grandparents' house.

Some weeks later, after waiting daily for her parents' return, she realized on her own (because no adults had spoken with her) that her mother and her father had died. Consequently, when her three brothers disappeared one day, she took for granted that they also were dead. The resulting emotional paralysis that McCarthy describes in herself as a child of six was exacerbated by the abusive five years she endured after being sent to join her brothers.

Unwilling to take on the raising of four children, her grandparents had hired their great-aunt Margaret and her husband, "uncle Myers," to care for them in a dilapidated house two blocks away. Shabbily clothed, ill fed, beaten regularly (with no apparent pattern other than if anyone "misbehaved," then that child and all of his or her older siblings were whipped), McCarthy and her brothers learned that no one was to be trusted. No explanations were given for the adults' behaviors. Instead, their "role models" were erratic, irrational, manipulative, and self-involved.

Being rescued by their maternal grandfather Preston, apparently not because of the abuse McCarthy and her oldest brother had detailed but because McCarthy was not wearing her glasses (a punishment for falling and breaking them), was both a relief and a source of bewilderment to McCarthy. Another puzzle was the fact that she remained temporarily with her maternal grandparents while the boys were sent to boarding school (the youngest, Sheridan, later than the others).

Although satire is noticeably absent in *Memories of a Catholic Girlhood*, irony is used most effectively in highlighting McCarthy's internal processes as she copes with different environments. For example, in order to gain positive attention at a Catholic all-girls boarding school, the author evaluates several plans and chooses to announce just before a retreat that she has "lost" her faith. In the process of her arguments with two priests, however, she realizes that what she thought was simply an attention-getting lie is actually the truth. To make the problem even more complex, she must now pretend for the rest of her stay at this school that she has found her lost faith so that she can receive Eucharist with the other girls.

The impact of her early dehumanizing experiences as well as of those school years when she could not overcome her "outsider" feelings was to color McCarthy's life in both her satiric writing style and her detachments from people. *Memories of a Catholic Girlhood* is a poignant chronicle of debasement, the search for meaning, and survival.

SUMMARY

McCarthy's literary career was fraught with controversy. Her novels that earned the greatest public acclaim received the worst critical response. Nevertheless, through satire, she continued to fictionalize the people and the events in her life out of her fascination with human motivation.

Writing primarily about the intelligentsia, she has nevertheless managed to capture the imagination of the American public and the attention of honored American literary institutions. Her attention to detail, her painstaking research, her rapier wit, and her understated use of humorous devices fuse into a literary style uniquely her own.

Kathleen Mills

BIBLIOGRAPHY

By the Author

LONG FICTION:
The Oasis, 1949
The Groves of Academe, 1952

A Charmed Life, 1955
The Group, 1963
Birds of America, 1971
Cannibals and Missionaries, 1979

SHORT FICTION:
The Company She Keeps, 1942
Cast a Cold Eye, 1950
The Hounds of Summer, and Other Stories, 1981

NONFICTION:
Sights and Spectacles, 1937-1956, 1956
Venice Observed, 1956
Memories of a Catholic Girlhood, 1957
The Stones of Florence, 1959
On the Contrary: Articles of Belief, 1961
Mary McCarthy's Theatre Chronicles, 1937-1962, 1963
Vietnam, 1967
Hanoi, 1968
The Writing on the Wall, and Other Literary Essays, 1970
Medina, 1972
The Seventeenth Degree, 1974
The Mask of State, 1974
Ideas and the Novel, 1980
Occasional Prose, 1985
How I Grew, 1987
Intellectual Memoirs: New York, 1936-1938, 1992
Between Friends: The Correspondence of Hannah Arendt and Mary McCarthy, 1949-1975, 1995 (Carol Brightman, editor)
A Bolt from the Blue, and Other Essays, 2002 (A. O. Scott, editor)

DISCUSSION TOPICS

- Many Catholics reacted negatively to Mary McCarthy's *Memories of a Catholic Girlhood.* Several decades later, does this kind of reaction seem justified?

- Discuss McCarthy's use of irony in *The Groves of Academe,* beginning with its title.

- Is it unfortunate for McCarthy's reputation that she is best known for *The Group*?

- What features of McCarthy's style are most responsible for her success as a novelist?

- Do the autobiographical elements in McCarthy's novels generally enhance or detract from them?

About the Author

Abrams, Sabrina Fuchs. *Mary McCarthy: Gender, Politics, and the Postwar Intellectual.* New York: Peter Lang, 2004.

Auchincloss, Louis. *Pioneers and Caretakers: A Study of Nine American Novelists.* Minneapolis: University of Minnesota Press, 1961.

Brightman, Carol. *Writing Dangerously: Mary McCarthy and Her World.* New York: Clarkson Potter, 1992.

Epstein, Joseph. "Mary McCarthy in Retrospect." *Commentary* 95 (May, 1993): 41-47.

Gelderman, Carol W. *Mary McCarthy: A Life.* New York: St. Martin's Press, 1988.

Grumbach, Doris. *The Company She Kept.* New York: Coward, McCann, 1967.

Kiernan, Frances. *Seeing Mary Plain: A Life of Mary McCarthy.* New York: W. W. Norton, 2000.

McKenzie, Barbara. *Mary McCarthy.* New York: Twayne, 1966.

Pierpont, Claudia Roth. *Passionate Minds: Women Rewriting the World.* New York: Alfred A. Knopf, 2000.

Stock, Irvin. *Mary McCarthy.* Minneapolis: University of Minnesota Press, 1968.

Stwertka, Eve, and Margo Viscusi, eds. *Twenty-four Ways of Looking at Mary McCarthy: The Writer and Her Work.* Westport, Conn.: Greenwood Press, 1996.

Wilford, Hugh. "An Oasis: The New York Intellectuals in the Late 1940's." *Journal of American Studies* 28 (August, 1994): 209-223.

Frank McCourt

Born: Brooklyn, New York
August 19, 1930

*In his two memoirs, McCourt writes about his difficult upbring-
ing in New York City and Limerick, Ireland, during the Great
Depression and World War II and his adulthood after his return
to the United States at the age of nineteen.*

Gasper Tringale/Scribner

Biography

Frank McCourt was born in Brooklyn, New York,
on August 19, 1930, to Irish immigrant parents. His
father, Malachy McCourt, was born in Northern
Ireland. Although the consumption of alcohol was
prohibited at the time, New York's illegal but
widely tolerated speakeasies became the focus of
Malachy's life. By any measurement he was an alcoholic, liable to abandon work and family at any
time for a drink, or several.

Frank McCourt's mother, Angela Sheehan, was
from the city of Limerick in western Ireland and
grew up in a slum. Her father had abandoned the
family just weeks before she was born. She immigrated to New York in November, 1929, just after
the crash of the U.S. stock market, and met
Malachy shortly after her arrival. Attracted to each
other in spite of the objections of Angela's cousins,
who did not trust the Northern Irish, Angela became pregnant. Her family forced Malachy to
marry Angela, and the two wed in March, 1930.
Frank, their first son, was born in August and was
named after Saint Francis of Assisi. A year later, a
second son, Malachy, was born to the McCourts,
followed two years later by twins, Eugene and Oliver, and then a daughter, Margaret, who died in infancy. Michael was born six years after Frank, and a
last child, Alfie, was born about 1940. Malachy, Sr.,

could not find or hold employment, and the family
returned to Ireland.

Life in a Limerick slum during the 1930's was
even worse than that in a Brooklyn flat. Malachy
continued to drink, and the burden of feeding and
clothing her children fell on Angela, who unhappily relied on charity. The McCourts shared with a
dozen other families an outdoor privy, which was
situated just outside the McCourts' door; the
stench was overpowering. In the winter the ground
floor of their apartment flooded, and the family
moved upstairs, to what they called Italy. With the
senior McCourt frequently absent, Frank would
steal food from shops and doorsteps. Local Catholic priests inspired fear in their young parishioners,
in this life and for the next, rather than comfort
and solace.

During his childhood, Frank almost lost his eyesight, and he suffered from typhoid. While hospitalized, he developed a love of literature. His escape from reality was through American films, but
the McCourt brothers saw those films as reality, the
American reality to which Frank longed to return.

Although one of his teachers urged him to attend a grammar school or high school, Frank was
rejected because of his poverty. Instead, at the age
of fourteen, he took a position at the post office delivering telegrams, a common means of communication in the 1930's. Finally, after ruthlessly hoard-
ing money, he returned to New York at the age
of nineteen in 1949. With his limited education,
McCourt could only obtain casual labor or menial
jobs on the docks and in hotels. With the outbreak
of the Korean War in 1950, he was drafted into the
United States Army.

Qualifying for the G.I. Bill after his discharge, he enrolled at New York University. He had literary ambitions but was reluctant to write about his own background because of the shame he associated with it. After graduation, he became a teacher in the New York City public school system, first at the rough McKee Vocational High School on Staten Island, then at Seward Park High School in lower-east Manhattan, and finally for eighteen years at the prestigious Stuyvesant High School. His brothers Malachy and Michael followed Frank to New York in the 1950's, and Angela and Alfie, the youngest sibling, came in 1959. The senior McCourt remained in Northern Ireland, and Frank saw his father only twice before Malachy's death in 1985. Angela died in 1981. She was cremated and her ashes taken back to Limerick.

McCourt began work on a novel in the 1960's, titled "If You Live in the Lane," but abandoned it. Through the years he jotted down his memories of his early life, remembrances that he used in writing *Angela's Ashes* (1996), a surprise best seller. McCourt was awarded the Pulitzer Prize in biography, the National Book Critics Circle Award, and the *Los Angeles Times* Book Award. *'Tis*, (1999) also a best seller, followed *Angela's Ashes*, relating McCourt's story after he returned to the United States.

ANALYSIS

McCourt became a successful writer at an age when retirement beckons the majority. After a long teaching career, during which he taught creative writing to high school students, McCourt turned to his own life as the subject for his two memoirs, *Angela's Ashes* and *'Tis*. At first in New York, he attempted to hide his difficult childhood from others. While a student in a writing class at New York University, he was asked to write about an incident in his past. McCourt described sharing a collapsed bed, smelling of urine, with his three brothers. The instructor gave the composition high marks and asked McCourt to read it aloud to the class. He could not: He was too ashamed. Over the following decades, McCourt would write down incidents he recalled from his childhood and, with the encouragement of his third wife, Ellen, began what became *Angela's Ashes*, which originally was to be a single-volume work.

Angela's Ashes and *'Tis* are written in the first-person voice, as are most memoirs. However, early in *Angela's Ashes* a wonderful transition occurs in the narrative. At the beginning, McCourt writes in the first-person voice about the past as the past, as history, where he tells of his parents' backgrounds in Ireland, their arrivals in New York, their first meeting, and subsequent marriage. Then, about twenty pages into his story, McCourt switches from narrating the past as history to narrating the past as the present in telling a vignette that occurred when he was three years old and on a seesaw with his brother Malachy. Frank got off the seesaw, causing Malachy at the high end to tumble to the ground, hurting himself, with Frank getting the blame from Angela, his mother. It is not the incident which is memorable, a common enough occurrence in childhood, but the author's voice that captivates the reader.

From that point on, McCourt tells the story of his life as if he was experiencing it today rather than from the perspective of several decades. He explained later that writing it was like putting on a glove, and he retained that present sense of narrative immediacy throughout the memoir. McCourt's life, particularly the years in Limerick, was filled with horrendous experiences, as have been the lives of many others. It is McCourt's use of that present perspective and matter-of-fact narrative tone that prevents his memoirs from being merely stories of one appalling event after another.

Both *Angela's Ashes* and its sequel, *'Tis*, are told chronologically, although the former is more anecdotal, depending upon what themes or subjects are paramount at any given moment. Among the several themes that run through McCourt's memoirs are religion and patriotism. Irish Catholicism was a product of centuries of Ireland's being dominated by England and its Protestant Church of Ireland. For many, being Irish meant being Catholic. The Catholic Church in Ireland, however, was an autocratic institution, and religion permeated Irish life.

Frank and his brothers are baptized and confirmed in the Church, but the priests inspire little besides fear in young Frank. To sin, whether by stealing food or masturbating, is to take the first, inevitable step toward Hell. When a priest says it is a glorious thing to die for one's religion, Frank silently wonders why so many big people have not died for their faith if such is the goal. His father often says that to die for Ireland is a magnificent objective, particularly when he comes home drunk at night and wakes the boys, requiring them to sing patriotic songs. Both Church and father seem to demand and expect sacrificial deaths.

Frank's earliest books are Church books, including lives of the saints and worship missals. When Frank's father takes him to their local parish church to apply to be an altar boy, Frank is rejected because he is only a boy from the slums, while the Church wants middle-class boys as altar boys. When Frank's teacher urges that he attend high school, the Christian Brothers order rejects him. At the time he wrote *Angela's Ashes*, McCourt stated that although he admired some individual priests and nuns, he found the institutional Church despicable. He expressed the same attitude toward radical Irish nationalism as represented by the Irish Republic Army, in which his father had fought in the 1920's.

A predominant theme is that of grinding poverty, exacerbated by alcoholism. The elder McCourt was addicted to alcohol long before Frank was born. After he learned that Angela was pregnant, he intended to flee New York for San Francisco, but he got so drunk he missed his train. The McCourt family's return to Ireland and the slums of Limerick mires the family in perpetual poverty. They survive on charity from the St. Vincent de Paul Society or on the government dole, picking up pieces of coal from the streets in order to heat their home and cook, with bread and tea the ordinary meal.

In school, the teachers enforce discipline with leather straps and wooden canes, and education for most ends at age thirteen or fourteen. On the McCourts' street, there is a single outdoors lavatory for a dozen families, located immediately adjacent to the McCourt apartment. As a consequence, Frank almost dies of typhoid, spending several months in the hospital. When the shoes of the McCourt boys wear out, soles and heels are replaced by pieces of bicycle tires. When Malachy McCourt, Sr., is able to obtain a job, his wages rarely arrive at home. He drinks all of his salary away, establishing a pattern that persists when he goes to work in England during World War II.

Frank loves his father, but given the repression of emotions typical of Irish society at that time, he cannot dare express that love. Appropriately, given the commanding presence of religion, Frank compares his father to the Holy Trinity: his father reads the paper and drinks tea in the morning, he tells stories and hears the boys' prayers at night, and he is drunk too often. In *'Tis*, which relates Frank's life after returning to America, his father plays little role, remaining in England and then in Northern Ireland, but there is no escaping from the threat of alcohol. Frank's brothers all work and drink in bars and pubs, and his brother Malachy eventually becomes a spokesman for Alcoholics Anonymous.

ANGELA'S ASHES

First published: 1996
Type of work: Memoir

McCourt relates the story of his childhood in Limerick, Ireland, during the Great Depression and World War II.

Angela's Ashes was written after McCourt had retired from teaching creative writing. He had jotted down his memories of various events and vignettes over the years and had unsuccessfully attempted to write a novel about his early life. When he began writing *Angela's Ashes*, he envisioned that it would be one volume, culminating with his mother's death and cremation in 1981, thus the title, but it concluded instead with McCourt's return to America in 1949 when he was nineteen.

The book begins with the separate arrivals of McCourt's parents in New York—Angela from Limerick and Malachy from Northern Ireland—their marriage, and the births of their first four children. Frank, the oldest, was conceived before his parents' marriage, an event which traumatized him when he learned about it years later. The first pages of *Angela's Ashes* are written from the first-person viewpoint but from the perspective of when the work was composed in the 1990's. Then the author, by accident he claimed, began

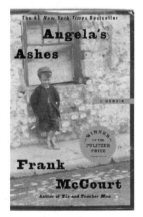

telling his story through the eyes of his young self, a technique that gives immediacy to the work.

Angela's Ashes relates the events of Frank's life until he was nineteen. He was born during the Great Depression, and the family's return to Ireland when he was four was no solution to the family's economic crisis. Settling in the Limerick slum where Angela grew up, the McCourts struggled with a litany of tribulations, including the deaths of three of Frank's younger siblings, his alcoholic father's inability to get and keep jobs, his mother's depression due to the deaths of her children, and the almost impossible task of surviving with no income, little food, and miserable housing.

The McCourt boys attended Leamy's National School, an institution for educating slum children to the age of thirteen or fourteen. Upon finishing school they would take menial jobs, such as Frank did when he delivered telegrams. The teachers were brutal taskmasters, but a few were also inspiring. At least one recognized Frank's literary bent, encouraging him to pursue his education—an impossibility given the family's economic plight and class status. The Catholic Church played a major role in Frank's life, not often for the better, as the fear of damnation pursued him during his childhood and afterward.

Frank lost his virginity to an older girl, and when she soon died from a heart condition, he feared that she had gone to Hell. At the age of seventeen or eighteen, he took a position writing debt collection letters for an old woman, and when she died he stole a few pounds, adding to the money he had previously saved. All together, his funds then totaled enough to pay for ship passage to America, his birthplace, so familiar to him through Hollywood films.

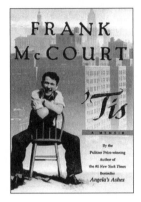

He knew almost no one other than a pedophile priest who had befriended him on the ship, and who arranged a job for McCourt through his contacts with the local Democratic Party, sweeping and mopping at the Biltmore Hotel. McCourt felt isolated and alienated in the land of his birth. The upper-class college students who frequented the Biltmore stood in contrast to his own lack of education, and, compounded by his continuing eye problems, his Irish brogue, and general poverty, gave him feelings of inferiority.

It is the Korean War that McCourt credits for his escape. Drafted into the Army in spite of his bad eyes, he was sent to Germany, where he eventually became a battalion clerk. After his discharge, with the aid of the G.I. Bill, he enrolled in New York University, in spite of lacking a high school education. While there, he met his first of three wives, Alberta, called Mike, a middle-class Episcopalian from Rhode Island. She is the only one of McCourt's wives mentioned in *'Tis*. Theirs was a contentious relationship even before marriage, which produced McCourt's only child, his daughter, Maggie.

After graduation, McCourt found a teaching position in a working-class high school on Staten Island, and his comments about the lack of preparation and interest of his students and the cynical and pessimistic attitude of his fellow teachers express timeless themes. McCourt earned an M.A. degree, taught remedial courses at a community college, and eventually obtained a position in one of New York City's most prestigious high schools, where he taught creative writing to college-bound students. His brothers Malachy and Michael followed him to New York, with Malachy becoming something of a celebrity, famous for his popular bar and his appearances on television. McCourt's mother, Angela, and his youngest brother, Alfie, arrived from Ireland, ostensibly for a visit, but they stayed.

Angela was unhappy about everything in America, from tea bags to the taste of lettuce, much to Frank's frustration. His father, Malachy, came over

---

'Tis

First published: 1999
Type of work: Memoir

McCourt continues his memoir, beginning with his return to the United States in 1949.

'Tis begins where *Angela's Ashes* ends, with the arrival of McCourt in New York in September, 1949.

in the 1960's, but his drinking drove him back to Northern Ireland. Angela died in 1981, Malachy in 1985. In that latter year, the McCourt brothers, relatives, and friends took Angela's ashes back to Limerick, distributing them on the family grave site, while saying a Hail Mary prayer. Frank, himself long estranged from the Catholic Church, noted that Angela truly deserved the presence of a priest, a proper farewell for a mother of seven.

SUMMARY

Frank McCourt initially hoped that if *Angela's Ashes* was published it would get a brief review, but it became instead a runaway best seller and was awarded the Pulitzer Prize and made into a successful film. *'Tis* also became a best seller, although most critics did not find that it had the compelling qualities of its predecessor.

In addition to his storytelling abilities and narrative technique, McCourt can also credit his success to the fact that his memoirs are in the tradition of the Horatio Alger novels of the nineteenth century, where the hero overcame any obstacle through luck and pluck. Of course, McCourt's work is much more brutally realistic than most earlier accounts of poverty, and his explicit description of sexual repression, the corrupting power of the clergy, and widespread alcoholism do not reflect the writings of the Victorian era.

Eugene Larson

BIBLIOGRAPHY

By the Author

NONFICTION:
Angela's Ashes, 1996
'Tis, 1999
Ireland Ever, 2003 (photographs by Jill Freedman; text with Malachy McCourt)

DRAMA:
A Couple of Blaguards, pr. 1984 (with Malachy McCourt)
The Irish and How They Got That Way, pr. 1997

About the Author

Ascheron, Neal. "Ceremony of Innocence." *The New York Review of Books* 44, no. 12 (July 17, 1997): 24-26.

Donoghue, Denis. "Some Day I'll Be Out of the Rain." *The New York Times Book Review*, September 15, 1996, 16.

Foster, R. F. "Tisn't: The Million-Dollar Blarney of the McCourts." *The New Republic*, November 1, 1999, 29.

Hughes, Carolyn T. "Looking Forward to the Past: A Profile of Frank McCourt." *Poet and Writers Magazine* 27, no. 5 (September/October, 1999): 22-29.

Shannon, Christopher. "Rising from the Ashes." *First Things*, no. 75 (August/September, 1997): 68-70.

Sullivan, Robert. "The Seanachie." *The New York Times Magazine*, September 1, 1996, 24-27.

DISCUSSION TOPICS

- What is the connection between alcoholism and poverty in Frank McCourt's memoirs?

- How do Hollywood films condition McCourt's perception of the United States?

- Is the dysfunctional nature of the McCourt family a product of the poverty engendered by the Great Depression or the result of other causes, such as the nature of Irish society in the early twentieth century?

- What is the relationship between the Catholic Church and Irish patriotism in McCourt's memoirs?

- Do the members of the McCourt family love one another? If so, how do they show it? If not, how can the reader see that?

Carson McCullers

Born: Columbus, Georgia
February 19, 1917
Died: Nyack, New York
September 29, 1967

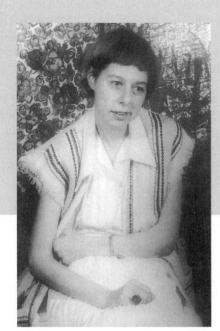
Library of Congress

For her haunting tales of love and loneliness told in her own evocative style, McCullers is considered one of America's exceptional writers.

BIOGRAPHY

Born Lula Carson Smith, McCullers was raised in a town near a big Army post in rural southwest Georgia by a successful jeweler and a remarkable mother who encouraged her genius. An aloof, precocious child, she longed to be rich and famous and live in the snowy North. By the age of eight years, she was producing little plays with neighbor children. At ten she took piano lessons and aspired to play concerts onstage. It is said that she read every worthwhile book in the local library. At fifteen, she came down with rheumatic fever, misdiagnosed at the time, which led to debilitating illnesses later.

After high school, her parents sold heirloom jewelry so she could sail to New York and study at the prestigious Juilliard School of music. Unfortunately, the money was lost on the subway, and she was forced to work odd jobs to pay for courses in creative writing. During a summer vacation in Georgia, Carson was introduced to Reeves McCullers, a charming, handsome, and intelligent soldier who soon left the Army to join her at Columbia University. When she took ill, Reeves brought her home, where they were married on September 20, 1937. McCullers followed her husband to Charlotte, where he found work as a debt collector, and then to Fayetteville, an Army town much like Columbus. There she finished her first novel, *The Heart Is a Lonely Hunter* (1940), and wrote her second, *Reflections in a Golden Eye* (1941), not for publication, she later said, but for fun.

The Heart Is a Lonely Hunter changed their lives forever. McCullers lived the rest of her life as a literary celebrity. They moved to New York and began to mingle with other artists and celebrities. At the Bread Loaf Writers' Conference, the Yaddo Artists Colony, and elsewhere, McCullers befriended writers such as W. H. Auden, Eudora Welty, Louis Untermeyer, Tennessee Williams, Truman Capote, Klaus Mann, and Arthur Miller as well as actress Marilyn Monroe, composer David Diamond, and Swiss socialite Annemarie Clarac-Schwarzenbach, for whom Carson felt a special affinity. In September, 1940, McCullers left her husband to live with Auden, dancer Gypsy Rose Lee, and magazine editor George Davis in Brooklyn Heights.

On a trip to Georgia that winter, McCullers suffered strokes that impaired her vision. Seeking a reconciliation, Reeves brought her back to New York in April. There they embarked upon a complex triangular love affair with Diamond. After Reeves left her for him, McCullers sued for divorce but continued to see both of them. Poor health kept her from living with Diamond in Mexico, so she returned to Yaddo and wrote *The Ballad of the Sad Café* (1943).

After the divorce, Reeves reenlisted in the Army, was wounded in the invasion of Normandy and decorated for bravery, and returned to the United States. On March 19, 1945, Carson and Reeves were remarried in a civil ceremony. They set sail for Europe after *The Member of the Wedding* was published in 1946 and the Guggenheim Foundation awarded her a second grant. She was enthusiastically received by major writers in Rome and Paris. In August and November, 1946, she was paralyzed on the left side by strokes. Her recuperation was followed by another separation. In March, 1948, Carson attempted suicide and was briefly placed in a psychiatric clinic in Manhattan. Soon restored to her mother's care, she was reunited with Reeves by summer's end.

Convinced by Tennessee Williams to adapt *The Member of the Wedding* for the stage, McCullers found herself the toast of Broadway in 1950. Winner of the New York Drama Critics Circle Award, she sold the film rights for $75,000 and headed for Europe. Reeves stowed away on the ship. They bought a house near Paris, but their marriage could not be saved. When he proposed a double suicide, Carson fled for her life; Reeves killed himself on November 19, 1953.

McCullers continued writing and lecturing in the United States, but there were more setbacks. Devastated by her mother's death in 1955, she was further weakened by pleurisy, cancer, pneumonia, and several surgeries, including a radical mastectomy. Under the care of psychiatrist Mary Mercer, McCullers continued to write until pain prevented her from completing her signature. She lived to see the success of Edward Albee's adaptation of *The Ballad of the Sad Café* on Broadway and the beginning of film production of her first two novels. On August 15, 1967, she suffered a massive brain hemorrhage that left her comatose until her death several weeks later.

ANALYSIS

Spiritual isolation is the abiding theme of Carson McCullers's fiction. At the core of modern life, she saw a tragic failure of individuals to connect with one another emotionally, to return love, or to commit themselves to a socially edifying pattern of shared values. Her characters struggle through agonies of psychic stress to realize the radical loneliness in their lives. Sexual deviation, violence, and sexual initiation in adolescence move them to their personal crises.

Typically, her characters live in perfectly normal surroundings, such as a small mill town or an Army post in peacetime, but her revelation of their inner lives is so penetrating and their psychic turmoil is so grotesque that they seem to inhabit a world of existential dread. Overwrought inward obsessions define characters such as Weldon Penderton, Mick Kelly, or Frankie Addams, though their predicaments may appear absurd to ordinary people. Perhaps no American writer since Edgar Allan Poe has painted the mental landscape as well as McCullers; she has deftly delineated the subtle nuances of psychic states lying along the continuum linking psychosis and neurosis with normalcy.

Her relation to the literary tradition of southern gothic fiction is easily misunderstood. It is true that her characters include deaf-mutes, lunatics, criminals, fanatics, a giant in love with a dwarf, eunuchs, perverts, and variously mutilated, disfigured, and misshapen people; yet, the grotesquery in this gallery was not designed merely for sensational effect or regional humor. McCullers uses her bizarre characters to demonstrate how intricately the usual and the unusual are entangled in human nature, and, as a result, how delicate is that balance of wildly divergent impulses called normality. To overemphasize the grotesquery in her fiction may obscure one of her most valuable insights: Spiritual isolation is a universal condition of modern humankind and not the result of individual eccentricity.

A radical inability to connect meaningfully with others traps McCullers's most memorable characters within themselves. Her best characters yearn to find meaning in life and to carve out a victorious place in the order of things. Mick Kelly aspires to master the cosmic harmonies of music and find fame on the concert stage. Doctor Copeland works to free blacks from the bondage of segregation. Others seek fulfillment in the rigid patterns of military life or the emotional concord of a good marriage.

Instead, they become deracinated souls, isolated from one another and cut off from the meaning they seek from life. Mick Kelly winds up behind a counter at a ten-cent store. Doctor Copeland is beaten by the police and alienated by his own family. Although some characters and situations in McCullers's fiction reveal the glories of unselfish love, the warmth of domestic accord, and the capacity for courage in ordinary people, her plots tend to exacerbate rather than resolve antagonisms that divide people, and the prevailing mood is one of existential angst.

A critic once complained that *The Member of the Wedding* was without a beginning, middle, or end. McCullers's fiction does depend upon character revelation, a lyrical style, and narratorial bearing more than a story line. Far from being plot-ridden, her stories are musically structured. She once told her publisher that *The Heart Is a Lonely Hunter* was composed like a fugue, with theme and counter-theme developed contrapuntally as characters interact in mingled harmony. The emotional pace and tone of *The Ballad of the Sad Café* and *The Member of the Wedding* are established by abrupt beginnings, long middles, and brief, haunting codas. The sound of music often sets the mood, reveals a character, or makes a point. For example, the rapture of a classical concerto transports Alison Langdon and her houseboy, Anacleto; a deaf-mute's radio plays unheard; and the harmony of a chain gang's song lifts each member's soul.

A distinctive lyrical quality pervades language as well as structure in McCullers's tales. Simple but intense, humorous yet sympathetic, elegant but never high-flown, her storytelling voice is capable of interweaving an utterly realistic narrative and wild descriptions and preposterous details. An uncanny instinct for colloquial idiom makes her tone ring perfectly clear and sweet, without a trace of sentimentality or judgmental dogma.

Some critics who admire her individual works have been disappointed with her career. They say that she limited her work to a narrow range, sociologically and intellectually, relying too much on characters like herself. Given that she worked within self-imposed limits and against odds beyond her control, however, McCullers achieved spectacular success. Her career was foreshortened by crippling pain and early death, but each of the books she wrote in her twenties sold more than half a million copies, and all were adapted to stage or screen or both. If she focused on the heart rather than the intellect, and on people rather than society, she succeeded nevertheless in illuminating the lonely depths of the souls of modern men and women made tragically incomplete by the failure of love.

THE HEART IS A LONELY HUNTER

First published: 1940
Type of work: Novel

In a small southern town, four lonely people look to a deaf-mute for understanding and friendship.

The Heart Is a Lonely Hunter was the result of a strange creative process. Bedridden for weeks, McCullers wrote some character sketches. One day, in a flash of inspiration, she announced to her mother that the story would revolve around a deaf-mute named Singer to whom others pour out their hearts. The novel grew organically, without a controlling plot.

In part 1, the five main characters are introduced. Always polite, immaculately clean, and soberly attired, John Singer is oddly paired with Spiros Antonapoulos, a fat, retarded deaf-mute. After illness requires him to stop drinking wine, Antonapoulos develops antisocial habits. Singer offers excuses to the police, but his friend is committed to an insane asylum.

At an all-night café owned by Buff Brannon, Singer meets the radical drifter Jake Blount and the respected black doctor Benedict Copeland, men who hold Marxist views and aspire to revolution. Despite sharing similar views, their personalities are quite different. Blount is, by turns, a well-spoken fanatic and a swaggering, violent drunk. He accuses capitalists of liking pigs more than people, because people cannot be sold as sausage. People in the café, except for Singer and Brannon, dismiss such talk as drunken ranting. By contrast, Doctor Copeland is quite dignified and high-minded and is a well-read student of the philosopher Baruch Spinoza. Single-mindedly devoted to the "strong, true purpose" of desegregation, Copeland uses his brain rather than his heart and thus alienates potential allies such

as Blount and his own family. In their different ways, Blount and Copeland allow fanaticism to dry up their powers of love.

Mick Kelly, a talented yet lonely girl of thirteen, is the most fully drawn character. Her family runs the shabby boardinghouse where Singer lives. To him she opens the "inside room" of her being, confiding in him her innermost feelings and aspirations.

In part 2, frustrations abound. Mick's experiences are tragically disappointing. To prove that she is like other girls, she throws a carefully orchestrated party but then finds herself delighted when order breaks down and guests go running through the neighborhood.

After her younger brother Bubber accidentally shoots Baby Wilson with a rifle and causes a superficial but bloody wound, Mick compounds Bubber's agony with talk of a child-sized electric chair awaiting him at Sing Sing. As a result, the boy is never his open, playful self again. Mick then has an embarrassing encounter with the boy next door. At the swimming hole, Mick dares him to strip naked, and he does. She does too, and they have sexual intercourse, only to feel guilt and shame afterward.

Doctor Copeland's struggle reaches a grim crisis when his son is tortured in prison by being tied up for three days with his legs in the air. Both feet are frozen and must be amputated. Demanding to lodge a complaint, Doctor Copeland is himself arrested, beaten, and kicked in the groin by the sheriff's deputies. Blount distributes leaflets calling on workers to revolt, but he succeeds only in provoking a race riot that leaves two blacks dead.

Buff Brannon is freed from a loveless marriage by his wife's death. In a bedroom rearranged not to remind him of her, he smokes his cigars, rocks in his chair, and thumbs the pages of his twenty-year collection of newspapers. Wearing his mother's gold ring and his wife's perfume, he retreats from the world of manly assertiveness into passive self-sufficiency.

One by one, these lonely hunters pour out their hearts to Singer, though he does not really understand them and wonders why they share inner secrets with him. The saddest scene occurs in his room, when they visit him all at the same time. He hopes they will enjoy the radio he bought for their pleasure, but they stand around nervously, unable to connect emotionally with one another. Singer's only friend is Antonapoulos, whom he visits with gifts that go unappreciated. When he arrives at the asylum one summer day, he learns that his friend has died. Heartbroken, he returns to his room and shoots himself in the heart.

Part 3 briefly tells what happens after Singer's suicide. More baffled by his death than his life, Brannon recognizes his own failure to love. Blount leaves town in the aftermath of the riot with forty dollars given to him by Brannon. Doctor Copeland gives up the struggle and moves in with rural relatives he had earlier scorned. Mick changes her mind about the "inside room" so lavishly furnished with dreams. She decides not to buy a piano, drops out of school, and goes to work at the ten-cent store.

Critics have disliked the novel's shapeless plot and crushing pessimism, but the author explores deep personal problems against the backdrop of a realistically drawn social landscape.

REFLECTIONS IN A GOLDEN EYE

First published: 1941
Type of work: Novel

Frustrated by impotence, deviance, and his wife's adultery, an Army officer murders an enlisted man.

Written in a matter of weeks, *Reflections in a Golden Eye* demonstrates the range of McCullers's talent. Here she goes beyond the realism that made her first novel so endearing and delves into a surreal world of dark, psychic impulses. Passions seethe beneath the rigid but fragile surface of military life on an Army post in peacetime. Six characters figure in the story.

Captain Weldon Penderton, an impotent, middle-aged man with homosexual inclinations, is married to the beautiful Leonora, daughter of the fort's former commander. Leonora is having an affair with a neighbor, Major Morris Langdon. Langdon's wife, Alison, cut off her own nipples with garden shears while mourning the death of a deformed baby. Morris and Leonora pass the time riding horseback and making love in a blackberry patch, while Alison, a virtual shut-in, spends her days listening to classical music with her Filipino houseboy, Anacleto.

Private Williams, a mysterious young man with an affinity for animals, becomes Leonora's favorite stable boy. He cares for her high-spirited stallion, Firebird. One afternoon, while Williams is sunbathing nude on a rock in the woods, Weldon, a poor horseman, takes Firebird out for a ride. As Williams looks on, the stallion breaks into a gallop that Weldon cannot control. Losing his balance, he slides out of the saddle and is dragged some distance. When Firebird finally stops, Weldon whips him viciously with the branch of a tree. Leonora soon discovers what has happened to her horse. During a party that evening, she gives her husband a sound thrashing with her riding crop in full view of the guests.

Much of the following action occurs, symbolically, at night. In the grip of a strange attraction, Weldon finds himself following Williams about the fort, gazing in through barracks windows for a glimpse of the youth. One night, Alison sees a shadowy figure entering the Pendertons' house. Thinking it is her husband, she investigates, only to discover that it is Williams on one of his visits to Leonora's bedroom, where he silently watches her sleep.

Alison delivers her hysterical report to Weldon, who refuses to believe it. When Alison announces her intention to file for divorce, Morris hastily has her committed to an insane asylum, where she commits suicide shortly after arrival. The story moves swiftly to its bizarre conclusion when, several nights later, Weldon happens upon Williams in Leonora's bedroom and shoots him. Only too late does he realize that he has destroyed the object of his strange fascination.

The novel explores a nightmarish world in which moral values have been lost. The loutish Morris Langdon, Leonora, and Private Williams live on an animalistic level of insensitivity and stupidity. Even their more imaginative counterparts, Alison, Anacleto, and Weldon, are doomed to destruction by their intensely convoluted emotions, self-loathing, and warped perceptions.

Moral direction and rational thinking have no part in the mad game played by the characters in this black comedy, for their visions of life are too distorted by personal suffering or emotional incapacity. Imagery in the novel plays tricks with perception: mirrors, windows, multifaceted eyes, the blur of colors Weldon sees as he hangs onto Firebird, and the grotesque reflections in the golden eye of Anacleto's ghastly green peacock. The characters themselves are never developed into fully human creations but remain abstract refractions of tragically incomplete psychic states.

THE MEMBER OF THE WEDDING

First published: 1946
Type of work: Novel

To escape the pains of adolescence, a lonely girl dreams of being united with her brother and his bride after the wedding.

In *The Member of the Wedding*, attention is concentrated on twelve-year-old Frankie Addams, her six-year-old cousin John Henry West, and Berenice Sadie Brown, a middle-aged black housekeeper. Their card-playing, eating, and talking in the kitchen during the last weekend of August constitute most of the action. It has been a bad summer for Frankie. Her best friend has moved away, she is too big to curl up beside her father in bed, and she belongs to no group. A lonely heart, she searches for "the we of me." In part 1, she latches onto the notion that she can join her brother and his bride after their wedding.

In part 2, she changes her name to F. Jasmine Addams and begins to believe that she belongs. She senses a fellow feeling with everyone she meets in town, including a soldier who buys her a drink at the Blue Moon and makes a date with her for that night.

Back home in the kitchen that afternoon, Berenice argues against Frankie's plans for the wedding. To show how foolishly people are served by unrealistic ideas of love, she tells of her four marriages. The first had been blissful, but, widowed, she married a succession of no-good men simply because they reminded her of her first husband. The last husband gouged out one of her eyes in a fight. Berenice's deep voice draws sympathy if not understanding from Frankie. Sometimes they break into song together, with John Henry's high notes sailing overhead and Frankie's voice harmonizing in the range between. They take turns pretending to be God. John Henry would remake the world with chocolate dirt and lemonade rain. Berenice would rid the world of war, hunger, and racism. Frankie likes Berenice's world, but she would also eliminate summer, enable people to change sexes at will, and start a worldwide club with membership certificates.

The long conversation does not resolve Frankie's inner turmoil. Having kept her rendezvous with the soldier a secret, she meets him at the Blue Moon on Saturday night. He uses a double-talk that is difficult for her to understand, but she accepts his invitation to his hotel room. After he throws her onto the bed, she knocks him out cold with a water pitcher and crawls down the fire escape, wondering if she has killed him.

Early the next morning, Frankie attends her brother's wedding, but her plan fails, because she cannot find words to ask if she can tag along. Finally, she must be dragged from the car so that the couple can make their getaway. Feeling worse than ever, she runs away that night, making it as far as the Blue Moon before a policeman recognizes her and restores her to her father.

The novel closes with a brief glimpse of moving day, when Frankie and her father go to live with relatives. She has a new best friend, a girl who likes reading poetry and pasting pictures in an art book. Now calling herself Frances, she is unmoved by the hardship that their relocation brings to Berenice and insensitive to the terrible death of John Henry from meningitis. The novel's ending shows that the girl's isolation is an ongoing condition, not the result of a dreary summer, a wrecked wedding, or a traumatic first date. With or without a best friend, Frankie remains seriously out of touch with the deepest feelings of those closest to her.

THE BALLAD OF THE SAD CAFÉ

First published: 1943 (serial), 1951 (book)
Type of work: Novella

A jilted husband returns to ruin his former wife's love affair with a hunchbacked dwarf.

A weird love story, *The Ballad of the Sad Café* was dedicated to David Diamond, her husband's lover. The story elevates elements of their triangular relationship to archetypal significance. Once a dingy old building in the middle of a town where "there is absolutely nothing to do," the café itself becomes a symbol of the human heart. Like a magic lantern, it may be lit by love—in this case, the love of a tall, muscular woman, Miss Amelia, for an itinerant hunchbacked dwarf, Cousin Lymon. Townsfolk are flabbergasted when Miss Amelia offers him room and board, for she has cared nothing for the love of men and seldom invited them inside except to trick them out of money. After three days, they suspect that she has killed him. When a delegation arrives to investigate, however, they are surprised to find Cousin Lymon strutting around as if he owned the place. Miss Amelia has been completely transformed. Once stingy and shrewd, she now treats them with 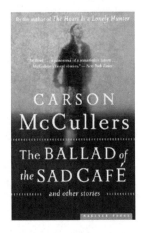 hospitality and generosity. Love has converted the town from boredom to joy, as the café hums with merriment and fellowship.

Six years later, the lantern is shattered when Miss Amelia's jilted husband, Marvin Macy, returns from prison. Years ago, their bizarre marriage had scandalized the town. On their wedding night, the bride bolted from the bedroom within half an hour. Whenever the groom came within reach, she gave him a violent drubbing. On the tenth day, he left town, vowing revenge. Before this marriage, Macy had been a terrible character, known as a defiler of young women and a brawler guilty of many crimes. In his pocket Macy carried the salted ear of a man he killed in a razor fight. His love for Miss Amelia transformed him, however, and he became religious and well mannered. His heart has been hardened, however, by his wife's rebuff.

When he returns, townsfolk expect trouble. To their surprise, Cousin Lymon falls madly in love with him. In fact, he makes a public spectacle of himself, following the handsome wastrel around and moaning when Macy snubs him. Miss Amelia bears this abuse with chagrin, until matters came to a head on Ground Hog Day. Miss Amelia squares off against Macy in a brutal fight. Physically an even match, they grapple destructively but indecisively until Cousin Lymon pounces on Miss Amelia and begins choking her. She is beaten before anyone realizes what has happened. Victorious, the two men wreck her moonshine still, ransack the café, and leave town together.

In humiliation, Miss Amelia's heart turns cold. She raises the price of everything to one dollar, and customers stop coming to the café. Brooding in solitude, she lets her hair grow ragged and her body become thin. Once again, the town reverts to empty dreariness in which "the soul rots with boredom."

In a noteworthy passage, the balladeer reflects upon love. At the heart of love's mystery, he finds a cruel paradox: Love is not a mutual experience, but very different for lover and beloved. The quality of love is determined solely by the lover, as the pairings in the story show. Macy is reformed by love for a woman who rejects him. She is similarly tempered by an unreciprocal feeling for the dwarf, who is himself transmogrified by an unrequited homosexual infatuation. Love proves no cure for radical loneliness of the soul, but rather intensifies its pain.

The story has a haunting, lyrical beauty. Characters are portrayed concretely, not dramatically. There is almost no dialogue, and virtually all events are related in flashback. The story is bracketed by references to the lyrical song of the chain gang. Perhaps Miss Amelia is more imprisoned by loneliness than the convicts are by chains, for their voices rise above their suffering and despair to recognize their unity.

SUMMARY

The southern writer William Faulkner said the only thing worth writing about is "the human heart in conflict with itself." By that standard, few have surpassed Carson McCullers, for she probed the tormented recesses of inner emotions. Tracking problems of loneliness and love to their lair within the heart, she found joy mingled with suffering so intense that her characters may seem grotesque. Nevertheless, her readers gain insights into life as it actually is lived. Neither sentimental nor moralistic, McCullers's novels make a more solid impact on the imagination than does merely sensational or experimental fiction.

John L. McLean

BIBLIOGRAPHY

By the Author

SHORT FICTION:
The Ballad of the Sad Café: The Novels and Stories of Carson McCullers, 1951
The Ballad of the Sad Café and Collected Short Stories, 1952, 1955
The Shorter Novels and Stories of Carson McCullers, 1972

LONG FICTION:
The Heart Is a Lonely Hunter, 1940
Reflections in a Golden Eye, 1941
The Ballad of the Sad Café, 1943 (serial), 1951 (book)
The Member of the Wedding, 1946
Clock Without Hands, 1961

DRAMA:

The Member of the Wedding, pr. 1950, pb. 1951 (adaptation of her novel)

The Square Root of Wonderful, pr. 1957, pb. 1958

NONFICTION:

Illumination and Night Glare: The Unfinished Autobiography of Carson McCullers, 1999 (Carlos L. Dews, editor)

CHILDREN'S LITERATURE:

Sweet as a Pickle and Clean as a Pig, 1964

MISCELLANEOUS:

The Mortgaged Heart, 1971 (short fiction, poetry, and essays; Margarita G. Smith, editor)

About the Author

Bloom, Harold, ed. *Carson McCullers.* New York: Chelsea House, 1986.

Carr, Virginia Spencer. *The Lonely Hunter: A Biography of Carson McCullers.* Garden City, N.Y.: Anchor Press, 2003.

_____. *Understanding Carson McCullers.* Columbia: University of South Carolina Press, 1990.

Clark, Beverly Lyon, and Melvin J. Friedman, eds. *Critical Essays on Carson McCullers.* New York: G. K. Hall, 1996.

Cook, Richard M. *Carson McCullers.* 1975. Reprint. New York: Frederick Ungar, 1984.

Evans, Oliver. *The Ballad of Carson McCullers: A Biography.* New York: Coward, McCann, 1966.

_____. "The Theme of Spiritual Isolation in Carson McCullers." In *South: Modern Southern Literature in Its Cultural Setting*, edited by Louis D. Rubin, Jr., and Robert D. Jacobs. Westport, Conn.: Greenwood Press, 1961.

Gleeson-White, Sarah. *Strange Bodies: Gender and Identity in the Novels of Carson McCullers.* Tuscaloosa: University of Alabama Press, 2003.

Graver, Lawrence. *Carson McCullers.* Minneapolis: University of Minnesota Press, 1969.

James, Judith Giblin. *Wunderkind: The Reputation of Carson McCullers, 1940-1990.* Columbia, S.C.: Camden House, 1995.

Jenkins, McKay. *The South in Black and White: Race, Sex, and Literature in the 1940's.* Chapel Hill: University of North Carolina Press, 1999.

McDowell, Margaret B. *Carson McCullers.* Boston: Twayne, 1980.

Savigneau, Josyane. *Carson McCullers: A Life.* Translated by Joan E. Howard. Boston: Houghton Mifflin, 2001.

Shapiro, Adrian M., Jackson R. Bryer, and Kathleen Field. *Carson McCullers: A Descriptive Listing and Annotated Bibliography of Criticism.* New York: Garland, 1980.

Tippins, Sherill. *February House.* Boston: Houghton Mifflin, 2005.

Walker, Sue. *It's Good Weather for Fudge: Conversing with Carson McCullers.* Montgomery, Ala.: NewSouth Books, 2003.

Westling, Louise. *Sacred Groves and Ravaged Gardens: The Fiction of Eudora Welty, Carson McCullers, and Flannery O'Connor.* Athens: University of Georgia Press, 1985.

DISCUSSION TOPICS

- Does the theme of loneliness in Carson McCullers's work equate with, or contradict, her social accomplishments?

- Are McCullers's literary themes typical of other twentieth century southern writers?

- What weakness is at the core of the character of Frankie Addams in *The Member of the Wedding*?

- Discuss the imagery of perception in *Reflections in a Golden Eye.*

- The dialogue in McCullers's novels is not remarkable, their significant conflicts of the inner variety. Given these facts, how does one account for the success of the plays based on them?

ROSS MACDONALD

Hal Boucher

Born: Los Gatos, California
December 13, 1915
Died: Santa Barbara, California
July 11, 1983

In a series of detective novels featuring private eye Lew Archer, Macdonald transcended the limitations of the genre, probing the enduring effects of crimes on both victims and their descendants.

BIOGRAPHY

Ross Macdonald was born Kenneth Millar in Los Gatos, California, on December 13, 1915, the son of John Macdonald Millar and Annie Moyer Millar. (He did not adopt the Macdonald pseudonym until 1956.) In 1919, the family moved to Vancouver, British Columbia, where his father (primarily a journalist) was a harbor pilot for a while. His parents separated the same year, and Macdonald (whose mother was a near invalid) lived with different Canadian relatives for about two years in 1928 and 1929 while attending St. John's, a boarding school in Winnipeg.

From there he went to Medicine Hat, Alberta, for a year to stay with an aunt, and then moved to Kitchener, Ontario, where he lived with his mother and grandmother and studied at Kitchener-Waterloo Collegiate and Vocational School. While there (1930-1932), he met Margaret Ellis Sturm, whom he would marry years later. Both published for the first time in the same issue of the school magazine, *The Grumbler*; Macdonald's story, a parody of Arthur Conan Doyle, featured a detective called Herlock Sholmes.

The 1932 death of his father gave Macdonald a legacy which enabled him to enter the University of Western Ontario; when his mother died in 1935, however, he left school and spent much of 1936 and 1937 traveling in Europe. Finally, on June 1, 1938, he received his A.B. degree and the next day

married Margaret Sturm. After attending summer school at the University of Michigan, they returned to Toronto, where Macdonald did graduate work at the Ontario College of Education. A daughter, Linda Jane, was born to the couple in June, 1939, and for the next two years Macdonald taught English at his former secondary school while returning to Michigan in the summers for graduate work. After Margaret (writing as Margaret Millar) published her first mystery novel, *The Invisible Worm*, in 1941, Macdonald was able to become a full-time graduate student at the University of Michigan, but induction in the U.S. Navy interrupted his studies in 1944. Immediately prior to his induction, he had completed his first novel, *The Dark Tunnel* (1944), a spy story; while serving as communications officer on the escort carrier *Shipley Bay* in the Pacific, he wrote *Trouble Follows Me* (1946).

When he returned to civilian life in March, 1946, Macdonald and his family settled in Santa Barbara, California, where he wrote two novels in less than nine months: *Blue City* (1947) and *The Three Roads* (1948). All these books were published under his real name, Kenneth Millar. After an abortive attempt at autobiographical fiction, he produced his first Lew Archer novel, *The Moving Target* (1949), using the name John Macdonald (his father's given names) to avoid competing with his wife, who had already published eight mysteries. While writing his early detective fiction—by *The Drowning Pool* in 1950, he had become John Ross Macdonald to distinguish himself from John D. MacDonald, another crime-fiction author—he completed his graduate work at Michigan, receiving the Ph.D. in 1952. His dissertation was a study of the psychological criticism of Samuel Taylor Coleridge, the nineteenth century English Romantic poet.

Between 1952 and 1956, Macdonald wrote a novel a year, with the name Ross Macdonald first appearing with *The Barbarous Coast* (1956). His seventeen-year-old daughter Linda's involvement in a vehicular homicide in 1956, for which she was sentenced to eight years of probation and ordered to undergo psychiatric care, led the Macdonalds to move to Menlo Park, California, where he as well as Linda underwent psychotherapy for a year. In 1970, he recalled this as a period when "seismic disturbances occurred in [his] life." He wrote: "My half-suppressed Canadian years, my whole childhood and youth, rose like a corpse from the bottom of the sea to comfort me." Because of the problem with his daughter and its aftermath, he said, "I've taken a step towards becoming the writer [Alfred Knopf, the publisher] would like to see me be."

After returning to Santa Barbara in the summer of 1957, Macdonald taught creative writing to adults and wrote book reviews for the *San Francisco Chronicle*. He also wrote *The Galton Case* (1959), the first of his books to develop variations on the Oedipus theme and the archetypal motif of the search for a father. Also in 1959, Linda Millar, then nineteen, disappeared for almost two weeks and was the object of a widespread and highly publicized search. Her difficult life (she died in 1970 at thirty-one) is reflected in a number of troubled girl characters who appear in the novels.

During the 1960's, Macdonald became involved in environmental issues, joining the Sierra Club and Audubon Society, cofounding Santa Barbara Citizens for Environmental Defense. Such concerns are manifest in such novels as *The Underground Man* (1971) and *Sleeping Beauty* (1973). In terms of his writing career, the decade began with *The Ferguson Affair,* a non-Archer mystery that had three hardcover printings in 1960, his biggest success thus far. In 1966, a popular film version of *The Moving Target* was released; called *Harper,* it starred Paul Newman. The decade concluded with *The Goodbye Look* (1969), Macdonald's first genuine best seller and his first novel to attract widespread critical attention.

The Underground Man in 1971 was the occasion for a front-page review by Eudora Welty in *The New York Times Book Review* and a *Newsweek* cover story. The book was adapted for a television film in 1974, the year in which the Mystery Writers of America gave Macdonald its Grand Master Award. Two years later, his twenty-fourth and last novel, *The Blue Hammer* (1976), was published, a best seller in the United States and abroad. By the close of the decade, Macdonald had begun to suffer the first symptoms of Alzheimer's disease, of which he died on July 11, 1983.

ANALYSIS

The traditional detective novel is a puzzle: It begins with a crime, proceeds through a search for a solution, and concludes with the culprit exposed. Characterization is minimal and often stereotypical, and there is little thematic development beyond the obvious: Crime does not pay, for the criminal never triumphs, and eventually normality is restored. Macdonald's work does not follow this pattern. By his fourth novel, Macdonald was writing complex studies of the human condition that had begun to move beyond genre fiction to the realm of mainstream literature. Though mysteries are central and a private detective is narrator and prime protagonist, Macdonald's multilayered narratives mainly examine the ways in which the past impinges upon the present and how people often are trapped by a heritage of which they are unaware.

Having begun as a spy novelist with *The Dark Tunnel* and *Trouble Follows Me*, Macdonald in 1947 published his first hard-boiled novel in the Raymond Chandler and Dashiell Hammett tradition: *Blue City*. Its exile theme and its inclusion of a search for a father foreshadow Macdonald's later works, including his fourth book, *The Three Roads*. The title recalls Sophocles' *Oidipous Tyrannos* (c. 429 B.C.E.; *Oedipus Tyrannus*, 1715), and the plot focuses upon the attempts of Macdonald's hero, Bret Taylor, to reestablish his identity by recalling his past after a wartime bout with amnesia. This is the first Macdonald book with California as the primary locale—a territory he would mine in his remaining twenty novels.

A year later, in *The Moving Target*, he introduces his private eye and narrator Lew Archer, who is featured in seventeen more novels and two story collections. Archer's name comes from Miles Archer, Sam Spade's murdered partner in Dashiell Hammett's *The Maltese Falcon* (1930). According to Macdonald, though, Archer is "patterned on Raymond Chandler's Marlowe," also a "semi-outsider . . . fascinated but not completely taken in by the customs of the natives." Unlike Chandler, Macdonald does not consider his detective to be the character who provides the "quality of redemption"; instead, he says, that quality "belongs to the whole work and is not the private property of one. . . . The detective-as-redeemer is a backward step in the direction of sentimental romance, and an oversimplified world of good guys and bad guys."

In 1973, after having written about Archer cases for almost a quarter of a century, Macdonald commented, "My narrator Archer's wider and less rigidly stylized range of expression, at least in more recent novels, is related to a central difference between him and Marlowe. Marlowe's voice is limited by his role as the hard-boiled hero." Archer, in fact, is an unusual private eye in many ways. For example, money is incidental to him, important mainly to pay the rent. Further, he invariably is drawn emotionally to one of his clients—not usually sexually but rather from a feeling of kinship with fellow sufferers, for he thinks that he "sometimes served as a catalyst for trouble, not unwillingly."

Though not obsessed with the past in the way his clients and suspects are, at one point he looks in a mirror and remarks that "all I could read was my own past, in the marks of erosion under my eyes." The past is a living presence that causes him to empathize with those who are its prisoners. Above all, Archer is a good listener who often solves cases because he learns so much from those who take him into their confidence and talk freely to him. Unlike most series detectives, Archer is neither static nor two-dimensional, for Macdonald expanded the persona over the years: Archer's moralizing and sermonizing tendencies increase in the later novels. While his ratiocinative instincts remain as sharp as ever, they are tempered by a greater sensitivity; he becomes more humane.

Macdonald's novels also developed as the years passed, with major thematic concerns surfacing. In *The Drowning Pool*, the themes of corporate greed and environmental destruction are central; they are motifs that figure prominently in such later books as *The Underground Man* and *Sleeping Beauty*. In *The Doomsters* (1958), Macdonald believed that he had made "a fairly clean break with the Chandler tradition, which it had taken some years to digest, and freed me to make my own approach to the crimes and sorrows of life." His most complex novel to that point, it has a plot (not simply a series of scenes in the Chandler manner) that presents a family saga as a means of dramatizing a theme. Furthermore, Archer for the first time becomes involved in the events and is not at all the detached private eye hired for a job.

The Doomsters leads directly to Macdonald's next novel, *The Galton Case*, his thirteenth, by which time he, by his own account, had "learned what every novelist has to learn: to convert his own life as it grows into his fiction as he writes." In writing it, he delved into his own past while maintaining aesthetic distance and gave a new dimension to what had become his customary concerns: the identity quest, greed, alienation, and the "pastness of the present."

In the eight novels of the following decade (all but the first, *The Ferguson Case* of 1960, featuring Lew Archer), the growth of Macdonald's plotting skills continues, whereas his characters remain superficial; the length limitations to which mystery genre writers had to conform may have mitigated against attempting both complex plotting and in-depth character development. In each of the books, his standard mix of posturing and duplicitous people—young victims, troubled women, arrogant yet insecure and unhappy rich people—confront resurrected pasts. An observation by Archer about one such person is applicable to many: "The mind that looked at me through his eyes was like muddy water continually stirred by fears and fantasies and old greed."

Macdonald's last novel of the decade, *The Goodbye Look*, was his first best seller and the first of his books to be reviewed on the front page of *The New York Times Book Review*, unusual for a mystery writer. Written during the Vietnam War, it has an antiwar theme in addition to Macdonald commonplaces. By this twenty-first of his novels (and the sixteenth Lew Archer novel), Macdonald's surer hands juggle his most complex plot to date, encompassing six different families whose paths cross over a quarter of a century.

Before being incapacitated by Alzheimer's disease, Macdonald wrote three more novels: *The Underground Man*, *Sleeping Beauty*, and *The Blue Hammer*, the first of which is generally considered his masterpiece. In addition to the recurring presence of familiar Macdonald motifs, there is in it a major focus upon the environment and ecological matters, the latter through means of a forest fire that rages during most of the book. The multiple plots, dealing with past and present events, are unified not only by the tight organization and overlapping of characters but also by their exemplification of the thematic underpinning, again involving the pastness of the present.

Sleeping Beauty is something of a sequel to its predecessor, focusing as it does upon the environment by means of an oil spill that is its primary symbol. The fragile link between people and nature, with human greed upsetting the necessary balance, is always in the background of the plot, which progresses through three generations of a family's corruption and concludes with a metaphorical linking of the human and natural tragedies. Also of interest in the novel is the suggestion that Lew Archer is faltering: Becoming too involved emotionally with a young woman, the "sleeping beauty" of the title, he unwittingly permits a murderer to commit suicide.

Macdonald's last novel, *The Blue Hammer*, which had its genesis in notebook entries written fourteen years before he completed it, is a fully realized delineation of the double motif and the need for self-realization; it is his most complex treatment of these and other standard motifs since *The Goodbye Look*. Critics complained about his reliance upon timeworn formulas and his reworking of previously used plots and characters, amounting to little more than a variation on old themes. Along with the sameness, however, there are significant differences. The Cain-Abel motif is new, and Archer is more introspective. Further, though he had been the consummate loner in so many novels over twenty-five years, the changes suggested in *Sleeping Beauty* lead in this novel to his first love affair, which not only ends in disappointment ("when she dropped out of sight, I felt the loss of part of myself") but also distracts him from his proper pursuits.

In *The Underground Man*, a minister sends a letter to a character whose search for his father initiates most of the key events, including the son's murder. The Reverend Riceyman's message, which Archer calls "good advice," can serve as a coda to most of the Macdonald canon: "The past can do very little for us—no more than it has already done, for good or ill—except in the end to release us. We must seek and accept release, and give release."

THE MOVING TARGET

First published: 1949
Type of work: Novel

Private detective Lew Archer's search for a kidnapped oilman leads to the exposure of an alien smuggling operation.

The Moving Target is a quickly paced mystery-adventure novel filled with chases, fights, and murders which Macdonald described as "a story clearly aspiring to be a movie," which it became: *Harper*, starring Paul Newman, in 1966. His fourth novel, it is a landmark in his career, marking as it does the debut of Lew Archer, a Los Angeles private detective patterned after Raymond Chandler's Philip Marlowe, with whom Archer shares a sense of righteousness. Archer, however, is more introspective and realistic. Being the narrator, he becomes the moral center of the book.

Linked as the book is to the "hard-boiled" detective fiction tradition, Archer is challenged by several dangerous physical encounters with adversaries. In one struggle: "I clubbed the gun and waited. The first two got bloody scalps. Then they swarmed over me, hung on my arms, kicked my legs from under me, kicked consciousness out of my head. . . . I came to fighting. My arms were pinned, my raw mouth kissing cement." In another encounter, "His fist struck the nape of my neck. Pain whistled through my body like splintered glass, and the night fell on me solidly again." A bit later he overcomes his captor, they fall into the water struggling, and Archer kills the man in self-defense. (In later novels, Archer's challenges become increasingly cerebral instead of physical, as he moves from his mid-thirties to middle age.)

With its Southern California setting and characters whom money, or the desire for it, corrupts, the novel anticipates the anti-acquisitiveness of later Macdonald books. At the very start, for example, Archer comes upon the oceanfront estates of Cabrillo Canyon and muses: "The light-blue haze . . . was like a thin smoke from slowly burning money. . . .

Private property: color guaranteed fast; will not shrink egos. I had never seen the Pacific look so small."

Though the plot is not as complex as those of later novels, it is multifaceted. The primary action, about the disappearance of Ralph Sampson, an oilman, is intertwined with a story line concerning a Mexican immigrant smuggling operation that Archer happens upon while tracking the kidnappers. Sampson does not appear until the end, when Archer finally discovers his body, but his personality pervades and motivates the action. Miranda, his daughter, recalls that he "started out with nothing . . . his father was a tenant farmer who never had land of his own." She understands, therefore, why Ralph wanted to own so much land, but she laments that "you'd think he'd be more sympathetic to poor people. . . . the strikers on the ranch, for instance."

Miranda is being courted by Alan Taggert, Sampson's pilot and surrogate son (replacing one killed in World War II), whose primary interest is her father's wealth, and this greed involves him in the ransom kidnapping of his employer. Ironically, Taggert is killed by a rival suitor, Sampson lawyer Albert Graves, a former district attorney who, having worked for millionaires so long, "saw his chance to be a millionaire himself" by marrying Miranda and killing his new father-in-law so he would not have to wait for access to his riches. Says Archer of his longtime friend and erstwhile colleague: "He wasn't looking down; he was looking up. Up to the houses in the hills where the big money lives. He was going to be big himself for a change, with a quarter of Sampson's millions."

THE GALTON CASE

First published: 1959
Type of work: Novel

An old woman's desire for reconciliation with her son and the appearance of a putative grandson involve Archer in a complex variation of the Oedipus theme.

According to Macdonald, he and young John Galton in *The Galton Case* have much in common, including "a sense of displacement, a feeling that,

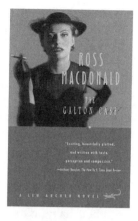

no matter where we were, we were on the alien side of some border. . . . like dubious claimants to a lost inheritance." Among Macdonald's notebook jottings about the novel is the statement, "Oedipus angry vs. parents for sending him away into a foreign country," and he has written that the book "was shaped not in imitation exactly, but in awareness of . . . early Greek models."

The action begins twenty years after Anthony Galton has dropped out of sight with his pregnant wife, a woman of dubious background whom his wealthy parents rejected. His elderly mother's attorney hires Lew Archer to solve the mystery, which the detective does easily, largely because of an extraordinary streak of good luck. Having ascertained that Galton became a poet with the pen name "John Brown," Archer locates the missing man's remains. This is only the beginning of the story, however, for Archer also happens upon a young man who may be Galton's son, a twenty-two-year-old calling himself John Brown, Jr., and bearing an uncanny resemblance to his supposed father. Archer suspects that he is an imposter, however, so with one case done, the private eye embarks on another—to establish the identity of John Brown, Jr.

Thus begins an odyssey taking Archer throughout California as well as to Nevada, Michigan, and Canada. Along the way he uncovers a conspiracy to dupe old Mrs. Galton and gain control of her wealth, a plan involving not only assorted gangsters and former convicts but also her trusted attorney. In typical Macdonald fashion, its origins go back decades, so Archer must delve through a tangled morass of tormented lives, along the way suffering a broken jaw and other physical traumas. Peeling away layers of the past, he ascertains that though John Brown, Jr., was part of the original plot, having been hired to play his role because he resembled Anthony Galton, he was not, after all, Theodore Fredericks of Pitt, Ontario: He really was John Galton.

Despite their many unusual twists and unexpected turns, the multiple plots are clearly linked, and they progress logically to their common conclusion. So much of Archer's success depends upon coincidence and sheer luck, however, that credibility sometimes is strained. This problem notwithstanding, *The Galton Case* is a compelling novel, for Macdonald maintains suspense throughout and paints memorable domestic scenes, not only in the Galton household but also between Gordon Sable (Mrs. Galton's attorney) and his alcoholic wife, and Mrs. Fredericks (John Galton's mother) and her alcoholic husband. The pair of tense meetings that Archer has with Marian Matheson (erstwhile maid of the fugitive young Galtons and their baby) advances his case and adds emotional power to the novel.

Macdonald is at his best, however, in scenes with Sheila Howell (daughter of Mrs. Galton's physician) and John Galton, who have fallen in love. The girl has an epic confrontation with her father, who doubts Galton's veracity; later, Archer locates the pair after they have fled together. This latter scene is an unaffectedly tender portrayal of young love, and the incident recalls the flight of John's parents years earlier. Further, on this occasion Archer sees old scars of childhood abuse on John's back, which remind him of marks reportedly seen on his mother's body decades ago.

Many of the characters are familiar Macdonald types, but standing apart from others is the boy who turns out to be the Galton heir after all. Handsome and personable, he seems from the start to be too good to be true, and indeed, at the beginning he is an excellent deceiver. His acting ability and careful preparation notwithstanding, the real reason that he is so convincing is that, unknown even to himself, he actually is the person he pretends to be. The man he knew as his father had actually murdered his real father, and his mother, who witnessed the crime, had married her husband's killer and remained silent for sixteen years lest Nelson Fredericks kill her son. Pretender though he is at the start, the boy is motivated by a desire to escape from a stifling environment, and despite his talent to deceive, he is honest with wealthy Ada Reichler, whom he meets while he is a student at the University of Michigan (where he is known as John Lindsay), taking her to Pitt so that she can see the kind of background from which he comes. At the end, he even is able to say to Mrs. Fredericks, "I don't hate you. . . . I'm sorry for you, Mother. And I'm sorry for what I've said." Having completed his

search, he is at peace with himself and everyone else.

While writing the book, Macdonald wrote to his publisher that he wanted it to be a transition work for him "out of the 'hard-boiled' realm. . . . [M]y ambition . . . is to write on serious themes." Despite the intent, much violence remains, but the thematic content is more fully developed than in earlier novels. One theme, already a standard in Macdonald's work, is the contrast between the haves and the have-nots, with Archer's disdain for the wealthy and greedy again in focus. This is subordinated to the identity theme, however, not only the son's search for his father (which would be Macdonald's concern in *The Underground Man*) but also the boy's quest to establish precisely who he is, which leads into still another common Macdonald theme, the intertwining of past and present. Near the close of *The Galton Case*, Marian Matheson asks Archer, "Is this trouble going to go on forever?" Finally, after twenty-three years, he can say, "We're coming to the end of it."

THE CHILL

First published: 1964
Type of work: Novel

A runaway bride and the murder of a woman professor lead to the reopening of old crimes and the discovery of changed identities.

The Chill, which won a British Crime Writers' Association Silver Dagger Award, begins with young Dolly Kincaid abandoning her husband the day after they are married. Alex Kincaid hires Lew Archer to find her, which Archer does effortlessly, but this turns out to be only the beginning of the story, involving a triple murder case extending back over many years. Young Alex, early in the story, remarks with awe to Archer: "It's almost as though history is repeating itself." Later, when someone says to him, "Anyway, it's all past history," Archer replies, "History is always connected with the present." On another occasion, he compares his present problem with earlier ones, "which opened up gradually like fissures in the firm ground of the present, cleaving far down through the strata of the past." The thematic and structural traits of *The Chill* place it in the Macdonald mainstream, a continuation of his contemporary Oedipal legend, but it is more complex than its predecessors, and it concludes with a stunning reversal that Archer happens upon only at the very end.

Dolly, the runaway bride, had witnessed the shooting of her mother years previously and testified against her father. Upon his release from San Quentin, he pleads his case to her, and she realizes that an unknown woman, not her father, had committed the crime. Rent by guilt, she flees her husband, Alex, and goes to a local college, supporting herself by assisting the dean's mother. Within a short time, Helen Haggerty, a French professor who serves as Dolly's adviser, is murdered, and Dolly finds the body. An emotional wreck, she is treated by a psychiatrist who had seen her as a child. Through therapy, she sorts out the confusions of past and present, resolving her doubts about herself and others.

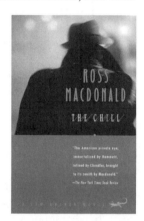

Meanwhile, Archer travels from California to Nevada and Missouri to do his own sorting and unraveling, and he finds that Haggerty also had witnessed a murder when she was a girl and was blackmailing Dean Bradshaw, an old beau. He also learns that Bradshaw had been leading at least two lives, hiding romantic liaisons from his elderly mother, with whom he lived. Haggerty's death leads Archer to delve into the long-ago death of Luke Deloney in Missouri, officially an accidental self-killing but actually a murder. As he peels away the layers of the past in an attempt to get at the truth about present events, Archer is confronted by new problems, with previously unknown people emerging and a bewildering sequence of events occurring. Roy Bradshaw becomes increasingly suspect, as the supposed facts of his life conflict: his excessive devotion to his mother, with whom he lives; his secret divorce from a woman called Letitia Macready; his similarly quiet marriage to his colleague Laura Sutherland; the summer tour of Europe that he never took, despite postcards home to Laura and his mother; and the many years of psychiatric care he underwent. In contrast, old Mrs. Bradshaw seems to be the epitome of stability, except for her obsessive attachment to her son.

At the very end, however, Archer sees that not even Mrs. Bradshaw is the matriarch he assumed she was. Signaling the startling revelation is Roy Bradshaw's cryptic statement, "I'm beginning to hate old women"; moments later, Archer sees a family picture and realizes that the Bradshaws are not mother and son but husband and wife. She had been Letitia Macready but pretended to have died in Europe to cover her murder of Deloney: She perpetrated the later charade to obscure her motive for murdering Helen McGree. It was she who killed Helen Haggerty out of fear that the younger woman was going to steal Roy. The ultimate irony is that she unintentionally kills Roy while going to murder his new wife.

After he has exposed the truth, Archer calls Letitia Osborne Macready Bradshaw an "old woman," and she snaps back, "You mustn't call me that. I'm not old. Don't look at my face, look into my eyes. You can see how young I am." He reflects: "She was still greedy for life." This senator's daughter also was greedy for love, money, and power; sustained by her fantasies, she permitted the obsessions to corrupt her and consequently ruin or destroy many lives. The morality tale, one of Macdonald's most successful books, concludes with Archer's "No more anything, Letitia." After decades, then, Archer has excised evil from society, and the survivors—particularly Dolly—can face the future confidently, secure in the knowledge that the past no longer holds secrets from them.

THE UNDERGROUND MAN

First published: 1971
Type of work: Novel

A son's attempts to learn the facts behind his father's long-ago disappearance dredge up the past and unleash a tragic sequence of events.

Like many other Macdonald novels, *The Underground Man* takes place primarily in the fictitious Santa Teresa, which bears more than a passing resemblance to Santa Barbara, where Macdonald lived for thirty-five years. Also typical is the fact that the action ranges widely throughout California.

Early in the book, Lew Archer becomes involved in the entangled affairs of a well-to-do Santa Teresa family split in marital disputes. Leo Broadhurst, scion of the clan, had vanished fifteen years earlier, leaving his wife for another woman, but then seemingly deserting the second woman as well. His son, consumed for years by the desire to find his father, finally advertises for information in a newspaper, but his reward offer succeeds only in dredging up the past and does not locate Broadhurst.

One reward seeker is Albert Sweetner, an escaped convict who had been a foster child of Edna Snow, onetime Broadhurst housekeeper. Sweetner's return revives a long-past scandal involving a teenage girl who is now a married woman. While the past closes in on these people and others, threatening their present lives, a raging forest fire also endangers them and their property and gives a sense of urgency to Archer's need to resolve the growing mystery—the flames are on the verge of destroying evidence.

During the few days that the action of the book covers, Archer learns that Broadhurst was a womanizer whose wife shot him; as he lay dying, Edna Snow finished him off with a knife—both exacting delayed revenge. By the end of the novel, events have moved full circle: The mystery of Leo Broadhurst's disappearance is solved, but his son dies in the process. Albert Sweetner also is killed, and another character commits suicide. There are positive futures for some others, but Lew Archer is the only one unchanged. He has not even made much money from his efforts. More than in any other Macdonald novel, the characters in *The Underground Man* have "all the years of their lives dragging behind them." Even Archer, nearing the close of the case, feels "shipwrecked on the shores of the past." At the end, Archer wishes for Leo Broadhurst's young grandson "a benign failure of memory."

Central to the novel are the quest and Oedipal motifs, which are most poignantly delineated in the character of Stanley, whose love-hate relationship with Leo is the motivating force of his life. As one character explains it, "he's angry at his father for abandoning him; at the same time he misses him and loves him." This omnipresence of the past is the primary theme of the work. The forest fire raging in the background of much of the action is a leitmotif serving as metaphor for one's alienation from one's fellows, from oneself, and from nature. It consumes everything in its path in the same wantonly destructive manner as the characters pursue their dreams or rebel against their nightmares.

Archer's first reaction to the blaze invokes war, alienated humanity's ultimate destructive act: "Under and through the smoke I caught glimpses of fire like the flashes of guns too far away to be heard. The illusion of war was completed by an old two-engine bomber, which flew in low over the mountain's shoulder." Later, when he reaches the Broadhurst ranch, Archer notices that the darkening fruit "hung down from their branches like green hand grenades." (War imagery is common in Macdonald's novels, a lasting effect of his experience in the Pacific during World War II.)

Counterpointing the symbolic squabbling of the jays in the opening scene of the book and the forest fire throughout is the rain at the end. By quenching the threatening blaze, the storm offers a purging of the old and a renewal of life. "When I went outside," Archer says, "the rain was coming down harder than ever. Water was running in the street, washing the detritus of summer downhill toward the sea." Further, the title of the novel recalls Fyodor Dostoevski's *Zapiski iz podpolya* (1864; *Notes from the Underground*, 1918); by calling attention to it, Macdonald leads the reader to see his themes of guilt and suffering in bolder relief.

With this twenty-second of his novels (the seventeenth with Lew Archer), Macdonald gained his long-sought recognition as successor to Chandler and Hammett in the hard-boiled school. At the same time, he was accepted as a serious novelist. *The Underground Man* is his major achievement, the work in which his worldview—including social commentary, mainly on environmental and ecological matters—is most fully and most memorably expressed. The several story lines in this novel are more skillfully developed and more unified than in any of his previous books, and the portrait of a corrupt society is especially memorable, with Archer's efforts revealing the venality behind the facade of propriety. Finally, despite echoes of earlier books, *The Underground Man* has its own voice and quality, and it perfectly combines timeless and timely themes.

SUMMARY

Writing as Ross Macdonald, Kenneth Millar produced a series of detective novels with plots more complex than is typical of the genre and characters more fully realized than is the usual practice. More important, his narratives are vehicles for themes, primarily variations on how people corrupt the American Dream by their greed and lack of vision.

Each of the novels is a tragedy, with the destruction, wrought from within the characters, unleashing avenging furies whose disastrous forces endure through generations. Through the efforts of Lew Archer, the moral center of almost all the tales, evil finally is purged, and the survivors can look forward to normal lives.

Gerald H. Strauss

BIBLIOGRAPHY

By the Author

LONG FICTION:

The Dark Tunnel, 1944 (as Kenneth Millar; pb. in England as *I Die Slowly*, 1955)

Trouble Follows Me, 1946 (as Millar; pb. in England as *Night Train*, 1955)

Blue City, 1947 (as Millar)

The Three Roads, 1948 (as Millar)

The Moving Target, 1949 (as John Macdonald; reissued as *Harper*, 1966)

The Drowning Pool, 1950 (as John Ross Macdonald)

The Way Some People Die, 1951 (as John Ross Macdonald)

The Ivory Grin, 1952 (as John Ross Macdonald; reissued as *Marked for Murder*, 1953)

Meet Me at the Morgue, 1953 (as John Ross Macdonald; pb. in England as *Experience with Evil*, 1954)

Find a Victim, 1954 (as John Ross Macdonald)

The Barbarous Coast, 1956

The Doomsters, 1958

The Galton Case, 1959

The Ferguson Affair, 1960

The Wycherly Woman, 1961

The Zebra-Striped Hearse, 1962

The Chill, 1964

The Far Side of the Dollar, 1965

Black Money, 1966

The Instant Enemy, 1968

The Goodbye Look, 1969

The Underground Man, 1971

Sleeping Beauty, 1973

The Blue Hammer, 1976

SHORT FICTION:

The Name Is Archer, 1955 (as John Ross Macdonald)

Lew Archer, Private Investigator, 1977

Strangers in Town: Three Newly Discovered Mysteries, 2001 (Tom Nolan, editor)

DISCUSSION TOPICS

- How does Ross Macdonald's Lew Archer differ from Dashiell Hammett's Philip Marlowe?

- How does Lew Archer change or develop over Macdonald's writing years?

- Which Macdonald novels best exemplify his environmental concerns?

- What makes Santa Barbara an effective locale for Macdonald's fictional purposes?

- How does Macdonald reconcile the claims of the genres of tragedy and detective fiction?

- Is *The Underground Man* an apt title for Macdonald's novel? Does he meet the challenge imposed by its implicit reference to Fyodor Dostoevski's novel?

NONFICTION:
On Crime Writing, 1973
Self-Portrait: Ceaselessly into the Past, 1981

About the Author

Bruccoli, Matthew J. *Ross Macdonald.* San Diego: Harcourt Brace Jovanovich, 1984.

Gale, Robert. *A Ross Macdonald Companion.* Westport, Conn.: Greenwood Press, 2002.

Mahan, Jeffrey H. *A Long Way from Solving That One: Psycho/Social and Ethical Implications of Ross Macdonald's Lew Archer Tales.* Lanham, Md.: University Press of America, 1990.

Nolan, Tom. *Ross Macdonald: A Biography.* New York: Scribner, 1999.

Schopen, Bernard A. *Ross Macdonald.* Boston: Twayne, 1990.

Sipper, Ralph B., ed. *Ross Macdonald: Inward Journey.* Santa Barbara, Calif.: Cordelia Editions, 1984.

Skinner, Robert E. *The Hard-Boiled Explicator: A Guide to the Study of Dashiell Hammett, Raymond Chandler, and Ross Macdonald.* Metuchen, N.J.: Scarecrow Press, 1985.

South Dakota Review 24 (Spring, 1986).

Speir, Jerry. *Ross Macdonald.* New York: Frederick Ungar, 1978.

Wolfe, Peter. *Dreamers Who Live Their Dreams: The World of Ross Macdonald's Novels.* Bowling Green, Ohio: Bowling Green University Press, 1976.

THOMAS McGUANE

Born: Wyandotte, Michigan
December 11, 1939

Recognized as a prose stylist in the tradition of Ernest Hemingway and F. Scott Fitzgerald, McGuane has produced masculine fiction that focuses on the problems of finding an acceptable place and vocation in the latter half of the twentieth century.

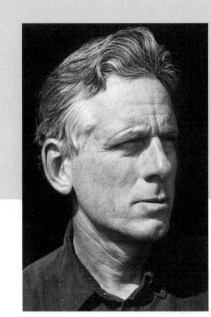
© Kurt Markus

BIOGRAPHY

Thomas Francis McGuane III was born in Wyandotte, Michigan, on December 11, 1939, to Thomas Francis II and Alice McGuane. His family contained some "fantastic storytellers," and McGuane inherited both the ability and the inclination to make storytelling his life. As a child, McGuane read nature books at his family's summer retreat, a fishing camp in northern Michigan that resembles the setting for his first novel, *The Sporting Club* (1969). His other passion, which he has also pursued since his childhood, is sportfishing, an activity that appears in most of his novels.

McGuane graduated from Cranbrook, an exclusive boarding school in Michigan. During his years there he once ran away to a Wyoming ranch owned by the father of a girlfriend and returned an avowed "sociopath." He later used this experience and the resulting attitude as the basis for his second novel, *The Bushwhacked Piano* (1971). His college career began on an unpromising note when he flunked out of the University of Michigan. He briefly attended Olivet College and then graduated from Michigan State University with honors. In 1965, he received his M.F.A. in playwriting from Yale University and spent the following academic year at Stanford University on a Wallace Stegner Fellowship. McGuane has supported himself by

writing screenplays, including *Rancho Deluxe* (1973), *Ninety-two in the Shade* (1975), *The Missouri Breaks* (1975), and (with Bud Shrake) *Tom Horn* (1980), and by directing *Ninety-two in the Shade*. Raising cutting horses brings in enough money to pay his ranch mortgage, and he has become an expert sport fisherman, sailor, and rodeo competitor.

Throughout his college career, McGuane avoided what have been considered the typical undergraduate excesses of alcohol and drugs to the point that he was called the "White Knight." In December of 1972, however, he lost control of his Porsche on an icy road en route to the Florida Keys, an accident that barely damaged the car but left McGuane so shaken that he could not speak for hours afterward. This brush with death made him see that art was not as important as life, and he abandoned what had been his relentless pursuit of writing. The following years were filled with tales of wild behavior, excessive drinking and drug use, and hasty marriages, encouraged in part by McGuane's involvement in screenwriting and directing in Hollywood. He had affairs with actresses Elizabeth Ashley and Margot Kidder and was divorced by his wife, Becky, after thirteen years of marriage when she learned that Kidder was pregnant. After nine months of marriage, Kidder and McGuane also were divorced.

McGuane admits his years of excessive behavior, but he maintains that the stories are exaggerated. Indeed, the amount of work that he produced indicates that close to 80 percent of his waking hours were spent writing and directing. His marriage in 1977 to Laurie Buffett (sister of singer Jimmy Buffett) helped stabilize his life, and since then he has approached both life and his art with greater balance.

McGuane's third novel, *Ninety-two in the Shade* (1973), draws on his experience sportfishing in the Keys. His fourth novel, *Panama* (1978), a departure from his first three, is a prolonged howl of despair from a washed-up rock star that reflects McGuane's own mixed feelings about his turbulent years in Hollywood. A more settled McGuane wrote three novels focusing on male restlessness in a country deteriorating into materialism and fads. *Nobody's Angel* (1982), *Something to Be Desired* (1984), and *Keep the Change* (1989) are set in the ranch country of Montana and feature protagonists who are looking for a way to live in a world that offers few satisfactory choices. *The Cadence of Grass,* an offbeat novel about a dysfunctional Montana family, was published in 2002

In *Nobody's Angel*, Patrick Fitzpatrick, disoriented by the deaths of his father and sister (recent events in McGuane's own life) fails to find a suitable answer to his search. The relatively upbeat conclusions of *Something to Be Desired* and *Keep the Change* reflect McGuane's satisfaction with his more orderly and settled life. He approaches his writing with energy and seriousness, but he receives equal pleasure from raising and training horses and successfully competing in rodeos.

An Outside Chance: Essays on Sport (1980) shows a slightly different side of McGuane than is revealed in his fiction. He is intensely interested in sport, especially fishing, and writes about it with a perception that most sportsmen and sportswriters do not possess. In 1986, McGuane published a collection of short stories, *To Skin a Cat;* the stories in this collection deal with the same concerns found in his novels, adapted to the more structured form of the short story.

ANALYSIS

The novels of McGuane reflect his interest and experience in playwriting and screenwriting. He gives readers visual images of moods, emotions, and action, and he refrains from simply telling readers what his characters are thinking, feeling, and doing. His characters speak tersely and rarely say explicitly how they feel. This spareness and terseness can be confusing to first-time readers of McGuane, especially as his worldview and the antics of his characters are definitely not mainstream.

Recognizing his themes and understanding his style and humor are necessary to readers' appreciation of the richness of McGuane's craft.

A consistent theme in all of McGuane's novels is father-son conflict. The father is a distant figure who, although respected and maybe even loved by his son, never has a warm relationship with his family. The son, the novel's protagonist, feels a sense of loss at not having a strong, concerned male as a guide and role model. In *Something to Be Desired*, the protagonist is himself a father, and he must work through his relationship with his son and try to avoid being the same kind of father that his had been. In three novels, surrogate fathers appear—C. J. Clovis in *The Bushwhacked Piano*, the grandfather in *Nobody's Angel*, and Otis Redwine in *Keep the Change*—but none of these older men has the strength of character that the real, but nonfunctioning, father has. This absence of the father leads in part to the unrest and aimless behavior of the protagonist as he searches for something to do and a way to act.

McGuane sees the twentieth century United States as a "declining snivelization." His protagonists search for the kind of America that young men used to grow up in, a lost primeval virtue that used to define American manhood. In *The Sporting Club*, one sees the vulgarity, weakness, and ineptness of wealthy Detroit businessmen as they pursue sport and "justice" at their hunting and fishing retreat. In *Ninety-two in the Shade*, Key West is filled with inept, arrogant suburbanites who demand trophy fish from their guides. Good fishing lanes are ruined by the earsplitting roar of military jets, mobile homes crowd the water's edge, and political corruption simmers just below the surface of daily life. In *Panama*, Chet Pomeroy returns to Key West to find changes that represent the general changes in the United States. A family jewelry store is now a moped rental shop, and a taco stand has replaced a small bookstore.

In the following three novels, the protagonists return to the ranch country of Montana to look for the values no longer sought by the schemers of Key West and Latin America. They discover that Montana and ranching have been invaded by the same forces that have ruined Key West. Patrick Fitzpatrick in *Nobody's Angel* discovers that men with Oklahoma oil money play at ranching. Lucien Taylor in *Something to Be Desired* becomes successful only by turning his ranch into a hot springs spa for the wealthy and aimless who travel around to the fashionable watering holes. Although Joe Starling (*Keep the Change*) is successful with one season of ranching, his work comes to nothing because of the scams of his uncle in a town that attaches to Joe the sins of his father. The only moral courses for these protagonists are to discover what to do by the process of elimination or to opt for lunacy.

Those same three protagonists are unable to be content with the lives they live, feeling that some romance is missing from their days. This dissatisfaction leads to aimless behavior and antics that are both bizarre and self-destructive. Patrick gives up, but Lucien and Joe find something that gives them a degree of satisfaction.

McGuane rarely comments on his characters' actions; bizarre behavior is simply presented as it happens. Vernor Stanton in *The Sporting Club* foments discord wherever he is; he is also, to a degree, self-destructive. Stealing a dignitaries' bus from a bridge-opening ceremony may seem to be no more than a juvenile prank, but it is also a comment on the pomposity of appointed officials and the ceremonies that surround them. When Thomas Skelton's father in *Ninety-two in the Shade* retreats to his bed for months, he is not a typical hypochondriac; he is actually sick of the world that allows his own father to become successful through political exploitation.

McGuane's humor resembles that of William Faulkner in "Spotted Horses," both in its physical nature and in the fact that it is used to ridicule. In *The Sporting Club*, Earl Olive's dynamiting of the main lodge, the flagpole, and the lifeguard chair sends a group of old men dashing in one direction in pursuit of the perpetrator, only to hear another blast to their rear. Wayne Codd's ineptness in spying on Ann Fitzgerald in *The Bushwhacked Piano* becomes slapstick when he falls off the roof with his pants down trying to photograph her in bed with Nicholas Payne. In *Something to Be Desired*, Lucien Taylor's efforts to dispose of the body of a customer who dies at his spa are hilarious to everyone but him and his employees, who become frustrated as one glitch after another prevents them from solving the problem.

THE SPORTING CLUB

First published: 1969
Type of work: Novel

Vernor Stanton and James Quinn expose the sordid origins and ancestors of an exclusive hunting and fishing club in northern Michigan.

McGuane used the woods of northern Michigan as the setting for his first novel, *The Sporting Club*. The Centennial Club, founded by distant ancestors of its present members, has been the retreat for highly paid Detroit executives and their families. Hunting and fishing are the accepted manly activities, while the women and children swim and lie in the sun. Into this setting come two characters who eventually destroy the club. James Quinn, who has rescued his father's business from the brink of bankruptcy, appears to be the ideal club member. He longs for the solitude of the woods and the established and honorable rituals of sport. He approaches fishing with care, expertise, and reverence, trying to cleanse himself of the stain of business and the attendant cutthroat competition. Returning to the club after an absence of several years is Vernor Stanton, a friend of Quinn from their adolescent days. Stanton is extremely wealthy and has cast himself apart from those who perform any of the normal tasks of upper-class American life. He wants to "make the world tense" and "foment discord."

Stanton's return is motivated by his desire to destroy the club and to convince the members that they are not the distinguished descendants of grand ancestors who founded the club on lofty ideals. To effect this goal, he must enlist the help of Quinn, who joined him in many a prank in the past. Quinn resists at first, mainly because he sees himself as a responsible businessman—too old, mature, and content to want to disrupt tradition. Stanton's challenges, the force of his personality, and the decadence of the present club members, though, change Quinn from a reluctant spectator into Stanton's accomplice. Stanton can be viewed as a knight in shining armor whose task is to rid the world of evil. Regardless of the reason the Centennial Club was founded, it increased its holdings by driving the surrounding families off their lands, often illegally, through bribes to political figures. Memberships are passed down from father to eldest son in biblical fashion, and most of the present owners act as though they are the rightful heirs of the club's glorious past.

Stanton's plan begins when he gets rid of Jack Olson, the club's manager, who has kept a perfect balance between wildlife, food supply, and hunting and fishing needs within the club's boundaries. When Olson leaves, he hires his replacement, Earl Olive, a man he met in a roadhouse bar. Olive enters with his people—bums, bikers, and floozies—who immediately clash with the club members. In retaliation for getting his nose broken in a duel with Stanton, Olive dynamites the dam, reducing the lake to swamp, and destroys the main building, the lifeguard stand, and the flagpole. Led by the militaristic Fortescu, the prominent club members decide to bring Olive to justice themselves.

A time capsule that is opened in honor of the club's centennial produces a photograph that reveals the decadence of the club's founders, at which point the present members reenact the sexual circus shown in the photograph. When outside authorities finally arrive to restore some semblance of order, Quinn is the only one sane enough to explain what happened. As an acknowledgment of its total destruction, the Centennial Club is put up for sale. Stanton immediately buys it, deeds Quinn's house to him, and uses the club for his own retreat.

In many ways *The Sporting Club* reflects the decadence of society in the same way that William Golding's *Lord of the Flies* (1954) does. Once they decide to solve the Olive problem themselves and shut out any outside help, the club members become irrational, authoritarian, and cruel. By the end, the club members and Olive's people are indistinguishable in their squalor and misuse of authority.

NINETY-TWO IN THE SHADE

First published: 1973
Type of work: Novel

Determined to be a fishing guide, Thomas Skelton pursues his dream in the face of a death threat from a violent, established guide.

McGuane's third novel, *Ninety-two in the Shade*, is set in steamy Key West in the world of sportfishing. On the surface, the plot deals with a turf battle between two fishing guides, old-timer Nichol Dance and newcomer Thomas Skelton. The real focus of the novel, though, is a common McGuane theme: the unrest of the protagonist (Skelton) and his search for something that will allow him to remain sane and escape the decadence of American civilization.

Thomas Skelton has quit college as a marine biology major and wants to become a fishing guide at his home of Key West. His despair at what he sees around him, however, has led to drug use, crazy behavior, and the process of discovering a career by elimination. Sportfishing seems to be the only occupation that will keep him sane. The only problem with his decision is that Nichol Dance, one of the guides west of Key Marathon, feels threatened enough to warn Skelton 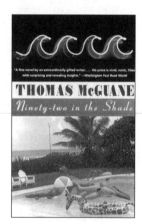 not to guide in Dance's territory. The conflict revolves around these two men: Dance feels that he must establish "credence"; Skelton feels that his only hope for sanity is to guide.

A series of events leads to a direct confrontation between Dance and Skelton. While in prison for attacking Ray the dockmaster, Dance sends his clients, the Rudleighs from Connecticut, to Skelton. During their excursion, Dance (released from prison because Ray did not die) "kidnaps" the Rudleighs from Skelton's skiff as both a practical joke and a warning. In retaliation, Skelton burns Dance's boat, his only possession of any value; Dance tells Skelton he will kill him if he guides west of Marathon.

Key West and guiding are the ends of the road for both men. Skelton knows that Dance is capable of carrying out his threat, but he orders his boat and continues his plan to guide because there is nothing else for him to do. Dance knows that killing Skelton will, at the least, put him in prison for life, but the alternatives (if Skelton guides) are suicide or loss of credence. Skelton's girlfriend, fa-

Thomas McGuane

ther, and grandfather all ineffectually try to dissuade him from his plan.

As in all McGuane's novels, there are problems between fathers and sons. In *Ninety-two in the Shade*, three generations of Skelton males are at odds with one another. Although Goldsboro Skelton finances his grandson's boat, Thomas is disgusted by his grandfather's lust for power and autocratic manner. Skelton's father feels the same way about Goldsboro and the world that Thomas does, and his method of coping is basically the same. He has also looked for a career by the process of elimination, finally withdrawing to a mosquito-net-covered bed where he watches television and plays works of Jean Sibelius and Hank Williams on his violin.

Skelton's behavior may seem aimless, nonproductive, and even harmful. The method behind his madness, however, is an effort to remain sane by not focusing on the deterioration around him. Skelton has come to Key West to find peace, but he must deal with trendy suburbanites, the Rudleighs, who force the guides to break the rules for sportfishing. He sees a former guide now working as a salad chef at Howard Johnson's because the bank foreclosed on his boat. One of the best fishing lanes is in the flight pattern for a military landing field, and the shattering roar of low-flying aircraft dominates everything at frequent intervals. As part of its efforts to promote tourism, the Chamber of Commerce holds a pie-eating contest in which the contestants gorge themselves to the point of vomiting, the winner to receive a day's guiding from Dance. Skelton can handle these intrusions into his world only by becoming completely involved with guiding.

Other signs of decadence are less obvious but insidious. Skelton's grandfather has become "successful" by exploiting the gaps that exist between deals for power and profit. His father is judged a crackpot and a failure for refusing to compete in a country he believes to be decadent. Within this setting, Skelton and Dance try to stay sane by doing the only thing left for them to do: work as fishing guides and protect their space.

SOMETHING TO BE DESIRED

First published: 1984
Type of work: Novel

Bored with life and lured by the possibility of wild sex and adventure, Lucien Taylor embarks on a voyage of self-discovery.

Something to Be Desired, McGuane's sixth novel, stands apart from his other novels in that the protagonist, Lucien Taylor, actually reaches a level of contentment and happiness—after abandoning his wife and young son. The "something to be desired," though, turns out to be exactly what he gave up, a life of domestic contentment with his wife, Suzanne, and his young son, James. The discovery process is filled with debauchery and aimless behavior, accompanied by a gradual increase in common sense and maturity and a huge increase in personal wealth.

Lucien's inability to tolerate contentment can be traced to his father, who ran off to Peru with a friend, Art Clancey. A high point in Lucien's life occurred when his father "kidnapped" him from school to camp in the mountains above Deadrock, Montana. Although the trip was a failure in one sense (they spent two days without food or shelter wandering in search of their campsite), Lucien was thrilled to be doing something with his father. When he discovered that his wife had loved Art Clancey (now dead), the elder Taylor had walked out of the house for good, leaving Lucien and his mother dependent on alimony, child support, and handouts from relatives.

During a successful career with the United States Intelligence Agency in Latin America, Lucien returns to Montana without his wife and son to find a more romantic life. He is abandoning what is generally understood as the good life: a beautiful woman who loves him, a son who desperately needs a father, and a good career that gives him the leisure to explore the culture of Latin America. Lucien is drawn to Montana by Emily, the lusty "dark" woman who would not marry him, when he hears that she has murdered her husband. He feels that she can supply his life with the passion, kinky sex, and romance that are missing. After Lucien posts her bail, Emily deeds him the ranch as collateral, which he then owns when she skips the country before her trial. With Emily gone, Lucien engages in aimless behavior and frequent but unsatisfying sex; he becomes the local joke in Deadrock.

The landscape and the physical ranch work keep Lucien from going completely crazy. He seems to recognize the value of the land and his good fortune in living on it. The rituals of mending fences, using horses for work, hunting and fishing begin to provide a small stabilizing force for Lucien.

At his lowest point, physically sick and contemplating suicide, Lucien decides to redeem himself and "set the world on fire." With a huge bank loan, he transforms the natural hot springs on the ranch into a health spa, complete with an airfield and exotic menus. The spa is wildly successful, attracting people whose behavior is as bizarre as Lucien's. Being surrounded by wealthy, dissipated, aimless, and eccentric clients allows him to see his own behavior from an objective perspective and to be more content with his own normality.

Lucien uses his success as a means of convincing Suzanne and James to visit, and it is during this visit that he discovers a fathering instinct, a desire to give James what his own father never gave him. Lucien grows up, casts off his self-destructive behavior, and can even reject Emily when she returns. He does not completely win back Suzanne and James by the novel's end, but the possibility is there for a total reconciliation if they can decide to trust him again.

KEEP THE CHANGE

First published: 1989
Type of work: Novel

Joe Starling tries to recover the family ranch in Montana after becoming disgusted with his aimless life in Florida as an illustrator of operation manuals.

Keep the Change is set primarily in Montana after a brief interlude in Key West and a dizzying dash across the United States. The plot concerns Joe Starling's attempt to reclaim his family's ranch after being unsuccessful as a painter in Florida. Starling is a typical McGuane protagonist, caught between his past and future, a man whose good intentions are often thwarted by his bad habits.

Losing the inspiration to paint and working as an illustrator of operation manuals causes Joe to feel disgusted with his rather comfortable life in Florida, where he lives with a ravishing Cuban beauty, Astrid. To escape, he borrows Astrid's car, a small pink convertible, for a trip to the grocery store and ends up in Montana. His destination is his family's ranch, left to him by his father and managed by his Aunt Lureen and her brother, Joe's Uncle Smitty. The property has been leased for years to a neighbor who wants to add it to his own spread. The ranch itself is in financial jeopardy, mainly because Smitty has been siphoning off the lease money for his own use and supposedly brokering seafood shipments from Texas. When Joe returns, he rejuvenates the ranch, rebuilding the springs and fence, buying calves, and eventually selling them at a substantial profit. This profit, however, the money necessary to keep the ranch afloat, is absorbed by Smitty's seafood scam and his general ability to run through a lot of money in a hurry.

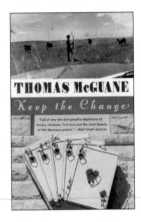

The father-son conflict in *Keep the Change* is typical of McGuane's work. Joe loved and admired his father, a distant and ruthless businessman who essentially sold out, even though he tried to instill in Joe a love of the land and a desire to keep the ranch in the family. When Joe returns to Montana to reclaim the ranch, he has to face the fact that his father was not liked by those who did business with him, and for those people the sins of the father are passed on to the son. The only real father figure Joe has had is Otis Rosewell, the foreman who supervised Joe when he was working for the neighboring rancher as a boy.

Joe courts his childhood sweetheart, Ellen Overstreet, as another way of trying to recapture the idyllic days of his past. On his return, he finds her married to his formal rival and sworn enemy, Billy Kelton, a hardworking but land-poor man who basically slaves for Ellen's father. Joe's relationship with Ellen is complicated by her present separation from Billy and the announcement that the father of Clara, her child, is really Joe and not Billy. The possibility of renewing an affair with Ellen leads to antic behavior, especially when she and Billy begin solving their marital problems, and Joe learns that Billy actually is Clara's father. Joe's antics are mild and short-lived for a McGuane protagonist, reflecting his ability to come to grips with his life.

In spite of the loss of the ranch, Joe seems to have wrested some meaning from his spiritual malaise. The novel ends, as does *Something to Be Desired*, on an unresolved but slightly upbeat note. This more mellow conclusion is a reflection of McGuane's changing style; it is less flashy and exudes a degree of warmth that is lacking in his earlier novels. He has not abandoned the dry wit, terse dialogue, and powerful descriptions of nature, but in *Keep the Change* they are integrated into the story and do not stand out as displays of verbal virtuosity.

SUMMARY

McGuane is a spokesman for what he sees as the decadence of the late twentieth century. His characters experience the confusion that results from the loss of strong masculine values in a world that supports and rewards cleverness and political power. They survive by looking askance at the world and searching for a vocation that will allow them to avoid seeing the deterioration around them. McGuane's humor and bizarre imagination make his novels as entertaining as they are thought-provoking and puzzling.

David Huntley

BIBLIOGRAPHY

By the Author

LONG FICTION:
The Sporting Club, 1969
The Bushwhacked Piano, 1971
Ninety-two in the Shade, 1973
Panama, 1978
Nobody's Angel, 1982
Something to Be Desired, 1984
Keep the Change, 1989
Nothing but Blue Skies, 1992
The Cadence of Grass, 2002

SHORT FICTION:
To Skin a Cat, 1986

SCREENPLAYS:
Rancho DeLuxe, 1973
Ninety-two in the Shade, 1975 (adaptation of his novel)
The Missouri Breaks, 1975
Tom Horn, 1980 (with Bud Shrake)

NONFICTION:
An Outside Chance: Essays on Sport, 1980
The Longest Silence: A Life in Fishing, 1999
Some Horses, 1999

About the Author
Bonetti, Kay. "Thomas McGuane." In *Conversations with American Novelists: The Best Interviews from the "Missouri Review" and the American Audio Prose Library*, edited by Kay Bonetti, Greg Michalson, Speer Morgan, Jo Sapp, and Sam Stowers. Columbia: University of Missouri Press, 1997.

DISCUSSION TOPICS

- How is fishing used as a metaphor in Thomas McGuane's fiction?
- McGuane's economic writing style has been compared to that of Ernest Hemingway. Are the two writers similar in other ways?
- What does McGuane's fiction say about relations between fathers and sons?
- What does McGuane's fiction say about being a man in contemporary America? Is he suggesting that something has been lost from American life?
- Describe the vision of the American West in McGuane's Montana novels.
- How is business corruption a consistent theme in McGuane's fiction?
- Compare two McGuane novels as voyages of self-discovery.

Carter, Allen Howard. "McGuane's First Three Novels: Games, Fun, Nemesis." *Critique* 17, no. 1 (1975): 91-104.

_____. "Speaking Against the Dark: Style as Theme in Thomas McGuane's *Nobody's Angel.*" *Modern Fiction Studies* 33, no. 2 (1987): 298.

Cook, Nancy S. "Investment in Place: Thomas McGuane in Montana." In *Old West-New West: Centennial Essays,* edited by Barbara Howard Meldrum. Moscow: University of Idaho Press, 1993.

Gregory, Sinda, and Larry McCaffery. "The Art of Fiction LXXXIX." *The Paris Review* 97 (Fall, 1988): 34-71.

Ingram, David. "Thomas McGuane: Nature, Environmentalism, and the American West." *Journal of American Studies* 29 (December, 1995): 423-439.

Klinkowitz, Jerome. *The New American Novel of Manners.* Athens: University of Georgia Press, 1986.

McClintock, James I. "'Unextended Selves' and 'Unformed Visions': Roman Catholicism in Thomas McGuane's Novels." *Renascence: Essays on Values in Literature* 49 (Winter, 1992): 139-152.

Masington, Charles G. "*Nobody's Angel:* Thomas McGuane's Vision of the Contemporary American West." *New Mexico Humanities Review* 6 (Fall, 1983): 49-55.

Minzesheimer, Bob. "McGuane Wrangles the Writing Life." *USA Today,* June 6, 2002, D7.

Morris, Gregory L. "How Ambivalence Won the West: Thomas McGuane and the Fiction of the New West." *Critique: Studies in Contemporary Fiction* 32 (Spring, 1991): 180-189.

Wallace, Jon. "The Language Plot in Thomas McGuane's *Ninety-Two in the Shade.*" *Critique* 29, no. 2 (1988): 111-120.

_____. *The Politics of Style: Language as Theme in the Fiction of Berger, McGuane, and McPherson.* Durango, Colo.: Hollowbrook, 1992.

Westrum, Dexter. *Thomas McGuane.* Boston: Twayne, 1991.

TERRY McMILLAN

Born: Port Huron, Michigan
October 18, 1951

McMillan's honest, realistic novels dramatize the struggles of African American women in their searches for love and commitment.

© Marion Ettlinger

BIOGRAPHY

Terry McMillan was born on October 18, 1951, in Port Huron, Michigan, a largely working-class town northeast of Detroit. Her father, Edward Lewis McMillan, a sanitation worker, was an alcoholic. Her mother, Madeline Tillman McMillan, a hardworking, determined woman, finally tired of being physically abused by her husband and divorced him. He died three years later, at the age of thirty-nine.

As the oldest of the five McMillan children, Terry had more than her share of responsibility. One of the jobs she took in order to contribute to the family income, however, brought her more than the meager $1.25 an hour she earned. When, at sixteen, she started shelving books at a local library, McMillan learned to love books. At first, seeing the classic works by writers such as the German novelist Thomas Mann and New England essayists Henry Thoreau and Ralph Waldo Emerson, she assumed that all authors were white. Only when she saw the picture of African American writer James Baldwin on the cover of a novel did she realize that blacks, too, could be writers. Even though she as yet had no idea of becoming a novelist herself, McMillan would come to consider this moment a turning point in her life.

At seventeen, McMillan decided that there was no future for her in Port Huron. Leaving her job as a keypunch operator, she headed for Los Angeles, where she found secretarial work and enrolled at Los Angeles City College. There, in a course on African American classics, she learned for the first time about the richness of her own heritage.

For a writer who was to be preoccupied with relationships, it was appropriate that McMillan's own first literary effort, a poem, was the result of an unhappy involvement with a man. Soon, she said, words began "turning into sentences." She decided to major in journalism at the University of California at Berkeley, and she also began writing fiction. In 1976, thanks to the novelist Ishmael Reed, she saw her first short story in print.

It was to be eight years, however, before McMillan's writing career would begin in earnest. First, she had to defeat her alcoholism and her drug habit, which had already begun to dominate her existence. After graduating from Berkeley in 1979, McMillan moved to New York City and enrolled in a master's program at Columbia University, then dropped out of graduate school and started working as a word processor with a law firm. In her free time, instead of writing, McMillan drank and took drugs with her boyfriend, Leonard Welch. Finally, on the eve of her thirtieth birthday, McMillan decided to change the direction of her life. She gave up cocaine and a few months later joined Alcoholics Anonymous and stopped drinking. In 1984, she had a son, Solomon. Several months later, seeing in her life the same pattern of abuse that she had observed in her own parents, McMillan broke off with Welch, resolving to make a new start for her baby and herself.

At the urging of friends in the Harlem Writers' Guild, McMillan had turned one of her short stories into a novel, *Mama*. After it was accepted by Houghton Mifflin for publication in 1987, the author realized that her publisher intended to promote it only minimally. With characteristic determination, McMillan sent three thousand letters to universities, colleges, book chains, and independent booksellers, set up her own promotional tour, and managed to get the first printing of her book sold before it was even published. Her success at this venture amazed Houghton Mifflin and made McMillan a legend in the publishing world.

In 1987, McMillan took a teaching position at the University of Wyoming in Laramie and began work on her second novel, *Disappearing Acts* (1989). Praised by critics, the book became a best seller and was optioned for film production. McMillan followed it with a collection, *Breaking Ice: An Anthology of Contemporary African-American Fiction* (1990), composed of fifty-seven selections by both established and relatively unknown black writers.

In August, 1990, a multimillion-dollar lawsuit was filed against McMillan and her publishers by Leonard Welch, who alleged that the character of Franklin Swift in *Disappearing Acts* was actually an unflattering picture of him. The case, however, was decided in McMillan's favor.

In 1990, McMillan had accepted a teaching position at the University of Arizona in Tucson, but in the fall of 1991, taking leave from the university, she moved to Danville, California. Her 1992 novel *Waiting to Exhale* was both a critical and popular success. The paperback rights alone brought the sum of $2.64 million, and Twentieth Century-Fox bought the film rights to the book. In the wake of her enormous success, however, McMillan commented that the amount of money she made would never be more important to her than being happy about her work and her life.

McMillan's next novel was to be entitled *A Day Late and a Dollar Short*. However, she had modeled the heroine of the story on her mother, and when Madeline McMillan died suddenly in 1993 after a severe asthma attack, the author had to put her work aside; it would not be published until 2001. The following year, McMillan's best friend, the novelist Doris Jean Austin, died of liver cancer. Too stricken to go on with her writing, McMillan decided to take an extended vacation. On the beach in Negril, Jamaica, she met Jonathan Plummer, a resort worker some twenty years her junior. Four months later, he followed her to the United States, moved into her mansion in Danville, California, and began attending college. He later became a pet groomer. Meanwhile, McMillan wrote their romantic story in the semiautobiographical book *How Stella Got Her Groove Back* (1996), which she dedicated to Plummer. On September 5, 1998, McMillan and Plummer were married on the beach in Hawaii. In January, 2005, however, McMillan filed for divorce, charging that Plummer had concealed his homosexuality from her until he knew that he would be approved for U.S. citizenship.

ANALYSIS

It has distressed some African American activists that McMillan does not focus on racism or social inequities. Although she sometimes touches on such matters, for example, having the heroine of *How Stella Got Her Groove Back* deplore the poverty that she sees in Jamaica, McMillan's primary emphasis is on personal fulfillment, particularly for black women. Mildred Peacock in *Mama* and Viola Price in *A Day Late and a Dollar Short* grew up at a time when African American women did not have the opportunities their daughters and granddaughters enjoy. As a result, they were trapped in poverty and abused by worthless men. Many of the black women of McMillan's generation are well-educated, upwardly mobile, bright women like the author herself, and therefore they have many more options. However, they too throw themselves away on men who do not deserve them, take refuge in addiction to drugs or alcohol, or simply resign themselves to loneliness. As McMillan herself moved into middle age, she began writing about the problems that women face in a society that puts a premium on youth. In focusing on personal matters rather than on ideology, McMillan has led the way for black women writers to produce realistic works based on their own experiences and observations, works that reflect the radically different world in which they live.

McMillan's defense against complaints about her use of profanity is, again, her insistence on realism. Her characters, she says, speak as they would in real life, and the fact that so many of her fans compare reading a McMillan novel to talking with their girlfriends supports the author's argument. By seeming simply to report her characters' thoughts and conversations, McMillan achieves an effect of immediacy that would be lost if she wrote in chaste, formal prose.

The most vehement criticisms of McMillan, however, concern her attitude toward African American men. A major theme in McMillan's novels is the difficulty that black women have in finding partners who are worthy of them. In contrast to her strong, responsible, independent women, McMillan's black male characters are weak and unreliable. They tend to define manliness in primitive terms of their power to subdue women or to seduce them.

Many of McMillan's men are like Crook Peacock in *Mama*, who makes a habit of getting drunk, breaking whatever fragile objects his wife treasures, and then giving her a thorough beating, which can be halted only by her agreeing to sexual intercourse. Even those male characters who do not descend to physical violence are only too willing to exploit the women who love them. In *Waiting to Exhale*, for example, a man in whom one of McMillan's heroines has invested three thousand dollars is repeatedly unfaithful to her, while the wealthy husband of another not only deserts his wife but also tries to escape with all of their property, heartlessly leaving her and their children in desperate financial straits.

Many of McMillan's male characters truly believe that they are worth supporting merely for their sexual skills. Even the relatively sympathetic Franklin Swift, who eventually reforms, seems through most of *Disappearing Acts* to be much better at talking about improving his lot in life than at doing anything about it. Admittedly, in the segments of the book that are written from Franklin's point of view rather than through the eyes of his long-suffering lover Zora Banks, McMillan makes it clear that not all of Franklin's problems are his own fault. It is difficult for an uneducated black man to get a job, and even when, through the quota systems, Franklin manages to do so, he is before long laid off, sold out by his own representative. Franklin cannot be accused of not trying; his flaw is that he gives up too easily. It is obvious that most of his problems could be solved if he took the trouble to get an education. Unlike the determined Zora, however, Franklin is too weak-willed to do so. It is easier to get drunk and let Zora worry about the bills.

Because the women in her novels are so much more impressive than the men, most of whom impress one as being essentially childish, McMillan is often accused of blatant "male-bashing." Again, her answer is that she is writing about things as they are, not as they ought to be. While her women characters do make some scathing comments about the men in their lives, McMillan does not believe that men cannot change; indeed, as a satirist, she is committed to point out their shortcomings in hope that at least some of them will improve. If it is a generational matter, then the answer might be found in *How Stella Got Her Groove Back*. The handsome young Jamaican in the story is sensitive, considerate, and ambitious. Moreover, as an open-minded, modern man, he has no trouble falling in love with a woman who is twenty years older. Ironically, the young man McMillan herself found in Jamaica, who later became her husband, proved to be a bitter disappointment. Her later books suggest that a woman may be better off settling for the love of children and the friendship of other women than in giving her heart to a man who, one way or another, is almost certain to break it.

MAMA

First published: 1987
Type of work: Novel

Despite personal disappointments and desperate poverty, a strong black woman gives her children a chance for a better future.

Mama, McMillan's first novel, is the story of an uneducated black woman living in the 1960's who possesses the strength to survive and the will to hope. Mildred Peacock, the protagonist of the story, is no saint. She swears, she drinks constantly, and whenever she has a good opportunity, she lets a good-looking man have sex with her. Her capacity for violence is established in the much-quoted first sentence of the book, "Mildred hid the ax beneath the mattress of the cot in the dining room."

As Mildred recalls the night she has just been through, it is clear that she might almost be justified in killing the man who has been her husband for the last ten years. Once again, her drunken husband has battered her, while the five children he professes to love cowered, terrified, waiting for the sounds of fighting to change to the sound of sexual intercourse. Because it is she who provides the financial and emotional support for the family, and her unfaithful husband comes home only to beat her, have sex, and father more children, Mildred finally decides that Crook is not worth keeping. She is going to get a divorce.

The rest of the novel shows how Mildred accomplishes the goal she has set for herself: to raise her children so that they will have a better life than hers. It is not an easy task. She has to deal with heartless employers, persistent rent collectors, and suspicious welfare workers as well as with her own weaknesses, particularly her needs for sex and alcohol. At one point, when her nerve pills are not enough, she has a nervous breakdown. However, she pulls herself together and rejoins the battle. At the end of the book, she sees all of her daughters settled, and she even has hopes for her prodigal son, who has sworn to stay away from the drugs that have caused him to land in prison.

In telling Mildred's story, McMillan alternates between two points of view, that of Mildred herself and that of her oldest daughter, Freda Peacock. Even though the two characters are often separated in the second half of the novel, each is always a part of the other's consciousness. Moreover, because mother and daughter share the same

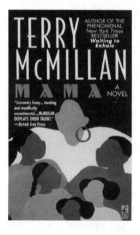

strengths, notably intelligence, determination, and an amazing capacity for hope, as well as the same weaknesses, including a susceptibility to addiction and a real talent for deluding themselves about men, the two lives often seem like one. Although it seems straightforward and simple, in fact *Mama* is intricately patterned and carefully choreographed, with the two main characters advancing and retreating until, at the end of the novel, they join in a touching expression of their love for each other.

DISAPPEARING ACTS

First published: 1989
Type of work: Novel

Two urban lovers with little in common except their feelings for each other move toward real commitment.

Disappearing Acts has been called an urban romance. It is, in essence, simply another New York City love story, as funny as the best works of Neil Simon. Underneath the wisecracks, the idiotic behavior, and the foolish misunderstandings that qualify McMillan's novel as a romantic comedy there is a serious exploration of the nature of human relationships.

It is never easy for one person to love another; when two people differ as much as the lovers in *Disappearing Acts*, it is particularly difficult. Zora Banks is an educated, ambitious black woman, a gifted singer and songwriter who is supporting herself temporarily by teaching music in a junior high school. Franklin Swift is a construction worker with a high school equivalency diploma who for years has been thinking about going to night school and starting his own business. He has as yet done nothing about it. As Zora soon finds out, however, there is more to Franklin than his striking good looks and his talent for lovemaking. He is responsible; he does his best to support the wife from whom he is not yet divorced and the two children he had with her. He is generous; early in their relationship, he surprises Zora with three hundred dollars so that she can get her piano out of layaway. He is intelligent; even though he never finished high school, he can beat Zora at every word game they play. Moreover, in his attitude toward woodworking, Franklin exhibits the same kind of artistic integrity that he so admires in Zora.

Nevertheless, there are problems that the lovers prefer not to face. Franklin is easily discouraged and too easily sinks into apathy. Furthermore, the two are not honest with each other. When he loses his job, Franklin lies to Zora. In turn, she does not warn him about her epilepsy; he learns about it only when she has a seizure. Even more important, when she becomes pregnant with Franklin's child, Zora has an abortion without even consulting him.

Ironically, it is after Zora decides to go through with another pregnancy that the relationship reaches a crisis. Still haunted by the rejection of his own mother, Franklin sees his new son as a rival for Zora's love. Soon he is threatening Zora, and after she makes him move out, he comes back and breaks up their apartment, then gets drunk and takes cocaine. Yet when he has reached rock bottom, it is his love for Zora that motivates Franklin to change. After months of struggle, he returns, bringing Zora as a gift no less than his own life, which he has finally begun to set in order.

Disappearing Acts is written as a series of monologues, some of them voiced by Zora and some by Franklin. The characters are so distinct that after the first two sections, McMillan does not even bother to head her chapters with the name of the speaker. Interestingly, she felt so strongly about this dual point of view that she changed publishers rather than change the structure of her book. When her editors pressured her to tell the entire story through Franklin's eyes, McMillan switched to another publisher. Obviously, she felt that both viewpoints were essential to her story. From the enthusiasm with which critics and readers have received *Disappearing Acts*, it is clear that McMillan's decision was the right one.

WAITING TO EXHALE

First published: 1992
Type of work: Novel

Four women friends support one another by sharing their uncertainties, their disappointments, their successes, and their dreams.

In several ways, *Waiting to Exhale* is quite different from McMillan's two earlier novels. Instead of two protagonists, there are four. Moreover, each of the twenty-eight chapters in *Waiting to Exhale* has its own provocative title, for example, "Venus in Virgo" and "Interstate Lust." Each also has the kind of beginning, middle, and end that one ordinarily finds in a short story. The novel proceeds from episode to episode, unified by the interaction among McMillan's four heroines, all of whom are success-ful women in their thirties living in Phoenix, Arizona, who are having trouble finding the right man.

Giving up on finding a man in Denver, Savannah Jackson quits her public-relations job and, with her cat and her art collection, moves to Phoenix, where she hopes to have better luck. From the beginning, however, the cards seem to be stacked against her. The good-looking man who agrees to drive her to Phoenix turns out to be a phony and a drug addict; the doctor out of her past who reappears in her life keeps stalling about the divorce he is supposedly considering; and the romantic San Franciscan she meets at a convention never returns her calls.

Meanwhile, Savannah's best friend, Bernadine Harris, has lost her husband of eleven years to a younger white woman. Although their marriage had long been dead, Bernadine had not expected to see the end of her comfortable lifestyle. She finds, however, that for months her husband has been transferring and concealing his assets so as to reduce the divorce settlement. Nothing makes Bernadine feel much better, not setting fire to her husband's BMW, not selling his restored antique car for a dollar, not even slapping his mistress. With the aid of her friends and the help of a determined lawyer, however, she finally gets a good settlement and even finds a fine man who wants to marry her.

Of all the friends, Robin Stokes is the one who seems most responsible for her own disasters. Good-hearted and generous, she is besotted with a man whose chief talent seems to be as a lover. Even though there is no possibility that this philanderer and parasite will settle down as a husband and father, she keeps taking him back. At the end of the novel, pregnant, Robin finally breaks off with him and decides instead to build her life around her baby.

For seventeen years, the fourth protagonist, Gloria Matthew, has done just what Robin plans to do. Ever since his birth, her son, Tarik, has been the center of her life. Whenever she feels lonely and empty, Gloria has made a habit of just eating a little more or working a little harder at the Oasis, the beauty shop that she owns. Ironically, not until she has nearly died from a heart attack, the direct result of poor diet and years of stress, does Gloria realize that, in fact, she is surrounded by people who love her: her three devoted women friends as well as her son, who is showing all the signs of fulfilling her hopes and expectations.

As far as the quest for worthy men is concerned, *Waiting to Exhale* must be said to end with probabilities, not with certainties. Yet there is one thing the protagonists can be sure of: From their friendship, they can draw the strength to face whatever life holds for them.

HOW STELLA GOT HER GROOVE BACK

First published: 1996
Type of work: Novel

On a vacation in Jamaica, the heroine meets a man half her age, falls in love with him, and finds that a holiday romance can evolve into lasting happiness.

In style, structure, and content, *How Stella Got Her Groove Back* is very different from any of Terry McMillan's other novels. This work is purely and simply a love story, and, as such, it is limited in scope. In fact, its primary focus is not on both lovers but on just one of them, the title character. Stella Payne is the first-person narrator, telling her story in a breathless, stream-of-consciousness narrative that does not have

either the complex structure or the more calculated style of McMillan's other books.

Stella is a forty-two-year-old woman who divorced her husband not because of any moral deficiencies on his part but because, over the years, their relationship had turned flat. In short, though she had once loved him, she now finds him boring. Without him, she still has a full life. She has a lucrative position as a security analyst, a luxurious home in Northern California, a BMW, a fat investment portfolio, a personal trainer, and the figure of a much younger

woman. She also has a sensible, eleven-year-old son, Quincy, who is both her greatest joy and her best friend.

With Quincy gone to visit his father, Stella decides to spend her vacation in Jamaica. Her sister Angela cannot believe that Stella would go anywhere alone, but Angela needs a man to tell her what to do; fortunately, she has a lawyer husband who is only too happy to perform that function. Stella's other sister, Vanessa, is all for the idea. She urges Stella to sleep with every man she can—but then, that is what the ebullient and irresponsible Vanessa would do.

With suitcases filled with new beach clothes, Stella takes off for Jamaica. On the beach near her hotel she meets Winston Shakespeare, a charming young man not quite twenty-one. Though the two are immediately attracted to each other, Stella tries to persuade herself that their relationship is merely a friendship. However, the first time they make love, she forgets the age difference, which in fact has never troubled Winston. Their passionate interludes are interrupted by Winston's leaving to take a job as a chef-trainee. At that point, Stella realizes that, at least for her, this may be more than just a fling. She is exhibiting all the symptoms of being desperately in love. However, she tries to resign herself to living without him.

Back in California, Stella finds that she has been fired. Since she is financially secure, she realizes that now she has the freedom to take her life in a different direction. She decides to return to Jamaica, this time taking along her son and her niece Chantel. Both young people throughly approve of Winston. Back in California, Stella throws caution to the winds and sends an airline ticket to Winston so that he can visit her on her own turf. The book ends with Stella's gleefully accepting Winston's proposal of marriage.

How Stella Got Her Groove Back has some of the same themes as McMillan's earlier books. Like *Mama*, it stresses the importance of family; Stella feels far more secure about marrying Winston after he obtains the approval of Quincy, Chantel, Vanessa, and even Angela. Like *Waiting to Exhale*, it points out the need for female friends; after Winston leaves for his job, Stella spends time with two other female vacationers and finds solace in their conversations. However, except for the language, the book might be classified as a romance, for it ends with the unrealistic assumption that the lovers will live happily ever after.

A Day Late and a Dollar Short

First published: 2001
Type of work: Novel

An aging matriarch spends her final weeks trying to transmit her wisdom to her flawed children and grandchildren.

With *A Day Late and a Dollar Short*, Terry McMillan returned to a familiar format. Like *Mama*, the new novel is the story of a large African American family dominated by a matriarch. In fact, Viola Price's extended family has so many members that, without the sketch of the family tree inside the cover of the hardback version of the book, it would be difficult for readers to follow the action. The novel is also confusing because there are six first-person narrators: Viola Price, her four children, and their father, Viola's former husband, Cecil. However, this approach has the advantage of making the characters more vivid and also more sympathetic. Despite their flaws, they all mean well. Moreover, for all their squabbling, they do have feelings for one another. Unfortunately, none of the children will face the truth about themselves and their lives, and Viola knows that, until they do, they will never fulfill the potential that she sees in all of them.

The most successful of Viola's children is her oldest daughter, Paris. It is Paris who frees her mother from financial worries, putting her into a new condominium and buying her the car that she desperately needs. However, Viola knows that Paris is desperately lonely. Moreover, she has taken to downing pills whenever she needs an additional spurt of energy. Viola's middle daughter, Charlotte, is also well off, but ever since she was a child, she has run on anger. She is too stingy to help her mother or anyone else in the family—but then, she has always yearned for proof that Viola loves her as much as she does Paris. Janelle, the youngest child, is too busy searching for herself to notice that her twelve-year-old daughter is being molested by her stepfather. Viola's only son, Lewis, is intelligent but hot-tempered and addicted to alcohol. As for Cecil, though Viola does not want him back, she does not like to see him victimized by his young girlfriend, who expects him to provide for her children and even for an unborn child that is almost certainly not his.

If *A Day Late and a Dollar Short* is about individual failures and family quarrels, it is also about courage. Whatever their shortcomings, every one of Viola's children and grandchildren has inherited some of her strength. They may experience rape, incest, addiction, illness, unwanted pregnancy, imprisonment, or heart-wrenching betrayal, but they pick themselves up and move on. What frustrates Viola is that, though they may survive, they all continue to evade the truth.

Then the unthinkable happens: Viola has one more attack of asthma, and this time she does not recover. Although inevitably Viola's death brings the family members together in one place, they still have not become the strong unit that she had always wanted them to be. Then Cecil reads the letter she had left for him, and the four children take turns reading each other's letters aloud. After the tears and laughter that follow, they begin making plans for their next reunion. From beyond the grave, Viola has taught them what they would not recognize as long as she was alive, that nothing is more important than family.

Summary

In a relatively short time, McMillan has established herself as a spokeswoman for a new generation. Although her major characters are black, McMillan's stories of bright, spunky, ambitious women who have everything they ever wanted—except the love of a good man—have evoked a warm response from women of all races.

McMillan justifies her use of profanity and her often unflattering portraits of men, as well as her inattention to racial and social issues, by insisting that she describes life as she sees it. However, though she is a realist, McMillan is not a pessimist. While her women are often disappointed in the men they love, they do find pleasure in their children, acceptance in their friendships with one another, and strength in family ties.

Rosemary M. Canfield Reisman

BIBLIOGRAPHY

By the Author

LONG FICTION:
Mama, 1987
Disappearing Acts, 1989
Waiting to Exhale, 1992
How Stella Got Her Groove Back, 1996
A Day Late and a Dollar Short, 2001
The Interruption of Everything, 2005

NONFICTION:
The Writer as Publicist, 1993 (with Marcia Biederman and Gary Aspenberg)

SCREENPLAYS:
Waiting to Exhale, 1995 (adaptation of her novel; with Ronald Bass)
How Stella Got Her Groove Back, 1998 (adaptation of her novel; with Bass)

EDITED TEXT:
Breaking Ice: An Anthology of Contemporary African-American Fiction, 1990

DISCUSSION TOPICS

- Why are some of the older women in Terry McMillan's novels described as matriarchs?

- What does McMillan suggest are the major flaws of black men? Which male characters in her fiction have the characteristics that make or would make them good husbands?

- How does sibling rivalry function in McMillan's novels?

- McMillan is often praised for her use of humor. How do her characters use humor to deal with their disappointments?

- How does McMillan show friendship between women as a liberating force in their lives?

- Why do you think McMillan's works are so popular with women readers? With African American women?

About the Author

Dandridge, Rita B. "Debunking the Beauty Myth in Terry McMillan's *Waiting to Exhale*." In *Language, Rhythm, and Sound: Black Popular Cultures into the Twenty-first Century*, edited by Joseph K. Adjaye and Adrienne R. Andrews. Pittsburgh: University of Pittsburgh Press, 1997.

_____. "Debunking the Motherhood Myth in Terry McMillan's *Mama*." *CLA Journal* 41, no. 4 (1998): 405-416.

Ellerby, Janet Mason. "Deposing the Man of the House: Terry McMillan Rewrites the Family." *MELUS* 22, no. 2 (June 1, 1997): 105-117.

Nunez, Elizabeth, and Brenda M. Greene. *Defining Ourselves: Black Writers in the 90's*. New York: P. Lang, 1999.

Patrick, Diane. *Terry McMillan: The Unauthorized Biography*. New York: St. Martin's Press, 1999.

Richards, Paulette. *Terry McMillan: A Critical Companion*. Westport, Conn.: Greenwood Press, 1999.

LARRY MCMURTRY

Born: Wichita Falls, Texas
June 3, 1936

McMurtry's novels examine the human consequences when the myth of the Old West, a central component in the American national mythology, loses force and can no longer shape people's lives.

BIOGRAPHY

Larry Jeff McMurtry was born on June 3, 1936, at Wichita Falls, Texas, twenty miles from his parents' home in Archer City, Texas (the Thalia of his books). McMurtry's grandparents had moved into Archer County in the 1880's and established their ranch along a cattle trail in north central Texas. The nine McMurtry boys (Larry's uncles and father, William Jefferson McMurtry) moved westward to work on the huge ranches in the Texas panhandle.

At family reunions, McMurtry heard his elders talk about the golden age of their youth and about such great ranchers and cowboys as Charles Goodnight, Teddy Blue, and Larry's own Uncle Johnny. His hard old uncles, withered and crippled by their long years of cowboying, had been present at the birth of the Western myth, and they lived long enough to see it die. The elder McMurtrys knew, as did Larry, that the new generation could not replace the old. He wrote:

> All of them lived to see the ideals of the faith degenerate, the rituals fall from use; the principal myth become corrupt. In my youth, when they were old men, I often heard them yearn aloud for the days when the rituals had all their power, when they themselves had enacted the pure, the original myth, and I know that they found it bitter to leave the land to which they were always faithful to the strange and godless heirs that they had bred.

McMurtry's books can be read as a parting wave to Old Man Goodnight, Teddy Blue, and Uncle Johnny.

Larry McMurtry and his family moved from the home ranch into the small town of Archer City. He was an honors student in high school and was active in many school activities, but the bitter love affair with the ranching country of his uncles found its companion in his own disillusionment with the small town. Small Texas towns, too, were dying, he later wrote, losing their bold and energetic people to the cities. McMurtry soon joined the migration to urban America. He graduated from North Texas State University in 1958 and received a master's degree from Rice University in Houston in 1960. Houston, San Francisco, and Washington, D.C., would be his principal places of residence in the future, until the late 1980's when he moved back to Archer City.

While he was at North Texas State, McMurtry began to write, finishing the first draft of *Horseman, Pass By* in 1958. He taught at various colleges for brief periods and worked as a "scout," locating rare books. In 1964, he moved to the Washington, D.C., area, where he opened a bookstore and continued scouting, traveling an average of about a hundred days a year.

Readers can see a pattern to McMurtry's books that matches the flow of his life. His first three books dealt with the small town of Thalia and the surrounding ranch country: *Horseman, Pass By* (1961), *Leaving Cheyenne* (1963), and *The Last Picture Show* (1966). He returned to Thalia in later books: *Texasville* (1987) and *Duane's Depressed* (1999). He wrote an urban or Houston series:

Moving On (1970), *All My Friends Are Going to Be Strangers* (1972), *Terms of Endearment* (1975), and *The Evening Star* (1992). Other books grouped themselves around displaced people who lived in a variety of settings: *Somebody's Darling* (1978), *Cadillac Jack* (1982), and *The Desert Rose* (1983), with its sequel, *The Late Child* (1995).

In later years, McMurtry returned to the ranch country in *Lonesome Dove* (1985), *Anything for Billy* (1988), *Some Can Whistle* (1989), and *Boone's Lick* (2000). He rounded out the story of *Lonesome Dove*'s Gus McCrae and Woodrow Call in *Streets of Laredo* (1993), *Dead Man's Walk* (1995), and *Comanche Moon* (1997). Several books of essays explain the themes of his fiction: *In a Narrow Grave: Essays on Texas* (1968); *Film Flam: Essays on Hollywood* (1987); and *Walter Benjamin at the Dairy Queen: Reflections at Sixty and Beyond* (1999). He published several nonfiction works: *It's Always We Rambled: An Essay on Rodeo* (1974); *Crazy Horse* (1999); *Sacagawea's Nickname: Essays on the American West* (2001); and *The Colonel and Little Missie: Buffalo Bill, Annie Oakley, and the Beginnings of Superstardom in America* (2005). He wrote books on his travels, *Roads: Driving America's Great Highways* (2000) and *Paradise* (2001). He published the novels *Buffalo Girls* in 1990; *Pretty Boy Floyd*, with Diana Ossana, in 1994; *Zeke and Ned*, also with Ossana, in 1997; and *Loop Group* in 2004. With all that, he had time to complete another series of books set in the Old West: *Sin Killer* (2002), *The Wandering Hill* (2003), *By Sorrow's River* (2003), and *Folly and Glory* (2004).

McMurtry did not struggle in obscurity. Several of his books were made into Academy Award-winning films: *Horseman, Pass By*, made into the 1963 film *Hud*; *The Last Picture Show* in 1971; and *Terms of Endearment* in 1983. He himself won an Academy Award for the screenplay to *Brokeback Mountain* (2005), written with Ossana and adapted from a story by Annie Proulx. *Lonesome Dove* brought McMurtry a Pulitzer Prize and was made into an outstanding television miniseries. His books have routinely become best sellers.

ANALYSIS

As a Texan who writes about Texas, McMurtry focuses on the Western myth of the cowboy and rancher, the cattle drives and the open plains. This myth shapes the self-conception of Texans and other westerners, and through films, books, and television it has also helped form the national self-image. When Larry's Uncle Johnny was five years old, he sat atop the McMurtry barn and watched cattle drives pass below. During his lifetime, the railroad made drives obsolete, as other machinery would largely replace the cowboy.

Years later, his young nephew Larry would explore in his fiction the meaning of the ending of the Old West, which continued to produce such powerful images in American culture. Larry McMurtry quickly found a national audience for his work, because all regions of the United States had at some time undergone a similar passage from frontier to town to city.

McMurtry closely analyzes the Western myth and its human products. The virtues of his rancher-uncles were great. They were independent men who had a deep sense of honor, justice, and respect for the land. Yet they were also intolerant, inflexible, and deeply contemptuous of anyone who did not conform to their values. They disdained such institutions of civilization as churches, schools, farms, and towns. Schools were jails, Larry's Uncle Jeff told him, and life was too short and sweet to lock oneself in jail. These men ridiculed any way of life or values but their own. Yet their way of life was dying, and their values were irrelevant to the more complex urban environment; the Old West did not give its people a usable past when they were forced into a new way of life. McMurtry, both victim and interpreter of this void, writes neither simple nostalgic elegies nor debunking exposés of his homeland; he writes instead of his bittersweet love affair with a homeland in which he found it difficult to live and from which he cannot easily depart.

Recurrent themes mark McMurtry's diverse body of work. Most of his characters have capacities that do not fit their circumstances. The mean-spirited and violent Hud in *Horseman, Pass By* lived in an age (the 1950's) that could not make use of his capacities; in an earlier age, his abilities might have made him a Charles Goodnight. In McMurtry's books, old ranch-country patriarchs struggle to maintain their dignity after their day has passed; strong women cope with weak, purposeless men who cannot find a meaningful role in modern society; young boys, growing up with tales of the old days, see no clear path to the future.

In McMurtry books, one often finds a theme of initiation, as young people pass from childhood into maturity, often introduced into adulthood through sex and death. Loneliness also is central to the life of McMurtry characters, whether they live on a ranch, go with their comrades on cattle drives, or live in towns or cities or on campuses. Marriage does not help end loneliness; failing or empty marriages litter McMurtry's books.

Women especially find themselves in situations that do not fit their capacities. The frontier or the small town offers them few opportunities outside their home, and their homes are filled with insensitive males living without purpose. When the patriarchy of the frontier collapsed, it was not replaced by a new social order based on healthy gender relations. McMurtry's strong women have more patience, wisdom, and optimism than men, but they are not socially oriented or educated enough to become feminists; they are earth-mother types.

HORSEMAN, PASS BY

First published: 1961
Type of work: Novel

Old rancher Homer Bannon and his stepson, Hud, are locked in conflict between frontier ranching values and Hud's materialistic values of oil-rich Texas.

Homer Bannon, the old cattleman in *Horseman, Pass By*, owns a ranch a few miles south of Thalia, Texas. In his eighties, he has spent his life building a cattle herd of exceptional quality. He is a prosperous rancher, whose joy comes in riding over his land among his cattle. Most of his affection goes to his land, not to his nagging second wife, Jewel, or to her son, Scott "Hud" Bannon. He loves his seventeen-year-old grandson, Lonnie, and tries to pass on to him his feeling for the land and for the traditions of the cowboy past.

Hud Bannon is the best and most reckless cowboy in Texas when he wants to be, Lonnie says, but the thirty-five-year-old Hud spends more time boozing and chasing wild women than working cattle. Hud values the land only for the money it can produce: He wants oil wells on the land, not cattle. Homer's resistance to having holes punched in the land by oil rigs seems to Hud to be mere senility.

Seventeen-year-old Lonnie is narrator of the story. He loves and respects his grandfather, but Homer's stories of the old ranching days can no longer satisfy the lonely and restless boy. At night, after everyone has gone to bed, Lonnie often climbs to the top of the windmill and sits, looking off at the lights of Thalia and Wichita Falls. The future confuses Lonnie. Neither Homer's traditional values nor Hud's materialism seems adequate. Even in love there is confusion. Halmea, the black cook, a strong, wise woman, understands Lonnie's loneliness and his sexual needs, but there is very little that an older, black woman, half sexual object and half mother-surrogate, can do for a young white boy living in Texas in 1954.

The action of the novel starts when one of Homer's cows dies. The state veterinarian tests the herd and finds it infected with the dreaded hoof-and-mouth disease. Homer's entire prize herd will have to be quarantined, then killed and buried. Before the results of the tests come back, a key conflict occurs. Hud wants to sell the herd before it is quarantined. Homer refuses to pass his problem along to some unsuspecting rancher. To Hud, Homer's moral uprightness is a sign of senility. Another defining conflict comes when the state veterinarian gives Homer the bad news and tries to ease the blow by telling him that he can sell some oil leases while he is waiting to rebuild his herd. Homer says:

> If there's oil down there these boys can get it sucked up after I'm under there with it. . . . I don't like it an' I don't aim to have it. I guess I'm a queer, contrary old bastard, but there'll be no holes punched in this land while I'm here. . . . What good's oil to me. . . . What can I do with . . . [oil wells]? I can't ride out ever day an' prowl amongst 'em, like I can my cattle. . . . I can't feel a smidgen a pride in 'em, cause they ain't none a my doin.

Homer's attitude toward oil confirms Hud's view that the old man is disintegrating, and Hud plots to take the ranch away.

With the herd slaughtered and buried in huge pits, Homer is physically and mentally exhausted. Hud explodes in frustration, raping Halmea, while Lonnie, beaten, watches. The climax comes when Homer falls and hurts himself. Hud and Lonnie find him writhing in pain. Lonnie goes for help. When he returns, he finds that Hud has shot and killed Homer. Did he shoot Homer to take the ranch or did he, in a flicker of love that he had once felt for the old man, kill him to stop his suffering? Lonnie does not know.

At the funeral, Lonnie feels reconciled to Homer's death, knowing that his grandfather is going back into the land he loved. He leaves the ranch, knowing that neither Homer nor Hud has left him a usable past. Perhaps he will become a wanderer, like so many of McMurtry's displaced characters.

THE LAST PICTURE SHOW

First published: 1966
Type of work: Novel

Young people confront conformity and purposeless life in a small Texas town.

Late at night, Lonnie Bannon of *Horseman, Pass By* would sit on top of his windmill and gaze off at the lights of Thalia, the small town that McMurtry describes in his third book, *The Last Picture Show.* There are more people in Thalia than on Lonnie's ranch, but they are equally lonely. People in Thalia in the early 1950's are caught between the dying countryside and the frightening pull of such booming cities as Dallas and Houston. Many people in Thalia had moved in from surrounding ranches (as the McMurtrys had moved to Archer City). Feeling under siege by the strange ways of the steadily encroaching urban United States, they impose their old ways on the town and try to crush any signs of nonconformity.

The story focuses on Sonny Crawford and his friend Duane Moore. It opens as the boys finish their last high school football game and continues over the following year as they search for a new path for themselves. Sam the Lion, once a rancher, now owns the town's movie theater, pool hall, and café. He acts as a father-surrogate for Sonny and Duane, and for other boys in need, including Billy, the mentally retarded boy that Sam took in and reared. Billy sweeps out Sam's businesses. If someone does not stop him, he sweeps to the edge of town and on into the empty countryside, as mindlessly occupied as the rest of the townspeople are as they go about their lives.

Duane dates the town beauty, Jacy Farrow, the daughter of oil-rich Lois and Gene Farrow. Jacy is a narcissistic, selfish young woman whose sense of self depends on the admiration and envy of others. She dates Duane only because he is a handsome high school athlete.

The story focuses mainly on Sonny, an innocent young man much like Lonnie Bannon. During this year, Sonny is initiated into manhood through a sexual relationship with Ruth Popper and through the death of Sam the Lion. Ruth Popper is an attractive woman who has had nearly all the life drained from her when she and Sonny begin an affair. She is the wife of football coach Herman Popper. Herman values a good shotgun more than he does a woman; Ruth tells Sonny, "The reason I'm so crazy is because nobody cares anything about me." Her affair with Sonny makes her see that she is not crazy and that she is an attractive woman.

Lois Farrow, Jacy's mother, is another strong woman who defies the mores of Thalia. The beautiful, rich Lois realizes a hard truth that many oil-rich 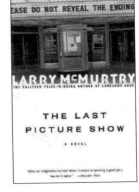 Texans confront: Having money does not fill life's emptiness. She fights off crushing boredom by drinking, having sex, and spending money. She also enjoys frightening men who cannot cope with assertive women. Both Ruth and Lois are examples of McMurtry characters whose capacities do not fit their situations.

Sonny matures enough to refuse to join the boys in their sexual escapades with heifers but not so much that the future becomes clearer to him. Nor does he mature enough to resist Jacy when she seduces him away from Ruth Popper. Duane, who had been away working in the oil fields, returns, fights with Sonny, and blinds him in one eye. Duane leaves for the Army. Jacy elopes with Sonny in order to be the center of attention. She knows that the Farrows will annul the marriage, which they do, and send her off to college before she wrecks the town.

The outside world intrudes into Thalia in various ways. It pulls Duane and Jacy away. Television provides too much competition for the picture show, and it closes. The closing of the movie theater is yet another disappointment for Sonny, following his loss of Sam the Lion, Jacy, Duane, and Ruth Popper. His final loss comes when Billy, blindly sweeping the street, is hit by a truck and killed. Later that day, Sonny tries to leave Thalia. He goes to the city limits and looks at the empty countryside: "He himself felt too empty. As empty as he felt and as empty as the country looked it was too risky going out into it." He looks back at Thalia: "From the road the town looked raw, scraped by the wind, as empty as the country. It didn't look like the town it had been when he was in high school, in the days of Sam the Lion." Sonny has matured, but not enough either to leave Thalia or to make a new, viable life in it. He returns to Ruth Popper; she takes him back, knowing he will not stay.

ALL MY FRIENDS ARE GOING TO BE STRANGERS

First published: 1972
Type of work: Novel

Young author Danny Deck comes to understand that he must choose between writing about life and living life as a good person and friend.

McMurtry has said that Danny Deck, his protagonist in his fourth novel, *All My Friends Are Going to Be Strangers*, is close to him in his sensibilities. In McMurtry's words: "It is true that the better you write the worse you live. The more of yourself you take out of real relationships and project into fantasy relationship the more the real relationships suffer."

In his fourth novel, McMurtry turns from the ranch country around Thalia and begins what has been called the Houston or urban trilogy. Danny Deck, a young student at Rice University, is from the ranching country around Archer City, Texas, but he has cast his lot with an urban way of life beyond the imagination of Homer Bannon or Sonny Crawford. As the novel opens, Danny meets tall, beautiful, remote Sally Bynum at a party in Austin and, immediately smitten, talks her into going back to Houston with him, where they marry. Sally, like

Jacy Farrow in *The Last Picture Show*, is self-centered; she is immune to both Danny's love and his anger. Within a month, Sally has walked out on him several times. In the midst of his perplexity, he receives a telegram from Random House telling him that it will publish his first novel, "The Restless Grass" (which in plot is similar to *Horseman, Pass By*). One dream is coming true, even as another may be taken away.

Danny's life is disjointed, because of both his sudden marriage and his publishing success. He turns to his best friends, Flap and Emma Horton. Emma's warm, bright kitchen provides him with a sense of order and normalcy, but she cannot keep Danny from feeling that he has been dislodged from his life in Houston and from his friends. Danny and Sally go to San Francisco, where his feelings of displacement grow. Sally, now pregnant, cuts him out of her life. He leaves, moving to a sleazy hotel, where he works on his second book.

Here his crisis deepens. More authors fill San Francisco than Danny knew even existed. He realizes that they cannot all be great and wonders whether he can be. If so, he wonders, at what cost? He meets Jill Peel, an intelligent and honest twenty-four-year-old artist who has won an Academy Award for her animated cartoons. She seems to love him but is sexually unresponsive, for reasons she will not explain. She is, she tells him, no longer a woman, only an artist. She has made for herself the decision that Danny is avoiding: to live for art rather than for friends or lovers.

Danny returns to Texas, where Sally has gone to have their baby. The trip begins a long, exhausting period of sleeplessness, alcohol, and drugs. Danny's life is out of control: "My life was no life. It was sort of a long confused drive."

If new ways of life in California have nothing for him, can he return to the ranch country of his ancestors? He visits his ninety-two-year-old Uncle Laredo, who, with his cook, Lorenzo, lives forty-seven miles off the paved road, deep in the harshest and most desolate country that Texas offers. Laredo owns a four-story, twenty-eight-room Victorian mansion, but he camps behind it and cooks out over an open fire. A hundred years earlier, Laredo would have been a legendary rancher; now he is a bitter parody of those men. He hates cattle and will not let them on his place; he raises goats, camels, and antelope. The half-crazed old man forces his ranch hands to occupy themselves by digging holes in the earth. In a parody of Homer Bannon and his love of the earth, Danny says about his uncle: "My own theory was that he dug the holes because he hated the earth and wanted to get in as many licks at it as he could, before he died." Danny leaves, not sure that he can get his life under control but convinced that Uncle Laredo's ranch "wasn't the Old West I liked to believe in—it was the bitter end of something. I knew I would never want to visit it again."

Increasingly out of control, Danny goes on to Austin and then to Houston, cutting ties with friends and acquaintances. He fights with Sally's family, ending any chance of having a relationship with his baby daughter. He has sex with Emma, betraying his friendship with Flap and undermining his friendship with her. "Emma and I couldn't talk. My life had gotten that awry. . . . A lot of hope had drained away."

He moves on, toward the Rio Grande Valley. He realizes that he is out of phase with his friends and that they all are going to be strangers. In return for that loss, he is an author—though probably not a great one. As the book ends, Danny, exhausted and distraught, is in the Rio Grande River, drowning the manuscript of his new novel.

TERMS OF ENDEARMENT

First published: 1975
Type of work: Novel

Aurora Greenway and Emma Horton, mother and daughter, buoyantly deal with the details of family life that make up the fabric of human existence.

Terms of Endearment finished the Houston trilogy on which Larry McMurtry had been working for a decade, although he later returned to finish the story of Aurora Greenway in *The Evening Star.* McMurtry had intended *Terms of Endearment* to be Emma Horton's book, but her mother, Aurora Greenway, took over. Once she had been invented as a character, it was difficult to keep Aurora under wraps. She is forty-nine years old and three years widowed; she is good-looking, plump, and self-centered. As the

story opens in Houston in 1967, Aurora is ticking off her standard list of complaints about her daughter: Emma is overweight (Aurora overlooks her own dietary sins), dresses poorly, and is married to a "drip."

Aurora is not really angry, Emma says: "Her mother hadn't really been on the attack; she had just been exercising her peculiar subtle genius for making everyone but herself seem vaguely in the wrong." Aurora goes to pieces—screaming and flailing the air with her hands and finally collapsing—when Emma tells her that she is pregnant with her first child. Aurora's blowup is not a result of concern for her daughter; it is a result of the fact that she is going to be a grandmother and is afraid that her suitors will drop her.

Aurora would have been an easy woman for readers to hate, but she turns into an attractive character as her irresistible, bubbling, and intelligent personality emerges. She is an "emphatic" woman—the kind that McMurtry's male characters are often drawn to and with whom they cannot cope. Her romantic life is confusing. She has various suitors begging her to marry them: a bank vice president, a retired general, a former opera star, and a wealthy playboy from Philadelphia. None can cope with her: "Only a saint could live with me," Aurora says, "and I can't live with a saint. Older men aren't up to me and younger men aren't interested." She cannot stand men who are frightened of her, and she cannot help frightening them. She wants domineering men but cannot stand to be dominated.

The only two people who can easily absorb Aurora's criticism are Emma and Rosie Dunlup. Emma sees life clearly. She understands and accepts her limitations and those of the people around her. Rosie has been Aurora's housekeeper for more than twenty years, every one marked by battle. The undaunted Rosie is the only one who can stand up to Aurora and return blow for verbal blow.

Aurora, Emma, and Rosie are tangled with men lesser than themselves; their capacities do not fit their situations. This is also true of the men: a general without any troops, an opera star with an injured throat, and a fiftyish, virginal oil millionaire, Vernon Dalhart, whom Aurora adds to her stable of suitors.

Plot is not very important. Emma has her baby. Rosie copes with a disintegrating marriage, and

Aurora has to choose among her suitors. Aurora solves her problem by not choosing. She allows the general to move in with her, but she forces him to allow her to retain her other admirers and pull them into a tight, continuing relationship with one another and with her (her sexual arrangement with the others is not clear). No one man is her equal, but the team together almost copes with her needs.

Part 2, only forty-seven pages long, jumps to the period from 1971 through 1976 and focuses on Emma's life in Des Moines, Iowa, and Kearney, Nebraska. Emma has three children, but her marriage with Flap has disintegrated. Flap is a failure in the academic world (he blames Emma for not nagging him to success) and has affairs with numerous co-eds. Emma has the strength and stability to have a couple of affairs, bringing some sexual fulfillment and emotional joy into her life.

Then Emma discovers that she has terminal cancer. Rosie, Aurora, and her suitors come to Emma to help her deal with dying. Emma dies with the dignity that she had always had; she does not cling tightly to life. Only Vernon Dalhart understands her needs fully: "He didn't demand that she live." She tries to help Flap cope with her approaching death, but she cannot even remember what the terms of endearment between them had been. Ten years later, Flap thinks of her one afternoon and thinks that "he had done something wrong, wrong, wrong, long ago." As Emma slips toward death, she has them bring Danny Deck's book to her; as the rest of the world fades, Danny returns to her memory. Emma is buried in Houston. Rosie and Aurora leave the cemetery together to take care of the three children, whom they are going to raise.

CADILLAC JACK

First published: 1982
Type of work: Novel

Antique scout Cadillac Jack McGriff balances his love for beautiful objects with his love of beautiful women.

In *Cadillac Jack*, McMurtry, drawing on his background as a scout locating rare editions of books, takes readers into the world of antique dealers and scouts, flea markets, auctions, and garage sales, a subculture that provides meaning to the lives of thousands of Americans. Like McMurtry, Cadillac Jack is a displaced Texan living in the Washington, D.C., area.

Jack McGriff—called Cadillac Jack because of his pearl-colored Cadillac—is an antique scout. He combs the United States, locating special items for dealers and collectors. As he gets older he gets pickier, only wanting exceptional items; he is no longer satisfied with the merely first-rate. Exceptional objects can be rare items, such as Billy the Kid's boots or Rudolph Valentino's silver cobra hubcaps, or they can be beautiful items such as the Sung vase he found in a junk barn in De Queen, Arkansas. Cadillac Jack is a legend in his subculture— doing what every flea-market and garage-sale addict dreams of doing: He finds treasure among junk. Jack paid $20 for the Sung vase and sold it for more than $100,000. He buys the objects that he falls in love with, but he keeps them only a short time. If he loses his discipline and cannot bring himself to sell what he buys, then he will become a collector or an antique dealer. He will have lost the calling that gives his life purpose.

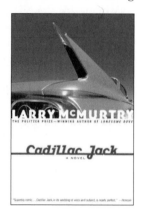

Cadillac Jack is not strong on plot. Jack does have a problem with women, however. He falls in love with nearly any (beautiful) woman who is in trouble. As the story opens, Jack has just met the beautiful social climber Cindy Sanders, who owns three fashionable shops, including an antique store. Cindy is a self-centered beauty, with little awareness of anyone or anything outside herself. Her beauty attracts Jack, and her antique shop seems to promise some common interest. Jack finds that she really has no knowledge or appreciation of antiques, but he thinks that if he can get her on his turf he can divert her from her fixation on dominating the Washington social scene. He proposes that she hold a boot show and exhibit an exotic collection that he can find for her, topped by Billy the Kid's boots.

Meanwhile, Jack meets Jean Arber and her two

charming daughters. Jean owns a little antique shop and knows her business. She is lovely and is a quiet, family-oriented woman. Jack also falls in love with her. This complicates matters, as Jack had not fallen out of love with Cindy—or his two former wives or various other girlfriends.

Jack and his loves provide a slim plot on which McMurtry can hang his satire of Washington. Jack attends parties with the nation's governmental and journalistic elite and finds most of them so bored and boring that it is often difficult to tell whether they are living or dead. Not many congressmen appear, evidently because they spend considerable time cavorting with the prostitutes at places such as Little Bomber's Lounge. In the background are the gray little bureaucrats inhabiting gray little cells in gray office buildings and apartments.

Some of McMurtry's characters are unforgettable. Boog Miller, a fat Texan with slicked-down hair, is a wheeler-dealer on the scale of Lyndon Johnson. He owns Winkler County, Texas, and all the oil underneath it. When he is not manipulating the politicians on Capitol Hill, he is enjoying the beauties at Little Bomber's or reading the works of historians and philosophers. Jack visits legendary collectors, among them Benny the Ghost, who materializes at auctions to buy the one good piece and then dematerializes. Jack is the only one who has visited Benny's five-story home jammed with twenty thousand to thirty thousand exceptional antiques.

Jack buys boots from the oil-rich, drug-crazed Little Joe Twine, who lives near Archer City, Texas. Little Joe is the most bizarre of the debris left in the wake of the collapse of the Old West, an extreme symbol of the empty lives of oil-rich, uneducated, former ranchers who have no purpose. He and his cowboys spend their days taking drugs and watching pornographic movies on Joe's wall-size television.

Jack's dream of a life with Cindy falls through when she marries a rich and powerful member of the Washington elite. His relationship with Jean falters when he destroys her trust by lying to her. Jack explains that he only lies to try to reach a higher and "happier truth," but Jean does not understand his ethical concept.

Jack finds peace and sanity by motion, by moving over the open road. The open range is no longer there, but thousands of miles of highway lie under the American sky. Jack leaves Washington for

points west. As he drives, he almost comes to an understanding of his relationship with beautiful women and with beautiful objects, he says, but then he starts thinking about the approaching city of St. Louis and loses interest in the question.

LONESOME DOVE

First published: 1985
Type of work: Novel

Augustus McCrae and Woodrow F. Call drive a herd of cattle from south Texas to Montana and establish the first ranch in that territory.

McMurtry dedicates *Lonesome Dove* to the nine McMurtry boys (his uncles and father) and tips his hat to Charles Goodnight, Teddy Blue, and the other cowboys of the Old West. The cattlemen helped civilize the West and, in the process, created a mythology that continues to shape the United States. That powerful American myth grew from a very brief era in United States history immediately after the Civil War, a twenty-year period of open range and cattle drives. That period and way of life gave birth to all the dominant images of the Old West.

McMurtry has his cowboys take their cattle right through the heartland of America, from Texas to Montana, along the frontier fault line between savagery and civilization. McMurtry quotes T. K. Whipple to define his theme: "Our forefathers had civilization inside themselves, the wild outside. We live in the civilization they created, but within us the wilderness still lingers. What they dreamed, we live, and what they lived, we dream."

This Pulitzer Prize-winning novel is a Western yarn in the old tradition, with cattle stampedes, Indian attacks, and the rescue of a beautiful woman by a heroic cowboy. It is exciting and funny and melancholy; the major criticism of the 850-page novel by many readers was that it was too short.

In the late 1870's, Augustus (Gus) McCrae and Woodrow F. Call, former officers in the Texas Rangers and friends for thirty years, are running the Hat Creek Cattle Company, located near the dilapidated little town of Lonesome Dove, hidden amid the mesquite thickets of south Texas on the Rio Grande River. Life drifts there, in the harsh terrain beneath the burning sun. Call, a man obsessed with duty, has no big tasks left. Gus, who can be gallant and heroic when the occasion demands, now is content to sit on his front porch, sip whiskey, and watch his two blue pigs eat rattlesnakes. Perhaps Gus and Call would have turned into Danny Deck's crazed Uncle Laredo if nothing had changed; however, Jake Spoon, an old friend from rangering days, arrives and tells Gus and Call that fortunes are going to be made in Montana, where the grass is deep, the water is bountiful, and the Army is about to tame the Indians.

Call decides that they should go north: There is no fun in south Texas anymore, and besides, there is a fortune to be made in Montana. Gus points out that Call never had any fun in his entire life and that he does not value money. Gus hopes the drive will be hard enough for Call: "You should have died in the line of duty, Woodrow. You'd know how to do that fine. The problem is you don't know how to live." Yet Gus agrees to go to Montana. There is nothing finer, he says, than riding a good horse into new country; besides, he realizes that he will get to see Clara Allen, the great love of his life, who had left sixteen years before and lives on the Platte River in Nebraska.

They gather cowboys for the drive. These include two former rangers, slow-thinking and steady Pea Eye Parker and the extraordinarily competent black man Joshua Deets. Young Newt Dobbs, Call's unacknowledged son, goes; he will be initiated into manhood on the journey. Other young cowboys join the drive, many of whom die along the trail. Jake Spoon refuses to punch cattle, but he trails along with the herd for protection and brings with him Lonesome Dove's only prostitute, Lorena Wood, who believes Jake's promise that he will take her to San Francisco.

If *Lonesome Dove* falls within the long tradition of celebration of the myth of the Old West, some literary critics see that McMurtry, while working from that mythology, also reconstructs it by building a firmer and more realistic foundation for it. The reality of the trail drive is almost unceasing discomfort due to heat, dust, rain, and injuries, with bad food and hard ground to look forward to at the end of a long day. Death is seldom glorious. It might come quickly, with a bolt of lightning, or horribly, from being washed into a tangle of water moccasins, or absurdly, as when the kindly Deets is killed

by a starving, frightened young Indian brave who thinks that the cowboy intends to steal an Indian baby. Some Western men idealize women, as the myth says, but hardship ages women, and lack of intellectual life starves their minds. Western chivalry does not prevent women from having to choose between starvation and prostitution. Some are traded for skunk skins; some are brutally raped.

As the herd moves northward, it crosses the Platte River, and Gus calls on Clara Allen, mother of two girls and wife of a man dying of a head injury. Gus is tempted to stay on the Platte, but his destiny is to ride on with his friend Call into the new land.

Together Gus and Call embody all the attributes of the mythological heroes pursuing a quest. Call displays courage and devotion to duty; he is a natural leader. Gus, gallant, courageous, and compassionate, is also a wise man who understands life and death. The land they are riding over is only a boneyard, he says, "but pretty in the sunlight." He tells Call that in wiping out the Indians in Texas, they had been on the wrong side. The Indians had been the interesting people, and Gus and Call had eliminated them to clear the way for bankers and lawyers. First as Rangers and then as ranchers opening Montana, Gus and Call help civilize the West, but that civilization has no place for them.

Gus reaches the beautiful open range of Montana. It is fitting that when he comes across one of the last herds of buffalo, he chases after it as a salute to a passing age and blunders into one of the few remaining bands of wild Indians. In the melee, an arrow lodges in his leg, and gangrene sets in. He gets to Miles City, where, while he is in a coma, a doctor amputates one leg. His other leg should also be removed, but Gus refuses to have it amputated, knowing that his refusal means his death.

Gus also understands that his friend is going to face the most dangerous crisis of his life. What does a hero do once he fulfills his quest? Gus will die a hero's death, but Call is condemned to live. As he lies dying, Gus does his friend a favor by asking that Call return his body three thousand miles to a picnic ground that he and Clara loved near Lonesome Dove: "It's the kind of job you was made for, that nobody else could do or even try. Now that the country is about settled, I don't know how you'll keep busy, Woodrow. But if you'll do this for me you'll be all right for another year, I guess." It was quite a party, he tells Call as he dies.

Call leaves Gus's body in Miles City until spring. He takes the herd on north, to Milk River, and finds the promised land in a beautiful valley with good grass and water. The men build a ranch as winter comes and continue to look to Call for leadership. Call goes through the motions of building a ranch, but his life now is without purpose. He is one of many McMurtry characters who have to pay the consequences of having lived past his day. In the spring, he turns the ranch over to Newt and makes the long trek back to Texas. He completes the task imposed by Gus, and when the book ends, Call is back in the near-empty Lonesome Dove, old and tired, without purpose or challenge.

STREETS OF LAREDO

First published: 1993
Type of work: Novel

Woodrow Call undertakes his final quest, to hunt down the murderous outlaws Joey Garza and Mox Mox.

In *Streets of Laredo*, Larry McMurtry completes the story of Captain Woodrow Call. As he is dying, Gus McCrae in *Lonesome Dove* warns his friend Call that their time has passed. In *Streets of Laredo*, McMurtry takes up Call's story some twenty years later. Captain Call is a legend in the West, a hero honored for helping make the border region of Texas and Mexico safe for settlers. The legend hides the reality that Call is now a bounty hunter, hired by the wealthy capitalists that he once despised. The legend also obscures the fact that Call is a small, frail, old man who removes the trigger guard from his rifle so that he can get his swollen, arthritic fingers on the trigger.

The story opens in San Antonio, when Call is hired by a railroad owner to hunt down Joey Garza, a train robber and psychopathic killer. Calls summons his old comrade, Pea Eye Parker, who farms in the Texas Panhandle and who is married to Lorena Wood. Pea Eye refuses to join Call. After thirty years of responding to Call's every order, Pea Eye stuns Call by placing his family ahead of his loyalty to the captain.

Word quickly spreads through the Rio Grande valley that Captain Call is hunting Garza. Tension mounts along the border as people wonder where the killer will strike next. Pea Eye Parker feels guilty for leaving Call to face Garza. He moves south to join Call. Shortly after this, Lorena learns that Call is not only chasing Garza but also facing Mox Mox, a crazed sadist who burns his victims alive. Lorena, terrified, rides south to find her husband. Meanwhile, Call, alone, attacks Mox Mox and his seven gang members. He kills six and wounds Mox Mox, who slinks away to die.

Call joins up with Lorena, and they make their way toward Pea Eye. Then, because of his failing eyesight and a moment of careless inattention, Call walks into an ambush. Joey Garza shoots him three times. Call is near death, and Lorena amputates his leg and carries him out of danger. A doctor later removes Call's right arm.

Garza besieges Pea Eye, and the old farmer draws on his courage to do what no one else has been able to do. He charges into the crazed killer's gunfire and inflicts wounds that eventually would have killed Joey, who makes his way home to Ojinaga, Mexico, where he dies in a final explosion of violence.

Order is restored to the border region, largely by the efforts of a woman and a farmer, Lorena and Pea Eye. Lorena brings the crippled Captain Call back to the Panhandle. Call becomes a silent recluse, living in a little cabin near Pea Eye and Lorena. The legendary Texas Ranger earns his keep by sharpening knives and scissors.

SUMMARY

McMurtry examines a central myth shaping American consciousness, that of the Old West, of the cowboys and ranchers, the cattle drives and open range. The myth took form from values that Americans brought with them to the West and then took on its own potent life to shape values in new ways. McMurtry also describes what happens to people who live on beyond the age and the social order that spawned the myth.

Ultimately, McMurtry is probing the American Dream. As one looks over his roster of purposeless lives and wrecked marriages, one might ask why American culture and society are not rich enough to provide the ingredients for meaningful lives when the heroic days pass.

William E. Pemberton

BIBLIOGRAPHY

By the Author

LONG FICTION:
Horseman, Pass By, 1961
Leaving Cheyenne, 1963
The Last Picture Show, 1966
Moving On, 1970
All My Friends Are Going to Be Strangers, 1972
Terms of Endearment, 1975
Somebody's Darling, 1978
Cadillac Jack, 1982
The Desert Rose, 1983
Lonesome Dove, 1985
Texasville, 1987
Anything for Billy, 1988
Some Can Whistle, 1989
Buffalo Girls, 1990
The Evening Star, 1992
Streets of Laredo, 1993
Pretty Boy Floyd, 1994 (with Diana Ossana)
The Late Child, 1995
Dead Man's Walk, 1995
Zeke and Ned, 1997 (with Ossana)
Comanche Moon, 1997
Duane's Depressed, 1999
Boone's Lick, 2000
Sin Killer, 2002
The Wandering Hill, 2003
By Sorrow's River, 2003
Folly and Glory, 2004
Loop Group, 2004

SCREENPLAY:
Brokeback Mountain, 2005 (with Diana Ossana; from a story by Annie Proulx)

NONFICTION:
In a Narrow Grave: Essays on Texas, 1968
It's Always We Rambled: An Essay on Rodeo, 1974
Film Flam: Essays on Hollywood, 1987
Crazy Horse, 1999
Walter Benjamin at the Dairy Queen: Reflections at Sixty and Beyond, 1999
Roads: Driving America's Great Highways, 2000
Paradise, 2001
Sacagawea's Nickname: Essays on the American West, 2001
The Colonel and Little Missie: Buffalo Bill, Annie Oakley, and the Beginnings of Superstardom in America, 2005

DISCUSSION TOPICS

- What is the myth of the Old West? How does it shape American history and society? How does it strengthen people? How does it fail them?

- Larry McMurtry's novels are sometimes read as elegies to the Old West. In what way is that true? Yet, despite their elegiac tone, McMurtry's works disavow simple nostalgia and refuse to romanticize life in the West. Discuss.

- McMurtry presents at least three types of male figures: admirable men such as Homer Bannon, Gus McCrae, and Woodrow Call; bad characters such as Hud and Jake Spoon; and unformed or confused young men such as Lonnie Bannon, Sonny Crawford, and Danny Deck. How did the myth of the Old West contribute to their successes and their failures?

- McMurtry presents readers with a diverse array of strong women. In what ways are they strong? Discuss their relationships with men. In what ways do both men and American society fail these women?

- McMurtry's characters often seem to have more capacities as human beings than society gives them opportunity to fulfill. How does this differ for men and women?

- Beneath McMurtry's snappy, humorous dialogue readers often find a bleak, dark view of life. Discuss.

Larry McMurtry

EDITED TEXT:
Still Wild: Short Fiction of the American West, 2000

About the Author

Busby, Mark. *Larry McMurtry and the West: An Ambivalent Relationship.* Denton: University of North Texas Press, 1995.

Lich, Lera Patrick Tyler. *Larry McMurtry's Texas: Evolution of the Myth.* Austin, Tex.: Eakin Press, 1987.

Neinstein, Raymond L. *The Ghost Country: A Study of the Novels of Larry McMurtry.* Berkeley, Calif.: Creative Arts, 1976.

Peavy, Charles D. *Larry McMurtry.* Boston: Twayne, 1977.

Reilly, John M. *Larry McMurtry: A Critical Companion.* Westport, Conn.: Greenwood Press, 2000.

Schmidt, Dorey, ed. *Larry McMurtry: Unredeemed Dreams.* Edinburg, Tex.: Pan American University Press, 1978.

NORMAN MAILER

Born: Long Branch, New Jersey
January 31, 1923

While there is no critical consensus on the stature of Mailer's novels, he is regarded as one of the most important fiction and nonfiction writers who have appeared since the end of World War II.

Library of Congress

BIOGRAPHY

Norman Mailer was born in Long Branch, New Jersey, on January 31, 1923, the son of Isaac ("Barney") and Fanny Mailer. Mailer's mother had family in business in Long Branch, but she and her husband soon moved to Brooklyn, where their son, Norman, and his younger sister, Barbara, attended public schools. Mailer has described his home life as deeply nurturing, with his mother taking the lead not only in caring for the children but also in earning the income (through an oil delivery business) that supported the family during the Depression when his father (an accountant) was sometimes out of work.

Mailer was a precocious child who did extremely well in school. Assembling an impressive model airplane collection and excelling in his mathematics and sciences courses, his early dream was to become an aeronautical engineer. Accepted at Harvard University in 1939 as an engineering student, Mailer was soon captivated by his writing courses, and by the end of his freshman year, he had determined to become a writer. He graduated in 1943 with an engineering major in deference to his parents' wish for him to have a degree that would qualify him for employment in a profession. He had already written several dozen stories and one unpublished novel. Waiting to be drafted for service in World War II, he wrote in eight months another novel, *A Transit to Narcissus* (published in facsimile in 1978).

Drafted in 1944, Mailer was assigned a number of desk jobs before volunteering as a rifleman so that he could get some experience in combat for the novel about the war that he wanted to write. Originally intended as a short account of a combat patrol, *The Naked and the Dead* (1948), Mailer's first published novel, developed into a long, complex study of the war, the military, and an impressive cross section of soldiers from all regions of the United States. It was hailed as the greatest fictional work to have come out of World War II, and Mailer found himself at twenty-five on the best-seller lists and launched as one of the most promising writers of his generation.

Mailer enjoyed his sudden celebrity, but it also frightened him, for he had not had time to develop his talent. Success had come with a rush. He floundered in the next few years, trying to find a subject as large as World War II, not wanting to repeat himself by writing a second war novel, but afraid that he did not have the experience yet for another major work. He traveled to Europe, visited Hollywood, and dabbled in radical politics. All these experiences found their place in his second novel, *Barbary Shore* (1951), which was heavily criticized as incoherent and excessively didactic. Searching for a new style that was less naturalistic than his first novel, Mailer had tried to write a political allegory that would reveal the fantastic, phantasmagoric, paranoid atmosphere of the Cold War years, when (as Mailer saw it) the United States and the Soviet Union tried to divide the world between them and regarded each other's actions with suspicion.

Demoralized and angered by the negative reviews of *Barbary Shore*, Mailer gradually cultivated a much more aggressive tone, taking on both political and literary establishments, identifying with rebels and hipsters, and defining a new style for himself—that of the engaged, controversial writer who in his own person embodied the conflicting temper of the times. His third novel, *The Deer Park* (1955), a study of Hollywood and the political atmosphere of the 1950's, had a difficult time with publishers, who shied away from its sexual explicitness, and Mailer turned increasingly to the essay form to express his opinions and his imaginative exploration of the American psyche in books such as *The Presidential Papers* (1963) and *Cannibals and Christians* (1966).

Mailer did not return to the novel until 1965, with the publication of *An American Dream*, a disturbing, first-person narrative about a hipster hero, Stephen Rojack, whose murder of his wife in the first chapter sets him off on a journey of self-testing and renewal. Several reviewers were outraged that Rojack not only was not caught or punished for his crime but also that the murder of a woman should become the foundation of a life-renewing quest— especially as only a few years earlier Mailer himself had been incarcerated in Bellevue Hospital in New York City after stabbing his second wife, Adele Morales.

From this point, it became difficult for critics to separate Mailer's public and private life, especially since Mailer—after the indifferent reception of his next novel, *Why Are We in Vietnam?* (1967)—turned to nonfiction, in which his life and personal voice came to the fore. In *The Armies of the Night: History as a Novel, the Novel as History* (1968), *Miami and the Siege of Chicago: An Informal History of the Republican and Democratic Conventions of 1968* (1969), *Of a Fire on the Moon* (1970), *St. George and the Godfather* (1972), *Marilyn* (1973), and *The Fight* (1975), Mailer covered a protest march on the Pentagon, political conventions, the moon shot, the life of a famous actress, and the Muhammad Ali-George Frazier world boxing championship bout in an inimitable voice and sense of participation that made him and his subjects all of a piece, as though they were part of one continuous nonfiction novel about contemporary life.

Although certain subjects were well within his imaginative grasp—such as the march on the Pen-

tagon, which could be described as though it were a war filled with moments of intense action and exquisite character revelation—others eluded him— such as the highly technological, impersonal, and even bureaucratic way the astronauts prepared for their trip into space. As comprehensive and subtle as Mailer's voice had become, he was unable to treat every subject with equal skill, and he (as well as the critics) eventually tired of the way the Mailer ego impressed itself upon everything.

In response to this long period of autobiographical work, Mailer decided to treat the story of Gary Gilmore, a convicted killer who gripped Americans' imagination by refusing to appeal his death sentence and by demanding that the state of Utah execute him, in a scrupulously objective narrative devoid of his usual baroque, metaphorical style. As a result, *The Executioner's Song* (1979) was hailed as a triumph, a return to the panoramic social novel that first earned Mailer his high reputation.

Ancient Evenings (1983), a tour-de-force history of ancient Egypt, *Tough Guys Don't Dance* (1984), a murder mystery, and *Harlot's Ghost* (1991), a spy mystery, are all novels that draw upon the fund of ideas Mailer has developed in more than forty years of exploring the meaning of human identity—the individual's relationship not only to society but also to the universe—for Mailer believes it is possible for the novelist to express both the consciousness of his or her time and an awareness of the eternity, of which a single time and place are only a part. *Oswald's Tale: An American Mystery* (1995) and *The Gospel According to the Son* (1997) followed the publication of *Harlot's Ghost*.

Analysis

Mailer has often said that it was his reading of James T. Farrell, especially of Farrell's Studs Lonigan novels (1932-1935), that made him want to become a writer. Farrell wrote in a naturalistic style, vividly describing the society in which a young Irish boy grows up, matures, and dies. An urban novelist, concerned with how institutions press upon individuals, Farrell traced the story of an individual, Studs Lonigan, who dreamed of distinction but died in misery. What gripped Mailer was the idea that literature could be made from a young man's quest for an identity while at the same time exploring the societal forces that conspire against individuality.

Mailer's early short fiction before *The Naked and the Dead* featured young men caught in extremity—in war, in poverty, or in their travels when they threw in with rugged types and tested their mettle. The ethnicities and social backgrounds of his characters were important in defining their senses of the world and in determining their behavior. This is most clearly the case in "A Calculus at Heaven" (1942), set in the Pacific war theater, in which each character stands for a social type and class:

Bowen Hilliard, the captain, Ivy Leaguer and frustrated artist, who looks to war for some kind of resolution of his unfulfilled life; Dalucci, an Italian, working-class midwesterner, puzzled by his ineffectual life and wondering what it is all about; Wexler, a Jewish boy from New Jersey, proud of his football career and spoiling to show his Army buddies how tough a soldier he can be. These types and others foreshadow the panoramic method of *The Naked and the Dead*, in which Mailer presents a range of characters meant to represent the United States' diversity and to describe the conditions of society.

Mailer's style in this early fiction and in *The Naked and the Dead* was derivative of American writers Farrell, Ernest Hemingway, and John Dos Passos. Indeed, one of the appealing elements of *The Naked and the Dead* is Mailer's deft blending of styles and points of view. Like Hemingway, he is concerned with the fate of individuals, but he links the fate of isolated characters to the destiny of society, showing (as Dos Passos would) how individual character and social class are connected. Like Farrell, who made the Irish neighborhoods of Chicago a graphic part of his fiction so that Studs was brought into high relief by his surroundings, Mailer made the story of men in war gripping by describing in riveting detail what it was like to slog through the terrain of the Philippines.

Ultimately, it was the influence of Hemingway that prevailed when Mailer decided, after the great success of his first published novel, that it was not enough to know his characters and their environment and to describe them faithfully. He had to have a great theme and significant events by which to measure himself as a writer. *Barbary Shore* and *The Deer Park* thus take on Cold War politics and the motion-picture industry as counters against which his characters must seek their true identities and philosophies. Neither Mailer's second nor third novel is entirely satisfying because of his difficulty in creating a credible first-person voice. He was drawn to this mode of narration after deciding he no longer had the confidence of the third-person narrator he had used to sum up society in *The Naked and the Dead*.

The flaw he had trouble rectifying in *Barbary Shore* and *The Deer Park* was precisely that Mikey Lovett and Sergius O'Shaugnessy, his first-person narrators, were so tentative about themselves. Self-doubt increased the drama of their own quests for identity, but it also lent a certain vagueness and lack of color to the narratives, so that neither Lovett nor O'Shaugnessy was quite believable. They lacked the complex, idiosyncratic style Mailer was to develop in *Advertisements for Myself* (1959).

When Mailer decided to use himself—his troubles, his doubts, his conceits—his style developed and prospered. His theme was still the same, the trials of the individual in his confrontation with society, but now that confrontation was much more convincingly portrayed in the light of a complicated and often comic personality willing to delve very deeply into his own faults and follies. The impact of Mailer's fiction is palpable in *An American Dream*, in which the first-person narrator, Stephen Rojack, has a mind that is as agile as Mailer's own.

In *The Armies of the Night*, Mailer's discovery of himself as a character capable of representing the conflicting forces of the country receives its most effective treatment. The style is successful because it is Mailer's third-person commentary on himself as he takes up the protest against the Vietnam War by joining a march on the Pentagon. Referring to himself as a "left Conservative" is a canny way of expressing the contradictions in himself, of the middle-aged writer who is reluctant to give up his privileges to play the part of dissenter and yet who realizes that his creative power and insight often come when he finds himself in opposition to the status quo.

None of Mailer's subsequent nonfiction equals the complexity of *The Armies of the Night*, although *Miami and the Siege of Chicago, Of a Fire on the Moon, Marilyn,* and *The Fight* all contain extended passages that rival his best autobiographical work. *The Executioner's Song*, however, marks a return to the naturalistic method of *The Naked and the Dead*. Its cast of characters, depiction of the western landscape, and evocation of the eastern interests that turn Gilmore's story into a media event far outclass his first novel's understanding of society and politics.

Embedded in *The Executioner's Song* is a quest to understand the very underpinnings of human identity, of the way the American character is related to human nature, and of the way life in the twentieth century United States was but an extension of the eternity of which Gilmore, for example, is sure he partakes. Notions of reincarnation and of karma inform much of Mailer s fiction and nonfiction since the early 1960's; they culminate in *Ancient Evenings*, in which he creates a time and a land (ancient Egypt) that function on magic, telepathy, and reincarnation.

THE NAKED AND THE DEAD

First published: 1948
Type of work: Novel

General Cummings sends a patrol to scale Mount Anaka as part of a strategy to destroy Japanese resistance on the island of Anopopei.

The Naked and the Dead, Mailer's first published novel, was hailed for its riveting depiction of men in war, beset not only by the vicissitudes of battle but also by their social backgrounds and personal problems. Mailer put his brief combat experience to good use, beginning his novel by describing what it feels like to travel on a troop ship, cooped up with men from every part of the United States, anticipating combat but not knowing what it would really be like, and reflecting on life back home—traumatic childhood incidents, plans that were never accomplished, and dreams that remain unfulfilled.

Nearly half of the novel is used to build up the complex social context of the soldiers who will be picked for the dangerous mission to scale Mount Anaka behind enemy lines. In characters such as Roth and Goldstein, Mailer reveals the anti-Semitism rampant in the Army and the efforts of Jews either to ignore the prejudice or to prove their courage and loyalty. Slowly the soldiers on patrol learn to work together as a unit, even as Mailer interrupts the narrative of their approach to the mountain with flashbacks to their civilian lives. Detailed ac-

counts of the irascible Gallagher's life in Boston, easy-going Wilson's love life in the South, and Croft's rather sadistic life in Texas punctuate the conflict and the cooperation of the men on patrol.

Juxtaposed with the lives of common soldiers are the stories of the officers, the higher-ups who give the orders and plot the strategy of the war. General Cummings, a deeply conservative and aloof man, the product of a troubled childhood and of a first-class education, seeks to mold his army into an instrument of his own will. He is opposed in this by Harvard-educated Lieutenant Hearn, who rejects Cummings's incipient fascism and disputes his authority. Attracted by Hearn's intelligence, Cummings does not believe that Hearn really takes his liberal scruples seriously. Cummings is lonely and would like to groom a protégé, but when Hearn proves resistant and goes so far as mashing his cigarette into the immaculate floor of the fastidious general's tent, Cummings decides to teach Hearn a lesson by dispatching him as leader of the patrol charged with climbing Mount Anaka as part of the plan to surprise the Japanese and to take the island of Anopopei away from them.

On patrol, Hearn learns what it means to lead men. He would rather not be a dictator, but Croft—used to having his own way with the men—becomes an adversary. Just when Hearn believes he may have established his dominance, Croft leads him into a Japanese ambush, and Hearn is quickly killed by a bullet. Cruelly driving the men up the mountain, the maniacal Croft is clearly the counterpart of Cummings, certain that he can impose a pattern on history and make it subordinate to his will. The whole mission finally collapses when the exhausted men accidentally stumble into a beehive and are stung into a terrified run down the mountain.

Eventually Japanese resistance crumbles—not because of Cummings's strategy but merely because of exhaustion. Cummings is not even present when his second-in-charge, Major Dalleson, a competent but unimaginative officer, has to take responsibility for handling the rout of the Japanese. Both Cummings and Croft are thwarted, but neither the disaffected men on patrol nor the liberalism represented by Hearn suggest an effective counter to the reactionary forces that appear to be still in control at the end of the novel.

AN AMERICAN DREAM

First published: 1965
Type of work: Novel

Stephen Rojack, a psychology professor and television personality, murders his wife, Deborah, and sets off on a heroic quest of rebirth.

Several reviewers of *An American Dream* were outraged at the premise of the novel: A man murders his wife and not only gets away with the crime but also actually becomes a better man, finding a new inner strength and appetite for life. Feminist critics attacked Mailer for his misogyny, professing to see a pattern in much of his work that demeaned women while elevating the heroic nature of men. Other critics simply found the novel itself unpersuasive and Rojack a rather ridiculous specimen—like Mailer himself, out to establish some concept of heroism that said more about the deficiencies of the author than about the society or the characters Mailer was ostensibly treating.

Later critics of the novel were much more sympathetic, praising the novel for its stylistic virtuosity and courage in probing the tensions and violence of contemporary life. They were willing to grant Mailer his subject matter and believed that it was beside the point to fret about the morality of Rojack's murder. Mailer had not presented it as simply good or evil but as an act that reflects Rojack's desperation and extreme desire. He both loves and hates Deborah, and their physical struggle that results in his strangling her is caused by his sudden urge to relieve himself of the grip she has held on his life.

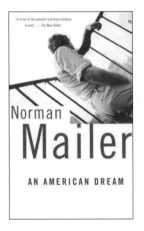

Deborah is vicious. She reminds her husband of everything he has not accomplished, and her words wound a man who came out of the war a hero and with the same kind of promise that put him into politics with John F. Kennedy in Congress. Rojack's career, however, had not prospered. His stature as an eccentric professor of psychology and television personality is scorned by his wealthy wife, who turns to more prominent men—perhaps even to Kennedy himself, she seems to imply in referring to her lovers.

The point about Rojack's murder is that it forces him to act on his own, to become his own man, and to jettison all supports—such as his reliance on Deborah and on her father to help him return to politics. In order to justify himself, Rojack engages in the most extravagant actions—toughing out a confrontation with gangsters when he becomes interested in Cherry, one of their girlfriends, stomping and throwing Shago Martin (Cherry's former lover) down the stairs, confronting his father-in-law, Barney Oswald Kelly, who would just as soon have Rojack killed for what he suspects Rojack has done to Deborah, and walking the parapet outside Kelly's apartment in an almost mystical effort to prove his courage.

Much of this seems foolhardy, even ridiculous, by the very naturalistic standards of character development that Mailer had adopted in *The Naked and the Dead*. Yet Mailer stubbornly sticks by his character's excessive actions, implying that the only way Rojack can remake himself is to seek the death of his former self. The result is a character that transcends the boundaries of social background and individual pathology. Rojack comes to believe that he can indeed become another man, can invent a new style for himself.

The extent to which Rojack will ultimately succeed in sustaining a new identity is not clear. The novel leaves him on the road, traveling to Yucatan, mourning the death of Cherry, who has gotten caught in the revenge of her former lover's friends seeking to murder Rojack for his roughing up of Shago Martin. Rojack has attained his new life at enormous cost to himself and has done nothing to ameliorate the evil of society's powerful figures, like Kelly.

THE ARMIES OF THE NIGHT

First published: 1968
Type of work: Novel

A reluctant Mailer joins the march on the Pentagon to protest the Vietnam War and to show solidarity with a younger generation of dissenters.

With *The Armies of the Night*, Mailer received the best reviews since the publication of *The Naked and the Dead*. Reviewers found his third-person treatment of himself as a character utterly convincing. Mailer's narration seemed so credible because he dealt with all the important aspects of his character in conjunction with the complexity of events surrounding the march on the Pentagon. In other words, his original aim in *The Naked and the Dead* of showing the convergence of character and society was amply demonstrated in a mature, comic, and subtle work.

Mailer begins *The Armies of the Night* with his own reluctant agreement to participate in the march. He is at home trying to write when he gets a call from Mitchell Goodman, a friend urging him to come to Washington. At first, Mailer is petulant, advising Goodman that it behooves writers to write, not to engage in events that only take them away from their work. Mailer has to admit to himself, however, that he is not writing anything important at the moment and that he is really looking for excuses to duck a commitment.

Mailer's ambivalence and early efforts to dominate events result in his drunken antics as master of ceremonies at the Ambassador Theater, where Robert Lowell, Dwight Macdonald, Paul Goodman, and other literary luminaries have gathered to read their work and to express their support for the march on the Pentagon. Mailer makes a spectacle of himself by trying to act the role of a literary Lyndon Johnson, trying to bully the crowd and mold it—like General Cummings—into an instrument of his will. This is a new generation, however, impressed with Mailer but hardly willing to have him dominate events. He is booed as much as he is cheered.

Sobering up and realizing that his attitudes toward draft resisters are ambivalent, Mailer joins the marchers with a newfound sense of modesty, hoping only to be arrested and quickly released to make a symbolic point. Instead, he is detained for many hours and is forced to probe his feelings about himself and about his middle-class life. *The Armies of the Night* becomes, in part, a coming to terms with his middle-aged self and his left conservatism, which is sympathetic to the young protestors but is not willing to take revolutionary action to change the fundamental bases of society. Instead, Mailer is comfortable moving within the power structure, trying to bore from within and examine its complacent beliefs and his own sometimes fatuous convictions.

The first half of *The Armies of the Night*, then, is what Mailer calls "the novel as history." Through his personal lens, events unfold and are interpreted in the novelist's quest for meaning. The

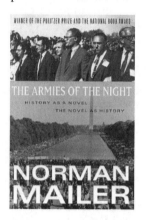

second and shorter half of *The Armies of the Night*, "history as a novel," is a more objective study of accounts of the march on the Pentagon, which shows how the march was planned and reported; it dwells on the discrepancies of press reports and demonstrates that those who purport to write "history," no less than those who write novels, make constructs of events—imaginative projections of what they think happened, of what they saw from different points of view. The armies in Mailer's title refer, therefore, not only to the clash between the protestors and the guardsmen at the Pentagon but also to different modes of perception. History and the novel are distinct genres, but they also have more in common than their practitioners are usually willing to admit. In writing both history and a novel, Mailer combines fiction's immediacy and drama with history's documentary quest for verification.

THE EXECUTIONER'S SONG

First published: 1979
Type of work: Novel

A vivid third-person account of the life and execution of murderer Gary Gilmore and of the societal forces that inform and are attracted to his singular story.

The Executioner's Song appeared at a time when critics (and Mailer himself) had become tired of the way his personality tended to dominate everything he wrote. He wanted to find a subject that would be bigger than his ego and that would force him to write in a different style. Presented with a massive amount of material by Larry Schiller, who had bought the rights to Gilmore's story, Mailer found that he had hundreds of characters to work with, speaking on tape and in documents that amounted to a massive social novel which would ultimately cover virtually every region in the United States through the voices of people describing their involvement in Gilmore's life.

Conducting new interviews and immersing himself in the thousands of pages of court record and press coverage, Mailer developed an objective, precise, spare voice that had the ring of authenticity, for it was a voice that did not seem to make any more of the experience than what a reader could observe in the accounts on the page.

The Executioner's Song is divided into two parts, "Western Voices" and "Eastern Voices." The first part begins with the release of Gilmore from prison and the efforts of his relatives to find him a decent job and place to live. Gilmore has trouble adjusting, coping with the everyday necessities of working, shopping, eating, and so on. He falls in love with Nicole Baker, a young woman he is sure he has met in another life, and whom he binds to himself with an intensity that drives him to despair when she leaves him. Committing two murders for no apparent reason—except for the implication that he shoots two clean-cut Mormon men rather than turn the gun on himself and Nicole—Gilmore decides in prison that he should be executed.

The second part of *The Executioner's Song* details the media attention that Gilmore's resolution to die inspires. Gilmore is articulate, determined, and contemptuous of the state. His defiance and his willingness to accept punishment fires the public imagination and provokes the interest of Schiller, who sees both book and film possibilities in Gilmore's saga. In many ways, Schiller becomes Mailer's surrogate, for in his previous books Mailer has put himself forward as the sensibility reporting on and shaping events. Now it is Schiller who assembles every piece of the story, getting exclusive rights and dealing directly with Gilmore. As in Mailer's use of the third-person voice to describe himself in *The Armies of the Night*, his third-person depiction of Schiller is a brilliant way of showing how the reporter both reflects and shapes the events he covers.

A huge critical and popular success, *The Executioner's Song* was praised as a great social novel giving a panoramic view of the United States. Mailer confessed that he could not have invented better characters. They were presented with a density and wealth of social detail that surpassed those of *The Naked and the Dead*, thus making *The Executioner's Song* a comprehensive and convincing work.

SUMMARY

Many critics have suggested that Mailer's greatest achievement has been in nonfiction, where he has had a plot ready-made and a cast of characters about whom he can report with uncanny accuracy and insight. At the same time, in turning to nonfiction he has adapted the techniques of fiction to show how much of history—once it is reported—can be seen as a novel. To dismiss his novels, however, would be a mistake, as *The Naked and the Dead* and *An American Dream*, for example, express and often superbly realize the way he has tried to shift between and balance the countervailing forces of the individual and society.

Carl Rollyson

BIBLIOGRAPHY

By the Author

LONG FICTION:
The Naked and the Dead, 1948
Barbary Shore, 1951
The Deer Park, 1955
An American Dream, 1965
Why Are We in Vietnam?, 1967
The Armies of the Night: History as a Novel, the Novel as History, 1968
Marilyn, 1973
The Executioner's Song, 1979
Of Women and Their Elegance, 1980
Ancient Evenings, 1983
Tough Guys Don't Dance, 1984
Harlot's Ghost, 1991
Oswald's Tale: An American Mystery, 1995
The Gospel According to the Son, 1997

SHORT FICTION:
New Short Novels 2, 1956
The Short Fiction of Norman Mailer, 1967

DRAMA:
The Deer Park: A Play, pb. 1967

SCREENPLAY:
Tough Guys Don't Dance, 1987

POETRY:
Deaths for the Ladies and Other Disasters, 1962

NONFICTION:
The White Negro, 1957
The Presidential Papers, 1963
Cannibals and Christians, 1966
The Bullfight, 1967
The Idol and the Octopus: Political Writings on the Kennedy and Johnson Administrations, 1968
Miami and the Siege of Chicago: An Informal History of the Republican and Democratic Conventions of 1968, 1969
Of a Fire on the Moon, 1970
The Prisoner of Sex, 1971
The Long Patrol: Twenty-five Years of Writing from the Work of Norman Mailer, 1971 (Robert Lucid, editor)
Existential Errands, 1972
St. George and the Godfather, 1972
The Faith of Graffiti, 1974 (with Mervyn Kurlansky and Jon Naar)
The Fight, 1975
Some Honorable Men: Political Conventions, 1960-1972, 1975
Genius and Lust: A Journey Through the Major Writings of Henry Miller, 1976
Pieces and Pontifications, 1982

DISCUSSION TOPICS

- *The Naked and the Dead* has been called the greatest American novel about World War II. What does it say about war and military life?

- Some have claimed that Norman Mailer's nonfiction writing is superior to his fiction. Argue for or against this assertion.

- How does Mailer explore the conflict between the individual and society?

- Mailer has often been criticized for his failure to create well-developed female characters. Is this complaint valid?

- Discuss the political commentary in Mailer's writings. Does a unified picture of American politics emerge?

- How does *The Armies of the Night* comment on the concept of history?

Portrait of Picasso as a Young Man, 1995 (also known as *Pablo and Fernande: Portrait of Picasso as a Young Man,* 1994)

The Spooky Art: Thoughts on Writing, 2003

Why Are We at War?, 2003

MISCELLANEOUS:

Advertisements for Myself, 1959

The Time of Our Time, 1998

Modest Gifts: Poems and Drawings, 2003

About the Author

Adams, Laura, ed. *Will the Real Norman Mailer Please Stand Up?* Port Washington, N.Y.: Kennikat Press, 1974.

Bloom, Harold, ed. *Norman Mailer.* Philadelphia: Chelsea House, 2003.

Braudy, Leo, ed. *Norman Mailer: A Collection of Critical Essays.* Englewood Cliffs, N.J.: Prentice-Hall, 1972.

Castronovo, David. "Norman Mailer as Midcentury Advertisement." *New England Review: Middlebury Series* 24 (2003): 179-194.

Denby, David. "The Contender." *The New Yorker* 74 (April 20, 1998): 60-66, 68-71.

Glenday, Michael K. *Norman Mailer.* New York: St. Martin's Press, 1995.

Gordon, Andrew. *An American Dreamer: A Psychoanalytic Study of the Fiction of Norman Mailer.* London: Associated University Presses, 1980.

Kimball, Roger. "Norman Mailer's American Dream." *New Criterion* 16 (November, 1997): 4-10.

Leeds, Barry H. "Norman Mailer: Politically Incorrect?" *English Record* 51 (Winter, 2001): 10-25.

Lennon, J. Michael. "A Conversation with Norman Mailer." *New England Review: Middlebury Series* 20 (Summer, 1999): 138-148.

_____, ed. *Conversations with Norman Mailer.* Jackson: University Press of Mississippi, 1988.

_____. *Critical Essays on Norman Mailer.* Boston: G. K. Hall, 1986.

Levine, Andrea. "The (Jewish) White Negro: Norman Mailer's Racial Bodies." *MELUS* 28 (Summer, 2003): 59-81.

Lucid, Robert F., ed. *Norman Mailer: The Man and His Work.* Boston: Little, Brown, 1971.

McCann, Sean. "The Imperiled Republic: Norman Mailer and the Poetics of Anti-Liberalism." *ELH* 67 (Spring, 2000): 293-336.

Manso, Peter. *Mailer: His Life and Times.* New York: Simon & Schuster, 1985.

Merrill, Robert. *Norman Mailer Revisted.* New York: Twayne, 1992.

Mills, Hilary. *Norman Mailer: A Biography.* New York: Empire Books, 1982.

Poirier, Richard. *Norman Mailer.* New York: Viking Press, 1972.

Solotaroff, Robert. *Down Mailer's Way.* Urbana: University of Illinois Press, 1974.

Wenke, Joseph. *Mailer's America.* Hanover, N.H.: University Press of New England, 1987.

BERNARD MALAMUD

Born: Brooklyn, New York
    April 26, 1914
Died: New York, New York
    March 18, 1986

Universally recognized as one of America's greatest writers, Malamud transcends the Jewish experience to champion the triumph of the human spirit.

© Jerry Bauer

BIOGRAPHY

Bernard Malamud was born on April 26, 1914, in Brooklyn, New York. The older of two sons of Max and Bertha (Fidelman) Malamud, who had emigrated from Russia in the early twentieth century and ran a grocery store, he enjoyed a relatively happy childhood. Both Yiddish and English were spoken in the Malamud household, and a great emphasis was placed on the cultural aspects of Judaism. Malamud's early years were spent going to the Yiddish theater on Manhattan's Second Avenue and reading novels by such favorites as Horatio Alger. Doubtless his later writings were influenced also by his father's stories of life in czarist Russia.

Malamud's father and teachers encouraged young Bernard to develop his obvious talent for storytelling. One of his most cherished gifts he received at age nine; it was the multivolume *Book of Knowledge* encyclopedia that his father gave him after the boy's recovery from pneumonia. Many of his boyhood nights were spent in the back room of the family store, putting on paper the stories he made up to amuse his friends. He would later confess a lifelong love for short fiction even over the novel, because, as he said "if one begins early in life to make up and tell stories, he has a better chance to be heard out if he keeps them short." His interest in literature continued through high school at Erasmus Hall in Brooklyn, where he was an editor

of the literary magazine and was involved in dramatic productions.

In 1936 Malamud graduated with a B.A. from City College of New York. He had written a few stories while in college, and after graduation he continued to write in the little spare time he had from jobs in a factory, a variety of stores, and as a clerk with the Census Bureau in Washington, D.C. While working on an M.A. at Columbia University, he taught English at Erasmus Hall Evening High School, devoting his days to studying and writing. He continued his teaching at Erasmus for several years after receiving his graduate degree in 1942.

In 1945, Malamud married Ann de Chiara. His father was quite upset by Malamud's marrying a gentile but was later reconciled—on the birth of the couple's son, Paul. During the 1940's, Malamud's stories appeared in several noncommercial magazines, a fact that made him happy even though he received no payment. In 1949, he sold "The Cost of Living" to Pearl Kazin at *Harper's Bazaar.* In that same year, he and his family left New York for Corvallis, Oregon, where he had accepted a position at Oregon State University.

A lifelong city dweller, Malamud was overwhelmed by the vastness of the Pacific Northwest. Although it took him a while to get his bearings, the change of scenery and lifestyle permitted him a new perspective on his life and his writing. In those early years at Oregon State he developed a weekly routine that allowed much time for writing: He taught three days a week and wrote four. This disciplined approach helped him zero in on those things about which he really yearned to write. His teaching was not totally satisfying because, without a Ph.D., he was allowed to teach composition but not literature. His most gratifying teaching came during a night workshop in the short story, which he offered for townspeople who wanted to take a writing course. Malamud later admitted that he did not care what he taught as long as he had time to write. Some of his fondest memories of those early days at Oregon State were of his wife pushing the baby stroller as she handed him lunchtime sandwiches through the window of the Quonset hut where he wrote and taught. During those years, his work appeared in such noted magazines as *Partisan Review* and *Commentary* in addition to *Harper's Bazaar.*

In 1952 his first novel, *The Natural,* appeared to mixed reviews. Some critics were put off by what they saw as an obscure use of symbolism, while others applauded its masterful use of fable and its art of ancient storytelling in a modern voice. In 1956, the *Partisan Review* made Malamud a fellow in fiction and recommended him for a Rockefeller Grant, which allowed him to take a leave of absence from Oregon State to spend a year in Europe. In 1957, his next novel, *The Assistant,* was published. More Jewish in its characters and theme than *The Natural,* this work firmly established him as a major American writer. Malamud was presented with the Daroff Memorial Award and the Rosenthal Award of the National Institute of Arts and Letters for his second novel.

In 1958, thirteen of Malamud's previously published short stories appeared in his first collection, *The Magic Barrel.* Including such notable short stories as "The Magic Barrel," "Angel Levine," and "The Last Mohican," the collection strengthened Malamud's position as a major Jewish voice in American letters. *The Magic Barrel* won a National Book Award in 1959. A fellow in the Ford Foundation's humanities and arts program from 1959 to 1961, Malamud wrote his third novel, *A New Life* (1961). Also in 1961 he left Oregon State to take a position in language and literature at Bennington College in Vermont, where he taught for more than twenty years, with the exception of a two-year visiting lectureship at Harvard University from 1966 to 1968.

In 1963, he published another collection of short stories, *Idiots First,* followed by his fourth novel, *The Fixer,* in 1966. *The Fixer,* which won him a second National Book Award and a Pulitzer Prize in 1967, was researched by a trip to Russia and six months of uninterrupted study.

From 1969 until his death in 1986, Malamud continued to publish both novels and short stories. His works include *Pictures of Fidelman: An Exhibition* (1969), a collection of stories about one character; *The Tenants* (1971), a novel about the conflicts between an old Jewish writer and a young black one; *Rembrandt's Hat* (1973), another collection of stories; *Dubin's Lives* (1979), a novel about a writer at midlife; *God's Grace* (1982), a novel; *The Stories of Bernard Malamud* (1983), another collection; and a host of stories published separately in prestigious magazines.

Additional awards and honors included Vermont's 1979 Governor's Award for Excellence in the Arts, the Brandeis Creative Arts Award (1981), and the American Academy and Institute of Arts and Letters' Gold Medal in Fiction (1983). From 1979 to 1981 Malamud was president of the PEN (International Association of Poets, Playwrights, Editors, Essayists, and Novelists) American Center. He died in Manhattan on March 18, 1986.

ANALYSIS

Malamud first came to prominence during the late 1950's and early 1960's, a period when trends in fiction centered on the "new novel." In part, Malamud's writings can be seen as a reaction to this school, which devalued form, presented weak, atypical characters, offered a negative view about the future of humankind, and often provided an amoral view of the world. Taking an opposite stance, Malamud was absolutely adamant about the role of fiction: "The purpose of the writer is to keep civilization from destroying itself. But without preachment. Artists cannot be ministers. As soon as they attempt it, they destroy their artistry."

Indeed, Malamud's literary roots extend deeply into the nineteenth century narrative method. He is foremost a storyteller. "I feel that story is the basic element of fiction," he claimed, "though that idea is not popular with disciples of the 'new novel.'" He admitted to being influenced by the great European realists such as Gustave Flaubert, Thomas Hardy, Anton Chekhov, Leo Tolstoy, and Stendhal as well as modern Americans such as Ernest Hemingway and William Faulkner. Malamud tells a story in the traditional manner. He was a great believer in form, which he called an "absolute necessity . . . the basis of literature." At the heart of every story stands character. In fact, Malamud is devoted to the development of the individual:

> The sell-out of personality is just tremendous. Our most important natural resource is Man. The times cry out for men of imagination and hope. Instead, our fiction is loaded with sickness, homosexuality, fragmented man, "other-directed" man. It should be filled with love and beauty and hope. We are underselling Man.

Like his literary forebears, especially the American writers, Malamud favors the initiation story. A typical Malamud story follows the maturation pattern: A young man who has led an unfulfilled life fraught with failed relationships, undeveloped emotions, and questionable morality undertakes a journey. Most often this odyssey involves physical movement—from a rural setting to a city, or the reverse. There, the young man encounters a series of father figures—some false and some true—and by asking questions, suffering for past inadequacies, facing new experiences, and accepting responsibility for himself, he grows.

The quintessential Malamud format, then, is mythic. Joseph Campbell, the eminent scholar and myth critic, reduced the basic structure of myth to "separation-initiation-return." Certainly Malamud's most familiar protagonists follow this pattern. Roy Hobbs and Yakov Bok separate from their bucolic innocence for the urban experience, S. Levin departs New York City for a small town in rural Oregon, and Frank Alpine journeys from the West to New York City. All four protagonists are male, young, and without parents; furthermore, all four search for father surrogates to guide them through the difficult passage to adulthood. In their new worlds they are initiated through a series of trials; encountering deception, often in the form of female temptresses, they make mistake after mistake and are forced to suffer.

Iris Lemon, the heroine of *The Natural*, teaches the essential Malamud lesson when she says, "We have two lives, Roy, the life we learn with and the life we live with after that. Suffering is what brings us toward happiness." The returns are varied. Each novel ends after a decisive moment in which the youthful protagonist is at the threshold of maturity.

Roy Hobbs cuts off his involvement with gamblers by returning the bribery money and stalking off. Frank Alpine replaces Morris Bober in his tomb of a grocery store. S. Levin loads up the car with his new family to return to the East. Yakov Bok leaves the prison cell of his self for a trial, now willing to shoulder the load of communal suffering. While these novels are open-ended (the reader has no idea of any protagonist's ultimate fate), the important thing is that these characters have come to sense who they are, have clarified their relationship to the world, and have willingly accepted their responsibility.

Ultimately, in the battle between humanism and nihilism, Malamud's novels are an affirmation of life. As Malamud himself has said, "Literature, since it values man by describing him, tends toward morality. . . . Art celebrates life and gives us our measure." Though starting in the gloom, all of his lead characters search for "possibilities," "a better life," "a new life," "opportunities," and, to some degree, they find them. They may live in a modern wasteland—a world of suffering, toil, and degradation—but they persist. They learn to turn suffering into a positive value rather than letting it crush them. His schlemiels prosper.

While Malamud's heritage is undeniably Jewish (his father was a Jewish immigrant, and, like Sholom Aleichem and I. L. Peretz, he is part of the tradition of Yiddish storytelling), to see him as wholly a fixture in the so-called Jewish Literary Renaissance is to limit him. "I write about Jews because I know them," he says. "But more important, I write about them because Jews are absolutely the very stuff of drama." Malamud does not envision the Jew as unique, as primarily a product of the Judaistic culture and consciousness in the manner of Saul Bellow and Philip Roth. The Jew is a metaphor for all people, a modern-day Everyman—as Malamud's oft-quoted remark "All men are Jews" suggests. As a humanist, Malamud seeks through his synecdochic method to examine the whole human race.

Malamud's works are essentially an affirmation of the community of humankind. Despite his protagonists' varying ethnic, geographic, educational, and national backgrounds, Malamud emphasizes not their differences but their similarities. His plots, themes, characters, and mythic underpinnings all combine to stress the essential community of humanity. Moreover, Malamud is full of hope: "My premise is that we will not destroy each other. My premise is that we will live on. We will seek a better life. We may not become better, but at least we will seek betterment."

THE NATURAL

First published: 1952
Type of work: Novel

In the modern world, heroism is a difficult struggle for a young man.

The Natural, Malamud's first novel, initially received mixed reviews but is now generally regarded as a superb piece of literature. The novel is both an anomaly for and an introduction to the author. The book differs from the typical Malamud novel: Its style is not as realistic; its central protagonist, Roy Hobbs, is not Jewish; it closes on a note of defeat; and it centers on a sport, professional baseball. As such, *The Natural* is generally viewed in the top echelon of sports novels, such as Robert Coover's *The Universal Baseball Association, Inc., J. Henry Waugh, Prop.* (1968) and Mark Harris's *Bang the Drum Slowly* (1956). *The Natural* is also one of the two Malamud books to have been made into a film (though in this case, to ensure the film's popularity, the ending is more optimistic, with Hobbs's hit winning the play-off). The book follows the traditional Malamud initiation story pattern, has a mythic structure, uses an Everyman figure as protagonist, and utilizes a mixed tone of comedy and tragedy.

The Natural has many levels. On the surface, it is a sports book about the rise and fall of Roy Hobbs, a young man with the potential to be a baseball superstar and hero. Malamud knows the diamond sport, and he has infused his tale with actual events from baseball lore. With his being an orphan, his tendency to overeat, and his hitting a homerun for a dying boy, Hobbs is obviously based on Babe Ruth. Hobbs's being shot in a hotel room by a deranged woman echoes the fate of Eddie Waitkus, and his ultimate succumbing to the gamblers' desire to throw a game is highly reminiscent of Shoeless Joe Jackson. Thus, Hobbs symbolizes the best and the worst baseball has to offer.

On another level *The Natural* is an initiation story. Roy Hobbs, whose name means "bumpkin king," is a white-faced pitcher one year out of the Northwest High School League. After striking out the American League batting champion, he hubristically announces that he wishes to be "the best there ever was in the game." His pride and immaturity bring him a silver bullet in a Chicago hotel room. Fifteen years later he tries the major leagues again, but his carnal lust, materialism, and immaturity lead him to throw a game. At the novel's conclusion, Hobbs, feeling old and grimy and filled with overwhelming self-hatred, realizes that "I never did learn anything out of my past life, now I have to suffer again."

On perhaps the deepest level, Roy Hobbs is the archetypal protagonist on a heroic quest. Malamud borrows from many legends but mostly from the Grail myth. Like Sir Perceval, the youthful Hobbs sets out alone for the Grail (baseball championship) armed with a marvelous weapon—his bat, Wonderboy (seemingly magical and carved from a lightning-blasted tree). Along the way, he tries to aid a dying Fisher King figure, Pop Fisher (manager of the New York Knights). Unable to discern the temptresses (Memo Paris and Harriet Bird) from the Lady-in-the-Lake (Iris Lemon)—that is, to see the distinction between carnal lust and true love—Hobbs succumbs to the evil figure (Judge Goodwill Banner) in the Chapel Perilous (here the Judge's dark tower). Hence, Hobbs is not granted a vision of the Grail (the right to play in the World Series), and neither the urban wasteland nor the dying Fisher King is saved or replaced.

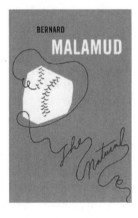

On a psychological level, Hobbs never matures. Narcissistically fixated on his athletic career, he mistakenly pursues the sterile and feeble-breasted (Memo Paris and Harriet Bird) instead of the fertile Iris Lemon, who is pregnant with his child, and who appropriately breaks his phallic symbol, Wonderboy. Hobbs, though in his thirties, is likewise a broken child. Though aided by various father figures (scout Sam Simpson and Pop Fisher), he is unable to become a real father himself. On a moral level, Malamud stresses Hobbs's failure to develop a suitable moral code. The protagonist is preoccupied with himself. Unable to recognize the need to live for other people (Iris Lemon, Pop Fisher, or his public) as well as the value of love, self-sacrifice, and suffering, Hobbs ends up alone, defeated.

The Natural is a book of blends. The reality of American baseball is mixed with heroic myth. Moments of sheer terror are rendered in a very poetic style. When Harriet Bird shoots Roy Hobbs, the narrator's description is vivid, almost lyrical: "The bullet cut a silver line across the water. He sought with his bare hands to catch it, but it eluded him and, to his horror, bounced into his gut." At the same time, however, the narrator seems detached and ironic: "She pulled the trigger (thrum of bull fiddle)." *The Natural*, then, is much more highly symbolic and lyrical than Malamud's later novels, closer to the traditions of the romance than the realistic novel. Rather than being viewed as flawed, even inconsistent, the novel is probably best read as an experiment, a harbinger of forms and themes that in later works will be better rendered.

THE ASSISTANT

First published: 1957
Type of work: Novel

After a series of mistakes, a man matures through suffering and the acceptance of responsibility.

The Assistant, Malamud's critically acclaimed second novel, is a realistic look at the Jewish community. Malamud, however, transcends the Jewish experience by revealing on a universal moral level what it means to be a man. His protagonist learns about the regeneration of the self and the process of individual redemption.

The focal point of this initiation novel is Frank Alpine, a twenty-five-year-old orphan who has recently come from the West to New York City. Typical of his always making the wrong decision, Frank falls in with a thug and helps him rob and beat a poor Jewish grocery store owner, Morris Bober.

Later, after falling in love with the grocer's daughter, Helen, Frank rescues her from a would-be rapist (the same thug) but then completes the act of rape himself. Clearly at the nadir of his existence and unknowledgable about himself, Frank finally begins to learn.

Deciding that he is, after all, "a man of stern morality," Frank takes the place of the grocer he injured. He works sixteen hours a day in the grocery, supplements this with a night job, and secretly gives the Bober family money from his savings account. He also cuts his ties to Ward Minogue, the thug, and stops his voyeuristic behavior toward the woman he loves, Helen Bober. Through discipline, love, and suffering, Frank becomes a responsible adult such that even Helen realizes that "he had changed into somebody else, no longer what he had been." Appropriately, at the end of the novel, Frank has himself circumcised and, after Passover, becomes a Jew.

On the surface, Malamud seems to be suggesting the moral supremacy of the Jewish belief; however, the writer does several things to suggest that he is really interested in establishing a general humanistic code of ethics. First, Frank's role model, Morris Bober, is not an orthodox Jew (he never goes to synagogue and fails to follow the dietary code). Second, Frank actually traces the Catholic pattern of sainthood; Malamud takes care to indicate that Frank parallels his namesake, Saint Francis of Assisi. Early in the novel, Frank describes Saint Francis as a man of poverty feeding birds in a natural setting. By the middle of the novel, Helen notices Frank in the park feeding peanuts to pigeons. On the last page, Frank has a vision of himself as Saint Francis working in poverty in the grocery store. Third, Malamud has Frank follow the mythic pattern of the questing knight. As he journeys through the blighted land, Frank asks the traditional questions, faces the various temptations, and ultimately replaces the dead king. As a result, Frank embodies the basic patterns of moral growth in Western culture, not only Jewish law.

Another pattern used by Malamud is that of the father replacing the son. Morris's grocery is repeatedly described in negative images—a prison, a cave, a tomb, and a coffin. Later, when Frank takes over the store, he uses the same imagery, even going so far as to say that, like Morris, he has a perpetual stink (failure) in his nose. At Morris's funeral,

Frank falls into the grocer's grave and must climb out. Like Morris, Frank uses the grocery to help Ida, Morris's widow, survive and to help Helen attain her desire—going to college.

The Assistant is also a muted criticism of the American Dream. Morris, a Russian immigrant who has come to America to seek his fortune, is instead buried (first in his grocery store, and then in the ground) a poor man. Morris's problem is that he is an honest man who, despite Frank's prodding, refuses to cheat his customers. Morris is foiled against Charlie, his former partner who cheated him, and Julius Karp, who trades on people's miseries with a liquor store and lies to Morris about to whom he will rent his property. Because they lack scruples, Charlie and Julius have become rich.

Frank Alpine is not the novel's only "child" of a family. One reason Malamud uses the omniscient method of narration is to explore other characters. In fact, the novel employs several other father-child relationships. Much of the novel focuses on Helen Bober, who has had to relinquish her dream of college and work as a menial secretary at Levenspiel's Louisville Panties and Bras to support her father. Unable to develop her possibilities, she has become very unhappy. Similarly, Louis Karp is unable to take over his father's liquor store, Nat Pearl seems to be a perpetual law student, and Ward Minogue, in reaction to his father, a police detective, has turned to a life of crime.

Ironically, the only successful transmission of knowledge from father to son is through Morris to his surrogate son, Frank, the orphan.

Perhaps the real strength of this novel lies in Malamud's ability to make his fictional universe so real. One way he accomplishes this is his steady flow of minor characters: Breitbart, the light-bulb peddler; Al Marcus, the paper-bag salesman stricken with cancer; Nick Fuso, the upstairs tenant. Malamud carefully describes the gray-haired Polish woman who appears every morning at 6:00 A.M. to buy her three-cent roll. The Yiddish speech patterns ring true: when Leo the cakeman says, "Bad all over," Morris replies, "Here is the worst." The language is replete with words such as *schmerz* and *landsleit*.

A NEW LIFE

First published: 1961
Type of work: Novel

After a painful struggle toward self-definition, a man ironically gains freedom and triumph by choosing responsibility and defeat.

A New Life continues Malamud's treatment, begun in *The Natural* and refined in *The Assistant*, of the search for self-definition. This most picaresque of his works follows the struggles of S. Levin, a young professor from New York who hopes to redeem what he perceives as a failed life through relocation to a technical college in the Northwest. Set in the 1950's, the novel substitutes the mythic placelessness of Malamud's earlier novels with a Stendhalian realism replete with topical allusions to the Cold War, McCarthyism, and liberalism versus loyalty oaths.

The novel is actually two books in one. On one level, *A New Life* functions as a satire on academic life. Amid a world of drab parties, hateful faculty meetings, and dull classes, Malamud introduces a cast of mentally crippled faculty members whose only goal seems to be to hang onto their jobs no matter what sacrifices of intellectual or moral principle must be made. The students are no better; they find little interest in things intellectual and see no ethical problem with cheating to pass their classes. On the second, and more important, level, Malamud deals with his ever-present theme of the quest. The characters and incidents that Levin encounters at Cascadia College are the obstacles in his mythic journey to self-discovery. As in all Malamud's novels, the hero must ultimately make a choice that will determine his destiny. In *A New Life* this choice involves, as always, a definition of freedom. To complete his quest, Levin must come to terms with the suffering involved in gaining true freedom.

Malamud's satirical pen is sharp, with barbs directed both at the academic establishment and at his hero's excessive idealism. From Levin's arrival in Eastchester, the home of Cascadia College, it is apparent that this former drunkard and professed liberal is out of his element in the stifling atmosphere of this land-grant institution devoted to giving its students a practical education. He is told flatly that the liberal arts (which he believes "feed our hearts") have no place in the school's conservative English department, devoted to drilling students with the anachronistic chairman's text, *The Elements of Grammar.*

Against this backdrop Levin encounters a series of disillusionments as he attempts to shape a new life filled with success in his academic career and a oneness with the beauties of the natural world. Be it teaching, departmental relationships, or encounters with nature, Levin's lofty expectations arising from his overblown, often comic romanticism doom him to comic failure. A modern-day Don Quixote, he sees his efforts to impose his ideals on an insensitive world end in bumbling disaster: Attempting to inspire his students with his own enthusiasm for learning, he lectures with his fly unzipped; thinking he has found a role model in a "liberal" colleague, he discovers only an arch antifeminist reduced to trivial causes such as opposing "indiscriminate garbage dumping and dogs that run loose and murder his chickens." Filled with an intoxicating joy in the beauties of a pastoral scene, he steps in cow dung.

Indeed, Malamud fashions Levin as a more intense version of Roy Hobbs or Frank Alpine—the hero who is his own worst enemy. Levin's attempts to escape the ghosts of a failed love affair, the suicide of his mother, and a two-year lapse into drunkenness have proved futile. Relocation to another part of the United States and a beard grown over the face he cannot stand to look at fail to exorcise the old self that haunts his every action. Levin is given to fitful dreams and long bouts of melancholy in his room. So intense are these battles between what he desires and what he realizes he must accept instead that Levin at times seems at the point of insanity.

Levin's disillusionment with the academic life leads to loneliness and a need for female companionship. Even in the arena of love, however, Levin's romanticism dooms him to an almost clownlike failure. Counseled during his first meeting with the departmental chairman against sexual escapades with women from town, colleagues, students, or faculty wives, Levin launches into a series of affairs with exactly these types—with predictable results. His conquest of a waitress in a barn is interrupted by her boyfriend, who steals their clothes. His liaison with Avis Fliss, a single member of the department, ends abruptly in his office one night when, during frantic foreplay, he discovers her damaged breast and becomes impotent. Even his consummated affair with Nadalee Hammerstand, a student, ultimately ends in disappointment, when, after a madcap journey involving comic confrontations straight from a picaresque adventure, he arrives at their rendezvous by the ocean only to encounter a series of slapstick events that ruin any chance of sexual fulfillment.

The novel's turning point comes when Levin, a failure both academically and with women, falls in love with Pauline, the wife of Gerald Gilley, the director of composition and the antithesis of everything for which Levin stands. It is through his relationship with Pauline that Levin discovers who he is and gains the courage to break free from the bonds of his false idealism. After months of struggle, during which Levin (torn between his romantic ideas and practical reality) rejects Pauline and then takes her back, the affair culminates when Levin agrees to tell Gilley about the relationship. His admission, during the heat of his campaign against Gilley for department chairman, leads to his dismissal from Cascadia.

His future uncertain, Levin must confront Gilley to ask for custody of the Gilleys' adopted children. After failing to dissuade the aspiring husband and father by detailing all the problems Levin is bringing upon himself with such a neurotic woman and endlessly sick children, Gilley places a final stipulation on his willingness to let them go: Levin must renounce the teaching profession. When Levin agrees, Gilley asks him why he is willing to shoulder such a burden. Levin's answer, "Because I can, you son of a bitch," marks him as the Malamudian hero who finds freedom in the acceptance of responsibility, inner triumph in outward defeat.

THE FIXER

First published: 1966
Type of work: Novel

Against a backdrop of early twentieth century Russia, a man gains self-definition by accepting suffering as a means to freedom.

The Fixer is perhaps Malamud's finest novel. A best seller and Literary Guild selection, it won for him both the Pulitzer Prize and the National Book Award for fiction. In addition, it was cited for excellence by the American Library Association and was adapted into a film. Malamud continues his theme of the quest for self-definition.

The Fixer, however, replaces the more modern settings of his earlier novels with the historical backdrop of early twentieth century Russia. The novel's plot is based on an incident that occurred in 1911 in Kiev, the setting for most of the book. The work is by no means a slavish reportage of actual events; rather, Malamud uses the situation of Mendel Beiliss, a Kiev worker who was imprisoned for the ritual murder of a Christian boy, as the basis for his fictional account of the struggles of his hero, Yakov Bok.

Underlying the plot of *The Fixer* is Malamud's familiar attempt to define true freedom in an insensitive, seemingly irrational world. Yakov Bok, a poor fixer (or handyman), grows disenchanted with his humble life in a run-down village. An orphan who was taught his trade in an orphanage and apprenticed at age ten, Bok has served in the Russian army and taught himself some history, geography, science, and arithmetic in addition to learning the Russian language on his own. Considering himself a freethinker, he feels trapped in his situation (even his childless wife has deserted him) and longs for the new opportunities that life in the city might afford. He sells all that he owns except his tools and a few books, then journeys to what he believes will be freedom in Kiev.

Malamud uses Bok's journey to reveal the character's basic humanity. For all his shortcomings, Bok is a good man, and it is his spirit of giving that constantly embroils him in trouble. Like Roy Hobbs, Frank Alpine, and S. Levin, Bok is his own worst enemy. At times his troubles are comical; feeling sorry for an old woman walking on the road to Kiev, he offers her a ride in his run-down cart only to have the cart break down under their weight.

At other times, however, his humanity leads him into more devastating circumstances. His false imprisonment for the ritual murder of a Christian boy is a direct result of his rescuing the anti-Semite Nikolai Maximovitch from smothering in the snow after passing out in a drunken stupor and his sheltering an old Jew suffering from the cold. Maximovitch, at first thankful for the rescue and not knowing Bok is a Jew (a fact Bok conceals), gives his savior a room in his house and a job managing his brickworks. Later, however, after discovering Bok's Jewishness and hearing the false accusations of assault by his daughter, who has tried unsuccessfully to seduce Bok, Maximovitch acts as a central witness against Bok in the death of the boy. Bok's sheltering of the old Jew also provides evidence against him when the situation is misinterpreted by the authorities.

The majority of the novel treats Bok's imprisonment. For more than three years he endures almost unbearable physical and mental suffering. Paramount to his anguish, of course, is the injustice of his fate; an innocent man, he has been cast into the prison's hellish confines with little chance to defend himself and with little real hope of being cleared of the charges. Bok's isolation becomes a time for reading and reflection, as he attempts to understand his role in such an irrational situation.

Malamud uses a well-drawn cast of characters to aid Bok in his movement toward self-definition. During his confinement Bok comes in contact with people from the outside, as well as those of the prison community, who offer either torment or support. Each of these minor characters contributes to Bok's understanding of himself and his relationship to the world in which he must live.

Perhaps Bok's most important visitors are the two members of his family. Shmuel, the skinny old peddler with the talent for selling the seemingly worthless, attempts to get his son-in-law to open his heart to God and accept some responsibility for all his troubles. Tugging at the Jewishness which Bok has earlier tried so hard to deny, Shmuel claims that even in the face of great trouble God will always provide, if only a person will let him. For all his efforts, however, a disappointed Shmuel finally leaves his son-in-law.

It is left to Raisl, Bok's unfaithful wife, to help him open the door to understanding the nature of suffering and responsibility. At the novel's beginning, she has deserted Bok for a stranger she met at the village inn, leaving her husband with feelings of anger and guilt because she failed to bear him a child. Ironically, she visits Bok in prison with the sole purpose of getting him to sign a paper acknowledging his paternity of a child she has conceived by another man. Raisl's comment, "Whoever acts the father is the father," helps bring about Bok's epiphany on the relationship between responsibility and freedom.

He comes to a realization that only through accepting the sometimes irrational suffering that responsibility to others brings can one find true freedom. No longer fearful of his prison cell, he concludes that the freedom he has so long sought is, in reality, a state of mind that must be actively pursued. At the novel's conclusion he drinks in the crowd's cheers as he heads to trial, a hero of the downtrodden. With a newly discovered spirit he shouts, "Where there's no fight for it there's no freedom."

"THE MAGIC BARREL"

First published: 1954 (collected in *The Magic Barrel*, 1958)
Type of work: Short story

In this story, love is a redemptive force earned through suffering and self-knowledge.

"The Magic Barrel" is another fantasy; this one mixes elements of the traditional fairy tale with Jewish folklore. Like most fairy tales, the story begins with "Not long ago there lived . . ." Leo Finkle, the rabbinical student searching for a wife, is the prince; Salzman, the marriage broker with the magic barrel and sudden appearances, is the supernatural agent; and Stella, his prostitute daughter, is the princess. As in a typical fairy tale, the prince finally meets the princess and through the intervention of the supernatural agent has a chance at a happy ending.

The fairy tale combines with elements from Jewish folklore. The characters are stereotypic: the

marriage broker, the schlemiel, and the poor daughter. The setting is the usual lower-class milieu. With Leo helping Salzman at the end, the plot has the familiar reversal. Even the theme is the easily recognizable one of redemptive rebirth through love. Malamud also infuses the story with humor. Aside from the stock characters and stock situations, he uses puns, hyperbole, and juxtaposition (women are described in the jargon of a used-car salesman).

The story is also social criticism directed at the Jews. Leo Finkle has learned the Jewish law but not his own feelings. He takes refuge in his self-pity, he wants a wife not for love but for social prestige, and he uses his religion to hide from life.

"ANGEL LEVINE"

First published: 1955 (collected in *The Complete Stories*, 1997)
Type of work: Short story

In recognizing another's divine essence as well as the bond of brotherhood between himself and another, a man is redeemed.

"Angel Levine," part fable and part fantasy, is yet another example of Malamud's brotherhood theme. The New Yorker Manischevitz, a typical Malamudian Job-like victim, seeks relief from his suffering and aid for his sick wife, Fanny. In the Malamudian world, help comes from human rather than divine sources, represented here by a Jewish black man/angel, Angel Levine. Manischevitz can only wonder why God has failed to send him help in the form of a white person. The tailor's subsequent refusal of aid, which is saturated with egotistical pride, fails to lead to relief.

Eventually, Manischevitz, in pursuit of aid, roams into Harlem, where, finding Angel Levine in Bella's bar, he overhears the essential Malamudian lesson about the divine spark in all people: "It de speerit," said the old man. "From de speerit arize de man. . . . God put the spirit in all things."

Colorblind at last, Manischevitz can now believe that the same spirit dwells within every human, uniting all. Manischevitz is rewarded by the sight of a dark figure flying with dark wings. The final meaning of his experience he conveys to Fanny when he admits, "Believe me, there are Jews everywhere." Here he is Malamud's *raisonneur* mouthing the familiar theme of brotherhood.

"THE GERMAN REFUGEE"

First published: 1963 (collected in *The Complete Stories*, 1997)
Type of work: Short story

A teacher of communication ironically fails to communicate with his language student.

"The German Refugee," one of the few first-person stories in the Malamud canon, illustrates the familiar theme of brotherhood. The narrator, Martin Goldberg, relates his attempts to teach English to a German refugee, Oskar Gassner, who is to give a lecture in English about American poet Walt Whitman's relationship to certain German poets.

Two distinct stories emerge: Oskar's anguish and his failure to learn English, as well as the irony of the narrator's failure to understand why. While Martin teaches Oskar English, the German army begins its summer push of 1939. What the narrator fails to realize is his student's deep involvement with his former country's fate and that of his non-Jewish wife, whom he left there.

Malamud emphasizes the irony through the references to Whitman. Oskar ends up teaching the important lesson when he declares about the poet that "it wasn't the love of death they [German poets] had got from Whitman . . . but it was most of all his feeling for *Brudermensch*, his humanity." When Oskar successfully delivers his speech, the narrator feels only a sense of pride at what he taught the refugee, not the bonds of *Brudermensch*, that have developed between them. When Oskar commits suicide, the narrator never sees that he is partially responsible.

SUMMARY

Although undeniably part of the Jewish Literary Renaissance, Malamud is quintessentially a humanist. His novels and short stories, quite possibly some of the finest literary achievements of the latter half of the twentieth century, argue for the dignity and common bonds of all people. Occasionally experimental, Malamud basically uses traditional forms to stress traditional values. "My work, all of it," he claims, "is an idea of dedication to the human. If you don't respect man, you cannot respect my work."

Hal Charles

BIBLIOGRAPHY

By the Author

SHORT FICTION:
The Magic Barrel, 1958
Idiots First, 1963
Pictures of Fidelman: An Exhibition, 1969
Rembrandt's Hat, 1973
The Stories of Bernard Malamud, 1983
The People, and Uncollected Stories, 1989
The Complete Stories, 1997 (Robert Giroux, editor)

LONG FICTION:
The Natural, 1952
The Assistant, 1957
A New Life, 1961
The Fixer, 1966
The Tenants, 1971
Dubin's Lives, 1979
God's Grace, 1982
The People, 1989

NONFICTION:

Talking Horse: Bernard Malamud on Life and Work, 1996 (Alan Cheuse and Nicholas Delbanco, editors)

About the Author

Abramson, Edward A. *Bernard Malamud Revisited.* New York: Twayne, 1993.

Astro, Richard, and Jackson J. Benson, eds. *The Fiction of Bernard Malamud.* Corvallis: Oregon State University Press, 1977.

Avery, Evelyn, ed. *The Magic Worlds of Bernard Malamud.* Albany: State University of New York Press, 2001.

Bloom, Harold, ed. *Bernard Malamud.* New York: Chelsea House, 2000.

Davis, Philip. *Experimental Essays on the Novels of Bernard Malamud: Malamud's People.* Lewiston, N.Y.: Edwin Mellen Press, 1995.

Field, Leslie A., and Joyce W. Field, eds. *Bernard Malamud: A Collection of Critical Essays.* Rev. ed. Englewood Cliffs, N.J.: Prentice-Hall, 1975.

_____. *Bernard Malamud and the Critics.* New York: New York University Press, 1970.

Nisly, L. Lamar. *Impossible to Say: Representing Religious Mystery in Fiction by Malamud, Percy, Ozick, and O'Connor.* Westport, Conn.: Greenwood Press, 2002.

Ochshorn, Kathleen. *The Heart's Essential Landscape: Bernard Malamud's Hero.* New York: Peter Lang, 1990.

Richman, Sidney. *Bernard Malamud.* Boston: Twayne, 1966.

Salzberg, Joel, ed. *Critical Essays on Bernard Malamud.* Boston: G. K. Hall, 1987.

Sío-Castiñeira, Begoña. *The Short Stories of Bernard Malamud: In Search of Jewish Post-immigrant Identity.* New York: Peter Lang, 1998.

DISCUSSION TOPICS

- At the time Bernard Malamud wrote *The Natural*, critics did not take baseball novels very seriously. What did Malamud inject into his novel that forced critics to take notice?

- How is the theme of the American Dream presented in *The Assistant*?

- On what shortcomings of the academic world does Malamud concentrate in *The Assistant*?

- What historic events and conditions of early twentieth century Russia are important in *The Fixer*?

- By what techniques does Malamud universalize his recognizably Jewish characters and conflicts?

Brigette Lacombe

DAVID MAMET

Born: Chicago, Illinois
November 30, 1947

Capturing the rhythms and idioms of working-class American speech and dramatizing the business world in conflict with personal values, Mamet has enriched the stage with penetrating character studies of postmodern life.

BIOGRAPHY

To call David Mamet a "Chicago boy, bred and born" would not be entirely accurate, but he did live the formative years of his childhood and youth in the embrace of that giant Midwestern hub of the free enterprise system—the "hog butcher of America." Mamet was reared by his mother, who was a teacher, and his father, who was a labor lawyer, in a Jewish neighborhood on the South Side of Chicago, and attended grade school and high school in the city. Following his parents' divorce when he was eleven, Mamet lived with his mother and sister, his high school education then split between a suburban high school and Francis W. Parker School in Chicago.

Various odd jobs taught Mamet how the working world operated and exposed him to the rough and colorful language of the streets. Much has been made of his early experience at Second City (an improvisational comedy group) as a busboy, where he saw the improvisational artists and, more important, learned the language of the stage. As a backstage volunteer in neighborhood playhouses, he furthered his interest in the theatrical world. His father, Bernard, a Chicago lawyer, was an early influence in Mamet's sensitivity to the musical rhythms of natural language

Although his father had a law degree in mind for Mamet, the young high school graduate preferred the broadening education of Goddard College in Vermont (where he received a B.A. in English in 1969), where the liberal arts were taught in an experimental atmosphere. He intentionally interrupted his graduate education to spend more than a year in New York City, taking acting classes at the Neighborhood Playhouse by day and working at night as house manager for an Off-Broadway musical, the long-running success *The Fantasticks* (1960). This coincidence, together with his earlier accidental discovery of Second City in Chicago, convinced him that the theater world had something to offer him, and although he was never successful as an actor, he continued in the theater from that time on.

Mamet's stage writing had begun in college with a musical revue called *Camel*, but his first serious stage effort was *Lakeboat* (1970), written on demand for an acting class he was teaching at Marlboro College. When that teaching job was over, Mamet returned to Chicago for a series of nontheater jobs; once again, his sensitivity to the rhythms of business was to stay with him during his playwriting hours. Especially notable was his stint with a real estate development company selling Florida lots from Chicago, an experience that was to be dramatized in Mamet's Pulitzer Prize-winning play, *Glengarry Glen Ross* (1983). College teaching still appealed to him, however, and he returned to Vermont, this time to his alma mater, Goddard College, where for three years he taught theater and served as artist-in-residence. During these years his writing became more clearly articulated, and he began to write scenes for his students to work with in acting classes.

As an offshoot of his combining actor training with playwriting, he formed the St. Nicholas Company, but he moved to Chicago in 1972, where this company, under the name St. Nicholas Players, was re-formed in 1974. Mamet began in earnest his grassroots research into the nature of human discourse, wandering the streets of the city, visiting his father's law offices, trying out on paper the dialogues and ideas that flooded into his head. From that period came *Duck Variations* (1972), produced in Vermont in 1972, a nondramatic dialogue between two elderly gentlemen sitting on a park bench watching and feeding ducks. Its form helped Mamet find a writing style that freed him from elaborate stage directions and the other paraphernalia of stage scripting, allowing him to concentrate on the spoken (and unspoken) rhythms of speech and pause, and at the same time giving actors the respect they deserved for finding the sense of the line without parenthetical assistance.

Similar in style is *Sexual Perversity in Chicago* (1974), again essentially a series of simple dialogues, in bars and on the beach, in which the two main characters reveal the complexity of their relationships without directly addressing them. In this play, more elaborate than *Duck Variations*, three of the four characters share the dialogue series from time to time. There is also a love relationship in this play, a theme Mamet would not examine again until *The Woods* (1977). Mamet combined these two plays as his first attempt at a New York success, at the Off-Off-Broadway showcase house St. Clements Theatre, in 1975. It moved to the Off-Broadway Cherry Lane Theatre in 1976, opening June 16, and Mamet enjoyed his first recognition from the difficult New York theater community.

Back in Chicago, Mamet's play *American Buffalo* had been staged with great success in 1975 at Stage 2, an adjunct to the Goodman Theatre, a prestigious not-for-profit theater. The three-character play moved to Broadway in early 1977; in that same year Mamet married actress Lindsay Crouse. The play marks the beginning of an important new theme for Mamet (although *Sexual Perversity in Chicago* hinted at the possibilities): the examination of the world of business and enterprise. Here, three crooks plan a burglary, but the setting and plot are larger metaphors for the absence of moral principle in business. Far from a symbolic play, it is an ultrarealistic look at the lifestyles of its three colorful, if self-destructive, characters.

A period of intense playwriting and production activity followed. Of the plays of these few years, which included *Dark Pony* (1977), *The Water Engine* (1977), and *Mr. Happiness* (1978), perhaps the most completely realized was *A Life in the Theatre* (1977), a two-character drama about the waxing and waning of two theater actors' careers; this story, too, is told in the short-scene, blackout style that had already worked so well for Mamet. The mise-en-scène of backstage theater life, with its combination of art and commodity, continued his study of the conflict of business and friendship (or, as some critics view the play, an exploration of love).

A steady stream of powerful plays began to emerge from Mamet's imagination. Occasionally suffering from adverse critical opinion, they nevertheless contain potent characterizations and stunningly convincing dialogue. *Lone Canoe* (1979), a musical/historical study of Indian life versus advancing civilization, for example, was not successful but continued the daring verbal experimentation that has come to be associated with Mamet's work. *Edmond* (1982) is a dark look at the descent of an average man, from his tame married life to a new if subterranean view of love in a prison.

In 1984, after a run in London, *Glengarry Glen Ross* came to Broadway, an event that announced the maturing of Mamet's work. Here, he had found his voice and his subject and joined them in a powerful, unforgettable theater experience. That year it won for him the esteemed Pulitzer Prize, as well as the virtually unanimous praise of the New York critics. As well, *Glengarry Glen Ross* would, over two decades later, win the Tony award for the Best Revival of a Play in 2005. *Speed-the-Plow* (1988), another three-character play, examines the world of Hollywood film "product" development (a world to which Mamet had been introduced through his screenplay for the 1981 remake of *The Postman Always Rings Twice*). The production of *Speed-the-Plow* dominated the press because of the presence of pop star Madonna, and much of the criticism and publicity centered on her rare stage appearance. Whether the play itself carries the full weight of Mamet's talent is a matter of critical debate, but some of the dialogue illustrates Mamet at his best.

Mamet's screenplays have been successful as well. Often working on rewriting classic films, such as *We're No Angels* (1989), starring Robert De Niro and Sean Penn, and *The Postman Always Rings Twice* for director Bob Rafelson, Mamet has also written original screenplays, such as *American Buffalo* (a play of pawn shop enterprising that he wrote in 1975, which went to the screen in 1996) and *House of Games* (1987), in which his wife, Crouse, starred. Mamet has adapted other writers' works for the screen, such as *The Verdict* (1982), directed by Sydney Lumet, from Barry Reed's 1980 novel of the same name. He has had his stage plays adapted, such as *About Last Night* (1986), directed by Edward Zwick and starring Rob Lowe and Demi Moore, based on Mamet's 1974 classic *Sexual Perversity in Chicago*. He has also directed numerous films, among them a 1994 version of his play *Oleanna* (1992), which had earned him a Drama Desk Award nomination for Outstanding New Play.

Further screenplays have included such blockbusters as *The Untouchables* (1987), starring Kevin Costner and Sean Connery; *Hoffa* (1992), directed by Danny DeVito and starring Jack Nicholson; *The Edge* (1997), starring Anthony Hopkins; and *Wag the Dog* (1997), a frighteningly realistic take on waging a war to deflect attention from a president's sex scandal, staged by a Washington spin doctor and a Hollywood producer played by Dustin Hoffman and De Niro, respectively.

ANALYSIS

In Mamet's dialogue, the American language of informal discourse becomes a tool for combat and defense, a song of near meanings, and a sanctuary in slang for the dangerous exposure to true feeling. He has perhaps caught the rhythms of the spoken language as no one has since William Shakespeare, and his characters are true to their speech. He is often compared to Eugene O'Neill, and some critics believe that he surpasses that great American playwright in his ability to make believable the speech patterns of common street life. Several observers of Mamet's canon have used a musical analogy, calling his dialogue "Chicago jazz" or "a fugue" otherwise underlining the sense of rhythm that his speeches seem to evoke.

Some critics, while noting the strength of the dialogue, interpret the talking scenes as static or undramatic. While it is true that "action" in its basic sense is often missing or concentrated at the end of the plays, the "action" inside the dialogue is complex and multilayered. All speech is, in fact, "speech-act," the establishing of relational strategies by means of speech. The dialogue in a Mamet play, then, is a series of defenses, justifications, explanations, probing into opinions, and establishing common ground; and underneath all the talk is action as dramatic as any more obvious or physical action. Mamet's characters admit, deny, offer, accept, deceive, sell, plead, reveal, and conceal in their language. Many times, as critics have noted, the dialogue conceals the emotional content of the scene, as though (in Voltaire's words) "words conceal meaning." In this respect, Mamet, more than any other contemporary playwright, finds his true genre in stage writing in which the action is carried almost exclusively in the character dialogue.

Mamet's views of personal relationships, a theme important to his work, are easily revealed in the content and the mise-en-scène of his plays: Love is treated not as a gentle or honest relationship but as a hard-fought conclusion. Usually love is seen as it collapses, as a relationship breaks apart. In *Sexual Perversity in Chicago*, for example, the getting together of Dan and Deborah takes place briefly and almost offstage; their break-up, however, is open and on the stage. Even the scene in which Deborah moves in with Dan is not placed in a neutral or happy setting but in her former apartment, with her former roommate Joan angrily concealing her own bitterness and unhappiness with a series of smart-aleck rejoinders. In every play, love is shown in off-handed, negatively connoted scenes.

Where Mamet stands in terms of business and enterprise is not so easily revealed in a single examination of one play or scene. While it is certainly true that the shoddy, "grifter" side of business takes center stage, the question remains whether Mamet applauds that attitude or finds fault with it. In one sense, the dynamics of a business transaction are like drama, but in another sense, the phoniness and false intentions of business dealings are antithetical to true communication. Mamet has chosen to dramatize the inability or reluctance of the characters to enter into an honest negotiation and at the same time their willingness to join in friendships and bonds that transcend simple business dealings.

In the play *Glengarry Glen Ross*, Roma's best scene is a brutally honest rephrasing of the principles of existentialism, and for a moment the audience thinks that this is Mamet himself speaking. When Roma turns salesman, however, the audience realizes that his apparent frankness was only the warm-up to the duplicitous business of selling Florida property to an unwilling restaurant owner. *The Water Engine* dramatizes the inventor's dilemma of finding financial security without selling out to the free enterprise system; both this idea and the theme of *Speed-the-Plow* are reminiscent of some themes of playwright Sam Shepard in this respect, showing the artist at odds with the world of enterprise.

More viscerally important than either love or business is Mamet's prevailing theme of language as defense, as shield against encroachment by honest emotion. In *American Buffalo*, the affection between Donny and Bobby is never spoken of outright, but it is there in Donny's long-suffering patience, in his attempt to include Bobby in the scheme (against Teach's wishes), and his defense of Bobby when Teach hurts him in the final scene. Teach is all alone in the world, with no friends; even Ruthie, an offstage presence, hurts his feelings when he asks for a piece of her toast. Bobby and Donny, however, have developed an awkward, unspoken father/son relationship in the dingy setting of the junk store. Bobby's devotion to Donny (as witnessed by his attempts to buy the coin) is an example of how simple, less articulate people show their affection. Donny, on the other hand, a bridge between the world of business and deceit and the world of human interaction, has none of the verbal brittleness of Teach. Teach is all words; he is adept at using talking as a shield, a defense, and an aggressive agent.

While the harsh language of virtually all the characters suggests that Mamet is always coarse in his treatment of relationships, it is a mistake to see Mamet's plays as devoid of warmth. The play *A Life in the Theatre* is touching in many instances, and at base is a pas-de-deux of two like souls. Told poignantly and sensitively, it is a graceful work. While not entirely devoid of the rough language of Mamet's other plays, the dialogue moves through a more sophisticated vocabulary, because the characters are educated actors in the midst of the world of theater rather than people in a working-class environment.

The Woods is a love story as well, despite the harshness of its conclusion. *Sexual Perversity in Chicago*, on the surface about the coming together and breaking apart of the couples, is also a story of male bonding, however crude and insensitive Bernie is

to Dan's problems. It is a play about the inability to love, and as such shows the influence of Samuel Beckett, Harold Pinter, and other absurdists, showing characters caught in the dilemma of a need for love and a world that sees love as a weakness. In the big city life that pervades Mamet's work, love has no permanent place. In fact, business is not so much a subject as a metaphor for all human relationships: intimate contact for personal gain, duplicity and deceit for protection. The love stories are always concerned with implied and stated contracts, with the unspoken rules with an ineffable morality that transcends the gutter talk of the dialogue itself.

Storytelling is an art both for Mamet's characters and for Mamet himself. In every play, at least one long monologue is devoted to telling a story of the past, both as protective device and as a form of bravado on the part of the speaker, to hide or to reveal his inner self. It is as though the speaker tells his story to avoid revealing himself, yet reveals himself at the same time accidentally. Whether that can be said of Mamet himself is open to question. An open, talkative, witty, and accessible personality, Mamet often appears with a large cigar, a "prop" behind which he successfully hides his personal life.

AMERICAN BUFFALO

First produced: 1975 (first published, 1976)
Type of work: Play

Three petty thieves try to steal back a possibly valuable buffalo nickel from the man who purchased it.

The scene is a sleazy junk store, run by Donny, in a run-down urban setting. Donny runs the shop in a low key, using Bobby to run errands for him. The world of the shop is cluttered and arbitrary, an organic construction rather than a carefully designed one. The financial stakes are low here; an occasional sale to a passerby is enough to sustain the two men in their unambitious lives.

Into this mix comes Teach—angry, "wired," full of venomous energy—with a plan, a scheme, a project of the will (to use Henrik Ibsen's term). It is not enough for Teach to plan and carry out the crime;

his innate secretiveness, paranoia, and distrust must extend to his partners, Donny and an offstage figure (Fletch) who eventually deserts the project. Teach brings an anger with him that has become emblematic of the kind of vicious energy that drives Mamet's plays forward. One sees the same kind of energy in Bernie (*Sexual Perversity in Chicago*) and in Roma (*Glengarry Glen Ross*), although Roma is closer to a hero than other destructive Mamet characters.

Driving the minor-key greed of the two more passive characters (Bobby is slightly simple, helpful, and, in a scheme of his own, determined to please Donny) is the possibility of stealing back a coin Donny sold to a customer some time previously. Apparently the coin, a buffalo-head nickel, has some value, because the customer paid fifty dollars for it. Rather than taking delight in Donny's windfall, Teach sees the customer as a cheat who probably knows the coin was worth even more. Thus, as a kind of angry revenge, they can steal the coin back with a clear conscience—the customer has somehow turned into the villain, and the trio become, in their own minds, the Robin Hood-like righters of wrongs.

What goes wrong with the burglary is distrust and lack of sophistication. First, the victim is not away from the house; the thieves have been misinformed by Bobby, because he left his observation post. Also, their silent partner has not shown up, and they suspect that he has preceded them in the theft and betrayed them. In fact, he is in the hospital, but they do not believe the story. At the end of the play, Donny shows that he is not another Teach but a friend of a more compassionate order.

The play is not exactly an indictment of all business. The question of trust, of partnership, is examined, and the conclusion is double-sided. The agreements between Donny and Teach are suspect because they are based on distrust; however, the relationship between Donny and Bobby is more genuine. In the opening scene, when Bobby is sent to get food for Donny, there is a sense that the way business works best is by trust—Donny tells Bobby to buy some food for himself as well and does not quibble about the money.

When Teach enters, his first lament is about an incident that occurred in the same restaurant—an argument over half a piece of toast. While the scenes are immediate and dynamic, on reflection

they represent two ways of "doing business" (which for Mamet means joining in any relationship). Either the business arrangement is the only connection between partners, in which case duplicity and trickery are parts of the agreement, or else the business arrangement is part of a larger relationship, one of affection and mutual trust, in which case the automatic self-serving attitudes of the business person have no place.

Now widely done on the regional stage, this play is often the center of controversy regarding appropriate stage language for more conservative audiences. Its success as drama has invariably won the argument in favor of language verisimilitude, and the rest of Mamet's works have subsequently been widely accepted.

GLENGARRY GLEN ROSS

First produced: 1983 (first published, 1983)
Type of work: Play

High-pressure Florida real estate salesmen fight for leads to promising clients, losing their own principles and values in the process.

In this play, Mamet has found his strongest metaphor for the complexity of human relationships. A group of salesmen, vying for "leads" to hot prospects for a Florida land scheme, make use of language not only to "close" their prospects but also to obfuscate their actual intentions, which include robbing the "leads" from the real estate office. On the surface, every salesman is a man for himself, and the last emotion one would expect is friendship and loyalty among them. They can only judge their success by the sales they make, and the "board" of the contest is the measurement of that success. The best leads get the best closes, and if a man is too far down on the list of persons getting leads, he never has a chance to catch up. In this respect, the play is reminiscent of Arthur Miller's *Death of a Salesman* (1949), because the American Dream of success is separated from the method, from the moral premise behind success.

The first-act scenes in the restaurant are hard-edged dialogues, almost monologues with a responding listener. Moss and Aaronow, whom the audience originally suspects for the office break-ins, are an example of the intimidation relationship in which Mamet excels. Aaronow is drawn into the robbery by dint of Moss's ability to "sell" his guilt to him. As in *American Buffalo*, the criminal turns his crime around into a sort of revenge against someone who did not play by the rules— here it is Moss, showing Aaranow that to steal the leads is a just punishment for Williamson, whose job is to give the leads out. Williamson, it is noted, has never closed a sale, has never been out there in the field, but is a pawn of the offstage owners, Mitch and Murray.

In a sense, there is something besides Florida real estate being sold: reputation, one's place on the sales board, even one's loyalty to the police, are all for sale. At the center of the play is Roma's and Levene's friendship, despite their competition for the Cadillac. When they are both winners, when the sales are closing, they share a frenetic energy and understanding of the almost sexual exaltation of success. When Levene defends Roma to Williamson, the audience sees a side of him that is soft and more likeable; however, the revealing of that very softness is the undoing of Levene, when he accidentally lets Williamson know that he was the actual burglar in the previous night's incident. Williamson immediately pounces on the flaw, and Levene is discovered as the crook. In the meantime, Roma does not even realize what his friend has done for him, as he pursues a lost sale.

The fast-talking world of Florida (and Arizona) real estate sales is a world where the men function only in direct proportion to their ability to hide themselves, to seek the fast buck. It is a hollow relationship but one with certain unspoken rules. The three-day rule, in which a customer has three days to cancel his deal, is a rule imposed from outside. The customers who are never serious, such as the Indians and the Nyborg family (famous for writing bad checks), are looked down on by the salesmen as unfair players, as wastes of time. Stealing the leads and selling them to a competitor is a way of breaking the rules of the business they are in, but more importantly, it confuses the order of success among the men.

Mamet found inspiration from his own brief work in such a sales office and from "those guys you see on planes" who are the businessmen at work, artificial in their own relationships, competing daily,

either directly or indirectly, for the same dollar. Very little daydreaming is actually done about spending the money, about eventually relaxing and enjoying the fruits of their labors. At the moment, like racehorses, they are in the race, and every bit of energy must go into winning it.

Events such as Levene's triumphant entrance and depiction of his grand sale to Bruce and Harriet Nyborg (underscored by Aaranow's disgruntled "I had them on River Glen") are the highlights of these men's lives—the moments when they can announce their successes to one another. The fact that the Nyborg deal will fall through when the check is shown to be fraudulent caps the deadly day of deceit and hopelessness in the ruined office. The other deal gone sour, the sale to Lingk, occurs at the office itself, when Lingk, prompted by his less gullible wife, demands a retraction of the deal. The support character of the detective, Baylen, the only one not involved in the real estate scheme as seller or buyer, is not fully developed—he represents a "finding out," a revealing not of who broke the law but who broke the unwritten code by which these men work.

The storytelling abilities of Mamet's characters, especially the salesmen, are a reflection of Mamet's own ability to tell a good story. The quick-talking defense mechanism of the salesman prevents real contact. As in *American Buffalo*, where the physical object of the buffalo nickel is a carefully chosen symbol (of the lost American West, perhaps, as one critic notes), so the valueless Florida real estate the men are hawking is a symbol of the uselessness at base of the efforts of the men and their world. What they have to sell is worthless; their lives are made worthless as a result.

SPEED-THE-PLOW

First produced: 1988 (first published, 1988)
Type of work: Play

A pair of motion picture producers decide whether to make a sure-fire hit or a high-risk but thematically valuable script recommended by their temporary secretary.

In this play, the question of the worth of a commodity is made the center of the conflict. Far from being useless, worthless property, as in *Glengarry Glen Ross*, here the "product" is a film script more or less guaranteed to make money versus a very questionable project that has no real value but is valuable to the spirit of the men involved.

Bobby Gould, a newly promoted production executive, is visited by an old "friend and associate," Charlie Fox. Gould has "a new deal" with the money man, Ross (offstage). In a power position, Gould is constantly "promoted" by other producers who want him to approve their film deals. He is wary of being "promoted," but Fox, an old friend and business associate, brings him a perfect project—a name actor has agreed to "cross the street." Fox does not "go through channels"—a metaphor for the disguises, the safeguards between people and their emotions—not because he trusts his friendship with Gould, but because he is sure that his film opportunity will appeal to Gould on a business level.

Money versus people is the theme, as Gould and Fox themselves agree: When the "deal" starts to slip away, what are the real values? The question of loyalty and friendship versus the world of business, as in *Glengarry Glen Ross* and *American Buffalo*, comes up again. "It's only words unless they're true," says Fox. Another property, by an Eastern philosopher, has taken the fancy of Karen, a temporary secretary, who visits Gould and sleeps with him in exchange for consideration of the new project.

The audience must consider whether Gould was truly converted to the new book or was tricked into believing in the ideas of the book. The theme that concerns Mamet once again is the interface of business (by which he means cold, distrustful relationships with unwritten rules) and friendship (by which he means trust without boundaries). Two scripts compete for one "green light" from the head of the studio. One script, clearly a moneymaker, is trite and exploitive and imitative. The other script is a large idea from an Eastern author, purveying a notion that radiation was sent by God to change the world. Its value as box-office revenue is very questionable, but Karen's explanation of it, coupled with her offer of sexual gratification, is too much for Gould, and he changes his mind in favor of the radiation book. When his friendship with Fox, a friendship bordering on "old boy" camaraderie, is threatened, Fox shows Gould that Karen was simply using him for her own ambitions.

When Gould sends Karen away and goes to the meeting with Fox, the audience realizes that Gould has abandoned his soul and his only chance for true greatness. On the other hand, the duplicity and confused nature of love is also in question: If Karen had been clearly the good influence, the play would have been melodramatic, but with Karen's motives under question, the play becomes much more insightful and complex. This sense of possible betrayal, coupled with a swing in power from one person to another, is at the base of the play's drama.

Karen is an unusual character for Mamet—an attractive woman who presents the idea of noble principles to an otherwise superficially insensitive businessman. Usually the women in Mamet's plays are impediments to a man's business, asking for personal commitment (as in *The Woods*) in place of the retreat of the emotions that Mamet sees as a masculine trait. Here, again, the woman is asking the man to be himself, to go against the rules of business (including the first rule of guarding himself from damage in friendship), to project himself outside the safe business deal into a film based on belief. Where Mamet stands on the question of real value is not immediately clear, as the radiation text in question is at once profound and nonsensical. As in all of his plays to date, Mamet stays neutral regarding the nature of truly principled action.

OLEANNA

First produced: 1992 (first published, 1993)
Type of work: Play

This play examines the sociopolitical ambiguity and explosiveness of an academic relationship between a female student and a male professor.

In this play, sexual harassment is at the epicenter, but the harassment is dubious, interpreted, skewed, absurdly subliminal if even present, as each of the two characters—John, a professor about to take tenure, and Carol, a student struggling with more than grades—defend their interpretations of the language of the student-professor dynamic.

Confused and at the end of her academic rope, Carol comes to John's office to express concerns about failing his course. A male arm around female shoulders, a bargain to come to the office to learn all she can from all he knows, and the grade will become an A, and a tension is established that carries the play. Yet all is not quite so simple as an offer to show that she can study hard and prove herself deserving of the almighty A. With each well-intended appointment, Carol arrives, but John is on the phone, or takes a phone call, or makes a phone call. In the middle of Carol's sentences, the phone will ring. John will put her off at key intellectual moments to talk to his wife about the new house that they plan to buy (once he is tenured). John makes Carol wait while he finishes phone discussions regarding logistics of the house. John stops their study sessions to answer the questions that the caller has about the house.

So the phone—clearly the symbol of the power of language and the power to interrupt, intercept, interject, or mute the language of the less important student—ushers in the true themes of *Oleanna*, themes of language, restrictions of language, power, and power through language. Nowhere in the play while the curtain is up does John sexually harass Carol. Yet his impervious position of power and his manner of espousing antiacademia, lecturing the attentive note-taking Carol, and interrupting repeatedly her attempts to take power by using the language from which she is distanced from the start, impel the student to challenge John in the only way that she can to turn the desks: She uses language, that which she has claimed is inaccessible to her, to bring him down. She accuses him of raping her, maligns his direction, and seethes venom about being a former victim and about having the power to take the case to the cutting place—the tenure committee—in a manner that elicits the basest of unnatural and natural responses at once: John resorts to violence, to lifting his office chair over his head, at the ready to bring it crashing down over her head.

THE OLD NEIGHBORHOOD

First produced: 1997 (first published, 1998; includes *The Disappearance of the Jews*, 1983, *Jolly*, 1989, and *Deeny*, 1989)
Type of work: Play

A penetrating study of reconciliation—of geographical place, of family members, and of attempts at self-identity.

That David Mamet is a master of language is once again utterly apparent in this play, but what is also clear is Mamet is a linguophile. The redemption comes by way of Bobby returning to his old neighborhood, by way of the communing and commiserating of a family culture, and ultimately by way of dialogue that hums, spits, stutters, and stalls. Intentional and realistic, the spoken words are as evocative as the pauses to express the ineffable.

Bobby Gould has come home, returning to his old Chicago neighborhood ("to get Comfort"), where he converses with his boyhood buddy Joey in act 1 ("The Disappearance of the Jews"), with sister Jolly and her husband Carl in act 2 ("Jolly"), and with a past lover, perhaps still loved, in act 3 ("Deeny"). While the present points toward the question of the future, the past is the focus.

In act 1, a dolorous exchange of "woulda-coulda-shoulda" is the bonding agent. Bobby would love to have been in Hollywood in the 1920's. Joey would have loved living in the shtetl. Joey would lose his wife to old age, and the people of town would bake for him. They would have been smart Jews. They would have been free. However, the characters are not free. The true freedom is only in the words, in the essence of their epic and allusive storytelling and in their heroic plans for a future trip, which surely will release them into a pleasant memory.

In act 2, brother and sister futz with the tethers of their childhoods, reminiscing about a Christmas that they are still tied up in by an overbearing mother who controlled them with gifts that they did not want or need, with words that they can never forget, with actions that control their todays, bastardizing even the most idyllic of childhood moments.

In act 3, the past is revisited, again in the keenest of dialogue—Bob's subtle and uttering agreements and Deeny's thoughtful, philosophical pleasantries. There is a suspension of agony, finally, in conversation that, controlled by Deeny, is more visionary than revisionary. Though that is the precise effect. While Joey of act 1 has claimed they "have no connection," denying even that of what could have been or what could still be, Deeny brings a connectedness—by way of truth and dreamy possibility of truth, by way of well-founded and solid love (which she desires and Bobby is capable of providing), and by way of, essentially, the connection made by talk, by words, by realistic speech between humans, whatever their dilemma or despair.

SUMMARY

Mamet's plays might appear on the surface to be all rough language, superficial relationships, static or absent plots, and unpleasant characters, but they deserve a closer look. The language is often quite beautiful when heard with a sensitive ear to the sensitivity of the rhythms of ordinary speech. Relationships that appear to be superficial are, in fact, deep and complex. Actions of a very subtle kind drive the plays forward, embedded in speech and in unspoken bonding. Often, the violent climax of the play comes as an inevitable release of tensions built up through the whole play's structure. Mamet can never be said to be loveable, but behind his facades and protections, he is an astute observer of the human parade and, ultimately, a believer in life.

Thomas J. Taylor; updated by Roxanne McDonald

BIBLIOGRAPHY

By the Author

DRAMA:
Camel, pr. 1968
Lakeboat, pr. 1970, revised pr. 1980, pb. 1981
Duck Variations, pr. 1972, pb. 1977
Sexual Perversity in Chicago, pr. 1974, pb. 1977
Squirrels, pr. 1974, pb. 1982
American Buffalo, pr. 1975, pb. 1976
Reunion, pr. 1976, pb. 1979
A Life in the Theatre, pr., pb. 1977
The Revenge of the Space Pandas, pr. 1977, pb. 1978 (one act; children's play)
The Water Engine, pr. 1977, pb. 1978
Dark Pony, pr. 1977, pb. 1979
The Woods, pr. 1977, pb. 1979
Mr. Happiness, pr., pb. 1978
Lone Canoe, pr. 1979 (music and lyrics by Alaric Jans)
The Sanctity of Marriage, pr. 1979, pb. 1982
Donny March, pr. 1981
The Poet and the Rent, pr., pb. 1981 (children's play)
A Sermon, pr., pb. 1981
Short Plays and Monologues, pb. 1981
Edmond, pr. 1982, pb. 1983
Glengarry Glen Ross, pr., pb. 1983
The Disappearance of the Jews, pr. 1983, pb. 1987 (one act)
Red River, pr. 1983 (adaptation of Pierre Laville's play)
Goldberg Street: Short Plays and Monologues, pb. 1985
The Shawl, pr., pb. 1985

David Mamet

A Collection of Dramatic Sketches and Monologues, pb. 1985

Vint, pr. 1985, pb. 1986 (adaptation of Anton Chekhov's short story)

The Cherry Orchard, pr., pb. 1986 (adaptation of Chekhov's play)

Three Children's Plays, pb. 1986

Three Jewish Plays, pb. 1987

Speed-the-Plow, pr., pb. 1988

Uncle Vanya, pr., pb. 1988 (adaptation of Chekhov's play)

Bobby Gould in Hell, pr. 1989, pb. 1991 (one act)

Three Sisters, pr., pb. 1990 (adaptation of Chekhov's play)

Oh Hell: Two One-Act Plays, pb. 1991

Oleanna, pr. 1992, pb. 1993

The Cryptogram, pr., pb. 1994

No One Will Be Immune, and Other Plays and Pieces, pb. 1994

Plays, pb. 1994-2002 (4 volumes)

An Interview, pr., pb. 1995 (one act)

The Old Neighborhood, pr. 1997, pb. 1998 (includes *The Disappearance of the Jews, Jolly*, and *Deeny*)

Boston Marriage, pr. 1999, pb. 2001

Faustus, a Play, pb. 2004

SCREENPLAYS:

The Postman Always Rings Twice, 1981 (adaptation of James M. Cain's novel)

The Verdict, 1982 (adaptation of Barry Reed's novel)

The Untouchables, 1987

House of Games, 1987

Things Change, 1988

We're No Angels, 1989

Glengarry Glen Ross, 1992 (adaptation of his play)

Hoffa, 1992

Oleanna, 1994 (adaptation of his play)

Vanya on 42nd Street, 1994

American Buffalo, 1996 (adaptation of his play)

The Edge, 1997

The Spanish Prisoner, 1997

Wag the Dog, 1997 (with Hilary Henkins; adaptation of Larry Beinhart's novel *American Hero*)

The Winslow Boy, 1999 (adaptation of Terrence Rattigan's play)

State and Main, 2000

The Heist, 2001

LONG FICTION:

The Village, 1994

The Old Religion, 1997

Wilson: A Consideration of the Sources, 2000

DISCUSSION TOPICS

- How is David Mamet's *American Buffalo* a study of American capitalism?

- What are the symbolic implications of the buffalo in *American Buffalo*?

- Consider acts 1 and 2 of *Glengarry Glen Ross*. How does the structure of each differ, and how does that structure contribute to the play as a whole?

- How do the salesmen in *Glengarry Glen Ross* each meet the expectations and challenges of the business world? Who perpetuates and who defies the conventions of ethical and unethical business strategies?

- How does the telephone function in *Oleanna*?

- Consider the physical characteristics, acts, and gestures of Carol and John in *Oleanna*. How do they contribute to characterization and plot development?

- In *The Old Neighborhood*, how are Bobby Gould's name and identity problematic?

- What do the characters of *The Old Neighborhood* seek?

POETRY:
The Hero Pony, 1990
The Chinaman, 1999

TELEPLAYS:
Five Television Plays, 1990
A Life in the Theatre, 1993 (adaptation of his play)

RADIO PLAYS:
Prairie du Chien, 1978
Cross Patch, 1985
Goldberg Street, 1985

NONFICTION:
Writing in Restaurants, 1986
Some Freaks, 1989
On Directing Film, 1991
The Cabin: Reminiscence and Diversions, 1992
The Village, 1994
A Whore's Profession: Notes and Essays, 1994
Make-Believe Town: Essays and Remembrances, 1996
True and False: Heresy and Common Sense for the Actor, 1997
Three Uses of the Knife: On the Nature and Purpose of Drama, 1998
Jafsie and John Henry: Essays on Hollywood, Bad Boys, and Six Hours of Perfect Poker, 1999
On Acting, 1999
Five Cities of Refuge: Weekly Reflections on Genesis, Exodus, Leviticus, Numbers, and Deuteronomy, 2003 (with Lawrence Kushner)

CHILDREN'S LITERATURE:
The Owl, 1987
Warm and Cold, 1988 (with Donald Sultan)
Passover, 1995
The Duck and the Goat, 1996
Bar Mitzvah, 1999 (with Sultan)
Henrietta, 1999

About the Author

Bigsby, C. W. E. *Beyond Broadway.* Vol. 3 in *A Critical Introduction to Twentieth Century American Drama.* Cambridge, England: Cambridge University Press, 1985.

_____. *David Mamet.* London: Methuen, 1985.

Cohn, Ruby. *New American Dramatists: 1960-1980.* New York: Grove Press, 1982.

Dean, Anne. *David Mamet: Language as Dramatic Action.* Rutherford, N.J.: Fairleigh Dickinson University Press, 1990.

Mamet, David. *Writing in Restaurants.* New York: Penguin Books, 1986.

Ruas, Charles. *Conversations with American Writers.* London: Quartet Books, 1986.

PAULE MARSHALL

Born: Brooklyn, New York
April 9, 1929

Marshall introduces a rich West Indian perspective into the body of African American literature, examining cross-cultural conflicts between individuals and their societies.

Courtesy, Augusta State University

BIOGRAPHY

Paule Marshall was born in Brooklyn as Valenza Pauline Burke, one of three children of Samuel and Ada Burke, immigrants from the island of Barbados. Her father, whom she dearly loved, was unskilled but dreamed of a better life. Eventually, he left the family to join the "kingdom" of black religious leader Father Divine in Harlem. Her mother worked as a domestic servant. Marshall credits her early interest in language and stories to "the poets in the kitchen," her mother's Barbadian friends who gathered in the basement kitchen of her brownstone house after work to have a cup of tea or cocoa and discuss their lives.

At the age of nine, Marshall visited Barbados, where she first met her maternal grandmother, an impressive ancestral figure who appears in many of Marshall's works. Her story "To Da-duh, in Memoriam" (1967) is a nearly autobiographical account of this visit. Inspired by the beauty of the islands, she began to write poetry, and on her return began a period of intense reading. By accident, she discovered the poetry of Paul Laurence Dunbar, the first African American author whose work she had ever read, and this experience gave her the courage to think of becoming a writer.

In 1950, Marshall married Kenneth E. Marshall. Three years later, she graduated Phi Beta Kappa, cum laude, from Brooklyn College. Her first published story, "The Valley Between" (1954), reflects her own struggle as a wife and mother with her desire for education and a writing career. Marshall worked in New York public libraries and from 1953 to 1956 was the only woman staff writer for *Our World* magazine, traveling on assignment to Brazil and the West Indies.

While doing postgraduate work at Hunter College in 1955, Marshall began her autobiographical novel *Brown Girl, Brownstones* (1959), completing it in Barbados. A television adaptation of the novel was presented on the Columbia Broadcasting System (CBS) the following year. At first, the book was treated as a book for juveniles and was largely ignored. Since its reissue by the Feminist Press in 1981, however, it has been considered a classic female *Bildungsroman*.

A Guggenheim Fellowship awarded in 1960 allowed Marshall to complete and publish a collection of four novellas, *Soul Clap Hands and Sing* (1961). This book marked a significant shift in her work: Each novella is written from a male character's perception and bears a political subtext.

In the 1960's, black women writers remained largely unread. Marshall, divorced in 1963, determined to support herself and her son, Evan-Keith, by writing rather than by teaching, and she was thus dependent on grants. In the eight years it took to complete her ambitious second novel, *The Chosen Place, the Timeless People* (1969), she received the Rosenthal Award from the National Institute of Arts and Letters (1962) and grants from the Ford Foundation (1964) and the National Endowment for the Arts (1967).

In 1970, Marshall entered an "open and innovative marriage" with Nourry Menard, a relationship that allowed her more freedom to write. A journey to West Africa in 1977 gave her a broader perspective and strengthened her awareness of African influences in her own life. Three years later, she traveled to East Africa, where she was welcomed as a native daughter.

Marshall became more widely known in the 1980's. A collection of earlier work, *Reena, and Other Stories*, appeared in 1983 and was republished in 1985 as *Merle: A Novella and Other Stories*. The book includes her autobiographical essay "From the Poets in the Kitchen" (1983), initially published in *The New York Times Book Review*, and the novella *Merle*. Adapted and rewritten from *The Chosen Place, the Timeless People, Merle* further defines Marshall's favorite and most fascinating character, the charismatic West Indian Merle Kinbona.

A third novel, *Praisesong for the Widow*, was also published in 1983. Set in the islands of Grenada and Carriacou, it won the Before Columbus American Book Award the following year. In 1991, *Daughters* appeared, a novel that draws strong parallels between the lives of women, past and present, in New York and the West Indies. *The Fisher King* (2000), Marshall's fifth novel, focuses on a small boy's restoration of two families that have been estranged for years because of prejudice and misunderstanding.

In addition to her writing career, Marshall has taught at a number of colleges, including Yale University, Virginia Commonwealth University in Richmond, the University of California at Berkeley, and the Iowa Writers' Workshop. She holds the Helen Gould Sheppard Chair of Literature and Culture at New York University. Among her many honors are the John Dos Passos Award for Literature, the American Book Award, and a MacArthur Fellowship.

ANALYSIS

One of Marshall's unquestioned strengths is her skill with language, especially the colorful West Indian dialects. She has identified herself as trilingual, at ease with the dialect of Barbados, the African American dialect of Harlem, and the "proper" English she spoke at school. She believes that her sense of language is an African characteristic, triggered by listening to her mother's friends, who "did marvelous things with the English language.... They brought to bear the few African words and cadences that they remembered and they infused

and enriched it." In "From the Poets in the Kitchen," Marshall confesses that she longed to possess the same power with words. Her evocative scene at the beginning of the 1961 novella *Barbados* affirms her mastery of that power: "Dawn, like the night which had preceded it, came from the sea. In a white mist tumbling like spume over the fishing boats leaving the island and the hunched, ghost shapes of the fishermen. In a white, wet wind breathing over the villages scattered amid the tall canes."

Marshall is not a static writer, for each book presents a new challenge. *Reena, and Other Stories* demonstrates in one volume her increasing command of language between 1954 and 1983. *Brown Girl, Brownstones* is seen primarily through the viewpoint of the girl Selina, but the novellas of *Soul Clap Hands and Sing* are perceived through their male protagonists. Marshall's longest novel, *The Chosen Place, the Timeless People*, is lushly overwritten, encompassing the voices of many characters, whereas *Praisesong for the Widow* is taut and compact. *Daughters* employs some experimental techniques—a poetic slash between words to mark direct thought, an occasional shift into present tense. In *The Fisher King*, a novel in which bloodlines from Africa, the Caribbean, and the United States come together in the child Sonny, the male characters again attain equal significance with the female.

Marshall's themes include the individual quest for identity and the need for community, as well as a recognition of individual interconnectedness with the past. In her work, the desire to establish an identity is always linked to integration within a larger community, and her concept of community spreads outward from Brooklyn to encompass the entire African world. A character's sense of community is then strengthened by an awareness of communal history.

Discovering her historical past, first in Barbados, later in Africa, gave Marshall that communal view that was so healing, and her characters seek similar discoveries. In *Brown Girl, Brownstones*, Selina Boyce longs to break away from her family to become her own person, but she does so by determining to go to Barbados, her ancestral home. In *The Chosen Place, the Timeless People*, the American Jew Saul Amron finds himself embraced by the community of Bournehills and is then better able to come to terms with his own history. In *Daughters*,

Ursa Mackenzie breaks away from her father's influence only to become aware of the community of daughters to which she, her mother, and every other woman belong.

All of Marshall's major characters find they must explore their collective, as well as their personal, history. One way to connect with the past is through ritual, especially dance, and Marshall uses it often. Examples include the social rituals of the Barbadian Association in *Brown Girl, Brownstones*, the pigsticking ritual of the cane workers and the Carnival reenactment of Cuffee Ned's revolt in *The Chosen Place, the Timeless People*, and the collective ritual of the Carriacou Big Drum in *Praisesong for the Widow*. In contrast, *The Fisher King* demonstrates that the personal history of each individual character informs the collective history of all.

Another major concern of Marshall's work is the need for social change. One of her most political novels is *The Chosen Place, the Timeless People*, which examines the social and economic problems of Bournehills, a hard-luck section of a small Caribbean island where the shadows of slave and master have not been fully obliterated. A number of references are made to thirty pounds sterling, the former price of a slave. Merle Kinbona reminds her American guests that nine million Africans died on their journey to the New World, and the raging sea below her Cassia House will never forget them. Yet the major tension now is between the oppressive British owner of the sugarcane mill and the exploited native workers, known locally as the "Little Fella." The many sociopolitical tensions of *Daughters* are reflected in the Caribbean politician Primus Mackenzie and his African American wife, Estelle, through their conflicting views on what is best for the people of Triunion and for their daughter, Ursa.

Marshall questions not only British capitalism, as seen in Bournehills, but American materialism. *Brown Girl, Brownstones'* Silla Boyce succumbs to the American Dream of ownership, sacrificing her husband, her daughters, and much of her humanity. Mr. Watford of *Barbados* loses his human tenderness in his pride of possession. From a different perspective, *The Fisher King* deplores the materialism of some of the American characters, as opposed to others who have chosen to live in Europe.

Marshall also addresses the control that society has had over women. In her own world, men were the ones who held power. Elsewhere, she notes the triple invisibility of her mother's Barbadian friends, her mentors in America, who were black, female, and foreign. In a 1979 interview, she stated, "I wanted to turn that around. I wanted women to be the centers of power." By emphasizing the role of the black woman in her community, Marshall anticipated popular culture by twenty years. She believes that her role as a writer is to tell the truth about her community, to counteract negative stereotypes of African Americans, and to offer a model for young black women.

BROWN GIRL, BROWNSTONES

First published: 1959
Type of work: Novel

A young girl of West Indian ancestry comes of age in 1940's Brooklyn, discovering her identity to be apart from, yet defined by, her parents and her culture.

Brown Girl, Brownstones, Marshall's first novel, is the story of Selina Boyce, the daughter of Barbadian immigrants, and her journey to womanhood. At ten, Selina resists her awkwardly changing body, uncomfortable yet fascinated by a dawning sexual awareness. Marshall writes candidly about women's bodies, menstruation, and sexuality at a time when writers, especially women, were not encouraged to be so frank.

This initiation novel brings Selina into much more than physical womanhood. She must also develop emotionally and mentally; she must learn humiliation, grief, understanding, and the courage to be herself. Many characters guide Selina through her approaching womanhood: the voluptuous boarder Suggie; Miss Thompson, an elderly southern hairdresser who serves as comforter and surrogate mother and whose foot bears an ulcerous "life-sore" as a direct result of racism; Selina's schoolmate Beryl; and, of course, her parents. A final guide is Clive, a sometime artist whose major lesson for her is to learn to leave him.

Selina's real and ongoing conflict is with her mother, a blank, formidable woman. Eventually, Selina learns to understand her mother better, but she never completely overcomes her anger at her mother's treatment of her father. Selina also recognizes that a part of her is determined and ruthless, too. She is her mother's daughter as well as her father's.

A second plot line follows the complex struggle between Selina's parents. Deighton, her charming yet doomed father, was a cosseted child who was sent to college in Barbados to become a teacher. His proud refusal to be treated as second-class, his insistence that the white world must see him as an equal, leads him to grandiose, ill-fated schemes. Silla, her mother, comes from a background of rural poverty and is determined to survive in "this man country" by acquiring property and renting to tenants. Her strength allows the family to survive as she moves from domestic work into a wartime job as a lathe operator. Silla, however, is weakened by her unquestioning embrace of American materialism. When she realizes that her husband's dreams will never allow him to share her practical goals, she betrays him by acts that devastate the family.

The faded elegance of the Brooklyn brownstone that the Boyce family shares with other tenants symbolizes the changing neighborhood of the 1940's. Upstairs lies the disabled Miss Mary, the death-in-life white servant of the building's former owners, whispering of her dead lover and the vanished past. Next to her lives good-time Suggie, who lures a succession of strange men to her room on weekends to obliterate the loneliness and frustration of her life as a maid to a white family.

Marshall's West Indian characters are, as always, her strength. Their rich dialect leaps off the page. They add an extra dimension to the novel by virtue of their customs, idioms, and intense desire for better lives.

SOUL CLAP HANDS AND SING

First published: 1961
Type of work: Four novellas

Four aging men, each in a different country, face mortality and their incomplete lives.

The title and thematic center of *Soul Clap Hands and Sing* are taken from William Butler Yeats's

poem "Sailing to Byzantium": "An aged man is but a paltry thing,/ A tattered coat upon a stick, unless/ Soul clap its hands and sing." The male protagonists of these novellas are not singing. Each is middle-aged or older and has lived a life essentially empty of commitment; each reaches out tentatively and too late to another person.

In this collection, Marshall moves the setting beyond the United States to the islands of the Caribbean Sea and South America, deliberately assuming a male perspective. These stories concern not so much the age of the men but the parched condition of their souls.

Barbados is the first and shortest novella. Mr. Watford, thin, spare, and comfortably retired from his job in America, spends his days tending his coconut trees and scoffing at the young people and their political slogan, "The Old Order Shall Pass." A local shopkeeper urges Mr. Watford to support the unsteady economy by hiring a servant, but the girl he sends disturbs Mr. Watford, who is grudging and harsh with her, though he allows her to stay. Only when he sees her dancing with a young man does he begin to realize how jealous he is of her, and how lonely. He tries to approach the girl, but she spurns him, and he realizes that in his life "it had been love, terrible in its demand, which he had always fled."

In *Brooklyn*, Max Berman, a middle-aged Jewish professor undone by the Communist-baiting of the 1950's and his self-imposed isolation, is physically attracted to his young African American student and suggests she visit his country home. She reluctantly agrees. He fantasizes a romantic idyll based upon his power over her, but she, who has always quietly sidestepped life, determines to face her fear of him head on. Refusing his advances, she becomes aware of her own strength, and he is humiliated.

The appropriately named Gerald Motley, of British, Hindu, and African ancestry, is the protagonist of *British Guiana*. Educated in England and privileged because of his light skin, he is the first man of color to become program director for British Guiana Broadcasting. Now in his sixties, he has allowed himself to become a figurehead, spending most of his time in a hotel bar. Ironically, Motley fails to recognize his reflection in the mirror, and thus himself. He too has rejected love—for the angry young man who has become his protégé and for Sybil, the woman who tries to save him.

Finally, *Brazil* introduces the small, dark figure of comic O Grande Caliban, who with his foil, tall blond Miranda, has been a fixture of Rio de Janeiro's nightlife for thirty-five years. Caliban, preparing to retire, is shocked to learn that his real identity has been absorbed by his comic persona. Even his new young wife does not know his true name. A symbolic search leads him from his former mentor Nacimento, who cannot recognize him, to his gaudy and aging mistress Miranda, who knows him only as Caliban. His real self unrecognized by present, past, or future, Caliban destroys Miranda's apartment in despairing fury.

PRAISESONG FOR THE WIDOW

First published: 1983
Type of work: Novel

A middle-class African American widow rediscovers her personal and ancestral past through her visit to a small Caribbean island.

In *Praisesong for the Widow*, Avey Johnson and two friends are in the midst of a Caribbean cruise, which her friends have urged upon her, when Avey suddenly feels that she cannot continue. Without explanation, she disembarks at Granada, knowing only that she must get back to her immaculate home in North White Plains, New York. Instead, she finds herself walking too far down the beach in the heat and seeks refuge in a small bar. Lebert Joseph, the lame and ancient owner, urges her to stay for an extra day to join the annual excursion to his native island of Carriacou. There, the Big Drum celebration is held to honor the Old Parents, the Long-time People: "Each year this time they does look for us to come and give them their remembrance."

The novel reiterates Marshall's concern with "the need for black people to make the psychological and spiritual journey back through their past." On her journey, Avey recalls the hard but rewarding years with her husband, Jay, on Halsey Street in Brooklyn, before they moved to the respectability of White Plains. She remembers her childhood visits to her father's great-aunt in South Carolina and the old woman's thrilling story of Ibo Landing, of slaves who turned their backs on the New World and walked home across the sea. Lebert also reminds her of her heritage by pointedly asking her, "And what you is?" He does not mean American but rather wants to know her African tribal heritage.

A dual vision of reality is particularly evident here. The great-aunt tells Avey that "those pureborn Africans was peoples my gran' said could see in more ways than one." Modest Avey is also Avatara (incarnation), named for and by the great-aunt's grandmother in a vision. Her passionate husband, Jay, becomes the severe businessman Jerome Johnson, almost a stranger. When she looks at Jerome's face in his coffin, to her horror Avey sees another pale, thin-lipped face superimposed on his—the face of some white ancestor. Even the polished splendor of her White Plains dining room reminds her of the museum of the dead at the foot of Mount Pelee on Martinique.

On her sea journey to Carriacou, Avey is violently and symbolically purged. She is placed in the deckhouse, reminiscent of a slave ship's hold, and senses she is not alone; she must remember and reenact the journey of her African ancestors.

After Avey is ceremonially purified, the enigmatic Lebert guides her through the rituals of the Big Drum, the Beg Pardon, the Nations Dance. One critic identifies him as "the incarnation of the African deity Legba—trickster, guardian of the crossroads where all ways meet." This beloved figure served as a link between humans and gods and was vital to many rituals. Thus the Big Drum is real but mythic, the Nations Dance is modern but timeless. When Avey joins the final dance, she recognizes it as one performed by her great-aunt's people in South Carolina, and she remembers the steps. *Praisesong for the Widow* connects Avey Johnson, a modern black American, with her worldwide African heritage, her present life with an ancient past, so that she is finally made whole.

DAUGHTERS

First published: 1991
Type of work: Novel

Torn between the island traditions of her father and her mother's idealistic faith in social justice, a woman seeks direction in her life and community with other women.

Paule Marshall's sprawling novel *Daughters* presents another of her conflicted characters, the thirtyish urban professional Ursa Mackenzie, who is straddling two worlds: New York, where she lives and works, and the fictional Caribbean island of Triunion, where she spent her first fourteen years. Not only does she embody the clash of two cultures and the weight of history, but on a personal level she must find her own way. Choosing direct involvement over statistics, Ursa has just resigned her well-paid job with a consumer research group in or-

der to assist the African American candidate for mayor in a nearby city. Her father, Primus Mackenzie, a powerful Triunion politician known to everyone as "the PM," disapproves of her new career, but her liberal African American mother Estelle is pleased.

Ursa shares an uneasy connection with her parents and a failing relationship with a former lover, but she maintains a much stronger bond with her best friend and guide, Viney Daniels, an assistant vice president at Metropolitan Life and the mother of an exemplary son. Viney warns Ursa, "You can't hear your own self, your own voice trying to tell you which way to go, what to do with your life." A distorted version of their close friendship is mirrored by Astral Forde, the Creole manager of the PM's faded hotel for retired tourists, and her impoverished friend Malvern, who never manages to rise.

In fact, Ursa frequently views her life as "a series of double exposures," with "everything superimposed on everything else." From her dual vision of

parallel scandals in the Caribbean and the United States by politicians who ignore the needs of their black citizens, she learns to make connections. Her mayoral candidate, like her beloved father, has become a puppet for the moneyed interests that have always controlled politics.

Throughout her novel, Marshall works with a complex astronomical metaphor that often seems forced. The petite Ursa—whose unusual name suggests the constellation Ursa Minor, the Little Bear or Little Dipper that guided escaping slaves northward—was named for her formidable grandmother, Ursa Major, a matriarch highly respected in Triunion. The elder woman's physically imposing son (sun) is the PM, who employs a loyal family servant named Celestine and is married to tiny Estelle (star) and whose customary keep-miss, or mistress, is Astral. These women "form another constellation" around him.

Marshall emphasizes the many ways in which women form connections: through blood, through history, through shared experience. In addition, inspired by a statue of rebellious slaves on Triunion, Ursa seeks to complete her once-rejected master's thesis showing how black men and women worked together as equals during this rebellion. The reconciliation of these modern daughters—their united love, anger, and desire to reform a corrupt political system—enables them to renew the PM's health and energy, returning him to his youthful dream of improving the lives of his people.

THE FISHER KING

First published: 2000
Type of work: Novel

The advent of a small boy, the descendant of black expatriate musicians in Paris, begins to heal their dysfunctional families in Brooklyn.

In *The Fisher King*, eight-year-old Sonny Payne arrives in the United States with Hattie Carmichael, an American expatriate who has cared for him in Paris since his birth, when his parents disappeared. Hattie, once a scorned foster child, grudgingly returns to Brooklyn in response to a letter from Edgar Payne, a wealthy real estate developer and brother of the great jazz pianist Sonny-Rett Payne, Sonny's grandfather Edgar has asked her to bring the boy for a memorial concert that will honor Sonny-Rett on the fifteenth anniversary of his death in Paris, when he was detained in a Metro station by suspicious police. Apparently he argued with them and tried to leave, fell or was pushed down the stone steps, hit his head, and died.

Honoring the wishes of Sonny's deceased grandparents, Hattie has refused all previous contact with his American family, so the boy must become acquainted with his personal history. His ancient great-grandmothers, who live across the street from each other but never speak, embody the ongoing resentment between West Indian immigrants and African Americans. Sonny-Rett's mother, Ulene Payne, an unkempt and angry woman with Parkinson's disease, encouraged her talented son to study European classical music but barred him from her home when he turned to American jazz, that "Sodom and Gomorrah music." Sonny is a little afraid of her but thrilled by the player piano that she allows him to touch.

His other great-grandmother, Florence McCullum-Jones, is a pretentious woman who considers herself superior to immigrants such as Ulene. Florence proudly shows Sonny her heritage: the magnolia tree planted by her father after he was driven from the South by envious whites. Her beautiful, shallow daughter Cherisse, Hattie's dear friend, became Sonny-Rett's wife, a union that both families bitterly opposed. When the couple severed all ties and fled to Europe in 1949, Hattie, who was in love with both, joined them to become Sonny-Rett's manager. At the crucial memorial concert, Hattie, as ancestral figure, teacher and historian, narrates her memories of Sonny-Rett, recalling how his very first transcendent, twenty-minute solo at the local jazz club stunned the audience. While Sonny-Rett's music reveals the details of his life, young Sonny is also able to connect with his past from the loving testimony of his grandfather's friends.

Although a cynical Edgar Payne believes that "nothing's pure. . . . Nothing's wholly selfless," Sonny is as uncorrupted as the Arthurian knight Perceval, who healed the wounded Fisher King, keeper of the Holy Grail. Sonny, a budding artist, likes to draw knights, castles, and fortresses in his notebook, adding a sketch of himself in full armor at the corner of every page. To his young cousins who marvel at his drawings, he explains that this figure protects his injured grandfather, who safely rests inside the fortress as the Fisher King once did. While his grandfather's bloody head wounds mend, Sonny carefully transfers him to each new fort he draws. In his innocence, he likewise begins to heal the bitterness and pain of his divided family.

SUMMARY

Marshall has incorporated into her work her personal struggle as a black woman and black writer living in a society that undercut her sense of self and her concern for social change. Her books explore the individual search for identity as well as the simultaneous need for integration within a larger community and a deeper awareness of the past. Her vivid portrayal of West Indian American life contributes to a better understanding of the multiple aspects of the African American experience.

Joanne McCarthy

BIBLIOGRAPHY

By the Author

LONG FICTION:
Brown Girl, Brownstones, 1959
The Chosen Place, the Timeless People, 1969
Praisesong for the Widow, 1983
Daughters, 1991
The Fisher King, 2000

SHORT FICTION:
Soul Clap Hands and Sing, 1961
Reena, and Other Stories, 1983 (also known as *Merle: A Novella and Other Stories,* 1985)

About the Author

Busia, Abene P. A. "What Is Your Nation? Reconnecting Africa and Her Diaspora Through Paule Marshall's *Praisesong for the Widow.*" In *Changing Our Own Words: Essays on Criticism, Theory, and Writing by Black Women,* edited by Cheryl A. Wall. New Brunswick, N.J.: Rutgers University Press, 1989.

Denniston, Dorothy Hamer. *The Fiction of Paule Marshall: Reconstructions of History, Culture, and Gender.* Knoxville: University of Tennessee Press, 1995.

_____. "Paule Marshall." In *Black Women in America,* edited by Darlene Clark Hine. 2d ed. New York: Oxford University Press, 2005.

Ferguson, Moira. "Of Bears and Bearings: Paule Marshall's Diverse *Daughters.*" *MELUS* 24, no. 1 (Spring, 1999): 177.

Marshall, Paule. "An Interview with Paule Marshall." Interview by Daryl Cumber Dance. *Southern Review* 28, no. 1 (1992): 1-20.

Schaeffer, Susan Fromberg. "Cutting Herself Free." *The New York Times Book Review,* October 27, 1991, 3, 29.

Spencer, Suzette A. "Truth and Reconciliation." *The Women's Review of Books* 18, no. 4 (January, 2001): 15.

DISCUSSION TOPICS

- How is Paule Marshall's great theme, the search for identity, shown in her work?

- Are Marshall's characters always aware of their history? Does learning more about their history necessarily affect her characters?

- Compare any one of Marshall's West Indian characters with a corresponding African American character. Do you notice any significant differences between them?

- How does Marshall transcend traditional stereotypes in her characters? Does she ever use stereotypes? If so, what effect do they produce?

- Discuss the role of the ancestor figure in Marshall's work. Is one always present?

- Does Marshall's frequent use of West Indian dialect or fragments of other languages (French, for example) add to or detract from her story?

BOBBIE ANN MASON

Born: Mayfield, Kentucky
May 1, 1940

Most of Mason's stories and novels examine culture shock—the effects of contemporary social changes on the residents of small towns or farms in Western Kentucky.

Jymi Bolden

BIOGRAPHY

Bobbie Ann Mason was born in Mayfield, Kentucky, on May 1, 1940. Her parents, Wilburn A. and Christianna Lee Mason, operated a small dairy farm, and Mason's writing frequently reflects this rural heritage. Mason did farm chores but also explored popular culture. In 1954, she became the national president of the Hilltoppers fan club and attended concerts by this musical group throughout the South and Midwest. As editor and chief author of *Hilltopper Topics*, the fan club newsletter, Mason also displayed an early interest in writing.

After graduating from Mayfield High School, Mason attended the University of Kentucky, where she studied English and wrote for the school newspaper. During the summers she also worked as a reporter for her hometown newspaper, the *Mayfield Messenger.* Mason earned a B.A. degree in 1962 and was soon employed by Ideal Publishing Company in New York City as a writer for fan magazines. In moving from rural Kentucky to a big city and taking on the job of interviewing famous actors and musicians, Mason described herself as a victim of culture shock.

In 1963, Mason left New York City to enter graduate school at the State University of New York at Binghamton, and in 1966, she received an M.A. in English. Later that year she entered a Ph.D. program at the University of Connecticut. There

she met Roger Rawlings, whom she married on April 12, 1969.

Mason received her Ph.D. in 1972 and began teaching at Mansfield State College in Pennsylvania. Mason's doctoral dissertation focused on Vladimir Nabokov, an author whose works are very different from Mason's but whose intricate style she greatly admires. Her first book, *Nabokov's Garden: A Guide to "Ada"* (1974), is a scholarly work based on her dissertation. In 1975, she published a strikingly different scholarly book, *The Girl Sleuth*, in which Mason examines the self-reliant heroines of her favorite childhood books—Nancy Drew and other young female detectives. Thus, Mason's experiences and her writings at this point in life display an unusual mixture of rural simplicity and urban sophistication, of popular culture and academic analysis.

In 1979, Mason gave up her teaching job and began to write full time. Although as a student she had contributed some stories to the University of Kentucky literary magazine, her first significant success as a writer of fiction did not come until February 18, 1980, when the *New Yorker* published her story "Offerings." On October 20, 1980, the *New Yorker* published a second story, "Shiloh," and Mason soon became a regular contributor of both fiction and nonfiction. Mason's first collection of short stories, *Shiloh, and Other Stories*, appeared in 1982. It received the Ernest Hemingway Foundation Award and was nominated for the PEN/Faulkner Award.

Mason's first novel, *In Country* (1985), focused on the lingering effects within the United States of the Vietnam War. In 1983, during a visit to the Vietnam Veterans Memorial in Washington, D.C., Mason had found in the list of names on the wall a variation on her own name—Bobby G. Mason. This accidental discovery, implying that she and other civilians at home were also casualties of the war, inspired the final section of *In Country*, where the book's main characters make a pilgrimage to the memorial. In 1985, Mason also published "Big Bertha Stories," a poignant account of how war experiences affected one soldier and his family. In 1989, Warner Bros. released a film version of *In Country*, and Mason received from the Vietnam Veterans of America a citation honoring her for increasing public understanding of the consequences of the war.

In 1988, Mason published *Spence + Lila*, a novella whose unusual title identifies the two main characters and suggests, typographically, their close relationship. The aging married couple, who resemble Mason's own parents, must deal with Lila's breast cancer. Throughout the experience their love remains quiet and undemonstrative but still sustaining.

During the 1980's, Mason published numerous stories in *The New Yorker*, *The Atlantic Monthly*, *Harper's*, and other journals. The title story of her second collection of stories, *Love Life* (1989), focuses on love, and other stories in the volume present variations on that emotion.

In 1990, after a long residence in the Northeast, Mason moved back to Kentucky. In 1995, she received an honorary doctorate from the University of Kentucky, and she subsequently became a writer-in-residence there. This move back home apparently inspired Mason to contemplate her past. In 1999, she published *Clear Springs: A Memoir*. As the title of this book suggests, it describes some of the family and regional sources from which Mason's inspiration as a writer has flowed.

Mason continued to publish both fiction and nonfiction into the twenty-first century; several short stories were collected in *Zigzagging Down a Wild Trail* in 2001. In 2002, she published a biography of Elvis Presley in the Penguin Lives series. This sensitive treatment of a troubled music icon displayed Mason's continuing interest in popular culture and those who create it.

ANALYSIS

An early reviewer of *Shiloh, and Other Stories* described Mason's typical setting as a "ruburb." This coined word—a fusion of "rural" and "urban"—identifies not only a place but also a significant conflict in Mason's fiction. Most of her characters reside on the boundary between old ways—the presumed safety and simplicity of the country—and new modes of behavior that frequently bring confusion and isolation. When Mason herself left Kentucky to take her first full-time job in New York City, she described herself as a victim of culture shock. She was the country girl forced to adjust to the radically different big city. Mason's characters may not travel far from their small-town Kentucky homes, but radical changes do invade their pastoral world. In the story "Lying Doggo," for example, a young woman exclaims that she once shelled corn for the chickens and listened to the songs of Hank Williams but now she is expected to know the appropriate wine for every meal.

With the introduction of Wal-Marts and countless tract houses, the appearance of small towns and farms is indeed dramatically altered. In fact, Leroy Moffitt in "Shiloh" compares the new subdivisions that spread across the landscape to oil slicks. Along with these physical alterations come even more disturbing personal and social changes—such as recreational drug use, divorce, and trauma after combat in Vietnam.

One of Mason's primary strategies for documenting such change is her frequent allusion to popular culture, especially songs, television shows, and films. For example, *In Country* begins with a quotation from Bruce Springsteen's "Born in the U.S.A." that aptly describes the fire still burning within many war veterans. "Graveyard Day" refers to two sharply contrasting television shows—*The Waltons*, a nostalgic tribute to an ideal American family, and *All in the Family*, a more realistic series that refuses to gloss over family problems. In the story, the unconventional family that is watching *The Waltons* turns their television off in the middle of the program, as if to suggest that such storybook families have also suffered a premature ending. In "Shiloh," the Moffitts' infant son dies while they are at the local drive-in watching a double feature of *Dr. Strangelove* and *Lover Come Back*. The first film provides a commentary on the surreal nature of their relationship after the baby's death, and the second emphasizes their need for reconciliation and mutual support.

Mason describes various passages through life to show how characters of different generations deal with significant changes. Her most characteristic stories show young adults confronting divorce and related family problems. In "Residents and Transients," for example, Mary is separated from her husband and sees herself as much like a rabbit smashed on the highway but still attempting to hop. Both Mary and the rabbit keep trying to move forward but are powerless to do so. Elderly protagonists are also confused and thwarted. The retired couple in "The Ocean" have sold the family farm and set out in a new camper for Florida, but they become lost both literally and metaphorically. In asking the way to 65, they are requesting both directions to the proper interstate highway and guidance toward meaningful old age. Mason's fiction also includes adolescent rites of passage. For example, "Detroit Skyline, 1949" describes the pain of initiation into a puzzling adult world. Here a young girl must confront, in her mother's sudden miscarriage, the combined mysteries of sexuality and mortality.

The novel *Feather Crowns* (1993) is a departure from Mason's usual focus on contemporary society. Set in 1900 in western Kentucky, this book describes the births, and deaths shortly afterward, of quintuplets. The title refers to a nest of feathers formed in a pillow by the impression of a baby's head—interpreted as a sign that the baby is blessed. Although such settings and events are atypical for Mason, the novel displays a familiar Mason theme—the shock of radical change. The parents of the quintuplets must adjust not only to the remarkable births but also to the throngs of reporters and curious spectators who invade their home seeking glimpses and souvenirs of the babies.

"SHILOH"

First published: 1980 (collected in *Shiloh, and Other Stories*, 1982)
Type of work: Short story

After Leroy Moffitt wrecks his tractor-trailer rig, he and his wife Norma Jean attempt to solve problems in their marriage that they have ignored for years.

Although "Shiloh" was the second story that Mason published, it remains one of her most popular and

is a good example of her typical characters and themes. The story focuses on a troubled marriage—on wreckage and attempts to rebuild. For most of his marriage Leroy was on the road as a truck driver. Now, after a serious accident, his wrecked truck sits idle in his backyard while he recovers from a leg injury. For the first time he and his wife Norma Jean must deal with another terrible accident that occurred sixteen years earlier—the death of their infant son Randy. As Norma Jean lifts weights and Leroy does needlepoint, they must also deal with reversed gender roles and other sweeping social changes that have affected their small town.

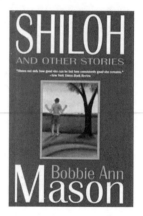

Leroy tries to cope by assembling craft kits—a B-17 Flying Fortress, a model-truck lamp, a log cabin made from Popsicle sticks. After constructing the miniature cabin, Leroy hopes to construct a real cabin as a home for himself and Norma Jean. In all these actions, Leroy attempts to make many small parts fit together—to create an orderly whole that is lacking in his own life. In aspiring to raise a cabin, Leroy also reverts to a presumably less turbulent time in the past.

When Leroy and Norma Jean cannot reconstruct their lives at home, they head for Shiloh on a second honeymoon. Ironically, in an attempt to find peace, they visit a battlefield, one of the bloodiest of the Civil War. The story ends ambiguously as Norma Jean stands on a bluff looking out over the Tennessee River and Leroy struggles to catch up with her. With her clear focus on the opposite shore, Norma Jean will surely deal with her present problems and move on. Whether or not Leroy will accompany her remains unclear.

"GRAVEYARD DAY"

First published: 1982 (collected in *Shiloh, and Other Stories*, 1982)
Type of work: Short story

Frightened by her own divorce and the fragmentation of families all around her, Waldeen is unwilling to commit to her boyfriend, Joe McClain, until she observes the care with which he cleans his family's cemetery.

The title "Graveyard Day" refers to the time set aside each year for cleaning and maintenance of a family cemetery. While many contemporary families break apart, this activity demonstrates Joe McClain's dedication to his kin and his close connection even with those who are no longer alive. As he carefully tends the graves of his dead relatives, he convinces Waldeen that she can build a new relationship with him.

Throughout the story Mason presents several unconventional families. After Waldeen's divorce, she and her daughter Holly constitute a family, but the roles of parent and child are reversed as Holly frequently reprimands her mother. Joe spends most evenings with Waldeen and Holly, and these three try to form another family configuration. In still another variation, C. W. Redmon and Betty Mathis live together but avoid marriage because Betty does not want children. To satisfy his own need for a more extensive family, C. W. borrows Holly and takes her fishing. In all these situations, the family unit is more temporary than abiding. Indeed, a reference to television emphasizes the constantly shifting nature of family relationships. As Holly and her pseudo-father Joe play cards, they laugh like contestants on *Let's Make a Deal.* The game show analogy suggests that their merriment may be transient and that family arrangements are always subject to renegotiation.

At the graveyard, Waldeen realizes that if she marries Joe (and stays married long enough) they will both be buried there with his family. As she imagines their common headstone, she begins to feel that the promise of marriage is symbolized not by a diamond ring but by a burial plot. Thus, in the middle of a cemetery, she finds hope for a new life. If she pursues a fuller relationship with Joe, she can perhaps forge new family links that will endure.

IN COUNTRY

First published: 1985
Type of work: Novel

During the summer after her high school graduation, Sam Hughes approaches maturity by exploring the Vietnam War experiences of her dead father, while her uncle Emmett Smith tries to heal his own psychic wounds from that same war.

The two main characters of *In Country* are Sam Hughes, a seventeen-year-old girl from Hopewell, Kentucky, and her uncle, Emmett Smith, a Vietnam War veteran. Emmett becomes a surrogate parent for Sam because her father died in Vietnam before her birth and her mother has remarried and established a new family miles away in Lexington. Sam and Emmett live together in a decrepit house and form another of Mason's unconventional modern families.

With these two main characters Mason combines the themes of initiation and recovery. In the course of the summer, Sam comes of age, and Emmett simultaneously attempts to resolve the residual problems from his military service in Vietnam.

Sam moves toward maturity by examining the past—primarily the war that took the father she never knew. The search for a father is a common motif in initiation stories since knowing one's heritage may help to define one's sense of self. Sam tries to clarify her identity by reading old letters and journal entries written by her father, by briefly dating a Vietnam War veteran, and by staging a mock military exercise at a nearby swamp that she thinks may display topography much like that of Vietnam.

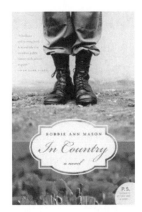

Emmett attempts to fix his battered psyche by

using construction or reconstruction techniques similar to those in other Mason stories such as "Shiloh" and "The Rookers." He repairs defects in physical objects, such as toasters and hair dryers, in hopes that such actions will help him to fix internal flaws. He also digs deep trenches around his house to correct problems in the foundation. A neighbor jokingly suggests that Emmett may be digging to China, and he is indeed trying to uncover and solve psychological problems that originated on the other side of the world.

Sam and Emmett come together most evenings to watch reruns of *M*A*S*H*—another good example of Mason's use of popular culture to underscore her themes. Although this television series actually deals with an army surgical hospital in the Korean War, it shows injuries and deaths similar to those in Vietnam. More important, for Emmett it helps to put the horrors of war in perspective by juxtaposing them with the irrepressible humor of Captain Hawkeye Pierce.

The most significant episode in the novel for both Emmett and Sam is a pilgrimage near the end of the summer. Along with Sam's grandmother, the two main characters journey to Washington, D.C., to visit the newly dedicated Vietnam War Memorial. Visiting this site provides further insight for Sam and closure for Emmett. As they approach the Memorial, its influence (like that of the war) is still negative because it looks like a giant boomerang and a black gash in the earth. Soon, however, comforting images emerge as they see flowers blooming out of cracks in the wall. In scanning the list of casualties, Sam finds her own name included, just as Mason did on her own visit to the Memorial. Since the names Sam Hughes and Bobbie Mason are both relatively common and also gender ambiguous, their occurrence in a list of largely male war casualties is hardly surprising. This coincidence, however, demonstrates that the victims of war were not just combatants but also many people left at home—young and old, male and female.

At the end of her pilgrimage, Sam touches both the letters of her father's name and those of her own as inscribed in the stone wall. In finally locating her father, she has also found herself. In the final sentence of *In Country*, Emmett sits like a statue of Buddha serenely contemplating the wall. Long after the war was officially over, he has finally found some personal peace.

SUMMARY

Bobbie Ann Mason's fiction documents an era of change in the rural South. Her slice of this world—the fictional town of Hopewell, Kentucky, where many of her works are set—displays the conflict between old values that are often supportive and new modes of behavior that may be both liberating and disturbing. To anchor these conflicts in their contemporary setting and to reinforce her themes, Mason uses numerous references to popular culture.

Albert E. Wilhelm

BIBLIOGRAPHY

By the Author

LONG FICTION:
In Country, 1985
Spence + Lila, 1988
Feather Crowns, 1993
An Atomic Romance, 2005

SHORT FICTION:
Shiloh, and Other Stories, 1982
Love Life, 1989
Midnight Magic: Selected Stories of Bobbie Ann Mason, 1998
Zigzagging Down a Wild Trail, 2001

NONFICTION:

*Nabokov's Garden: A Guide to "Ada," * 1974

The Girl Sleuth: A Feminist Guide to the Bobbsey Twins, Nancy Drew, and Their Sisters, 1975, 1995

Clear Springs: A Memoir, 1999

Elvis Presley, 2002

About the Author

Brinkmeyer, Robert H., Jr. "Finding One's History: Bobbie Ann Mason and Contemporary Southern Literature." *Southern Literary Journal* 19 (Spring, 1987): 22-33.

Flora, Joseph M. "Bobbie Ann Mason." In *Contemporary Fiction Writers of the South,* edited by Joseph M. Flora and Robert Bain. Westport, Conn.: Greenwood Press, 1993.

Price, Joanna. *Understanding Bobbie Ann Mason.* Columbia: University of South Carolina Press, 2000.

Ryan, Maureen. "Stopping Places: Bobbie Ann Mason's Short Stories." In *Women Writers of the Contemporary South,* edited by Peggy Whitman Prenshaw. Jackson: University Press of Mississippi, 1984.

Wilhelm, Albert. *Bobbie Ann Mason: A Study of the Short Fiction.* New York: Twayne, 1998

DISCUSSION TOPICS

- How do Bobbie Ann Mason's characters deal with change?

- How does Mason portray the contemporary American family?

- How does Mason portray women, especially women of different generations?

- How do the settings of Mason's stories and novels influence the characters who live in or travel to those locations?

- How do details of popular culture (such as references to music, films, and television programs) contribute to Mason's fiction?

- How did the Vietnam War, as depicted in Mason's fiction, affect the soldiers who fought there and those who remained at home?

- In what ways does Sam mature during the summer portrayed in *In Country*?

EDGAR LEE MASTERS

Born: Garnett, Kansas
August 23, 1868
Died: Melrose Park, Pennsylvania
March 5, 1950

Masters owes his literary fame almost exclusively to the finely crafted epitaphs in his 1915 book of poems, Spoon River Anthology.

BIOGRAPHY

Edgar Lee Masters was born on August 23, 1869, in Garnett, Kansas. He was the son of Emma and Hardin Masters, who hailed from Illinois. When he was still an infant, his parents returned to their home state. Masters spent his childhood and adolescence in the Sangamon Valley of central Illinois, largely in the towns of Petersburg and Lewiston.

In Petersburg, Hardin Masters developed a successful law practice and was elected several times to local political offices. In his 1936 autobiography, *Across Spoon River*, Edgar Lee Masters recalled that his parents had argued very frequently. He felt more loved by his grandmother than by either of his parents. Although Masters admired his mother's refinement and interest in literature, he resented her harsh criticism. His relationship with his father was strained. He appreciated his father's intelligence but thought that Hardin Masters was excessively concerned with law and politics and remained emotionally distant from his wife and children. The most painful event of his childhood was the death in 1878 of his five-year-old brother Alex from diphtheria. When he wrote his autobiography almost six decades after Alex's death, Edgar Lee Masters still felt intense grief.

After his undergraduate studies at Knox College in Illinois, he moved to Chicago and studied law. He was admitted to the bar in 1891, and he practiced law for four decades in Chicago. In 1898, he married Helen Jenkins, with whom he had two daughters, Marcia and Madeline, and one son, Hardin (who published in 1978 a very personal series of reflections on the family life and career of his father). Helen divorced Edgar Lee Masters in 1923, presumably because of his numerous adulterous affairs. After his divorce, Masters almost never wrote of his first wife. In his 1936 autobiography, he referred by their first names to sixteen of his mistresses, but the index to *Across Spoon River* contains no reference to Helen Masters.

In 1926, Masters married Ellen Coyne; they had one son, Hilary. They moved to New York in 1931, where they lived for most of the last two decades of his life. During the 1930's and 1940's, Masters became an important figure in New York literary circles. He became ill in the late 1940's and died on March 5, 1950, in a convalescent home near Philadelphia.

Masters was a prolific writer. Between 1898 and 1942, he published more than fifty books in such diverse genres as poetry, autobiography, theater, biography, and short fiction, but he has remained famous solely for his *Spoon River Anthology* (1915). His autobiography, *Across Spoon River*, shows him to be a rather vain, libidinous, and unsympathetic person. Hardin Masters assured his readers that his two sisters, Marcia and Madeline, felt very alienated from their father for decades after the 1923 divorce.

When he wrote in his own literary voice, Masters was a terribly repetitious writer. In *Spoon River Anthology*, however, he composed 246 epitaphs, which revealed the extraordinarily diverse ways in which dead inhabitants perceived the reality of life in the mythical village of Spoon River. Although this very moving and well-structured book of poems clearly owes much to Masters's own experiences in the Sangamon Valley of central Illinois, the feelings of joy, frustration, anger, grief, and love that it expresses have moved readers not only in the United States but in many other countries as well. Hardin Masters wrote with evident pride in 1978 that his father's masterpiece had been reprinted more than one hundred times and had been translated into numerous foreign languages.

ANALYSIS

After the publication of *Spoon River Anthology* in 1915, several critics believed that Edgar Lee Masters would develop into a major visionary poet. His later books of poetry, including his 1920 *Domesday Book* and its 1929 sequel, *The Fate of the Jury: An Epilogue to Domesday Book*, reminded numerous readers, however, of narrative techniques and stylistic devices that he had used with greater diversity and effectiveness in *Spoon River Anthology*. Although less original than *Spoon River Anthology*, his other works in such diverse genres as poetry, biography, autobiography, fiction, and drama are certainly not negligible.

Although he did publish more than fifty books, his major works written after 1915 were his long narrative poems, *Domesday Book* and *The Fate of the Jury*, his autobiography, *Across Spoon River*, and his biographies of Abraham Lincoln (1931) and Walt Whitman (1937). In his autobiography, he referred to himself as "an omnivorous reader" who admired not only American literature but also the Greek classics and works of modern writers of his own literary sensitivities. He identified closely with German poet Johann Wolfgang von Goethe and frequently praised Goethe's ability to see through appearances and grasp the essence of reality. In his biography of Walt Whitman, he affirmed that Whitman had been the American Goethe. Masters argued that Whitman had expressed with unsurpassed clarity profound aspects of the American experience just as Goethe had explored the true nature of the German spirit.

Masters may well have exaggerated similarities between Goethe and Whitman, but he did help readers to understand why Whitman was the preeminent American visionary poet. Although Masters also wrote books on such important Americans as Abraham Lincoln, Vachel Lindsay, and Mark Twain, these are highly impressionistic works that tell a reader more about Masters's views on American culture than they do about their subjects.

After his *Spoon River Anthology*, Masters wrote two major poetic works: *Domesday Book* and *The Fate of the Jury*. Critics have frequently compared the *Domesday Book* to Robert Browning's *The Ring and the Book* (1868-1869). Both narrative poems describe legal proceedings undertaken to determine the cause of a woman's death and relevant details about her life. Masters denied even having read *The Ring and the Book* before 1920, but the critic John Flanagan has argued that "the denial seems a bit disingenuous."

In his *Domesday Book*, Masters used his extensive experience as a lawyer in order to show how a county coroner named Merival and the members of his coroner's jury obtained testimony from diverse witnesses before concluding that Elenor Murray, whose body had been found in a wooded area, had died from natural causes. The *Fate of the Jury* describes the emotional suffering endured by Merival and the members of the jury in the years that followed their deliberations concerning the death of Elenor Murray.

In one sense *Domesday Book* reveals very effective uses of deductive reasoning in order to show that a crime had not been committed. As a detective story, the *Domesday Book* is very successful, but Masters believed that this book about the hopes, loves, and suffering of Elenor Murray and those who knew her somehow constituted "a census spiritual" of American society. Masters was clearly sincere, but he never shows convincingly that his remarks on Elenor Murray represent profound insights into the nature of American culture. A reader is left with the impression that Masters made excessive claims for the significance of the book.

Although the characters in *Domesday Book* and *The Fate of the Jury* come from diverse social classes and have very different personalities, these books are very repetitive and do not always retain the reader's interest. Masters presents a consistently pessimistic view of life, society, politics, and the law.

Once readers realize that Masters did not believe in the existence of true love, honest businessmen, or upright lawyers, they are not surprised that his characters behave in a terribly predictable manner. Despite initial positive reactions to the *Domesday Book* and *The Fate of the Jury*, these books have not aged well. They merely serve to remind readers that the *Spoon River Anthology* was Masters's only aesthetically successful work.

SPOON RIVER ANTHOLOGY

First published: 1915
Type of work: Poetry

Interconnected epitaphs spoken by people buried in the local cemetery tell of life in the fictional town of Spoon River, Illinois.

Spoon River Anthology encourages and almost demands the rereadings of epitaphs, because almost all these poems make references to characters and events mentioned in other poems. The reader soon comes to appreciate that each inhabitant of Spoon River expresses a partial and very personal perception of reality. The speakers, who are all now dead, will never understand that their views of themselves differ greatly from the opinions held by their fellow villagers. Each rereading of epitaphs helps one to see beyond appearances in order to discover the hidden and complex emotional and social realities in this village.

Spoon River Anthology is certainly not merely a work of historical interest about life in small American towns in the late nineteenth and early twentieth centuries. These 246 epitaphs express a microcosm of almost any town—be it in the United States or elsewhere—from any century. Successive generations of readers have discovered many different levels of meaning in these poems.

Masters began this book with a powerful poem titled "The Hill." As its title suggests, this poem is spoken by the cemetery itself, which is located on a hill overlooking the town. The cemetery asks repeatedly "where" certain villagers now are; the answer is not that they are in Heaven. The cemetery repeatedly answers its own question by responding: "All, all are sleeping on the hill." This eternal "sleep" has brought little consolation to those whose lives were filled with unhappiness. The solitude and loneliness of those "whom life had crushed" have become permanent.

Although the dead speakers in the *Spoon River Anthology* are extremely diverse in their social backgrounds and personalities, Masters included several similar sets of poems that are spoken by spouses and by other members of the same family. These series of poems show clearly that personality conflicts or an unwillingness to communicate can doom a marriage to failure. Some critics have suggested that Masters was thinking about his own unhappy first marriage or of the profound incompatibility of his parents.

Among the most effective epitaphs spoken by spouses are those by Mr. and Mrs. Benjamin Painter. He was a successful but vain lawyer who would have the reader believe that he was the innocent victim of an insensitive wife who forced him to leave their house and to live "in a room back of a dingy office." Such an explanation, however, is not plausible. Despite divorce or separation, a wealthy lawyer would rarely have to live in such unbecoming quarters. Readers sense that Benjamin Painter is concealing an important fact.

Masters describes Mrs. Painter as a lady "with delicate tastes" who could not stand his alcoholism or crude behavior. Separation was essential for her emotional well-being. Despite their wealth, the Painters were bitterly unhappy and lonely people. Benjamin felt so alienated that he asked to be buried not near other family members but with his dog, Nig, whom he describes as his "constant companion, bed-fellow, comrade in drink." This lawyer whom most people in Spoon River admired so highly was, in fact, a psychologically unstable man with a serious drinking problem.

Readers come to empathize with his wife, whom the townspeople considered to be a snob. The druggist Trainor expresses a curious assessment of the Painters. He affirms that they were "Good in themselves, but evil toward each other: He oxygen, she hydrogen." This chemical comparison suggests that the Painters might have attained happiness and inner peace if they had never married each other.

Although the Painters clearly had a disastrous marriage, it would be wrong to conclude that Masters presented a consistently negative view of love and marriage. A very moving epitaph is spoken by a couple named simply "William and Emily." Their surnames, social class, and professions are irrelevant; they represent any couple whose mutual love matured over the years. Emily and William speak with one voice. Their love for each other began with "the glow of youthful passion" and grew until they both started "to fade away together." They feel, however, no anger at death. They aged together in mutual love, and it seemed only natural to them that the "fire" of passion and life be extinguished "gradually, faintly, delicately." Emily and William felt inner peace when it was their turn to leave "the familiar room" of their earthly abode in order to live together for eternity.

The love of which Emily and William speak may refer also to one's family and to society as a whole. Love of country is a theme frequently treated in the *Spoon River Anthology*. Masters never confused love of country with admiration for politicians. He was a Populist and consistently questioned the motives of politicians and members of the ruling class. He

portrayed the leading figures in Spoon River, such as Mayor Blood, the circuit judge, Judge Somers, and state legislator Adam Weinrauch, as amoral individuals who abused their authority for personal gain by selling their votes or judicial decisions to the highest bidders. These vain men still do not understand why the townspeople held them in such low esteem. While they possessed power they were feared; in death, however, these members of the ruling class have received poetic justice.

The self-righteous Judge Somers is angry because he was buried in an unmarked grave, whereas an impressive marble tombstone was erected over the grave of the town drunkard, Chase Henry, who is amused by this unexpected and undeserved honor. He was a Catholic, but the local Catholic priest would not permit the burial of Henry in consecrated ground. For reasons that Henry has never understood, certain Protestants took umbrage at this decision and decided to

honor him with an expensive tombstone. Chase Henry appreciated the irony of this situation. He tells his listeners: "Take note, ye prudent and pious souls,/ Of the cross-currents in life/ Which bring honor to the dead, who lived in shame." Henry knows that his tombstone, topped with a large urn, means nothing. It was erected by irrational people angered by the priest's refusal to permit the burial of Chase Henry in a Catholic cemetery.

Another speaker also knows all too well that one should not mistake appearance for reality. Barney Hainsfeather was a Jewish businessman whom the Christians in Spoon River never really accepted as their equal. Because of an absurd error, Barney Hainsfeather is now buried in the Protestant cemetery of Spoon River, whereas the body of John Allen was sent to the Hebrew Cemetery in Chicago. Barney and John both died when the train to Peoria crashed and burned; their bodies were burnt beyond recognition. Barney now finds himself under a tombstone with Christian prayers carved in the marble. He concludes his epitaph with this lament: "It was bad enough to run a clothing store in this town,/ But to be buried here—*ach*!"

Although Masters had a healthy distrust of those who possessed political power, he did remain an extraordinary idealist. Masters felt that people would become and remain morally upright if they avoided the destructive temptations of power and wealth. He firmly believed that wealth and power would corrupt almost anyone. One could object that Abraham Lincoln governed wisely without compromising his moral principles. Masters would argue that Lincoln was the exception and not the rule among politicians.

Perhaps the most famous epitaph in the *Spoon River Anthology* is the one spoken by Anne Rutledge, whom Lincoln had loved before his marriage to Mary Todd. In her simplicity and honesty, Anne Rutledge imagines that her altruistic love for Lincoln inspired in him a desire to uphold the ideals of "justice and truth" on which American society is based. In a mysterious but real way her love for Lincoln and his love for humanity made possible "the forgiveness of millions towards millions." Love alone put an end to the hatred provoked by the American Civil War. Without love, a republic "shining with justice and truth" would have ceased to be meaningful to many citizens. Anne Rutledge ends her epitaph with these eloquent lines:

I am Anne Rutledge who sleep beneath these weeds,
Beloved in life of Abraham Lincoln,
Wedded to him, not through union,
But through separation.
Bloom forever, O Republic,
From the dust of my bosom!

A mystical and almost religious union connects all those, both great and small, who live their lives so that the republic may flourish for the good of all of its citizens.

SUMMARY

Masters's literary reputation rests solely on his 1915 masterpiece, *Spoon River Anthology*. Its 246 epitaphs constitute a unique contribution to American literature. The fictional speakers present very personal perceptions of what life in Spoon River meant to them. Readers come to the realization that Spoon River represents any small town in America or elsewhere. For generations, readers have appreciated the refined artistry by which Masters gave each speaker a unique poetic voice.

Edmund J. Campion

DISCUSSION TOPICS

- *Spoon River Anthology* was originally conceived as a novel. What makes the form that Edgar Lee Masters finally chose so effective?

- Consider *Spoon River Anthology* as a work of social criticism.

- Some critics have seen Masters himself in the character Percival Sharp. How plausible is this theory?

- What is the function of the epilogue to *Spoon River Anthology*? Is it necessary or even desirable?

- Masters was an admirer of Walt Whitman. How does his handling of free-verse lines and rhythms differ from Whitman's?

BIBLIOGRAPHY

By the Author

POETRY:
A Book of Verses, 1898
The Blood of the Prophets, 1905
Songs and Sonnets, 1910
Songs and Sonnets, Second Series, 1912
Spoon River Anthology, 1915
Songs and Satires, 1916
The Great Valley, 1916
Toward the Gulf, 1918
Starved Rock, 1919
Domesday Book, 1920
The Open Sea, 1921
The New Spoon River, 1924
Selected Poems, 1925
The Fate of the Jury: An Epilogue to Domesday Book, 1929
Lichee Nuts, 1930
The Serpent in the Wilderness, 1933
Invisible Landscapes, 1935
The Golden Fleece of California, 1936
Poems of People, 1936

The New World, 1937
More People, 1939
Illinois Poem, 1941
Along the Illinois, 1942
The Harmony of Deeper Music: Posthumous Poems, 1976

LONG FICTION:
Mitch Miller, 1920
Children of the Market Place, 1922
The Nuptial Flight, 1923
Skeeters Kirby, 1923
Mirage, 1924
Kit O'Brien, 1927
The Tide of Time, 1937

DRAMA:
Althea, pb. 1907
The Trifler, pb. 1908
The Leaves of the Tree, pb. 1909
Eileen, pb. 1910
The Locket, pb. 1910
The Bread of Idleness, pb. 1911
Lee: A Dramatic Poem, pb. 1926
Jack Kelso, pb. 1928
Gettysburg, Manila, Acoma, pb. 1930
Godbey, pb. 1931
Dramatic Duologues, pb. 1934
Richmond, pb. 1934

NONFICTION:
Levy Mayer and the New Industrial Era, 1927
Lincoln, the Man, 1931
The Tale of Chicago, 1933
Vachel Lindsay: A Poet in America, 1935
Across Spoon River, 1936
Walt Whitman, 1937
Mark Twain, a Portrait, 1938
The Sangamon, 1942

About the Author

Flanagan, John T. *Edgar Lee Masters: The Spoon River Poet and His Critics*. Metuchen, N.J.: Scarecrow Press, 1974.

Hallwas, John E., and Dennis J. Reader, eds. *The Vision of the Land: Studies of Vachel Lindsay, Edgar Lee Masters, and Carl Sandburg*. Macomb: Western Illinois University Press, 1976.

Masters, Hardin Wallace. *Edgar Lee Masters: A Biographical Sketchbook About a Famous American Author*. Rutherford, N.J.: Fairleigh Dickinson University Press, 1978.

Primeau, Ronald. *Beyond Spoon River: The Legacy of Edgar Lee Masters*. Austin: University of Texas Press, 1981.

Russell, Herbert K. *Edgar Lee Masters: A Biography*. Urbana: University of Illinois Press, 2001.

Vatron, Michael. *America's Literary Revolt*. Freeport, N.Y.: Books for Libraries Press, 1969.

Wrenn, John H., and Margaret M. Wrenn. *Edgar Lee Masters*. Boston: Twayne, 1983.

PETER MATTHIESSEN

Born: New York, New York
May 22, 1927

Naturalist Matthiessen's principal concern is with humankind's place in and impact on the natural world—in particular with its negative impact on the balance of life on earth.

Courtesy, University of California
at Santa Barbara Libraries

BIOGRAPHY

Peter Matthiessen was born in New York City to Erard A. and Elizabeth C. Matthiessen on May 22, 1927. He developed his lifelong interest in nature and the environment early in life. His father, an architect, was a trustee of the National Audubon Society, and Peter soon developed a passion for the natural world, spending much of his youth in the Connecticut and New York countryside.

After serving in the United States Navy, Matthiessen attended the Sorbonne, University of Paris, from 1948 to 1949 and received a B.A. from Yale University in 1950. After teaching creative writing at Yale in 1950, he returned to Paris and developed friendships with a variety of American expatriate writers, including James Baldwin, Richard Wright, William Styron, Terry Southern, and Irwin Shaw. With Harold L. Humes, Matthiessen founded the *Paris Review* in 1951. He married Patricia Southgate in 1951; they divorced in 1958. In 1963 he married Deborah Love, who died in 1972. In 1980 he married Patricia Eckhart; they live on Long Island, New York.

While in Paris, Matthiessen wrote his first novel, *Race Rock* (1954). His other novels include *Partisans* (1955), *Raditzer* (1961), *At Play in the Fields of the Lord* (1965), *Far Tortuga* (1975), and a trilogy about the Florida Everglades, which includes *Killing Mister Watson* (1990), *Lost Man's River* (1997), and *Bone*

by Bone (1999). Matthiessen has published two collections of short stories, *On the River Styx, and Other Stories* in 1998 and *Midnight Turning Gray* in 1984.

Matthiessen worked as a commercial fisherman and a captain of a deep-sea charter fishing boat between 1954 and 1956. He has traveled widely, and these experiences—as well as his lifelong commitment to sharing his concern for the preservation of the wild—inform all of his writings. In 1956, Matthiessen took off on his first lengthy trip with the intention of visiting every wildlife refuge in the United States, because he wanted to see his country's untamed places before they all disappeared. This journey resulted in *Wildlife in America* (1959). Since then, he has made anthropological and natural history expeditions to Alaska, the Canadian Northwest Territories, Peru, New Guinea, Africa, Nicaragua, and Nepal.

Since the 1961 publication of *The Cloud Forest: A Chronicle of the South American Wilderness*, Matthiessen has produced many books that reflect his interests in human and natural history, including *The Shorebirds of North America* (1967), *Oomingmak: The Expedition to the Musk Ox Island in the Bering Sea* (1967), and *Blue Meridian: The Search for the Great White Shark* (1971). *The Tree Where Man Was Born: The African Experience* (1972) examines the people and animals of East Africa; *Sand Rivers* (1981) focuses on a trek he made in one of Africa's largest remaining game preserves, the Selous Game Reserve. *The Snow Leopard* (1978) describes his Nepal trek; this book won both the National Book Award for contemporary thought (1979) and the American Book Award for its paperback edition (1980).

Matthiessen also writes about human history, particularly about current events that reflect issues which he sees as being central to the environmental and political problems that humankind now faces. *Sal Si Puedes: Cesar Chavez and the New American Revolution* (1970) examines the farm labor organizer's efforts to gain equality for American migrant workers. *In the Spirit of Crazy Horse* (1983) looks at the issue of racism as it has affected American Indians; *Indian Country* (1984) further explores this same topic.

Matthiessen won recognition for *Sand Rivers*, which received both the John Burroughs Medal and the African Wildlife Leadership Foundation Award in 1982 and the gold medal for distinction in natural history from the Academy of Natural Sciences in 1985. In addition, Matthiessen received the American Academy Award (1963), a National Institute/American Academy of Arts and Letters grant for *The Cloud Forest* and *Under the Mountain Wall: A Chronicle of Two Seasons in the Stone Age* (1962), and National Book Award nominations for *At Play in the Fields of the Lord* and *The Tree Where Man Was Born*. His book *Wildlife in America* is in the permanent collection of the White House library. Matthiessen has also contributed many articles, essays, and short stories to such publications as *The New Yorker, The New York Review of Books, The Atlantic, Esquire, Audubon, Newsweek*, and *The Saturday Evening Post*.

ANALYSIS

Matthiessen is considered one of America's foremost environmental writers. Both his fiction and nonfiction devote themselves to considerations of the fragile planet humans share with other life-forms. Matthiessen's subject is life on earth; he takes his materials wherever he finds them, no matter how remote the locale. His writing reflects his passion for travel, his interest in human nature—both innocent and destructive—and his commitment to calling others' attention to the pressing problems associated with the environment. Yet, although Matthiessen characterizes himself as a romantic, he does not give into what could be a temptation to romanticize nature: He describes both the beauty and the brutality of the natural world.

Matthiessen is especially noted for his unflinching consideration of the damage that industrial imperialism is causing or is about to cause the world's fragile ecosystem, in particular, damage to those underdeveloped or undeveloped portions of the globe most vulnerable to the devastating effects of such things as clear-cutting, pollution, and overpopulation. Thus, the journeys that Matthiessen shares with his readers are not simply travelogues for armchair tourists wishing to see exotic places; rather, his books first challenge his reader to think about what they see and, second, ask them to develop a shared concern for the continued well-being of a threatened environment, ecosystem, or ancient culture that he describes. His books again and again reflect his fear that industrial greed threatens to wipe out cultures, creatures, and whole geographical areas. Such fiction as *At Play in the Fields of the Lord* and *Far Tortuga* and most of his nonfiction, such as *Indian Country, Sand Rivers*, and *Men's Lives: The Surfmen and Baymen of the South Fork* (1986), take this perspective as their controlling focus.

Wildlife in America launched Matthiessen's career as a traveler to far places, an activity that was to be the main thrust of his life for the following twenty years. His travels inform all of his work, fiction and nonfiction alike. For example, *Far Tortuga* chronicles the voyage of a Caribbean turtling schooner. Yet Matthiessen does not always write of faraway places; he also addresses the problems faced by the vanishing or victimized cultures of North America with the same intensity that he brings to his exploration of the more remote corners of the world. While such a book as *Under the Mountain Wall: A Chronicle of Two Seasons in the Stone Age* looks at the culture of the New Guinea Kurelu tribe, *Sal Si Puedes: Cesar Chavez and the New American Revolution* focuses on Chavez's work to organize migrant workers in California. Books such as *The Cloud Forest: A Chronicle of the South American Wilderness* and *Oomingmak: The Expedition to the Musk Ox Island in the Bering Sea* examine cultures far from the immediate influence of the United States, but in his books *In the Spirit of Crazy Horse* and *Indian Country*, Matthiessen examines the effects of the modern age on American Indian cultures and peoples.

Always present in Matthiessen's nonfiction is a strong sense of the writer's personality. Matthiessen is not an invisible observer clinically reporting what he sees; his personal voice and the strength of his commitment can be heard very clearly in all that he writes. His far-flung travels not only afford him the opportunity to show his readers other cultures and locales, but they also allow him to reveal his own personality, his emotions, and the interior journeying for which the external expedition is an emblem. *The Snow Leopard* is perhaps the best example of this aspect of Matthiessen's writing; in it he journeys through Nepal with George Schaller, a wildlife biologist on the trail of the endangered snow leopard. The book is as much—if not more—about Matthiessen's need to find internal answers and silence as it is about the two men's pursuit of the leopard. The book details Matthiessen's struggle to achieve an interior peace and acceptance; the leopard eventually becomes an externalized version of that elusive Zen silence.

Besides *The Snow Leopard*, Matthiessen has written another autobiographical work, *Nine-Headed Dragon River: Zen Journals 1969-1982* (1985) which discusses his journey toward and practice of the Zen philosophy and way of life.

Matthiessen's fiction explores the moral landscape in much the same way that his nonfiction examines humankind's lack of moral commitment to the planet on which it lives. For example, his second novel, *Partisans*, reflects the liberal Left's disillusionment with communism. Set in Paris, it concerns American newsman Barney Sand's search for Jacobi, a communist who has been rejected by his own people. *Raditzer* examines the ambiguities associated with the friendship of two Navy men during World War II: the narrator, Charles Stark, and the morally corrupt Raditzer. Matthiessen confesses that Joseph Conrad and Fyodor Dostoevski have been major influences on his writing. *Raditzer* reflects the same moral focus and bleak interior landscapes so often the focus of both these writers. Critics see his subsequent novel, *At Play in the Fields of the Lord*, as expressing these same interests.

AT PLAY IN THE FIELDS OF THE LORD

First published: 1965
Type of work: Novel

Contact with a modern civilization can only bring about the destruction of primitive cultures.

At Play in the Fields of the Lord, set in the jungles of South America, has received much critical recognition. An aboriginal tribe of Amazonian Indians—the Niaruna—lives so far up the headwaters of the Amazon that they have never seen "modern" men, except the anthropologist who has been there to observe them. Once discovered, however, they become the focus of a number of groups' attempts to bring civilization to them. The Niaruna will never be the same after foreigners come on the scene, but neither will the Americans who go there. This novel expresses Matthiessen's central concern with the negative impact that modern technology has, not only on the less "advanced" cultures on which it encroaches but also on the people who take their own advantages for granted. The book also describes the tension that arises when the innocent "savages" are confronted by an essentially corrupt civilization—in this case, Catholic and Baptist missionaries and two American mercenaries.

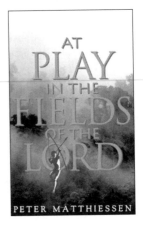

The Niaruna are causing problems for the governor of their state; although they usually live peacefully in their remote villages, they occasionally cause trouble for the civilized South American Indians who are their neighbors. The prefect of Oriente State wants them "pacified" by whatever means is effective. Although he personally favors bombing the Niaruna and driving them across his country's borders, he cannot afford a scandal. Because he holds two American soldiers of fortune as detainees (Wolfie and Moon), he coerces them into taking the job.

Not only does *At Play in the Fields of the Lord* show readers what can happen to the Indians once they are introduced to the twentieth century, it also examines the effect that going into the jungle has on people who have always taken modern conveniences for granted. In the jungle, many pretensions are stripped away, and people such as the (perhaps well-intentioned) missionaries cannot handle the result. Being face-to-face with nature and primitive tribes can terrify, as it does Hazel Quarrier, wife of Martin, one of the Baptist missionaries. While most of the characters are far from mad, they do show the effects of their removal from the protective shelter of the modern world. The piranhas, the filth and disease, the local infighting, the brutality of the Niaruna, and their own innate brutality all conspire to test these characters in ways they have never imagined possible in their "safe" modern world. The portrait Matthiessen offers is hardly flattering, for, although the Niaruna are predictably changed from their encounters with foreigners, the people who come to civilize them—mercenaries and missionaries alike—are affected in more savage ways.

It is not the missionaries who offer the most complicated response to the Niaruna; Lewis Meriwether Moon, a Cheyenne Indian who grew up on an American reservation and who has since become a soldier of fortune, displays the most complicated response to these people. At first he looks on fulfilling the prefect's demands to subdue the Niaruna as merely another job. Yet, once he becomes involved with these other Indians, he begins to see himself as their savior. In them he sees his own people; under the influence of a hallucinogenic drug, Moon hijacks a plane originally intended for bombing the tribe and parachutes into the Niaruna's forest. They look upon him as a sort of god; he struggles to live like a native but has trouble walking barefoot. Completely alienated by his experiences at home, he dreams of successfully leading the Niaruna in their battle to defend their territory. Given Matthiessen's pessimistic outlook, it comes as no surprise that Moon fails in his efforts to organize the Niaruna's resistance to the missionaries and the prefect.

Matthiessen clearly believes that the downfall of these remote cultures will only be a matter of time and that, no matter how well-intentioned the people who go to them are, contact with the outside modern world will destroy them. Even in the modern desire to "do good" lies the destruction of the world's remaining innocence and the debasement of the very people who thought that their work would help.

FAR TORTUGA

First published: 1975
Type of work: Novel

A crew of Caribbean fishermen battle against nature in their hunt for turtles.

In *Far Tortuga*, Matthiessen blends poetic form with the novel to create a hybrid whose form helps to tell the story of the crew of the schooner *Lillias Eden* and their search for the elusive green turtles. The story is one familiar to readers of tales of the sea: people against the elements. Raib Avers, the captain of the decrepit turtle-fishing boat, is determined to prove that he is the best captain alive in the Caribbean; his driving will endangers the lives of his entire crew and is strongly reminiscent of perhaps the most famous sailor, Herman Melville's Captain Ahab of *Moby Dick* (1851). Like Ahab, Captain Avers is angry, compelled, and reckless with the lives of those who work alongside him. His desire to find the turtles is responsible not only for his own death but also for those of all but one of his crew.

Hoping to use the money earned from a good haul to refit his boat, Avers sets out without a chronometer, life jackets, fire extinguishers, or a radio capable of calling for help. The boat and crew are doomed from the start. The crew seems typical of such a story: a drunk, a stowaway, a stranger, a malcontent, and so on. Captain Avers is determined that his plans will succeed despite the fears of his crew. In the end, piracy, shipwreck, and the death of all but one person are what occur. Critics liken Matthiessen not only to Melville but also to Joseph Conrad, who is famous for his brutally pessimistic stories of men who go to sea.

Far Tortuga resembles Matthiessen's other work in that it, too, is about the people of a dying culture. The book demonstrates Matthiessen's careful observations and understanding of the area about which he writes: In 1967, he spent an extensive period of time sailing with the turtle fishermen of the Grand Caymans. *Far Tortuga* describes these people's way of life and examines a livelihood that is rapidly vanishing and a locale that has now been exploited and irreversibly altered by the tourist industry, at the expense of the indigenous culture.

The novel provides stunning descriptions of the native wildlife, sea, and weather, all related in Caribbean dialect. Matthiessen follows the crew of the *Lillias Eden* as they leave Grand Cayman Island to go after turtles in the southwest Caribbean off the coast of Nicaragua. Because it is the end of the turtle season, Avers and his crew are unable to locate many of the creatures; frustrated, he heads for Far Tortuga, the name given by West Indian turtle-fishing men to an island supposedly located south of Cuba that is reputed to be the last sanctuary for green turtles. It is also a place that may or may not exist, one that is not even recorded on modern charts. Whether or not the *Lillias Eden* actually ever arrives there is not clear.

As a novel, *Far Tortuga* is experimental; Matthiessen forgoes many of the conventional strategies of fiction. The book is organized as a series of conversations in which the speakers are never identified by name; a reader must learn to recognize the different dialects and speech mannerisms in order to know who is talking. Matthiessen also does not allow himself the luxury of describing the characters' physical or emotional states; all the reader has to go on is the conversations that are reported.

In addition to this spare form of reporting, Matthiessen experiments with the physical form of the book. In the early pages of the novel, Matthiessen includes a ship's manifest and a diagram of the *Lillias Eden*'s layout. This provides the only real description of the boat, and it is up to the reader to interpret the information that has been given. The book's endpapers offer charts for the area where the *Lillias Eden* sails; the reader must use them to follow the course of the boat as Captain Avers searches farther and farther afield for the turtles. Elsewhere, Matthiessen draws a straight line to indicate the horizon; he surrounds words with a page of white space; he indicates the death of a shipwrecked crew member with a black blot with the character's name under it on an otherwise blank page. These tactics serve to eliminate the author almost completely from the book. For some readers such strategies will be troublesome, yet these techniques capture the feel of the journey, the isolation, and the futility. They also make *Far Tortuga* a novel that some critics have called a cross between poetry and novel.

THE SNOW LEOPARD

First published: 1978
Type of work: Nonfiction

The search for the elusive snow leopard mirrors a spiritual quest for inner peace.

Unlike his earlier books, Matthiessen's *The Snow Leopard* is intensely personal, revealing the writer himself—the individual who is so passionately interested in understanding the world around him, who is committed to imparting the knowledge that he does gain to interested readers. In his earlier work, Matthiessen the person was always remote—an observer who let his descriptions speak for themselves. In *The Snow Leopard*, however, what he describes is both his journey through Island Nepal and his quest to find inner peace.

In 1973, he accompanied wildlife biologist George Schaller on a trek to the Crystal Mountain in northern Nepal, near its border with Tibet. Schaller, a dry, stoic man, is intent on locating a herd of bharal—blue sheep, a rare animal that could be a close ancestor of both sheep and goats that had lived twenty million years ago. The trek covered over 250 miles and took Matthiessen, Schaller, and their sherpa guides over snow- and ice-covered mountain passes, through breathlessly high elevations to the Land of Dolpo. Not only did they intend to find the blue sheep, they also had hopes of sighting the rare snow leopard, a creature that is seldom seen and about which little was known.

Much of *The Snow Leopard* is Matthiessen's recounting of this trek, based on the extensive journal he kept while in Nepal. As such, his travel narrative is in the tradition of such explorers as Sir Richard Burton, Sir Henry Morton Stanley, and Sir Ernest Henry Shackleton. Matthiessen brings the reader face-to-face with the land and the people of Nepal. One learns precisely what it was like trekking in harsh weather, living in a small tent, dealing with the native population, and existing in an environment whose enormity dwarfs its human inhabitants.

Although Matthiessen makes use of his trained observer's eye to create a detailed picture of the Himalayas' natural history, *The Snow Leopard* is much more than a travelogue. Matthiessen is as interested in chronicling his interior spiritual quest as he is in describing his and Schaller's search for the snow leopard. A year prior to his departure on this trip, Matthiessen's second wife, Deborah Love, had died a brutal death from cancer. His trek through Nepal becomes a means by which he searches for peace and healing. A student of Zen Buddhism, Matthiessen looked upon his turmoil as a Zen problem in achieving inner quiet. He sought to capture a sense of unity with the natural world around him, a world that included the death of the woman he had loved.

The Snow Leopard attempts to explain the manner in which such inner Zen harmony is achieved. If one goes looking for a preconceived answer, one will be disappointed; it is necessary to become almost passive and allow whatever the answer is to emerge of its own accord, prompted by one's experiences on the journey. That is what Matthiessen attempted to do in Nepal. The snow leopard itself becomes the emblem for that quest: It is a creature that both Matthiessen and Schaller very much wish to see, yet it remains hidden, almost refusing to show itself precisely because they are looking for it. Similarly, as long as Matthiessen struggled with the fact of his wife's death, he could not attain inner harmony.

At the book's conclusion, the snow leopard has never been seen: There is some indication that it may have fleetingly appeared, but Matthiessen can never be sure. In fact, it is no longer important that the leopard was not sighted, for the journey's real purpose had not been to find it. In looking for one thing—the snow leopard—Matthiessen found something he had despaired of ever attaining: acceptance of Deborah's death, the Zen perspective that the world is as it should be.

As in his other books, Matthiessen here takes the opportunity to examine the Western attitude toward the world and toward nature. He reflects on his fellow Americans' desire both to love nature and to subdue it for the sake of "progress" and monetary gain. This type of progress is one Matthiessen always questions vigorously and one he ends up rejecting as wrongheaded. While some critics find *The Snow Leopard* to be less satisfying than Matthiessen's earlier books, they confess that what causes them the most trouble is the mystical vision quest that is a key aspect of the book, the sections that may make the book difficult to under-

stand but, at the same time, are what lend it such an intensely personal tone.

INDIAN COUNTRY

First published: 1984
Type of work: Nonfiction

In fragmenting American Indian cultures, Americans have destroyed their last contact with primal nature.

The themes of vanishing wilderness, of a world in which humans are only an insignificant part, and of the rape of the land are all a part of Matthiessen's *Indian Country*. In that sense, the book reflects concerns he has expressed earlier in his writing career. This time, Matthiessen tackles a subject closer to home: the loss of Native American lands and traditions. Matthiessen sees the American Indians as the last representatives of a life tied to the land and in harmony with nature.

Juxtaposed with that is American capitalism: big business taking over more and more of the land and destroying more and more of the environment in its greed for materials and profit. Most victimized by this voracious appetite, Matthiessen feels, are the Native American tribes, whose best interests have not been represented by the Bureau of Indian Affairs (BIA).

Indian Country begins in inland Florida, with Americans Indians in conflict with the American energy industry. Matthiessen then visits reservations in Florida, Tennessee, New York, California, North and South Dakota, and the Southwest. Included among the tribes that he visits are the Hopi, Navajo, Cherokee, Mohawk, Muskeegee, Sioux, Apache, and Comanche. With the help of an Indian "guide," Craig Carpenter, who describes himself as a detribalized Mohawk in search of genuine Native American culture, Matthiessen finds people whose culture is dying, whose young people are leaving, and whose land is desolate and difficult. The people seem to be split into two groups: the traditionals, who want to preserve the old ways, and the tribals, who wish to achieve some blending with the white culture. Not only do the Native Americans appear to be at odds with the whites, whom Matthiessen portrays as selfish opportunists, they also seem to be divided among themselves. For Matthiessen, the BIA, which should work to protect Indian interests, is only another means by which these indigenous cultures and their lands are rapidly being destroyed.

Once again, Matthiessen is a moralist whose main objective is to alert readers to the damage done to the environment at the hands of greedy capitalist technocrats. Wherever he looks on Native American land, Matthiessen sees evidence of the encroachment of destructive technologies: Energy conglomerates steal or buy oil and mineral rights and leave behind a landscape littered with strip-mine debris, poisonous uranium tailings, and oil rigs. Matthiessen views the American Indians as the representatives of the way in which life should be lived: in harmony with nature.

Some critics observe that, unlike his earlier books, in *Indian Country* Matthiessen shows a tendency to idealize his subject, presenting the Native Americans as the symbol for all that is noble and pure, ignoring the fact that these peoples are not simple savages but are members of a variety of complex and confusing cultures in which the environment as much as the people themselves seem to be threatened. Matthiessen does not make an attempt to draw distinctions between the more than three hundred separate tribes, ignoring the very different social, religious, economic, political, and environmental circumstances that differentiate these peoples. The book has also been criticized both because he has chosen to exclude anthropological and historical sources from his work and because he does not discuss key internal issues that American Indian tribes now face, such as the role of tribal members living off the reservation or the concerns of tribal members of mixed race.

KILLING MISTER WATSON

First published: 1990
Type of work: Novel

Edgar J. Watson is murdered by more than twenty of his neighbors, a number of whom now recount the varying stories leading up to the event.

The central characters of Peter Matthiessen's *Killing Mister Watson* are based on Edgar J. Watson, who lived between 1855 and 1910 and farmed in the Florida Everglades, and the "Queen of the Outlaws," Belle Starr. Watson liked to brag about his having killed fifty-seven men; however, he was only accused of one such crime: the 1889 death of Belle Starr in Fort Smith, Arkansas, who was found dead after a disagreement with Watson over some land.

In the novel, Watson and others recount their versions of events that involve Watson, forming a collage of opinion and versions of what Watson may or may not have done. However, even though Watson was never brought to trial for Starr's murder, he left Arkansas for the remote regions of the Everglades, where he raised pigs and otherwise supported himself off the land. Despite the cloud of doubt in Arkansas, Watson seemed to fit in as a welcome member of the Everglades, and he settled in to begin farming in Chatham Bend. Watson remains to the end of the novel a paradox: a man who boasted of a violent past, yet in his new "incarnation" as a Florida farmer, a devoted family man and a man generally regarded by his neighbors as a pillar of his community. Thus it is startling when, some thirty years after arriving in Florida, more than twenty of his neighbors—upstanding men of the nearby town of Chokoloske—meet him at that town's boat landing on October 24, 1910, gunning him down in a barrage of bullets.

Matthiessen has woven the novel from a combination of the historical record and the myths and rumors that have come to surround Watson's life and death. The narrative structure that Matthiessen employs underscores the disparities: events are narrated in different voices, and no two narrators agree as to who exactly Edgar J. Watson was or whether he got what he deserved. Yet the mystery is why so many men would join together to murder him in such a public fashion. It seems that Watson was a better businessman than many people had known: He apparently has been systematically murdering his field hands rather than paying them the wages that they earned. The main character is revealed through the accounts of twelve narrators to be a vicious, brutal owner who victimized those who could not defend themselves and for whom no real legal recourse existed at the time, given that they were poor and black and that Watson was powerful and white.

In this regard, as one narrator in the novel, Chokoloskee postmaster Mamie Smallwood, points out, Watson's behavior in regard to his hired hands is simply a "local" South Florida version of what was happening at the hands of Americans in many formerly Spanish colonies.

Killing Mister Watson is the first novel in what would eventually become a trilogy addressing the mysteries surrounding Watson's life, apparent sociopathic behavior, and subsequent public murder. In the second novel, *Lost Man's River* (1997), the focus shifts to Watson's son, Lucius, and his attempts to learn the truth about what kind of man his father really was and to unravel the mysteries surrounding the elder Watson's murder. In the final novel in the series, *Bone by Bone* (1999), Edgar Watson "returns" to recount his own version of events. By this time, at least thirteen other versions of Watson have been presented by the other narrators of the previous two books, so the "truth" of Watson, the motivations behind his brutal murders of his farmworkers—if indeed he did so—remain an enigma.

SUMMARY

One of the most respected modern American writers expressing natural history and environmental concerns, Matthiessen focuses on threatened and vanishing environments and on human cultures. He sees modern technology as the chief threat and cause of destruction. He has traveled widely and brings his careful attention to everything that he observes and records. His writing is powerful and evocative, and does not shy away from unpleasantness. Matthiessen can hardly be called a writer of simple travelogues or "nature books,"for his work also records his pursuit of moral vision, reflecting his own deep journeyings—interior explorations that take place while he contemplates and reports.

Melissa E. Barth

BIBLIOGRAPHY

By the Author

LONG FICTION:
Race Rock, 1954
Partisans, 1955
Raditzer, 1961
At Play in the Fields of the Lord, 1965
Far Tortuga, 1975
Killing Mister Watson, 1990
Lost Man's River, 1997
Bone by Bone, 1999

SHORT FICTION:
Midnight Turning Gray, 1984
On the River Styx, and Other Stories, 1989

NONFICTION:
Wildlife in America, 1959
The Cloud Forest: A Chronicle of the South American Wilderness, 1961
Under the Mountain Wall: A Chronicle of Two Seasons in the Stone Age, 1962
The Shorebirds of North America, 1967
Oomingmak: The Expedition to the Musk Ox Island in the Bering Sea, 1967
Sal Si Puedes: Cesar Chavez and the New American Revolution, 1970
Blue Meridian: The Search for the Great White Shark, 1971

Peter Matthiessen

Everglades: Selections from the Writings of Peter Matthiessen, 1971 (Paul Brooks, editor)

The Tree Where Man Was Born: The African Experience, 1972

The Wind Birds, 1973

The Snow Leopard, 1978

Sand Rivers, 1981

In the Spirit of Crazy Horse, 1983

Indian Country, 1984

Midnight Turning Gray, 1984

Nine-Headed Dragon River: Zen Journals 1969-1982, 1985

Men's Lives: The Surfmen and Baymen of the South Fork, 1986

African Silences, 1991

Tigers in the Snow, 1991

Baikal: Sacred Sea of Siberia, 1992

Shadows of Africa, 1992

East of Lo Monthang: In the Land of Mustang, 1995

An African Trilogy, 2000 (includes extracts from *The Tree Where Man Was Born*, *African Silences*, and *Sand Rivers*)

The Peter Matthiessen Reader: Nonfiction, 1959-1961, 2000 (McKay Jenkins, editor)

The Birds of Heaven: Travels with Cranes, 2001

End of the Earth: Voyaging to Antarctica, 2003

CHILDREN'S LITERATURE:
Seal Pool, 1972

About the Author

Dowie, William. *Peter Matthiessen*. Boston: Twayne, 1991.

Gabriel, Trip. "The Nature of Peter Matthiessen." *The New York Times Magazine* 10 (June, 1990): 30-31, 42, 94-98.

Holland, Patrick, and Graham Huggan. "Postmodern Itineraries." In *Tourists with Typewriters*, edited by Holland. Ann Arbor: University of Michigan Press, 1998.

Matthiessen, Peter. "An Interview with Peter Matthiessen." Interview by Kay Bonetti. *Missouri Review* 12, no. 12 (1989): 109-124.

Norman, Howard. "Peter Matthiessen: The Art of Fiction CLVII." *The Paris Review* 150 (Spring, 1999): 186-215.

Payne, David G. "Peter Matthiessen." In *American Nature Writers*, edited by John Elder. Vol. 2. New York: Scribner's, 1996.

Roberson, William H. *Peter Matthiessen: An Annotated Bibliography*. Jefferson, N.C.: McFarland, 2001.

Ross-Bryant, Lynn. "The Self in Nature: Four American Autobiographies." *Soundings: An Interdisiplinary Journal* 80, no. 1 (Spring, 1997): 83-104.

Shnayerson, Michael. "Higher Matthiessen." *Vanity Fair* 54 (December, 1991): 114-132.

DISCUSSION TOPICS

- Peter Matthiessen often writes unflatteringly about the U.S. government. In what ways does he think that the United States failed in its obligations to the native people of the Americas?

- Matthiessen is often characterized as an environmental writer. What purpose does such a writer have in crafting books for his readers? What "enemies" does Matthiessen identify in this type of writing? Do you believe that it is possible for writers such as Matthiessen to make a difference in people's attitudes about environmental issues?

- Are there instances in which it is right for people to take the law into their own hands, as the men of the Everglades did with Mr. Watson?

- Is it possible, given the nature of the multiple versions of the story of Edgar J. Watson recounted in *Killing Mister Watson*, to ever know the "truth" about a particular event?

- For what reasons did Matthiessen choose to write about his search for the snow leopard? In what ways does *The Snow Leopard* work on a variety of different thematic levels? If these levels interconnect, in what ways do they do so? For what purpose?

- In what ways does the novel *Far Tortuga* function as a parable? In what ways can this be said of much of Matthiessen's writing?

HERMAN MELVILLE

Born: New York, New York
    August 1, 1819
Died: New York, New York
    September 28, 1891

Although the full value of Melville's literary achievement was unrecognized until a half-century after his death, he has become known as one of the greatest American novelists of the nineteenth century.

Library of Congress

BIOGRAPHY

Herman Melvill, who did not add the final *e* to his name until after his father's death, was born in New York City on August 1, 1819, to Allan and Maria Melvill. His father, a relatively prosperous merchant and importer, was an open-minded, optimistic man whose Unitarian beliefs contrasted with his wife's sterner Calvinism. Melville's grandfathers were both Revolutionary War heroes: Thomas Melvill had participated in the Boston Tea Party, and Peter Gansevoort had led the forces that defended Fort Stanwix.

In 1830, Allan Melvill went bankrupt and was forced to move his family up the Hudson River to Albany, New York. Two years later he died, leaving his eldest son, Gansevoort, to support Maria and the seven younger children. When Gansevoort's fur business failed during the Panic of 1837, Herman Melville abandoned any hope for further formal education and began a frustrating search for steady employment. He worked as a bank clerk, a farm laborer, and a schoolteacher. He briefly studied surveying in the hope of being employed on the Erie Canal. When this prospect failed, Melville signed on as "boy" aboard the merchant ship *St. Lawrence* for a voyage to Liverpool, England.

After returning from Liverpool, Melville traveled to Illinois in another unsuccessful effort to find employment and once again tried teaching.

On the last day of 1840, unable to find another opportunity, he signed on as a common sailor aboard the whaling ship *Acushnet*, bound for the South Seas. After eighteen months of hard labor, short rations, and harsh treatment at sea, Melville and a companion jumped ship at Nuku Hiva in the Marquesas Islands. For about three weeks Melville lived with the reputedly cannibalistic Typee tribe before being picked up by the Australian whaler *Lucy Ann*. Conditions aboard the *Lucy Ann* were even worse than they had been aboard the *Acushnet*, and Melville became involved in a mutinous work stoppage that landed him in a Tahitian jail. He and a companion escaped and, after traveling about the nearby islands, he shipped out on the whaler *Charles and Henry*, from which he was discharged in Hawaii in 1843. Concerned that he would once again be arrested, Melville signed on to the warship *United States* and was released from service when the ship docked in Boston in October of 1844.

Almost immediately, Melville began to write of his adventures in the South Seas. *Typee: A Peep at Polynesian Life* (1846) was a great critical success, although Melville's American publishers pressured him to remove several passages in which he had condemned the behavior of missionaries. His second book, *Omoo: A Narrative of Adventures in the South Seas* (1847), was completed after his marriage to Elizabeth Shaw, daughter of Lemuel Shaw, chief justice of the Massachusetts Supreme Court. Like its predecessor, *Omoo* was well received, and although Melville did not make much money from either of his first two books, he was understandably confident about his literary future.

After publishing *Mardi, and a Voyage Thither* (1849), an allegory of political satire that was rejected by the reading public because of its experimental approach, Melville quickly wrote two realistic narratives based on his sea experiences, *Red-burn: His First Voyage* (1849) and *White-Jacket: Or, The World in a Man-of-War* (1850). In 1850 Melville purchased a home, called Arrowhead, near Pittsfield, Massachusetts. There he became friends with Nathaniel Hawthorne.

During his first year at Arrowhead, Melville completed his masterpiece, *Moby Dick: Or, The Whale* (1851); however, the work did not win recognition nor earn for him the money he needed to support his growing family. Desperately, Melville tried to imitate the successful romances of the era by publishing *Pierre: Or, The Ambiguities* (1852), but the work, which hinted at incest and attacked the hypocrisy of Christian moralists, brought Melville scathing reviews that generally concluded the author had gone mad.

With the serial publication of *Israel Potter: His Fifty Years of Exile* (1854-1855), Melville entered a brief period in which he contributed fiction to the leading monthly magazines of his day. Stories such as "Bartleby the Scrivener" (1853) and "Benito Cereno" (1855) appeared in *Putnam's* and *Harper's* before being published in a collection, *The Piazza Tales* (1856). *The Confidence Man: His Masquerade* (1857), Melville's dark picture of the United States on the brink of civil war, was the last of his prose fiction to be published during his lifetime.

Concerned for his son-in-law's health and sanity, Judge Shaw financed a trip to Europe and the Middle East for Melville. When he returned, Melville unsuccessfully tried for three years to support his family on the lecture circuit, finally selling Arrowhead in 1863 and moving to New York City. There his frustrating search for employment ended when he accepted a position as a customs inspector in 1866, but the difficult years had taken a toll. In 1867, believing that Melville had become mentally ill, Elizabeth threatened to leave him. In that same year, their son Malcolm killed himself at the age of eighteen.

Melville kept his position as a customs inspector for nineteen years until a small legacy allowed him to retire in 1886. During his time at the custom

house, Melville abandoned fiction and turned instead to poetry. He published *Battle-Pieces and Aspects of the War* (1866), *Clarel: A Poem and Pilgrimage in the Holy Land* (1876), *John Marr and Other Sailors* (1888), and *Timoleon* (1891) in small private editions. The manuscript of *Billy Budd, Foretopman* (1924), which Melville evidently wrote during the last five years of his life, was discovered after his death of a heart attack on September 28, 1891. The work was not published until Melville was "rediscovered" in the 1920's.

ANALYSIS

Melville died in 1891, a forgotten author. His death came almost forty years after he had stopped publishing fiction and more than thirty years before the discovery of the manuscript of *Billy Budd* and its posthumous publication began the revival of the author's literary reputation. By the middle of the twentieth century, the significance of his work was recognized, and his novel *Moby Dick* was viewed as one of America's literary masterpieces. Although Melville's poetry has received increasingly favorable attention, his literary reputation is firmly based on the remarkable series of novels and stories that he created over eleven years during the 1840's and 1850's. Although his fiction is varied, written in different genres, for different purposes, and with differing degrees of success, Melville's work is unified by themes and techniques that allow readers to trace the remarkable development of his literary skills during this brief period.

Using the term "theme" in its broadest sense, all Melville's major themes spring from his lifelong concern with the question of authority. His treatment of this subject would be less interesting if he had been a polemicist arguing from a set viewpoint. Instead, Melville explored ideas and was often driven between opposing viewpoints. One of his favorite transitional words was "nevertheless," an indication of the contrariness of his thinking. Because Melville was open and sympathetic to sometimes contradictory ideas, the themes that derive from his interest in the limits and applicability of authority are far-ranging, touching on questions of self-awareness, civil obedience, and moral verities.

Individual liberty is one recurrent theme that derives from Melville's interest in authority. Writing at a time when slavery was the most discussed political issue in the United States, Melville examined the struggle for personal liberty from a variety of viewpoints, acknowledging the necessity of liberty to human development while warning against its abuse. Melville's young protagonists strain against the limitations imposed by authoritarian rule, usually represented by tyrannical ship captains. They also dream of escaping the moralistic restrictions of societal codes. Ironically, their positions as common seamen make Melville's protagonists both rootless wanderers of the open seas and victims of the most repressive working conditions in nineteenth century America.

The books also demonstrate that individual liberty depends upon freedom from want. *Redburn's* portrayal of a mother and child starving in the streets of Liverpool and *Typee's* exposition on the benefits of a moneyless society exemplify Melville's indictment of capitalism's inequality. Yet Melville also showed the dangers of individual liberty. For characters such as Captain Ahab in *Moby Dick*, Taji in *Mardi*, or Pierre in *Pierre*, the pursuit of personal desire becomes a monomania that cuts off the possibility of happiness. Bartleby's preference not to work is a sign of despair. For Melville, the idea of individual liberty implied the dark possibility of misanthropy, madness, and alienation. Worst of all, it could mean becoming a renegade, a person who cuts himself off from his societal and familial connections.

The extent to which an individual should subordinate personal desires in order to be civilly obedient is another theme that evolves from Melville's consideration of authority. Melville's novels demonstrate his sensitivity to the social ills of his time and his commitment to protesting injustice. He chastised Christians for supporting the imperialistic and racist actions of missionaries in *Omoo*, satirized the inefficiency of bureaucrats in *Mardi*, deplored governments' failures to meliorate urban poverty in *Redburn*, argued against the naval policy of flogging in *White-Jacket*, criticized the United States' failure to support its veterans adequately in *Israel Potter*, questioned the conditions of women factory workers in "The Tartarus of Maids," and exposed the exploitative working conditions of seamen in several books.

Melville's anger was, however, tempered by the terrible threat of civil war and the violent rebellions that were changing European governments.

Although sympathetic to rebels and dissenters, Melville feared rebellion that could become anarchy. Thus, in *Typee* and *Omoo*, his protagonists elect to return to the oppressive seafaring exploitation from which they have escaped. In the epilogue to *White-Jacket*, Melville urged his reader to reject mutiny even if the ship of state seemed mishandled. In "Benito Cereno" he contrasted the evil of slavery with the darker evil of anarchy. In *Billy Budd* he sympathized with Captain Vere's terrible decision to hang Billy Budd for the accidental murder of Claggart because the larger issue of order in society took precedent.

Divine authority was another important theme for Melville. After being visited by Melville in Liverpool in 1856, Nathaniel Hawthorne wrote that Melville "can neither believe, nor, be comfortable in his unbelief; and is too honest and courageous not to try to do one or the other." Melville could not ignore the reality of evil in the world nor could he easily accept the authority of a paternalistic God; thus, he imagined a character such as Ahab, who tries to strike at the mystery of omniscience in the form of the white whale, but he showed how such unbending pride leads to destruction. Like his weary pilgrim in *Carel*, Melville unsuccessfully pursued a divine authority that he could accept wholeheartedly.

Melville's prose is enriched and complicated by his use of symbolism and allusion. His best books provide readers with symbols of provocative resonance: the tattooed bars on the faces of the Typees, the delicate glass ship in *Redburn*, the protagonist's odd jacket in *White-Jacket*, the mysterious and ominous white whale in *Moby Dick*, and the blank walls outside the lawyer's windows in "Bartleby the Scrivener." In his early work, Melville freely used informative passages taken from other sea narratives or scientific works, exposition that he interjected to increase his narratives' credibility and to respond to his readers' desire for information about the exotic lands and people he was describing. In later works, Melville's writing is more allusive, reflecting his voracious reading in theology, history, philosophy, and literature.

Most of Melville's novels can be read as initiation tales in which young, innocent, and idealistic men, who are orphaned by circumstances or conscious choice, brave the tempests of the world's open seas. Yet Melville wrote with incredible range, and his novels use the themes and techniques of many genres: the gothic romance of *Typee*, the picaresque satire of *Omoo*, the fantasy and allegory of *Mardi*, the social commentary of *Redburn* and *White-Jacket*, the patriotic tale of *Israel Potter*, the sentimental romance of *Pierre*, and the absurdist drama of *The Confidence Man*.

In some cases Melville was desperately trying to find an audience, for he was always short of money, and his writing never paid his expenses. In a letter to his friend Nathaniel Hawthorne, Melville complained that "dollars damn me.... What I feel most moved to write, that is banned,—it will not pay. Yet, altogether, write the *other* way I cannot. So the product is a final hash, and all my books are botches." Perhaps the diversity of Melville's work is best explained by his consuming desire to go beyond what he had previously written. Soon after completing *Moby Dick*, he wrote to Hawthorne, "Lord, when shall we be done with growing? As long as we have anything more to do, we have done nothing. So, now, let us add Moby Dick to our blessing, and step from that. Leviathan is not the biggest fish;—I have heard of Krakens."

TYPEE

First published: 1846
Type of work: Novel

After living among the inhabitants of a tropical island, a young deserter from a whaling ship returns to the society he has initially spurned.

Typee: A Peep at Polynesian Life is based on Melville's experiences in the South Seas, specifically his desertion of the whaling ship *Acushnet* in the Marquesas Islands and his subsequent stay with a tribe of reputedly cannibalistic islanders. He wrote the novel when he was twenty-five, soon after returning from his sea journeys, and he later told his friend Nathaniel Hawthorne that "from my twenty-fifth year I date my life." The reviews of this first novel were almost unanimously favorable, convincing Melville that he was going to be a literary success.

Typee is narrated by a dreamy young sailor who is weary of the conditions aboard the whaling ship *Dolly*. He combats the tedium of the voyage by constructing fantasies of tropical adventures. When the *Dolly* anchors in Nuku Hiva harbor in the Marquesas Islands, the sailor convinces himself and a companion named Toby to ignore the fearful tales of murderous cannibals and jump ship. Their escape from the ship to the island's interior is a harrowing and symbolic initiation rite, forcing the young deserters to survive chills, fever, hunger, and perilous heights in order to earn their entry into the enigmatic paradise of Typee Valley. Their trial ends when they exhibit their determination by leaping from a cliff into the top of a tree in the valley below.

In Typee valley they discover a society free from the necessity of work and the restrictions of "civilized" moral codes. They are taken in by the tribe. The protagonist, who names himself Tommo, is adopted by a family which provides for all of his needs. Tommo and Toby spend their time learning about the valley and bathing with the young women of the tribe. Tommo develops a special relationship with the beautiful Fayaway, and the young couple share blissful canoe trips on the valley's lagoon.

Tommo, however, cannot trust this tropical paradise. A mysterious leg injury, suffered during his escape, plagues him throughout his stay with the Typee, functioning as a measure of his psychological state, particularly his continuing suspicions of the natives' cannibalistic intentions. Tommo's fears are heightened by the linguistic barriers that make full communications impossible and by a series of ambiguous events that fuel his gothic imagination.

After Toby is allowed to leave the valley, Tommo's anxiety increases, and when the Typees begin to pressure him to be tattooed, Tommo panics. The tattooed facial bands seem like racial prison bars to Tommo. Although he repeatedly argues the superiority of Typeean culture and praises the beauty and gentleness of the Typees themselves, the thought of becoming one of them and cutting himself off from his own cultural heritage drives him to escape.

Because of his leg, Tommo must be assisted in his escape. Fayaway, his adopted father, Marheyo, and his Typeean friend and guide Kory-Kory take him to the beach, where a ship has been sighted. Their reluctant assistance and their obvious sadness at his departure exemplify the selfless innocence of the Typee, but the cannibalistic side of the tribe is represented by Mow-Mow, a fierce chief who has opposed letting Tommo leave. Mow-Mow tries to prevent Tommo's escape by swimming after the longboat that has picked him up. When Mow-Mow reaches the longboat, Tommo slashes the savage's throat with a boat hook, baptizing himself in blood in order to return to so-called civilization.

Typee is Melville's first effort at portraying the enigmatic character of moral truth. Despite the melodrama of its conclusion, which might lead some readers to assume that Mow-Mow's desperate pursuit discloses the true barbarism of the Typee, *Typee* does not solve the basic enigma of good and evil. Instead, it suggests that any moral judgment is relative and open to question.

The novel's romantic narrative is interrupted by informative chapters that explain native customs and argue the merits of Typeean culture. Although these expository interruptions offer an alternate way of viewing Typee Valley, their connection to the narrative is sometimes artificial. Indeed, many of these chapters were added after the completion of the manuscript, in response to the publisher's concern for authenticity.

MOBY DICK

First published: 1851
Type of work: Novel

A young seaman survives a disastrous whaling journey led by a megalomaniacal captain who is pursuing a powerful white whale.

Moby Dick: Or, The Whale is Melville's masterpiece, the book in which he most thoroughly used his experiences in the South Seas to examine the human condition and the metaphysical questions that were at the center of the author's troubled worldview. From the novel's famous opening line, "Call me Ishmael," the reader is addressed directly by the book's youthful but embittered narrator. Unlike many of Melville's youthful narrators, Ishmael is not presented as a young innocent, although he does face an initiation into the ways of the world. Instead, he is depicted as a young man with a past,

who takes to the sea to avoid taking some more drastic action in response to the difficulties he has faced.

Ishmael comes to New Bedford, Massachusetts, to sign on to a whaling ship, but before sailing he is confronted with comic and foreboding events that suggest the broad range of the novel. First, Ishmael shares a bed with a tattooed South Seas islander named Queequeg. Despite his initial comic horror, Ishmael demonstrates his open-mindedness by overcoming his fears and becoming friends with the cannibal.

Ishmael also attends the famous whaleman's chapel, where he hears Father Mapple deliver a sermon based on the story of Jonah and the whale, a sermon that emphasizes the dangers of human pride. After selecting the *Pequod*, a ship named after an Indian tribe that was massacred by the Puritans, the narrator and his new pagan companion are confronted by a strange old man who warns them of dangers to come.

The *Pequod* sails on Christmas, but Captain Ahab remains in his cabin for many days. Meanwhile, the ship is managed by the three mates, Starbuck, Stubb, and Flask. Ishmael describes the careful hierarchy of the ship, whose ethnically diverse crew composes a microcosmic vision of the world. When Ahab does reveal himself to the crew, his scarred face and whalebone peg leg present a sobering image of a physically and mentally damaged man.

Ishmael, who is reflective and open to all ideas, provides the reader with a wealth of information regarding whales, whaling, and whaling ships. His approach to the gathering of knowledge is eclectic, ranging from scientific classification to imaginative association. As the *Pequod*'s crew hunts for whales and Ahab hunts for Moby Dick, Ishmael hunts for meaning.

In the pivotal chapter, titled "The Quarter-Deck," Ahab reveals his purpose to the men. In a masterful display of persuasive oratory, he stirs the crew to dedicate themselves to assist him in his vengeful pursuit of the white whale and nails a gold doubloon to the mast as the prize to the man who sights Moby Dick. When Starbuck, whose name suggests his struggle against fate, questions Ahab's personal pursuit of vengeance against a dumb animal, Ahab reveals his belief that the world is operated by a malicious force that works through visible objects. Thus, Ahab's quest is not only a matter of individual vengeance but an effort to strike at the controlling force of nature.

During the journey around the Cape of Good Hope and across the Indian Ocean, the *Pequod*'s crew lowers boats to pursue whales. Ahab then reveals the special boat led by the demonic Fedallah, which he has kept hidden. The *Pequod* also meets other vessels. Before the novel is over, the *Pequod* has met nine other ships (*Goney, Town-Ho, Jereboam, Jungfrau, Bouton-de-rose, Samuel Enderby, Bachelor, Rachel*, and *Delight*), and each meeting adds perspective to Ahab's mad quest. As he begins to hear direct testimony about the white whale from sailors on other ships, Ahab's obsession intensifies. He orders his men to ignore opportunities to capture other whales and frantically studies his charts.

Before the final, tragic confrontation, the African American cabin boy, Pip, is lost overboard and goes insane before he is finally rescued by the *Pequod*. Touched by the lad's condition, Ahab takes Pip under his personal care, and Pip returns Ahab's kindness with an innocent devotion that almost distracts Ahab from his vengeful course. It is clear that in order to persevere in his quest, Ahab must sever all ties of human affection.

In the end, the crew of the *Pequod* wages a three-day battle against Moby Dick, a struggle that concludes with the whale's destruction of the ship and all the crew except Ishmael. The narrator ironically escapes aboard Queequeg's coffin and survives to tell the tale.

Moby Dick is an expansive book in which Melville uses diverse styles. The book incorporates a wide range of dialects and rhetorical models as different as the new sermon and the tall tale. As in *Typee* and other earlier novels, Melville inserts autonomous chapters, such as the chapter on cetology, that interrupt the narrative; in *Moby Dick*, however, the interrelation of these chapters to the themes of the book is closer. Moreover, most of the autonomous chapters in *Moby Dick* use a particular subject, object, or event to present Ishmael's musings on the meaning of experience.

"BARTLEBY THE SCRIVENER"

First published: 1853 (collected in *The Piazza Tales*, 1856)
Type of work: Short story

A confident and self-satisfied lawyer discovers the limits of his melioristic impulses.

"Bartleby the Scrivener: A Story of Wall Street" was one of the first stories that Melville published during the brief period when his work was accepted by the major periodicals. It has become his most widely known story, praised for being ahead of its time. The story focuses on a prosperous lawyer, who prides himself on being a "safe man."

Ensconced in his Wall Street law offices, the lawyer manages an office of complementary contrasting scriveners (law copyists) who represent opposing types. The lawyer works around the limitations of his employees in the optimistic belief that his is the enlightened and most effective way to lead life. In effect, he attempts to avoid conflict and promotes compromise. He stands as a representative of nineteenth century American optimism, an outlook that Melville questioned in much of his writing.

When a cadaverous man named Bartleby approaches him for employment, the lawyer, pressed for extra help at the time, gladly puts the new employee to work. Bartleby is clearly capable of doing acceptable work, but before long he exhibits an annoying refusal to engage in certain tedious activities, such as proofreading documents. Pressed for time, the lawyer works around this unusual refusal, but before long he discovers that Bartleby is living in the offices at night, subsisting on ginger nuts that he stores in his desk. The lawyer's uneasiness is compounded when Bartleby begins to refuse all work, refuses to leave the premises, and spends much time staring out a window at the brick wall only inches away from him.

The lawyer's melioristic optimism is pushed to the limit. He tries to discuss the situation with Bartleby, attempts reasoning with him, even attempts bribing him. He invites him to stay at his home. Bartleby's maddening response is always the same: "I would prefer not to." The lawyer eventually surrenders, trying to escape his responsibility for this strange, broken human being by moving his offices and leaving Bartleby behind, but before long the new residents of the building are complaining about the strange character who lives in the hallways. The lawyer renounces any responsibility, and Bartleby is hauled off to the Tombs, the city prison, where he is surrounded by walls such as those he stared at from the lawyer's window.

The lawyer tries to bribe a jailer to assure that Bartleby is treated well, but upon his return weeks later, he discovers that Bartleby has been refusing to eat and has died of malnutrition. At the story's end, when the lawyer sighs "Ah Bartleby! Ah humanity!" the reader recognizes the universal implications of the story and knows that the lawyer will be unable to approach life with the same simplistic optimism he had before.

As an epilogue of sorts, the narrator adds a bit of information about Bartleby's past, explaining that he had been previously employed in the dead letter office of the post office. In this position he was repeatedly faced with the tragedies of miscommunication. This revelation should not serve as an easy explanation for Bartleby's condition, however, for Melville's story depicts the mystery of despair and argues that some suffering is beyond melioration. Melville's "story of Wall Street" has been praised for its modernity. Certainly the tale foreshadows the twentieth and twenty-first century theme of urban alienation and describes a dehumanized environment of brick and mortar that is shut off from the consolations of the natural world.

"BENITO CERENO"

First published: 1855 (collected in *The Piazza Tales*, 1856)
Type of work: Short story

An optimistic sea captain is deceived by a cunning and diabolical slave.

Melville's story "Benito Cereno" was originally published serially in three parts. There is some indication that he considered making it into a novel but was discouraged by his potential publisher. Melville drew much of his material from Amaso Delano's *A Narrative of Voyages and Travels in the Northern and Southern Hemispheres* (1817); in fact, much of the court deposition material is transcribed exactly from the original.

The story is set in August of 1799 off the coast of Chile, where the "singularly undistrustful" captain of an American sealer, *Bachelor's Delight*, Amaso Delano, comes upon an erratically sailing ship that is flying no colors. Against the advice of his mate, Delano approaches the mysterious vessel in a longboat and discovers that she is the *San Dominick*, a Spanish merchant ship carrying slaves from Buenos Aires to Lima. Upon boarding her, Delano meets the captain, Benito Cereno, an invalid who tells Delano a tale of the disease and the bad sailing weather that has killed much of his crew.

Delano is puzzled by the lack of discipline on the ship, the mysterious actions of the crew and slaves, the oversolicitousness of the servant Babo, and the mercurial behavior of Don Benito, who switches from gentleness to harshness without warning. Delano studies the unusual mix of sailors and slaves on deck, sensing that all is not as it seems; however, he is unable to reach any reasonable conclusion about the situation.

Although he takes pride in his enlightened attitude toward the Africans on board, Delano's racist assumptions regarding the limited capabilities of blacks lead him to suspect that the Spaniard is plotting some evil. In general, Delano has no capacity to discern evil, and his ethical blindness, which parallels the pragmatic optimism of nineteenth century America, prevents Delano from perceiving the situation until the truth is thrust upon him. Like the lawyer in "Bartleby the Scrivener," Delano is an optimist who is indisposed to countenance evil; therefore, he repeatedly assures himself that his suspicions are illusory.

After resupplying the *San Dominick*, Delano prepares to depart and promises to tow the disabled ship to safe anchor next to the *Bachelor's Delight*. As Delano casts off, Don Benito leaps into the longboat, pursued by the knife-wielding Babo. For a moment, Delano believes that he is being attacked by Don Benito, but a "flash of revelation" makes the situation clear. He realizes that the slaves have rebelled, killed most of the Spaniards, and are plotting to capture Delano's ship in order to continue their journey to freedom. Their leader, Babo, is revealed to be a cunning and violent deceiver rather than the loyal servant that Delano had imagined him to be.

Delano overcomes Babo, rallies his crew, and manages to overwhelm the slaves who hold the *San Dominick*. The rebellious slaves are brought to trial, and the last portion of the story is a reconstruction of the court proceedings, retelling the narrative in cold, legalistic terms. Cereno is ruined by the experience. Delano's efforts to console the Spaniard are futile, and Don Benito retires to a monastery, where he soon dies. Babo is executed, but his head, which is placed on a pole, still smiles in warning after death. The story shows that evil—dark metaphysical evil, an evil that cannot be repaired, meliorated, or ignored—is real in the world. Don Benito recognizes this, and the realization crushes him. Delano's optimism is tempered but not conquered by the experience.

The story uses color imagery to emphasize the idea that truth is difficult to interpret. White represents good, although, as in the case of the skeleton that the murderous slaves place on the *San Dominick*'s figurehead, good is sometimes in decay. Black represents evil, although the story also recognizes the correctness of the slaves' impulse toward freedom and disputes the stereotype of blacks as incompetent and happy-go-lucky. Gray is the other frequently used color in the story, and it represents the ambiguous mix of good and evil that faces humankind in the world.

THE CONFIDENCE MAN

First published: 1857
Type of work: Novel

A masterful confidence man toys with a ship full of passengers on a journey down the Mississippi River.

The action of Melville's *The Confidence Man: His Masquerade* takes place on April Fool's Day aboard the *Fidèle*, a steamship heading down the Mississippi River. The novel introduces the reader to a bewildering array of characters, one of whom is a skilled confidence man who appears throughout the book in a variety of disguises.

The theme of *The Confidence Man* is trust—the limits of belief in society. Melville examines the heart of humankind and finds it as corrupt as Mark Twain did in his later works. Aboard the *Fidèle*, which is presented as a microcosm of human society, with an incredible diversity of human types, self-interest is the only human motivation. Perhaps more disconcerting is the near impossibility of ascertaining the true character of anyone on board. The protean confidence man is only the prime example of the rule of pretense. The world of *The Confidence Man* is a world of deception and deceit; each of the confidence man's swindles demands that the dupe display confidence, and each parallels the Fall of Man. The confidence man toys with his victims until he discovers the weakness that he can use against them.

The confidence man appears in a bewildering series of disguises: a mute wearing cream colors, a crippled African American beggar named Black Guinea, a Man with a Weed, an agent from the Seminole Widow and Orphan Asylum, the president of the Black Rapids Coal Company, an herb doctor who sells Omni-Balsamic Reinvigorator and Samaritan Pain Dissuader, the Happy Bone Setter, an agent for the Philosophical Intelligence Office, the Cosmopolitan (who wears a strange outfit pieced together from the national costumes of several nations), and Frank Goodman.

The novel also presents a number of recognizable regional types, particularly the rough-and-ready westerner and the sly Yankee peddler, and frequently sets one region's representative against another. Melville provides scant clues for the reader to determine the identity of these characters, thus placing the reader in a position similar to that of the confidence man's victims, who are sometimes accosted by more than one of his manifestations.

There is very little action in the novel, which consists almost entirely of the confidence man's discussions with his victims. Thus, the narrative consists of the dialectical working of ideas. The passengers with whom he interacts are themselves shown to be engaged in a variety of confidence games; at least, they are frequently shown to be self-interested people who rarely reveal their true thoughts or intentions. As in any confidence game, the novel's protagonist is able to play on the selfish motives or inflated egos of his victims.

For the most part, the confidence man is successful, but his monetary gain is generally slight. The fact that he works so hard for little gain emphasizes the book's contention that evil has its own purposes. His toughest opponents are westerners such as Pitch and Charles Arnold Noble, who are hardened against the human geniality on which the confidence man feeds, or soulless intellectuals such as Mark Winsome, Melville's scathing caricature of Ralph Waldo Emerson. Thus, the novel seems to maintain that the only defenses against deception are misanthropy or vacuousness.

As the work nears its conclusion, the confidence man goes below decks, where he discovers an old man reading the Bible by the dim light of a single lamp. Around the cabin in the darkness are other men in berths, whose comments interrupt the confidence man's conversation with the old man. After buying a counterfeit detector and a money belt from an innocent-looking boy and subsequently realizing that he has been sold inferior merchandise, the old man is led away by the confidence man, who extinguishes the lone remaining light in the cabin, ending the book in smoky darkness.

Critics have struggled with *The Confidence Man,* and perhaps no other book of Melville's has been judged as variously. Some view it as Melville's greatest achievement next to *Moby Dick*; others maintain that it is a brilliant failure, a "non-novel" lacking plot or character development. It has been read as social criticism, religious allegory, and a commentary on the history of optimistic philosophy.

BILLY BUDD, FORETOPMAN

First published: 1924
Type of work: Novella

A ship's captain sentences a young seaman to hang for accidentally killing an officer.

Billy Budd, Foretopman was written during Melville's final years. He may have begun it after reading "The Mutiny on the *Somers*" in *The American Magazine* in June, 1888. Melville's cousin Guert Gansevoort had been a lieutenant on the U.S. brig-of-war *Somers* in 1842 and had been a member of the military court that condemned a young seaman accused of mutiny. Melville may have wanted an opportunity to reinterpret the situation.

The manuscript was discovered after his death, and it was not published until 1924. Many critics have suggested that *Billy Budd* represents Melville's most mature vision of the metaphysical questions that troubled him throughout his life. They suggest that in this novella Melville came as close as he could to reconciling the confrontation between free will and authority.

William Budd is a young, handsome sailor aboard the *Rights-of-Man* who is impressed into service aboard H.M.S. *Indomitable* in 1797. Although the ironically named ships comment on the tyranny of such an act, Budd accepts his enforced change of ships with good spirits. Indeed, Budd is a character of remarkable innocence. Neither stupid nor weak, he nevertheless is untouched by the knowledge of evil. He is an image of man before the Fall, marred only by his tragic flaw, a tendency to lose the capacity to speak during times of emotional stress.

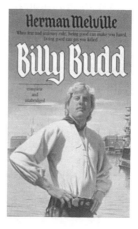

The captain of Budd's new ship, Captain Vere, is a thoughtful, well-read man who takes an immediate liking to his new recruit, but the *Indomitable*'s master-at-arms, Claggart, is a different case. From the start, Claggart, an embodiment of satanic malice toward virtue, shows an unreasoning dislike for the new recruit, whom he mockingly calls Baby Budd. Unable to conceive of innocence such as Budd's, Claggart assumes that Budd returns his hatred, and he plots the young sailor's downfall. Unable to taunt or tempt Budd into actual crime, Claggart baldly accuses him of mutinous activities. Budd, who is unable to speak in response to the accusation, strikes Claggart in the temple and kills him.

Captain Vere is left with a terrible decision. It is a time of war, and Vere accepts the importance of maintaining authority. Recent mutinies aboard other British warships make his decision more critical. Vere can see no way to avoid hanging Budd, and he makes it clear to the officers who convene to decide Budd's fate that they cannot respond to human sympathies but that they must perform their duty to preserve order and the rule of law. If

Budd can be seen as an image of Adam before the Fall, and Claggart can be seen as an image of Satan, Vere can be seen as a model of God, a stern but righteous father. He orders the execution, but the story portrays Vere as a sensitive man who sentences Budd to die despite his deep sympathy for the boy. Before being executed, Billy cries out "God bless Captain Vere!" and his final act of forgiveness is echoed by the crew assembled to witness the execution.

Soon after Budd's execution, the *Indomitable* engages another ship in battle, and Vere receives a fatal wound. As he dies, he murmurs the name Billy Budd, but his final words are affectionate and sad rather than remorseful, for he knows that he has played his tragic part faithfully. *Billy Budd* is Melville's final examination of authority, and in the story he resigns himself to the tragic necessity for authority to preserve the greater good, even at the expense of individual rights.

CLAREL: A POEM AND PILGRIMAGE IN THE HOLY LAND

First published: 1876
Type of work: Poem

A young intellectual fails to find spiritual regeneration during a tour of the Holy Land.

Melville wrote *Clarel: A Poem and Pilgrimage in the Holy Land* during the twenty years following his journey to Europe and the Middle East in 1856-1857. Just as Elizabeth Melville hoped that her husband's extended tour would ease his debilitating depression, Clarel, the protagonist of the narrative poem, searches for spiritual renewal, attempting to regain the faith that he has lost during his years of study.

The poem is divided into four parts, and each part culminates in death. In part 1, Clarel is repulsed by the barrenness of Jerusalem and overwhelmed by feelings of loneliness. His need for a companion is answered when he meets Ruth, falls in love with her, and impulsively asks for her hand in marriage. Their courtship is interrupted by the death of Ruth's father, and Clarel decides to pass

the time of mourning by joining an odd assortment of pilgrims who are traveling toward the Dead Sea.

In part 2, Clarel and the other pilgrims journey through the wilderness. His companions represent a range of opinions, and much of the poem recounts their discussion of theological matters. Set amid the formidable and barren landscape of the Siddom Gorge, part 2 builds toward the group's encampment on the shores of the Dead Sea. There the aged mystic Nehemiah, who has been traveling with them, dies after having a visionary dream and walking into the water.

In part 3, the pilgrims travel to Mar Saba, the ancient monastery and oasis. In Mar Saba, the starkness of their journey is relieved by the conviviality of the monks, the comfortable quarters, and the plentiful food and drink. The humanism of this center of Christian belief stands in contrast to the closed doors and dust-covered shrines of Jerusalem that Clarel had first encountered. However, this part of the poem also ends in death, as the pilgrims discover the corpse of Montmain, one of their companions, with its eyes open, staring at the sacred palm.

In part 4, the pilgrims return to Jerusalem, completing their symbolic circular path. Clarel, who has had second thoughts regarding his betrothal to Ruth while on his journey and has even exhibited some homosexual interest in Vine, one of his companions, discovers that Ruth has died while he has been traveling. Confused and alone, Clarel is last seen joining another band of pilgrims.

Critics have argued over the implications of the poem's epilogue. Some see in it a Melville who, near the end of his life, had made peace with the conflict between disbelief and belief. Others, however, see in it a reaffirmation of Melville's lifelong inability to resolve the conflict and a conviction that it could not be resolved.

SUMMARY

As perfumes were made from the ambergris formed in the intestines of whales, so Melville transformed his gritty experience as a sailor into a body of fiction that addresses the most difficult questions of human existence. Thus, *Moby Dick*, a lengthy and often obscure story about the anachronistic business of hunting whales, transcends its limitations to stand as one of America's proudest contributions to world literature.

Melville's determination to explore the meaning of existence through his fiction, his ability to transform the objects and events he describes into resonant symbols of profound metaphysical significance, and his unbiased examination of the social questions of his time compose his greatness.

Carl Brucker

BIBLIOGRAPHY

By the Author

LONG FICTION:
Typee: A Peep at Polynesian Life, 1846
Omoo: A Narrative of Adventures in the South Seas, 1847
Mardi, and a Voyage Thither, 1849
Redburn: His First Voyage, 1849
White-Jacket: Or, The World in a Man-of-War, 1850
Moby Dick: Or, The Whale, 1851
Pierre: Or, The Ambiguities, 1852
Israel Potter: His Fifty Years of Exile, 1855
The Confidence Man: His Masquerade, 1857
Billy Budd, Foretopman, 1924

SHORT FICTION:
The Piazza Tales, 1856
The Apple-Tree Table, and Other Sketches, 1922

POETRY:
Battle-Pieces and Aspects of the War, 1866
Clarel: A Poem and Pilgrimage in the Holy Land, 1876
John Marr and Other Sailors, 1888
Timoleon, 1891
The Works of Herman Melville, 1922-1924 (volumes 15 and 16)
The Poems of Herman Melville, 1976, revised 2000

NONFICTION:
Journal up the Straits, 1935
Journal of a Visit to London and the Continent, 1948
The Letters of Herman Melville, 1960 (Merrill R. Davis and William H. Gilman, editors)

MISCELLANEOUS:
Tales, Poems, and Other Writings, 2001 (John Bryant, editor)

About the Author

Bloom, Harold, ed. *Herman Melville.* Philadelphia: Chelsea House, 2003.

Branch, Watson G., ed. *Melville: The Critical Heritage.* Boston: Routledge & Kegan Paul, 1974.

Davey, Michael J., ed. *A Routledge Literary Sourcebook on Herman Melville's "Moby Dick."* New York: Routledge, 2004.

Dryden, Edgar A. *Monumental Melville: The Formation of a Literary Career.* Stanford, Calif.: Stanford University Press, 2004.

DISCUSSION TOPICS

- In what ways did Herman Melville's first two commercially successful novels become misfortunes for him?

- What traits of Captain Ahab in *Moby Dick* make him such a memorable character? Can this character be comprehended or is he ultimately mysterious?

- What does the white whale in *Moby Dick* symbolize?

- In "Bartleby the Scrivener," why does Bartleby "prefer not to"?

- What characteristics of modern Manhattan are already present or adumbrated in "Bartleby the Scrivener"?

- Discuss lack of imagination as a weakness in the lawyer in "Bartleby the Scrivener" and Captain Delano in *Benito Cereno.*

- Does Captain Vere make the right decision in *Billy Budd, Foretopman*? Do Billy's final words cast any light on the matter?

- Did Melville make his mature works too ambiguous?

Hardwick, Elizabeth. *Herman Melville*. New York: Viking Press, 2000.

Heflin, Wilson L. *Herman Melville's Whaling Years*. Edited by Mary K. Bercaw Edwards and Thomas Farel Heffernan. Nashville: Vanderbilt University Press, 2004.

Higgins, Brian, and Hershel Parker, eds. *Critical Essays on Herman Melville's "Moby Dick."* New York: G. K. Hall, 1992.

Johnson, Claudia Durst. *Understanding Melville's Short Fiction: A Student Casebook to Issues, Sources, and Historical Documents*. Westport, Conn.: Greenwood Press, 2005.

Levine, Robert S., ed. *The Cambridge Companion to Herman Melville*. New York: Cambridge University Press, 1998.

Parker, Hershel. *Herman Melville: A Biography—Volume 1, 1819-1851*. Baltimore: Johns Hopkins University Press, 1996.

_____. *Herman Melville: A Biography—Volume 2, 1851-1891*. Baltimore: Johns Hopkins University Press, 2002.

Robertson-Lorant, Laurie. *Melville: A Biography*. New York: Clarkson N. Potter, 1996.

JAMES MERRILL

Born: New York, New York
March 3, 1926
Died: Tucson, Arizona
February 6, 1995

Merrill was recognized in his twenties as a skilled young poet; he continued to publish poetry of more and more significance. His career reached a high point with his epic trilogy, The Changing Light at Sandover, *published in 1982.*

Library of Congress

BIOGRAPHY

James Merrill was born in New York City, the son of Helen (Ingram) Merrill and Charles E. Merrill, one of the founders of the brokerage firm Merrill, Lynch, Pierce, Fenner, and (at one time) Beane. His parents divorced before his eleventh birthday, at which time he discovered a love for opera and music.

Merrill attended Lawrenceville School in New Jersey, where he began to write, privately printing *Jim's Book: A Collection of Poems and Short Stories*. After graduation, he entered Amherst College, but after a year there, he entered the U.S. Army, in which he served another year (1944-1945). He then returned to Amherst, where he was elected to Phi Beta Kappa, had various poems published, and starred in a school production of Jean Cocteau's *Orphee* (pr. 1926, pb. 1927). He wrote a senior thesis on Marcel Proust, the famous modernist French novelist, a writer who was always to have much influence on him. Merrill received his B.A. summa cum laude in 1948 and stayed on to teach a year at Amherst, then left to become a writer. He decided that Manhattan was not the proper atmosphere in which to write, so he first traveled throughout Europe, finally settling down in a house he purchased in Stonington, Connecticut, in 1954. In the mid-1960's he bought another house in Athens, Greece. Throughout these years he shared both houses with his companion, David Jackson.

Merrill published his first book of poems, *First*

Poems, in 1951. The book was well received and launched him on a lifelong career of writing. Before publishing another book of poems, he wrote two plays, *The Immortal Husband* (pr. 1955, pb. 1956) and *The Bait* (pr. 1953, pb. 1960), and a novel, *The Seraglio* (1957). *The Bait* was acted Off-Broadway in 1953. *The Immortal Husband* was presented at the Theatre de Lys in Greenwich Village in February, 1955; reviewers found it well written but confusing.

Merrill's novel *The Seraglio* received mixed reviews: It was considered to have style, humor, and shape but to be shallow in character and insubstantial in story. Although these attempts in forms other than poetry led to comparative failure, these works do illustrate Merrill's skill in narrative and dramatic writing which would later inform some of his most ambitious attempts and better achievements; after these partial failures he temporarily swore off prose.

Very soon after, Merrill published his next book of verse, which was enthusiastically received; it was titled *The Country of a Thousand Years of Peace, and Other Poems* (1959). The country is Switzerland. Earlier Merrill had met a young Dutch writer, Hans Lodeizen, and had become close friends with him. Lodeizen became ill with leukemia, and Merrill visited him in the hospital in Switzerland. Lodeizen was very ill and soon died; the title poem of the volume is an elegy written for him.

During the 1960's and 1970's, Merrill, living both in Connecticut and Athens, published five more books of poetry and was often lauded as one of the top poets of the time. He published *Water Street* in 1962, *Nights and Days* in 1966, *The Fire Screen* in 1969, *Braving the Elements* in 1972, and *The Yellow Pages: Fifty-nine Poems*, made up of previously uncollected poems, in 1974. *Nights and Days* won the National Book Award for poetry in 1967. Although reviewers of his earlier poems praised his verbal and formal skills, they often criticized him for lacking serious subject matter. These were the days of the Vietnam War protests, it should be noted, and many a poet was criticized for lacking "relevance" to the events of the day and the troubles of the times. Later in the 1970's, the critics found that his poems took on more substance and that his "relevance" quotient was rising.

Merrill's next book was quite a departure. Called *Divine Comedies* (1976), it contained six somewhat long poems and three short ones, followed by the "Book of Ephraim." The latter purported to be an account of a conversation, through a Ouija board (and with the help of David Jackson), with a first century Greek slave named Ephraim, who worked on the staff of the emperor Tiberius and was later strangled to death while still young for attempting to make love to the young Caligula. The poem is an amazing tour de force, primarily because it immediately engages the reader's interest and curiosity and because the poetic writing (both of "Ephraim" and Merrill) is so good. The book won the Pulitzer Prize in poetry.

Two sequels immediately followed "The Book of Ephraim": *Mirabell: Books of Number* (1978), which won the National Book Award for Poetry, and *Scripts for the Pageant* (1980), which won the Bollingen Prize. The three poems were later combined with a "coda" and published in 1982 as *The Changing Light at Sandover* (1982), a trilogy of poems based on Merrill's and Jackson's encounters with a Ouija board. It won the 1983 National Book Critics Circle Award. Merrill then published more volumes of poetry, including *From the First Nine: Poems, 1946-1976* (1982), *Santorini: Stopping the Leak* (1982), *Souvenirs* (1984), *Bronze* (1984), *Late Settings* (1985), *The Inner Room* (1988), and *A Scattering of Salts* (1995). Merrill died in 1995 one month shy of his sixty-ninth birthday.

ANALYSIS

Merrill's work is considered difficult, but he did not write difficult poetry to forbid the reader access to his work; he was a poet with W. H. Auden's sense: one who simply liked to have fun with words and was deeply sensitive to the multiple valences, the mercurial surfaces, that words present. Merrill's early poetry was often labeled as being merely clever. Indeed, the early poems are among the small number of true modernist poems written in the United States along with those of Wallace Stevens, the great American poet of the 1920's and 1930's. These poems are congeries of imagery surrounding a central intuition, often not clearly stated, creating a feeling where none existed before.

Unfortunately for Merrill, the age of the modernist poets was passing, and the critics lamented the lack of substance in his work. Indeed, many of his early poems (such as "The Mirror") are symbols of the relationship between poetry and its subject. The reigning poetic fashion of the 1970's was confessional poetry: trying to make some personal experience relevant for society. Perhaps this fashion inspired Merrill. He began writing longer poems, more influenced by the narrative technique he had shown in his early novel, *The Seraglio*, and they began to be about Merrill's deeper life, rather than chance meetings and symbolist confrontations.

"Broken Home," for example, is a reminiscence of his parents' divorce and of his own frightening Oedipal encounter with his mother. In this period, certain images dominate. Fire imagery increases in importance; the house becomes a synecdoche for the identity of its occupants. Most of all, the mirror comes to the fore as an image of poetry, that reflection of reality that is supposed to tell readers something about themselves. The image appears everywhere in Merrill's poetry—subtly, as a pond, a lake, skies, or even broken glass, or directly, as in the earlier poem "The Mirror."

After Merrill set up his winter home in Athens, the landscapes of his poetry became more and more Greek and more mythological. The Greek house gets its own treatment, especially after a fire forced its thorough reconditioning. Merrill begins to combine his mythic sense with a perhaps even stronger animism, and one hears a black mesa and a stream bank speak in soliloquy. Intimations of immortality appear here and there in his poems, as long poems appear more frequently.

All of this seems like a preparation for *The Changing Light at Sandover*, certainly the most individual book of poetry published in the United States since Walt Whitman's *Leaves of Grass* (1855). The technique of this book, of transcribing (actually, more or less editing) the messages of the Ouija board into poetry, allows Merrill the freedom to create a dramatic epic. The voices of the Ouija board bear witness to a world of the spirit to which Merrill the witness can act as either a skeptic or a believer, and a true dialogue can be set up between the voices of the board and the reflections and responses of the poet.

Dotted throughout *The Changing Light at Sandover* are set pieces showing some remarkable prosodic advances over his earlier poetry. He had always shown a skill at creating unique verse forms, often some combination of quatrains in tetrameter or pentameter, especially with his favorite rhyme scheme (*abba*), but with the long poem came some even more memorable set pieces. For example, there is the W section of "The Book of Ephraim," written in a masterful terza rima, reinforcing its allusions to Dante, the medieval Italian epic poet. These allusions begin with the title of the book, *Divine Comedies*, in which "The Book of Ephraim" first appeared.

There is a section of pentameters with random rhymes reminiscent of the meditative poems of W. H. Auden, the brilliant modern British American writer. *Scripts for the Pageant* contains a modernist set piece called "House in Athens," written in six-line stanzas of trochaic trimeter broken by a fourth line in pentameter, rhymed haphazardly, sometimes with consonance.

The same book also includes a poem, "Samos," written in the form of a medieval canzone or sestina, with five twelve-line stanzas repeating the sounds of "sense," "light," "water," "fire," and "land," arranged *abaacaaddaee*. The sounds change in each stanza so that a different sound ends the first line of each one.

On the surface, Merrill's poetry is difficult, exploiting the modernist device of not specifying his nouns—his characters and places. His goal is to render, as exactly as possible, the movements of the human spirit in its encounter with reality, the world, or other people. In doing so, he acts as if the word as medium contains the realities it names. His work, as a result, has a profound civilizing function. Merrill also wants to know how he feels toward (and among) his own poetry, that wisdom of the

imagination which gives value to life. He stands in a line of great writers, including Auden and Proust, who taught him how each sensation is a seed which, if properly nurtured, can turn into a work of art.

"THE BROKEN HOME"

First published: 1965 (collected in *Collected Poems, James Merrill*, 2001)
Type of work: Poem

Merrill reminisces about his old house and his parents' divorce.

"The Broken Home" uses a unique form, a combination of seven different types of sonnet, to explore the meaning of family in the life of a child. The first sonnet is unrhymed and begins with the apparent genesis of the poem: He is going home one night and sees a family through the windows of the apartment above his. He goes to his own room and, trying to read a book of maxims, asks if his lonely life has any value.

The second sonnet, written in pentameters and rhyming *abba cddc effe gg*, talks about his father's world. His father had two goals—sex and business—and a desire to "win." "Time was money." He married "every thirteen years," but when he was seventy, he died: "Money was not time."

The third sonnet is in a sort of free verse, rhymed *abba cddc efg efg*. It comments on what Merrill says was a popular "act" when he was a boy. A woman would accost a famous man and, after calling him names, would demand that he give women the vote; he would, in return, implicitly tell her to go back to homemaking. The last three lines of the sonnet turn it into an allegory of what Merrill feels is the eternal battle of the sexes between "Father Time and Mother Earth." He begins to see his own parents' divorce as part of a larger rift in the world between the male and female principles, a theme he will further develop in his famous trilogy.

The fourth sonnet is written in a sort of tetrameter, rhyming *abba bccb dee bdb*, and is the celebrated center of the poem. The young boy, led by his dog, enters the bedroom of his distraught mother; she is in bed, sleeping, "clad in taboos." He wonders if she is dead; she jumps and reaches for him, and he runs from the room in terror. This Oedipal incident seems to color the whole poem. The fifth sonnet is again in free verse, rhyming *abc db cdc eee fef*; the rhyme scheme includes many slant rhymes. The poem centers on the conceit of a lead toy soldier. The parents decide to separate; he feels that they were full of passions but that everything is now cold and heavy.

The sixth sonnet, rhyming (or slant rhyming) *abba cddc eff ghh*, tells what he believes is the result of his parents' divorce: He refuses to be like his father, active and competitive, or like his mother, nurturing, a gardener.

The last sonnet is the closest to the Petrarchan model, rhyming *abab cdcd efg efg*. The octave celebrates the whole event, telling of the little boy and his dog frozen back in time. The sestet points out that the house is now a boarding school; perhaps its inhabitants will learn more there than he did. The poem is not didactic or condemnatory; it merely delineates a history and relates it to today and to the world.

"18 WEST 11TH STREET"

First published: 1972 (collected in *Braving the Elements*, 1972)
Type of work: Poem

The poet treats an accidental bomb explosion by antiwar protesters as symbolic of humankind's troubles.

"18 West 11th Street" seems to have been inspired by a newspaper report: Certain anti-Vietnam War protesters had a house blow up around them while they were trying to make bombs. The only survivor was a young woman named Cathy Wilkerson, seen running from the building naked and covered with blood.

The poem is one of Merrill's most difficult—at least partially because it tries to tell three stories at once. The first is the story of the bombing: The five revolutionaries are fed up with society and its warmongering leaders. They have given up trying to use words to get their message across and are now resorting to bombs, a means of "incommunication." Instead of bombing "The Establishment,"

however, they end up bombing themselves, leaving only the unfortunate woman, fleeing naked and wounded into the night.

The second story turns on a marvelous coincidence: 18 West 11th Street was Merrill's childhood home. The story is of little Jimmy coming down with a cold on his birthday. The story is not clear, but the mood is one of disappointment: No one seems to care except the maid. The Merrills had three children, making the total official population of the house five. The story also makes much use of fires, mirrors, furniture, a "parterre" or garden, and a clock on the mantel. There are references to a mysterious woman who seems to be a double object of affection, and the story hangs heavy with the lack of communication.

The third story is the myth of the Garden of Eden. The house's garden, with its one tree made leafless by the explosion, becomes the primal garden. The woman escaping was heard to exclaim the name "Adam" as she was running away, so the poem suggests that lack of communication, leading to an explosion, is the proper mythical explanation for all humankind's ills. When one can no longer communicate with others, one resorts to violence of some kind, whether civil, domestic, or religious. Further, the poem suggests that the division is incurable and that therefore these explosions are inevitable.

The poem seems to be grow from the two lines at the exact center of the poem printed in capital letters:

NIX ON PEACE BID PROPHET STONED
FIVE FEARED DEAD IN BOMBED DWELLING.

The opening line points out that there is no peace, blaming it on President Richard Nixon. The prophet seems to be the revolutionaries, who listed smoking marijuana as part of their sins against society. The five dead in the dwelling are also Merrill's family. The boy on his birthday apparently rattled off some poems to his family which were "duds"— they were ignored by his family members.

The poem is written in a series of tercets emphasizing the triple nature of the theme, and the style is gnomic; it takes the concept of functional ambiguity to its extremes, all the while resembling the notes of a mad newspaper reporter on a fast-breaking story. Each word seems to try, by the use of pun and multiple meaning, to apply to all three stories, making the puzzling out of the poem difficult in the extreme.

THE CHANGING LIGHT AT SANDOVER

First published: 1982
Type of work: Long poem

An encounter with a spirit on a Ouija board leads to a 560-page poem consisting of conversation with spirits and commentary by the poet.

The Changing Light at Sandover is one of the more remarkable poetic works to have been published in the West since T. S. Eliot's *The Waste Land* (1922). Its genesis is interesting enough: James Merrill and his lover, David Jackson, had been experimenting with a Ouija board with little result when, one day in 1955, a spirit named Ephraim answered the ritual question: "Who's there?" After a long time conversing with Ephraim, Merrill decided to take the notes he took from their "conversations" and turn them into a poem. The resulting work, "The Book of Ephraim," contains a series of twenty-six poems, each beginning with a separate letter of the alphabet, one for each of the twenty-six capital letters on the board.

Merrill solves the difficult problem of separating the words of the "spirits" from his own by putting the former in capital letters; words of people other than himself are in italics. Each of the poems uses a slightly different poetic form, so the longer poem can be viewed as a book of forms. Narrative sections fall into blank verse, and didactic commentary tends to slip into heroic couplets. There are meditative sections that use stanza forms reminiscent of Percy Bysshe Shelley or William Wordsworth, the great British romantic poets of the nineteenth century, and there is a section of 127 lines in terza rima, the length of a typical Dantean canto, that narrates a long discussion on life and art with his nephew.

The primary problem of the poem is that of what credence one should be expected to give to the garbled transmissions of a Ouija board. Merrill tackles the problem in various ways: He sees his psy-chiatrist, who calls the exercise a folie à deux, an attempt by him and his lover to communicate on some higher plane. He also expresses his own skepticism, pointing out that Ephraim knows no more about what he says than Merrill or Jackson does. Yet the tone of the poem in some way demands belief if it is not to break down into an elaborate folly.

"The Book of Ephraim" also contains large sections of a very murky novel concerning characters in the southwestern United States who are trying to settle on a remote piece of land. Ephraim at one time tells Merrill to forget it, but Ephraim is somehow in the novel himself, for the heroine of the book carries around a Ouija board. There are many other things in *The Changing Light at Sandover*, such as tributes to Merrill's friends Auden, Maya Deren, and Maria Mitsotáki and to Merrill's mother. There is a beautiful elegy for Venice, the dying city, and the discussion with his nephew on art. Ephraim himself is a springboard to many other things.

With book 2, *Mirabell: Books of Number*, all is quite different. The spirits "write" most of this book; moreover, they seem to demand belief much more than they did in "The Book of Ephraim." One meets new spirits here—fourteen black batlike creatures who claim to be creatures of a past world; they also claim to be speaking "science" rather than merely reporting otherworldly gossip, as Ephraim did. Their "science," however, turns out to be as metaphorical as the account of creation in the Bible, despite an elaborate numbering scheme which owes more to Pythagoras, the ancient Greek numerological philosopher, than it does to Einstein. In fact, their chief spokesman is first called 741. Later, he changes his bat form and becomes a peacock; Merrill then names him Mirabell, after the hero in *The Way of the World* (1700) by William Congreve, the witty seventeenth century British playwright. Mirabell elab-

orates a system of creation and salvation through what he calls "labwork" and "V" work, and describes the creation of soul substance out of materials from former humans, animals, and trees. He posits five super-souls who guide the world, being reincarnated in each generation, and hints at higher beings, including those in charge—called 00, god B (for biology), and in the end, a guardian of the sun, Michael.

The poem is divided into ten sections headed by the ten numerals on the Ouija board, 0 through 9. Sprinkled throughout are more delightful lyrics, odes, elegies, and didactic couplets. The book ends with a glorious and peremptory speech by the white angel of the sun, Michael, who apparently announces that Jackson and Merrill must stay even longer, for there is more work to be done.

The third section is called "Scripts for the Pageant"; it is the longest and most complex of the three sections, taking up exactly half of *The Changing Light at Sandover*. It is here that one learns, for the first time, what "Sandover" means: Merrill's childhood home, after he moved out of it, was turned into a boarding school called Sandover, and the central dining room became a ballroom. While Jackson and Merrill operate the Ouija board at Stonington, the spirits gather, by means of an antique mirror, in the ballroom at Sandover, a "place of learning." The result is the "pageant" that is part of the trilogy.

If the form of the first book was conversational and the second, catechetical, the third book is epic-dramatic. The speakers' names are often lined up at the left margin as one would expect in a playbook, and the style has been raised. The book is organized, again according to the Ouija board, into ten "YES" sections, five "&" sections, and ten "NO" sections. The book, like the two others, is dotted here and there with set pieces, stanzaic blank verse, and terza rima—the latter, like the two sections in terza rima before it, ending with the word "stars," a quiet but effective tribute to Dante. Then comes a piece called "Samos," opening the "&" section, a beautiful double canzone in the medieval manner, celebrating the desire of poets everywhere to make the best of the material they are given.

In content, there is immense variety: The reader meets the four archangels who rule the four elements of Earth, from whose struggles comes the drama of human history. The reader then learns the names of the five super-souls: Akhnaton, Nefertiti, Homer, Montezuma, and Plato; then one discovers that Maria Mitsotáki was Plato reincarnate and that she will be reborn in India soon as a Hindu sage. One learns that god B has a twin sister, whom humans call Nature and whom readers meet at Sandover dressed like a Victorian belle. God B himself speaks, saying that his children (Michael and Gabriel) have shown the light and dark: Make a V work out of it, he says to Merrill.

The entire book ends with a coda: Auden and Maria will be released from their waiting room when Jackson and Merrill break the mirror; they do so, and the correspondents say goodbye to one another. There is one more scene, however; Merrill gathers at the ballroom at Sandover with all those who took part in the pageant. They await his reading of the book the reader has just finished.

"LOSING THE MARBLES"

First published: 1988 (collected in *Inner Room*, 1988)
Type of work: Poem

This poem is a meditation on old age, concentrating on the aspects of decaying mental and physical abilities.

"Losing the Marbles" is a seven-part poem meditating on the various aspects of old age, especially as they relate to poetry. Section 1 is written in the manner of a romantic meditation, indicating the impetus for the poem. The poet has lost his date-calendar and cannot remember what he is supposed to do that day—nor can he remember what he and his friends discussed at lunch. He comments: "another marble gone." Then he remembers; they were describing what each one's "Heaven" would be. His was to be an acrobat in old Greece when the Parthenon was a living building. The coming of dusk brings to mind a line of the famous twentieth century Welsh poet, Dylan Thomas: "Rage, rage against the dying of the light." He puns, saying that evenings were graces allowing a man to tumble gracefully "into thyme,/ *Out* of time."

Section 2 is in the style of a metaphysical ode. Complicated metaphors fill it—a storm like a silver car, a rivulet of ink in which the poet must dip, mouth-to-mouth resuscitation by means of the *Golden Treasury*. It is an ironic comment on the inability of poetry to stem the storm of old age. Section 3 at first is a puzzle: It is a series of disconnected phrases arranged helter-skelter on the page. It seems to be describing a passionate sexual encounter at first, then it modulates into a lament not only for the body's ineptitude but also for the good memories that present failures obscure.

Section 4 is in rhymed couplets. It begins by insisting that old age should not blot out the artistic achievements of the past. "My text is Mind," he says. He first points out the monetary value of even an inch of a Cézanne canvas, and then creates what appears to be the central aphorism of the poem: "Art furnishes a counterfeit/ Heaven" where ideas are immortalized, even if those who hold them cannot be. The section concludes with puns on marble ("All stone once dressed asks to be worn"; "topless women" choose worn stones at the beach "To use as men upon their checkerboards").

Section 5 solves the puzzle of section 3: It is written in modified sapphics and contains, in the exact same spot on the page, all the words of section 3. It turns out to be a rational comment on the passion and lament of section 3. It begins by pointing out that the human body is the preferred symbol of young poets and that a majority of them scorn "decrepitude/ in any form." In old age, the body "plunders what we cannot," and the poem presents images of death. Merrill concludes that old poets learn how to make poems of homecomings, even though the "marble" for such works comes from "no further off/ than infancy."

Section 6 begins with three stanzas in ballad form, pointing out that "pattern and intent" make up for aphasia. The second half is in free verse and chronicles the return from a voyage on an ocean liner. The passengers are full of gossip, especially about friends who have "flipped" or who have died; but, they say, do not mention death.

Section 7 is in blank verse and relates that the poet's lover gave him a pack of marbles for his birthday, and he in response embedded them in the slats about the pool. The pool then is described as a "compact, blue, dancing,/ Lit-from-beneath oubliette." Both the marbles and the pool reflect the stars, and the poet sits near them talking about the heavens (as in section 1). The pool and the marbles become an image for art of all kinds which, by reflecting the heavens above, provides spiritual knowledge nowhere else available.

SUMMARY

Merrill had ensured his place in the line of great American poets. He began as a disciple of the Symbolist poets and, after publishing a series of books of very good small poems, launched into deep waters with a major work, *The Changing Light at Sandover*. Although the content of the book irritates many, the deeper subject matter and the poetic skills with which it treated make most who read it respect it as a grand attempt. Merrill was a successful postmodernist poet in that he pushed poetry past its Symbolist stage to a place where it can deal with the questions of his time.

Robert W. Peckham

BIBLIOGRAPHY

By the Author

POETRY:
The Black Swan, and Other Poems, 1946
First Poems, 1951
The Country of a Thousand Years of Peace, and Other Poems, 1959, revised edition 1970
Water Street, 1962
Nights and Days, 1966
The Fire Screen, 1969
Braving the Elements, 1972
The Yellow Pages: Fifty-nine Poems, 1974
Divine Comedies, 1976

Mirabell: Books of Number, 1978
Scripts for the Pageant, 1980
The Changing Light at Sandover, 1982
From the First Nine: Poems, 1946-1976, 1982
Santorini: Stopping the Leak, 1982
Bronze, 1984
Souvenirs, 1984
Late Settings, 1985
The Inner Room, 1988
A Scattering of Salts, 1995
Collected Poems, James Merrill, 2001

LONG FICTION:
The Seraglio, 1957
The (Diblos) Notebook, 1965

DRAMA:
The Bait, pr. 1953, pb. 1960
The Immortal Husband, pr. 1955, pb. 1956
The Image Maker, pr., pb. 1986

NONFICTION:
Recitative, 1986
A Different Person: A Memoir, 1993

> ## DISCUSSION TOPICS
>
> - How does *The Seraglio* reflect the thematic concerns of James Merrill's poetry?
>
> - Merrill has been criticized for the lack of substance in his poetry. Is this complaint valid?
>
> - How is the spiritual world used as a metaphor in *The Changing Light at Sandover*?
>
> - What does "Losing the Marbles" say about old age?
>
> - Merrill's poetry is often described as difficult. Can a case be made that this difficulty is central to his method?

About the Author

Adams, Don. *James Merrill's Poetic Quest.* Westport, Conn.: Greenwood Press, 1997.

Berger, Charles, ed. *James Merrill: Essays in Criticism.* Ithaca, N.Y.: Cornell University Press, 1983.

Bloom, Harold, ed. *James Merrill.* New York: Chelsea House, 1985.

Halpern, Nick. *Everyday and Poetic: The Poetry of Lowell, Ammons, Merrill, and Rich.* Madison: University of Wisconsin Press, 2003.

Hammer, Langdon. "Merrill and Stevens." *Wallace Stevens Journal: A Publication of the Wallace Stevens Society* 28 (Fall, 2004): 295-302.

Lurie, Alison. *Familiar Spirits: A Memoir of James Merrill and David Jackson.* New York: Viking, 2001.

Materer, Timothy. *James Merrill's Apocalypse.* Ithaca, N.Y.: Cornell University Press, 2000.

Moffett, Judith. *James Merrill: An Introduction to the Poetry.* Rev. ed. New York: Columbia University Press, 1984.

Polito, Robert. *A Reader's Guide to "The Changing Light at Sandover."* Ann Arbor: University of Michigan Press, 1994.

Rotella, Guy, ed. *Critical Essays on James Merrill.* New York: G. K. Hall, 1996.

Vendler, Helen. "Ardor and Artifice: The Mozartian Touch of a Master Poet." *New Yorker* 77 (March 12, 2001): 100-104.

White, Heather. "An Interview with James Merrill." *Ploughshares* 21 (Winter, 1995/1996): 190-195.

Yenser, Stephen. *The Consuming Myth: The Work of James Merrill.* Cambridge, Mass.: Harvard University Press, 1987.

W. S. MERWIN

Born: New York, New York
September 30, 1927

One of the leading American poets of his generation, Merwin has won most of the major honors for poetry and translation.

Matthew Carlos Schwartz

BIOGRAPHY

William Stanley Merwin was raised and educated in Union City, New Jersey, and Scranton, Pennsylvania. His father was a Presbyterian minister, and it is said that some of Merwin's first writings were hymns. He was educated at Princeton University and studied writing under John Berryman and R. P. Blackmur. After postgraduate studies in romance languages, he traveled throughout England, France and Spain. Settling on the island of Majorca in 1950, he worked as a tutor to Robert Graves's sons. Merwin was quite successful in placing his early work and publishing his first volume, *A Mask for Janus*, in 1952. Merwin received the Yale Series of Younger Poets Award for this volume, which had been selected by W. H. Auden. From 1951 to 1955, he lived in London, supporting himself by writing for British radio and television and translating Spanish and French classics. His second volume of poetry, *The Dancing Bears*, was published in 1954.

After 1954, he supplemented his income through a series of literary fellowships. In 1956, he returned to the United States and wrote plays for the Poets' Theatre in Cambridge, Massachusetts. *Green with Beasts* came out in 1956, and four years later he published *The Drunk in the Furnace*. By 1966, he was able to issue his first *Collected Poems*.

This first collection marks the first phase of his career, during which he worked mainly with traditional forms, heavily symbolic imagery, conventional rhetoric, and literary allusions. This phase is usually described as heavily influenced by T. S. Eliot and Ezra Pound, though the hand of the Irish poet William Butler Yeats can also be detected. Merwin's work in these years is formidably intellectual, typical of these models. He is also attracted to themes related to the disintegration of personality in the face of modern stresses and to the loss of traditional order. Yet he manages a charming recasting of a fairy tale as a ballad in "East of the Sun and West of the Moon," from *The Dancing Bears*, and several poems, conspicuously "Leviathan," in *Green with Beasts*, show him simply reveling in language.

The first collection also disclosed a change in direction, primarily in *The Drunk in the Furnace*. Several striking poems track his reactions to the aging of his grandparents and to his impending sense of loss of all that they represent. The title poem consolidates several of his preoccupations: Both individual and environment are castoffs of the world that humans have made, and both stand as criticisms of it. Merwin developed these patterns further in *The Moving Target* (1963). Here the forms were flexed almost to the breaking point, and the language became at best personal and at extreme elliptical. Yet his characteristic themes—loss, death, disorientation, disintegration—remained constant. What changed was Merwin's voice, which was more evasive and subtle.

Still, although this volume signals change, it did little to prepare readers for *The Lice*, Merwin's most celebrated book, which appeared in 1967. In it, the poet appeared to have completely abandoned the former starting points of his poetry, substituting for them mental attitudes from an altogether alien tradition, almost as if an orthodox priest should suddenly embrace Shintoism. Careful reading, however, shows that the divergence is more apparent than real. The disintegrations of values, traditions, and cultural unity is within the language itself. What recourse does a poet have in the collapse of communication? If language itself fails, then poetry becomes an exercise in solipsism, and the poet seems to be speaking to himself. If the poet still persists in poetry, it can only mean that some hope remains of eventually making a connection. Merwin persists, his words now often sounding like voices heard vaguely in dreams but bearing all the fright of dreams at the same time.

Subsequent volumes—*The Carrier of Ladders* (1970; awarded the Pulitzer Prize), *Writings to an Unfinished Accompaniment* (1973), *The Compass Flower* (1977), *Feathers from the Hill* (1978), *Opening the Hand* (1983), and *The Rain in the Trees* (1988)— primarily follow the leads established in the 1960's, although in the later works Merwin seems to be returning to earlier, temporarily abandoned forms and traditions, or experimenting with classical oriental forms. In the late 1970's, he settled in Hawaii, where he has continued to work.

His awards are numerous and various, including the Aiken Taylor Award for Modern American Poetry, the Bollingen Prize, the Govenor's Award for Literature of the State of Hawaii, a Ford Foundation grant, the Wallace Stevens Award, the Shelley Memorial Award, the PEN Translation Prize, the Lila Wallace-Reader's Digest Writers' Award, and the Ruth Lilly Poetry Prize. Merwin has also received fellowships from the Guggenheim Foundation, the Academy of American Poets, the National Endowment for the Arts (NEA), and the Rockefeller Foundation. He has also served as chancellor of the Academy of American Poets.

Merwin was named the Poetry Consultant to the Library of Congress for 1999-2000, jointly with Louise Glück and Rita Dove. He received the 2004 Lannan Lifetime Achievement Award, and his poetry collection *Migration: New and Selected Poems* (2005) won the National Book Award. He served a five-year term as judge of the Yale Series of Younger Poets from 1997 to 2002.

ANALYSIS

The poetry of W. S. Merwin is diverse in its form and content and has been well received since his first publication, *A Mask for Janus*. As stated above,

Merwin's early poetry is traditional and formal. These poems are in regular formal measures and employ conventional rhetorical devices; the tone is distant and sophisticated; the voice is cultivated. Even more popular patterns, such as the ballad form in "Ballad of John Cable and Three Gentlemen," are formalized: This is a literary ballad, alluding to medieval folk-song tradition.

Merwin's second volume, *The Dancing Bears*, is also predominantly formal. Its touchstone poem, "East of the Sun and West of the Moon," recasts the traditional folk tale of the same title, dealing with a peasant's daughter given in marriage to a white bear who lives at the end of time and visits her only after dark. Merwin transforms this into a triple allegory of the nature of love, the responsibility of humans to the past and their heritage, and the function of literature. Other poems in the volume expand a recurring theme of life as continual self-proving and obligation to the past.

Green with Beasts contains further exercises with formal structures. These are all deftly turned, fashioned by the hands of a master—but a master who paradoxically seems less assured of the permanence of his work. Merwin repeatedly turns in this book to images of incompleteness, of frustrated energies. "The Master" laments the lot of those doomed to work in the shadow of genius, especially when that genius is not humanly admirable. "Saint Sebastian," likewise, is a delicately wrought sonnet, but its subject is a Christian martyr cut down before his prime, shown in the act of entering death. The subject contradicts the artistic premise of the style.

The formal structures in *The Drunk in the Furnace* are similar to those used earlier, though simpler; the same is true of the themes. The voice, however, has changed. Early in the book, the poem "Odysseus" sets the tone. This voice is quiet, reflective, showing an Odysseus musing over his restlessness, an Odysseus so perplexed between undifferentiated choices that he can hardly make up his mind. The plaint informs the book, appearing over and over in various guises. For example, in a series of poems on his aging and dying grandparents, Merwin repeatedly attempts to come to terms with the part his life plays in the pattern of theirs—and then with whether there is any pattern in theirs at all. The book closes with "The Drunk in the Furnace"; the image of a vagrant howling in a makeshift shelter parallels that of the hesitant Odysseus.

In *The Moving Target*, Merwin almost completely drops the public voice and turns introspective, as if he has despaired of open discourse. The poems themselves turn bleak, once their protective shells are breached. "Lemuel's Blessing" is based on an eighteenth century poem by a madman in which Lemuel "blesses" his readers with the wolf—that is, with a curse. Merwin feels that the only appropriate blessing for a race bent on destroying itself is cursing. Similarly, "The Saint of the Upland" laments that his worshipers have learned nothing from him.

The Lice, probably the most praised book of Merwin's career, extends this approach; in fact, it carries the poetry of hopelessness about as far as it can go and reduces Merwin's formal patterns to the level of contextless, broken mutterings. Everything here is fragmented, indrawn, muted. "The Gods," for example, addresses nonexistent beings, for humans have developed into things no god would have the patience to endure. There are a few moments of relief, as when the song of birds at dawn in "How We Are Spared" raises the light in the sky, which can only be a sign of hope, but there is no clue to hope of what. The visions of this book cleanse the eyes and mind, though only by searing.

The Carrier of Ladders brought the poet the Pulitzer Prize and celebrity. It continues the difficult vein opened in the two previous books, though with some tempering. Some of the poems even show a partial return to his earlier, more straightforward style. "The Judgment of Paris" presents a relatively direct account of a standard myth, even if it does slant it negatively. One group of poems dealing with the American West acts almost like a nucleus for the book. In them, the speakers show awareness both of the beauty of the landscape and of the ugliness that humans have brought in their migration. This divided reaction probes the depth of the pain that the poet is both registering and disguising. "The Removal" attests this, in its dedication "to the endless tribe." The poet himself is one of them; in speaking to them, though, he cannot help recalling the destruction they bring, nor can he help reminding them of that.

Writings to an Unfinished Accompaniment contains further examinations of internal states of awareness and further attempts at frustrated communication. In these poems, however, Merwin seems less desperate and more accepting than he had

been. Some of these poems even seem playful; "Tool" and "The Unwritten" show a zest in wordplay long absent from his work. Other figures also appear here, breaking into the void previous poems had spun around the isolated individual. At this point, the turn is slight, hardly noticeable. "Finding a Teacher" is elliptical, almost impersonal, but the poem's speaker does end up staying for a meal. "The Search" carries the process further, describing how the speaker's world grows silent when he suddenly becomes aware of the absence of the other. The book ends with "Gift," in which the speaker acknowledges the existence of hope and the possibility of giving oneself to another.

This slight turning becomes more definite in subsequent books. *The Compass Flower, Feathers from the Hill*, and *Finding the Islands* all mark both a reacceptance—or at least a reacknowledgment—of others and the external world and a return to poems as made objects rather than the expression of emotional states. The two latter books, in fact, contain explicit love poetry, quite distinct from anything else the poet has done. In *Finding the Islands*, Merwin composes exclusively in stripped-to-the-bone, unpunctuated triplets. Yet he includes nothing from these books in his *Selected Poems*, which could indicate that he intends to discard them. Nevertheless, the change in direction seems clear. *Opening the Hand* makes it definite: "Sheridan" is a reexamination of the Civil War general's consciousness during the Battle of Cedar Creek, "Questions to Tourists Stopped by a Pineapple Field" is a marvelous send-up of typically inane tourist-guide conversation, and "Black Jewel" recaptures the timeless timekeeping of crickets. *The Rain in the Trees* includes a number of fine lyrics that have won the admiration of critics.

THE DRUNK IN THE FURNACE

First published: 1960
Type of work: Poetry

In a series of dramatic portraits and monologues, Merwin shows that human failures stem primarily from internal deficiencies.

With *The Drunk in the Furnace*, Merwin intensified and expanded his earlier position that human beings had become increasingly subject to divorce from their environment and from their integrating spiritual centers. The book is enclosed by two defining figures, a Greek warrior-hero and a street person, who reflect for Merwin the typical human situation. The first is the title character in "Odysseus," the epic wandering hero of the Homeric poems, about whom Alfred, Lord Tennyson had written two poems in the high Victorian mode projecting Odysseus's role as the model male hero, the man whose will admits no obstacles to his quest.

Merwin's Odysseus character is internally and externally a wanderer. This represents a dilemma that cannot seem to be resolved regardless of what choice the hero makes. Merwin exemplifies this conflict in his poem in the way the hero often cannot remember who caused his wandering and where his destination lies. Ultimately, the hero must come to terms with his internal conflict before he can externally find his home.

"One Eye" considers the probable consequences of the proverb "In the country of the blind the one-eyed man is king." Commonly, this saying is taken to summarize folk wisdom, that one can capitalize on one's advantages by choosing one's objective audience carefully. Things do not work out this way in Merwin's world. Although One-Eye at first finds immediate acceptance, his situation quickly begins to pall. As king, he discovers his subjects rich in goods from which he cannot profit, such as their intricate music. Worse, he learns that he cannot share his gift, his advantage, with them: No matter what he does, they will never see. In the end, he cannot save them from their common human fate. He is powerless to change the fundamental conditions of their lives and death.

Merwin uses the image of the singing derelict from the title poem to close this volume. The poem actually begins with the image of the abandoned furnace, cast off to add its litter of decay to an already poisonous creek. This illustrates Merwin's view of what humans do to themselves, progressively contaminating their environment until it can no longer support life. The drunk, equally cast out by society, appropriately houses himself in this pile of junk, from which he serenades the community. The good people ignore him, for good or evil, but their children cannot keep from gaping at him and, the poet says, studying him. What they learn is the human way: casting out and refusing, even to

their own harm. Merwin at this point holds out little hope.

THE MOVING TARGET

First published: 1963
Type of work: Poetry

In more personal and less formal poems, Merwin examines the bleak options left for humans in a world they have desolated.

The Moving Target catalogs Merwin's ventures into the dark void of possibility available to humans. As before, Merwin finds little hope. "Noah's Raven," for example, explains why that bird did not return to the ark with the message that the deluge had passed, that God would once again establish his covenant with humans. On leaving, it realized it had nothing more in common with humans; their kinds would henceforth be alienated. By refusing to bring back empty promises, the raven signifies that it sees little hope. Similarly, "Dead Hand" illustrates in two lines that this most human of organs continues to clutch even after death; its only value to anyone resides in the metal and mineral of its rings.

"Lemuel's Blessing" develops from an allusion to Christopher Smart, an eighteenth century poet who suffered from religious mania and was considered insane. Merwin suggests that only madmen can see accurately in a world that has chosen madness as a way of life. Smart prayed that Lemuel "bless with the wolf," the traditional and mythical enemy of humans—arguing, that is, that releasing wolves on humans would paradoxically purge them of their own beastliness. He goes on to call the wolf a "dog without a master," hinting that humans are destroying themselves by failing to practice the mastery for which they were created. Finally, he notes that the Lord will care for the wolves of the desert, implying that humans who have chosen to abandon nature deserve no such care. All these points tally with Merwin's theme. The poem goes on to show humans reveling in the dogginess of their lives.

In "The Saint of the Uplands," the saint laments that his message has fallen on deaf ears, in two ways. He is no more than his followers, hence undeserving of being considered a saint, and he has no more to give them than they can find for themselves. Yet instead of learning that simple point, they persist in building a shrine to him, in which they perpetuate their ignorance. Perhaps the most striking poem in the book is "The Crossways of the World etc.," which certainly prefigures the next turn in Merwin's development. Unlike his earlier work with its broken lines, stanzas, and phrases, it looks like abbreviated, interrupted, and unpatterned musings. The imagery is entirely of loss and failed connections, which reflects the overwhelming sense of devastation in Merwin's vision of human reality.

THE CARRIER OF LADDERS

First published: 1970
Type of work: Poetry

Still working with broken forms, Merwin finds evidence of human significance.

The metaphor implicit in the title of *The Carrier of Ladders* signals a change, however slight, in Merwin's orientation and attitudes: Only humans carry ladders, and their object in so doing is to rise, to climb to a new level, even if they do not know exactly what they will find there. The poems in the volume mostly build on this premise. The opening poem, "Teachers," sets the pattern. The speaker is not clear about much. His surroundings witness mostly pain, but he finds some solace in sleep, and sleep brings dreams in which he remembers learning from books of voyages, the "sure tellings" that taught him. Where they led or may lead is dark, but the speaker values these teachers.

"The Judgment of Paris" re-creates the ancient Greek myth in which three goddesses compete for mastery before Paris; the decision Paris makes leads to the Trojan War. Merwin suggests that the contest was rigged: Any decision Paris would have made would have led to destruction. Human beings, Merwin suggests, are naturally defective and they cannot avoid self-destructive behavior. Ultimately, this is what makes humans interesting. This idea is appropriate to its subject. One of Homer's themes, picked up by the Greek dramatists afterward, is that humans bring suffering down on themselves but that this suffering engenders com-

passion, which promotes unity. Merwin ends the poem with an image of Helen picking a flower with roots that allay pain, concluding that it is also human to relieve suffering.

One section of this volume consists of poems dealing with the westward movement in American history. Merwin certainly does not see this as a glorious episode in the United States' history. While admitting the intoxication of the quest, the poet is fully aware of how much past and present destruction was implicit in it. In "Other Travellers to this River," he conjures up the early travel writer William Bartram—who popularized the notion of "conquering" the new land—to draw the contrast between the intensity of his vision and the damage done to the land. "Western Country" carries this further by suggesting that the conquest itself is illusory as well as wrongheaded: The land is not to be conquered but revered. In attempting to conquer, humans are also discrediting and damaging themselves. Still, Merwin's voice here is less strident than saddened, as if he has learned to accept the necessity of loss and the human experience.

"LAMENT FOR THE MAKERS"

First published: 1996 (collected in *The River Sound*, 1999)
Type of work: Poem

Merwin presents a survey of twentieth century poets' deaths and contributions to the poet and poetry.

"Lament for the Makers" was a poem published as an epitaph to W. S. Merwin's anthology *Lament for the Makers* and was later republished in *The River Sound* (1999). The poem exhibits a loose iambic tetrameter with many meter variations in couplet form. The second couplet in each stanza always rhymes with "me," the last word in each stanza. This directly correlates with William Dunbar's sixteenth century poem "Lament for the Makers." Dunbar's poem similarly consists of stanzas with two rhyming couplets and every fourth line ending in "me." Dunbar's last line is "Timor Mortis Conturbat me," which roughly translates as "the fear of death troubles me." This allusion and structure create Merwin's poem, which laments the death of various twentieth century poets. Through the accumulation of these deaths, Merwin inevitably questions his own life and accomplishments.

Merwin incorporates the death of each author with a reference to his life or writing. For instance, "on the rimless wheel in turn/ Eliot spun." T. S. Eliot died on January 4, 1965, and Eliot instructed that his ashes be buried at the church of St. Michael, East Coker, England. On his plaque are the lines from Eliot's "East Coker" in *Four Quartets* (1943): "In my beginning is my end [. . .] In my end is my beginning." The important image employed throughout the *Four Quartets* is the symbol of a wheel, as in the wheel of fortune or fate, and the prevailing theme is that the path to glory lies in the stillness at the center of the turning wheel. Thus, Merwin's allusion is rich and complex in the way in which the symbol of a wheel coincides with Eliot and one of his major poems and the way in which the action of a wheel spinning leads into the image of a car spinning out of control. Randall Jarrell, who also died in 1965, was "borne/ off by a car" and killed in the accident.

What seems to be a dark and ominous message in this poem about dying authors and the presence of death for the poet is juxtaposed with the "secret" and the "changeless overtone" that is likened to a note of music, and the poet is always "trying to find where it comes from/ and to what words it may come." This search for the precise word to describe that secret seems to be the act of the poet seeking to describe the essence of life. Though the words themselves cannot keep a poet alive, and "the clear note they were hearing/ never promised anything," Merwin leaves the reader with hope that the note can always be heard.

"A GIVEN DAY"

First published: 1996 (collected in *The Vixen*, 1996)
Type of work: Poem

This is a poem of memory about waking at first light and what may come in the new day.

"A Given Day" is the final poem in *The Vixen*. It is written in the same form as all the poems in that collection, and all the poems seem to flow into one

another with similar tones and images, so that the reader who reaches "A Given Day" has already experienced many days in this lyrical narrative. As with many other poems in *The Vixen*, "A Given Day" returns to autumn, but here the speaker in the poem is waking at first light. Where once the speaker was concerned with darkness or shadows, as in "Ancestral Voices," now the poem is concentrated on that moment of dawn.

There is no punctuation, and the first word is the only capitalized one. This poem is the beginning of a new day in which the poet remembers daily things—walking on a bridge, "thinking of a friend while she was still alive," being in a room with friends, and the eyes of animals. These small things are fused into each other like in a dream. Each line is enjambed into the next line, and each image flows into the next image. In the end, the rising day and all memory leads onward to winter. The reader might feel a sense of relief as the dying season of autumn finally comes to a close, for winter is a time of rest.

"LOSING A LANGUAGE"

First published: 1988 (collected in *The Rain in the Trees*, 1988)
Type of work: Poem

This poem recounts the loss of language, poetry, and the precise knowledge of things.

The title of this poem sets the tone of loss, and the first two lines qualify the loss of a language in the way "the old still remember something they could say." The poem exemplifies instances in which words that could once describe a particular situation, "standing in mist by a haunted tree" or "The verb for I," do not exist in contemporary language. This poem can also be a lament for the act of finding the precise word, the mot juste of the twentieth century modernists, and in the contemporary generation, "everywhere instead of a name there is a lie."

The poet seems to be referring to the euphemistic nature of contemporary language, political correctness, and maybe even contemporary poetry. When the poet states, "nothing that is here is known," one senses that without the words to name or describe a thing, one loses the knowledge of that thing, so that the loss of language is also the loss of knowledge. The end of the poem presents the reader with two images, extinct feathers and "the rain we saw," which seems to be the poet's attempt at rescuing the precise knowledge of things through poetry. Instead of explaining the loss of language in common terms, the poet offers two potent images to exemplify the feeling of loss, leaving the reader with a profound emotion.

SUMMARY

W. S. Merwin is a widely accomplished poet and translator, and he has won praise for his craftsmanship and searing vision. These traits are evident in every stage of his poetry, which has evolved through an extremely wide range. Of the poets of his generation, he is most remarkable, perhaps, for his insights into the spiritual desolation of post-industrial human society, into the cost in spirit of technological gains. His expressions are often complicated and uncompromising in his assessment of human pride, but his great poems acknowledge the human experience and truths of humanity.

James Livingston; updated by Matthew Nickel

BIBLIOGRAPHY

By the Author

POETRY:
A Mask for Janus, 1952
The Dancing Bears, 1954
Green with Beasts, 1956
The Drunk in the Furnace, 1960
The Moving Target, 1963
The Lice, 1967
Animae, 1969
The Carrier of Ladders, 1970
Writings to an Unfinished Accompaniment, 1973
The First Four Books of Poems, 1975
The Compass Flower, 1977
Feathers from the Hill, 1978
Finding the Islands, 1982
Opening the Hand, 1983
Koa, 1988
The Rain in the Trees, 1988
Selected Poems, 1988
The Second Four Books of Poems, 1993
Travels, 1993
The Vixen, 1996
Flower and Hand: Poems, 1977-1983, 1997
The Folding Cliffs: A Narrative, 1998
The River Sound: Poems, 1999
The Pupil, 2001
Present Company, 2005
Migration: New and Selected Poems, 2005

DRAMA:
Darkling Child, pr. 1956
Favor Island, pr. 1957
The Gilded Nest, pr. 1961

TELEPLAY:
Huckleberry Finn, 1953

RADIO PLAYS:
Rumpelstiltskin, 1951
Pageant of Cain, 1952

NONFICTION:
The Miner's Pale Children, 1970
Houses and Travellers, 1977
Unframed Originals, 1982
Regions of Memory: Uncollected Prose, 1949-1982, 1987
  (Cary Nelson, editor)
The Lost Upland, 1992
The Mays of Ventadorn, 2002
The Ends of the Earth: Essays, 2004
Summer Doorways, 2005

TRANSLATIONS:
The Poem of the Cid, 1959
Satires, 1961 (of Persius)
Spanish Ballads, 1961
Lazarillo de Tormes, 1962
The Song of Roland, 1963
Selected Translations, 1948-1968, 1968
Products of the Perfected Civilization: Selected Writings of Chamfort, 1969 (of Sébastian Roch Nicolas Chamfort)
Transparence of the World: Poems, 1968 (of Jean Follain)
Twenty Love Poems and a Song of Despair, 1969 (of Pablo Neruda)
Voices, 1969, 1988 (of Antonio Porchia)
Asian Figures, 1973 (of various Asian pieces)
Selected Poems, 1973, 1989 (of Osip Mandelstam; with Clarence Brown)
Iphigenia at Aulis, 1978 (of Euripides; with George E. Dimock, Jr.)
Selected Translations, 1968-1978, 1979
Four French Plays, 1985
From the Spanish Morning, 1985 (of Spanish ballads, Lope de Rueda's prose play *Eufemia*, and *Vida de Lazarillo de Tormes*)
Vertical Poetry, 1988 (of Roberto Juarroz)
Sun at Midnight (poems by Muso Soseki with Soiku Shigematsu), 1989
Pieces of Shadow: Selected Poems of Jaime Sabines, 1996
East Window: The Asian Translations, 1998
Purgatorio, 2000 (of Dante)
The Life of Lazarillo de Tormes: His Fortunes and Adversities, 2005

DISCUSSION TOPICS

- How does W. S. Merwin treat the past in any of his poems? What roles do tradition and literature play in his poetry?

- Select four different poets whom Merwin mentions in "Lament for the Makers." Identify for what each poet was mainly known and his manner of death. How does Merwin incorporate each poet's life and death into his "lament"?

- Does William Dunbar's repeated "Timor Mortis Conturbat me" (the fear of death troubles me) in his sixteenth century poem "Lament for the Makers" relate to Merwin's "Lament for the Makers"? Does Merwin offer any consolation in his poem? How?

- How does Merwin use natural images in "A Given Day"? What does the image "flowers of winter" mean, and how does this image affect the whole poem?

- Compare Merwin's poem "Losing a Language" with the early twentieth century poem "Ars Poetica" by Archibald MacLeish. What kind of structural similarities exist between the two poems? Do Merwin's poetry and images exemplify MacLeish's idea of what a poem must be?

- In "Losing a Language," what does "when there is a voice at the door it is foreign/ everywhere instead of a name there is a lie" mean?

ANTHOLOGY:

Lament for the Makers: A Memorial Anthology, 1996

About the Author

Bloom, Harold, ed. *W. S. Merwin*. Philadelphia: Chelsea House, 2004.

Byers, Thomas G. *What I Cannot Say: Self, Word, and World in Whitman, Stevens, and Merwin*. Urbana: University of Illinois Press, 1989.

Christhilf, Mark. *W. S. Merwin, the Mythmaker*. Columbia: University of Missouri Press, 1986.

Davis, Cheri. *W. S. Merwin*. Boston: Twayne, 1981.

Hix, H. L. *Understanding W. S. Merwin*. Columbia: University of South Carolina Press, 1997.

Hoeppner, Edward Haworth. *Echoes and Moving Fields: Structure and Subjectivity in the Poetry of W. S. Merwin and John Ashbery*. Lewisburg, Pa.: Bucknell University Press, 1994.

Mark, Irwin, ed. *Many Mountains Moving: A Tribute to W. S. Merwin*. Boulder, Colo.: Many Mountains Moving, 2002.

Merwin, W. S. *Unframed Originals*. New York: Atheneum, 1982.

Nelson, Cary, and Ed Folsom, eds. *W. S. Merwin: Essays on the Poetry*. Urbana: University of Illinois Press, 1987.

Scigaj, Leonard M. *Sustainable Poetry: Four American Ecopoets*. Lexington: University of Kentucky Press, 1999.

Shaw, Robert B., ed. *American Poetry Since 1960: Some Critical Perspectives*. Chester Springs, Pa.: Dufour, 1974.

JAMES A. MICHENER

Born: New York, New York
February 3, 1907?
Died: Austin, Texas
October 16, 1997

Known as one of the most popular writers of the twentieth century, Michener is generally considered to be among the best writers of historical fiction.

© John Kings

BIOGRAPHY

James Albert Michener claimed to have been born in New York City on February 3, 1907, although the actual history of his birth is obscure. Abandoned as an infant in Doylestown, Pennsylvania, he was adopted by a Quaker woman, Mabel Michener, who boarded children and who may have been his birth mother. She supported the children in her care by taking in laundry and by sewing buttonholes; James helped make ends meet as a child by working as a soda boy, paperboy, and hotel watchman. Nevertheless, the Michener family was evicted frequently, and James spent four months in the poorhouse. Mabel made these bad times bearable for James by instilling in her adopted son a love for books and music. He also acquired a sympathy for poor people and an admiration for hard work that resurfaced years later in his novels.

Michener was enrolled in Doylestown Grammar School but was overcome with wanderlust at the age of fourteen, an impulse that would remain with him. After bumming his way across forty-five states and staying with more than fifty families, Michener returned to high school and became a sports columnist and an amusement-park spotter at fifteen. Even though he was very active in basketball, baseball, tennis, and acting, Michener graduated first in his class and was awarded a scholarship to

Swarthmore College; he graduated summa cum laude and Phi Beta Kappa in 1929.

Michener continued to pursue his intellectual goals after college. A traveling scholarship, the Lippincott Award, sent him to St. Andrew's University in Scotland. While in Europe, he also found time to collect rare songs in the Hebrides, study painting in Siena, Italy, tour Spain, and ship out as a seaman in the British merchant marine. Returning to the United States in 1933, Michener taught English for three years at a Quaker institution called George School near Philadelphia. After marrying Patti Koon in 1935, he became a professor at Colorado State Teachers College in Greeley. In 1936, he began his six-year tenure with the educational press, which marked the beginning of his writing career. In 1940, he became a visiting history professor at Harvard University and then a textbook editor at Macmillan in New York.

Michener's promising career at Macmillan was interrupted by the bombing of Pearl Harbor. After he enlisted in the Navy, Michener's ability as a writer came to the attention of his superiors, and he was sent to officers' school, where he was trained for service in the Mediterranean theater. Ironically, though, when Michener requested active duty, he was sent to the Pacific region. He visited forty-nine Pacific islands, collecting material for a novel about the South Pacific. Eventually, he became senior historical officer for the area from New Guinea to Tahiti. At the end of the war, Michener was discharged with the rank of lieutenant commander, and he returned to his position at Macmillan.

Michener's career as a novelist began in 1946 with the publication of two chapters of his South Pacific novel in *The Saturday Evening Post*. He was still working in Macmillan's educational department when *Tales of the South Pacific* was published in 1947 and won the Pulitzer Prize. That same year, he divorced his first wife and married Vange A. Nord, a *Time* magazine writer and interior decorator. Financial liberation for Michener came both from the sale of the rights for what would become the 1949 musical and the 1958 film *South Pacific* and from his appointment as roving reporter for *Reader's Digest*. Nevertheless, he continued to work at Macmillan while working on his second novel, *The Fires of Spring* (1949), until a literary agent, Helen Straus, persuaded him to quit his job and become a full-time writer.

The knowledge of Asia that Michener had displayed in his first two novels led to other responsibilities. In 1953, he was named president of the Asia Institute, the only graduate school in the United States devoted exclusively to training in Asian affairs. In 1954, he also helped to found the Fund for Asia, a nonprofit organization that he disbanded two years later. After Vange sued for divorce, Michener married a Japanese American woman named Marl Sabusawa in 1955; she died of cancer in 1994.

A series of global reporting assignments soon followed. The National Broadcasting Company (NBC) sent him to Java, Bali, Malay, Cambodia, Vietnam, Thailand, and Burma in 1956 to film a documentary. That same year, *Reader's Digest* sent him to Hungary to cover the Hungarian Revolution, an experience that he recorded in *The Bridge at Andau* in 1957.

Between writing novels, Michener also found time for politics. He had supported Adlai Stevenson's bid for the presidency in 1956 and pleaded for the election of John A. Burns for governor of Hawaii in 1959. Michener's own political career began in 1962, when he ran unsuccessfully for congress from the Eighth Congressional District in Pennsylvania. Between 1967 and 1968, he served as secretary of the Pennsylvania Constitutional Convention and head of the Pennsylvania electors.

Two books were the direct product of his involvement in politics during the 1960's: *Report of the County Chairman* (1961) and *The Drifters* (1971). Michener's political activity continued in the

1970's, with his appointment to the United States Advisory Commission on Information (1970-1974) and his trip to China with President Richard Nixon in 1972. On February 1, 1979, Michener testified before the U.S. Senate on the topic of space exploration.

Michener contributed millions of dollars to universities and institutes in the 1980's, to give back a little of what he believed he had received from education. He also reached out to universities in an entirely different way during that decade. To assist with the writing of *Texas* (1985) and *Alaska* (1988), he asked university students from those states to help him with the mammoth task of conducting the necessary research. He also increased his publication pace: He wrote eleven books between 1986 and 1991. He continued to travel; in 1989, for example, he went to Havana, Cuba, to collect facts for *Caribbean* (1989). As a testament to his continuing popularity, *Caribbean* received a first printing of thirty-five thousand copies, the largest in the history of Random House. Before his death he moved to Texas, where his use of the University of Texas library may have prompted him to donate more than thirty-seven million dollars to the university. He died of renal failure in 1997.

ANALYSIS

Michener is certainly one of the most successful and unique writers of fiction of the twentieth century. Unlike many best-selling authors, Michener amassed a huge following, not by filling his novels with gratuitous sex and violence, but by writing huge, carefully researched books that create their own universes. Each of his epic novels gives the reader a *Weltanschauung*, or a view of life, through the myriad details he presents pertaining to the history, archaeology, religion, language, geology, wildlife, agriculture, and social and economic lore of a region. Michener's background as an educator is reflected in this factual quality of his books, which has made each one a "history course" for the average American, many of whom have little time or interest to delve into history books. By reading Michener's novels, one can learn a great deal without much effort.

It is the epic quality of Michener's fiction, however, that has brought him under fire from the critics. His desire to involve his characters in as many historical events as possible results in what many perceive to be contrived situations. In addition, the vast time frames that his novels span give Michener little room for character development. Thus, his characters are often stereotypes or one-dimensional beings who converse in somewhat stilted dialogue. Even though Michener has never claimed to be a stylist such as John Updike or Saul Bellow, critics have lambasted his workmanlike prose, which is devoid of paradox, irony, or ambiguity. Moreover, because Michener interprets facts as he gives them, he has been accused of preaching to his readers, telling them how to think about historical events.

Michener's mass appeal, however, indicates that the general public has overlooked these shortcomings. Not only do many people feel enlightened by his facts, but they are also enthralled by his themes. The fact that Michener possessed a blend of liberal and conservative tendencies helped him reach out to a broad audience.

Racial discrimination is a moral issue in all of Michener's novels except for *The Bridges at Toko-Ri* (1953) and *The Drifters*. In *Hawaii* (1959), Michener attributes the zeal of the missionaries and their descendants in Hawaii to an implicit belief in the superiority of white Christianity and the ways of the Western world. This ideological conflict intensifies with the arrival of Chinese, Japanese, and Polynesian immigrants to Japan. In *The Source* (1965), Michener points out that the Hebrews' faith in their status as God's Chosen People bolstered their spirits and prevented them from capitulating in the face of overwhelming opposition; however, in the modern world, Michener argues, this archaic (even egotistical) way of thinking is still nurturing ancient antagonism between the Jews and the Arabs. *Centennial* (1974) dramatizes the decimation of the Indians in nineteenth century America and the exploitation of the Japanese and Mexican field laborers in the twentieth century to demonstrate the bigotry that accompanied the winning of the West. In these novels and others, Michener demonstrates that because discrimination diminishes the potential of a large segment of a society, the society as a whole suffers for it.

The environmental issue is another major target of Michener. In many of his novels, he discusses the fragile bond that exists between the land and the people who live on it. *Hawaii* dramatizes the drastic changes that take place in the lives of the inhabitants through the depletion of the islands' only nat-

ural commodity, sandalwood. Arrogance, Michener says, is primarily responsible for the failed promise of paradise in *The Source, The Covenant* (1980), and *Texas*. Although the environmental crisis is only one of several issues in these novels, it is at the core of *Centennial*. Throughout that novel, Michener demonstrates that respect for the land is essential if humans expect it to support them in the twenty-first century.

Michener's conservative leanings manifest themselves in his solid belief in the Puritan work ethic. The slothful natives in *Hawaii* lose control of their islands to the more industrious Chinese and Japanese. In *Centennial*, Michener applauds the resourcefulness and ingenuity of immigrants such as Potato Brumbaugh and his Japanese and Mexican workers who are able to coax productivity out of a barren land. In fact, Michener is so convinced of the enabling power of hard work that even some of his villains, such as the soldier Skimmerhorn in *Centennial* and the pirate Bonfleur in *Chesapeake* (1978), command respect because they are men who are able to achieve their goals through the sheer force of their own will. If a society such as those that existed in Virginia (*Chesapeake*) and Hawaii (*Hawaii*) begins using slaves to do all the work, moral and economic bankruptcy soon follow. Michener clearly admires the self-made millionaires in *Hawaii* and *Centennial* who, he argues, are entitled to their vast riches because they, like Michener himself, pulled themselves up from humble beginnings.

Finally, Michener's emphasis on the wisdom and courage of the young reflects his acceptance of change as a fact of life. Adherence to tradition is commendable, Michener says, but such behavior also impedes progress, causing rigid societies to stagnate and die. It is the freethinkers, such as the children of the Japanese immigrants in *Hawaii*, who revitalize their culture by changing with the times. Such changes, Michener warns, must not be made impulsively; many of his heroes and heroines reach a point where they have to decide which values are worthy of preservation.

TALES OF THE SOUTH PACIFIC

First published: 1947
Type of work: Novel

In the face of overwhelming odds, American military personnel display amazing courage before and during combat.

Michener's first novel, *Tales of the South Pacific,* appears at first to be a collection of nineteen casually related episodes. Upon closer inspection, however, a coherence becomes apparent, produced by a chorus of common themes and characters that resonate throughout the work. In this way, Michener's novel is reminiscent of William Faulkner's *Go Down, Moses* (1942), which achieves unity through the same devices. The classification of the book, though, is still so nebulous that the Pulitzer Prize authorities felt compelled to change the category of "novel" to "fiction in book form" before awarding it the Pulitzer Prize in 1948.

Michener is more successful at attaining narrative unity in this book than he is in most of the others, largely because *Tales of the South Pacific* is so much shorter. The unidentified first-person narrator describes himself as a "paper-work sailor." The observations that he makes in the first two tales, "The South Pacific" and "Coral Sea," reveal Michener's primary goal, which is to discuss the human side of World War II.

Although several stories, such as the first two, are no more than journalistic sketches, "Mutiny" has true literary merit. The narrator has been sent to Norfolk Island to oversee the cutting down of a strip of pine trees so that an airstrip can be built. The title refers both to Charles Nordhoff and James Norman Hall's *Mutiny on the Bounty* (1932) and to the resistance of an old lady named Teta Christian and a retarded fifteen-year-old girl; both of their ancestors migrated to Norfolk Island from Pitcairn Island in 1856 and planted most of the pines. The organic symbol of the trees, a "cathedral of pines," is contrasted with the cold, heartless, mechanistic symbol, the bulldozers, one of which is blown up by the two women. Through Tony Fry, a sympathetic Navy lieutenant, Michener is saying that victory is hollow if the spirit of free individuals is trampled.

"Our Heroine" is one of two stories on which the musical *South Pacific* was based. Nellie Forbush is attracted to a wealthy French planter named Emile DeBecque. Although she is enchanted by the bright hues of the foliage on the island, however, she has trouble accepting the same variations in DeBecque's eight illegitimate children. This is the first appearance of what was to become a major theme in Michener's later novels: the need for racial tolerance.

The effects of long periods of inaction on virile young men are demonstrated in the next three stories. In "Dry Rot," eight hundred men who are afflicted with a fungus growth also "itch" for action with the enemy and, in a different sense, with women. "Fo' Dollar" is the second story that inspired *South Pacific.* After the young woman he had been writing to in "Dry Rot" dies, the frustrated Joe Cable falls in love with a beautiful Tonkinese woman named Liat; however, he cannot marry her because he is to be part of the invasion of Kuralei. The theme of racial intolerance resurfaces in Cable's reluctance to bring Liat back to the United States and in the way Liat is ridiculed by the young French women at the convent.

Bus Adams is the narrator of "A Boar's Tooth" and "Those Who Fraternize" and is the main character in "Wine for the Mess at Segi." In "A Boar's Tooth," a gruesome native ritual reminds Dr. Benoway of the revolting emphasis that all religions place on appurtenances, such as the importance some American churches place on the height of a church steeple. In "Wine for the Mess at Segi," the dangers that the men encounter in their search for whiskey provide as much relief from boredom as does the whiskey itself. "Those Who Fraternize," which is narrated by Bus Adams, focuses on the desperate attempts of four of the half-caste DeBecque sisters to attain security by marrying sailors. The futility of trying to establish permanent, meaningful relationships during wartime is underscored by the fact that all the girls' lovers are killed in battle.

The stir-crazy sailors finally encounter the enemy in the last four stories—"The Strike," "Frisco," "The Landing on Kuralei," and "The Cemetery at Hoga Point." Even though the narrator is personally involved, his commentary is oddly restrained. The commander of the Navy Supply Depot in "The Strike" is Captain Kelley, a no-nonsense officer who likes to imitate Captain Bligh in *Mutiny on the*

Bounty. Unlike the descendants of the mutineers in "The Mutiny," sailors such as Polikopf rebel against authority by burlesquing naval life.

In "Frisco," the crew of a landing craft headed for Kuralei form a loose bond through their shared memories of the last American city in which they spent time. "The Landing on Kuralei" is a minute-by-minute account of the American assault, during which more than nine hundred Japanese and more than two hundred American soldiers are killed. The narrator fully comprehends the sense-lessness of war when he discovers that the coura-geous Tony Fry is killed during the landing and that the cowardly Bill Harbison has avoided the conflict altogether. The elegiac tone of "A Ceme-tery at Hoga Point" is tempered by the assertions of the narrator and the two black gravediggers that there will never be a shortage of good men when duty calls.

Even though *Tales of the South Pacific* was consid-ered by many critics to be a poor choice for the Pu-litzer Prize in 1947, the novel is noteworthy for its small-scale approach to an epic conflict. The Pa-cific theater of war as recorded in this book is a learning experience for both the readers and the military personnel. Michener implies that people such as Nellie Forbush and Joe Cable survive by questioning the values that they brought with them and adapting to their new circumstances.

HAWAII

First published: 1959
Type of work: Novel

The history of Hawaii illustrates Michener's belief that all civilizations advance at racial crossroads.

Hawaii, the first of Michener's "blockbuster" nov-els, was also the first of a new type of historical novel. Although Honoré de Balzac, Émile Zola, and John Dos Passos had all written novels that span several decades, none of their works had the epic scope of *Hawaii*, which covered several hun-dred years of human history. Another innovation was the attention that Michener paid to historical accuracy, which makes the novel as instructional as it is entertaining.

The novel begins with the birth of the Hawaiian islands in a section titled "From the Boundless Deep." These "new" lands, totally devoid of life, can be tamed only by the arrival of what the narrator terms a "new breed" of people. This first-person narrator, whose identity is unknown until the end of the novel, is Hoxworth Hale, a direct descendant of several of the families depicted in the novel.

The second section, "From the Sun-Swept La-goon," deals with the first human inhabitants. In the ninth century, King Tamatoa and his younger brother flee Bora Bora in the middle of the night for fear that they will be sacrificed to a new god, Oro. Blown off course by a terrible storm, they land on a mountainous island that appears to be habit-able. Many of the rituals that the missionaries will confront hundreds of years later are introduced in this section.

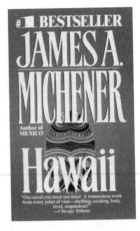

The narrator then jumps forward one thousand years to document the arrival of the first Cauca-sians—missionaries from Yale University. The title of this section, "From the Farms of Bitterness," re-fers to the "fire and brimstone" that Abner Hale, the stereotyped embodiment of Calvinistic Con-gregationalism, preaches as he converts the na-tives. Hale's preaching also makes subtle refer-ences to the inherent superiority of the white race and Western culture. By contrast, Hale's wife, Jerusha, preaches a message of love in the school which she sets up to bring literacy to the islands. In a few short years, Jerusha dies from overwork, a fit-ting death for the woman from whose body would spring a line of men and women who would devote their lives to bringing "civilization" to the islands.

To introduce the arrival of the Chinese immi-grants in "From the Starving Village," Michener begins with the birth in 1847 of one of the most fas-cinating characters in the novel, Nyuk Tsin. In 1865, her parents are killed by the invading Tar-tars; soon thereafter, Nyuk is abducted. A Punti cook named Mun Ki, who works at the brothel where Nyuk has been sold into prostitution, de-cides to take her with him to Hawaii, where he intends to sell her. During the ocean voyage that Mun Ki and Nyuk share with three hundred other conscripted Chinese, Mun Ki appreciates Nyuk's potential as a good wife, even though she is a Haaku. Both people, Michener says, are victims of tradition.

Once in Hawaii, Mun Ki and Nyuk Tsin are not in John Whipple's employ for very long before they absorb the old Yankee virtues of thrift, family solidarity, scholarliness, and common sense. Nyuk's willingness to spend her off hours earning money to buy land convinces Whipple that the Chinese will revitalize the indolent Hawaiians. Yet Nyuk's most sterling qualities become apparent only after Mun Ki contracts leprosy and is sent to a leper colony; Nyuk goes there with him. Like Jerusha Hale, Nyuk Tsin and the other "kokuas" who accompany their diseased relatives to the leper colony demonstrate that the word "love" has what Michener calls a "tangible reality." Just before he dies, Mun Ki, in one of the only sentimental scenes in the novel, calls Nyuk his real wife, a belated acknowledgment of her worthiness.

When Nyuk returns to Honolulu, the first thing she does is to reunite herself with her sons, who have been cared for by a charitable Hawaiian woman named Apikela. In time, all of Nyuk's sons, including the one who was adopted by the governor while she was at the leper colony, become community leaders.

Despite the increasing fortunes of the Chinese, the haoles, or whites, control Hawaii during the remainder of the nineteenth century. Rafer Hoxworth's grandson, "Wild" Whipple, stands for all the ruthless American entrepreneurs of the nineteenth century. Michener's re-creation of the deposing of Queen Liiuokalani and the admission of Hawaii as a territory by U.S. president William McKinley takes liberties with the facts.

Michener's love of the Japanese is evident throughout the entirety of "From the Inland Sea." His account of the beauties of the Inland Sea and the island of Kauai has a lyrical quality that is quite striking. One of the workmen imported from Hiroshima, Kamejiro Sakagawa, exhibits persistence, obedience, endurance, and industriousness in all the menial jobs that he is given. Of all the Japanese characters in this section, he is the best developed. Another quality that Michener admires in the Japanese, their patriotism, drives four of Sakagawa's

sons to enlist in the 222d Combat Team (the fictional equivalent of the 442d). Racial discrimination is a major theme in this section. World War II marks the decline of the whites and the emergence of the Asians as the ruling class in Hawaii.

The final section of the book, "The Golden Men," is generally considered to be the weakest. Instead of developing each scene, Michener provides brief synopses of a staggering number of postwar conditions in Hawaii. Many readers were offended by his portrayal of a descendant of generations of Hawaii residents as a surfer who preys on wealthy women. The title of this section refers to Hawaii's population. The narrator recapitulates the ancestor worship and the insistence on racial purity by all the races in Hawaii and then, on the last page, observes that all Hawaiians are "products of the mind," the beneficiaries of the cross-fertilization of ideas from different cultures.

Hawaii is the novel on which Michener's reputation most firmly rests. Although critics still complained about his "cardboard characters," they were impressed by the scope and narrative power of his novel. Charles Sutton dubbed him the "Pepys of the Pacific," after the seventeenth century English diarist Samuel Pepys. In addition, the ending of *Hawaii* is much more satisfying than those of Michener's other novels. Whereas the evidence of disorder and unreason contradicts the narrator's optimistic affirmation about the future in books such as *Centennial*, Hoxworth Hale's prediction regarding the ultimate unity in which all people will live seems to be warranted by the novel it concludes.

THE SOURCE

First published: 1965
Type of work: Novel

Suffering and obedience to the law characterize the development of the Jewish culture.

Of all Michener's novels, *The Source* is certainly the most ambitious and complex. Conceived while Michener was on a visit to Israel, the novel traces the history of the Jews from their primitive origins thousands of years ago to the establishment of Israel in 1948. The chapters in each stage of the history illustrated are, for the most part, independent narratives; however, like *Hawaii*, partial continuity is achieved through the repetition of familiar family names.

In *The Source*, Michener employs a variation on the narrative technique that he used in *Hawaii*. The historical events in *The Source* are put into contemporary perspective by a frame story that is set in 1964. In the frame story, a team of three archaeologists is excavating a Tell, or mound, at the site of the fictional crossroads of the ancient world called Makor, or the Source, because of its spring. The narratives correspond with the unearthing of each successive level of human habitation, beginning with the earliest level—Level XV. At the end of each chapter, the archaeologists evaluate the finds that correspond to the events that have previously been related.

The chapter titled "The Bee Eater" begins in 9831 B.C.E. and introduces Ur, the progenitor of

the Family of Ur that appears in the following four chapters. Ur is primarily a hunter, but his son's experiments with planting presage a new way of life for Ur's descendants. When his son-in-law is killed by a wild boar, Ur begins probing the mysteries of life and death by asking himself questions such as "Why do I live?" By the year 2202 B.C.E., the people of Makor have attempted to answer those

questions by creating gods, in "Of Death and Life." When the time comes for Urbaal to sacrifice his first-born son to the Canaanite god of Death, he does so willingly in spite of the protests of his wife.

"An Old Man and His God" introduces the Haibiru, who are the forerunners of the Hebrews. After arriving in Makor, the Haibiru diplomatically respect the local gods but cling to the belief that El Shaddai is the most powerful god. This theological conflict is dramatized in the dilemma faced by the leader of the Haibiru, Zadok, whose granddaughter is impregnated by Zibeon, the son of the Canaanite leader.

The third historical chapter, "Psalm of the Hoopoe Bird," takes place during the reign of David. By this time, El Shaddai has been replaced by Yaweh, who controls the heavens and the hearts of humanity. A descendant of Zibeon named Jabaal is an engineer who builds a massive tunnel that King David places below the more abstract accomplishment of a psalmist named Gershon. In 1964, though, the rediscovered tunnel is itself hailed as a psalm of those who do God's work.

In "The Voice of Gomer," a theme that had been an undercurrent in the previous chapters—suffering for one's religious beliefs—receives its first major exposition. Gomer, a poor widow, becomes a heroine because she does as Yahweh commands, regardless of the hardships she must endure. When Yahweh tells her to defy the governor and drive out the priestess-prostitutes of Baal, she does so. Imprisoned in a well shaft, Gomer predicts that Yahweh will use the Babylonians to punish the Hebrews for their pagan ways. The Jews' passive acceptance of God's punishment becomes an integral part of their character.

"King of the Jews" is the only chapter of the novel that is told in the first-person voice. The narrator is a Roman soldier named Myrmex who admires his superior, Herod, because Herod kills his beloved Jewish wife when ordered to; however, obedience, Michener implies, is admirable only when the command is from God. Although Myrmex does not construe Herod's disfigurement by a horrible disease to be a sort of divine punishment, the evidence provided by the author forces the reader to draw this conclusion. Five hundred years later, the Jews continue to resist any attempt to change their beliefs. In "Yigal and the Three Generals," the Jews organize a successful protest against the bringing of a statue of the god Caligula to Makor. For their defiance of Nero, many are crucified.

The harshness of Jewish law is exposed in "The Law," which is set in the Byzantine period. Rabbi Asher declares Menahem a bastard because his widowed mother remarries before the fifteen-year waiting period has elapsed. Barred from participating in Jewish rituals, Menahem converts to Christianity. While the arrival of the Muslims in 635 C.E. does not disperse the Jews, it does add to their suffering in "A Day in the Life of a Desert Rider." After eight hundred Jews of Medina are beheaded for refusing to convert, military units are dispatched all over the Middle East to do the same everywhere, if need be, to spread Islam. The next two chapters recount the invasion of the Holy Land by the Crusaders. In "Volkmar," Michener draws a clear parallel between the slaughter of Jews in Europe and in the Middle East in the eleventh century and the systematic extermination of European Jews by Adolf Hitler in the twentieth century. Two hundred years later, in "The Fires of Ma Coeur," the Crusaders are on the decline.

The first example of "modern" persecution occurs in the chapter titled "The Saintly Men of Safed." The three men who take center stage in this episode are saintly because each suffers mightily for his belief. Michener's description of the tortures endured by Jews in the Spanish Inquisition is just as horrifying as his explanation of the shocking plight of the lepers in *Hawaii*. The chapter ends with Michener's observation that Judaism has had a tendency to be protected from common understanding when too much emphasis is placed on mysticism and legalism.

The need for religious tolerance is the central theme of "Twilight of an Empire." In 1880, a Russian Jew named Schumuel Hacohen attempts to escape the anti-Semitic atmosphere of his homeland by establishing a colony of transplanted Russian and Polish Jews along the Jordan River. The once-dispersed Jews return to their homeland in larger numbers than ever before. "Rebbe Itzik and the Sabra," the last of the historical narratives, is an account of the evacuation of the British from Palestine. The chapter ends with the Jews' assertion that they will never again submit to oppression or dispersion, thereby adding a new dimension to the Jewish character.

The novel comes full circle in the last chapter with the discovery of the well and prehistoric flints by the archaeologists in the frame story. The Jews' strict adherence to tradition, Michener says, has been a heavy burden, but it has preserved and defined the Jewish character through the centuries. The novel ends with the optimistic pronouncement that the Arabs and Jews are closer than they realize because they share land and the same partnership with God.

CENTENNIAL

First published: 1974
Type of work: Novel

Violent conflict, heroic struggles, and cruel injustice characterize the lives of the people and the animals that inhabit Colorado throughout its turbulent history.

Published two years after his nonfiction examination of the Kent State University shootings—*Kent State: What Happened and Why* (1971)—*Centennial* returns to the genre upon which Michener's reputation rests. Like *Hawaii* and *The Source*, *Centennial* is a fascinating blend of historical fact and fiction. Unlike his previous novels, though, which are set in exotic lands, *Centennial* takes place in the continental United States.

In *Centennial*, Michener employs the same type of narrative artifice that he used in *The Source*, but which he believed was unnecessary in *Chesapeake*, *The Covenant*, and *Space* (1982). The contemporary presenter of the historical episodes in this novel is the fictional Professor Lewis Vernor, who is commissioned by *US* magazine to validate a series of articles on a town in Colorado called Centennial.

As in *Hawaii*, Michener provides a dramatic and historically verifiable explanation of how the land was created and populated. It is in his exposition of the prehistory of Colorado that Michener introduces two themes that run through the entire novel: the survival of the fittest and the persistence of the past into the present. The first human inhabitants of Colorado followed the woolly mammoths across a land bridge from Asia to Alaska thirteen thousand years ago. Michener then moves to the second half of the eighteenth century to introduce the progenitor of many of the characters in the novel, Lame Beaver, who inadvertently makes the area attractive to white men when his golden bullet falls into their hands.

Despite the plethora of Indian lore that Michener provides, Lame Beaver's story is strangely uninteresting. The thrilling exploits of the first two white men who come on the scene, however—Jacques Pasquinel, a trapper, and Alexander McKeag, a fugitive from Scotland—help to bring the novel alive in chapter 5. McKeag, Pasquinel's fellow trapper, is a much more complex character; he breaks with Pasquinel after a knife fight with Pasquinel's half-breed son, Jake. This dispute foreshadows the racial tensions that permeate the remainder of the novel.

The following two chapters document the two forces that contributed to the vanquishing of the culture of the American Indians: the settlers and the United States government. The central character of chapter 7 is Levi Zendt, a former member of a Pennsylvania Dutch community who is ostracized for flirting with his brother's girlfriend. In his flight from injustice, Levi bears an ironic resemblance to the Indians in chapter 8 who are forced to leave their homeland after their treaties are broken. The courage of Levi and his sixteen-year-old bride, Elly, is underscored by their naïveté, which is revealed early by Levi's insistence that horses be used instead of oxen to pull his huge Conestoga wagon. Thus, his journey is also a rite of passage, and his tutors are the people who join with them. After Elly dies, he starts a store that becomes the focal point of the town of Zendt's Farm, later renamed Centennial.

In chapter 7, the whites are firmly established as the dominant race in Colorado by the machinations of the U.S. government and the instrument of its will, the U.S. Cavalry. The domination of the whites is ratified in a treaty during the Civil War that reduces the Indians' lands to forty-acre allotments on reservations. The degradation of the Indians culminates in a massacre of the Arapaho that is instigated by the fanatical Frank Skimmerhorn.

The novel then moves to its third phase, the civilizing of the West. Chapter 8 is probably the most successful because of its unity and because of the verisimilitude that is achieved by its detailed and authentic portrayal of life on the range. In order to stock the 670,000 acres of range, a transplanted Englishman, Oliver Seccombe, hires a Confederate general and the son of the infamous Frank Skimmerhorn to drive longhorn cattle from Texas to Colorado. The story focuses on a fourteen-year-old boy named Jim Lloyd. Because of Jim's inexperience as a cowboy and his overall naïveté, it is appropriate that the reader view the trip through his eyes. Throughout the drive, Jim exhibits those qualities that Michener contends were essential in the winning of the West: responsibility, courage, and skill.

Chapter 9 dramatizes the struggles among the various forces of civilization to control the prairie. An immigrant from the Ukraine named Hans Brumbaugh finds farming to be more profitable after he begins irrigating the land to produce potatoes first, then beets. Although Oliver Seccombe maintains an uneasy truce with Brumbaugh, he declares war against the sheep herders and their leader, Messmore Garrett. The tragedy of this conflict is pointed out by Paul Garrett years later, as he observes Hereford cows and sheep grazing together with no apparent harm to the grass.

Michener's epic narrative culminates in chapter 11, which illustrates what Michener calls the "dark side of western history." To make ends meet, a destitute actress named Maude Wendell lures a Swede to her bedroom in hopes of blackmailing him. When he protests, she kills him, and she and her son conceal the corpse in an ancient beaver cave. Ironically, the Wendells prosper: Maude becomes a socialite, and her husband and son become unscrupulous real estate agents.

Chapters 12 and 13, which bring the novel into the twentieth century, add a whole new set of characters. Chapter 13 concerns the efforts of Mervin Wendel, the railroad, and an agronomist named Dr. Thomas Dole Creevey to attract farmers to Colorado in 1911. Despite the warnings of Lloyd and Brumbaugh, the immigrants implement Dr. Creevey's system of dry farming, only to find the promise of the first few years shattered by crop failure in the 1920's and by the dust storms of the 1930's.

Like chapter 1, chapter 14 is composed entirely of the frame narrative. In Paul Garrett, Professor Vernor finds a man who epitomizes the history of the West. In Garrett, the genetic strains of many of the main characters converge (although a bit too conveniently to be believable). Yet Paul is also a product of the West in his love and respect for the land. Another frontier quality, courage, surfaces in Paul's decision to marry a Mexican woman despite the social constraints prohibiting such a union.

Paul acts as Professor Vernor's guide and introduces him to changing aspects of the West. Looking to the future, Paul tells Professor Vernor that Colorado will be in trouble if it does not acknowledge the fact that humankind and nature have always existed in precarious balance and begin protecting all of its components.

Despite its shortcomings, *Centennial* is an impressive work. The novel clearly benefits from the years that Michener spent in Colorado. The desert scenes, for example, are much more vividly described than are the desert scenes in his earlier *The Covenant*. Michener must also be praised for avoiding the big, easy subjects such as gold mining and railroad building and choosing, instead, the more challenging subjects such as irrigation and farming.

CHESAPEAKE

First published: 1978
Type of work: Novel

The history of the Eastern Shore of Maryland from 1583 to 1978 demonstrates the need for religious tolerance, personal integrity, and respect for the environment.

In *Chesapeake*, another sprawling novel, this one covering four hundred years and four major families, Michener abandoned his usual narrative practice of providing several points of view and used the third-person omniscient point of view. He also shaped his novel by dividing it into fourteen "episodes" with their own chapters. The first seven voyages concern the settlement of the Eastern Shore, first by Pentaquod, a peaceful member of the warlike Susquehannock tribe who settles among the Nanticokes, and then by the three white families that dominate the remainder of the novel. The Steeds are Catholics who settle on Devon Island and eventually become landed gentry. The Turlocks are distinctly lower-class people who spring from indentured stock and adapt to the land. The Paxmores are peace-loving ("pax") Quakers who have fled New England religious persecution. The fourth Family, the Cates, are the children of slaves. Michener uses the families and the landscape to demonstrate familiar themes. Devon Island, seat of the Steed family's colonial power, erodes, despite humankind's efforts to slow or stem the erosion, and finally disappears at the end of the novel after Pusey Paxmore's funeral and the hurricane that follows it. Pusey—descended from the moral center of the novel, the Paxmores—has just finished serving time for involvement in the Watergate

scandal. The Steed family also declines, much like the Southern families in the plays of Tennessee Williams. The Paxmores live, appropriately, at Peace Cliff. The Nanticokes, whom the Turlocks have assisted, eventually vanish when Tciblento dies, showing how the white man's intolerance, exploitation, and racism have destroyed indigenous tribes.

There are so many characters that few are drawn in any detail. One exception is Rosalind Janney, who marries Fitzhugh Steed and finds that she must administer both the house and the plantation. She also is the driving force behind seeing that the infamous pirate Bonfleur ("good flower"), ironically named, is brought to justice and hanged. When "wayward" women are whipped, as is the custom, she bares her own back and effectively puts an end to the practice. She is perhaps the feminist in the novel.

As is his practice, Michener also includes historical characters (Thomas Jefferson, John Smith, Henry Clay, Daniel Webster, and George Washington make cameo appearances) and historical events. Teach Turlock, Simon Steed, and Levin Paxmore unite to take on the British, primarily at sea; and Michener tells his readers more than they want to know about boat building. Similarly, in the Civil War material, the intricate details of the Underground Railroad, particularly as it relates to the Paxmores, are given.

Michener also devotes chapters to nonhuman characters: geese and crabs, both identified with the Eastern Shore. The goose Onk-or, his mate, and their flock are threatened by the huge guns capable of killing several birds with one shot. Conservation is not an Eastern Shore practice, whether it concerns birds or crabs. Michener also personifies the crab as "Jimmy," the name given by Shoremen to male crabs. While providing a wealth of detail about geese and crabs, Michener also demonstrates the interconnectedness between the human world and the world of nature.

SUMMARY

In terms of book sales, Michener was one of the most successful American writers of the twentieth century. The immense popularity of his novels is made all the more amazing by the fact that the subjects of his novels are not in tune with what the public generally seemed to want. People read Michener's novels not only to escape but also to learn. Each of his massive, epic novels reflects his obsession with geographic and historical detail.

Although his characters are, for the most part, stereotyped representatives of certain types of people, his most heroic characters embody those virtues that Michener has tried to cultivate in himself: hard work, courage, resourcefulness, and independence.

Alan Brown; updated by Thomas L. Erskine

BIBLIOGRAPHY

By the Author

LONG FICTION:
Tales of the South Pacific, 1947
The Fires of Spring, 1949
The Bridges at Toko-Ri, 1953
Sayonara, 1954
The Bridge at Andau, 1954
Hawaii, 1959
Caravans, 1963
The Source, 1965
The Drifters, 1971
Centennial, 1974
Chesapeake, 1978
The Covenant, 1980
Space, 1982
Poland, 1983
Texas, 1985
Legacy, 1987
Alaska, 1988
Journey, 1988
Caribbean, 1989
The Eagle and the Raven, 1990
The Novel, 1991
Mexico, 1992
Recessional, 1994
Miracle in Seville, 1995

SHORT FICTION:
Return to Paradise, 1951
Creatures of the Kingdom: Stories of Animals, 1993

NONFICTION:
Proposals for an Experimental Future of the Social Sciences: Proposals for an Experimental Social Studies Curriculum, 1939 (with Harold Long)
The Unit in the Social Studies, 1940
The Voice of Asia, 1951

DISCUSSION TOPICS

- Discuss the relations between the Native Americans and white settlers in *Chesapeake* and *Centennial*.

- Discuss the conflict between progress and the environment in James Michener's novels.

- Most of Michener's major characters are men. Discuss Michener's female characters in terms of their "feminism."

- What accounts for the decline of Michener's important families?

- Discuss Michener's depiction of Quakers and the Quaker religion in *Chesapeake*.

The Floating World, 1954
Selected Writings, 1957
Rascals in Paradise, 1957 (with A. Grove Day)
Japanese Prints from the Early Masters to the Modern, 1959
Report of the County Chairman, 1961
The Modern Japanese Print: An Appreciation, 1962
Iberia: Spanish Travels and Reflections, 1968
Presidential Lottery: The Reckless Gamble in Our Electoral System, 1969
The Quality of Life, 1970
Facing East: The Art of Jack Levine, 1970
Kent State: What Happened and Why, 1971
A Michener Miscellany, 1950-1970, 1973
About "Centennial": Some Notes on the Novel, 1974
Sports in America, 1976
In Search of Centennial: A Journey, 1978
Testimony, 1983
Collectors, Forgers, and a Writer: A Memoir, 1983
Six Days in Havana, 1989
Pilgrimage: A Memoir of Poland and Rome, 1990
My Lost Mexico, 1992
The World Is My Home: A Memoir, 1992
Literary Reflections: Michener on Michener, Hemingway, Capote, and Others, 1993
William Penn, 1994
This Noble Land, 1996
A Century of Sonnets, 1997
Talking with Michener, 1999 (interviews; with Lawrence Grobel)

EDITED TEXT:
The Hokusai Sketchbooks: Selections from the Manga, 1958

About the Author

Anthony, Arthur. "Avoiding Nostalgia: James Michener's *The Bridge at Andau*." *Literature and the Arts* 5, no. 1 (Spring/Summer, 1993): 47-53.

Becker, George. *James A. Michener*. New York: Frederick Ungar, 1983.

Beidler, Philip D. "*South Pacific* and American Remembering: Or, 'Josh, We're Going to Buy This Son of a Bitch!'" *Journal of American Studies* 27, no. 2 (August, 1993): 207-222.

Bell, Pearl K. "James Michener's Docudramas." *Commentary* 71 (April, 1981): 71-73.

Grobel, Lawrence. *Talking with Michener*. Jackson: University Press of Mississippi, 1999.

Hayes, John P. *James Michener: A Biography*. New York: Bobbs-Merrill, 1984.

Hines, Samuel M., Jr. "Political Change in America: Perspectives from the Popular Historical Novels of Michener and Vidal." In *Political Mythology and Popular Fiction*, edited by Ernest J. Yanarella and Lee Seligman. New York: Greenwood Press, 1988.

Michener, James. "Historical Fiction." *American Heritage* 33 (April/May, 1982): 44-48.

Osterholm, J. Roger. "Michener's *Space*, the Novel and Miniseries: A Study in Popular Culture." *Journal of Popular Culture* 23, no. 3 (Winter, 1989): 51-64.

Severson, Marilyn S. *James A. Michener: A Critical Companion*. New York: Greenwood Press, 1996.

Library of Congress

EDNA ST. VINCENT MILLAY

Born: Rockland, Maine
February 22, 1892
Died: Austerlitz, New York
October 19, 1950

The first woman to win the Pulitzer Prize in poetry, Millay became the lyrical voice of the Jazz Age by expressing a modern romantic sensibility in traditional verse forms.

BIOGRAPHY

Great fame and wealth were victories Edna St. Vincent Millay won over the hardships, neglect, and poverty of her childhood. The eldest of three daughters born to Henry and Cora Millay, she was named after St. Vincent's Hospital, where Cora's brother had just miraculously recovered from unconsciousness after being trapped in the hold of a ship for ten days without food or water. When Vincent, as her family called her, was only eight years old, her father left home, never to pay the five dollars a week in child support ordered after the divorce. That same year the three daughters nearly died of typhoid fever. Forced to eke out a living as a country nurse and a weaver of hair for wigs, Cora was gone for days at a time, leaving Vincent to care for herself and two sisters, Norma and Kathleen.

To relieve the loneliness and drudgery, when their loving mother was home she entertained the children with music and poetry, nurturing the talents that enabled Vincent to escape the domestic duties that deterred many women from independence and success. Millay later recalled the moment she fell in love with poetry. Turning the pages of her mother's large volume of William Shakespeare's plays, she was overwhelmed by Romeo's death speech on Juliet's beauty.

Such early experiences pointed the way to themes which she later explored in her poems: love and loss, nature and change, life and death, art and beauty, justice, equality, and the predicament of women in American society.

Her literary abilities surfaced in high school in Camden, Maine, where she edited the student newspaper and wrote some poems published in *St. Nicholas Magazine*. Then in 1911, on a visit to attend her ill father, she began "Renascence," the poem which would make her famous. She submitted it to a contest sponsored by the New York publisher Mitchell Kennerley. Although she did not win the prize, the poem's publication in *The Lyric Year* (1912) attracted the attention of famous poets and literary critics.

Millay was offered a scholarship to Smith College, but she went to Vassar instead because its student body was more diverse, with women from around the world. There she acted in school plays, wrote a drama called *The Princess Marries the Page* (1932), and earned a bachelor's degree, though she was barred from the graduation ceremony in 1917 for persistently breaking the college's rules.

Next she traveled to Greenwich Village, where she joined the Provincetown Players and met Floyd Dell and Max Eastman, editors of a radical magazine, *The Masses*, which was then under indictment for discouraging enlistment in the armed forces during World War I. Though juries failed to convict the publishers, their magazine went out of business. Love affairs with Dell, Edmund Wilson, Arthur Davison Ficke, and others drew Millay closer to the leftist literary and political avant-garde in New York. She wrote and directed an antiwar play, *Aria da Capo* (1920), began writing short stories (under the pseudonym Nancy Boyd), and continued to publish poems in popular magazines.

Then came *A Few Figs from Thistles* (1920). Its poems were saucy, defiant, witty little works sharply differing in tone from the serious, mystical "Renascence." A generation of young people found a metaphor for their own lifestyles in the surprising image in "First Fig:"

> My candle burns at both ends;
> It will not last the night;
> But ah, my foes, and oh, my friends—
> It gives a lovely light!

Dash guilt and sorrow, Millay was telling women; instead, seize the day with the boldness of men. Love must be free, not bound by unbreakable vows. Such gallant verse made her the most widely read poet in the United States.

Newly earned fame and money enabled her to travel from Greenwich Village to Rome, Vienna, Hungary, Albania, England, and the Left Bank in Paris. From time to time and place to place she engaged in notorious love affairs with women as well as with men. Her health was failing, however, and in 1922 her mother joined Millay as a traveling companion, at one point using her knowledge of herbs to help her daughter terminate a pregnancy.

Then, with the publication of *The Harp-Weaver, and Other Poems* (1923), Millay became the first woman to win the Pulitzer Prize in poetry. She embarked on highly successful reading tours around the United States and readings of her poetry on the new medium of radio. One of the most famous women in America, she received honorary doctorates, won more prizes for her poetry, and continued to publish poems, plays, and prose.

On July 18, 1923, she entered into an open marriage with a debonair Dutchman, Eugen Jan Boissevain, who provided financial security and relieved her of domestic chores. The newlyweds toured Asia and returned to live the rest of their lives on a 700-acre farm called Steepletop near Austerlitz, New York.

Millay went back to Europe to collaborate with Pulitzer Prize-winning poet George Dillon on *The Flowers of Evil*, a translation of Charles Baudelaire's *Les Fleurs du mal* (1936). Her adulterous affair with Dillon set the background for her *Fatal Interview* (1931). The strength of her affection for him is captured in lines she wrote on a note below his telephone number:

> Let us be fools & love forever,
> There was a woman, if tales be true,
> Who shattered Troy for a shepherd boy,
> Less beautiful than you.

In the late 1920's Millay threw herself back into social causes. She joined a protest march to plead for mercy for Nicola Sacco and Bartolomeo Vanzetti, a pair of labor agitators and draft-dodgers who were convicted for murder on evidence later refuted. Millay met personally with the governor of Massachusetts, who nevertheless refused to pardon the men or commute their sentences. They were executed in 1927.

Two catastrophes befell Millay in 1936. While she was at work on a verse drama, *Conversation at Midnight* (1937), a hotel fire on Sanibel Island, Florida, consumed her manuscripts. Also, she was accidentally flung from the passenger seat of a car, thereby suffering a back injury which caused years of pain and an eventual addiction to morphine.

As Nazi armies swept through Europe in the late 1930's and early 1940's, stealing a large part of Boissevain's fortune as plunder, Millay joined the war effort, publishing several volumes of propaganda and making many public speeches.

Then in 1944 her pen was stilled by a nervous breakdown. After her husband died in 1949 of a stroke after surgery for lung cancer, Millay sank. Her lifeless body was found at the foot of a staircase in her home on October 19, 1950.

ANALYSIS

Millay matured artistically at an early age and devoted her whole life to the conscientious exercise of her literary gift. A supremely lyrical poet, she wrote brief verses charged with feeling. Readers of her poetry find themselves overhearing, as it were, the passionate declarations and confessions of a plain, honest person with whom they can easily identify. Millay found a voice all her own: witty, insightful, straightforward, clear as a whistle, familiar and yet formal. She uses witty rhymes, well modulated assonance and alliteration, and finely crafted phrases with perfect diction. Outspoken in her advocacy of personal individuality and social justice, Millay expressed the post-Victorian morality of the

Jazz Age in the traditional vocabulary and verse forms of the former era.

Written when she was nineteen years old, the poem that established her fame, "Renascence," is a Wordsworthian song of praise to the infinite unseen power in nature and its connection to the human spirit. "The soul can split the sky in two," she cries, "And let the face of God shine through." Romantic joy proceeds from freedom; Millay celebrated that credo from the beginning to the end of her career. Ever true to the ideals of high Romanticism, Millay worships the transient yet transcendent beauty of nature. She was season-wise, attuned to the vagaries of nature's changing forces and forms. Without a specific theology or religion, she worships the eternal made manifest in the temporal realm. "Euclid alone," she averred, "has looked on Beauty bare." The poet praises abstract beauty, for while others have delighted in beautiful things aplenty, only the original genius of geometry has reached all the way to the abstract essence of beauty, "nothing, intricately drawn nowhere." This idealistic Romanticism was, nonetheless, in her renditions, realistic. She could find beauty in the toad or the slimy marsh no less than in sunset or flower.

Her modern wisdom could accommodate impermanence, loss, and change. Conservatives were shocked by her condoning infidelity in love, but it was essential to her philosophy of life. A lover should delight in the happiness of a day, or a month, or a half of a year, without allowing rancor or remorse to spoil the rest of the relationship. The heart must learn what the head knows, that love may not last. It surely cannot outlast the freedom in which it was born, even if the chains are forged by a religious vow of marriage.

Therein lay the conundrum at the core of Millay's life and literary work. The stance of a libertine is difficult, especially for a woman of that era. How could a woman, no matter how talented, escape from male domination and the inert cultural expectation that women serve as vessels to bear and nurture the ensuing generations? Attempts to live free from the customary constraints were met with ridicule, humiliation, and even assault. So, for a woman who would devote her life to poetry, the predicament was particularly acute. In her life, Millay found a successful solution to this problem in her open marriage with a loving and supportive husband. In her poetry and prose, she demands for a woman the same liberty as a man enjoys to create an independent, radiant identity of one's own.

Millay's passion for liberty was artistically united with a passion for order, as her preference for and mastery of traditional forms of poetry attest. Her brief lyrics compress passion to maximum intensity. Especially in the sonnet she found a verse form that can effectively impose order upon turbulent emotion and render it understandable. The sonnet's fourteen iambic lines give a poet the room to develop a thought, and they lend a regular rhythm to her utterance. As well as any poet, Millay mastered the Shakespearean sonnet with its three cross-rhymed quatrains and a bombastic closing couplet.

Although Millay hit her artistic stride early and found fame in youth, she fell out of favor with literary critics because she was modern without being a modernist. She did, occasionally, experiment with blank verse and free verse, but she did not adhere to the program of modernist contemporaries who rejected traditional poetry and sentimental verse. Her humor, optimism, whimsy, compassion, musicality, and way of revealing herself confounded the principles of Ezra Pound, T. S. Eliot, the New Critics, and other modernists whose preferences shaped the judgment of mid-twentieth century literary critics and anthologists. The *New Oxford Book of American Verse* (1976) did not include a single one of her poems.

Since that time Millay's artistic reputation has been revived, and, by more sympathetic academicians and the general public, she is regarded as something of an oasis in the wasteland of modernism. She has been studied as a force that advanced the congeries of various artistic, social, political, and ethical sensibilities usually associated with feminism.

A FEW FIGS FROM THISTLES

First published: 1920
Type of work: Poetry

Postwar disillusionment is thwarted by cynical yet light verse.

This slim volume of four sonnets and nineteen other brief lyrics overturned the tone of high seriousness in Millay's early poem "Renascence" and delighted a broader range of readers. The poet's new, plucky persona pricks the pretensions of stodgy moralists by ridiculing domesticity, remorse, and what she calls "pious planning."

In "The Penitent" she reconsiders the feeling of guilt brought on by a little sin and concludes that, if her sorrow is not genuine, she "might as well be glad!" In "The Merry Maid" she finds compensation for a broken heart in being freed from care. She hungers for a lover "wanton, light and false" but gives fair warning that she would leave him immediately except that she admires his beauty. "Oh, think not I am faithful to a vow!" she declares. "Faithless am I save to love's self alone."

There is much more than impudence in Millay's few figs. She justifies her wantonness as the psychological result of best wishes bestowed upon her by parents with contradictory personalities. "What should I be but a prophet and a liar," she asks, "Whose mother was a leprechaun, whose father

was a friar?" Hers would be of no common sort but a dual personality, "a harlot and a nun" combined into one. She strikes a note heard in later works as well. "What should I be but just what I am?" Here, in modern dress, reappears the high Romantic insistence on the autonomy of the individual following his or her own intuition.

Millay works a twist on the ancient poetical theme *carpe diem*. In her treatment, a woman—be she a merry maid, a penitent, a singing-woman, a philosopher, or the poet's own persona—must have the freedom and drive to seize pleasure during youth, before dreary duty and responsibility can tame her energy. Petulantly refusing to let "Sleep's dull knife" cut her day in half, she commands Time only to take away from the other end of her life, leaving youth unhampered.

THE HARP-WEAVER, AND OTHER POEMS

First published: 1923
Type of work: Poetry

Technically brilliant verses express deeper feeling with greater emotional maturity.

Dedicated to Millay's mother, this collection of thirty-nine sonnets, "The Ballad of the Harp-Weaver," and twenty-seven other short poems was awarded the Pulitzer Prize. It displays the poet at work in a more serious vein on the perplexities of life and love and particularly on the struggle of the artist to find eternal truths obscured by changing nature.

The eponymous ballad fathoms the currents of maternal love and self-sacrifice. Too poor to buy clothing for her son, a mother weaves on her harp clothes fit for a prince, singing in "a daft way" as she works her magic. The situation clearly represents Cora Millay's talents as a poet and a weaver. At poem's end, the mother, looking not a day older than nineteen years, is found with fingers "Frozen dead" in her harp.

Several of the lyrics probe the problematical aspects of erotic love. It delights, but it cloys. The poet likens its joys to those of wine, noting that as thirst augments wine's pleasures, so desire intensifies love's thrills. Love exercises sovereignty over the lover and the beloved, but the thralldom expires with the season. Millay's persona is satisfied to let love's play end with the summer and knows well that love dies in little ways, with hurtful words and lies. She even blesses Death for taking a lover in the full bloom of youth because it "cuts in marble/ What would have sunk to dust!"

The seventeen-sonnet sequence titled "Sonnets from an Ungrafted Tree" reflects upon the self-sacrifice of a wife who tends a dying husband long after their love has withered away. She looks upon him as a stranger sleeping in a familiar bed. The poet captures the agony of lingering time in a memorable metaphor likening the man to a clock, the "mainspring being broken in his mind." For all the despair and hopelessness of her situation, she manages to escape bitterness by feeling relief in having been unburdened of love and by experiencing the rapture of "making mean and ugly objects fair."

FATAL INTERVIEW

First published: 1931
Type of work: Poetry

A sonnet sequence explores the course of a doomed love affair.

The poet reached the peak of her powers in this sequence of fifty-two sonnets which deliver much unhappy wisdom on the perplexities of a failed love affair closely resembling that of Millay and Dillon. The first and last sonnets allude to the myth of Endymion and Selene, a goddess who falls in love with a handsome mortal. The poet's persona suffers love in the ancient way, on a grand scale like that of Cleopatra or Cressida.

The central problem, though, is as modern as it is ancient. The beloved defies possession even as the lover must possess. The poet's persona feels condemned to "drag [Love's] noisy chain" even as she longs to bind her beloved to her. Yet "what you cannot do," she tells him, "Is bow me down." In the twentieth sonnet the poet states it another way by declaring that beauty cannot be bought, even if it has been paid for. Likening erotic love of beauty to the freedom of a bird's flight, she reminds lovers that the turtle dove has never even heard of possessive love.

Thus these lovers begin their affair in freedom, "not in a ring" or a marriage vow to be forever faithful. In an unforgettable vignette, Millay depicts giving her love as generously as a country girl carries apples in her skirt and gives them all to her beau. The poet extols the ecstasy of love's consummation. "Heart," she encourages her lover,

> have no pity on this house of bone:
> Shake it with dancing, break it down with joy.
> No man holds mortgage on it; it is your own . . .

Millay, though, was wise enough to understand that Time is an enemy, whether by making the hours of love fly by, or by lengthening the day of grief, or by sapping beauty and strength away. She faces the facts in these, perhaps her most poignant lines:

> Love is not all; it is not meat or drink
> Nor slumber nor a roof against the rain,
> Nor yet a floating spar to men that sink
> And rise and sink and rise and sink again . . .

There may come a time when love either turns false or grows cold. Millay's philosophy of love offers a remedy for the anguish of lost love. The broken heart is a heart no more. It can be consoled by letting go, by being relieved of care, by realizing that "the bankrupt heart is free."

So the poet advises young lovers, in the phrase she coined, to burn their candles at both ends, so that all possible joy can be had before old age converts that unspent energy to doubts, fears, and feeble compromises.

SUMMARY

From the rugged quarry of her own life Millay hewed verbal gems of wisdom which teach modern youths the hard truths about life and love. She was the spokeswoman of her generation, and her poetry epitomized the new sensibility of the era, yet her voice speaks to all people for all time. Her spirit and her artistic achievement have been compared to the greatest women, and men, who ever wrote, from Sappho to Shakespeare. Among American poets, she ranks with Emily Dickinson, though in some respects they were of different temperaments; Dickinson, poet of the unlived life; Millay, poet of the exact opposite.

Though Millay's literary talent ripened in youth, it grew ever brighter with age. She became more outspoken as she penetrated more deeply the follies of twentieth century people and nations. Her faith in freedom, personal as well as political, never faltered. She delighted in the vigorous pursuit of happiness and the fearless expression of one's own individuality. In the face of the rigid conventions of her day, she championed the rights of women to do the same.

John L. McLean

BIBLIOGRAPHY

By the Author

POETRY:

Renascence, and Other Poems, 1917
A Few Figs from Thistles, 1920
Second April, 1921
The Ballad of the Harp-Weaver, 1922
The Harp-Weaver, and Other Poems, 1923
The Buck in the Snow, and Other Poems, 1928
Edna St. Vincent Millay's Poems Selected for Young People, 1929
Fatal Interview, 1931
Wine from These Grapes, 1934
Conversation at Midnight, 1937
Huntsman, What Quarry?, 1939
Make Bright the Arrows, 1940
There Are No Islands Any More, 1940
Invocation to the Muses, 1941
Collected Sonnets, 1941
The Murder of Lidice, 1942
Collected Lyrics, 1943
Poem and Prayer for an Invading Army, 1944
Mine the Harvest, 1954
Collected Poems, 1956

DRAMA:

The Princess Marries the Page, pr. 1917, pb. 1932
Two Slatterns and a King, pr. 1917, pb. 1921
Aria da Capo, pr. 1919, pb. 1920
The Lamp and the Bell, pr., pb. 1921
The Wall of Dominoes, pb. 1921
Three Plays, pb. 1926
The King's Henchman, pr., pb. 1927 (libretto; music by Deems Taylor)
Conversation at Midnight, pb. 1937, pr. 1961

NONFICTION:

Distressing Dialogues, 1924 (as Nancy Boyd)
Letters, 1952

TRANSLATION:

The Flowers of Evil, 1936 (of Charles Baudelaire)

About the Author

Brittin, Norman A. *Edna St. Vincent Millay.* Rev. ed. Boston: G. K. Hall, 1982.

Freedman, Diane P., ed. *Millay at One Hundred: A Critical Reappraisal.* Carbondale: Southern Illinois University Press, 1995.

Milford, Nancy. *Savage Beauty: The Life of Edna St. Vincent Millay.* New York: Random House, 2002.

Nierman, Judith. *Edna St. Vincent Millay: A Reference Guide.* Boston: G. K. Hall, 1977.

Thesing, William B., ed. *Critical Essays on Edna St. Vincent Millay.* New York: G. K. Hall, 1993.

DISCUSSION TOPICS

- How did World War I affect Edna St. Vincent Millay's social consciousness?

- What was Millay's attitude toward marriage?

- How does Millay use events and images from nature to describe human emotions?

- Why did Millay prefer the sonnet and other traditional poetic forms to free verse and other experiments of modernists such as Ezra Pound and T. S. Eliot?

- How did Millay contribute to the development of feminism?

ARTHUR MILLER

Born: New York, New York
October 17, 1915
Died: Roxbury, Connecticut
February 10, 2005

Clearly one of America's foremost dramatists, Miller has consistently penetrated the American consciousness and gained worldwide recognition for his probing dramas focusing on social awareness and individual liberty.

Inge Morath/Magnum

BIOGRAPHY

Arthur Miller, son of Jewish immigrants, was born on October 17, 1915, in New York City. His father, Isadore, born in Austria, ran a prosperous garment business, and his mother, Augusta Barnett Miller, was a schoolteacher. When his father's firm began to fail in 1928, the Millers moved to a suburban area of Brooklyn, an area that would be the model for the settings of *All My Sons* (1947) and *Death of a Salesman* (1949). From his mother, Miller inherited a strong sense of mysticism that would inform much of his later work. As a young boy, Miller resented his father's withdrawal, which was caused by his business failure. The figure of the failed father would later play a significant role in Miller's writing.

The young Miller came of age during the Depression of the 1930's. Seeing once-prosperous people on the streets begging for work affected him deeply. To him, the Depression signified the failure of a capitalist system of government and the tragedy of a generation of people who frequently blamed this failure on themselves. The events of the Depression and their impact on personal success and failure led Miller to probe individuals' relationship to their work and to consider critically the price they must pay for success or for their lack of it.

Like Biff Loman in *Death of a Salesman*, Miller was more athlete than scholar. His reading consisted largely of adventure stories and some of Charles Dickens's novels. Unable to get into college, he worked for his father, where he first became moved by the plight of salesmen. After rotating through a series of odd jobs, Miller worked in an automobile parts warehouse, where his savings from a low-paying job enabled him to save enough money to enroll in the University of Michigan. He relates this experience in *A Memory of Two Mondays* (1955).

While working, Miller became an avid reader and was especially impressed by Fyodor Dostoevski's *Bratya Karamazovy* (1879-1880; *The Brothers Karamazov*, 1912), a novel that focuses on a failed fatherland of fraternal rivalry. It contained the trial motif that Miller frequently returned to as a controlling theme in his own writing. Through sheer persistence, Miller finally convinced admissions officers at the University of Michigan to admit him. At the university, he became interested in social causes and began to develop a strong liberal philosophy. He studied playwriting under Kenneth Rowe and won two successive Avery Hopgood Awards, one in 1936 for *Honors at Dawn* and another in 1937 for *No Villain*.

In 1938, he won the Theater Guild National Award for *They Too Arise*. Following the style of the 1930's, Miller's early plays focused on young idealists struggling to eliminate social injustice. After college, he worked for the Federal Theater Project and wrote radio scripts. In 1944, he portrayed the feelings of the ordinary soldier in his screenplay "The Story of GI Joe" but was thwarted by motion-picture executives who wanted him to romanticize his work.

That same year, he had his first Broadway production, *The Man Who Had All the Luck* (1944), but his drama of a man dismayed by his incredible success was unconvincing and was not well received by critics or audiences. In 1947, Miller finally achieved success on Broadway with *All My Sons*, a better controlled and more topical work than *The Man Who Had All the Luck*, which had closed after four performances and had saddled Miller with a debt of over fifty thousand dollars. In 1949, *Death of a Salesman* achieved unprecedented critical acclaim and established Miller as a significant American playwright.

Disturbed by such repressive elements of the 1950's as the Cold War, the scare tactics of Senator Joseph McCarthy, and the betrayal by his onetime liberal friends who cited names before the House Committee on Un-American Activities, Miller wrote *The Crucible* (1953), which connected the witch-hunts of seventeenth century Salem, Massachusetts, to the often irresponsible search for communists in the 1950's. *The Crucible*, however, did not achieve immediate success. His next works were two one-acts, *A Memory of Two Mondays* and *A View from the Bridge* (both 1955). An expanded version of *A View from the Bridge* (1956) tells the story of Eddie Carbone, a longshoreman who, driven by incestuous desires for his niece, informs on his niece's boyfriend and other illegal immigrants living with him. Miller here shows how those who persecute others often have their own personal, hidden agendas, as was the case with McCarthy and his henchmen.

The mid-1950's were troubling times for Miller. After divorcing his first wife, Mary Grace Slattery, Miller married film star Marilyn Monroe in 1956 and became involved in her turbulent life and career. He was also cited for contempt of Congress for refusing to name names before the House Committee on Un-American Activities. Although he was acquitted on appeal, this ordeal exacted a financial and emotional toll on him. In 1961, his marriage to Monroe ended in divorce, and, in 1962, he married Ingeborg Morath, a *Magnum* photographer.

After a nine-year hiatus from the American stage, Miller wrote *After the Fall* (1964) and *Incident at Vichy* (1964). Both plays analyze the universal guilt associated with the genocide of the Jews. Miller returned to the form of family drama with *The Price* (1968), a drama depicting the rivalry of two brothers.

Continuing to experiment, Miller wrote *The Creation of the World and Other Business* (1972), a comedy based on Genesis; *The Archbishop's Ceiling* (1977), a play about power and oppression in a European communist country; *The American Clock* (1980), a montage view of the Depression focusing on the trials of one family; and *Danger: Memory!* (pb. 1986, pr. 1987), two short symbolic dramas exploring the mysteries hidden in past actions. Although these dramas failed to receive the critical acclaim of his earlier works, the continual revivals of his dramas, both on stage and on television, and his burgeoning international reputation kept Miller in the forefront of American theater.

In the early twenty-first century, having had an impressive career that spanned six decades, Arthur Miller was ill with cancer and heart trouble, and he was receiving hospice care in the Manhattan apartment of his sister, Joan Miller Copeland. At his request, he was moved by ambulance to his home in Roxbury, Connecticut, where he died a few days later, on February 10, 2005, succumbing finally to heart failure. His last play, *Finishing the Picture*, was produced in the fall of 2004.

ANALYSIS

A serious dramatist who believed in drama's ability to bring about change, Miller explored both the social and psychological dimensions of his characters. For him, individual dilemmas always grew out of the crucial social contexts that confront average people. He is much concerned with how individual morality is influenced by the social pressure that press unrelentingly upon them. His dramas attempt to go beyond being merely simple pieces or self-absorbed psychological studies to deal in depth with moral and ethical issues. He was interested in how ordinary individuals can live in unity and harmony with their fellow humans without sacrificing their own dignity.

In most of Miller's dramas, the family is the central unit through which he presented and explored social and ethical issues. Central to Miller's family drama is the image of the failed father. In selling out his fellow men to protect his family business, Joe Keller in *All My Sons* indirectly causes the death of his own son, Larry. In *Death of a Salesman*, Willy Loman forces his false dream on his son, with disastrous consequences. Both fathers commit suicide. Quentin's father in *After the Fall*, like Victor Franz's father in *The Price* and Moe Baum in *The American Clock*, lose money in the Depression and go into devastating psychological declines.

The sons in Miller's writing often strive to break their bonds with their fathers. Chris Keller, like Biff Loman, becomes disillusioned with his father's false values. Quentin sees through his father's phoniness, and Victor realizes his father's betrayal. The father often represents the misguided and self-centered dream of material success that must be attained at any cost. The sons must break away from their fathers and their fathers' worlds if they are to realize their own identities and lead more authentic lives.

In the family dramas, the mother has two sides. Kate Keller, like Linda Loman, both supports and defends her husband at all costs. In Miller's later plays, the mothers refuse to accept the failure of their husbands. Quentin's mother treats the father with contempt, and Victor's mother vomits on his bankrupt father. Although the mother may be a source of stability in support of the father, she can also be a source of disillusionment.

Although some critics disagree, Miller sees his common heroes as tragic figures willing to sacrifice everything for their convictions even though their convictions are often based on false ideals or on private delusions. Willy Loman is a washed-up salesman; Eddie Carbone, a troubled longshoreman; and John Proctor, a simple farmer. Each is willing to die for his beliefs. Miller's heroes proudly confirm their individual identity. Willy screams, "I am Willy Loman." Eddie must defend his name, and John Proctor in *The Crucible* would rather die than lend his name to an evil cause. Naming names and accusing others is a serious offense. Dying anonymously in death camps is an abomination.

Miller's heroes are not victims of inexorable social forces. Ultimately, they bear the responsibility for their own actions. Embedded in them is a sense of guilt, usually for sexual infidelity. Willy's affair in a Boston hotel room haunts him, and Proctor's adultery fills him with shame. Proctor, like Quentin, stands accused before his wife. The Puritan strain of sexual guilt, a recurring theme in American literature, is an undercurrent in Miller's work.

Guilt for Miller, however, extends beyond sexual transgressions. It is centered in a more serious crime: betrayal, either of oneself or of others. Miller's characters often live in worlds of illusion and denial, and those who escape from tragedy must undergo a process of self-discovery. In Miller's cosmos, individuals must act upon their own consciences without betraying their fellow humans for private gain.

His plays, which often involve litigation, put society itself on trial. In a post-Holocaust world, no one is innocent. After the Depression, a shadow has been cast on capitalism and its promise of salvation through material prosperity. Socialism, which once held out the dream of a universal brotherhood, has given way to totalitarianism. In this fallen world, the individual must learn how to live with dignity and honesty against a backdrop of disillusionment.

Although labeled a realist, Miller has experimented with a number of innovative dramatic techniques. In *Death of a Salesman*, he intersperses time sequences from the past and present without using flashbacks. In *After the Fall*, he employs expressionistic stage techniques in a stream-of-consciousness narrative. The device of a narrator in *After the Fall* and *A View from the Bridge* and the authorial comments in *The Crucible* introduce a distancing effect to his dramas. The montage effect in *The American Clock* and the Pinteresque absurdist style employed in *Danger: Memory!* demonstrate his ability to handle a variety of dramatic styles.

Miller's poetic use of idiomatic speech and his subtle deployment of dramatic symbols clearly indicate that his drama has moved far beyond photographic realism. Using a variety of approaches, Miller most often juxtaposes the past actions of his characters with the ethical dilemmas in which they find themselves. Through this technique, they are forced to define themselves in terms both of their social situations and of their moral convictions.

As Miller realized that his life was winding down, he felt compelled to write a final play, *Finishing the Picture*, to answer some of the questions that the public had about his life. This play, produced just months before his death, marked the end of a highly productive career.

FOCUS

First published: 1945
Type of work: Novel

In this novel, the first of only two in Miller's career, the protagonist learns to let go of his prejudices.

Arthur Miller's first play, *The Man Who Had All the Luck*, closed after only four performances in 1944, although in the same year, Miller received the Theatre Guild National Award. In this play, Miller was concerned with how people can find a spiritual home in an outside world that often is corrupt and destructive. It was essentially this concern that he explored in his first novel, *Focus*.

Initially, Lawrence Newman, a corporate personnel manager, is much concerned with propriety, with external appearances, as Willy Loman was in *Death of a Salesman*. The corporation for which he works gives him the sense of security that he needs, as does his neighborhood in Queens, where he is dependably loyal to the standards of behavior expected by his employers and by his neighbors.

Newman is racially intolerant. He builds his own self-esteem most effectively by categorizing people and filling groups in his mind with those whom he deems inferior to him. As he rides the subway to work every day, he observes the people around him, placing them conveniently into the categories that he has created. He places Jews in the column labeled "Avarice" and, by so doing, feels better about himself because he is a Gentile. Yet this sort of categorization goes still further. When he reads racist statements etched on the wall of the subway station or when he reads in the newspaper about the destruction of a synagogue by vandals, his heart races slightly because he feels that he is not alone and that, just possibly, a movement based on racial superiority is about to get underway.

Even though Newman supports his company's policy of anti-Semitic racial policies, he is demoted, which leaves him bewildered. By now, however, Gertrude has added a new dimension—sex—to his life. He had deplored what he thought to be the blatant sexuality of Jews as he observed them from his subway set, but now he is himself an eager participant in what he had deplored in them. His rigid world begins to seem ridiculous to him. His comfort zone has been breached.

His first sexual adventure with Gertrude emboldens Lawrence to the point that he protests his demotion. He begins to feel what it is like to be a Jew when he gets eyeglasses that make him look Jewish and result in his being the butt of anti-Semitic comments in his racially discriminatory workplace. He gradually begins to see Jews as individuals rather than as broad, generalized types.

His epiphany comes in the form of a dream in which he envisions a carousel revolving on a plot of land above an underground factory. Through this dream, he comes to realize that beneath surfaces one may also find something deeper, something not necessarily good. His most heroic moment comes in his own Queens neighborhood when a group of anti-Semitic hooligans attack the only Jewish resident in the block and Newman (whose name suggests the change that has taken place in him) comes to the aid of the neighbor. When the police arrive, they presume that Newman is a Jew, and he does not correct them.

In the course of his gradual transformation, Lawrence Newman is forced to realize that racial prejudices adversely affect not only their targets but also their perpetrators. He also realizes that those who are racially prejudiced eventually become the very caricatures that their racial categorizing has created of the groups on which they look with contempt.

ALL MY SONS

First produced: 1947 (first published, 1947)
Type of work: Play

A man who sacrifices the lives of others for personal wealth becomes responsible for the death of his own son.

All My Sons is a realistic drama with tragic overtones. The play is tightly structured. It takes place in a single day and a single place. Following the tradition of playwright Henrik Ibsen, Miller slowly unravels past events to reveal a moral wrong or sinister crime. Joe Keller is a prosperous manufacturer enjoying the fruits of his wealth. He is a jovial man with a loyal wife, Kate, and a devoted son, Chris, who will inherit his father's business. Miller said that he started the first scenes slowly, without much action, but he plants unmistakable hints of menace early in the play.

Despite its realistic tone, the play has the air of a fatalistic tragedy. Larry, Joe's son, was missing in action in World War II. After three years, he is presumed dead, yet Kate refuses to accept his death. As son, brother, and lover, Larry's haunting presence overshadows the entire action. The night before the play opens, a storm knocks down Larry's memorial apple tree, a sign of hidden guilt and the fall from innocence. Anne, Larry's old girlfriend, is staying in his room, which still contains Larry's clothes and his freshly polished shoes. Chris wants to marry Anne, but he is not sure that she has accepted Larry's death. Even after Anne has accepted his proposal, Chris still kisses her more as Larry's brother than as her fiancé. Also, as long as Kate will not accept Larry's death, Chris cannot have his mother's blessing to marry Anne.

Larry's death is linked to a hidden crime: Joe Keller knowingly sold defective engines to the Army, causing the deaths of twenty-one pilots. Joe has pushed the blame onto his innocent partner, who is serving a jail sentence. Kate will not accept Larry's death because Larry's death will point to Joe as the murderer of his own son. Because Larry did not fly any of the defective planes, Joe considers himself innocent in his son's death; Anne, however, reveals a letter from Larry in which Larry condemns his father for the deaths of the pilots and declares his intent to fly a suicide mission. Joe, who bears responsibility for his own son's death as well as for the deaths of the other pilots, commits suicide.

In *All My Sons*, Miller explores the hidden order of the universe. The crime that Keller tried to avoid comes back to haunt him. His dead son's voice condemns him from the grave. Although this play has been criticized for its melodramatic effects, *All My Sons* adds a tragic dimension to a realistic drama.

DEATH OF A SALESMAN

First produced: 1949 (first published, 1949)
Type of work: Play

An unsuccessful salesman relives his past, trying to discover the reasons for his failure, then commits suicide in order to leave his son his negligible insurance money.

More effectively than any other American drama, *Death of a Salesman* probes the nature of the American Dream and its promise of success. America was established as a new Eden, a place where one could transform the wilderness into a paradise of riches. The American myth created the pioneer hero who moved with ease to greener pastures. One side of Willy Loman is firmly grounded in this myth.

Willy's father was a traveling man who got rich peddling gadgets in South Dakota and then headed for Alaska. Willy's brother Ben is a true adventurer who walks into the jungles of Africa at seventeen and comes out rich. Ben, who is constantly on the move, shunning civilization and its laws, is the self-reliant hero of the American myth who conquers the wilderness and makes his fortune. As a salesman, Willy also sees himself as an adventurer who opens up new territories in New England— once the original frontier.

The play focuses on a longing for the lost Eden. Willy admires the scenery on his trips to New England. He longs to smell the lilacs and wisteria that once grew in his suburban idyll, now overshadowed by dingy apartment buildings. He wants to build a house in the country where he can raise chickens and grow things. In the end, this American Adam is reduced to the tragic figure of a down-and-out salesman planting lettuce in a barren garden in the dead of night as he deteriorates mentally and contemplates suicide.

The theme of the Edenic garden coincides with the theme of the outdoorsman and the Western myth of open spaces. Willy is not only a gardener who, like Henry David Thoreau, wants to remain close to nature; he is also a man who can chop down branches, build porches, and remodel ceilings. His sons long to leave cramped offices and go swimming. Biff wants to go west to raise horses or to be a carpenter.

Willy holds onto two other American myths. The myth of "having it made" is embodied in Dave Singleman, who at eighty-four can sit back and make sales from his hotel room. Dave is the popular hero whose funeral attracts throngs of his loyal customers. Dave projects the image of the man who has "made it" in the system and who can make money effortlessly. The second American myth to which Willy subscribes is the "get rich quick" scheme. Like Ben, he hopes to find diamonds. He encourages his sons to establish a million-dollar sporting goods business with no capital and little experience.

Willy has based his notion of success on popularity and appearances, but Willy himself does not make a good appearance. Both he and his sons are out of place in a competitive world. The business world is changing; old promises are worthless. When Willy is no longer productive, he is fired. In the end, he "sells" his life for a twenty-thousand-dollar insurance policy in order to stake his son's fortune. His death becomes merely another "get rich quick" scheme. Charley and Bernard, Willy's neighbors, prove that success can be achieved, but for Willy Loman, who has absorbed too many American Dreams, the system inevitably becomes destructive.

In 1949, *Death of a Salesman* won the New York Drama Critics Circle Award and the Pulitzer Prize. The play ran for 742 performances. In 1966, a television production played to seventeen million people. In 1975, it was successfully produced at the Circle in the Square theater with George C. Scott in the lead, and in 1984, it played Broadway again with Dustin Hoffman in the lead. In 1985, Hoffman was featured in another television production of the play. *Death of a Salesman* has been produced around the world. In his book *"Salesman" in Beijing* (1984), Miller documents an unprecedented Chinese production. The play still appears in most college anthologies and continues to be taught as an American classic.

THE CRUCIBLE

First produced: 1953 (first published, 1953)
Type of work: Play

In a repressive Puritan society that is executing innocent people as witches, a simple farmer refuses to barter his conscience for his life.

The Crucible is about the right to act upon one's individual conscience. In Puritan New England, Roger Williams, the founder of Rhode Island, demanded his right to act according to his personal conscience. In the nineteenth century, Henry David Thoreau considered the exercising of this right a moral obligation, even if exercising it resulted in breaking the law. The individual's right to follow his conscience is part of the American heritage. In *The Crucible*, Miller shows how an ordinary individual living in a repressive community gains tragic stature by sacrificing his life rather than betraying his conscience.

Salem is a divided and disturbed community. Hidden behind its sacred crusade are the petty grievances of the self-interested and the vengeful. The town's minister, the Reverend Paris, is desperately trying to stabilize his power and is more interested in maintaining his social position than in ministering to his congregation. When his daughter Betty, with Abigail Williams, Tituba, and other young girls, is seen dancing naked in the forest, he fears the scandal will bring down his ministry. Thomas Putnam is disturbed because he wants an excuse to confiscate his neighbor's land. His wife, Ann, is jealous of Rebecca Nurse, who has more children than she. Abigail Williams consciously seeks to avenge herself on Elizabeth Proctor, who dismissed her from the Proctors' service.

Miller clearly shows that in a community like this, which is at odds with itself, all that is needed to ignite hysteria is the specter of Satan, the epitome of insidious evil behind which small-minded people hide their own hostility and their quest for power. Soon experts such as John Hale are brought to Salem to find evil, even where it does not exist. Next, a high court invested with infallible judgment acts on the testimony of finger-pointing witnesses who indiscriminately accuse innocent people. Miller shows how judges at a purge trial lead witnesses to give the appropriate testimony. Tituba, a Barbados native, confesses to witchcraft because she knows what the authorities want to hear. The young girls accuse innocent people to deflect blame from themselves and to gain power and publicity.

In this climate of hysteria, John Proctor, a simple farmer, is called upon to act. Proctor, an independent man who is not afraid to oppose his minister and to work on the Sabbath, knows that the young girls are lying. At first, Proctor is reluctant to act. He withdraws from the town and tries to prevent his wife from incriminating herself. He not only knows that the young girls are making a sham of human justice but also knows that, deep down, he does not believe in witches—yet he will not confess to this heretical view.

Moreover, Proctor is a guilty man, a sinner, with hidden sin gnawing at his conscience. He has betrayed his wife and has committed adultery with Abigail Williams, so he also faces the judgment of his wife and has shaken her trust in him. Miller follows a theme in American literature, one that is especially pronounced in the works of Nathaniel Hawthorne. This theme examines the ways that private sin and nagging guilt intermingle with public sin. To save his wife and the town, Proctor must discredit Abigail, but to do so, he would have to expose his own guilt.

Proctor's battle with the court is doomed, for the repressive court is implacable. He first tries to present concrete evidence, but in the Puritan court such evidence is suspect. A list of character witnesses becomes a source for suspicion and further interrogation. To question the court is blasphemy. In times of political and religious hysteria, everyone, including the witnesses, is on trial. Mary Warren, a young girl who strives to act justly and responsibly, breaks down under the pressure of the court and the hysterical antics of Abigail. Proctor tries to expose Abigail as a morally loose woman and openly implicates himself as an adulterer, but his wife lies to protect him. Even though Governor Danforth can see that the accusations of witchcraft are questionable, he continues to commit himself to a course of injustice rather than admit a mistake and discredit the court.

Not being a saint like Rebecca Nurse, Proctor is willing to lie and confess to witchcraft so that he can live and raise his family. However, when he is asked to name names and sign a public confession, his conscience will not allow him to ruin the names of others or to have his name used to justify evil. Only if he can retain his individual dignity can he pass on to his children anything of value. Proctor, an ordinary man, takes extraordinary action and is resigned to dying for his convictions.

The Crucible opened on Broadway in 1953 to a lukewarm reception, but it was later revived Off-Broadway with more success. Jean-Paul Sartre wrote the screenplay for the French film version of *The Crucible, Les Sorcieres de Salem* (1955). In 1961, *The Crucible* was converted into an opera, and in 1967, it was adapted for television with George C. Scott in the lead role. *The Crucible* is Miller's most frequently produced work both in the United States and abroad.

AFTER THE FALL

First produced: 1964 (first published, 1964)
Type of work: Play

When a lawyer relives scenes from his past that test his ability to relate to the women in his life, he is forced to accept responsibility for his actions.

After the Fall demonstrates one man's struggle to survive in a fallen world. The fall from Eden is a recurrent theme in American literature—America, after all, was established as a kind of New World Garden, a bountiful paradise that would yield endless riches. It would bring forth an ideal community in which all individuals could live together in harmony and prosperity. The possibility of a fallen Eden, however, always lurked in the Puritan commitment to the individual's natural propensity for evil. Some of the greatest American authors—Nathaniel Hawthorne, Herman Melville, Henry James, and William Faulkner—have treated the theme of the fall. In *After the Fall*, Miller explores this theme in the light of the modern world.

Quentin, the main character, who feels that there is no God to judge his actions, is an alienated man. He tries to plead his case to a sympathetic listener who is neither seen nor heard.

Quentin, a once-successful lawyer, examines his own conscience and becomes aware of his own fall from innocence. Through Quentin, Miller explores the historical context which has led humanity into a state of universal guilt. With his new girlfriend, Holga, Quentin visits a Nazi concentration camp. At the site, he is amazed to realize that human beings created such atrocities to slaughter nameless victims. According to Miller's ethics, a hero dies affirming his identity by retaining the dignity of his name. Anonymous slaughter is anathema. The atrocities of the camps have made everyone, especially the survivors, guilty. Innocence is no longer possible, for the Holocaust of the Jews has violated all the principles of Judeo-Christian morality. The image of the concentration camp haunts Quentin throughout the play, a constant reminder that the world has fallen.

Quentin also experiences the guilt inherent in being part of a family. His father went bankrupt in the Depression, another symbol of the fall—a fall from economic stability that changed the American system and made once-successful men feel guilty for their own falls from prosperity. Quentin's mother blames his father for the father's failure to avoid economic disaster. Quentin becomes an accomplice as he begins to share her contempt for his father, inherent in which is the message that he himself must succeed. Dan is the brother who has remained loyal to the family, while Quentin, who sees through his father's phoniness, has separated himself from the family. In his quest for self-knowledge, Quentin tries to go beyond blaming his troubles on the actions of his parents. Quentin tries to see family life as part of a fallen world in which betrayal and loss of faith prevail.

Quentin defends his friend Lou, caught up in the national hysteria promoted by the investigations of the House Committee on Un-American Activities, another sign of the fall. The American system is being distorted by petty publicity seekers who have no conscience about destroying people's lives. People break faith and name names in absurd public confessions. They compromise their consciences for economic security.

The guilt, however, lies not only with the Committee. Lou, who once believed in the ideals of a communist brotherhood, has written a book distorting the facts about Russian life. The great idealistic cause of leftist sympathizers, such as Lou and Mickey, has been a fraud. The utopian vision that has been so much a part of the American consciousness has again failed; everyone is a "separate person." Mickey is willing to betray Lou; Max, Quentin's boss, will not easily tolerate Quentin's support of a communist. Quentin finds himself stymied by the breach of communal fidelity and is groping for answers in a fallen world.

Another sign of the fall from Eden is seen in the sexual fall and in the presence of Eve as temptress and betrayer. In *After the Fall*, betrayal has its locus in women. Quentin comes to realize that his wife, Louise, is not his innocent, unfilled Eve. Quentin's mother holds his father in contempt and refuses to share in the responsibility for their failure. Louise tries to separate herself from Quentin and to maintain her innocence. Maggie, the star singer whom Quentin subsequently marries, always sees herself as an innocent victim and forces Quentin to realize that he cannot save her from herself. The women in Quentin's life are judgmental and often label men as idiots. Only through Holga, a survivor of the Nazi concentration camps, does the alienated Quentin learn to accept the responsibility for his actions and to persevere.

After the Fall was partially inspired by Albert Camus's *La Chute* (1956; *The Fall*, 1957), which Miller saw as a book about troubles with women and about the impossibility of rescuing a woman who does not want to be rescued. The critics, however, could not divorce Miller's play from its author. Miller was accused of being cheap and sensational in publicly exploiting his relationship with Marilyn Monroe. The play was labeled a self-indulgent confession. Others found it confusing and uneven. Miller, in turn, accused the critics of not seeing beyond certain autobiographical allusions in order to penetrate the deeper meaning of the play. *After the Fall* opened on January 23, 1964, as the first production of the new Lincoln Center Repertory Theater. The play was adapted for television in 1974 and was revived Off-Broadway in 1984, with Frank Langella in the leading role.

THE PRICE

First produced: 1968 (first published, 1968)
Type of work: Play

This play revisits much of the territory that was part of Miller's social consciousness throughout his career as a dramatist.

The Price involves two brothers, Victor and Walter, and focuses on the distribution of their dead parents' belongings, all housed in a ten-room brownstone. The secondhand furniture broker, Solomon, has offered a thousand dollars for these belongings, and Victor has reached a tentative agreement with him, although his wife and brother both urge him to hold out for three times the amount offered.

The play involves family secrets and duplicity. The brothers' father, who had been reasonably prosperous, suffered the fate of many during the Great Depression of the 1930's and was reduced to living at a bare subsistence level. He made his sons realize that he did not have the wherewithal to send them to college. Victor accepted his fathers' penury at face value, but Walter, who suspected that his father had squirreled away some money to increase his own sense of security, struggled to continue his education, eventually becoming a surgeon. Victor, meanwhile, became a police officer and, during the action of the play, has served on the police force for twenty-eight years.

As Walter's fortunes increased, Victor at one point approached his brother, requesting a five-hundred-dollar loan so that he could continue his education. Walter, however, although he was easily able to spare the money, would not make the loan because of his suspicion, which proved to be quite accurate, that their father was hiding money from his sons.

Victor was always loyal to his father, even though his wife, Esther, wished that he might be slightly less loyal and might do something that would enable the two of them to lead more comfortable existences. Victor, who is scrupulously honest, could certainly use the money from the sale of his father's assets, but he insists that the proceeds be shared equally with Walter, who has little need for them. Indeed, Walter suggests that the brothers simply donate their father's effects to the Salvation Army in his name so that he might take a tax write-off that he would share with Victor. Victor, however, feels that he has made a commitment to Solomon and that he must honor that commitment.

Walter's monetary success has done little to provide him with a happy life. He suffered a nervous collapse and had to be confined to a mental institution for some time. His wife has divorced him. Nevertheless, Victor begins to question whether his family's life was worth the sacrifices he made to sustain it when Walter defected from his father's house.

Walter offers Victor, soon to retire, a job as a hospital administrator. Victor wonders if he is too old to embark on a new career, but then he thinks of the eighty-nine-year-old Solomon, who, in buying out the estate of the brothers' father for a thousand dollars, is setting himself up in a new furniture venture. As the play ends, Walter has come to view himself and Victor as two halves of the same person. Raised in the same household, they were forced to invent their identities when their father suffered business reverses. A bifurcation took place as each went in his own direction.

SUMMARY

Miller examined both the psychological and sociological makeup of his troubled characters. His heroes are common men who relentlessly pursue either their firm convictions or their misguided illusions. Using family relationships as starting points, Miller's plays confront moral dilemmas, focusing on the individual's responsibility to be true to himself or herself as well as part of the human race. His concern with the ordinary individual's struggle for self-definition in a troubled world not only made him a renowned American playwright but gained for him a worldwide reputation as well. He is one of the most frequently studied playwrights in the American canon.

Paul Rosefeldt; updated by R. Baird Shuman

BIBLIOGRAPHY

By the Author

DRAMA:

Honors at Dawn, pr. 1936

No Villain, pr. 1937

The Man Who Had All the Luck, pr. 1944, pb. 1989

All My Sons, pr., pb. 1947

Death of a Salesman, pr., pb. 1949

An Enemy of the People, pr. 1950, pb. 1951 (adaptation of Henrik Ibsen's play)

The Crucible, pr., pb. 1953

A Memory of Two Mondays, pr., pb. 1955

A View from the Bridge, pr., pb. 1955 (one-act version)

A View from the Bridge, pr. 1956, pb. 1957 (two-act version)

Collected Plays, pb. 1957 (includes *All My Sons, Death of a Salesman, The Crucible, A Memory of Two Mondays,* and *A View from the Bridge*)

After the Fall, pr., pb. 1964

Incident at Vichy, pr. 1964, pb. 1965

The Price, pr., pb. 1968

The Creation of the World and Other Business, pr. 1972, pb. 1973

The Archbishop's Ceiling, pr. 1977, pb. 1984

The American Clock, pr. 1980, pb. 1982

Arthur Miller's Collected Plays, Volume II, pb. 1981 (includes *The Misfits, After the Fall, Incident at Vichy, The Price, The Creation of the World and Other Business,* and *Playing for Time*)

Two-Way Mirror, pb. 1984

Danger: Memory!, pb. 1986, pr. 1987

Plays, pb. 1988-1995 (5 volumes)

The Ride Down Mt. Morgan, pr., pb. 1991

The Last Yankee, pb. 1991, pr. 1993

Broken Glass, pr., pb. 1994

Mr. Peter's Connections, pr. 1998, pb. 1999

Resurrection Blues, pr. 2002

Finishing the Picture, pr. 2004

LONG FICTION:

Focus, 1945

The Misfits, 1961

SHORT FICTION:

I Don't Need You Any More, 1967

Homely Girl, A Life, and Other Stories, 1995

DISCUSSION TOPICS

- What ethical compromises do some of the major characters in Arthur Miller's plays make? Why do they make such compromises?

- Discuss the role that personal and societal failure play in some Miller plays that you have read.

- Discuss the roles that parent-child and husband-wife relationships play in the Miller plays that you have read.

- Discuss Miller's concern with the nature of guilt as reflected in his writing.

- To what extent do his main characters bear responsibility for their own actions?

- Discuss the interplay between reality and fantasy in one or more of Miller's plays.

- What specific elements of historical events play a part in Miller's writing?

- What effect do social pressures have on at least three of his major characters?

Arthur Miller

SCREENPLAYS:
The Misfits, 1961
Everybody Wins, 1990
The Crucible, 1996 (adaptation of his play)

TELEPLAY:
Playing for Time, 1980

NONFICTION:
Situation Normal, 1944
In Russia, 1969 (photo essay; with Inge Morath)
In the Country, 1977 (photo essay; with Morath)
The Theater Essays of Arthur Miller, 1978, revised and expanded 1996 (Robert A. Martin, editor)
Chinese Encounters, 1979 (photo essay; with Morath)
"Salesman" in Beijing, 1984
Conversations with Arthur Miller, 1987 (Matthew C. Roudané, editor)
Conversations with Arthur Miller, 2002 (Mel Gussow, editor)
Spain, 1987
Timebends: A Life, 1987
Arthur Miller and Company, 1990 (Christopher Bigsby, editor)
The Crucible in History, and Other Essays, 2000
Echoes Down the Corridor: Collected Essays, 1947-2000, 2000
On Politics and the Art of Acting, 2001

MISCELLANEOUS:
The Portable Arthur Miller, 1995 (Christopher Bigsby, editor)

About the Author

Bloom, Harold, ed. *The Crucible: Annotated and with an Introduction by Harold Bloom.* Philadelphia: Chelsea House, 1999.

Brater, Enoch, ed. *Arthur Miller's America: Theater and Culture in a Time of Change.* Ann Arbor: University of Michigan Press, 2005.

Carson, Neil. *Arthur Miller.* London: Macmillan, 1982.

Gottfried, Martin. *Arthur Miller: His Life and Work.* Cambridge, Mass.: Da Capo Press, 2003.

Korrey, Stefani. *Arthur Miller's Life and Literature: An Annotated and Comprehensive Guide.* Lanham, Md.: Scarecrow Press, 2000.

Martin, Robert A., ed. *Arthur Miller: New Perspectives.* Englewood Cliffs, N.J.: Prentice-Hall, 1982.

Miller, Arthur. *Timebends: A Life.* New York: Grove Press, 1987.

Moss, Leonard. *Arthur Miller.* Rev. ed. Boston: Twayne, 1980.

Schlueter, June, and James K. Flanagan. *Arthur Miller.* New York: Frederick Ungar, 1987.

Larry Colwell

HENRY MILLER

Born: New York, New York
December 26, 1891
Died: Pacific Palisades, California
June 7, 1980

Writing with enormous energy and unparalleled frankness in a style derived from extensive self-education and a sharp ear for the American vernacular, Miller extended the boundaries of imaginative prose while bringing psycho-surrealism into American fiction.

BIOGRAPHY

Henry Valentine Miller was born in the Yorkville section of Manhattan's Upper East Side the day after Christmas in 1891. His father, Heinrich Miller, was an affable raconteur who ran a tailor shop, while his mother, Louis Marie Nieting, liked the stability and order of a stolid community of merchants and conventional shops. Before Miller was a year old, his family moved across the East River to the Williamsburg section of Brooklyn, where young Henry spoke German until he entered school. He was a good student, ranking second in his high school class, and upon graduation in 1909, he entered City College of New York but dropped out after only one term.

For the next few years, he worked at a variety of jobs, traveled to California (where he met Emma Goldman), read widely, and began to dream of becoming a writer. Financial restrictions kept pulling him back to Brooklyn and his parents' home, and after a number of affairs, he married Beatrice Wickens, a piano teacher, in 1917. Two years later, his daughter Barbara was born, and in that same year, his first written works were published—a few reviews for a small short-story magazine called *The Black Cat*, based in Salem, Massachusetts.

Miller succeeded in getting a job as an employment manager for Western Union Telegraph Company in 1920, a position he used as the basis for the first part of *Tropic of Capricorn* (1939), and over a three-week vacation in 1922, he wrote the manuscript for a novel to be called *Clipped Wings*, about telegraph messengers. The novel was never published, but he felt that March 22, 1922, was his "first day of being a writer."

In 1924, he divorced Wickens when he met June Smith, a dancer in a Brooklyn club; June was the basis for the Mara/Mona figure of Miller's autobiographical romances. Miller and Smith were married as soon as his divorce was granted, and for the next few years, he tried several methods of earning a living while unsuccessfully pursuing a career as a writer. In 1927, while his wife was traveling in Europe with a female friend, Miller wrote a twenty-six-page outline of what would become *The Rosy Crucifixion* epic—including *Tropic of Capricorn, Sexus* (1949), *Plexus* (1953), and *Nexus* (1960)—and began a revised version of his Western Union novel, retitled *Moloch*, which was never published.

One of his wife's male friends sent the Millers to Europe in 1928 to find a publisher, but Miller was uncomfortable there, and as his marriage was beginning to deteriorate, he returned to the United States. There he began a third novel in 1929 called *Crazy Cock*, which was also never published. As his marriage drifted toward a complete collapse in 1930, Miller returned to Paris alone to begin a decade of expatriatism. He subsisted on handouts, the generosity of friends, and occasional newspaper work. Although the first wave of that period's American expatriates had returned to the United States, Miller became friends with an interesting

1751

group of international avant-garde artists. In 1931, the year he began his intense friendship with Anaïs Nin, he started another novel, which he saw as a "Parisian notebook" and which was to appear eventually as *Tropic of Cancer* (1934).

Miller's wife arrived unexpectedly in Paris in October, 1931, and while she and Miller were unable to rescue their marriage, her involvement with Nin led to the transformation of the Miller/Nin relationship from one of mutual admiration and encouragement to a secret sexual attachment as well. Nin and Miller corresponded steadily throughout the 1930's, and Nin provided the money from a personal loan to assist in the publication of *Tropic of Cancer*. The book was widely admired by some leading literary figures, such as Ezra Pound and T. S. Eliot (who wrote that it was "a rather magnificent piece of work"), but because of its sexual expressiveness, it was banned in every English-speaking country.

Miller divorced Smith in 1934 and returned briefly to New York in 1935 before spending the remainder of the decade in Europe, where he wrote *Black Spring* (1936), a book of essays called *Max and the White Phagocytes* (1938), a study of D. H. Lawrence which was not published until 1980, and *Tropic of Capricorn*. As World War II threatened to engulf Europe, Miller left Paris (with a ticket purchased by Nin) to visit the British writer Lawrence Durrell in Greece, which became the setting for his rhapsodic travel journal, *The Colossus of Maroussi: Or, The Spirit of Greece* (1941).

Arriving in New York in 1940, broke and unable to find an American publisher for the books he had been writing, Miller toured the United States with the artist Abraham Rattner, a trip which became the basis for *The Air-Conditioned Nightmare* (1945). In the early 1940's, Miller began to write the trilogy that formed the body of *The Rosy Crucifixion*, the epic account of his life with June Smith in the 1920's. James Laughlin, the visionary American publisher of New Directions Press, began to send Miller steady advances against royalties for books he could legally publish in the United States.

Miller journeyed to the West Coast in 1944, hoping to find some kind of work in Hollywood, and when this failed, he settled in the rugged California coastal country of Big Sur and married Janina Lepska. Miller's daughter Valentine was born in 1945, and although *Tropic of Cancer* had been sell-

ing steadily in Europe, Miller was unable to collect any royalties and continued to struggle financially. When *Sexus* was published in 1949, the year after Miller's son Tony was born, the extreme frankness of its account of sexual behavior upset even some of his longtime supporters such as Durrell, and in 1950, the book was banned worldwide.

Miller and Lepska were divorced in 1952, the year he wrote *The Books in My Life*, and in the following year, Miller married Eve McClure. During the 1950's, Miller was gradually being recognized by some conventional critics as an important writer, and the publication of *Big Sur and the Oranges of Hieronymus Bosch* in 1957 enabled readers to see his more genial, less rebellious side. He was elected to the National Institute of Arts and Letters in 1958 and concluded his exploration of his life in the 1920's with *Nexus* in 1960, although he maintained for many years that there would be a sequel.

Barney Rosset of Grove Press challenged the restrictions on the rights of writers and publishers by issuing *Tropic of Cancer* in an American edition in 1961, and the book immediately became a best seller. Miller and McClure were divorced in 1963, and *Tropic of Cancer* was finally ruled not to be obscene after two years of trials. Miller bought a residence in Pacific Palisades in the mid-1960's and began to publish shorter books of recollections and reflections with Noel Young's Capra Press. In 1967 he married Hoki Tokuda. The marriage lasted three years and led to Miller's *Insomnia: Or, The Devil at Large* (1970), and he spent the 1970's writing only on occasion but finally being celebrated by friends and admirers who recognized him as an honored sage and important figure in American literary history.

ANALYSIS

Miller's work was misunderstood from the very beginning not only because of its startling candor and sexual explicitness but also because Miller was one of the foremost exponents of many of the modernist techniques which traditional commentators were unprepared to evaluate or understand. For one thing, Miller (like artist Pablo Picasso and the composer Igor Stravinsky) challenged the limits of conventional composition, refusing to be bound by the "rules" of unity or the linear demands of chronology. His books were not exactly novels or autobiographies or journals or essays but instead blended those forms into a mutant or hybrid amalgam which combined some of the elements of various genres generally kept separate.

Also, Miller's literary voice ranged from the conversational to the oratorical, with many variants along the scale, and his use of language ranged from his mastery of American colloquial speech to his proficiency with many different modes of rhetorical declaration. At the root of all these elements, Miller drew on—indeed, plunged into—the depths of his subconscious mind in an effort to create as complete and accurate a picture of his sensibility as it evolved across the middle decades of the twentieth century as his means allowed. The narrative consciousness of his "autonovels" was an archetype of the artist-as-hero, a replacement for the more traditional adventurer, athlete, soldier, or industrialist of earlier American fiction, and because this artist/hero grew and changed with the author, he was never completely captured in any single volume Miller wrote.

For this reason, critics have often suggested that Miller's books lack form and structure, but Miller worked throughout his career from a rough outline he developed in the 1920's, a sprawling chart which mapped the direction of two progressive narratives. The first and more specific one would be an epic of artistic and emotional development, in which the extraordinary sexual maelstrom he inhabited with June Smith would be explored in unprecedented depth. This track was called "Capricorn" in his notes, and eventually came to include *Tropic of Capricorn, Sexus, Plexus* (which was a failure), and *Nexus* and remained incomplete in Miller's mind until his death. The other track, which eventually disclosed its form as it was written, derived from Miller's ideas about how an artist might live in an ideal social community. It had its origins in the world of childhood which he recalled as a kind of paradise he had lost long ago and hoped to regain in another form through the self's revelation in artistic perceptions.

Miller took as his model Walt Whitman's "Song of Myself" (1855), and the form of the work is determined by the collision of the phenomena of the universe and the evolving artistic consciousness of the author. This track began with *Tropic of Cancer*, a book which declared the fully formed but still developing self of the author in opposition to a landscape of blight and erosion; it then moved both back toward a dreamlike past in *Black Spring* and outward to a more congenial environment in *The Colossus of Maroussi*. Eventually it moved on to a semi-conclusion in *Big Sur and the Oranges of Hieronymus Bosch*; this track actually includes many of Miller's letters to Durrell, Nin, and others.

In the first group (a triad if *Plexus* is discarded), the author is the prime agent of the action, a character in flux whose future is unclear, whose present is in turmoil, and whose life is instinctual, immediate, and often psychologically devastating. In the second group, a quartet, the author is more of an observer than an actor, prepared by the events of the triad to comment on, evoke and describe, and evaluate everything he sees.

The crucial link between the two tracks is the fact that the triad should explain the artist who erupts into being and song in *Tropic of Cancer*, but in *Nexus*, the tone and mood of the narration (Miller writing in 1960) is hardly like the defiant snarl that proclaims a unique, dangerous, and compelling new creation. This failure of sorts is typical of Miller's inability to realize his aspirations completely, but the mysteries that remain are a part of the appeal of his work, and the struggle toward clarity and self-understanding is as fascinating in its dead ends and tortured turnings as in its occasional moments of satisfaction and fulfillment. Miller's attempts to understand and express the feminine equivalent of his traditionally masculine sensibility is part of a goal he never really reaches, but—as is the case in much modernist art—the journey is as important to the traveler as the destination.

Two additional related factors further complicate Miller's work. One is his use of the "I" narrator, a device which was valuable for the process of self-creation but confusing to critics who tended to assume that there was a fairly specific equivalence between the author and his central character. Miller however maintained, "If I lie a bit now and then it is mainly in the interest of truth," and his essential point is that any technique for establishing "reality" is appropriate and justified.

Similarly, many readers have been troubled by his treatment of women. In actuality, the attitudes of various male characters are not representative of the author at all, and in many cases, they are used as indications of the failure of the speaker to find love and his neurotic retreat into physical gratification as a substitute for a more complete relationship. It is necessary to see passages which exhibit anxiety and hatred as reflecting a national psychosis that is part of the society Miller constantly criticizes in his desire to see a utopian America. This does not mean that Miller is entirely free from some of the attitudes he expresses but that, as in most aspects of his work, everything is more complex than any single instance might suggest.

TROPIC OF CANCER

First published: 1934
Type of work: Novel

Fortified with gleeful anger and the energy of creative awareness, an underground artist prowls the streets of Paris recording human erosion and redemptive beauty.

Even after the close of the twentieth century, *Tropic of Cancer* still has the power to startle and overwhelm a reader. Its wild, violent language, its immense force, its radiant paeans to the historic beauty of Paris, and its unsettling descriptions of a society in an advanced state of decomposition reflect a bottom dog's sense of the world that is still relevant and disturbing.

Even the fairly explicit sexual passages retain the power to shock and disturb, not because of their pornographic content but because they show the psychotic self-absorption of people ruined by social stratification and personal egocentricity. Miller wrote the book as a declaration of his own survival after a wrenching psychic experience, and his exuberant embrace of nearly every aspect of existence is a reflection of his discovery that he had found a voice and a form appropriate to the ideas and ambitions he had been harboring for his entire adult life. Before the book was published, Nin read the manuscript and accurately described the protagonist as "the mould-breaker . . . the revolutionist," and the revolution Miller was proclaiming was part of the modernist enterprise of challenging conventional but no longer viable authority.

One aspect of this challenge was the form of the book itself. It was begun originally as a kind of journal called "Paris and Me," and Miller eventually divided the book into fifteen sections. It has little character development, however, beyond the narrator's personal journey, a discontinuous sense of chronology, no plot in any familiar sense, no real dramatic events, and no conclusion. Instead, the narrative drifts and drives from "the fall of my second year in Paris" (in 1929) and continues in rhythmic lurches to the spring of 1931, but time is elastic. Days and months have no particular meaning, as the narrator has no regular job or any other specific schedule. This enables him to roam freely, at random primarily, so that he is able to avoid all the traps which have led his companions to spiritual destruction.

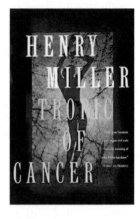

Certain motifs recur throughout the book. There are many scenes of male bonding, including men eating, drinking, arguing, complaining, and womanizing together. One of the most striking among these is section 8, in which Miller describes Van Norden, a nonspiritual man, as a mechanical monster who is something of a double for the protagonist. These sections are often bracketed with descriptions of women from the perspective of male lust. In passages such as the one in section 3, where the protagonist celebrates the qualities of Germaine, a whore he finds admirable, Miller is criticizing the narrowness and self-centered posturing of the men in the book. These passages are often also apostrophes to the mythic beauty and mysterious power of Woman, what Norman Mailer calls Miller's "utter adoration," reflecting "man's sense of awe."

A third motif includes an introduction of the comic into almost everything so that mundane difficulties become a source of humor rather than a cause for concern. This capacity for appreciating the comic aspect of a generally frustrating and discouraging pattern of searching for food, love, friendship, and so on is what separates the protagonist from nearly everyone else, and this gives Miller, as his fourth motif, a pure vision of ecstasy generated by the almost delirious contemplation of beauty in many forms, particularly in the city itself.

Section 13 offers Miller's powerful tribute to artist Henri Matisse, constructed in terms of the artist's use of light—a continuing fascination for Miller, who sets it against the darkness and sterility of the cancerous world. The fact that the protagonist can emerge from a realm of human decomposition with his sense of wonder at the phenomena of the universe intact is what makes the book exhilarating in spite of all the failure it examines. As the book moves toward a conclusion, or at least an ending or stopping, Miller becomes more and more rhapsodic, exclaiming "I love everything that flows," in a tribute to writer James Joyce.

On the last pages of the book, after a bizarre interlude spent teaching at a boys' school in Dijon (a job Nin helped Miller obtain), the protagonist steps out of a doomed culture and into a landscape of serenity. For a moment, as he regards the River Seine, he is able to imagine himself merging with the great flow of cosmic energy that animates the universe, his own manic energy temporarily spent and his psychic demons relegated to the realm he has left. The culmination of the artist's development at the end of *Tropic of Cancer* is, as Jay Martin says, proof that he is now the man who can write the book.

TROPIC OF CAPRICORN

First published: 1939
Type of work: Novel

A man is rescued from a desolate existence by a woman whose romantic allure is as powerful as it is mysterious.

Henry Miller planned to explore his relationship with June Smith in a multivolume proto-epic that covered his life in the 1920's in extraordinary detail. While his plans were never completely carried out, *Tropic of Capricorn* is the first book in the series, an introduction to the world in which he was living and a prologue to the later volumes, which concentrate on his life with Smith. It is divided into three parts, beginning with the protagonist employed by the Cosmodemonic Telegraph Company, an apt name for the metaphorical conceit he developed to dramatize the bureaucratic insanity of modern

industrial society. As an employment manager, the protagonist is able to meet and describe a staggering variety of people, representative of a full range of strange and fascinating characters in the United States.

After the failure of his marriage, the narrator is thrown into a kind of sexual psychic hell that almost destroys his mental stability. Then, he is redeemed by a woman he barely knows but who promises to lead him from, as Jay Martin puts it, "the Inferno of civilization and the Purgatorio of sensuality into the Paradiso of the liberated imagination." The book concludes with the protagonist so totally absorbed by his idealized sense of love that it is clear that he is on the verge of further psychic calamity, but the aura of romance is so great that it overwhelms everything else, including judgment and perspective.

BIG SUR AND THE ORANGES OF HIERONYMUS BOSCH

First published: 1957
Type of work: Journal

Toward the end of his career, a writer finds peace and serenity amid personal and public distraction in a landscape of wonder.

In 1944, Miller settled in what he called "my first real home in America," a cabin on Partington Ridge, located in the rugged beauty of the Big Sur region of the California coast. He lived there for the following twelve years, and in *Big Sur and the Oranges of Hieronymus Bosch*, he tried to combine his vision of an ideal community with the somewhat less perfect situation of his life. In a painfully honest and often mundane report of his day-to-day life as a writer, parent, counselor, and local explorer, Miller produced what Norman Mailer calls a "wise record" of psychic survival. Still dedicated to his work (this is the time when Miller wrote *Sexus*, the heart of the triad that covers his life in the 1920's), Miller was not as animated by the fire of wrath that drove his earlier work, and much of what he covers is amusing but not widely significant.

For readers familiar with Miller's life and work, the book is like visiting an old friend, and Miller's sense of style and language is still impressive enough to make his descriptions of the landscape and his observations about the world captivating. Except for the last hundred pages, though, there is little narrative suspense, and Miller's occasional pronouncements as the sage of Big Sur, the center of an artistic gathering of serious and talented writers, are dissipated by frequent homilies and banal commentary. Too often, the genial ironist becomes the coy famous writer (as in references to "my quaint biographical romances"), but in the last part of the book, originally published separately as

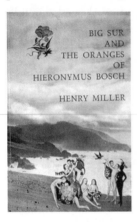

"The Devil in Paradise," Miller provides the only real portrait of evil in his work.

A visit from an old acquaintance from his Paris days, the astrologer Conrad Moricand, brings an infusion of Old World decadence into this New World of semi-innocence. Moricand is a monster of self-obsession, vain, supercilious, and haughty, and

Miller presents him as a parasitical creature controlled totally by an icy egotism. The contrast between the two men is an effective demonstration of how far Miller himself is now from the cancerous world of the 1930's when he began his "song" and how much more he is capable of creating than the erotica which made him notorious.

SUMMARY

Miller became famous for the wrong reasons and stayed famous for the right ones. Although his books have never been studied in American schools, he is one of the United States' most widely read authors. Beyond the shock of his examinations of previously forbidden aspects of human behavior, readers have discovered his erudition, his insight into every aspect of human nature, his mastery of an appealing style of expression (what George Orwell called his "friendly American voice"), and his judicious critique of contemporary society. His work, although uneven, eccentric, sprawling, and not always tasteful, remains compelling in accordance with Ezra Pound's definition of literature—"News that stays news."

Leon Lewis

BIBLIOGRAPHY

By the Author

LONG FICTION:
Tropic of Cancer, 1934
Black Spring, 1936
Tropic of Capricorn, 1939
The Rosy Crucifixion, 1949-1960, 1963 (includes *Sexus,* 1949, 2 volumes; *Plexus,* 1953, 2 volumes; *Nexus,* 1960)
Quiet Days in Clichy, 1956

DRAMA:
Just Wild About Harry: A Melo-Melo in Seven Scenes, pb. 1963

NONFICTION:
Aller Retour New York, 1935
What Are You Going to Do About Alf?, 1935
Max and the White Phagocytes, 1938
Money and How It Gets That Way, 1938
The Cosmological Eye, 1939
Hamlet, 1939, 1941 (2 volumes; with Michael Fraenkel)
The World of Sex, 1940, 1957
The Colossus of Maroussi: Or, The Spirit of Greece, 1941

The Wisdom of the Heart, 1941

The Angel Is My Watermark, 1944 (originally published in *Black Spring*)

Murder the Murderer, 1944

The Plight of the Creative Artist in the United States of America, 1944

Semblance of a Devoted Past, 1944

The Air-Conditioned Nightmare, 1945

The Amazing and Invariable Beauford Delaney, 1945

Echolalis: Reproductions of Water Colors by Henry Miller, 1945

Henry Miller Miscellanea, 1945

Obscenity and the Law of Reflection, 1945

Why Abstract?, 1945 (with Hilaire Hiler and William Saroyan)

Maurizius Forever, 1945

Patchen: Man of Anger and Light, with a Letter to God by Kenneth Patchen, 1946

Of, by and About Henry Miller: A Collection of Pieces by Miller, Herbert Read, and Others, 1947

Portrait of General Grant, 1947

Remember to Remember, 1947

Varda: The Master Builder, 1947

The Smile at the Foot of the Ladder, 1948

The Waters Reglitterized, 1950

The Books in My Life, 1952

Nights of Love and Laughter, 1955 (Kenneth Rexroth, editor)

Argument About Astrology, 1956

A Devil in Paradise: The Story of Conrad Mourand, Born Paris, 7 or 7:15 p.m., January 17, 1887, Died Paris, 10:30 p.m., August 31, 1954, 1956

The Time of the Assassins: A Story of Rimbaud, 1956

Big Sur and the Oranges of Hieronymus Bosch, 1957

The Red Notebook, 1958

The Intimate Henry Miller, 1959 (Lawrence Clark Powell, editor)

The Henry Miller Reader, 1959 (Lawrence Durrell, editor)

Reunion in Barcelona: A Letter to Alfred Perlès, 1959

To Paint Is to Love Again, 1960

The Michael Fraenkel-Henry Miller Correspondence, Called Hamlet, 1962 (2 volumes)

Stand Still Like the Hummingbird, 1962

Watercolors, Drawings, and His Essay "The Angel Is My Watermark," 1962

Books Tangent to Circle: Reviews, 1963

Lawrence Durrell and Henry Miller: A Private Correspondence, 1963 (George Wickes, editor)

Greece, 1964

Henry Miller on Writing, 1964 (Thomas H. Moore, editor)

Letters to Anaïs Nin, 1965

Selected Prose, 1965 (2 volumes)

Order and Chaos chez Hans Reichel, 1966

Writer and Critic: A Correspondence, 1968 (with W. A. Gordon)

Collector's Quest: The Correspondence of Henry Miller and J. Rivers Childs, 1947-1965, 1968

Insomnia: Or, The Devil at Large, 1970

DISCUSSION TOPICS

- Which compositional habits of Henry Miller make generic criticism of his works difficult or even futile?

- Can Miller be defended against the charge that his novels lack form or structure?

- Analyze and characterize the "I" in *Tropic of Capricorn*.

- Has the sexual content of Miller's novels been more enticement or distraction to serious readers?

- Is Norman Mailer correct in calling Miller's attitude toward women one of "utter adoration"?

My Life and Times, 1971 (Bradley Smith, editor)
Henry Miller in Conversation with Georges Belmont, 1972
Journey to an Unknown Land, 1972
On Turning Eighty, 1972
Reflections on the Death of Mishima, 1972
First Impressions of Greece, 1973
Reflections on the Maurizius Case, 1974
Letters of Henry Miller and Wallace Fowlie, 1943-1972, 1975
The Nightmare Notebook, 1975
Books of Friends: A Tribute to Friends of Long Ago, 1976
Four Visions of America, 1977 (with others)
Gliding into the Everglades, and Other Essays, 1977
Sextet, 1977
Henry Miller: Years of Trial and Triumph, 1978
My Bike and Other Friends, 1978
An Open Letter to Stroker!, 1978 (Irving Stetner, editor)
Some Friends, 1978
Joey: A Loving Portrait of Alfred Perlès Together with Some Bizarre Episodes Relating to the Other Sex, 1979
Notes on "Aaron's Rod" and Other Notes on Lawrence from the Paris Notebooks of Henry Miller, 1980 (Seamus Cooney, editor)
The World of Lawrence: A Passionate Appreciation, 1980 (Evelyn J. Hinz and John J. Teumissen, editors)
Reflections, 1981
The Paintings of Henry Miller, 1982
From Your Capricorn Friend: Henry Miller and the "Stroker," 1978-1980, 1984
Dear, Dear Brenda, 1986
Letters by Henry Miller to Hoki Takuda Miller, 1986
A Literate Passion: Letters of Anaïs Nin and Henry Miller, 1987
The Durrell-Miller Letters, 1935-1980, 1988
Henry Miller's Hamlet Letters, 1988
Henry Miller and James Laughlin: Selected Letters, 1996 (Wickes, editor)

About the Author

Brown, J. D. *Henry Miller.* New York: Frederick Ungar, 1986.

Dearborn, Mary V. *The Happiest Man Alive.* New York: Simon & Schuster, 1992.

Ferguson, Robert. *Henry Miller: A Life.* New York: Norton, 1991.

Gottesman, Ronald, ed. *Critical Essays on Henry Miller.* New York: G. K. Hall, 1992.

Jahshan, Paul. *Henry Miller and the Surrealist Discourse of Excess: A Poststructuralist Reading.* New York: P. Lang, 2001.

Lewis, Leon. *Henry Miller: The Major Writings.* New York: Schocken Books/Random House, 1986.

Martin, Jay. *Always Merry and Bright: The Life of Henry Miller.* Santa Barbara, Calif.: Capra Press, 1978.

Mathieu, Bertrand. *Orpheus in Brooklyn: Orphism, Rimbaud, and Henry Miller.* Paris: Mouton, 1976.

Mitchel, Edward, ed. *Henry Miller: Three Decades of Criticism.* New York: New York University Press, 1971.

Widmer, Kingsley. *Henry Miller.* Rev. ed. Boston: Twayne, 1990.

N. SCOTT MOMADAY

Courtesy, Lewis and Clark College

Born: Lawton, Oklahoma
February 27, 1934

Of Kiowa-Cherokee ancestry, Momaday successfully transmutes the rhythms and the power of the American Indian oral (storytelling) tradition into sophisticated American multicultural poetry, fiction, and autobiography.

BIOGRAPHY

Born in the Kiowa and Comanche Indian Hospital, Momaday was registered as having seven-eighths Indian blood (with the remaining one-eighth attributable to pioneer ancestry); his name was registered as Novarro Scotte Mammedaty, born to Mayme Scott (Natachee) and Alfred Morris (Huan-toa) Mammedaty. It was Momaday's father who simplified the surname to its current spelling.

American Indians believe that the act of naming has the special significance of bringing the named one into existence and helping to chart his or her life course. Momaday has been granted the gifts of three separate namings. At six months of age, he was given his first Indian name by Pohd-lohk, stepfather of Mammedaty, Momaday's grandfather, who died of Bright's disease two years before Momaday was born. Devil's Tower (Tsoai), Wyoming, according to Kiowa oral tradition a sacred site of mystical power, was the basis by which he was named Tsoai-talee (Rock Tree Boy) by the old man. Before Momaday was five, a Sioux elder gave him his second Indian name, Wanbli Wanjila (Eagle Alone). Later in his life he received yet a third name, Tso-Toh-Haw (Kiowa for Red Mountain).

Momaday's mother was a teacher and a writer; his father, a teacher and an artist. Throughout Momaday's early years, his mother shared her love of English literature with him. Although his par-

ents raised him to view English as his first language, they also encouraged him to immerse himself in the tribal cultures of the reservations on which they lived. Consequently, Momaday sees his childhood as an enriching experience. He considers his early formal education, however, including attendance at several Catholic schools, as unremarkable and substandard. At twelve, Momaday moved with his parents to Jemez Pueblo, New Mexico, which remained his home until his senior year in high school. For his graduation year, Momaday decided to seek a more rigorous education at Augusta Military School, Virginia, in preparation for college.

In 1958, Momaday was awarded his A.B. in English from the University of New Mexico. Although he thinks of himself primarily as a poet, he has stated that until his graduate studies at Stanford University he knew little about classical poetic perspectives; he received his Ph.D. from Stanford in 1963. There, Momaday credits Yvor Winters, a professor and a friend, with having a profound influence upon his writing and, in fact, suggesting that he draw on the storytelling traditions of his ancestry to find his artistic voice. In addition to his 1959 Stanford University creative writing fellowship, in 1962 Momaday won the Academy of American Poets prize for his syllabic poem "The Bear." The images and associations of that poem (influenced by William Faulkner's "The Bear") recur throughout his canon.

Having written his doctoral dissertation on the poet Frederick Goddard Tuckerman, Momaday served as editor for the 1965 Oxford University Press edition of *The Complete Poems of Frederick Goddard Tuckerman*. Since that time, the bulk of

Momaday's prose and poetry has reflected both his Native American heritage and the Southwestern landscape.

After holding an assistant professorship for two years at the Santa Barbara campus of the University of California, Momaday was awarded a 1966-1967 Guggenheim Fellowship. During this time, he wrote and published a limited edition of Kiowa folklore, *The Journey of Tai-me* (1967). A revised edition, with illustrations by his artist father, appeared in 1969 under the title *The Way to Rainy Mountain*. Describing a personal quest inspired by the death of his grandmother, Aho, Momaday's chronicle of Kiowa tribal history from emergence to demise coalesces racial memory, legend, and personal experience into a life-giving renewal of Kiowa spirituality.

Momaday has stated that for those few years he focused on prose writing, setting aside his poetry. One of the results was the 1969 Pulitzer Prize for *House Made of Dawn* (1968), his first published novel, written intermittently over a period of two years. *House Made of Dawn* is a nonchronological presentation of human growth through the main character's isolation and alienation and his ultimate healing restoration.

Momaday regards teaching creative writing as an ideal profession for a writer because of the flexible college schedule that means time for writing, for example four or five hours in the early morning, followed by afternoon classes. Despite being a self-proclaimed unhurried writer, during his years at Stanford University (from 1973 to 1982) as a full professor, Momaday published three major works as well as articles for periodicals. He also traveled to Russia for a stint teaching at Moscow State University.

The early to mid-1970's marked Momaday's return to poetry and art as forms of expression. His first two publications following *The Way to Rainy Mountain* were collections of his poetry, *Angle of Geese, and Other Poems* (1974) and *The Gourd Dancer* (1976), which he illustrated himself. As an artist, Momaday has sketched in both graphite and pen-and-ink. He has also worked in acrylic and in watercolor. For Momaday, the spontaneous process of creating visual pieces is in direct counterpoint to the intense deliberation with which he writes.

Published in 1976 and labeled autobiography, *The Names: A Memoir* contains far more than is traditional for that genre. American Indian oral tradition functions in part to perpetuate tribal legend and memory through the telling of its stories. Once the stories have been truly heard, they become part of the listener's experience. Supplementing his text with pictures from his mother's family album, Momaday has transformed the tradition into a visual recounting.

Momaday's profound attachment to the Southwest is clear. Since 1982, he has served as a full professor in the University of Arizona's English department, a move he has described as coming home again. In 1989, Momaday published *The Ancient Child*, a novel based upon a Kiowa legend that had long fascinated him, the legend of Devil's Tower and the boy who becomes a bear. At the same time, Momaday explores the role of art in modern and traditional societies, explores the way in which artistic vision grows, expands, matures, and transmutates. An allusion to Emil Nolde's painting *Sternenwandler,* or *Wanderer Among the Stars*, suggests the novel's concern with not just an ethnic view of the artist, but a cross-cultural view: those who must look deeply within themselves and dare to experiment with new forms in order to live up to their potential. Through allusions to Norse mythology ("Loki"), Latin etymology, the philosophy of John Locke, and Grace Moon's 1926 children's book about Navajo/Pueblo life, Momaday intentionally carries his vision beyond the limitations of ethnocentricity.

He has since written *Circle of Wonder: A Native American Christmas Story* (1994) and a play, *The Indolent Boys* (1994). *The Man Made of Words: Essays, Stories, and Passages* (1998) has spawned much critical discussion of his goals and methods. His *In the Bear's House* (1999) combines artwork, verse, and prose in an artistic mix that Momaday has made his own; sets up a philosophical debate between Urset, the original bear, and Yahweh; includes poems about bears (even one on a Moscow subway); and retells the Kiowa story of the boy transformed into a bear while chasing his seven sisters.

Although he has declined to function in an official capacity as a spokesman on Native American issues, Momaday is an active reviewer of topics related to the American Indian. In his storytelling pieces for periodicals, he has also shared such unique personal experiences as his membership in the Gourd Dance Society, the Taimpe, which performs an annual celebration in Oklahoma.

ANALYSIS

Momaday's vital identification with the Southwest and with Native American nations (particularly the Kiowa) is consistently reflected in his choice of locations, subject matter, and protagonists. Momaday is unwilling to write about anything that he has not examined and does not know intimately, and his focus is restrained yet powerful. He does not speak Kiowa, but he has made his Kiowa heritage a stepping-stone to understanding broader multicultural experiences. He sees in the mixed blood of his people and their ability to adapt to new situations hope for their survival, not as the Plains warriors of the past but as modern artists, thinkers, and community members with a whole sense of themselves and their place, not only in the Native American world but in the world at large as well. Thus, he regularly draws parallels between world mythologies and gives his stories a texture and a depth that promise more than an ethnic vision.

Momaday has described himself as a "word walker," a storyteller who uses language on his life's journey in a way that transcends dimensions. If language is as powerful as Momaday believes, the spoken word can create a new reality, with precision, awareness, and harmony with the rhythms of nature essential to their appropriate expression. For him, words have an integrity that brings insight and vitality. Consequently, Momaday's distinctive juxtaposition of what may initially appear to be fragmented scenes is actually designed to reveal essences rather than simple chronological sequences. In *House Made of Dawn*, for example, the shattering of Abel's body after his beating by Martinez is dramatically reinforced by the abrupt intrusion of prison memories, childhood experiences, and a peyote ceremony.

Such is the Native American concept of "seeing"—to recognize the facet of creation existing on this plane and beyond to its essence as an integral part of the Great Mystery (God). Momaday's central concern is humankind's harmonious and awe-filled relationship with all existence. When humankind denies this relationship or responsibility for it, the inevitable results are isolation, alienation, and disintegration. The blindness motif in *House Made of Dawn* is only one example of the consequences of self-alienation or other forms of alienation.

To Momaday, any separation from nature deteriorates the human spirit. Lack of positive female relationships, disregard for ancestral heritage, and denial of tribal memory can hasten an individual's, or a culture's, demise. As a result, Momaday moves repeatedly from crises to vividly detailed descriptions of landscapes, because he believes that an intimate connection with "place" is vital to human awareness and understanding. In *The Way to Rainy Mountain*, the historical description of an important ceremonial teepee's destruction by fire is followed by a slow, soothing description of silence and shadow at day's end.

Light and shadow, sound and silence, circular imagery, water and animal symbolism, and the four directions of the Medicine Wheel recur, thematic and stylistic instruments with which the author heightens his reader's awareness of the interconnectedness of life. According to American Indian philosophy, the Medicine Wheel reflects the process of life from birth to death. Each direction possesses its own integral characteristics. The healing of Abel's dawn run at the conclusion of *House Made of Dawn* exemplifies Momaday's use of Medicine Wheel symbolism. The color for the East is the red of dawn; its season spring; its spiritual quality understanding; its animal totem the eagle, a representation of a direct connection to the Great Mystery achieved as the result of successful passage through major life crises.

Momaday's prose writing style is most often described as lyrical. This quality is evidenced in his stress upon the rhythm and sound of his word choices, designed to reflect both the content and the substance of his subject matter. The following brief passage from *The Way to Rainy Mountain* describes dawn's stillness: "It is cold and clear and deep like water. It takes hold of you and will not let you go." The mystical quality of this language deftly projects the author's sense of wonder and reverence.

Although he has written in traditional iambic form, Momaday's most compelling poetry is either chant or syllabic rather than metered. A chant, such as "Plain-view: 2," involves what might appear in print as monotonous repetition; however, when it is read aloud as if to the beat of an Indian ceremonial drum, its impact increases dramatically. Despite the classification of his poetry as experimental, the chant is firmly rooted in Native American oral tradition. Use of parallelism and repetition increases the power of the words. Furthermore, these techniques serve as memory aids for the listeners so that other levels of awareness may be more easily attained.

Syllabic poetry, such as "The Bear," depends upon a specific pattern of syllables per line, concrete imagery, and most often the use of rhyme. The advantages of this poetic form are that its rhythms are less artificial than a fully metered poem and that the phraseology is less cluttered and more direct. For Momaday, syllabic poetry appears to reflect more accurately his mystical awareness of, and attunement to, the elements of nature.

Even in the most dire of circumstances, such as the demise of the Kiowa tribal identity, Momaday's Native American vision enables him to surge toward the hope of resurrection and rebirth. One foundation upon which he bases his perception of life is the historical failure of externally imposed restrictions to alter internal value systems. Recognizing the exigency of establishing a tribal/family memory, whether experienced or imagined, is another. The final step that he repeatedly presents in his writing is accepting the responsibility to feel wonder and joy in communion with the "giveaway" that is this universe.

imagination to create artificial barriers rather than accepting what already exists. A second technique is the fragmentation of their capacity to penetrate directly to the essence, so that they can deny it.

In stanza 2, Momaday expresses his incredulity regarding human insensitivity. That anyone could so delude himself as to misperceive the grandeur of the bear, one of nature's most graced, appears to be beyond the parameters of Momaday's belief system. To the author, the aged bear is a warrior, a moral animal with courage and dignity.

The absolute stillness of stanza 3 is a striking poetic device to reinforce the bear's immense power. He dominates without action. Thoughtful and discerning, he does not react. He waits. Mythic healer and destroyer, he simultaneously exists in all times, all dimensions.

The bear's power in the physical world is now limited by age and injury. The consequent imbalance of his spiritual and his bodily potency is symbolic of his imminent return to the Earth Mother. In the final stanza, the bear has magically disappeared, without apparent sound or movement. Nature, in the form of buzzards, shows her respect.

"THE BEAR"

First published: 1961 (collected in *In the Presence of the Sun: Stories and Poems, 1961-1991*, 1992)
Type of work: Poem

Unrecognized by humans who are out of harmony with nature, the bear is a moral animal in balance with the physical and spiritual world.

"The Bear," winner of the 1962 Academy of American Poets prize, is a five-stanza syllabic poem. Momaday devotes the first two stanzas to the question of the processes employed by humans to distort their visions of the natural world. The remaining three stanzas depict the bear without distortion, as an integral element in the cycle of life.

Humans consciously pervert their perception of the bear because of their unwillingness to face the potential of what they might have been had they opted for nature rather than civilization. One of the defenses that humans favor is the misuse of their

HOUSE MADE OF DAWN

First published: 1968
Type of work: Novel

An alienated young American Indian undergoes the initiation trials crucial to his reemergence as an actualized human being.

House Made of Dawn, Momaday's first novel, is divided into four major sections with dated chapter subheadings. In keeping with the Native American sense of history, the narrative is episodic rather than chronological. Thus, Momaday evokes both a sense of timelessness and a concentration on the essence of each experiential piece, gradually forming a healing pattern for Abel, the protagonist, as he moves toward an internal congruence with the earth.

Part 1, "The Longhair," opens and closes with Francisco, Abel's grandfather. A drunken Abel arrives by bus and is taken home. The ensuing flashbacks from Abel's childhood are both pleasant and fearful. His lack of attunement with nature is evidenced when, as a young child, he refuses to accept the moaning of the wind and responds instead with fear. The death of his brother Vidal is juxtaposed with Abel's coming-of-age rites.

Memories of the Eagle Watchers Society, survivors whom disaster had molded into medicine men, are next to surface. Abel catches a great eagle during the hunt but cries when he thinks of the implications of its captivity. Recognizing that the bird is no longer able to retain its natural state of grace, he strangles it. Once again, death is paralleled to life.

As the novel continues, Father Olquin, a priest fascinated by the perverted journal of Fray Nicholas, whom he sees as a saint, and Mrs. Martin St. John are introduced. Despite her pregnancy, Angela St. John plots to seduce Abel. Neither of these antagonists has made appropriate life accommodations for his or her role. Abel himself is too spiritually fragmented to meld with the rhythms of his horse in the annual rooster-snatching contest. The evil albino, however, retrieves the rooster and beats Abel with it. Thus, Abel is directly confronted with his alienation from himself and others.

Following a description of the unique gifts of animals to the land, Abel begins to reexperience nature's rhythms but discovers that he is not yet healed enough to have words for a creation song. Nevertheless, he does have the power to bed Angela, who sees in him the bear, thereby starting down her own path of healing, which is reinforced by her craving for the cleansing rain. Abel kills the albino, then kneels beside him to honor the dying process and to soak in the purifying rain.

Part 2, "The Priest of the Sun," is set in Los Angeles. The Right Reverend John Big Bluff Tosamah opens a serious sermon on the power of the word and how modern people have diluted that power, but midstream he begins to interject his own dilutions in the form of colloquialisms, irony, and blatant humor.

Readers receive their first indication of Abel's critical physical condition as he lies near the water. He flashes back to his childhood healing by Josie, a medicine woman, and to his trial for the albino's murder. Still, Abel has no words. Instead, he coughs blood, as an owl, the sharp-sighted night bird, watches.

Remembrance of the dawn runners against evil and death unblocks Abel's awareness. He recognizes his isolation from self and from creation and, now open for healing, returns to the water. The peyote episode is also curative, as Ben Benally is revealed as healer through his vision of the horses and the "house made of dawn."

Abel remembers Josie's nurturance after his mother had died. He realizes that his generalized chronic fear is paralyzing his potential for integration. Flashing back to a time when he had wanted to share the extraordinary sight of twenty-four geese rising in formation from the river, Abel relives Millie's story of abandonment, isolation, and grief. Then he rises to journey home. As Abel travels, Tosamah reveals the story of the Kiowa migration and the steps that led to their demise. Part 2 concludes with Tosamah's tale of the sojourn to Rainy Mountain.

Ben Benally narrates part 3, in Los Angeles, after he has given Abel his own coat for Abel's train ride home. The night before, Ben had created a future in words for the two men so similar in background that they could be brothers. He had privately sung the healing "House Made of Dawn" chant. Considering Abel's history in Los Angeles, Ben concludes that Abel did not fit. He interacted little with others and appeared withdrawn, lost. After his failed drunken attack on Tosamah, during which the other poker players laughed, Abel had isolated himself totally.

The tension of the foregoing scenes is alleviated by the comic story of the venerable Indian who fell into the river. Moreover, this story bridges to the "Turquoise Woman's Son" song, a chant to restore wholeness to the incomplete, the means by which Abel prepares for change. Angela's brief street appearance introduces her to Ben, who will call her while Abel is recovering in the hospital. The symbolism of Abel's reappearance after three days lends credibility to the theory that he is progressing toward wholeness. Similarly, Angela's tale of the bear and the maiden represents her healing connection to the Earth Mother.

Part 4, "The Dawn Runner," in Walatowa (which means Village of the Bear), opens as Abel returns to his dying grandfather. After spending two days in a drunken stupor, Abel acknowledges the chronic state of his own illness. Even though he wants to speak to his grandfather, once again he has no words. Francisco, however, does. Transmission of his own honorable experiences on the bear hunt empowers Abel.

After his grandfather dies, Abel prepares him for burial and notifies Father Olquin. Although the priest has almost deluded himself into believing that he has successfully adapted to the Indian culture surrounding him, his protestations of understanding ring false. In fact, Father Olquin's capacity for self-deception has increased. Preparing for his own dawn run to wholeness, Abel rubs his upper body with ashes. Then, as dawn strikes the horizon, he runs beyond his own pain, beyond evil, beyond death. By repeating the words of Ben's healing song, Abel indicates his acceptance of integration with nature.

THE WAY TO RAINY MOUNTAIN

First published: 1969
Type of work: History and folklore

Momaday recounts Kiowa legend and history from tribal memory.

The Way to Rainy Mountain, illustrated by Al Momaday, is both a eulogy for the demise of an active tribal identity and a celebration of the potential for its perpetuity in individual tribal consciousness. Divided into three major parts, "The Setting Out," "The Going On," and the "Closing In," the text has twenty-four numbered sections.

Each section is also separated into three passages, clearly delineated by three unique typescripts. Until section 20, the first passage is a translation of Kiowa myth, the second concerns Kiowa history, and the third is written from the author's own experience. (Momaday's sources for the first two excerpts originate in both familial and tribal heritage.) A gradual composite begins to form as the author claims the elements for his own mythic heritage.

The book both begins and ends with a poem. The introductory poem, "Headwater," is a lyric description of the Kiowa emergence into the world. The Kiowa became what they dreamed. They were what they saw. Coming down from the mountains, never an agrarian people, the tribe adapted to its new environment as nomadic warriors and horsemen. Although they learned quickly from the Crow and were befriended by Tai-me, who became the focal point of their Sun Dance culture, the Kiowa did not long flourish. Tribal division and a series of disasters in the 1800's decimated the tribe. A meteor shower was taken to symbolize the destruction of the old ways. Epidemics raged. The buffalo and the Kiowa horses were massacred. Their slow surrender to the soldiers at Fort Sill was spiritually devastating to tribal consciousness.

The myth of the arrowmaker in section 13 is a recurrent theme in Momaday's writing. Artistry and precision are aesthetically essential to an appropriate balance with nature. They are also essential to survival. Because the arrowmaker is a craftsman, he knows that his arrow will fly true. His stalking awareness (as much a part of the Native American tradition as is dreaming) alerts him to an alien presence. Taking "right action" and moving cautiously, the arrowmaker allows the stranger the opportunity to declare his intentions. When the stranger does not, he becomes the enemy. Momaday uses ambiguity to heighten curiosity, and the anonymity of this fallen presence is intriguing.

The warrior society of section 3 illustrates Momaday's emphasis upon mastery and right action. If an individual is attuned to both self and surroundings, self-aware but not self-preoccupied, then his or her behaviors will be effortless and true. The dog that leads the warriors is not as attuned to his own nature as is the dreamer who counsels him simply to be a dog.

The concluding poem, "Rainy Mountain Cemetery," eulogizes the ancient ones who have traveled to dimensions beyond this earthly existence. That they had survived is not the issue; those left behind blend the ancestral memories with their personal identities in order to preserve the collective tribal consciousness.

THE NAMES: A MEMOIR

First published: 1976
Type of work: Autobiography

A narrated account of the writer's experiences, both actual and metaphysical.

The Names: A Memoir differs from the traditional autobiographical account in both its approach and its subject matter. Again, Momaday has structured his writing to reflect the essence rather than the chronology. Across a cultural continuum of his and own and his ancestors' experiences, Momaday weaves imaginative re-creations.

Naming is a process by which one identifies and reinforces predominant characteristics of a situation or an individual. In this memoir, Momaday sustains a mythic familial and tribal consciousness by naming the significant events that shape their distinctive spirit. For Momaday, active participation in a life experience does not necessarily imply that he is the protagonist in that event. He adheres to the Native American beliefs in the timelessness of the universe and the vital union of the physical and the spiritual worlds.

Therefore, Momaday's memoir serves two purposes. First, his assimilation of the collective memory through his contribution as a listener in the oral tradition perpetuates the heritage of his people. Second, his sharing of this heritage by creating an avenue to express oral traditions through the written word increases the tribe. His memories become the reader's memories.

As Momaday studies a picture of Mammedaty, the grandfather who died two years before the author was born, Momaday experiences with full sensory impact the great Sun Dance giveaway in which a young boy joyfully led his black horse into the circle for Mammedaty. The author describes the feel of his own hands upon the horse. In the time-ridden physical universe, this event is an impossibility; in dimensions of the metaphysical universe, it is a reality.

Employing visual symbolism as a catalyst to shifting levels of awareness is a technique crucial to Momaday's potency. Minute detail of landscapes, animal behaviors, and characteristics of the aged in a synesthetic presentation of his emotional response evoke like awarenesses in his readers. The genealogy of his family nurtures in others their own histories.

Directly and succinctly, Momaday reaffirms the timelessness of his universe with the statement, "Notions of the past and future are essentially notions of the present." Similarly, family trees are mirrors rather than extensions of an individual. Momaday then names the idea that he is defining himself, thereby giving physical existence to the process. The subsequent flow of his stream-of-consciousness musings is uninterrupted by punctuation. His paragraphing confirms that the only boundaries he places upon his creation of self are those of ideas.

In the epilogue, Momaday closes the metaphysical circle of his Kiowa identity with his return to the hollow log from which the Kiowa entered this world.

THE ANCIENT CHILD

First published: 1989
Type of work: Novel

A commercially successful Kiowa painter must discover his familial and tribal heritage in order to evolve as an artist and as a human being.

The title *The Ancient Child* refers to the Kiowa creation story of a boy who, while chasing his seven sisters, turns into a bear. Frightened, they climb a giant tree and become the constellation the Seven Sisters. The boy/bear pursues but cannot climb so high. His slide back down the tree leaves claw marks that, when the tree falls and its clawed trunk petrifies, appear as the slashes on the Devil's Tower, Tsoai-talee. Tsoai-talee is also Momaday's Kiowa name, so he is connected to both sacred land and bear power. Within the context of the story, his alter ego Locke "Loki" Setman, or Set, can find inner peace only if he, like the boy of the myth, finds his spirit identity and is transformed by wrestling with the bear within him, The creation story is connected with another ancient tale of a male child who mysteriously appears in a village; no one knows who he is, but in their memories he is transmuted into a bear cub so that villagers can comfort themselves with an identity that makes sense of their failure to otherwise identify him. Likewise Locke Setman, whose name means Walking Bear or Bear Above, is unknown to the Native Americans whom he encounters in Navajo areas and must become "Bear" in order to gain his place and his native identity. Thus, ancient and modern merge and the stories of the past recur in new forms.

Locke Setman's parents died during his childhood, so he has been cut off from family and tribal land. He is a highly successful San Francisco painter whose agent is pushing his art in Europe and arranging showings in Paris, with the condition that Setman continue to paint as he had done in the past. However, as an artist, Setman is evolving into a better artist, one whose works may well be much less commercially successful but will enable Setman to experiment artistically, stretch his vision, and discover his artistic identity. When he goes to his Grandmother Kopemah's funeral (she remembered the last Sun Dance), he meets a beautiful young relative, Grey, who has learned medicine woman ways from his grandmother. She appears to him in different, disturbing forms that puzzle and intrigue him, and before he leaves, she passes to him a medicine bundle containing powerful bear parts and crystals. They work on him mysteriously until he turns sick and violent, and his present mistress, who realizes that he cannot love her until he discovers his own inner self, brings him to Grey.

Grey takes him to Navajo territory, where contact with the land helps restore his inner peace, and, with the aid of powerful Navajo women, he recovers a sense of manhood and of self that he did not know he was missing. He marries Grey and impregnates her, and she gives up her youthful time projections of being Billy the Kid's lover and inspiration; instead, she focuses on the reality of marriage to a modern man with ancient powers. Setman's art evolves as he is gradually transformed into the Bear of Kiowa myth, "a mythic embodiment of the wilderness."

There are clearly autobiographical elements at work here, as Momaday illustrates his own evolution into an expressionist artist through the growth of Setman, hence the artistic focus of the book headings: "Planes," "Lines," "Shapes," and "Shadows."

IN THE PRESENCE OF THE SUN: STORIES AND POEMS, 1961-1991

First published: 1992
Type of work: Poetry and short stories

The title, from related poems entitled "In the Presence of the Sun: A Gathering of Shields," recalls the spirit world, the Sun Dance, the warrior tradition, and the heart of Kiowa belief and culture.

This collection contains four main sections, the first twenty-nine previously published works (including the poems "The Bear," "The Angle of Geese," and "The Gourd Dancer") and the last twenty-seven new poems. The middle sections are "The Strange and True Story of My Life with Billy the Kid" (a set of verses written by the nineteen-year-old Navajo-Kiowa shaman named Grey in *The Ancient Child*) and the shield poems.

Momaday contrasts death in nature with mainstream ideas of death in "Angle of Geese," pays homage to his grandfather and the traditions by which he lived in "The Gourd Dancer," and explores the nature of myth in the Billy the Kid poems. A New Mexico legend, Billy the Kid embodies the violence of the Old West (his eyes are without expression) and the seductiveness of the outlaw hero, but he offers no future despite his occasional sensitivities (such as coming prepared with a plug of tobacco to share with an elderly friend when he himself does not chew tobacco). The poems trace Henry McCarty/Billy the Kid's progress toward his destiny, the final meeting with Pat Garrett.

The imagistic prose collection entitled "A Gathering of Shields" begins with a tribute to the spiritual, cultural, and artistic value of the Plains Indian shield and includes ink drawings of the shields gathered for a ritual ceremony. The stories number sixteen, an intentional heightening of the power of the sacred number four. The shields are more than the tools of warriors: They embody the best and worst of those who created and carried them. Some, such as "The Shield That Was Touched by Pretty Mouth," "The Shield That Was Looked After by Dogs," and "The Shield That Was Brought Down from Tsoai," carry great power because of the history of their bearers. Others, such as "The Shield of Which the Less Said the Better," are of no value: This shield, taken by soldiers and sold in Clinton, Oklahoma, for seventeen dollars, lost its value despite its antiquity. That the final shield, "The Shield of Two Dreams," reflects the dream of the father passed on to the daughter fits with Momaday's idea of tradition passed on but modified to fit new contexts and new social values. These shields embody their individual creator, his contribution to the survival of the group, and the spirit that he leaves behind.

Of the newer poems, "The Great Fillmore Street Buffalo Drive" captures a historical moment of final slaughter as a buffalo herd is driven to a senseless death on Pacific Coast boulders, but one buffalo "dreams" back to a canyon wall and disappears into shadow, at one with nature. Poems such as "Wreckage" and "Mogollon Morning" that place the poet amid canyon walls and rock, learning from the light and shadows, are Momaday at his best. In "At Risk," the poet discovers his connections with ancient cave painters and finds his own face mirrored in the masks of ancient animals dancing on cave walls. This poem is an apt close to a collection that, as a unit, suggests the author's struggle to find a poetic voice, an identity that reflects his multicultural essence.

SUMMARY

An award-winning poet, novelist, autobiographer, and scriptwriter, Momaday has concentrated his literary attention on that which he holds closest to his heart: the southwestern landscape, his American Indian heritage, artistic endeavor, and a synthesis of cultures. The minute detail of his passages on human and nonhuman facets of nature is masterful. His reverence for nature and his insistence that all humankind must recognize its responsibility to heal the physical and spiritual earth drive his works. He argues in varied ways that humans must first balance themselves in relation to their universe. A pioneer in creating new means through which to share Native American oral tradition, Momaday reshapes conventional written forms to serve his ends.

Kathleen Mills; updated by Gina Macdonald

BIBLIOGRAPHY

By the Author

POETRY:
Angle of Geese, and Other Poems, 1974
The Gourd Dancer, 1976

LONG FICTION:
House Made of Dawn, 1968
The Ancient Child, 1989

DRAMA:
The Indolent Boys, pr. 1994

NONFICTION:
"The Morality of Indian Hating," 1964
The Journey of Tai-me, 1967 (memoir; revised as *The Way to Rainy Mountain,* 1969)
"The Man Made of Words," 1970
Colorado: Summer, Fall, Winter, Spring, 1973 (with David Muench)
The Names: A Memoir, 1976
Ancestral Voice: Conversations with N. Scott Momaday, 1989 (with Charles L. Woodard)

CHILDREN'S LITERATURE:
Circle of Wonder: A Native American Christmas Story, 1994

EDITED TEXT:
The Complete Poems of Frederick Goddard Tuckerman, 1965

MISCELLANEOUS:
In the Presence of the Sun: Stories and Poems, 1961-1991, 1992
The Man Made of Words: Essays, Stories, and Passages, 1998
In the Bear's House, 1999

About the Author

Barry, Nora. Review of *Ancestral Voice: Conversations with N. Scott Momaday. MELUS* 16 (December 22, 1989): 115-117.

Douglas, Christopher. "The Flawed Design: American Imperialism in N. Scott Momaday's *House Made of Dawn* and Cormac McCarthy's *Blood Meridian." Critique: Studies in Contemporary Fiction* 45 (Fall, 2003): 3-24.

Isernhagen, Hartwig. *Momaday, Vizenor, Armstrong: Conversations on American Indian Writing.* Norman: University of Oklahoma Press, 1999.

Owen, Louis. *Other Destinies: Reading the American Indian Novel.* Norman: University of Oklahoma Press, 1992.

Roemer, Kenneth, ed. *Approaches to Teaching Momaday's "The Way to Rainy Mountain."* New York: Modern Language Association of America, 1988.

Scarberry-Garcia, Susan. *Landmarks of Healing: A Study of "House Made of Dawn."* Albuquerque: University of New Mexico Press, 1990.

Scenters-Zapico, John. "Cross-Cultural Mediations: Language, Storytelling, History, and Self as Enthymematic Premises in the Novels of N. Scott Momaday." *The American Indian Quarterly* 21 (June 22, 1997): 499.

Schubnell, Matthias. "Locke Setman, Emil Nolde, and the Search for Expression in N. Scott Momaday's *The Ancient Child." The American Indian Quarterly* 18 (September 22, 1994): 468-480.

Stevens, Jason W. "Bear, Outlaw, and Storyteller: American Frontier Mythology and Ethnic Subjectivity of N. Scott Momaday." *American Literature* 73 (September, 2001): 599-631.

DISCUSSION TOPICS

- The bear is a powerful figure that runs throughout N. Scott Momaday's canon and is associated with the author himself. What are the characteristics of the bear? What is its function in the book or poems that you have read?

- What is the Kiowa creation story of the Seven Sisters constellation and of the Devil's Tower? How does Momaday personalize that story and make it part of his life?

- *The Ancient Child* is the story of a San Francisco artist. What in the structure, the language, and the content of the book keep readers focused on the artistic? What type of artistic evolution does the main character, Locke Setman, undergo?

- Billy the Kid is a recurring figure in Momaday's books and poems. What do readers learn about him, his real life, and the fantasy life that Momaday creates for him? Is it hard to draw the line between fact and fiction?

- Although Momaday's modern Indians return to their heritage to find themselves, he does not advocate a return to a lost past. Instead, his traditional characters have a place in the modern world. Choose two such characters and illustrate the two sides of their natures, the traditional and the modern.

- In *The Way to Rainy Mountain,* Momaday describes the history of the Kiowa in order to delineate their character as a people. What does the history that he describes reveal about the Kiowa? What do you think his message is to modern Kiowas?

- Some have called Momaday a purely Native American author, but others describe him as a multicultural author speaking of a wider experience than that of one ethnic group. What values does Momaday advocate and what issues does he address that speak to a cross-cultural audience?

Doubleday

BRIAN MOORE

Born: Belfast, Northern Ireland
August 25, 1921
Died: Malibu, California
January 11, 1999

Moore used his Roman Catholic background to examine spiritual, ethical, and social issues in what has become a quietly impressive canon of novels.

BIOGRAPHY

Brian Moore was born in Belfast as the fourth child in a family of nine. His father, James Bernard Moore, had made his way through medical school on scholarships to become a prominent surgeon. He had not married until he was fifty, and he died when Brian was eighteen. Moore recalled his father as an exacting man, impatient with failure, who put great pressure on his children to excel in their schooling. The son's response was to focus on failed or marginal characters in his fiction; he has said that he regards failure as "a more intense distillation [than success] of that self you are."

Moore was educated at Newington Elementary School and St. Malachy's Diocesan College, both in Belfast. He bitterly recalled his formal education as old-fashioned, rigid, and harshly disciplinary, with canings for the slightest infractions. In *The Feast of Lupercal* (1957), he draws an acrid portrait of St. Malachy's in his Ardath College, where clerical masters prevent students from developing independent minds. His feelings about his Jesuit education are related to the ambivalence he has about religious belief.

The Moore family had originally been Protestant, but Brian's paternal grandfather converted late in life to Catholicism. Brian was raised a Catholic, only to be stunned when his mother confessed her unbelief on her deathbed. From his youth, he was an unbeliever, yet all his life he remained fascinated by the role faith plays in people's lives. In most of his novels, he has dramatized what he regards as the suffocating weight of Irish Catholicism's moral flaws.

After having failed in mathematics, Moore left college in 1938 without taking a degree. For a year he took courses at the University of London's Belfast branch. In 1940, he joined Belfast's Air Raid Precautions Unit and National Fire Service, gaining experiences he would delineate in *The Emperor of Ice-Cream* (1965). In 1943, he joined the British Ministry of War Transport and accompanied the Allied Occupation Forces into North Africa, France, Italy, and Germany. In 1945, he worked for the United Nations Relief and Rehabilitation Administration Economic Mission in Warsaw, then traveled as a freelance reporter in Scandinavia and France.

Moore returned to England in 1947 but emigrated to Canada the following year. From 1948 to 1952, he reported for the *Montreal Gazette* and also had several pulp novels published under an assumed name. In 1953, he became a Canadian citizen, and he retained his Canadian citizenship even after moving to the United States in 1959. In 1955, Moore issued his first serious—and perhaps still best—novel, *The Lonely Passion of Judith Hearne.* The book won him Britain's Authors' Club First Novel Award.

From 1959 to 1962, Moore resided in New York City, living partly on a Guggenheim Fellowship while writing *The Luck of Ginger Coffey* (1960, set in Montreal) and *An Answer from Limbo* (1962, set in

New York). In 1963, he moved to Los Angeles to write the screenplay for *The Luck of Ginger Coffey*, then to write *Torn Curtain* for Alfred Hitchcock. In 1964, he settled in Malibu with his second wife, Jean Denney. His first marriage, to Jacqueline Sirois, had lasted from 1951 to 1957. In Southern California, Moore wrote occasional film scripts and travel articles and taught as an adjunct professor at the University of California, Los Angeles, but he devoted the bulk of his time to his novels. He was essentially a loner who gave few interviews and enjoyed his international status, living in California yet retaining his Canadian citizenship while writing, more often than not, about Ireland's taboo-ridden, backward society.

ANALYSIS

Even though Moore wrote many highly praised novels, he was rarely considered in books or essays dealing with contemporary fiction. Such British peers as John Fowles, Doris Lessing, Iris Murdoch, Kingsley Amis, Anthony Burgess, Anthony Powell, William Golding, Muriel Spark, and Julian Barnes have received far more attention. Moore's limitations have been noted: His canvas was often small, his subject matter was usually restricted, he seldom broke new ground in either theme or technique, he sometimes yielded to temptation by writing slick melodramas, and he seemed unable to create a masterwork that would show his powers at their highest level.

Granting all this, a powerful case can be made for the view that Moore was one of the most distinguished voices in modern fiction. His prose is clear, spare, taut, apparently flat yet cumulatively lyrical, with a rare metaphor producing a powerful impact. His highly accessible books teem with convincing details and are populated by characters who speak and act vividly. His tonal command can mix the poignant with the droll, the sardonic with the tragic. He mastered a matrix of substantial themes that include failure, loneliness, loss, exile, and meaninglessness. Moore excelled in dramatizing crisis points in which people are compelled to confront the core of their lives, which are often led in quiet desperation.

Moore was not a popular writer, as his subject matter is unexciting and his treatment of it pessimistic and never sensational. Except for sexual affection, emotional intimacy between men and women did not engage his imagination. Over and over again, he strikes his deepest notes in the chords of parental relationships, risking sentimentality to arrive at ordinary truths of behavior in such novels as *The Luck of Ginger Coffey, An Answer from Limbo, The Emperor of Ice-Cream,* and *Fergus* (1970). Whereas other modern writers fizz, soar, and flash on stylistic sprees, Moore's voice remains quiet and sober. His consistently high artistry earned him a solid reputation among other writers—Graham Greene called Moore his favorite living novelist—but his preoccupation with personal defeat, renunciation, and unhappiness cost him the wide readership his talent deserves.

On the literary horizon, Moore cast himself as a shadowy presence, because his fiction cannot be conveniently classified. He chose to reject what he acidly termed, in an interview, "Barthian byways . . . Borgesian mazes . . . Beckett's crossroads." He was averse to such symbolic fiction as Saul Bellow's *Henderson the Rain King* (1959) and such philosophic narratives as Bellow's *Herzog* (1964). He also expressed his distaste for the school of the New Novel inspired by Nathalie Sarraute and Alain Robbe-Grillet, and he dismissed the postmodern works of such writers as Vladimir Nabokov, Italo Calvino, and Thomas Pynchon as lacking a sense of real life.

Real life is what Moore's fiction focuses on: the ordinary, frequently dull, always recognizable world in which parents and relatives, friends and enemies all live. His fictive mode is that of such realistic probers of the ethical life as George Eliot, Henry James, and E. M. Forster. By far the leading influence on his work, however, is the example of James Joyce.

Like Joyce, Moore chose to write about Ireland from the perspective of exile. Joyce's obsession with Irish paralysis and death is comparable to Moore's preoccupation with Belfast's stagnation and decay. Moore's first two novels, *The Lonely Passion of Judith Hearne* and *The Feast of Lupercal,* are directly indebted to Joyce's great collection of his stories, *Dubliners* (1914). The protagonists of both books are "outcast from life's feast," like Maria in "Clay" or Mr. Duffy in "A Painful Case." In several interviews, Moore stated that he found the experimental Joyce of *Ulysses* (1922) and *Finnegan's Wake* (1939) to be "inimitable," but the Joyce who celebrates life's commonplaces was his prime mentor.

In 1993, Moore surprised many of his readers by issuing, for his first time, a political novel, *No Other Life*. The book deals with a messianic Catholic priest's rise and fall from power on a corrupt, poverty-stricken Caribbean island; the parallels to Jean-Bertrand Aristide's career are numerous. Yet the work is only superficially a *roman à clef*. It focuses on the relationship between a French Canadian missionary, Father Paul, and his brilliant black protégé, Jeannot. Father Paul nourishes Jeannot's soul and promotes his career until Jeannot becomes the leader of the island's dispossessed, only to be forced into exile. The book becomes a meditation on the struggle between religious and temporal faith, spiritual doctrine and public deeds. Moore finds himself, after all, once more in his familiar domain.

THE LONELY PASSION OF JUDITH HEARNE

First published: 1955
Type of work: Novel

A fortyish Irish spinster loses her last hope for a husband, her faith, and her mind.

In *The Lonely Passion of Judith Hearne*, Moore's first novel, he introduces all the themes that will flower in his distinguished career. He takes a large risk by making his protagonist an unmarried, plain, narrow-minded woman over forty who is impoverished, lonely, conventionally pious, and secretly alcoholic. He is tender with her, even inviting the reader to like her as he describes in impressive detail her confused interior life. Honoré de Balzac would have made her a villain, as he did the brooding title character in *La Cousine Bette* (1846; *Cousin Bette*); Flannery O'Connor would have mocked her with gothic glee; Eudora Welty would have drawn her comically; F. Scott Fitzgerald, Ernest Hemingway, and William Faulkner would not have imagined her; Vladimir Nabokov would have disdained her.

Joyce, though, might have joined Moore in empathizing with Judith Hearne as a loser whose fate is determined by the suffocating weight of Irish banality, hypocrisy, and empty religiosity. Hearne is an aging, long-faced Belfast music teacher with barely one hundred pounds a year to her name, in a land where a good man is almost impossible to find. Yet she longs for such a husband, and the merciless way in which her hope is broken makes for the action of Moore's most moving novel.

Before the book's present time, Hearne has spent years caring for her aunt, a selfish, domineering woman whose life, like that of Eveline's mother in the *Dubliners* tale, lays a crazy spell on her. In dour, drab, and dreadful Belfast, spinster Hearne has been evicted from a series of boarding homes because of her drinking. She ends up in a house run by a malicious, slimy-voiced woman whose son is a Machiavellian lout. The landlady's vulgar brother, James Patrick Madden, has returned from New York and is rumored to be rich; it turns out that the only fortune he ever made was a small sum compensating him for having been run down by a city bus. His American occupation was that of a doorman.

Madden is equally deluded about Hearne: Her air of high breeding and an expensive wristwatch given her by her aunt lead him to hope that she is wealthy and might finance his scheme to open a hamburger joint for Yankee tourists. As their mutual illusions crumble, Hearne locks herself in her room and opens her secreted cache of whiskey. Later, she beseeches God in a dark, empty church; God gives her no sign. In despair, Hearne withdraws her meager savings from the bank, checks into Belfast's best hotel, and goes on a bitter binge.

Moore skillfully balanced Hearne's understandable drive to fulfill her sexual and social needs with the repressive institutional forces in Belfast that deny and taunt, humiliate and defeat her. He superbly chronicled her movement from hope to despair to nihilism. Knowing the grim truth leaves her emotionally and spiritually bankrupt, hopelessly tangled in the net of her lace-curtain destiny. Hearne's passion mounts to unrelieved suffering, too pathetic even for tragedy.

AN ANSWER FROM LIMBO

First published: 1962
Type of work: Novel

An examination of an ambitious writer's commitment to his career at the price of destroying his family.

In *An Answer from Limbo*, Brendan Tierney, a thirty-year-old Irishman who has emigrated to New York City, is supporting himself, his wife, and their two bratty children by working for a magazine while also trying to write his first novel. Moved to competitive action by a younger friend's announcement that his own novel will soon be published, Brendan hits on what he regards as a great solution to speeding his creative career: He brings his mother from Belfast to look after the children, encourages his wife, Jane, to take a job, quits his own, and devotes himself unreservedly to his novel.

Brendan's maneuvers prove as simplistic as they are selfish. Mother Tierney turns out not to be the simple, stalwart person she appears to be. Her dreams and fantasies reveal a troubled heart and mind as she, with her unquestioning Catholic faith, comes to live among pagans as an unpaid, overworked servant, made to feel like an exploited intruder. Jane Tierney looks on religion as a vulgar superstition while employing psychoanalytic jargon as her dogma. Hers is a spiritual emptiness that she seeks to fill by having a humiliating affair with the office creep.

As for Brendan, his ruthless ambition to become a successful writer—rich, socially prominent, sexually magnetic—permits him to rationalize his sacrifice of his family to his work; he is certain that he is offering himself on the altar of art, as such authors as Gustave Flaubert and Thomas Mann have done. When he tells his mother that he has made art his religion, she only laughs at him. Moore is careful not to inform the reader whether or not Brendan has literary talent, saying only that a publisher does accept his novel. Brendan refuses to acknowledge his responsibility for the circumstances of his mother's death (she suffers a broken hip and a stroke and experiences two days of agonizing pain in an impersonal, unfeeling environment). At her funeral, he has an unusual crisis of self-understanding:

Is my belief in my talent any less of an act of superstitious faith than my mother's belief in the power of indulgences? And, as for the ethics of my creed, how do I know that my talent justifies the sacrifices I have asked of others in its name?

On the book's final pages, Brendan admits to himself that more powerful than his grief over his mother's death is his author's drive to observe the graveside scene carefully so he can write about it someday. He confesses, "I have altered beyond all self-recognition. I have lost and sacrificed myself."

An Answer from Limbo is Moore's most disturbing as well as one of his finest novels. The book is about cultural alienation, as Mrs. Tierney finds herself uprooted from her Irish Catholic norms in the secular wasteland of North America. It is about the emotional limbo in which Jane is cast, as she realizes that her husband and children do not love her, nor she them. It is, above all, about the consequences of a dehumanizing obsession, a private ambition that ends up ruining the writer as well as those around him.

THE DOCTOR'S WIFE

First published: 1976
Type of work: Novel

An Irish doctor's wife has a liaison with a young American and ends up leaving both her husband and her lover.

The temptation is powerful to compare *The Doctor's Wife* to Flaubert's *Madame Bovary* (1857): The protagonists of both novels are married to provincial doctors, have convulsively passionate affairs with younger lovers, and engage in the subterfuges and stratagems that adulterous relationships necessitate. Yet the differences between the heroines are important: Emma Bovary was bored and unhappy in her incompatible marriage long before she encountered Rodolphe and Léon; Moore's Sheila is seemingly satisfied to be married to Dr. Kevin Redden and looks forward to a second honeymoon, when they plan to revisit Villefranche in the French Riviera.

Sheila's overworked husband is unable to join her for medical reasons, however, and when she visits her good friend Peg in Paris, she soon finds herself involved, emotionally and, in a few days, sexually, with a wholesome, handsome, charming American graduate student, Tom Lowry, who, at twenty-six, is eleven years her junior. It turns out that Kevin is rigid, anti-intellectual, unadventurous, unimaginative, and just plain unable to understand her. Moore links Dr. Redden with his native Belfast: bleak, rainy, repressive, bitter, bombed, and barricaded. Villefranche stands, in stark contrast, for a lover's paradise: sunny, sexual, self-indulgent, beautiful, uncomplicated, a world away from the blight of Ireland. Tom follows Sheila there, she discourages her husband from joining her, and soon she and Tom are joyously united.

Kevin Redden's suspicions darken to irrational rage as he finally confronts his candid wife in her hotel room and ends up raping her. Their marriage is over, but Sheila decides not to accompany the adoring Tom to the United States. She is a person of moral integrity who feels, in a Jamesian mode of moral renunciation, that she must not derive personal profit from her decision to abandon her husband. Moore dramatizes Sheila's psychological crisis in spiritual terms: She has attained a state of grace during the Villefranche episode, but, according to her Catholic outlook, she must enter purgatory to expiate her venial sins. She chooses an uncertain new life in London, where she can shed her past yet continue her penance for having betrayed both her husband and her lover. Moore, with his sober artistry, has created in Sheila Redden a heroine of a depth, intensity, and subtlety rare in contemporary fiction.

BLACK ROBE

First published: 1985
Type of work: Novel

A Jesuit missionary in the seventeenth century is sent into the wilds of Canada to convert the native inhabitants and in turn must confront an internal wilderness.

In a radical departure from earlier fictions, Moore situated this novel in the Quebec province of Canada in 1635, yet the novel features another portrait of a character struggling with a lonely passion. The novel centers on Father Laforgue, a young French Jesuit, who approaches missionary work among the "Savages" (the European name for the native inhabitants) of North America with overwhelming zeal.

As in the case of each of Moore's historical novels, Laforgue is modeled after an actual figure, Father Noel Chabanel, though Laforgue becomes a vehicle for Moore to explore long-standing themes and concerns. Perhaps the most crucial of these is the theme of faith. In Laforgue, Moore paints a portrait of man whose life, his very being, is informed by a deep, ravishing faith in something beyond himself. In many of his novels, Moore examined the loss of faith, the sense of vacuousness that comes without any sense of deep and abiding belief. Laforgue is, in fact, so dedicated and convinced of his beliefs that he longs for martyrdom and the opportunity for self-sacrifice. Thus, the location of action in the seventeenth century allows for a revealing counterpoint to the contemporary period in which lives are largely lived without any larger system of belief.

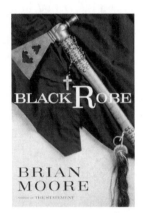

This is not to suggest, however, that Moore's dissatisfaction with the Catholic Church has suddenly vanished. Father Laforgue is so convinced of his spiritual rectitude that he stands in judgment of other Europeans in the New World and of the Savages. Intolerance and bigotry are firmly in place, as colonizers—in this case religious imperialists—attempt to impose their views on a people they blithely regard as inferior. Laforgue regards the Savages as barbaric, and in converting them, he will bring them into the light of Christianity and enlightenment. The novel, however, is constructed to challenge these convenient stereotypes without valorizing one culture or system of belief over the other.

Thus the Savages regard the Jesuits with suspicion and their own sense of superiority. Each culture, as seen in the eyes of the other, is full of superstition and sorcery, yet each is based on a dedication to the supernatural and some form of afterlife. The novel's most compelling transformation is Laforgue's movement from spiritual complacency to a deep sense of questioning not only the Savages but also his own comfortable assumptions about people and his religion.

By the novel's conclusion, Laforgue's assurance gives way to acceptance of difference. Where initially he seeks to baptize and save one soul after another, he yields to a ceremony of mass baptism. In the midst of ritual, he arrives at genuine, individual prayer, asking God to spare the Savages and questioning if God indeed loves humans. Salvation becomes Laforgue's, but not through traditional and accepted means.

THE STATEMENT

First published: 1995
Type of work: Novel

A former Vichy government operative convicted of war crimes continues to evade capture as he hides in one church and monastery after another.

Moore continues to explore the possibilities of the historical novel by writing a political thriller that is as entertaining as it is thought-provoking. An elderly man, Pierre Brossard, is pursued by a nameless figure in southern France. The reader is led to believe that Brossard, because of his age, is a defenseless victim until he suddenly brandishes a pistol, shoots his pursuer, and rolls his car off a high mountain road. Among the dead man's possessions is a document indicating that Brossard is a former chief in the Vichy government responsible for the execution of fourteen Jews in 1944. The novel quickly evolves into an intricate game of cat and mouse as government officials search and Brossard hides in one monastery or abbey after another.

The novel offers a sophisticated psychological study of a depraved soul in torment. On the surface, the central situation—a Nazi sympathizer escaping justice—does not provoke sympathy in most readers. Yet Moore so finely developed his character that Brossard is by turns thoroughly contemptible and oddly pitiable. Through much of

the novel the reader cannot determine whether Brossard is a depraved killer or a victim of overzealous officials looking to place blame on a convenient scapegoat. In a clever dream sequence the reader eventually learns that Brossard is all that his accusers have contended.

Brossard is not only a study in persecution but an example of a thoroughly self-absorbed creature as well. His life revolves around simple Darwinian self-preservation and self-justification. He has convinced himself that he is a hero, one who stood up for the true France, battling infidels and remaining loyal to the misunderstood Marshal Philippe Pétain. Because of the support he has enjoyed for so long from the Catholic Church, he is further convinced of his moral superiority.

In emphasizing Brossard's relationship with the Catholic Church, Moore once more explored his ambivalent feelings about religion and Catholicism in general. Moore often vacillated in his attitudes about Catholicism, and an interesting counterpoint is *The Color of Blood* (1987), another political thriller set in an unidentified Eastern European country dominated by a totalitarian regime. A radical wing of the Church encourages revolution, while the protagonist, Cardinal Bem, is a centrist dedicated to what he believes is God's will and the best interests of the laity. Consequently, he opposes rebellion yet resists collaboration with the state, and the novel suggests, in spite of Moore's oft-stated contempt for the Church's control of its followers, that as long as the Church is led by selfless men like Bem, it can be a genuine force for the betterment of humankind.

In *The Statement,* however, the Catholic Church and its leaders represent self-serving mendacity and political manipulation. Historically the Church, from Pope Pius XII down to parish priests, supported the Vichy government because of its opposition to communism. After the war, many members of the Church aided Vichy collaborators in evading the law. As Moore makes eminently clear, the Church is not simply a bastion of spiritual high-mindedness but a sophisticated and often ruthless institution that is well versed in the language of political intrigue.

THE MAGICIAN'S WIFE

First published: 1997
Type of work: Novel

France's leading magician travels to Algeria to perform for the local Muslim leaders and dissuade them from opposing France's imperialistic machinations.

Moore once more engaged his imagination with history, and as he did in *Black Robe* and *Lies of Silence* (1990), as he grapples with the effects of colonialism and effects of political and cultural exploitation. His novels shuttle among eras and different nations and cultures; in this novel, action is situated in mid-nineteenth century France and Algeria, revealing the origins of France's domination of North Africa.

The magician's wife of the title is Emmeline Lambert, an intelligent woman eclipsed by her husband's celebrity and her gender's marginal influence in French aristocratic circles. Her husband is summoned to Emperor Napoléon III's winter palace for what appears to be royal performance but is actually a political maneuver. Lambert is dispatched to Algeria to hoodwink a local leader into suspending a jihad that would rout Europeans from his country. Just when it appears that his charade has succeeded, his wife, acting out of disgust and an act of conscience, confesses the chicanery to the leader, and her husband is shot and paralyzed.

The theme of deception is paramount. Lambert, though celebrated and famous, is actually a cheap fraud, and like other frauds in Moore's works, he is a morally vapid figure. Witnessing his self-absorption and chicanery, Emmeline realizes that her marriage is the product of trickery. The man she believed possessed nobility of spirit is an empty vessel. The aristocrats at the emperor's palace represent another collection of impostors and predatory exploiters. Worst of all is the emperor, whose hapless foreign policy is the furthest thing from his ancestor's world-altering adventures.

Moore returns one last time to his concern with the role of faith in human life. Emmeline contrasts the empty formalism of Catholicism and its rituals with the prayers of the Muslims. In Algeria, she finds profound, genuine intensity of belief, where people, no matter how elevated or ordinary, are informed by a belief in the power and immanence of God in their lives. Then a Muslim leader forestalls his jihad not because he is overwhelmed by Lambert's prestidigitation but because of a conviction of his own moral superiority that needs no outward show to confirm its force.

SUMMARY

Brian Moore may never attract a wide public, but he is admired by discerning readers for his intelligent and sensitive command of such dark aspects of human nature as guilt, disillusionment, unfulfillment, loneliness, betrayal, and misunderstanding. He tenderly yet unsparingly created characters who are outcast from life's usual joys and who forlornly seek a spiritual beatitude they will find unattainable. Himself a lapsed Catholic and self-exile from Ireland, Moore nevertheless revisited the struggles of people who are religiously tormented and morally baffled, either as victims of a puritan, taboo-ridden, benighted Belfast or as strangers to a hedonistic, dehumanizing, aimless United States. His quietly impressive body of work earned him a place among the English-speaking world's best writers of minor rank.

Gerhard Brand; updated by David W. Madden

BIBLIOGRAPHY

By the Author

LONG FICTION:
Judith Hearne, 1955 (pb. in U.S. as *The Lonely Passion of Judith Hearne*)
The Feast of Lupercal, 1957

Brian Moore

The Luck of Ginger Coffey, 1960
An Answer from Limbo, 1962
The Emperor of Ice-Cream, 1965
I Am Mary Dunne, 1968
Fergus, 1970
Catholics, 1972
The Great Victorian Collection, 1975
The Doctor's Wife, 1976
The Mangan Inheritance, 1979
The Temptation of Eileen Hughes, 1981
Cold Heaven, 1983
Black Robe, 1985
The Colour of Blood, 1987 (pb. in U.S. as *The Color of Blood*)
Lies of Silence, 1990
No Other Life, 1993
The Statement, 1995
The Magician's Wife, 1997

SCREENPLAYS:

The Luck of Ginger Coffey, 1963 (adaptation of his novel)
Torn Curtain, 1966
The Slave, 1967
Catholics, 1973 (adaptation of his novel)
Black Robe, 1991 (adaptation of his novel)

NONFICTION:

Canada, 1963
The Revolution Script, 1971

> ## DISCUSSION TOPICS
>
> - Consider the role that fantasy plays in Brian Moore's fiction.
>
> - What significance does setting have in his novels?
>
> - Moore's work seems to defy convenient categories. Nevertheless, what fictional traditions inform his oeuvre?
>
> - Consider the theme of loneliness in a number of Moore's novels.
>
> - Moore was raised as a Roman Catholic. What role does Catholicism play in his works?
>
> - Analyze his treatment of the crisis of faith in his fiction.

About the Author

Craig, Patricia. *Brian Moore: A Biography.* London: Bloomsbury, 2002.

Dahlie, Hallvard. *Brian Moore.* Boston: Twayne, 1981.

Flood, Jeanne. *Brian Moore.* Lewisburg, Pa.: Bucknell University Press, 1974.

Foster, John Wilson. *Forces and Themes in Ulster Fiction.* Totowa, N.J.: Rowman and Littlefield, 1974.

Heaney, Liam. "Brian Moore: Novelist in Search of an Irish Identity." *Contemporary Review* 278 (2001): 230-235.

Hynson, Colin. "Brian Moore." *Book and Magazine Collector* 120 (1994): 62-69.

McSweeney, Kerry. *Four Contemporary Novelists.* Kingston, Canada: McGill-Queen's University Press, 1983.

Nichols, Celia. "Profiles of Irish Canadians: Brian Moore." *Canadian Journal of Irish Studies* 29, no. 2 (2003): 64-65.

O'Donoghue, Jo. *Brian Moore: A Critical Study.* Montreal: McGill-Queen's University Press, 1991.

Ricks, Christopher. "The Simple Excellence of Brian Moore." *New Statesman* 71 (February 18, 1966): 227-228.

Sampson, Denis. *Brian Moore: The Chameleon Novelist.* Dublin: Marino, 1998.

Sullivan, Robert. *A Matter of Faith: The Fiction of Brian Moore.* Westport, Conn.: Greenwood Press, 1996.

Library of Congress

MARIANNE MOORE

Born: Kirkwood, Missouri
November 15, 1887
Died: New York, New York
February 5, 1972

Acclaimed as one of the major American poets of the twentieth century, Moore is recognized for her innovations in poetic technique, use of detail, and exploration of paradox.

BIOGRAPHY

Marianne Craig Moore was born in her maternal grandfather's home in Kirkwood, near St. Louis, Missouri, on November 15, 1887. She never knew her father, an engineer and inventor, because earlier that same year he suffered a nervous breakdown and was committed to an institution. Her mother, Mary Warner Moore, and brother John then moved to Kirkwood to live with Marianne's grandfather, the Reverend John Riddle Warner, a Presbyterian minister.

Moore spent her first seven years in an affectionate, close-knit environment. Her grandfather and her mother encouraged serious reading and a tolerant attitude toward diverse religious beliefs. They both believed in the education of women. From her mother, she learned a verbal decorum and precision, but her mother's influence extended much further. Moore never married, and with the exception of her four years in college, she lived with her mother until the latter's death in 1947.

When Moore's grandfather died in 1894, her mother took the children to Carlisle, Pennsylvania, to live. Her small inheritance was insufficient to support the family, so she took a job as an English teacher at Metzger Institute for Girls, where her daughter began school in 1896. Moore especially remembered an art teacher who encouraged her to draw natural objects. She retained this interest throughout her life, and techniques of the visual arts influenced her poetic style.

Upon graduation in 1905, Moore entered Bryn Mawr College. Her first two years were difficult academically. During this time, she began to write poetry, and in 1907 the Bryn Mawr literary magazine published two poems, "To Come After a Sonnet" and "Under a Patched Sail." It published five more in her last two years of college. In those early poems Moore used run-on lines and a natural colloquial style, techniques that later became characteristic of her poetry. She said that she felt too immature to study English, but courses in comparative literature and art history opened her eyes to new developments in Europe in the early twentieth century. She majored in biology and histology. Later she commented that the precision, the disinterested logic, and the economy of statement in those laboratory studies enhanced her imagination. When she graduated in 1909 with an A.B. degree, she was uncertain as to her direction in life and said she would perhaps continue with her early interest in art and become a painter.

After graduation, Moore returned home and, during the next year, took a secretarial course. From 1911 to 1915 she taught business subjects at the United States Industrial Indian School in Carlisle. During these years, she continued to write, contributing ten poems to the Bryn Mawr alumnae magazine.

In 1915, two of her poems, "To the Soul of Military Progress" and "To a Man Working His Way

Through a Crowd," appeared in the April issue of the *Egoist*, a London literary magazine that was publishing the Irish writer James Joyce. With that, Moore burst upon the literary scene. During that same year, the *Egoist* published five more of her poems. Her work also appeared in the New York publication *Others* and in *Poetry*, a Chicago magazine.

The appearance of her work in these magazines coincided with other important events in her life. In 1916, she moved to New Jersey with her mother to keep house for her brother. During their stay in New Jersey, Moore made frequent trips to New York. In 1918, she and her mother moved to an apartment in Greenwich Village, where they lived until 1929. Moore worked briefly as a secretary and as a private teacher, while continuing to write. She also met artists and other writers such as William Carlos Williams and Wallace Stevens, who gathered at parties and frequented museums and galleries. During those years Moore published fewer poems. One, "The Fish" (1918), signaled a turning point in her development. She used the syllabic verse, stanzaic arrangement, and artist-like description that were later known as her unique style. She also wrote her well-known poem "Poetry," with its opening line, "I, too, dislike it."

At this time in her career her work began to be collected. Her first book, *Poems* (1921), containing twenty-four early pieces, was published without her knowledge by friends in England. In 1924, Moore assembled fifty-three of her own poems in *Observations*. This book received *The Dial* Award, which included $2,000 in prize money. Included were the long poem "Marriage," "The Octopus," and "Sea Unicorns and Land Unicorns." With this publication, she became an established poet, noted for range and versatility.

From 1921 to 1925, Moore worked as an assistant at a branch of the New York Public Library. In July, 1925, following publication of *Observations*, she became acting editor of *The Dial*. In 1926, she assumed full editorship, a job which she continued until *The Dial* ceased publication in July, 1929. In this capacity, Moore not only edited but also wrote editorials and more than a hundred reviews. Editing helped her to win recognition, so after the demise of *The Dial*, Moore was able to support herself and her mother by writing poetry, reviews, and essays.

They moved to a larger apartment in Brooklyn. In 1935, friends urged her to bring out *Selected Poems*, which included forty-two poems from *Observations* and nine others. It sold only 864 copies by 1942, but it contained some of her best verse: "The Steeple-Jack," "The Buffalo," and "The Jerboa." It also won the Ernest Hemingway Memorial Prize. In 1936, she published *The Pangolin, and Other Verse*. In 1940, she received the Shelley Memorial Award.

Other books followed, many of which included poems published in earlier books. *What Are Years* came out in 1941; *Nevertheless*, which won two prizes, appeared in 1944. In 1945, Moore received a Guggenheim Fellowship and in 1946, a joint grant from the American Academy of Arts and Letters and the National Institute of Arts and Letters. She then began translating seventeenth century French poet Jean de La Fontaine's *Fables*, a project which took eight years to complete.

The final illness and death of her mother in 1947 caused a significant change in Moore's poetry. Her grief for her lifelong companion was intense. *Collected Poems* (1951) was dedicated to her, and among the nine new poems was a brief elegy, "By Disposition of Angels." During the following seven years, Moore spent much of her time working on the fables and writing essays. In 1952, when modern poetry had begun to gain acceptance, she won the prestigious National Book Award, the Pulitzer Prize in poetry, and the Bollingen Prize. Her translation of La Fontaine's *Fables* came out in 1955. Also in 1955, she published *Predilections*, a group of twenty-two essays and reviews selected from pieces written beginning in 1916.

During the 1950's and 1960's, Moore's zest for learning and her lively responses on a wide range of subjects attracted a certain amount of public interest. Ford Motor Company asked her to suggest names for a new car. She continued to learn dances like the tango, and, famous for loving baseball, she threw out the first ball on opening day at Yankee Stadium in 1968. In 1966, she moved back to Greenwich Village.

In 1967, *The Complete Poems of Marianne Moore* appeared. This volume solidified her status as one of America's greatest poets, and in 1968 she received the National Medal for Literature. On February 5, 1972, she died in her sleep in her Greenwich Village apartment at the age of eighty-four.

ANALYSIS

Randall Jarrell, the modern American poet and critic, said that Marianne Moore discovered a new subject and a new structure for poetry. T. S. Eliot, the twentieth century British writer, felt that Moore was one of the few poets who have used the English language inventively. These sentiments are not unusual. Moore is a poet other writers admire. She had her early detractors because of her innovative rhythms and stark imagery. By the 1950's, however, when modernism became more widely accepted, Moore emerged as a major poet alongside William Carlos Williams and Wallace Stevens.

Moore's work has several distinct stylistic qualities and themes. Her main contribution is precise imagery created by a disciplined use of language. Throughout her career, she also dealt with discipline as a theme, advocating a set of values that included courage, independence, responsibility, and simplicity. Moore believed that humankind is besieged by threats to these principles and so must be constantly on guard. In many poems, particularly her later ones, she advocates creating emotional barriers to repel such threats. Throughout her career, Moore explored paradoxical situations, and seeming contradictions underlie many of her poems.

Tracing Moore's poetic career presents difficulties, for, as critic Bonnie Costello notes, her work does not conform to chronological development. Throughout her life, Moore continually revised. Each book she published contained reworked material, so each book includes different styles and themes. For example, her frequently anthologized work "Poetry" (1919), a statement of her belief in the honest and genuine in art, underwent three reworkings. The same holds true for many others. The verse that she wished to preserve appears in *The Complete Poems of Marianne Moore*, which conforms as closely as possible to her stylistic and thematic intentions.

Moore's precise style is one of controlled excitement. Her work affects the reader visually as well as emotionally and intellectually. She achieves this by presenting concrete images of ordinary objects. For example, in *The Pangolin, and Other Verse*, "The Pangolin" describes a scene near a willow tree where three hungry, wide-eyed mockingbirds as big as their mother wait for food. Whatever Moore's subject—fish, jerboa, octopus, nectarine, baseball, art—she gives clusters of precise, colorful images, always grounded in particulars. In "The Wood Weasel," the animal is an "inky thing/ adaptively whited with glistening/ goat fur." All Moore's images are visual, because she was interested in design and pattern as well as meaning.

Moore's prosody is also unique. Rather than the regular rhyme and rhythm of a form such as the sonnet, Moore uses syllabic verse. She counts the total syllables in a line and then arranges lines in balanced patterns. For example, in "The Frigate Pelican," the opening line of each stanza has fifteen syllables. This allows her to do a number of things. She is free to use normal prose syntax, and she frequently has the title as the first word in a poem. She can also use the run-on line. She is not under pressure to use masculine rhyme, because the stress can be on syllables other than the rhyming ones. She does rhyme words, but she works with internal correspondences more than end-rhymes.

Moore's basic unit, then, is the stanza rather than the line. She frequently parallels line length stanza by stanza. In "The Jerboa," for example, the third line of the first stanza has the same number of syllables as the third line of the second, third, and following stanzas. She indents to put together lines with end rhymes. This technique results in the stanzas themselves having a regularly controlled visual pattern on the page, one that is usually consistent within each poem. The pattern enhances the visual effect already created by her images. Even though the poems sometimes read like prose, they nevertheless require a dexterous reader. Because she valued restraint and precision, Moore sometimes omitted connections. She used ellipses and juxtapositions, and incorporated allusions, quotes, and other notes into the poetry.

Because Moore's style and subject matter are so precise, some critics classify her with the Imagists of the early twentieth century, who held precision as their watchword and believed that suitable poetic subject matter was whatever the senses experienced. Moore's poetry, however, differs from that of the Imagists. She not only describes things and what surrounds them literally but also merges that detail with what surrounds them imaginatively. Imagination was fundamental to Moore, and the reality she creates by fusing the two is where she finds her ethical principles. In "Apparition of Splendor" the porcupine is partially literal and partially imaginative. Combining these into one animal enables Moore to comment on her theme, order within chaos. Moore therefore takes the Imagists one step further by adding moral and intellectual convictions.

Moore developed certain themes early in her poetic career and continued working with them throughout her life. Humankind, she believed, lives in danger: People's ignorance of the significance of things and events makes them vulnerable. Nature is indifferent to people, so people must be hard and, like the cliff in "The Fish," must be on guard. One must armor oneself like the porcupine in "Apparition of Splendor," must be an "intruder," "insister," and "resister."

One form of protection is decorum and restraint, disciplines that avoid excesses in all areas of life. "Poetry" makes a strong case for stripping away all extraneous things and getting to what is honest; "The Octopus" reiterates this theme. Delight will arise from espousing values such as honesty, simplicity, and courage. Striving for them requires restraint, but the result, harmony with nature, will be protection in a harsh world.

As her career proceeded, Moore added poems that dealt with other themes, including the belief in a supreme being and the love and spiritual grace that results. "The Pangolin" details qualities of animals, architecture, and humanity, interrelating the power of grace in all their features. "What Are Years" is perhaps her most direct statement, and it shows that people can maintain the spiritual strength to keep going by being aware of something beyond the mortal.

Later in Moore's career, she also wrote poetry for particular occasions. "A Piece for Messr. Alston and Reese" (1956) was dedicated to the Brooklyn Dodgers baseball team; "To a Giraffe" she wrote for a book published in 1963 by the Steuben Glass Company. In this sort of poetry, she continued both her restrained experimental style and her thematic interests.

To speak of Moore's style and themes without mentioning her preoccupation with paradox would omit one of her major concerns. Even "Poetry" seems contradictory, as do such poems as "The Mind Is an Enchanting Thing." The paradoxes inherent in life are not problems to be solved, however: They present situations to be explored for whatever significance they present.

Moore's whole career was an exploration of these situations, whether literally or imaginatively experienced. The result is genuine poetry that renews the spirit, making her one of the greatest of the modernists.

"THE FISH"

First published: 1918 (collected in *Poems*, 1921)
Type of work: Poem

Sources of life contain forces of treachery and death that one must guard against even though one cannot completely understand them.

"The Fish" marked a turning point in Moore's development. Even though she would later write poems that were as good, critics note that she never excelled in achieving a more perfect integration of images and ideas. She creates precise images of natural things in terms that also denote human characteristics. These build upon one another to express an eternal truth—that all life forces contain death.

Moore always observed natural phenomena, both at first hand and in pictures and photographs. Her early education in art and the natural sciences provided her with a trained eye for details. In "The Fish," this observation results in images—colors, shapes, and textures—so precise that critic William Pratt included the poem in his book *The Imagist Poems* (1963), the definitive text on the Imagist movement. Like the Imagists, Moore bases the poem on common objects of nature. One fish "wades through black jade" as it moves near the treacherous cliff. The "sun,/ split like spun/ glass," invades every crevice, leaving nothing hidden. It reveals colors—the "turquoise sea/ of bodies" of fish, the "rice-grains" of jellyfish, and crabs like green lilies. Moore also introduces alien images such as "ash-heaps." These, like the verbs "wade" and "split," describe the surroundings, yet they also suggest natural and human forces of destruction.

She organizes these details so that they build to an ending that comments on the ethical significance of her images. In the first section, she describes the aquatic world surrounding the cliff:

fish, shells, barnacles, starfish, jellyfish, crabs, and toadstools. Following these images, she moves to a general statement about the nature of this world. "All/ external/ marks of abuse" show on the defiant cliff, all the physical signs of nature trying to destroy it; they show the foreboding presence of death within life. The sea, a source of life, also contains powers which threaten. Its creatures exist within it, unconscious of the magnitude of these forces; the cliff remains, a fortress against them. In the last stanza, Moore states the ethical significance of this scene. The cliff, a symbol of defiance and strength, can live on, existing and recording the history of abuses, even feeding upon this harshness.

This paradox, that life and death grow stronger at the same time, is one of Moore's favorite themes; "The Fish" contains some of her most important ideas. The cliff represents an ideal, the capacity of the courageous spirit not only to survive but also to prevail. The ocean, as it batters the cliff, represents the peril of existence that any life-form battles, but it also represents the source of all life. The fish and other creatures precariously balance between the two. All these images of life in the sea contain some hint of peril, suggesting nature's impersonal harshness and mysterious purpose. The verbs used in the images suggest unwelcome human intrusions— also forces of death. Like the cliff, human beings caught in this predicament should not hide but should face these forces defiantly. In the poem, Moore explores the human predicament, using the scene as a theater to expose ideas that are harder to clarify in a human context.

Her poetic techniques complement her ideas. The line breaks and stanzaic arrangements combine to keep the reader from scanning through too fast. It is a laborious, not an easy, movement, as is the interaction of the water and the cliff. Each stanza follows the same pattern. Each parallel line has the same syllabic count. The rhyme scheme is elaborate, but because of the run-on lines, it does not intrude. Moore also relies on the sounds to carry the meaning, quick consonants such as "crow-blue mussel-shells," rather than alliteration. She liked strict proportion and symmetry, so in each line and each stanza, she balances the key words.

This emphasis on pattern and stability in style further shows the precise integration of image and idea. The cliff is stable against constantly threatening forces; the poem itself has a strong formal arrangement. In "The Fish," Moore attempts to make sense out of the eternal problem of maintaining a resilient spirit in a world that nourishes yet also threatens at every turn. It is a theme with which she grappled her whole life, sometimes retreating to a position of hiding. Here, the ethical situation is clearly laid out imagistically. Like the cliff, humanity has no place to hide.

"POETRY"

First published: 1919 (collected in *Selected Poems*, 1935)
Type of work: Poem

A poet must present an object as itself but must also enhance it by imagination so that the poem illuminates a universal truth.

"Poetry," a poem Moore reworked several times, states her aesthetic beliefs. She published the first version in 1919, but in 1925 she stripped it from thirty lines to thirteen to comply with her principles of clarity and precision. In the *Selected Poems* of 1935, she returned it to the original. Then, in 1967, after she repudiated the syllabic verse she used in much of her poetry, she reduced it to the three lines that appear in *The Complete Poems of Marianne Moore* published that same year. (The original version appears in the "Notes" of that book.)

The poem is best known for the shocking first line, in which Moore states that she dislikes poetry. The remaining two lines of the 1967 version present some problems because she does not exemplify the word "genuine" after stating that there is "a place for the genuine" in poetry. In the original version, however, Moore illustrates precisely what poetry she repudiates and what poetry she admires.

Moore dislikes poetry that she calls "fiddle"— poetry written about stereotypical poetic subjects, such as nature, in high-sounding tones. Such works become so abstract, she says, that they cannot be understood. Poets who write this way, the "half-poets," take standard opinions as truth, then embroider them with pretty or overly intellectual language. The result is that truth, the "genuine," if it is there at all, becomes obscure.

What she admires and what she attempts in her own poems is, first, the presentation of objects for themselves. Things such as hands, eyes, and hair are honest subjects because they are useful things. She also develops images of things such as elephants pushing, horses rolling, and baseball fans cheering. Readers understand these subjects because they have experienced them. She renders her subjects accurately and precisely and then enhances them with the poetic imagination. The imagination rearranges the details, giving an aesthetic order so that the universal truths can emerge. Where the imaginative concept and the object rendered coincide lies pure realism of ideas.

If the rendering is precise and the imagination alive, readers will comprehend the truths and admire the poem because they understand it. A poet who writes this way is a "literalist of the imagination," a phrase Moore borrowed from the Irish poet William Butler Yeats. This poet will rise above trivial things to present true poetry, "imaginary gardens with real toads in them." Only those demanding raw material such as toads will even aspire to real poetry; only those with imagination will transform this raw material into truth.

This longer version follows Moore's common pattern. After the blunt opening, "I, too, dislike it," the beginning is casual in pace. To illustrate the abstract topic, she details specific images of people and nature. The poem reaches a climax in the next-to-last sentence. She ends offhandedly with a direct comment to summarize: If readers will not settle for less than the process she describes, then they are interested in real poetry.

Moore sets high standards, ones that she herself constantly sought through the revision process. Considering her emphasis on precise rendering of raw material before the poet synthesizes it by imagination, it is perhaps surprising that she so trimmed "Poetry" for the 1967 collection.

"THE JERBOA"

First published: 1932 (collected in *Selected Poems*, 1935)
Type of work: Poem

In art, as in life, the simple and natural things are virtuous; the extravagant and artificial are dangerous.

"The Jerboa" is a poem in two sections. In the first, Moore weaves together references to Egyptian art and the animals kept by Egypt's royal courts. In the second, she juxtaposes those articles of opulent living with the jerboa, a tiny desert rat which uses natural powers of survival. These contrasting images illustrate one of Moore's favorite themes: the value of the natural unity of form and function over the tendency of human cultures to perfect, transform, or possess nature, both in art and in life.

The opening stanza of the first section, "Too Much," contains the word "contrive," indicating that what follows will be unfavorable. Moore's images describe an honest picture of wasteful and artificial luxury. A crafter in ancient Rome fashions an indeterminate shape, a "pine cone/ or fir-cone," to serve as a fountain. Because Moore values precision, this indicates the first serious fault. This piece "passed for art" because it looked like something the ancient Egyptians would have liked for their courts.

The remaining fifteen stanzas describe the excesses of wealth, waste, and artificiality of the Egyptian pharaohs. They exploited animals by making them into possessions. They kept crocodiles and put baboons on the necks of giraffes to pick fruit.

They bred "dog-cats," unnatural creatures, to chase other small animals. They viewed all nature as theirs: impalas, ostriches, cranes, and geese. They liked "small things" and made playthings of nests of eggs and carved bone. These people destroyed the grace and form of nature by parodying it, by elevating some animals to the status of gods and degrading others.

Meanwhile, they were insensitive to human life. Slaves built colossi, dying in the process. Drought plagued the poor. Amid famine and death, the court kept dwarfs to make life a "fantasy." The whole environment, in fact, perverted what life should be. In games, they continued this masquerade by having men and women dress as each other. The pharaoh was the height of this fakeness, for he "gave his name" to images of serpents and beetles and was also named for them. He was no different from the other lifeless parodies.

The last three stanzas in "Too Much" are transitional. They introduce the pharaoh's mongoose, kept to kill snakes used in court rituals and games. This mongoose is restless under the restraint of its artificial existence. Unlike this animal, the jerboa has rest and joy in its desert home, "a shining silver house/ of sand" that lacks the artificial comforts of the court. Moore's meaning is clear: The life of the jerboa is preferable.

The second section, "Abundance," begins with a reference to Africanus, the native blacks who live like the jerboa when they are untouched by those motivated by greed and pride. Nine stanzas detailing the life of the jerboa follow. Moore does not moralize, but presents exhilarating images of an animal living harmoniously with its surroundings. Its color blends perfectly with the desert surroundings; it runs in a fashion that is musical. The jerboa approaches true artistry of simplicity and harmony.

Moore's poetic style enhances this theme. In the first section, the pace is slower, as though she wanted to make sure that the scorn in her lines is clear. The metrics of the second section are the same as the first—the same number of syllables in parallel lines, the same number of lines in stanzas, the same rhyme scheme. It moves faster, however; the imagery drawn from music and nature creates a lighter, more flowing effect. This contributes to the celebratory tone praising the animal that lives best because it lives in true harmony and true abundance rather than in artificial plenty.

In this poem, as in many others, Moore puts forth her value system by celebrating this uncomplicated life of an animal. Survival in the world depends on honesty in function and behavior, simplicity, modesty, and courage. Threats are everpresent, but the jerboa survives because it is fast, resourceful, and self-reliant; it is an ideal creature.

Human culture cannot realize this perfect condition, and Moore is aware of the paradoxical situation of the poet. In writing the poem she, too, has transformed the world to suit her purposes. What saves the poet from the same fate as the Egyptians is that she acknowledges that her comparisons are purely imaginary, having no power or authority. Instead, they allow the mind to imagine and pursue its own needs.

"THE MIND IS AN ENCHANTING THING"

First published: 1944 (collected in *Nevertheless*, 1944)
Type of work: Poem

The mind, a miracle of complexity and inconsistency, possesses the power to enchant and to be enchanted at the same time.

"The Mind Is an Enchanting Thing" appeared in the 1944 publication of *Nevertheless*. Both technically and thematically it is a central poem in Moore's work. In it, she uses intricate syllabic verse and stanzaic arrangements. Through a series of similes and metaphors, she alternates between details and generalities, integrating the two in the last line. The poems deals with a complex paradox: The mind is both subject and object, both enchanter and enchanted. It has the power to dissolve unities into multiplicities and also to synthesize those different facets into new unities. It has the power to transform dejection into joy, death into life. Moore is celebrating the miracle of the poetic process.

She introduces the paradox at the poem's beginning by changing a single syllable; the "enchanting" of the title becomes "enchanted" in the first line. A series of similes follows, each focusing on the contradiction inherent in being both subject and object. Having established the paradox, Moore uses an animal, the kiwi, to lead to the central part of the poem, the concept of the mind that "walks along with its eyes on the ground." Kiwi is the name New Zealand natives give to the apteryx, a flightless bird with a long beak that walks looking downward. It, too, is a paradox. It is a bird, but it does not fly. The mind is like the kiwi—it focuses intently, but it also "has memory's ear." It is in touch with the history it has stored, and in that sense, it can fly anywhere.

The sequence of similes that follows describes

strange phenomena that bring this contradiction to life: "Like the gyroscope's fall," and "like the dove-/ neck animated by/ sun." Forces of the universe move the gyroscope. Like the mind, it possesses those memories. The last line of the fourth stanza sums up these images: "It's conscientious inconsistency." Things are fixed and not fixed at the same time, just like the mind.

The concluding lines deal with the outcome of being a "conscientious inconsistency." The mind "tears off the veil" that the heart wears. Like the veil that separated the holy from the truly elect in the temple at Jerusalem, the veil the heart wears gets in the way of understanding. The veil represents certainty and, for Moore, the opposite of insight, so this process of liberating the heart to pursue truth is as important as the truth itself. The mind is also flexible. It resembles "unconfusion [that] submits/ its confusion to proof." Unlike King Herod, who refused to change his oath, the mind has nothing to do with death. Instead, the mind sustains life by its power to change sensation into understanding, to abstract from multiple detail by listening to inward as well as outward surroundings. The mind possesses all these powers and can delight itself even in a dull world; it perceives the unusual amid the ordinary. As long as it has these qualities, poetry is possible.

Moore enhances this theme by giving the poem a songlike quality. Changing "enchanting" to "enchanted" sets a rhythm. Throughout the poem, the hard consonants and rhyme scheme suggest a musical composition. Her reference to composer Domenico Scarlatti in the opening stanza reinforces this. Music liberates the spirit, but it is a controlled technical medium. Her prose technique, regular syllables per line and a precise stanzaic pattern, is also tightly controlled, yet Moore employs it to express a liberating idea.

Moore valued simplicity, and she attacked complex issues. The mind is worthy of celebration if it has faculties beyond simply perceiving stored memories. It can perceive hidden truths; it is not a weak, unchanging faculty but grows as life unfolds. It accepts the inevitable confusion of experience. Its connection with the spirit enables it to create poetry.

"IN THE PUBLIC GARDEN"

First published: 1958 (collected in *The Complete Poems of Marianne Moore*, 1967, 1981)
Type of work: Poem

Art has a public function, but the artist needs to retain a freedom of expression that exists in an absence of public demands.

Moore wrote "In the Public Garden" for the 1958 Boston Arts Festival, where she read the poem to an audience of five thousand people. In it, she considers art both in its public function and as an expression of individuality. To emphasize the importance of artistic freedom, she arranges her ideas in a series of paradoxes.

The first stanza introduces the duality. The festival "for all" takes place near Harvard University, which has made "education individual." Moore considers one individual, an "almost scriptural" taxicab driver who drove her to Cambridge. He wisely remarks: "They/ make some fine young men at Harvard." This comment suggests the beauties of the landscape, but Moore disrupts the reader's expectation by going backward from summer to spring to winter. She notes the weathervane with gold ball glittering atop Boston's Faneuil Hall in summer. Spring brings pear blossoms, pin-oak leaves, and iris. Winter, instead of death or hibernation, exhibits snowdrops "that smell like/ violets."

Moore next moves inside King's Chapel to contemplate gratitude. She quotes a traditional southern hymn about work as praise of God. A chapel and a festival are alike; they both involve an exchange. The festival-goer expects to get art or inspiration in exchange for pay or attention. Instead, Moore cites some unexpected givings: black sturgeon eggs, a camel, and, even more unusual, silence. Silence is as precious as freedom. This

comment leads to another unexpected statement, that freedom is for "self-discipline." In the next lines, Moore explores this paradox. She cites a quotation from President Dwight Eisenhower, who remarked that schools are for the "freedom to toil." She mentions the determination of prison inmates to gain their freedom by selling medicinal herbs, a strategy that would backfire if they themselves became ill.

At this point, Moore interrupts to return to the occasion at which she is speaking. She is grateful because the audience is there "to wish poetry well" by the fact of their attendance. She is grateful for religious, intellectual, and artistic freedom. She ends with that sentiment, now capitalizing "Art." Even though it is "admired in general," Art is "always actually personal." This is the exchange mentioned earlier. The artist, in exchange for self-discipline, receives silence, the absence of restraints. The public enjoys the freedom to hear the highly personal voice of the artist.

This poem typifies some of Moore's later works. She addresses the occasion, but she also continues to explore personal themes. The paradox of freedom as discipline is a central concern. She also refines stylistic devices. The syllabic verse is less exacting in the number of syllables per line than in her earlier poetry. She uses run-on lines but varies the regular five-line stanza by interjecting a three-line stanza at the point she addresses the occasion directly. Moore also employs an interesting rhyming device. She uses forty variations on a single rhyme, the "-al" found in "personal" and "festival." Perhaps she meant to suggest a pealing of bells appropriate to a celebration of artistic freedom. In varying her expected style to explore the truth of the paradox, she illustrates concretely what she went to Boston to say.

Summary

In keeping with the principle of restraint that she espoused throughout her career, Moore did not presume to have any extraordinary vision; critics and fellow poets have disagreed. James Dickey, an American poet and Moore's contemporary, believes that her poetry reached new conclusions. She accomplished this by weaving together particulars that people see but do not understand. To Dickey, her poetry presented moments of perception to renew the spirit.

Moore explored the nature of paradox. She insisted on strong values; determination and independence permeate all of her poems. She practiced the restraint that enables strong values to develop, devising new forms of poetic technique and constantly reworking to pare down to the simple yet elegant image and line.

Louise M. Stone

Bibliography

By the Author

POETRY:
Poems, 1921
Observations, 1924
Selected Poems, 1935
The Pangolin, and Other Verse, 1936
What Are Years, 1941
Nevertheless, 1944
Collected Poems, 1951
Like a Bulwark, 1956
O to Be a Dragon, 1959
Tell Me, Tell Me, 1966
The Complete Poems of Marianne Moore, 1967, 1981
Becoming Marianne Moore: The Early Poems, 1907-1924, 2002 (Robin G. Schulze, editor)
The Poems of Marianne Moore, 2003 (Grace Schulman, editor)

DRAMA:
The Absentee, pb. 1962

NONFICTION:
Predilections, 1955

TRANSLATION:
Selected Fables of La Fontaine, 1955 (of Jean de La Fontaine)

MISCELLANEOUS:
A Marianne Moore Reader, 1961
The Complete Prose of Marianne Moore, 1986

About the Author

Costello, Bonnie. *Marianne Moore: Imaginary Possessions*. Cambridge, Mass.: Harvard University Press, 1981.

Hadas, Pamela White. *Marianne Moore: Poet of Affection*. Syracuse, N.Y.: Syracuse University Press, 1977.

Joyce, Elisabeth W. *Cultural Critique and Abstraction: Marianne Moore and the Avant-Garde*. Lewisburg, Pa.: Bucknell University Press, 1998.

Miller, Christine. *Marianne Moore: Questions of Authority*. Cambridge, Mass.: Harvard University Press, 1995.

Molesworth, Charles. *Marianne Moore: A Literary Life*. New York: Atheneum, 1990.

Stamy, Cynthia. *Marianne Moore and China: Orientalism and a Writing of America*. Oxford, England: Oxford University Press, 1999.

Stapleton, Laurence. *Marianne Moore: The Poet's Advance*. 1978. Reprint. Princeton, N.J.: Princeton University Press, 1999.

Tomlinson, Charles, ed. *Marianne Moore: A Collection of Critical Essays*. Englewood Cliffs, N.J.: Prentice-Hall, 1969.

Willis, Patricia C., ed. *Marianne Moore*. Hanover, N.H.: University Press of New England, 1999.

DISCUSSION TOPICS

- Discuss the adjustment between precision and imagination in a poem such as "The Fish."
- What does Marianne Moore mean by beginning her poem "Poetry" with "I, too, dislike it"? How does the rest of the poem qualify this utterance?
- What is simple and what complex in "The Mind Is an Enchanting Thing"?
- Discuss the nature of the challenge facing Moore in presenting her poem "In the Public Garden" to an audience of five thousand people.
- Is paradox a matter mainly of contradiction or of unexpected truth as it appears in Moore's poems?
- How is Moore's prosody inventive and original?
- What does Moore's correspondence with the Ford Motor Company reveal about the relationship of the poetic and commercial sensibilities?

Jo Morris

WRIGHT MORRIS

Born: Central City, Nebraska
    January 6, 1910
Died: Mill Valley, California
    April 26, 1998

Morris's fiction, essays, and photographs convey his ideas about the human imagination as they depict the inhabitants of the Midwest.

BIOGRAPHY

Wright Morris was born in Central City, Nebraska, on January 6, 1910, the son of William Henry and Grace Osborn Morris. Morris's mother, the daughter of a Seventh-day Adventist preacher, was born on a farm near the south shore of the Platte River. Six days after Wright's birth, she died, leaving an emotional scar that would in one way or another shape the direction of all of his fiction. Morris never knew his mother, and she becomes a nebulous figure in his writings, often made conspicuous by her absence and frequently suggested by way of contrast with the many shallow, distant, and largely dysfunctional motherly types who people his novels.

William Morris had come to Nebraska from Ohio, lured west to work as a station agent for the Union Pacific railroad. The "jovial good-natured" man to whom Morris refers in his memoirs was also something of a speculator, never sticking with one job for long. Shortly after Grace's death, Will was remarried, to a young woman named Gertrude, left his position with the railroad, and took up chicken farming in an attempt to make a fortune supplying the railroad with day-old eggs. The enterprise failed when Morris's father lost his entire stock of pullets to a fatal disease. This episode appears, thinly disguised as fiction, in *The Works of Love* (1952).

In 1919, Morris relocated with his father to Omaha. William's fortunes continued to be bad, eventually leading Gertrude to abandon him and nine-year-old Wright, who by now was spending most of his time with the Mulligans, a foster family. In 1924, Morris and his father moved on to Chicago. Forced to live without much help from his father, who was struggling to find steady work, Morris learned rugged self-reliance the hard way, by supporting himself doing odd jobs and working at the local YMCA.

In 1926, in response to his father's need for a "new start," Morris made the first of several unsuccessful trips to and from California in search of better prospects. After returning to Chicago, Morris, though faced with virtually no home life, somehow managed to graduate from high school. In 1930, he enrolled in Pomona College in Claremont, California. In 1933, however, he left Pomona after deciding to spend some time traveling in Europe. After a soul-searching, adventurous year spent wandering in France, Italy, and Austria, Morris returned to the United States in 1934, convinced of his calling to become a writer.

By 1934, Morris had also married his first wife, Mary Ellen Finfrock, a teacher and native of Cleveland, Ohio. As early as 1936, Morris had begun to take photographs, which would later be published in his "photo-text" volumes, *The Inhabitants* (1946), *The Home Place* (1948), and *God's Country and My People* (1968). During the winter of 1941, while living in Los Angeles, Morris wrote his first novel, *My Uncle Dudley* (1942), a picaresque tale giving fictive form to Morris's many travels in the United States.

During the 1940's, Morris received the first two of his three Guggenheim Fellowships, allowing him to complete *The Inhabitants* and *The Home Place*. In addition to the two photo-texts and *My Uncle Dudley*, Morris found time to publish two other novels, *The Man Who Was There* (1945) and *The World in the Attic* (1949).

From 1944 to 1958, Morris lived in suburban Philadelphia, experiencing his most productive period and publishing some of his best work. The urban experience provided the impetus for *Man and Boy* (1951) and *The Deep Sleep* (1953). While in Philadelphia, Morris also became a neighbor and close friend to another Nebraskan, Loren Eiseley, the distinguished anthropologist, naturalist, and author of such books as *The Immense Journey* (1957), *The Firmament of Time* (1960), and *The Innocent Assassins* (1973). Eiseley's influence proved to be profound, and he helped Morris formulate aesthetic notions about people and nature—how human consciousness and intellectual growth depend on the ability to come to grips with one's past and the inevitable passage of time, a theme in much of Morris's fiction.

During the 1950's, Morris published *The Works of Love* (1952), a book that contains his quintessential statement not only about his father but also of the playing out of the American Dream of success on the Great Plains; *The Huge Season* (1954), a fictional account of his days at Pomona College; *The Field of Vision* (1956), a book that won the National Book Award; *Love Among the Cannibals* (1957), his most complete confrontation with the quotidian present; and *The Territory Ahead* (1958), an ambitious collection of essays on the major figures in American literature.

Morris ushered in the 1960's with the publication of what many feel to be his most sophisticated novel, *Ceremony in Lone Tree* (1960), a multivoiced narrative about how time, place, and perspective shape the American experience. In 1961, he divorced Finfrock and married Josephine Kantor, a Los Angeles art collector and dealer. In 1962, he published *What a Way to Go*, his first major novel about Europe, and began teaching creative writing at San Francisco State University, where he remained until he retired in 1975. In 1963, Morris released *Cause for Wonder*, another novel set in Europe; in 1965, *One Day*, a book about the effects of the Kennedy assassination on a small California

town; in 1967, *In Orbit*, a book about violence and crime in America's heartland; and in 1968, *A Bill of Rites, a Bill of Wrongs, a Bill of Goods*, a collection of social criticism and witty commentary about the contemporary scene.

During the 1970's and 1980's, Morris continued his impressive production of fine fiction and critical essays by publishing *Fire Sermon* (1971), *War Games* (1972), *A Life* (1973), and *About Fiction: Reverent Reflections on the Nature of Fiction with Irreverent Observations on Writers, Readers, and Other Abuses* (1975). After a brief stint in 1976 as novelist-in-residence at the University of Nebraska, Morris completed *The Fork River Space Project* in 1977 and went on to write *Plains Song, for Female Voices* (1980), a novel that earned for Morris the American Book Award for Fiction in 1981.

After 1981, Morris shifted his attention to the writing of his memoirs. Starting with *Will's Boy*, a story of Morris's childhood, he traced his maturation as a writer through successive autobiographical writings such as *Solo* (1983), a recapturing of his 1933-1934 *Wanderjahr* in Europe, and *A Cloak of Light* (1985), a memoir that covers the writer's middle years and ends with his second marriage (to Kantor).

ANALYSIS

In his long and productive literary career, Wright Morris's fictional practice remained consistent with the theoretical concerns he expresses in his essays and interviews. Morris was one of the few to combine the roles of novelist and literary critic, roles which frequently tend to diverge among twentieth century writers. His books on literature—*The Territory Ahead; a Bill of Rites, a Bill of Wrongs, a Bill of Goods; About Fiction;* and *Earthly Delights, Unearthly Adornments* (1978)—are perceptive studies that reveal many of his literary origins and aims. His novels, which are in many ways extensions of his theory, testify to Morris's unwavering belief in technique as an indispensable tool of the successful writer.

Although Morris's critical comments about fiction tend to be understated and somewhat implicit, they do suggest his profound interest in a number of artistic concerns. Foremost among these concerns are the nature and role of the artist, the writer's way of handling his material, the writer's relationship to literary tradition, the value of realism as a literary approach, and the importance of technique.

The best working definition Morris provides of the artist's role is found in this statement from *The Territory Ahead*:

Life, raw life, the kind we lead every day . . ., has the curious property of not seeming real *enough*. We have a need, however illusive, for a life that is more real than life. It lies in the imagination. Fiction would seem to be the way it is processed into reality. If this were not so we should have little excuse for art. Life, raw life, would be more than satisfactory in itself. But it seems to be the nature of man to transform—himself, if possible, and then the world around him—and the technique of this transformation is what we call art.

The passage introduces two key terms in Morris's theory—"transformation" and "reality." Generally speaking, Morris used transformation to signify the process through which unformed events, emotions, and memories—the writer's raw materials—are shaped into structured experience by the artist's imagination. The writer's role is thus to articulate experience and through such articulation build a form of reality that transcends the common plane of ordinary experience, resulting in the permanent capturing of transitory experience and feeling in the form of a work of art.

One of the reasons Morris made such strong claims for the imagination is that he sensed that the reservoir of raw material is dwindling. The workings of art, geographic expansion, and the mass media have all contributed to the exhaustion of untouched, virgin experience that fueled many early American writers. In creating material in the modern age, Morris sensed that many American artists too often have been guilty of misplacing artistic energy. To compensate for a dwindling supply of experience, too many writers have escaped into nostalgia to supply themselves with raw material missing from their own experiences. For Morris, the results of any sort of sentimental overindulgence in the past produces cliché, not art. Thus, all of his fiction represents a concerted effort to gain control over his material and to escape nostalgia by avoiding frozen and worn-out patterns of expression and behavior.

This is not to suggest that Morris completely eschewed literary tradition. In his view, tradition functions to prevent disorder and the pursuit of novelty for its own sake. He noted that an exclusive concern with newness often fails to produce the kind of art from which subsequent writers can learn. He felt that new artists must transmute their literary inheritances through technique and imagination so that what is of value is preserved and what is exhausted is not.

Even though Morris believed that literature should be in some sense representational, he was critical of some of the by-products of the drive toward realism. To Morris, a definition of realism meant more than a mere photographic rendering of the facts using the language of the vernacular. In his opinion, the successful writing of fiction requires that language be questioned, fashioned, and run through the processes of the imagination. Reality is never attained in art without being filtered through some subjective vision. As the critic G. B. Crump explains, "For Morris, the sense of life is indispensable in fiction, but it is not something that is given in the artist's materials, the automatic product of fidelity to the facts; it is achieved through his style, not through elimination of style."

Morris said in *About Fiction* that the writer's major task is to "make of this life what it failed to make of itself." To do so requires not only that the artist resist cliché, nostalgia, and vulgarity but also that he or she stand squarely in the present and face it for what it is, a place where Morris, quoting D. H. Lawrence in *The Territory Ahead*, says there is "no perfection, no consummation, nothing finished." In such a world, Morris sensed that the value of fiction is that it is, perhaps, the only means available for humanity to lend a sense of finish to the unfinished business of life. Morris firmly believed that a talented imagination can reveal the richness in almost any material. It is not essential that writers use a conspicuous style or parade their knowledge by making their works imitations of other novels. If a writer has talent and can realize his or her vision, the revelatory act will give fiction a sense of life and design on its own.

THE INHABITANTS

First published: 1946
Type of work: Prose with photographs

Through the combination of photographs and prose, Morris conceives an original vision of America's mythic past.

The Inhabitants, the first of Morris's volumes to combine photographs and prose, grew out of his preoccupation with the past. During the 1930's and 1940's, Morris began writing fiction using simple, compact visual cues to create "still" word pictures. After composing a number of such pictures, he concluded that he might actually photograph what he was describing in order more effectively to capture concrete detail and visible reality. What he was after was the look and feel of a specific time and place. To produce the look, he selected telling photographs from the many he had taken on his travels across the United States. For the feel, he used words. What resulted when Morris imaginatively synthesized his photographs and prose was the most experimental and innovative of Morris's four "photo-texts."

Technically, *The Inhabitants*, through its imaginative fusion of various points of view, anticipates many of the narrative devices Morris later employed in his multivoiced fictions of the 1950's and 1960's. As the critic Alan Trachtenberg points out in his 1962 essay, "The Craft of Vision," the book has a triangular structure that blends three separate strands: two narrative voices and the photographs. Each two-page spread has a monologue that announces the theme or argument of the book and occasionally meditates on the question of what an inhabitant is; a second voice—sometimes third person, sometimes first person, sometimes dialogue—provides a vernacular translation that narrates a particular example of what or who it is that "inhabits." Finally, the photographs provide the visual ambience or "look" of the artifacts or land depicted. The monologue maintains the continuity of the book by relating the many individual speakers to the whole and by reminding readers of the many divergent elements, as evidenced in the second voice, that represent the United States.

Essentially, Morris uses words to add another dimension to the visual cues provided by the pictures. In *The Inhabitants*, one of his intentions was to move his audience beyond the clichés of hard times, ruin, and alienation, commonplace in the photography of the Depression, into new recognitions spawned by variform perspectives on ordinary objects, artifacts, and environments. The words help overcome that problem by revealing the nature of the object or artifact.

Beyond the reading Morris gives to the photographs, however, exists another autonomous realm. The presence of the photographs authenticates the "thing itself" as an independent entity or essence that speaks using its own voice. Morris once referred to the houses, buildings, and artifacts he photographed as "secular icons" having a "holy meaning to give out." As such, the "thing" that Morris frames in his viewfinder has a metaphysical presence that goes beyond the mundane or superficial. Thus, Morris's photographs are usually concerned with significant abstract presentations, while his words are more concerned with personal interpretations.

When the photographs are coupled with textual voices, a balanced three-dimensional image emerges that represents a harmonious blend of reality and fiction. In *The Inhabitants*, authentication of time and place rapidly fading from sight shares equal status with imaginative presentation and textual revelation. Ultimately, the photograph gives, as Morris says in *Photographs and Words* (1982), an incomparable registry of "what is going, going, but not yet gone."

THE HUGE SEASON

First published: 1954
Type of work: Novel

Caught in the mundane present world of the 1950's, the protagonist, Peter Foley, finally faces and overcomes his obsession with the past.

The Huge Season is closely related to Morris's other novels in that it reflects one of his common themes: the hold of the past over the present. Where this book breaks fresh ground, however, is in its employment of raw material. It differs in that it is the first, and fullest, treatment that Morris gives to his experiences in college. Moreover, this is the first novel in which Morris shows a protagonist, Peter Foley, who actually escapes from the crippling forces of nostalgia and the mythic past.

In *The Huge Season*, the past is the 1920's, an artistically heroic age that produced such great writers as Ernest Hemingway, F. Scott Fitzgerald, and William Faulkner. When compared with the dull, seemingly unheroic 1950's, the past becomes magnified; in the minds of the main characters in the book—Montana Lou Baker, Jesse Proctor, Lundgren, and even Foley himself—it assumes blighting significance. All are, in a sense, captive to it and cannot free themselves from its compelling forces.

The central focus of the novel is one Charles Gans Lawrence, a tennis player and dormitory mate of Foley who, like Jay Gatsby in F. Scott Fitzgerald's *The Great Gatsby* (1925), has everything— money, good looks, and athletic ability. Lawrence, like Gatsby, proves to be psychologically dazzling. Exhibiting a tough, unpredictable compulsiveness, Lawrence fascinates his friends by performing audacious deeds. He first astounds them by becoming a superlative tennis player, despite the fact that he has one arm that is practically useless. Later, near the end of his sophomore year, Lawrence pulls another surprise by abruptly leaving college, apparently bored by it all, and going to Spain to become a bullfighter. Then, after being badly gored, he commits suicide, perhaps out of despair, perhaps to impress his friends, and he leaves what proves to be an indelible stamp on their imaginations.

The tension that Morris develops in the novel between past and present is filtered through the viewpoint of Foley, whose memory operates on two discrete levels. The present-day action, titled "Foley," is a third-person narrative that follows the events of a single day in which Jesse Proctor, an old friend of Foley, had testified before the Senate Committee on Un-American Activities. Foley travels to New York City, ostensibly intending to visit Proctor and Baker. In the process, however, he spends much of his time ruminating about the effects of his twenty-three-year mental captivity, dating from May 5, 1929, when Lawrence shot himself.

The past action of the 1920's is cast in a series of episodes contained in "The Captivity" sections.

Written in the first-person voice, it represents Foley's unfinished book manuscript about Lawrence. From a functional standpoint, the historical "Captivity" chapters chronicle actual historical events, while the "Foley" sections represent an attempt to find meaning in those events. In the end, they come together when Foley realizes that his captivity has been lifelong and that he has at last escaped from the pull of the past.

What causes this recognition is hinted at in an epiphanal moment that Foley experiences near the end of the book. Summing up the heroics of his generation, Foley asks himself:

> Did they lack conviction? No. . . . What they lacked was intention. They could shoot off guns, . . . jump from upper-floor windows, . . . or take sleeping pills to quiet the bloody cries of the interior. But they would not carry this war to the enemy. That led to action, action to evil, . . . and to the temporal kingdom rather than the eternal heavenly one. That led, in short, where they had no intention of ending up. The world of men here below. The God-awful mess men had made of it.

What Foley eventually recognizes is that life enhancement requires intention, which throughout the book Morris allies with conception, or the ability to make constructive use of the past. Survival in the present requires that one face facts, be they disconcerting or no, and try to put them to positive use. By the end Foley does so, and it grants him his emancipation.

THE FIELD OF VISION

First published: 1956
Type of work: Novel

On vacation in Mexico, five characters come to imaginative terms with their lives.

The Field of Vision, like *The Huge Season* and *The Inhabitants*, reflects Morris's struggle with the past. In this book, however, he is less concerned with how one escapes the past than he is with how one confronts and conceptualizes it. One of the most sophisticated and intricate of Morris's novels, *The Field of Vision* employs multiple perspectives to capture, group, and explore scattered fragments of the lives of five Americans.

What Morris reveals through the primary voices in the novel is largely a vision of failure. Virtually all the main characters are unable or unwilling to make constructive use of the past in order to cope effectively with everyday events. McKee, for example, prides himself in his common sense and adopts a conservative response to life; however, because he is unable to see beyond the superficial, he responds to the disconcerting present by retreating into the conventionality of middle-class values. Lois, McKee's wife, is conventional as well, marrying McKee because marriage provided an accepted pattern of behavior that protected her from her subverted darker desires. The McKees share material success—a big house and money—but no love. Both have rejected sex, and Lois remains "stiffly laced into her corset of character."

Scanlon, Lois's father, sees virtually nothing in the present. During the bullfight, he spends most of his time reminiscing about a wagon train that languished from thirst as it crossed Death Valley. An eighty-seven-year-old former plainsman, he saw the turn of the century but failed to turn with it, choosing to live his life isolated in a small Nebraska town. Gordon Boyd, an influential boyhood friend of McKee who once picked Ty Cobb's pocket and was the first to kiss Lois, was something of an audacious hero in his youth. Now, however, he is unemployed, and his outlandish antics hold more entertainment value than heroic inspiration. Finally, Dr. Lehmann, a psychiatrist whom Morris employs as a commentator on the characters' lives, sports a fake German accent and is more eccentric than the odd patients he treats.

To give structure to the central perspectives, Morris cast *The Field of Vision* in terms of a spectator's reaction to a bullfight and used the circle as the unifying device. The arena, a circular sandpit, is the central focus which elicits individual responses to the experience shared by the five main characters. The present events in the novel are brief, however, and are nearly inconsequential when compared to the past to which the characters repeatedly refer. The narrative technique is circular as well; it shifts from character to character, in round-robin fashion, according to the point of view presented.

One of the keys to interpreting *The Field of Vision* is found on the flyleaf to the first edition, on which Morris said that the book grew from the belief that the "imaginative act is man himself." Such a notion is reinforced in the book's epigraph, taken from John Milton: "The mind is its own place, and in itself/ Can make a Heav'n of Hell, a Hell of Heav'n." What Morris suggests is that reality, because it is evanescent and subjective, can best be captured by the inside workings of the human mind. Thus, each individual—for better or for worse—uses the imagination to give pattern and meaning to life.

LOVE AMONG THE CANNIBALS

First published: 1957
Type of work: Novel

The novel tells the story of two middle-aged Hollywood musicians who are members of a songwriting team, Macgregor and Horter, the "poor man's Rodgers and Hart."

Set entirely in the present and written exclusively using first-person narration, *Love Among the Cannibals* represents a refreshing comedic departure from the haunting multivoiced fiction characteristic of other Morris novels such as *The Huge Season, The Field of Vision,* and *Ceremony in Lone Tree.* One of the most readable and humorous novels in the Morris canon, this book was written and conceived more rapidly than any of his other works.

The story begins in 1950's Hollywood and features two men—Earl Horter, who composes lyrics for jukebox songs, and his piano-playing partner, Irwin K. Macgregor, referred to variously as a "first-class slob" and "second-class song writer." Both men are wayward World War II veterans who meet in California to work on a musical. While in the process of writing a number of songs and hanging out on the beach, the two pick up a couple of younger women and take them on a journey to Acapulco. The first is described as a "conventional" southern "chick," Miss Billie Harcum, who by the end of the story becomes Mac's dime-store bride. Eva, the second girl, is simply referred to as "the Greek." Like her biblical antecedent, Eve, Eva exudes an aura of mysterious, primitive sexuality, and she lures Horter into a brief and intense love affair that ends when she decides to drop him in favor of an aging professor of marine biology, Dr. Leggett.

In its essence, the book describes a love quest. However, instead of employing the overworked boy-meets-girl, boy-loses-girl, boy-gets-girl pattern of popular 1950's Hollywood plots, Morris uses *Love Among the Cannibals* as a vehicle for examining the consequences of breaking traditional boundaries and conventions, particularly sexual ones. Symbolically, this is figured through the border between California and Mexico. Once Horter and Mac cross it, their lives are propelled into a more primitive environment that forces them to exchange the coverings of their materialistic, cliché-ridden American identities for something that is ultimately more fleshy and vibrant. Similar to the fire-red convertible with green leather upholstery and built-in record player that is dismantled by the local natives after the car is abandoned on a remote Acapulco road, Horter and Mac are stripped by their experience with Billie and the Eva to the bedrock essentials of living in the immediate present.

For Earl in particular, this transformation brings him face-to-face with a life essence embodied in the Greek that, like Mexico, is "constantly in the process of becoming something else." Like a cannibal, he feeds on the energy she emits, hoping that he can in some way pierce through the earthly trappings of his unearthly desires. What she leaves him with is something far more significant than dreams of casual sex on a moonlight beach—a striking recognition of what essential love consists, "flesh feeding on flesh."

CEREMONY IN LONE TREE

First published: 1960
Type of work: Novel

Lone Tree, an abandoned Nebraska town, becomes the unlikely setting for a ceremony in honor of Tom Scanlon's ninetieth birthday.

Ceremony in Lone Tree is a continuation of the story begun in *The Field of Vision*. Once again, Morris uses many of the same characters he employed in the previous novel: Tom Scanlon, the man who lives his life in the past; McKee, the embodiment of middle-class conventionality; McKee's wife, Lois, a woman encased in her inhibitions; their grandson Gordon, the "infant Davy Crockett"; and Boyd, the "self-unmade man." This time, however, the scene is different. Instead of using Mexico, Morris employs the ghost town of Lone Tree as a setting.

To the five familiar faces Morris used in *The Field of Vision*, Morris adds Maxine Momeyer, Scanlon's second daughter; Maxine's husband, Bud; and daughter Etoile, who looks like a young Lois but has none of her inhibitions. The Momeyers have a nephew named Lee Roy, who uses his car to kill two taunting classmates and who shares local headlines with Charlie Munger, a murderer who slays ten innocent victims. In addition, Morris introduces Scanlon's third daughter, Edna; Edna's blustery husband, Clyde; little Gordon's inarticulate older brother, Calvin; Calvin's outspoken mother, Eileen; a character called "Daughter" (whom Boyd picks up in a restaurant in Nevada); and an unsuccessful writer of Westerns named Jennings.

By adding to the cast of characters and changing the setting, Morris is able to refine the vision of failure he introduced in *The Field of Vision*. Although *Ceremony in Lone Tree* has a number of comic moments—such as when Bud stalks and kills "Colonel" Ewing's expensive bull pup—and shares many of the same concerns with coming to grips with the past as were voiced in *The Field of Vision*, it digs deeper into the psychic center of its characters' patterns of behavior. In *Ceremony in Lone Tree*, for example, humans are portrayed as falling prey not only to nostalgia but also to dark impulses of violence and self-destruction.

In *Ceremony in Lone Tree*, Lee Roy and Charlie embody the extreme expression of such violent human impulses. By killing at random and without discretion, both express the irrational side of human nature and amplify a primitive impulse that the other characters subvert. For the McKees, Momeyers, and Ewings, this dark impulse is also the new dimension of the present and is a force to which they must awaken. Unfortunately, they do not, and choose to retreat, as in *The Field of Vision*, into the superficial.

Symbolically, Morris gives shape to this theme of destruction through the image of the atomic bomb:

> The past, whether one liked it or not, was all that one actually possessed. . . . The present was that moment of exchange—when all might be lost. Why risk it? Why not sleep on the money in the bank? . . . There was this flash, then the pillar of fire and the heat and the light of that moment illuminated for a fraction the flesh and bones of the present. Did these bones live? At that moment they did. The meeting point, the melting point of the past confronting the present. . . . [W]here it failed to ignite the present, it was dead.

This suggests precisely where the McKees, Momeyers, and, by implication, most Americans fail. For the most part, the past to which these characters subscribe is insubstantial and does very little to explain or illuminate uncomfortable present realities such as violence and the threat of nuclear destruction. To "live" requires constructive use of the past to combat the destructive elements of the present.

THE FORK RIVER SPACE PROJECT

First published: 1977
Type of work: Novel

Fork River, an abandoned Kansas town, becomes a site where a quasi-religious sect gathers, hoping to establish contact with extraterrestrials.

The Fork River Space Project is, unlike *Ceremony in Lone Tree* and *The Field of Vision*, a story of reconcilia-

tion and imaginative triumph. Early in his career, Morris often wrote about characters such as Foley, Proctor, or Boyd, who were at odds with society and frequently engaged their world with open hostility. In the novels written in his later years, however, Morris showed an increased affinity for characters who are at peace rather than at odds with their world. Kelcey, the narrator of *The Fork River Space Project*, is one such character, and his story of Harry Lorbeer, Lorbeer's partner Dahlberg, and their search for extraplanetary life illustrates Morris's firm belief in the regenerative power of the human imagination.

The story of the novel is filtered through the perceptions of Kelcey, who hires two handymen, Dahlberg and Lorbeer, to work on his Kansas house. Made curious by the eccentric work habits of both, Kelcey resolves to find out more about them. He discovers that Dahlberg is a writer of science-fiction stories. In addition, he finds that both spend their weekends in a ghost town named Fork River, where they lead a sect that believes the town to be the future site of a visit from outer space. The basis for such beliefs stems from a mysterious incident that left a huge crater in Fork River. According to legend, the event was caused by an outer-space vehicle that sucked the inhabitants of the town into the heavens. Another, more practical, theory posits that the mysterious formation was caused by a tornado. Dahlberg and Lorbeer, however, know that tornadoes never bore such scars into the earth and for that reason concede the phenomena to be extraterrestrial. Dahlberg, in fact, writes a story, "A Hole in Space," about the occurrence. Kelcey reads it and is impressed by its new vision of an unexplainable natural event.

What Dahlberg and Lorbeer hope to accomplish through their Sunday gatherings is to convince others that another visitation is possible. They believe, in essence, that if others believe, the mystery is more likely to repeat itself. Therefore, by presenting the facts of the case in an unconventional manner, they evolve a new and fresh perspective that they feel will reintroduce a sense of the mysterious into the event and will have the potential to expand the consciousness of the general populace.

In this incident, and a number of others throughout the book, Morris suggests some of his long-held beliefs about the nature of reality. In *Earthly De-*

lights, *Unearthly Adornments*, a book of critical commentary, he states that the American obsession with the "real" has had a depressing effect on the imagination. "In assuming we know what is real, and believing that is what we want, we have . . . measurably diminished 'reality,'" creating "more and more of what we know, and what we have," but "less of what we crave." In other words, the superficial materialism and relentless scientific fact-finding that dominate modern life have dried up the basic human sense of awe, mystery, and interest in the unknown. Thus, what Morris reveals through Kelcey's reaction to the Fork River Space Project is that the nature of reality is largely dependent on an imaginative construct that a number of people agree upon.

For some, especially those who look for empirical facts, Dahlberg and Lorbeer would seem to be mad. For others, such as Kelcey, there is something oddly life-enhancing about the enlarged vision these two men provide. Lorbeer and Dahlberg may be eccentric and somewhat lazy, but Kelcey senses that they have found a way to make constructive use of the imagination and are able to create a durable fiction by which to live from the fragmentary facts of their quotidian existence.

The Fork River Space Project, then, is about how mystery creates the effect of wonder and gives the imagination free rein to reformulate the essential facts. "On the mind's eye, or on the balls of the eyes, or wherever it is," Kelcey remarks, "we see what we imagine, or imagine what we see." By that statement, Morris emphasizes the notion that human conceptions of reality are more like fictions than facts, that ideas form conceptions, and that facts are arranged to fit such ideas. At bottom, the mysterious is what truly moves the imagination. When everything is known, the mind simply has no avenue for free play or growth, because the "soaring imagination" has been "leashed and hooded, like a falcon."

PLAINS SONG, FOR FEMALE VOICES

First published: 1980
Type of work: Novel

Plains Song, for Female Voices *covers three generations of Nebraska women in the Atkins family: Cora, Madge, and Sharon Rose Atkins.*

Plains Song, for Female Voices is the last novel Morris wrote and arguably one of his best. A fitting capstone to a distinguished literary career, the book received the prestigious American Book Award for Fiction in 1981. In this book, Morris returns to the Nebraska setting he had so painstakingly covered in previous Nebraska novels such as *The Home Place, The Works of Love,* and *Ceremony in Lone Tree.* This time, however, he tells his story through the eyes of three women, Cora, Madge, and Sharon Rose Atkins. In doing so, he employs third-person and omniscient narration to evoke a provocative and passionate view of women.

The only child of a widowed father and the matriarchal figure in the novel, Cora marries to please her father and moves west with her husband, Emerson. However, the thought of having sexual intercourse so terrifies Cora that she bites her knuckle to the bone during the first and last time she has sex with him. Their passionless relationship produces only a single child, Madge, who later marries a local Nebraska boy, Ned Kibbie. The other key character in the novel is Sharon Rose, the daughter of Emerson's brother, Orion, and Belle Rooney, the bride he transports from the Missouri Ozarks to Nebraska. After Belle's untimely death, Madge and Sharon grow up like sisters, even though they have markedly different temperaments. Madge embraces her domestic life and finds satisfaction in her role as wife and mother, but Sharon rejects the Plains and marriage altogether in favor of Chicago, music, and university life.

Although Cora seems to be an unlikely matriarch with little worldly experience, she is faithful to her heritage and embodies several key human values Morris had explored in earlier fiction about the Great Plains. In so doing, she becomes one of the most powerful forces in the novel, representing as she does the bedrock home-place values of hard work, abstinence, frugality, and independence. By contrast, Sharon stands in opposition to the figure Cora represents, and she realizes early on that such a life carries with it a number of limitations that stifle emotional and intellectual growth. As a substitute for marriage, Sharon finds solace in music, and to combat loneliness, she cultivates numerous friendships with women.

During the course of the novel, Sharon returns to Nebraska only three times, but the final visit is the most enlightening, coming as it does upon Cora's death. Although Sharon had rejected the life of her childhood, the passing of Cora awakens her sensibility to several profound realizations. Foremost among them is a newfound awareness of her own unshakable and subliminal emotional attachment to the Plains and a realization that the lives of women such as Cora, for all their foibles, can be valued, not merely for their integrity, but also for their refusal to submit wholly to masculine culture. More important, she learns that even though in her own life she has rejected traditional paternal values, she has not rejected humanity.

WILL'S BOY

First published: 1981
Type of work: Autobiography

Covering the years from 1910 to 1930, Morris describes his childhood, his father, and the Midwest before the Dust Bowl.

Will's Boy, an autobiography, reworks much of the same material that went into *The Works of Love*, a book with which Morris struggled through seven drafts between 1946 and 1951. However, in the more recent reconsideration of his boyhood, Morris for the first time makes a nonfictional attempt to resurrect his past. By limiting the scope of *Will's Boy* to the years between 1910 and 1930, Morris is able to trace significant events in his life from his birth in Central City, Nebraska, through his boyhood in Schuyler and Omaha, his teen years in Chicago, and on to his eventual enrollment in Pomona College.

In terms of action, Morris had a remarkable youth. His mother died shortly after he was born,

and his father, William Morris, a rambler with an eye for women, fine clothes, and money, moved from one town to another, married again, and drifted ever eastward. He dragged his son with him through a world of hotel lobbies, cafés, other women, foster parents, cars, and cross-country trips from Chicago to California and back again. Along the way, Morris showed an uncanny ability to take care of himself, finding a variety of jobs, including one at a Chicago YMCA that brought him into direct contact with street gangs and mobsters. Miraculously, he managed to make friendships, finish high school, and survive with almost no monetary or moral support from his father.

Concerning Will Morris, who is one of the central foci of the book, Morris passes subtle judgment, often relaying the pain of estrangement and conflict caused by his father's curious habits and ideas. For example, during Will's brief bachelorhood after the departure of Gertrude, his second wife, Morris, in a characteristic understatement, remarks that "we were almost companionable." His father rarely speaks candidly to his son, and Wright is repeatedly "farmed out" to relatives and other families. While staying with one such set of surrogate parents, the Mulligans, Morris's pride is severely injured by the fact that his father pays them either with bad checks or with nothing at all. Most of all, Wright is repelled by his father's loose ways with women and vividly recalls an uncomfortable moment when he caught him in bed with a young floozy. Although Morris calls his father a "kind man," he has "scorn" for him and recalls looking forward to living on his own.

The other major focus is Morris's missing mother, who haunts his memory. Her nonpresence represents an important gap in his experience. Morris puts it this way: "Six days after my birth my mother died. Having stated this bald fact I ponder its meaning. In the wings of my mind I hear voices . . . I see the ghosts of people without faces . . . My life begins, and will have its ending, in this abiding chronicle of real losses and imaginary gains."

Although the absence of his mother is painful, it is also a potent stimulant to the budding writer's imagination. Though Morris cannot replace her, he recognizes that had she lived, his life would have taken a different course, perhaps filled with "more than the wings of fiction."

Such memories as Morris has of his father and mother would seem to be fit materials for a sad, somber tale rather than one about the flights of youth. Morris, however, refuses to let the negative elements obliterate the positive ones. Consistent with a trend in his later fiction, Morris dwells on that which is life-enhancing, frequently using comic sections such as those about his stay with the Mulligans as a means to counter the senses of shame, dread, and grief that are found in his accounts of his father. The last pages of the book offer testimony to this tendency and give a sense of beginning rather than ending when they herald young Morris's arrival into adulthood with the engraving on the gates of Pomona College, "INCIPIT VITA NOVA": "Here begins a new life."

SUMMARY

Morris has been called "the least well-known and most widely appreciated" novelist in the United States today. A technical virtuoso, his unique combination of wry wit, spare rhetoric, vernacular precision, and narrative range distinguished him as one of the most original writers of his generation.

Though Morris's writings are all deeply concerned with the ways in which the past determines human behavior, he was equally preoccupied with finding ways to function constructively in the present and the future. Because he saw the imagination as the primary force that gives shape to experience, his novels applaud those characters who find ways to use it in gaining control over their lives.

Rodney P. Rice

BIBLIOGRAPHY

By the Author

LONG FICTION:
My Uncle Dudley, 1942
The Man Who Was There, 1945
The Home Place, 1948
The World in the Attic, 1949
Man and Boy, 1951
The Works of Love, 1952
The Deep Sleep, 1953
The Huge Season, 1954
The Field of Vision, 1956
Love Among the Cannibals, 1957
Ceremony in Lone Tree, 1960
What a Way to Go, 1962
Cause for Wonder, 1963
One Day, 1965
In Orbit, 1967
Fire Sermon, 1971
War Games, 1972
A Life, 1973
The Fork River Space Project, 1977
Plains Song, for Female Voices, 1980

SHORT FICTION:
Real Losses, Imaginary Gains, 1976
Collected Stories, 1948-1986, 1986

NONFICTION, ESSAYS, CRITICISM, AND PHOTO-TEXTS:
The Inhabitants, 1946
The Territory Ahead, 1958, 1963

A Bill of Rites, a Bill of Wrongs, a Bill of Goods, 1968
God's Country and My People, 1968
Love Affair: A Venetian Journal, 1972
About Fiction: Reverent Reflections on the Nature of Fiction with Irreverent Observations on Writers, Readers, and Other Abuses, 1975
Wright Morris: Structures and Artifacts, Photographs, 1933-1954, 1975
Earthly Delights, Unearthly Adornments: American Writers as Image-Makers, 1978
Will's Boy, 1981
Photographs and Words, 1982
Picture America, 1982
Solo: An American Dreamer in Europe, 1933-1934, 1983
A Cloak of Light: Writing My Life, 1985
Time Pieces: Photographs, Writing, and Memory, 1989

MISCELLANEOUS:
Wright Morris: A Reader, 1970

About the Author

Bird, Roy. *Wright Morris: Memory and Imagination.* New York: Peter Lang, 1985.

Booth, Wayne. "The Two Worlds in the Fiction of Wright Morris." *Sewanee Review* 65 (1957): 375-399.

Crump, G. B. *The Novels of Wright Morris: A Critical Interpretation.* Lincoln: University of Nebraska Press, 1978.

Howard, Leon. *Wright Morris.* Minneapolis: University of Minnesota Press, 1968.

Knoll, Robert E., ed. *Conversations with Wright Morris: Critical Views and Responses.* Lincoln: University of Nebraska Press, 1977.

Madden, David. *Wright Morris.* New York: Twayne, 1964.

Rice, Rodney. "Photographing the Ruins: Wright Morris and Midwestern Gothic." *MidAmerica* 25 (1998): 128-154.

Trachtenberg, Alan. "The Craft of Vision." *Critique* 4 (Winter, 1961): 41-55.

Trachtenberg, Alan, and Ralph Liebermann. *Distinctly American: The Photography of Wright Morris.* London: Merrell, 2002.

Wydeven, Joseph. *Wright Morris Revisited.* New York: Twayne, 1998.

DISCUSSION TOPICS

- How does the tension between past and present create conflict in Wright Morris's fiction?

- How does Morris use fiction to create a sense of time and place?

- How do photography and fiction commingle in his photo-texts?

- Why does Morris use multiple narrative techniques in his work?

- Many of his characters struggle to come to grips with experience (for example, Charlie Munger, Lois McKee, Cora Atkins, Tom Scanlon). How does Morris use such characters to develop themes in his fiction?

- Many of Morris's novels are comic. How does he create humor in his fiction?

- Morris has been called one of America's most original writers. What is original or novel in the way he creates fiction?

TONI MORRISON

Born: Lorain, Ohio
February 18, 1931

Morrison's novels develop a literary view of black American experience that is both fabulistic and realistic. She is the first African American writer to have won the Nobel Prize in Literature.

Stephen Chernin/Reuters/Landov

BIOGRAPHY

Chloe Anthony Wofford was born in Lorain, Ohio, on February 18, 1931, the second of George and Ramah Willis Wofford's four children. As an adult, Morrison was to view her father, who had been a child in Georgia in the early part of the twentieth century, as an antiwhite racist but also as someone who encouraged excellence and impressed upon his daughter a positive self-image to help her achieve such excellence. Her mother, on the other hand, maintained an optimistic, integrationist perspective, which was nevertheless tempered by a good deal of suspicion of the violence done by whites against blacks.

Morrison was an extremely bright child who, as the only black student in her class, was already able to read in the first grade, before any of her classmates. She studied Latin in high school and graduated with honors from the Lorain Public High School in 1949. She attended Howard University for four years, where she majored in English and started to go by the nickname "Toni."

Morrison graduated from Howard in 1953 with a B.A. in English and proceeded to graduate studies at Cornell University, where she wrote her master's thesis on Virginia Woolf and William Faulkner. She graduated with her M.A. in English in 1955 and began teaching at Texas Southern University that same year. In 1957, she returned to Howard as an instructor, and she married Harold Morrison, a Jamaican architect.

While a teacher at Howard, Morrison numbered among her students Houston A. Baker, Jr., who has since established himself as an important African American literary critic, African American poet Amiri Baraka (Leroi Jones), and Stokely Carmichael, the black power leader of the 1960's. As a member of a writing group there, she wrote a short story that was eventually to develop into her first novel. After the birth of two sons, Morrison resigned her teaching post, divorced her husband, and answered an ad in *The New York Review of Books* to become a textbook editor at L. W. Singer Publishing Company, a subsidiary of Random House, a job that entailed relocating to Syracuse, New York. In 1967, she was promoted to senior editor at Random House, where she worked often on black fiction. In this role, she helped develop the careers of black writers including novelists Toni Cade Bambara and Gayl Jones and black essayist and activist Angela Davis.

It was while living in Syracuse that Morrison returned to her short story about a black girl who wanted blue eyes. At the encouragement of Alan Rancler, an editor at Macmillan and later Holt, Rinehart, and Winston, she developed it into a novel which was published by Holt in 1970 as *The Bluest Eye*. It was generally well reviewed and immediately established Morrison as a writer of great talent. It was followed in 1973 by her second novel, *Sula*, a study of an intensely individualistic black woman, Sula, and her relationships to her closest friend, Nel, and to the community of "the Bottom," from which she is an outcast. It was also well reviewed (Sarah Blackburn called it "extravagantly beautiful" in *The New York Review of Books*) and was nominated for the National Book Award.

1799

It was probably her third novel, *Song of Solomon*, published in 1977, that established beyond any doubt that Morrison was a major American novelist. This powerful and often lyrically written novel, about a middle-class black man who is coerced by circumstances into searching for his ancestral roots in slavery, won for Morrison her largest audience to date and also won the National Book Critics Circle Award. Ironically, some of the same black, women critics who had been supporters of her first two novels were initially skeptical of this third one, feeling that she had strayed from the focus in her earlier novels on the societal forces which threaten black women specifically to write a more conventional narrative about a young man growing into wisdom.

Tar Baby, Morrison's fourth novel, published in 1981, may be the one which is least often read and which received the least critical attention. It traces the relationship between Jadine Childs, a black fashion model with a Europeanized background, and Son, a black Rastafarian. The conflict between Jadine's rather vague relationship to her African heritage and Son's more direct connection to his emerges as a major theme of the novel, one which remains to a large extent unresolved when the two separate at the end of the novel.

In 1984, Morrison left Random House after twenty years to become the Albert Schweitzer Professor of the Humanities at the State University of New York at Albany. In 1986, her first play, called *Dreaming Emmett*, premiered at Albany, and in 1987, her fifth novel, *Beloved*, was published by Alfred A. Knopf. It was widely proclaimed as her finest work to date, and many black writers and critics signed a letter of protest when *Beloved* was not awarded the National Book Award. It did, however, receive the Pulitzer Prize in fiction. In 1989, Morrison was appointed the Robert F. Goheen Professor in the Humanities at Princeton University.

In 1992, Morrison published *Jazz*, her sixth novel. In *Jazz*, Morrison continues her focus on African American history, moving from the slave era, which was the focus of *Beloved*, to the Jazz Age. *Jazz* is set in Harlem in 1926 and focuses upon an array of characters who ultimately cannot find completeness in their lives and their relationships. Joe Trace and his wife Violet are the central characters in the novel. Joe falls passionately in love with Dorcas, an eighteen-year-old girl. After his relationship with her ends, Joe shoots her "just to keep the feeling going." His wife Violet longs for the children she never had and even sees in Dorcas the daughter she never bore. The characters in *Jazz* are very much like the characters in a jazz or blues song. They live lives of desire, always painfully aware of both the beauty and the vanity of a desire that is never fulfilled. *Jazz* is a novel about the inescapability and the insatiability of human longings.

In 1993, Morrison became the first African American woman to win the Nobel Prize in Literature. In the award citation, the Nobel Committee called Morrison a writer "who in novels characterized by visionary force and poetic import, gives life to an essential aspect of American reality." In 1998, Morrison published her seventh novel, *Paradise*. For the third time, Morrison chose to use a very specific historical focus for her novel. Though she set her novel in the 1970's, she focuses on an all-black town in Oklahoma called Ruby. The town is based on a number of towns that were founded in the aftermath of the Civil War by blacks who went west looking not only for opportunity and land, but also for asylum from racial prejudice. The citizens of Ruby have isolated themselves from whites, but they have also isolated themselves from all types of corruption—sin, death, and what they call immorality. When the convent near their town becomes a haven for "lost" women, they attempt to protect themselves from corruption by destroying the women housed there. Their rejection of these women echoes the white rejection of blacks that was the central failing of American democracy. In order to face the consequences of their mistake, the town must change and in so doing face the reality of becoming a human community.

The central concerns of Morrison's fiction have always been the history of physical and economic violence against human beings, the disruption of positive black cultural traditions caused by white violence, and the amazing resilience of those traditions in the face of discrimination and persecution. Her focus has usually been primarily on the violence done to, and the cultural traditions of, black women, but increasingly her focus has extended to the price all human beings pay for violence and prejudice, both as perpetrators and as victims. In Morrison's world, cultural traditions become methods of holding society together in times of change, violence, and discrimination. Through the power of her writing, Morrison has succeeded in making the concerns of African Americans and all Americans who have participated in and been victimized by violence and discrimination central in American fiction.

Never one to sit on the sidelines, Morrison also engages the same issues in public lectures and in articles that have appeared in *The New York Times Magazine, Michigan Quarterly Review,* and elsewhere. Add to this her accomplishments as an editor and influential educator, and Morrison must be ranked with W. E. B. Du Bois and Langston Hughes as one of the most important and influential black writers of the twentieth century—and possibly as the most important black woman writer in American history.

ANALYSIS

The term "Magical Realism," often used to describe the fiction of Gabriel García Márquez, has also been applied to the fiction of Morrison. Though the thematic concerns of her work are in most other ways very different from those of Nobel laureate García Márquez, one does find in Morrison's fiction the same sense of the reality of magic, which (especially in her case) springs from a fundamental belief in the truth at the center of folklore.

The development of the use of folklore can be traced in Morrison's novels. It begins in *The Bluest Eye,* in which the sample from a child's reader that begins the novel is treated as a bit of contemporary folklore. It is an artificially constructed, white, middle-class folklore, however, which may not reveal a fundamental truth about anyone's life and which certainly does not apply to the lives of the black residents of Lorain, Ohio. Nevertheless, the main character, Pecola, is shown as having accepted the view of the world that this children's story encourages, even though it is a view which leaves no room for the realities of her life.

Sula, Morrison's second novel, incorporates characters that seem almost mythic, much as figures in folklore. There is the light-skinned man called Tar Baby and the three boys that Eva Peace takes into her household. Each one is named Dewey, and their identities begin to meld together. Perhaps most notably, there is the character Shadrack, who returned feebleminded from World War I and who becomes a mysterious hermit living on the edge of the black community of Medallion (called

"the Bottom"). He celebrates National Suicide Day each year. He eventually leads many within the community to their deaths in deserted tunnels near the town. Although the action in *Sula* is often strange and mysterious, it reflects the uncanny realism of myth.

It is in *Song of Solomon* that folklore, as such, comes explicitly to the foreground. Not only is there a minor character who appears as a ghost, but also the premise of the novel is adapted from African American folklore. The main character, Milkman Dead, uses a child's rhyme he overhears to uncover the secret of his own past, namely that his great-grandfather was one of the legendary men who supposedly escaped slavery by flying back to Africa. To become a complete person, Milkman not only has to make a connection to this folkloric ancestry but also must find how this ancestry can and cannot be applied to his own life.

Tar Baby explicitly continues the attempt to update and apply traditional black folklore to modern society and literature. The Rastafarian Son begins to perceive upper-class Jadine as a Tar Baby figure, someone who will trap him, and the last lines of the novel, describing Son running away "Lickety-split. Lickety-split," reinforce his connection to Brer Rabbit. It is probably in *Beloved* that Morrison uses magical and folkloric elements in the most fiercely original way.

Beloved concerns itself with the plight of Sethe, an escaped slave who, facing recapture, kills her youngest daughter rather than let that daughter grow up in slavery. The novel begins several years later, when Sethe and a surviving daughter, Denver, are living in the post-Civil War era in a house they believe to be haunted by this infant's ghost. Shortly after the haunting ceases, a young woman appears who introduces herself as "Beloved"—the only word on Sethe's daughter's gravestone.

Beloved is actually the first part of a trilogy of novels that Morrison would complete in the 1990's with *Jazz* and *Paradise.* In this trilogy Morrison moves her focus from folklore to history. In *Beloved,* she explores the history of slavery. In *Jazz,* she explores the history of the Jazz Age or the Harlem Renaissance. Finally, in *Paradise,* she explores a little-known fact of African American history: the founding of all-black towns in the West in the years following the end of the Civil War. All three of these novels are fictional, but each of them focuses upon important issues in the history of African Americans in this country: the human cost of surviving slavery, the improvisational nature of jazz and black life in the urban centers of the Northeast, and the desire to escape white discrimination by creating a kind of "paradise" where whites cannot enter. Each one of the novels is rich in the African American folklore and myths that she uses in her earlier novels, but they are also firmly rooted in history.

Whether dealing with folklore, music, or history, Morrison dramatizes both the difficulty and the joy of being black. The great miracle in her work is the miracle that exists throughout African American culture: that discrimination does not turn human beings into animals. Instead it empowers them to create magical and profound ways of surviving.

THE BLUEST EYE

First published: 1970
Type of work: Novel

A young black girl who wishes to have blue eyes is raped by her father and goes insane.

Morrison's first published novel, *The Bluest Eye*, is marked by much narrative experimentation and a dedication to exploring the struggles with dignity and violence that especially confront blacks. The wide-ranging narrative experimentation is something that, for the most part, her later novels would not continue; the themes with which it deals, however, were to remain important in all of her later works.

The novel begins with a brief sample story such as might be found in a typical child's reader about "Dick and Jane." This story is repeated twice, first without any punctuation, and a second time without even any spaces between the words, as if to suggest the unreasoning power that such stories have over the mind of the main character, Pecola Breedlove.

After this, the voice of the character who is the main narrator, Claudia McTeer, appears, and she very quickly summarizes the plot of the novel that follows: Pecola was raped by her father and became pregnant with a child who never grew. Claudia relates this from a child's point of view, calling the reader's attention not to the rape itself but to the marigold seeds that she and her sister, Frieda McTeer, planted at the same time but which never grew. In this way, the shock value of this rape is removed from the narrative and the focus of the novel is shifted away from what happened to why and how it happened.

The main body of the novel is broken into four sections, titled "Autumn," "Winter," "Summer," and "Fall." The first part of each section is narrated by Claudia and is followed by other parts, which are headed by quotations from the child's reader and are narrated from a variety of perspectives, usually in the third person. The first section begins in the autumn of 1940, in Lorain, Ohio. Shortly after Claudia and her sister Frieda recover from the flu, Pecola comes to stay with the McTeer family temporarily because her father, Cholly Breedlove, started a fire in their rented home, landing himself in jail and putting the rest of his family out of a home.

When Frieda offers Pecola a Shirley Temple mug from which to drink milk, the two girls discuss how "cu-ute" Shirley Temple is. Pecola drinks three quarts of milk in one day for the pleasure of looking at this mug. Pecola clearly idolizes Shirley Temple as the ideal girl, even though such a fair-skinned ideal leaves the dark-skinned, brown-eyed Pecola to be condemned as ugly. The reader later learns that Pecola's nightly prayer is for God to make her eyes beautiful and blue so that her family will be so impressed by them that they will never fight in front of them again.

In fact, this ideal is almost a mental inheritance from Pecola's mother, Pauline Breedlove, who adopted her own standards of beauty from the silver screen—to the point of taking Pecola's name from "Peola," a light-skinned girl of mixed race in the film *Imitation of Life* (1934).

While she is still staying with the McTeer family, Pecola begins menstruating. Learning that this means she can have a baby now, she asks Claudia, "How do you get somebody to love you?" Much of the rest of the novel is a presentation of different people's ways of asking and answering that question. Pecola herself takes her question to three prostitutes; they do not answer her question, but they do make her feel welcome. Pecola also buys some Mary Jane candies so she can experience, as she eats them, what it might be like to be lovely and loved, as the girl on the candy wrapper is. These two passages between them epitomize the idea that love is something which is packaged and sold—but only in imitations.

Some of the most engrossing passages of the novel are the ones that trace the personal histories of Cholly and Pauline Breedlove. One passage that is narrated alternately by a third-person narrator and by Pauline recalls the beginning of her relationship with Cholly and the deterioration of their marriage after they moved north to Ohio. It is clear that Cholly has become increasingly harsh over the years, but she nevertheless recalls their lovemaking fondly, and this fondness is part of why she stays with him.

Cholly's story leads directly to his rape of Pecola. At the funeral of his Aunt Jimmy, who raised him, he coaxes a cousin, Darlene, into having sex with him, but they are caught by a group of white men who point guns at them and tell them to keep going. This event lodges itself in Cholly's mind as an initial moment of depravity which always urges him on to other depravities. By the time he meets Pauline, the reader learns of a variety of crimes, including murder, of which he is guilty. His courting of her comes to look like only one more thing he did simply to prove that he could; his turning against her seems inevitable. His rape of Pecola is not excused, but it is seen as an extension of the early experience that forever linked violence and tenderness together for him. When, one evening while she is doing dishes, he glimpses Pecola's enormous longing for his affection, he feels that he "wanted to break her neck—but tenderly." He rapes her on the kitchen floor, then covers her with a blanket and leaves.

Pecola, pregnant, eventually takes her wish for blue eyes to Soaphead Church, a light-skinned West Indian man who supports himself as a "Reader, Advisor, and Interpreter of Dreams." He gives Pecola poison to feed to a lazy dog with the instructions that when the dog dies, she will have blue eyes. The next one sees of Pecola, she is clearly mad and is having a conversation with an imaginary friend who assures her how blue her eyes are.

The Bluest Eye ends with Claudia telling the reader that Pecola lives on as a beggar, picking through people's garbage. Claudia sees Pecola as a victim who was sacrificed by the entire community. The responsibility does not belong only to Cholly, who, she allows, tried in his destructive way to love her. Instead, the major responsibility for Pecola's victimization lies in the society into which she was born. Speaking for the novelist, Claudia wants to indict the way society encourages people such as Pecola and Cholly to measure themselves by arbitrary standards (such as race) that deny them individual value.

SULA

First published: 1973
Type of work: Novel

An unconventional black woman becomes an outcast in a black community.

Sula is a novel about the growth, development, and destruction of a person, a friendship, and a community. At the beginning of the novel, the hill on which the black community of Medallion, Ohio, lived (called "the Bottom," because the white farmer who gave it to a freed slave in return for services told him it was the bottom of heaven) has been deserted. The narrative as a whole sets out to tell why; along the way, one meets a striking variety of characters set against a harsh world.

Sula Peace's grandmother, Eva Peace, is one of the most remarkable characters in the novel. Left by her husband with three children to care for, she drops the children off with a neighbor and leaves town, to return a year and a half later missing one foot lost in a railroad accident, but with ten thousand dollars. When Sula is still young, Eva locks Plum, her son who had returned from World War I two years earlier, in his room and sets him on fire because he has become a drug addict. This is only the first of several shocking deaths.

As a child, Sula's closest friend is Nel Wright. In a scene that demonstrates the extent to which Sula has adapted to the violence of her surroundings, she slices off the tip of her own finger with a knife in front of some white boys who have been bothering Nel, as an unspoken threat of castration. At another time, when Sula and Nel are by the side of the river, they start teasing a young boy called Chicken Little. Sula swings Chicken around until he slips from her hands and sails, giggling, into the river—from which he never emerges. This incident forms a grim link between the two friends which separates them as much as it joins them. When the reader finds out that the sole witness to this event is Shadrack, a shell-shocked war veteran who (on the third day of every year) leads a National Suicide Day, a link seems to be made between Sula and Shadrack as outsiders.

The chaotic logic of calling a hill "the Bottom" dominates the novel. The random, violent deaths that appear throughout seem an extension of this logic, the point being that the initial act of greed and viciousness with which almost valueless land was given to a black man as valuable continues to shape and control the lives of the people who live there, preventing the establishment of any healthy social order. The result is that for Sula and Nel, the Bottom is less of a community than a furnace in which their souls are shaped.

The image of the Bottom as a furnace is supported not only by the fiery death of Plum but also by the similar death of Hannah, Sula's mother. When Eva looks out a window and sees that her oldest daughter, Hannah, has set herself on fire while setting a yard fire, she leaps from her room in an attempt to smother the flames covering Hannah. Hannah bolts and runs until someone douses her flames, much too late to save her life. Later, as Eva is in the hospital with her own injuries, she realizes that Sula had watched the whole thing passively. The implication is that Sula, as an inactive witness to her mother's death, shares some blame for it; as in *The Bluest Eye*, knowledge of a situation demands action.

At the end of part 1, Nel marries Jude Greene. Part 2 begins with Sula returning to the Bottom after having attended college. She arranges to have Eva removed to a nursing home and takes up residence in her house. After reestablishing her friendship with Nel, she then destroys it by seducing Jude. Sula does not understand the extent to which things have changed since they were young and shared boyfriends; Nel does not understand the extent to which things have not changed.

After her friendship with Nel ends, Sula lives in the Bottom as a pariah. She uses and discards a string of white and black men for sexual relations and so raises the wrath of the townspeople against her, until they come to think of her as evil. Ironically, Sula's "evil" presence in the town makes the parents more careful with their children, and

married women more devoted to their men. Sula herself does become obsessed with one man, Albert Jacks ("Ajax"), for a while, and even fantasizes that his body is made of gold, but he goes to an air show in Dayton and leaves her.

On Sula's deathbed, Nel tries to make up with her, but they get into a fight about the past. Nel accuses Sula of not respecting anyone else's values; Sula accuses Nel of not developing any values of her own. Though Nel has come by to help, she leaves Sula to die alone. Even so, Sula dies thinking, "It didn't even hurt. Wait'll I tell Nel." Shortly after Sula's death, Shadrack leads a National Suicide Day crowd down to some abandoned tunnels; the tunnels suddenly flood, killing much of the town, in the event that effectively ends the life of the Bottom.

The final section of the novel is set twenty-five years after Sula's death, in 1965. Nel goes to visit Eva Peace, who confuses her with Sula. After leaving Eva, Nel visits Sula's grave. As she leaves the cemetery, she calls out to Sula, overcome with grief for how much she has missed her childhood friend.

While Sula is living as an outcast in the Bottom, the narrator says that she is an artist who lacks the discipline of any art to sustain her. In *Sula*, Morrison has created a novel about a character who has the ability and the need to question a malformed society but who lacks the means to channel her rebellion into a constructive form. One of the formations Sula challenges is the one that sees marriage as the basic unit of society. For her, friendship with Nel is more fundamental than any relationship with a man. Twenty-five years after Sula's death, Nel realizes that friendship with Sula was always fundamental for her, too.

SONG OF SOLOMON

First published: 1977
Type of work: Novel

A middle-class black man growing up during a period of racial unrest uncovers his family's history.

Song of Solomon, for which Morrison won the National Book Critics Circle Award, is an enormously complex novel which, at the same time, is her most absolutely clear work; it may be her most popular book.

From the first lines of the book, the novel concerns itself with the idea of black men flying, an image it gets from black folktales which said that in the days of slavery, every now and then a slave would remember how to fly and would fly back to Africa. The main character of the novel, Macon Dead III (who picks up the name Milkman because his mother, Ruth Foster Dead, nurses him until he is past the age at which a child is usually weaned), is born the day after a black life insurance agent, Robert Smith, leaps to his death in an attempt to fly to Canada. When, as a very young man, Milkman

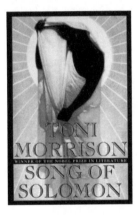

learns that he himself cannot fly, he loses all interest in the world.

From a young age, Milkman's closest friend is a boy who goes by the name of Guitar, who is a bit older and quicker than Milkman. It is Guitar who introduces Milkman to Milkman's own aunt, Pilate, whose name was chosen by her father at random out of the Bible (it suggests not only Pontius Pilate, but also the pilot of an airplane); she is the person who holds many of the keys to the knowledge Milkman will need to learn to fly.

Milkman's father, Macon, is the son of a freed slave who was killed for his land; he grew up as a harsh, greedy man, dedicated to making money. Milkman's mother is the adored daughter of the first black doctor in the town, a man who is memorialized in the name the black population still uses for one street: Not Doctor Street. Their marriage is animated by Macon's tirades against his wife and by little else.

Milkman grows up spoiled. He works for his father collecting rents and has a long and ongoing affair with his cousin Hagar, Pilate's granddaughter, which he never takes seriously—not even when Hagar tries to kill him for breaking up with her. Unlike his father, who consciously shapes his own attitudes toward people after the attitudes of the white people who persecuted his family in his youth,

Milkman unthinkingly adopts an attitude that allows him to use people.

When Milkman grows up, his father tells him about the feud that came between Pilate and himself as children. After their father was killed, they took refuge in a cave, where Macon assaulted and apparently killed a man carrying sacks of gold. Years later, Macon is still convinced that a sack Pilate has hanging in her living room contains that gold. Milkman and Guitar steal the sack; Milkman wants the money for himself, and Guitar wants the money for a black guerrilla organization he belongs to called the Seven Days, which is dedicated to killing one white person for every black person killed by a white. When the sack proves to contain nothing but rocks and bones, Milkman, Guitar, and Macon all remain convinced that Pilate did something with the money.

In part 2 of the novel, Milkman retraces Pilate's wandering as a child a half century after Macon and Pilate parted in the cave over the gold. He finds both an old woman who once sheltered the youngsters and the cave they hid in, but no gold, so he continues south to a town in Virginia called Shalimar, his grandfather's original hometown. In this way, the novel does a marvelous job of adapting a quest motif. In the process of looking for gold, Milkman, in fact, finds his own family's history, eventually learning (by deciphering a children's rhyme he overhears) that the town of Shalimar is named for his own great-grandfather, who supposedly flew back to Africa.

In the course of the quest, Milkman has become a less selfish person, and when Guitar, who has been tailing him, sees Milkman help another man load a heavy carton for shipping, he assumes that Milkman has found the gold and violated their arrangement. Thus, he begins to hunt Milkman with the intent of killing him. Milkman, however, has found his "gold" in the story of his great-grandfather's flight.

Having realized that Pilate's sack of bones contains her own father's remains (and not, as she thought, the remains of the white man she believed her brother had killed), Milkman flies back home to tell her, only to discover that Hagar has starved and fretted herself into a fatal fever over him. Milkman determines to care for Hagar's soul in death the way he never did in life, and he returns to Virginia with Pilate to bury her father's bones on the spot from which Shalimar (also called Solomon) is supposed to have leaped. Guitar is waiting for them across a narrow ravine, however, and shoots Pilate, intending to hit Milkman.

In the last paragraph, Milkman himself leaps across the narrow ravine, to the landing below, where Guitar is. It is a moment of pure inspiration that encompasses his entire history and heredity. To underscore the point, Morrison ends the novel with him in mid-air, flying toward Guitar.

Milkman's character development is triumphant but not without troubles. As his great-grandfather's flight, which the reader is free to think of as a real, magical flight, an escape from slavery, or a suicide, caused him to abandon an entire family, so Milkman's leap at the end might be read as an impetuous act that undercuts his intentions to be more responsible to people. The reader at the end has to make a leap of faith with Milkman, not only to assume Milkman will survive this leap but also to believe that he will be able to continue his personal growth when he gets back home. Nevertheless, the novel's triumph is unequivocal in its vivid demonstration of how links with the past can renew and guide the present.

BELOVED

First published: 1987
Type of work: Novel

A former slave meets a young woman who may be her daughter's ghost incarnated.

Morrison's novel *Beloved* is her single greatest novelistic achievement and is a tour through some of the nightmares created by slavery. When the novel begins in the post-Civil War era in 1873, Sethe, a former slave who escaped to the North while pregnant during the time of slavery, is living with her oldest daughter, Denver, in a house they both believe to be haunted by the ghost of the infant daughter Sethe killed when she was about to be recaptured (rather than let the daughter grow up in slavery). The novel is loosely based on the account of a former slave named Margaret Gamer who, as an escaped slave, tried to kill all of her children when they were captured in 1850 and succeeded in killing one; the novel is also a triumph of imagination.

When Paul D, who along with Sethe was a former slave at a plantation known as Sweet Home, comes to Sethe's house on 124 Bluestone Road and quickly becomes her lover, the ghost disappears. Very shortly thereafter, however, a well-dressed young woman about the age that Sethe's daughter would have been had she lived appears on the doorstep and introduces herself as "Beloved"—which is the only word on the gravestone that Sethe placed over her dead infant.

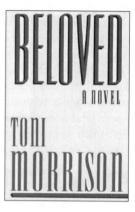

Paul D's reappearance and Beloved's sudden appearance force Sethe to confront the past locked away in what she calls her "rememory." She tells Paul D the story of spotting Schoolteacher, the cruel master of Sweet Home, and determining to put her babies "where they'd be safe"—that is, to death. What frightens Paul D more than anything else is her continued defense of her actions years later. Paul D is also forced by his meeting with Sethe to confront his own past. When he tells her, "You got two feet, Sethe, not four," to upbraid her for her infanticide, he is accusing her of acting like an animal. The comment seems to relate also to Paul D's past and his own struggle to retain his human dignity despite having been a slave and treated as a beast of burden for much of his life.

Beloved herself is presented as childlike and self-centered, very much like the petulant ghost that had haunted the house for years. Even when the narrative goes inside her head, it is not clear to what extent she is supposed to be literally the ghost of Sethe's daughter. Stamp Paid, a local black man, suggests that she might be the young woman who was kept locked up as a sex slave in a nearby town. Her own interior dialogue seems to suggest two separate minds at work, and perhaps the explanation most consistent with everything the novel contains is that Beloved is the escaped sex slave possessed by the ghost of Sethe's dead daughter. To see this explanation as a resolution to the puzzle presented by Beloved, however, would be to miss the force of Morrison's careful ambiguity. Beloved is a ghost, and, as Denver tells Paul D toward the end, something more; she is a person and something more. That something more is the key to unlocking the past to release the future.

As events draw to a climax—as Paul D becomes Beloved's lover and then moves out, as the household on 124 Bluestone becomes more removed from the outside community, and as Beloved demands almost obsessive attention—it is Denver, the daughter Sethe gave birth to while racing to freedom, whose future seems the most to be a prisoner to the past. It is unexpectedly Denver who finds the way to unlock the future for all of them, by getting a job that takes her outside her home. By working in the community, Denver reawakens in the community a sense of responsibility for Sethe, and they come together to try to exorcise Beloved—who is fat and maybe pregnant by now—from the house.

When members of the black community are gathered around the house at 124 Bluestone, Sethe sees Mr. Bodwin, her white landlord and Denver's employer, appear on horseback, looking a bit like Schoolteacher had two decades earlier when he had come for her. She tries to attack him with an ice pick but is intercepted. In the confusion, Beloved runs into the forest; later, there are reports of a madwoman having been spotted running naked. When it ends, Sethe seems finally to have given in to the despair that she had repressed for twenty years. Paul D tries to comfort her, however, and there is a strong suggestion that she is better off for being able to feel her despair.

In many ways, *Beloved* is a meditation on the ownership of human beings. Ironically, when Sethe kills her infant daughter to save her from slavery, she is committing the ultimate act of ownership—deciding that it is better for another person to die than live. She cannot help but repeat some of the sins of slavery, even in her reaction against it. The point is that slavery is so destructive that ending it is merely one step in healing the wounds it creates. Baby Suggs, Sethe's mother-in-law, who lived with Sethe for a while, seems to summarize the novel's theme early in the book when she says, "Not a house in the country ain't packed to the rafters with some dead Negro's grief." *Beloved* is a novel about healing such grief.

JAZZ

First published: 1992
Type of work: Novel

Much as in a blues or jazz song, Joe Trace's affair with Dorcas, a much younger woman, becomes an emblem of the unrequited desire so central in jazz and in life itself.

Much as in *Beloved* and in *Paradise*, Morrison focuses in *Jazz* on a particular period of African American history: the 1920's, sometimes called the Jazz Age. African Americans migrated in large numbers to urban areas of the Northeast in the early part of the twentieth century. They came to escape the racial discrimination so prevalent in the South and to find economic opportunity that urban centers in the Northeast promised. Their migration, sometimes called the Great Migration, created all-black areas in cities such as Chicago and New York City. Harlem is the most famous of these and is the setting for *Jazz*. The existence of large numbers of people of African descent in places such as Harlem created an explosion of African American art that became known as the Harlem Renaissance. A large part of this art was jazz, which gives Morrison the title of her novel and also the thematic center of her story. The economic opportunity that drew so many African Americans to the North never materialized, but the lives lived in the context of the city and the music are the subject of Morrison's novel.

Morrison's narrator gives to the reader the central plot on the opening page of the novel: "he fell for an eighteen-year-old girl with one of those deepdown, spooky loves that made him so sad and happy he shot her just to keep the feeling going." The "he" in this passage is Joe Trace. The eighteen-year-old girl is Dorcas. Joe Trace's wife, Violet, is the third party in the triangle. The narrator tells the reader, also on the first page of the novel, that Violet "cut her [Dorcas's] dead face" at the funeral. This sordid story is the center piece of the novel, and it bears an uncanny resemblance to the lurid "stories" of unrequited longing that are often at the center of blues and jazz songs.

All of the subplots in the novel follow the same pattern. Joe Trace seeks in Dorcas the mother he has sought all of his life but been unable to find. Similarly, Violet lost her mother to suicide and has always longed after her. She also longs for the children she has never been able to bear because of miscarriages and the busyness of city life. In some respects, she longs after Dorcas just as Joe has, for she is the child she never had. Dorcas herself is filled with longing for her parents who died in the East St. Louis race riots. Having been raised by the repressive Alice Manfred, Dorcas desires Joe and later Acton, a lover her own age. When Joe shoots her in jealousy, she ultimately bleeds to death, but she directs her last words to Joe: "There's only one apple," she says, implying that just as Adam and Eve, she and Joe have succumbed to the temptation to fulfill their longings; like Adam and Eve, they have failed.

Every other character in the novel conforms to this pattern of unrequited desire, even the narrator who desires the reader (*your fingers on and on, lifting, turning*) who desires to create characters that are in some way complete. However, the narrator confesses " I missed it altogether." What Morrison does not miss in this novel, however, is the feeling engendered by jazz. It is embodied in the orphanhood of all of the characters and embodied in this hauntingly lyrical description of urban life: "A colored man floats down out of the sky blowing a saxophone and below him, in the space between two buildings, a girl talks earnestly to a man in a straw hat."

PARADISE

First published: 1998
Type of work: Novel

An all-black town in Oklahoma must come to terms with its own persecution of outsiders.

Toni Morrison's *Paradise* explores a little-known fact of African American history: the migration of African Americans to the West after the Civil War. Like many whites who went west in the latter half of the nineteenth century, African Americans who migrated west sought a better life. In the case of African Americans, however, a central facet of that better life was isolation from white discrimination.

For that reason, black townships were formed in Oklahoma and Texas. Morrison's novel focuses upon a fictional township called Ruby in the state of Oklahoma during the 1970's. Ruby is actually the second township formed by the fictional community at the center of her novel. The first was named Haven and fell apart in the 1930's as cotton prices dropped and the town's population shrank because of limited opportunity and isolation. The founders of Ruby, who had descended from the founders of Haven, moved their town, bringing with them the oven which was at the center of Haven. They made the oven the centerpiece of Ruby. Inscribed upon its lip were the words the original founders had seen as the central tenet of their founding faith: "Beware the Furrow of His Brow." However, as a result of time and use, the words were now worn away so that some in town could only make out "The Furrow of His Brow" and others thought they might even read "Be the Furrow of His Brow."

On the outskirts of the town, there is a competing "paradise": a Convent that has fallen into disuse and become home to an array of wandering and desperate women, at least one of whom is white. The Convent has many characteristics that a reader would associate with various "havens" or paradises. Originally built as an "embezzler's folly," the convent was lavish and ornate with marble and teak flooring and fixtures and statuary that celebrated the sensual. It later became an Indian School, where Native American children were taught "to remember to forget." Finally, it had become a true Convent, home to nuns. Now only two of the nuns remain: Mother Magna, who is slowly dying, and Consolata, who is called Connie. Consolata (whose name suggests the word "consolation") sells the special peppers that grow only in the soil around the convent to the citizens of Ruby, presides over the death of Mother Magna, and takes in an array of desperate women who have nowhere else to go. She has ceased to practice her religion in any serious way because of an affair she had with Deacon Morgan, one of the twins (the other named Steward Morgan) who are central figures in Ruby and whose "powerful memories" hold intact the history and purpose of Ruby and Haven.

The novel begins as a group of men from Ruby (including both Deacon and Steward) attack the women at the Convent. The opening line reads,

"They shoot the white girl first." The men from Ruby believe that the Convent is a moral threat to the continued existence of Ruby. As the attack begins, Morrison shifts focus to the women who have come to the Convent. She traces the history of each woman, including Consolata. She also sets forth the history of the town, including the central conflict in town represented by the two ministers in town: the Reverend Misner, who believes in a loving, forgiving God, and the Reverend Pulliam, who believes in a God of wrath and vengeance. Morrison returns her focus to the attack on the Convent at the end of the novel. The men shoot and disperse the women, but when Roger Best, the undertaker, arrives for their bodies, they have vanished.

In the remainder of the novel, Morrison focuses not upon what happened to the bodies, but upon what happens to the town as its citizens attempt to deal with death and crime in their "paradise." Many of the women who supposedly died appear to those who rejected them earlier in life, but they appear for only a moment and then vanish, much as Christ appeared to believers after his crucifixion. As the novel ends, the Reverend Misner presides over the funeral of Save-Marie, a child who has died in Ruby. Though Morrison refuses to supply easy answers to what happened to the women at the Convent, she forces her readers to explore the limits that are placed on earthly paradises, limits that are embodied in the novel in death, hatred, crime, and murder occurring in a town founded to be perfect. Furthermore, the people who sought escape from discrimination have now become the discriminators.

SUMMARY

All of Morrison's work focuses on the attempts to construct a life out of the violence and destruction of the past. She emphasizes that the true violence of the past is something that takes courage to face, and not all of her characters can face it. Faulkner said that the past is never over; "it isn't even past." In Morrison's novels, the past pursues the present, and, unless people can face it, it will overtake the present and repeat itself in its worst aspects. However, in truly confronting the reality of death and violence, human beings create miraculous shadows that are impressed indelibly upon those who come after them in folklore, myth, music, and art.

Thomas Cassidy; updated by H. William Rice

BIBLIOGRAPHY

By the Author

LONG FICTION:
The Bluest Eye, 1970
Sula, 1973
Song of Solomon, 1977
Tar Baby, 1981
Beloved, 1987
Jazz, 1992
Paradise, 1998
Love, 2003

DRAMA:
Dreaming Emmett, pr. 1986

NONFICTION:
Playing in the Dark: Whiteness and the Literary Imagination, 1992
Conversations with Toni Morrison, 1994 (Danille Taylor-Guthrie, editor)
Birth of a Nation'hood: Gaze, Script, and Spectacle in the O. J. Simpson Case, 1997
Remember: The Journey to School Integration, 2004

CHILDREN'S LITERATURE:

The Big Box, 1999 (with Slade Morrison and Giselle Potter)

The Book of Mean People, 2002 (with Slade Morrison)

The Lion or the Mouse?, 2003 (with Slade Morrison)

The Ant or the Grasshopper?, 2003 (with Slade Morrison)

Remember: The Journey to School Integration, 2004

EDITED TEXTS:

To Die for the People: The Writings of Huey P. Newton, 1972

The Black Book: 300 Years of African American Life, 1974

Race-ing Justice, En-gendering Power: Essays on Anita Hill, Clarence Thomas, and the Construction of Social Reality, 1992

Deep Sightings and Rescue Missions: Fiction, Essays, and Conversations, 1996 (of Toni Cade Bambara)

About the Author

Carmean, Karen. *Toni Morrison's World of Fiction.* Troy: Whitson, 1995.

Christian, Barbara. *Black Women Novelists.* Westport, Conn.: Greenwood Press, 1980.

Furman, Jan, ed. *Toni Morrison's "Song of Solomon": A Casebook.* Cambridge: Oxford University Press, 2003.

Harris-Lopez, Trudier. *Fiction and Folklore: The Novels of Toni Morrison.* Knoxville: University of Tennessee Press, 1991.

McKay, Nellie, ed. *Critical Essays on Toni Morrison.* Boston: G. K. Hall, 1988.

McKay, Nellie, and William Andrews, eds. *"Beloved": A Casebook.* Cambridge: Oxford University Press, 1998.

Middleton, David L. *Toni Morrison: An Annotated Bibliography.* New York: Garland, 1987.

Morrison, Toni. "Unspeakable Things Unspoken: The Afro-American Presence in American Literature." *Michigan Quarterly Review* 28 (Winter, 1989): 1-33.

Page, Philip. *Dangerous Freedom: Fusion and Fragmentation in Toni Morrison's Novels.* Jackson: University Press of Mississippi, 1995.

Rice, H. William. *Toni Morrison and the American Tradition.* New York: Peter Lang, 1996.

Samuels, Wilfred D., and Clenora Hudson-Weems. *Toni Morrison.* Boston: Twayne, 1990.

Willis, Susan. "Eruptions of Funk: Historicizing Toni Morrison." In *Specifying.* Madison: University of Wisconsin Press, 1987.

DISCUSSION TOPICS

- Discuss the ways in which Toni Morrison's characters confront racism.

- Myth and folklore are the ways in which a culture or race learns to cope with existential problems such as death, war, violence, and disease. In a culture that has been enslaved, such devices enable people to survive the violence done to them and to their kind. What examples of these devices do readers find in Morrison's novels?

- Morrison is a novelist who is deeply involved in exploring the history of her people. Using the novels *Jazz*, *Paradise*, and *Love*, describe her use of history in her fiction.

- Morrison once said that she did not wish to write like white writers such as William Faulkner and Thomas Hardy. Rather, she sought to write fiction that was more like black music. In the light of that statement, what role does music play in Morrison's work?

- Ancestor figures appear in all of Morrison's novels. Describe three of these figures and explain their roles.

- African American experience of American culture is often difficult to describe. It is, in Morrison's words, "unspeakable." How does Morrison use language to speak about an unspeakable experience?

Courtesy, Allen & Unwin

WALTER MOSLEY

Born: Los Angeles, California
January 12, 1952

*In his mysteries and novels, Mosley emphasizes racial, ethi-
cal, and political themes that have been part of African
American literature for decades; his hard-boiled detective
novels blend the conventions of that genre with the themes
drawn from African American literature to produce mysteries that explore important racial themes.*

BIOGRAPHY

Walter Mosley was born on January 12, 1952, in
Los Angeles, to an African American father and a
white Jewish mother. Mosley's father had moved
from Texas to California and had been largely on
his own from the age of eight. Both of Mosley's parents worked in the field of education, and they provided him with a fine formal schooling. His father
also shared stories of the migration of many African Americans to California from the South during
the 1930's and 1940's. Mosley thus grew up steeped
in the history that would provide the distinctive
foundation for his novels featuring Easy Rawlins,
an African American who migrates to Los Angeles
after World War II.

In 1970, Mosley left home to attend Goddard
College in Vermont. He soon left Goddard but
stayed in Vermont, holding various jobs until he enrolled in Johnson State College, also in Vermont.
Mosley graduated from Johnson State in 1975 with
a degree in political science. After graduation, he
worked as a potter, a caterer, and a computer programmer. Moving to New York City in 1981, he continued to work as a computer programmer but
eventually decided to become a writer. Enrolling in
the City College of New York's writing program in
the mid-1980's, he achieved success with relative ra-
pidity. His first novel, *Devil in a Blue Dress* (1990),
which introduced Easy Rawlins, was nominated for
an Edgar Award by the Mystery Writers of America

and received a Shamus Award from the Private Eye
Writers of America. Other books in the Easy
Rawlins series are *A Red Death* (1991), *White Butterfly*
(1992), *Black Betty* (1994), *A Little Yellow Dog* (1996),
Gone Fishin' (1997), and *Bad Boy Brawly Brown*
(2002).

In 1996, Mosley's blues novel *RL's Dream* won the
Literary Award from the Black Caucus of the American Library Association. His collection of linked
stories about ex-con Socrates Fortlow *Always Outnumbered, Always Outgunned* (1998) has received
critical acclaim, with the story "The Thief" winning
an O. Henry Award in 1996. A second collection of
Socrates Fortlow stories, *Walkin' the Dog*, appeared
in 1999. In 1998, his first science-fiction novel, *Blue
Light*, was met with acclaim, and that year he won
the TransAfrica International Literary Prize. In
2001, Mosley returned to writing mystery fiction
with his Fearless Jones series. The series is set in Los
Angeles in the 1950's and features Paris Minton, a
secondhand book store owner, and his friend war
veteran Fearless Jones.

ANALYSIS

Mosley's mystery novels fall into the category of
hard-boiled detective stories. This genre is associated most often with Dashiell Hammett, Raymond
Chandler, and Ross Macdonald, pioneers who
transformed a popular form of entertainment into
world-recognized literature. By the time Mosley
started writing, there were dozens of successful authors working within the genre. In addition, the
once exclusively white male enclave of the private

eye had included several woman and African American detectives.

Easy Rawlins is not a licensed private investigator, but the unlicensed operative has a long lineage. The detective in Hammett's *The Glass Key* (1930), for example, is a friend of the primary suspect, and John D. MacDonald's Travis McGee and Lawrence Block's Matt Scudder are unlicensed agents who, like Easy Rawlins, do "favors" for people. There is also a related genre of hard-boiled novels that are stylistically similar to hard-boiled detective stories, only without a detective as protagonist. Prominent writers within this genre have included James Cain, Jim Thompson, David Goodis, and Harry Whittingham. Easy's first-person narrative and continual struggles with his inner self are reminiscent of many works in this latter genre, though Mosley's novels are definitely "whodunits" as well.

In both of its forms, the hard-boiled genre features a lean, hard style of language, suspense, fast-paced action, and psychological as well as social realism. As Raymond Chandler pointed out in his 1950 essay "The Simple Art of Murder," hard-boiled literature differs from the classical British detective story in its focus on the "mean streets" of America's cities and the real motives behind human behavior. Rather than inventing and unraveling puzzling crimes (for example, locked-door mysteries), hard-boiled writers explore the puzzles of the human heart.

The detective in hard-boiled literature is usually a lonely "knight," full of human flaws yet devoted to truth and justice. Unlike police officers, hard-boiled detectives are not limited by their bureaucratic positions or by the law. They are, however, limited. They often fail, and though they may note the world's injustices, they usually end up coping with them rather than bringing about instantaneous reform.

Mosley's series fits well into this genre. His style is lean and true to the streets. He presents Los Angeles in a conspicuously unidealized way. In addition, Easy is a loner who, despite his personal flaws, takes risks and bends rules to make the world more just. He also has a hunger for truth, though he is willing to lie if it serves his purpose.

Paris Minton and Fearless Jones of Mosley's second mystery series also fit this mold of the loner willing to take risks and bend the rules to create a kind of local justice. However, Minton and Jones are even more amateur as detectives, doing what they do to help others who seem helpless, but just as frequently they act as they do to help themselves when the system has failed.

What distinguishes Mosley's work, in addition to depth of characterization and sheer storytelling ability, is that he deals with issues of race, which pose many vexing problems of social justice. (Note the theme of color in Mosley's titles, as well as the fact that he begins his series with references to the colors of the American flag.) Following the lead of such prominent African American authors as Richard Wright, Ralph Ellison, and Chester Himes, Mosley explores problems of discrimination, black identity, and black alienation.

Mosley also treats the theme of violence. Easy Rawlins hesitates to use violence except in self-defense, yet he is saved more than once by his friend Mouse's willingness to use violence freely. Indeed, Easy seems to be incomplete without Mouse. Mouse's violence, however, also does not provide an answer. Left to himself, Mouse would drink, chase women, and occasionally shoot people. Violence is also an issue *Fearless Jones* (2001), again demonstrating an ambiguity about how violence fits into the social pattern.

Mosley's work has notable predecessors. Hammett explored the issue of race briefly in his short story "Nightshade" (anthologized in 1944), and Whittingham's 1961 novel *Journey into Violence* explores southern racism in a political context. Mosley's closest precursor, though, is Chester Himes. Himes's first novel, *If He Hollers, Let Him Go* (1945), takes place in Los Angeles and uses a hard-boiled prose style to explore issues of racial justice and black alienation. Himes's novel ends with the main character, Bob Jones, about to enter the Army in 1943. Mosley's Easy Rawlins is a World War II veteran who starts his tales just after the war. Moreover, Himes later made a name for himself by writing suspense novels featuring two black Harlem detectives who often play by their own rules.

What Mosley has fully demonstrated is the compatibility of two essentially radical literary perspectives. Although African American literature has been more overtly critical, the best hard-boiled work also challenges accepted beliefs about the justness of American society. With the successful marriage of these two literary perspectives, Mosley has produced eminently readable novels that resonate with meaning. Mosley's African American fiction also deals with issues of race, economics, and violence, depicting the difficulty of survival in the modern American culture where abuse and poverty affect all races. Violence is not depicted positively but presented as a failure of the society that must be addressed, as race and poverty issues must be addressed if society is to move forward.

DEVIL IN A BLUE DRESS

First published: 1990
Type of work: Novel

A black World War II veteran turns to the dangerous world of detective work when he loses his job in a factory.

Devil in a Blue Dress introduces readers to Ezekiel "Easy" Rawlins, the principal character in Mosley's detective novels. Easy is not a licensed detective; in fact, he is not a detective at all at the outset of the novel. It is 1948, and he is a young black veteran of World War II who has moved to the largely black Watts section of Los Angeles after growing up in a tough Houston neighborhood.

Circumstances conspire to put Easy in the detective business. He has lost his job at an aircraft factory after standing up to his white supervisor. Easy likens the plant to a plantation, but without his job there, he has no way to make the mortgage payments on his small house in Watts.

A solution arises when a bartender and former fighter named Joppy, also from Houston, introduces Easy to a menacing white man named Albright. Albright is searching for a white woman named Daphne Monet, who has been seen in Watts. According to Albright, Daphne's former lover merely wants to get in touch with her. Despite misgivings, Easy takes on the job of finding Daphne.

Soon a string of murders convinces Easy that he has gotten himself into something more dangerous than he imagined. The police rough him up. Desperate, Easy summons his friend Mouse from Houston to help. Mouse is Easy's best friend, but he is also the reason Easy left Houston. Mouse is a killer who, on one occasion, made Easy an accessory to murder. Easy leaves a message for Mouse. Not knowing what to expect, he then tries to handle the situation himself.

Daphne has been linked to a black gangster named Frank Johnson, whom Easy wants to avoid. He gets a break when Daphne calls and asks for his help. Instead of turning her over to Albright, Easy grants her request. When Daphne bolts again, Easy is sure that Albright means to harm her, even if his client does not. Easy believes that Albright is principally interested in thirty thousand dollars Daphne took when she disappeared.

In order to help Daphne, Easy tries to locate Frank Johnson. He returns home one day to find Johnson waiting for him. Suspicious about Easy's interest in his affairs, Johnson is about to kill Easy when Mouse appears and scares Johnson out of the house.

Daphne calls again, and Easy takes her to what he thinks is a safe haven, a motel owned by his Mexican American friend Primo. Daphne and Easy become lovers. Coming back from a meal, they find that Albright and two henchmen have tracked them down. Easy is knocked out, but when he comes to, he manages to find out Albright's address. He pursues Albright, leaving word for Mouse.

Easy finds that Daphne is being held by Albright and Joppy. They are trying to persuade her to tell them where the money is hidden. Easy tries to free Daphne, but he is once again about to be killed when Mouse comes to the rescue. Mouse mortally wounds Albright, kills Joppy, and makes Daphne (who, it turns out, is Frank Johnson's half sister) tell the whereabouts of the money. Mouse, Easy, and Daphne split the money three ways. Daphne leaves Easy because he now knows that she is not white. Indeed, she left her lover partly because a blackmailer threatened to expose her lineage. Easy is left to square things with the police. He implicates Joppy, Albright, and another murderer. Easy leaves Mouse out of his story; he also protects Daphne, who has killed the blackmailer.

Easy also has his compassionate side. He rescues a boy, Jesus, who has

been sexually abused by the blackmailer. He finds the boy a home with Primo and his wife. Easy cannot change the world, but he can make it better for one child.

A Red Death

First published: 1991
Type of work: Novel

Easy Rawlins is drawn into a case involving communists, a rogue federal agent, and the Federal Bureau of Investigation (FBI).

In *A Red Death*, it is now 1953, the period of McCarthyism. Easy has used the money he made in *Devil in a Blue Dress* to buy rental properties, which he owns secretly. He pretends to work for Mofass, his manager and rent collector. Trouble looms, however, when an Internal Revenue Service (IRS) agent named Lawrence targets Easy for investigation. Easy is soon facing the possibility of prison.

As if this is not enough, Etta Mae and LaMarque, Mouse's wife and son, come up from Houston. Etta Mae is estranged from Mouse and wants to live with Easy. Easy desires Etta Mae, but he knows that living with her might put him on a collision course with Mouse. Sure enough, Mouse appears in Watts, though he spends a night partying before looking up Easy. The delay gives Easy a chance to find an apartment for Etta Mae and LaMarque.

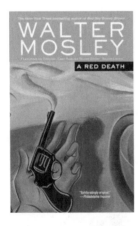

The situation with the IRS takes a twist during Easy's meeting with Lawrence. Desperate enough to respond violently, Easy is saved from drastic action when a Federal Bureau of Investigation (FBI) agent named Craxton offers to help. Craxton says that he will patch up Easy's problems with the IRS in return for help in nailing a union organizer and suspected communist named Chaim Wenzler. Wenzler, a Jew, is also active in several black churches, including one in Easy's neighborhood. Easy agrees to cooperate.

Easy meets Mouse in a bar. He tells Mouse the truth about Etta Mae and LaMarque, but he honors Etta Mae's request and refuses to tell Mouse her address. Mouse does not push the matter but warns that he will not wait forever to hear from Etta Mae.

The following morning, Easy finds the body of Poinsettia Jackson, one of his tenants, in her apartment. She appears to have hanged herself, which seems plausible in the light of her poor health and lack of money to pay rent. Easy, in fact, had been on the verge of letting Mofass evict her.

Easy takes Etta Mae to church the following Sunday morning. He hears an avid sermon against the waste of black youths in the Korean War, perhaps direct evidence of Chaim Wenzel's influence. Easy is introduced to Chaim. Despite himself, Easy likes the man.

Easy accompanies Etta Mae home. Displaying her divorce papers, she seduces him, and the two become lovers.

Easy begins to work with Chaim. The two become friendly; the only group that Chaim seems to be linked to is the National Association for the Advancement of Colored People, which Craxton quickly brands as "communist." Easy does learn from one of Chaim's former associates that Chaim has, quite by chance, come into possession of some classified documents. Easy now has enough on Chaim to satisfy the FBI.

Meanwhile, Lawrence refuses to go along with the FBI bargain and seals Easy's home. Easy is outraged, but he is restrained by sympathetic federal marshals. A call to Craxton gets the FBI agent to work directly with Lawrence's boss, who orders Lawrence not to bother Easy; Easy moves back into his house.

Two problems remain. Easy is Etta Mae's lover, and the threat of Mouse looms over him. Moreover, he has become close friends with Chaim, whom he has to betray if he is to keep Craxton happy and escape his tax problems. Together with the guilt he feels over Poinsettia's death, this situation drives Easy to drink one night while he is working at the church. Chaim and his daughter take Easy to the daughter's house to sleep off his drunk.

The next day, Easy again confronts death when the minister and his lover are found shot to death at the church. Easy calls the police, who seem suspicious of him now that he has been involved with two deaths.

Easy is picked up by the police, who now have evidence that Poinsettia was murdered; they have also learned that Easy owns the buildings run by Mofass. The presence of a black policeman, Quinten Naylor, does not keep Easy from being roughed up, but it does allow him to make a phone call to Craxton's office. Craxton gets him out of the lockup and puts him back on Chaim's case.

Chaim himself is then killed, however, and a shot is taken at Easy as he brings Chaim's daughter to his house to spend the night. Easy now thinks he knows the killer—Mofass, who has mysteriously disappeared. Enlisting the help of Mouse, Easy locates Mofass and is about to kill him. When, to Mouse's disgust, Easy hesitates, Mofass reveals that it is Lawrence who has done the killings in an attempt to get Easy's property. Mofass has helped because Lawrence had previously nailed him on a tax charge.

Working alone now, Easy locates the stolen classified documents and puts them into Lawrence's possession in order to save Chaim's reputation. He then arranges a meeting with Lawrence to check out Mofass's story. When Lawrence jumps him, Easy is once again saved by Mouse, who shoots Lawrence dead.

In the end, Etta Mae dumps Easy for Mouse. Easy is left with the orphan Jesus, who has come back to live with him. He forgives Mofass in the light of his own partial betrayals of Mouse, Chaim, and Poinsettia.

WHITE BUTTERFLY

First published: 1992
Type of work: Novel

Easy Rawlins investigates a series of brutal murders in Watts.

White Butterfly takes place in 1956. Easy is married and raising two children, an infant from his new marriage and Jesus, the orphan from the earlier books. This life is not idyllic, however; Easy has not told Regina, his wife, about his secret business holdings or about his detective work. Moreover, there are other important instances of miscommunication between the two that cloud the future of

their marriage. On the other hand, Easy is staying away from bars and living a cleaner, healthier life.

The situation worsens when Easy is approached—first by black policeman Quinten Naylor and then by a slew of high city officials—for help in tracing a serial murderer in Watts. This burst of attention is brought about by the appearance of a white victim. Up until this time, the victims have been black prostitutes and exotic dancers; the white victim, though, is a college student from a respectable family. Easy is bullied into helping when officials threaten to pin the crimes on Mouse.

Easy goes to work, frequenting bars and asking questions that lead him to a suspect but also to a surprising revelation: The white coed led a double life, coming to Watts to work as the "White Butterfly." When Easy reports this, he is told to discontinue his line of inquiry, partly because the girl's father is a former district attorney. Curiosity, though, gets the better of Easy. He speaks to the girl's mother, who is quite upset. The police chastise Easy and penalize him by arresting Mouse. Easy talks the police into releasing Mouse, and the two of them track the suspect, a black man, to San Francisco. They locate him just in time to witness his death in a bar fight staged by the local police. They learn that San Francisco has had a chain of similar murders about which the black population was never informed. The suspect's death becomes the final step in a massive cover-up.

Frustrated, Easy returns to Los Angeles; there, he learns that the white victim was the mother of a baby. When he puts the girl's parents in touch with the woman who is keeping the baby, he is arrested for extortion and appears to be hopelessly framed. Mouse comes up with bail money, and Easy reveals that the white coed was killed by her father.

Easy decides to be more open with Regina and to stop keeping secrets from her, but it is too late; Regina has run off with another man, taking Easy's daughter with her. Easy is left heartbroken, and he drinks heavily until Mouse and Jesus bring him back from the brink of self-destruction.

A subplot involves Mofass, who gets into trouble with white developers from whom he receives a bribe. While Easy will not bail Mofass out of trouble, the two do work together to get the upper hand over the white businessmen. Thus, while Easy's marriage fails, he is able to solidify his finances and, therefore, his independence.

RL's Dream

First published: 1995
Type of work: Novel

An old blues man, dying in New York City, is rescued from the street by a bitter young white woman, and each helps the other find a second chance.

RL's Dream opens with Atwater "Soupspoon" Wise, an old blues man, wracked with pain in his hip, his throat sore, making his way to his apartment in the East Village of New York City. Two young men come to evict Soupspoon, carrying him and his few belongings, including his red-enameled twelve-string Gibson guitar, out to the street.

As Soupspoon is being evicted, Kiki Waters, a twenty-something white woman from Arkansas, is on her way from the hospital to her East Village apartment, recovering from stab wounds inflicted by a black boy whom she stopped from attacking a schoolteacher. Randy, her sometimes boyfriend, helps her home.

At Kiki's building, they find Soupspoon sitting on the street while men continue dumping his things. The pathetic sight of Soupspoon being treated with such disrespect infuriates Kiki, and she insists on taking him to her apartment, where she cleans him up and makes him tea, which he drinks while she eats and drinks whiskey.

The first three chapters introduce three of the main characters of the novel: Soupspoon, Kiki, and Randy, Kiki's boyfriend who, with the help of his mother, has deceived himself into believing that he is not black. Race is a significant aspect of this novel. The other main character, who, although dead for fifty years and permeates Soupspoon's existence and the novel, is RL Johnson, the famous Delta bluesman with whom Soupspoon traveled and played when he was young.

Although the novel is told primarily from the points of view of Soupspoon and Kiki, reminiscences and dreams of both Kiki and Soupspoon demonstrate how events in the past shape the present. These looks into the past allow Mosley to tell the story of the blues.

When young, both Kiki and Soupspoon ran away from home—he to follow Robert Johnson and the blues, she to escape the sexual abuse of her father. Both were cared for by black women, not their mothers. The kindness of those outside one's family underscores the connectedness of humanity, despite differences in race and place.

Kiki takes Soupspoon to the hospital, but knowing he will need insurance to get treatment, Kiki returns to her job at the insurance company and tricks Fez, a man in the computer division who raped her friend the previous year, into letting her into the company's computer system, where she creates an insurance policy for Atwater Wise.

The doctors diagnose Soupspoon's hip pain as cancer and start him on treatment. During his illness and treatment, he dreams about or remembers his early life in Mississippi. When Kiki buys him a tape recorder, Soupspoon tells her about meeting and playing with Robert Johnson in Arcola, Mississippi. Soupspoon heard that Robert had died a few weeks after they separated. He tells Kiki that he has never played as well as he played with RL.

Soupspoon describes the blues as the music of the poor and downtrodden, but also the music of the devil. RL once told him that he could play so well because he traded his right eye to the devil for his ability to play the blues.

Soupspoon asks a friend who runs a gambling club if he can play the blues in his club. The friend agrees that when Soupspoon's "keemo" is over, he can play at the club. On a walk with Soupspoon, Kiki encounters the boy who stabbed her. All Kiki's pent up anger erupts when she catches the boy, and she threatens to kill him. Soupspoon intervenes, stopping Kiki from committing murder.

At the club, the patrons love Soupspoon and his music. The pain from the cancer seems to enhance his music; he is a real blues man again. At the second night's playing, a drunken Kiki is taken to her apartment by Randy and a friend. Fez is waiting there for revenge on Kiki and stabs Randy before Kiki shoots and kills him. She flees and eventually returns to Arkansas to find that her parents' deaths have made her wealthy. She marries and has four kids, often thinking of Soupspoon.

On his way home from the club that night, Soupspoon collapses on the street. He dies alone in the hospital but knows he has felt the blues again, and just before the end, he sees Robert Johnson.

"EQUAL OPPORTUNITY"

First published: 1998 (in *Always Outnumbered, Always Outgunned*)
Type of work: Short story

A fifty-eight-year-old black ex-convict in Los Angeles frightens the white managers in a large supermarket when he applies for a job and will not take no for an answer.

In "Equal Opportunity," ex-con Socrates Fortlow, the main character in the linked stories that make up the novel *Always Outnumbered, Always Outgunned*, tries for a job at a supermarket miles from his home in Watts. Twenty-seven years ago, Socrates killed two of his friends with his big hands. He travels to Venice Boulevard to apply for a job because he knows that he is considered a bum at the stores in his neighborhood, where he has been selling empty bottles to support himself. At the supermarket, he refuses to accept that his failure to have a phone, according to the white manager, disqualifies him from a job. He comes back four days in a row to see if he has been hired. He is told if he comes back on Monday, the police will be called.

Socrates returns on Monday and explains to two private security officers that he has not threatened anyone and feels he should be given a fair chance at a job. Socrates says that if the manager is scared, it is because she has not treated him fairly. The security officers decide he should get a job at the Santa Monica store since the manager there wants to "give guys a chance." Back in his neighborhood, Socrates and his friends celebrate his new job.

SUMMARY

Mosley has joined two worthy literary traditions in a fruitful partnership. He employs the form of the hard-boiled detective story to explore important racial themes in a suspenseful and eminently readable manner. His Easy Rawlins series also provides an accessible introduction to the history of Watts and of postwar America in general.

Mosley's African American novels take up the contributions of blacks in American culture, particularly the blues, but also look at the racial issues confronted by modern African Americans. He depicts these issues realistically, often showing violence as a part of them, but offers an idealistic vision of how such problems can be resolved if the races find ways to get beyond color.

Mosley presents a realistic look at poverty and violence, but he also projects a profound idealism. Mosley does a good job of exposing forms of racism, yet he rejects the temptation to brand all white people as bigots. The strength of his work lies in his refusal to offer simple solutions to the complex issues he raises.

Ira Smolensky; updated by Bonnie C. Plummer

BIBLIOGRAPHY

By the Author

LONG FICTION:
Devil in a Blue Dress, 1990
A Red Death, 1991
White Butterfly, 1992
Black Betty, 1994
RL's Dream, 1995
A Little Yellow Dog, 1996
Gone Fishin', 1997
Always Outnumbered, Always Outgunned, 1998
Blue Light, 1998
Walkin' the Dog, 1999
Fearless Jones, 2001
Bad Boy Brawly Brown, 2002
Fear Itself, 2003

The Man in My Basement, 2004
Little Scarlet, 2004

SHORT FICTION:
Futureland: Nine Stories of an Imminent World, 2001
Six Easy Pieces: Easy Rawlins Stories, 2003

NONFICTION:
Workin' on the Chain Gang: Shaking Off the Dead Hand of History, 2000
What Next: A Memoir Toward World Peace, 2003

EDITED TEXTS:
Black Genius: African American Solutions to African American Problems, 1999 (with others)
The Best American Short Stories, 2003, 2003 (with Katrina Kenison)

About the Author

Bunyan, Scott. "No Order from Chaos: The Absence of Chandler's Extra-legal Space in the Detective Fiction of Chester Himes and Walter Mosley." *Studies in the Novel* 35 (Fall, 2003): 339-365.

Carby, Hazel V. "Figuring the Future in Los(t) Angeles." *Comparative American Studies: An International Journal* 1 (March, 2003): 19-34.

Chandler, Raymond. *The Simple Art of Murder.* Boston: Houghton, 1950.

Geherin, David. *The American Private Eye: The Image in Fiction.* New York: Frederick Ungar, 1985.

Gray, W. Russel. "Hard-Boiled Black Easy: Genre Conventions in *A Red Death.*" *African American Review* 38 (Fall, 2004): 489-498.

Kennedy, Liam. "Black Noir: Race and Urban Space in Walter Mosley's Detective Fiction." In *Diversity and Detective Fiction,* edited by Kathleen Gregory Klein. Bowling Green, Ohio: Popular Press, 1999.

Levecq, Christine. "Blues Poetics and Blues Politics in Walter Mosley's *RL's Dream.*" *African American Review* 38 (Summer, 2004): 239-256.

Lomax, Sara M. "Double Agent Easy Rawlins: The Development of a Cultural Detective." *American Visions* 7 (April/May, 1992): 32-34.

Mason, Theodore O., Jr. "Walter Mosley's Easy Rawlins: The Detective and Afro-American Fiction." *Kenyon Review* 14 (Fall, 1992): 173-183.

Smith, David L. "Walter Mosley's *Blue Light:* (Double Consciousness) Squared." *Extrapolation: A Journal of Science Fiction and Fantasy* 42 (Spring, 2001): 7-26.

Young, Mary. "Walter Mosley, Detective Fiction, and Black Culture." *Journal of Popular Culture* 32 (Summer, 1998): 141-150.

DISCUSSION TOPICS

- What is Easy Rawlins's relationship to Mouse? Why does Easy seem unable to survive without Mouse?

- What does the Los Angeles setting symbolize to Easy and the other black people in the stories? What does Houston symbolize?

- How does Walter Mosley use children in the Easy Rawlins stories to build his characterization of Easy?

- Why does Mosley make Kiki in *RL's Dream* a victim of child abuse? How is the treatment of children a theme in the story?

- What do the blues represent to Soupspoon? What does Soupspoon mean when he says that the blues is the music of the devil?

- Why is the supermarket described in "Equal Opportunity" seen as a palace? If the supermarket is a palace, can Socrates be seen as a knight?

- Does the lie that Socrates tells about being an ex-con mean that he is a dishonest person or will be a bad employee?

Courtesy, Author

FARLEY MOWAT

Born: Belleville, Ontario, Canada
May 12, 1921

Mowat has written many books, including both fiction and nonfiction, but he is best known for his accounts of life in the Arctic, especially the two volumes describing the fate of the Ihalmiut Eskimos, People of the Deer *(1952) and* The Desperate People *(1959).*

BIOGRAPHY

Farley Mowat was born in Belleville, Ontario, on May 12, 1921, to Helen and Angus Mowat, both of Scottish ancestry. Farley was an adventurous child and a dedicated reader by age six. When Angus moved his family to Windsor in 1930, Farley was complementing James Fenimore Cooper and Ernest Thompson Seton with rambles around the city's hobo jungles and collections of wildlife (for example, Limpopo, a six-inch Florida alligator) and moths. A romantic move to Saskatchewan in a ship's cabin mounted on a Model T truck and a trip to Vancouver Island were followed in 1936 by an expedition to the Arctic with the ornithologist Frank Farley, his great-uncle, who taught him to collect bird nests and eggs on the tundra. Farley met his first Indians on this trip and was shocked by the brutal rifle assaults on the friendly whales around Churchill. In 1937, the Mowats resettled near Toronto, where Farley devoted much time to studying birds as a prelude to a two-month field trip to Saskatchewan to undertake an ornithological survey.

Mowat grew up fast during World War II, when he served as a brigade intelligence officer engaged in hard combat in Sicily and Italy. Discharged in 1946, he enrolled at the University of Toronto and in 1947 accompanied Francis Harper, a Pennsylvania biologist, to Canada's Keewatin District. Returning to Toronto that fall, Mowat married Frances Elizabeth Thornhill, a classmate. The trip with Harper inspired the first half of *People of the Deer* (1952), and a second trip, in 1948, partially funded by the Dominion Wildlife Service, exposed him to the suffering among the Ihalmiut that he was to recount in *The Desperate People* (1959). His long absences damaged his marriage, and in 1951, after two years in Palgrave, Ontario, in a house without running water, Fran was ready to leave. The publication in 1952 of *People of the Deer* provoked a controversy that reached the House of Parliament in Ottawa but to no effect, and the Ihalmiut were dismissed by Dr. A. E. Porsild of the Department of Resources and Northern Affairs as the product of Mowat's imagination.

During the 1950's, Mowat involved himself in left-wing causes; fathered a son, Robert Alexander, and adopted another, David; and struggled with his writing. He made his first visit to Newfoundland in 1957 but in 1958 was back in the Barrenlands investigating the plight of the Ihalmiut, a project that led to *The Desperate People*. With an old army friend, Mike Donovan, Mowat sailed in June, 1960, to the French-owned islands of Saint Pierre and Miquelon just off Newfoundland's northeast coast. He soon began an intense affair with a twenty-seven-year-old art student from Ontario, Claire Wheeler, and after an escapist interlude in England, they settled in at Burgeo, Newfoundland, where Mowat wrote the immensely successful *Never Cry Wolf* (1963). In 1965, Mowat obtained a Mexican divorce and soon married Claire before returning to Burgeo and starting a bitter feud with Joey Smallwood, the premier who had led Newfoundland into the Canadian Confederation. The Luddite Mowat opposed Smallwood's efforts to modernize, but he gave up this battle to travel to Siberia to study the Soviets' management of that great natural icebox.

The period from 1967 through 1977 demonstrated no coherent unity of purpose and was marked by travels to Europe, difficulties with publishers, outbursts of antagonism toward the United States for its Vietnam War, support for groups that opposed whale hunting and seal clubbing, and struggles with various writing projects. His relationship with his parents grew more complicated as Angus abandoned Helen for Barbara Hutchinson, a Toronto librarian. The filming of *Never Cry Wolf* in 1981 provided a pleasant interlude, as did a trip to Scandinavia with the governor-general of Canada Ed Schreyer and his wife. By 1984, two books decrying humankind's inhumanity to humans and to other animals—*And No Birds Sang* (1979) *and Sea of Slaughter* (1984)—had further boosted his huge success. (In 2001 there were 460 translations in twenty-four languages.) For Mowat, the 1980's and 1990's were replete with honors and more publications (*Virunga: The Passion of Dian Fossey* [1987] won many readers) but were also marred by an article, "A Real Whopper," that challenged the truthfulness of *People of the Deer* and *Never Cry Wolf*. From this attack, a consensus seems to have emerged that even though the books may have dealt lightly with the facts, they were badly needed statements about the plight of the Ihalmiut and the wolves. Whatever the case, Mowat remained, as one journalist characterized him, "a pint-sized dynamo."

ANALYSIS

Mowat's most discussed books, the ones that made his career, are the three accounts he wrote of life in the Arctic—*People of the Deer, The Desperate People,* and *Never Cry Wolf*—and the reader's first step in judging these works is to determine how much of them is truth, how much literary embroidery. The defense usually offered for Mowat's way of telling his stories is to admit, yes, there are inventions that violate the letter of the truth, but at the same time, these inventions are faithful to the spirit of the truth, a much higher goal. As one defender put it, Mowat

is concerned with reality, with truth, but with the underlying truths that are the concern of every creative artist. In his view, facts are important only as they relate to truth, and in themselves meaningless.

Closely connected to Mowat's sympathy for the wolf is *A Whale for the Killing* (1972), inspired by the fate of a whale trapped at Burgeo, Newfoundland, in 1967 and slaughtered by men with rifles. Of the whale's suffering, Mowat said,

An awesome mystery had intruded into the closely circumscribed order of our lives; one that we terrestrial bipeds could not fathom, and one, therefore, that we would react against with instinctive fear, violence and hatred.

This remark reveals the key to understanding Mowat's approach to nature and its creatures. A similar indignation informs *Sea of Slaughter,* a frontal attack on the destruction of numerous species from the oceans, and it explains his enthusiasm for writing *Virunga: The Passion of Dian Fossey.*

A persistent strain of contempt for bureaucracies colors many of Mowat's narratives, especially in his controversial account of Ottawa's treatment of the Ihalmiut in *People of the Deer,* as well as in his sharp criticism of Governor Smallwood's whaling policy in Newfoundland. The mere title of *Canada North Now: The Great Betrayal* (1976) speaks loudly on this point, as does *Rescue the Earth! Conversations with the Green Crusaders* (1990). In both these volumes, Mowat's political sympathies converge with his awe of the natural world.

Mowat owes much of his success to a plain style that carries incidents and characterizations along in a smooth narrative. In *The Desperate People,* for instance, the old Ihalmiut shaman Pommela emerges on the page in all his irascibility, and Pommela's rival leader, Owliktuk, stands out as a courageous leader of his group. Uncle Albert in *Never Cry Wolf* is an unforgettable and singular companion to Angeline and George and their cubs. However, what most distinguishes Mowat's depictions of people—and wolves—is his ability to enter imaginatively into their lives with a powerful human sympathy.

THE DESPERATE PEOPLE

First published: 1959
Type of work: Nonfiction

The author recounts the struggle for survival of the Ihalmiut Eskimos of the Keewatin District in the Canadian Northwest Territories.

The Desperate People describes the "virtual extinction" between 1952 and 1959 of the beleaguered Ihalmiuts in the inland plains known as the Barrengrounds. An appendix identifies by name all the Ihalmiut who were living in 1946 and either tells where they were living in 1958 or explains what happened to them. Of the 111 individuals, only 64 were known to be alive twelve years later, many of them at Rankin Inlet on the shore of Hudson Bay. Diphtheria was the commonest cause of death.

Due west of Hudson Bay, in the Canadian District of Keewatin, lies the Land of the Ihalmiut Eskimos, marked in the northwest by Dubawnt Lake and the Dubawnt River, in the southwest by Ennadai Lake, in the south by Nueltin Lake, and in the northeast by Yathkyed Lake. The Kazan River snakes down from the northeast to the southwest, and the tree line meanders around across the southern region. This is the home of the people christened by Farley Mowat as the People of the Deer in his book by that title. In 1912, the Ihalmiut, or "The Other People," as they knew themselves, were hit by an epidemic of what was probably influenza. This tragedy was followed in 1913 by the first trading post, an institution that introduced the tribes to Caucasian trinkets, flour, cloth, and "much other sorcery" that would convert the Ihalmiut to fox trappers. The introduction of rifles in return for fox pelts meant a rapid decrease in the caribou herds (the "deer" of Mowat's narratives are not the North American whitetail but caribou) and the disintegration of the people and their traditional way of life. Thus, by 1930, the Ihalmiut were reduced to four small groups, the largest being the People of the Little Hills, something above one hundred in number, clustered around Ennadai. The white trappers who swarmed into the Barrens in these years slaughtered the deer, poisoned the foxes with strychnine, and shoved the Ihalmiut aside. At the same time, the Ihalmiuts' traditional enemies, the

Idthen Eldeli, or Athapascan Indians, pushed northward to put pressure on the Ihalmiuts' southern flank. Thus, by 1932, the community numbered no more than two hundred across the whole region. In the winter of 1942-1943, forty-four people, a third of the survivors, died of hunger, leaving only about sixty Ihalmiut struggling along northeast of Ennadai.

Mowat flew into Windy Bay in May, 1947, with an unidentified male companion and befriended a lone Ihalmiut named Charles, who let him share his cabin. Through Charles, Mowat met the young shaman Ootek, his wife Howmik, and their daughter Kalak, as well as Ootek's neighbors Halo and his wife, Kikik. The natural leader of this group was Owliktuk, married to Nutaralik and father of their four children. Owliktuk's followers included Yaha, a good hunter; the fatalist Miki; and a fringe figure, Ohoto, husband of Nanuk. A nearby camp was under the control of the tyrannical shaman Pommela, spiritual guide to a small group including Katelo, Pommela's younger brother, and Katelo's twelve-year-old son; Onekwaw and his wife, Tabluk, and her daughter by a previous union; and Alekahaw, a "sly and clever opportunist." A third small camp, consisting of Hekwaw and his family, completed the Ihalmiuts when Mowat met them in the summer of 1947.

The Ihalmiuts' miseries were not alleviated much by the obtuseness of the government authorities, for whom Mowat harbors an obvious contempt. When a government plane flew in to the little outpost of starving survivors in the spring of 1948, it brought boxes marked "Eskimo Relief Supplies," a brutally disappointing collection of six sheet-metal stoves, several fox traps, one dozen large axes, and twenty galvanized-iron pails. Stoves and axes in a land of no trees revealed the minds of Ottawa officialdom. The best Mowat could do was give the Ihalmiut ten boxes of ammunition for their aging rifles and hope for the best. However, later, in August, Mowat procured one dozen .303 rifles and one thousand rounds of ammunition from the Canadian Army detachment at Churchill, along with a load of battle-dress trousers and jackets. In September, another plane landed with more ill-conceived supplies: a drum of rancid powdered milk, some flour and lard, and two large bales of discarded service underwear. However, this particular year ended happily, with Ohoto catching more than fifty fat deer for the coming winter and everyone enjoying a festive night before Mowat's departure.

A new challenge faced the Ihalmiut in 1949 when the Royal Canadian Corps of Signals decided to build a radio and meteorological station at Ennadai Lake and to bring in materials in the dead of winter on cat-trains, Caterpillar tractors towing strings of freight sleds. In the same year, an outbreak of poliomyelitis ravaged the Eskimo population all across the Keewatin District, killing some of the Ihalmiut, crippling another seventeen of them at the Padlei settlement, and maiming several of those in the camps led by Owliktuk and Pommela. The coming of the construction workers introduced novelty into the Ihalmiuts' lives, and the workers at first delighted in the diversion offered by the community, but Pommela's scrounging contributed to a weakening of warm feelings. The Ihalmiut expected the white workers to provide salvation from their destitution, but the government workers never understood the group's expectations, and the Ihalmiuts did not understand why their needs were ignored.

In early 1950, starvation began in the camps of Owliktuk and Pommela. Mowat explains the seeming indifference of the Canadian government to the dominance of the three "empires": the Hudson's Bay Company, whose dependence on fur trapping encouraged exploitation of the Eskimos; the missions run by the Roman Catholic Oblate organization and the Church of England, both of whom argued that salvation took precedence over health issues among the Eskimos; and the Royal Canadian Mounted Police, who saw their task as enforcing law among backward "natives." Moreover, the persistent image of the Eskimo as beaming primitives, happy in their igloos, slowed with the government's realization that these were a suffering people whose life expectancy was twenty-four years, whose infant mortality rate was 260 for every 1,000 live births, and whose risk of tuberculosis was one out of eight.

In 1948, the government approved a plan to relocate the Ihalmiut from Ennadai to Nueltin Lake, where they would work in a commercial fishery, and when the project opened in 1949, the trading post moved there from Churchill. The forty-seven surviving Ihalmiut were flown in on May 1, 1950, but their poverty and their fear of the Idthen Eldeli

prompted them to trek to Otter Lake that autumn. The 170 remaining Padliermiut were even worse off than the Ihalmiut and were saved only by the Hudson Bay post manager at Eskimo Point, who urged them to take refuge at the post. Even so, twenty-two Padliermiut starved that winter. The grand fishery project thus failed the Ihalmiut, who, by the spring of 1951, were back in their familiar Ennadai region.

Mowat reports that the Ihalmiuts' prospect of slow starvation was shared by all eleven or twelve thousand Eskimos scattered across Canada, and he contrasts Canada's neglect of them with the enlightened policies begun in 1952 by Denmark in Greenland. Ottawa's grasp of the crisis is reflected in its plan to make the Eskimos self-sufficient by carving pipe bowls out of soapstone. The collapse in prices for white fox pelts further left the Eskimos without a source of income and hastened their dependence on government assistance. The Ihalmiuts' misery—and Ottawa's indecisiveness, compounded by the persistent feeling of many Canadians—thus dragged on through the 1950's. However, when Mowat returned to Hudson Bay in August, 1958, he found a new rehabilitation settlement had been established near the mining outpost of Rankin Inlet, and thanks to the courage and insight of the mine manager, Andrew Easton, and the company president, Dr. W. W. Weber, Eskimos were enjoying employment on the same terms as other workers. Thus, Mowat's story ends with what he describes as the "near-miraculous transformation which has come over the Ihalmiut."

NEVER CRY WOLF

First published: 1963
Type of work: Natural history and autobiography

Lieutenant Mowat goes to the Keewatin District to study wolves for the Dominion Wildlife Service.

Never Cry Wolf is a short work (160 pages) that incorporates the truth about wolf behavior as Mowat interpreted it in his assignment to investigate "wolf-caribou-predator-prey relationships." He himself called it a "potboiler," and the Holt, Rinehart and Winston edition is marketed as juvenile literature complete with pedagogical materials. His critics sneered at the depiction of wolves as fanciful, but whatever the book's merit as a study of wolves, it sold more than 300,000 copies and established Mowat's reputation as a spokesman not only for wolves but also for nature in general.

As the narrator of *Never Cry Wolf*, Mowat is a young man whose vicissitudes are sometimes comic. His experience with his radio, for example, revealed an embarrassing gaffe by his Ottawa superiors: He had been supplied with an instrument meant for forest rangers and which had a range of only twenty miles. Nevertheless, Mowat rigged it up and sent his call sign, "Daisy Mae," crying out into the "darkling subarctic skies." As it turned out, he contacted an amateur operator in Peru, a Spanish speaker whose English was no better than Mowat's Spanish.

The substance of Mowat's story concerns his relationship with three wolves he names Angeline, her mate, George, and a solo male, Uncle Albert. One of his first discoveries was that wolves ate mice, of which there was a generous supply. The researcher's next step was to introduce mice into his own diet, and he created a dish he called Souris à la Crème. In many of his explorations, Mowat was accompanied by an Eskimo friend, Ootek, who interpreted wolf talk for him and helped track the three wolves and their cubs to their summer den. Mowat deflates some commonly accepted beliefs about wolves, especially the misconception that they always pose a threat to humans. Moreover, Ootek explains to him that a healthy adult caribou can easily outrun a wolf and that even a fawn is too fast for most predators. The wolf's usual victim is an aged or ailing doe, but even when successful, the hunter usually spends a long night traversing fifty to sixty miles of country.

Just before he returns to the city, Mowat hears George howling for his family, and it is to him "a voice which spoke of the lost world which once was ours before we chose the alien role. . . ."

SUMMARY

In a century that saw a rapid loss of habitat for both people and animals, Mowat stood up for those pushed to the margin by technology and population explosion. His name joins those of Rachel Carson and Dian Fossey, among others, who attempted to forestall the damage done by a sometimes blind and indifferent civilization.

Frank Day

BIBLIOGRAPHY

By the Author

NONFICTION:
People of the Deer, 1952, revised 1975 (sociology and autobiography)
The Dog Who Wouldn't Be, 1957 (autobiography)
The Desperate People, 1959, revised 1975 (sequel to *People of the Deer;* sociology and autobiography)
The Grey Seas Under, 1959
The Top of the World trilogy, 1960-1973 (natural history; includes *Ordeal by Ice,* 1960; *The Polar Passion,* 1967; and *Tundra,* 1973)
The Serpent's Coil, 1961
Owls in the Family, 1961 (autobiography)
Never Cry Wolf, 1963 (natural history and autobiography)
Canada North, 1967
The Boat Who Wouldn't Float, 1968 (natural history and autobiography)
Sibir: My Discovery of Siberia, 1970 (natural history and autobiography; pb. in the U.S. as *The Siberians,* 1970)

A Whale for the Killing, 1972
The Snow Walker, 1975
Canada North Now: The Great Betrayal, 1976
And No Birds Sang, 1979 (autobiography)
Sea of Slaughter, 1984 (natural history)
My Discovery of America, 1985 (autobiography)
Woman in the Mists: The Story of Dian Fossey and the Mountain Gorillas of Africa, 1987 (natural history and biography; also known by its Canadian title, *Virunga: The Passion of Dian Fossey*)
Rescue the Earth! Conversations with the Green Crusaders, 1990
No Man's River, 2004

About the Author

King, James. *Farley: The Life of Farley Mowat.* South Royalton, Vt.: Steerforth Press, 2002.

Lucas, Alec. *Farley Mowat.* Toronto: McClelland & Stewart, 1976.

Orange, John. *Writing the Squib: A Biography of Farley Mowat.* Toronto: ECW, 1993.

Thomas, Wendy, ed. *A Farley Mowat Reader.* Niwot, Colo.: Roberts Rinehart, 1997.

York, Lorraine. *Introducing Farley Mowat's "The Dog Who Wouldn't Be."* Canadian Fiction Series. Toronto: ECW, 1990.

DISCUSSION TOPICS

- Describe the relationship between the Ihalmiut and the caribou.

- What was the effect of fox trapping on Eskimo life?

- What impression does Farley Mowat give of Ottawa's attitude toward the Eskimos?

- What were the three "empires" that exerted so much influence on Eskimo life?

- Compare Owliktuk and Pommela as leaders.

- What factors led to the starvation of so many Ihalmiut?

- What are some of the humorous incidents in *Never Cry Wolf*?

- Describe the way in which the wolves hunted caribou.

- Describe Mowat's relationship with Angeline, George, and Uncle Albert.

Tom Victor

BHARATI MUKHERJEE

Born: Calcutta, West Bengal, India
July 27, 1940

Mukherjee's novels and short stories explore the experience and consciousness of South Asian immigrants, especially women, as they adjust to living in North America; they often redefine themselves and American society as well.

BIOGRAPHY

Bharati Mukherjee was born in Calcutta, India, on July 27, 1940, the daughter of pharmaceutical chemist Sudhir Lal Mukherjee and his wife, Bina (née Barrerjee). Mukherjee's was a comparatively wealthy Bengali Hindu Brahmin family, and during her early childhood they lived with their large extended family (numbering up to forty during wartime) in a flat in Ballygunge, a middle-class neighborhood of Calcutta. Life there was stable and somewhat insulated from the rough and tumble of Calcutta, but Mukherjee was aware of the homeless beggars roaming the streets, the funerals of freedom fighters during India's struggle for independence from British imperial rule, and the Hindu-Muslim riots at the partition of India and Pakistan. She enjoyed the affection of a loving father (who was fond of his three daughters despite his society's prevailing preference for sons), listened to the tales of her mother ("a powerful storyteller"), and feared the madness of an aunt.

When Mukherjee was eight, her father sent his three daughters to school in England and Switzerland. After three years of this experiment in European education, the sisters returned to Calcutta to live in a home set up within the compound of the pharmaceutical company partly owned by their father in suburban Cossipore. From there they attended a school staffed by Irish nuns; en route to school they sometimes had to run a gauntlet of strikers and picketers. When Mukherjee was eighteen, her father lost his partnership in his company and moved to Baroda (near Bombay), where he directed research and development at a chemical complex.

In 1959, Mukherjee earned a B.A. from the University of Calcutta, followed by an M.A. in 1961 from the University of Baroda. Even as a child, Mukherjee had felt the writer's vocation, and by the age of ten, she had already written an eighty-page novel—about English children in an English landscape. In 1961, Mukherjee enrolled in the Writers' Workshop at the University of Iowa, where she earned an M.F.A. (1963), followed by a Ph.D. in English and comparative literature in 1969.

Before leaving India, Mukherjee had promised her father to marry whomever the family chose for her. However, while at Iowa, Mukherjee met and married the Canadian writer Clark Blaise in a lunch-break wedding, and they have two sons. Both Mukherjee and Blaise have pursued successful careers as writers and university professors, having held appointments at several colleges, including McGill University in Montreal, Quebec, Canada; Skidmore College in upstate New York; Queens College, City University of New York; Columbia University; and the University of California at Berkeley. From 1966 to 1980, Mukherjee and her husband lived in Canada and became Canadian citizens. Mukherjee experienced several incidents of Canadian-style racism, however, about which she wrote eloquently in her prize-winning essay "An Invisible Woman" (published in *Saturday Night*, March, 1981), and in 1980, she and her husband decided to emigrate to the United States.

The couple are intensely interested in each other's writing and have collaborated on two nonfiction books. One, titled *Days and Nights in Calcutta* (1977; rev. 1986), is an autobiographical account of a year spent in India during 1973-1974. The other, *The Sorrow and the Terror: The Haunting Legacy of the Air India Tragedy* (1987), is a reportorial critique of the 1985 Air India crash in which Sikh terrorists allegedly blew up an airliner over the Atlantic.

ANALYSIS

Much of Mukherjee's fiction, like her nonfiction, has sprung from her personal background of growing up in South Asia interacting with her experience as an Asian woman immigrant in Canada and the United States. In developing the subject of the Indian diaspora to the West, Mukherjee has acknowledged the influence and example of the distinguished writer V. S. Naipaul, himself a Trinidadian of Indian descent who lives in England. Although Mukherjee admires Naipaul's exploration of the experience of exile, expatriation, and immigration, or as she puts it, "unhousement," "remaining unhoused," and "rehousement," there are wide differences in their outlooks and their sympathies. Typically, Mukherjee's protagonists are immigrant women of color from developing nations trying to make their ways in an economically advantaged society with a deplorable history of sexism and racism. Such characters are frequently objects of prejudice, exploitation, and violence that tend to brutalize and dehumanize them.

Unlike Naipaul, whose character analysis is colder and more sardonic, Mukherjee's sympathies lie, for the greater part, with such victims. Also unlike Naipaul's unremittingly ironic stance, Mukherjee often permits her characters to recover their humanity through love, especially love between man and woman—as in her novel *Jasmine* (1989) and her stories "Orbiting" and "Buried Lives," from *The Middleman, and Other Stories* (1988). Several of Mukherjee's characters are also able to empower themselves and shape their own identities, as is the case in *Jasmine* and the *Middleman* story "A Wife's Story." Mukherjee's treatment of the immigrant experience is therefore more optimistic than Naipaul's.

Though the Asian immigrant in the New World is her distinctive sphere of depiction, Mukherjee's earlier writing was greatly influenced by British authors such as Jane Austen and E. M. Forster. For example, the protagonist of her first novel, *The Tiger's Daughter* (1972), is a genteel and sensitive daughter of a wealthy Indian family—a character and a social milieu transposed into India from the mold of Austen. The descriptive style of Forster's *A Passage to India* (1924) echoes in the opening of Mukherjee's novel:

> The Catelli-Continental Hotel on Chowringhee Avenue, Calcutta, is the navel of the universe.... There is, of course, no escape from Calcutta.... Family after family moves from the provinces to its brutish center, and the center quivers a little, absorbs the bodies, digests them, and waits.

In the 1990's and afterward, however, Mukherjee vastly extended her fictional repertoire beyond an urbane realism to include forays into science fiction and historical romance, as in *The Holder of the World* (1993), as well as into the mystery thriller, as in *Desirable Daughters* (2002).

Irony is a persistent trait of Mukherjee's early work, an irony modeled consciously upon Naipaul's. This irony, expressing itself in the distance between author and protagonist, and between protagonist and her observed world, is already evident in *The Tiger's Daughter*, which records the impressions of a young and mainly passive Indian woman who has gone to the United States as a student, has married a white American, and is returning to her native Calcutta for a holiday visit. Through the subtle interplay between the protagonist's Westernized perspective, her memories of her Asian youth, and her inactivity, Mukherjee provides an ironic critique of upper-class Indian society, whose mores and vitality are crumbling like those in Anton Chekhov's *Vishnyovy sad* (1904; *The Cherry Orchard*, 1908)—Chekhov being another of Mukherjee's most admired authors.

The texture of Mukherjee's narratives is often enriched by patterns of repeated imagery and rendered intricate by literary allusions. In *Wife* (1975), for example, a dead mouse becomes an imagistic leitmotif symbolic of violence. In *Jasmine*, the repeated image of a dead dog occurs with chilling effectiveness, while allusions to Charlotte Brontë's *Jane Eyre* (1847) form a provocative subtext to the novel. Similarly, John Keats's "On a Grecian Urn" is a significant leitmotif in *The Holder of the World*, and the snake is an effective recurrent image in *Desirable Daughters*.

The locales, persons, idiom, and themes of Mukherjee's later work have increasingly taken on the traits of the American grain, especially traits along the lines of Jewish American writers about immigrant life such as Abraham Cahan, Henry Roth, Isaac Bashevis Singer, and Bernard Malamud. As she stated in 1985, "The book I dream of updating is no longer *A Passage to India*—it's *Call It Sleep*," Henry Roth's 1934 novel.

Certainly the narrative energy that infuses Mukherjee's later works is less genteel Anglo-Indian than raw American. For example, the beginning of the story "Angela" (in the 1985 collection *Darkness*) is a far cry from Austen: "Edith was here [in the hospital] to have her baby last November. The baby, if a girl, was supposed to be named Darlene after Mother, but Edith changed her mind at the last minute . . . while she was being shaved by the nurse."

Mukherjee unfalteringly captures the idiom and cadence of her protagonist-narrator as she speaks through the throat of an Atlanta sports fan and financial consultant in "Fighting for the Rebound" (from *The Middleman*):

I'm in bed watching the Vanilla Gorilla stick it to the Abilene Christians on some really obscure cable channel when Blanquita comes through the door wearing lavender sweats, and over them a frilly see-through apron . . . Okay, so maybe . . . she isn't a looker in the blondhair-smalltits-greatlegs way that Wendi was. Or Emilou, for that matter. But beautiful is how she makes me feel. Wendi was slow-growth. Emilou was strictly Chapter Eleven.

With her fast-paced, psychologically intriguing, and intellectually challenging narratives, Mukherjee provides valuable and moving insights into the too-often buried lives and unexpressed emotions of South Asians, especially South Asian women, who are making their way in a daunting New World of high technology, unruly mores, and random violence. Mukherjee is thus carving an important niche for herself and her primary subject matter, the South Asian diaspora to America, in the pluralist tradition of American letters.

WIFE

First published: 1975
Type of work: Novel

A young wife from Calcutta, India, migrates to New York City, goes insane, and kills her husband.

Wife, Mukherjee's second published novel, exemplifies the matter and manner of her early work. Unlike her first novel, *The Tiger's Daughter*, which is wholly set in India, most of *Wife* takes place in the United States. With a gentle irony that serves to alleviate and distance an otherwise pathetic protagonist, Mukherjee depicts the mental breakdown of a weak-minded young woman who cannot cope with the traumatic experience of immigration from the structured society of India to the liberated society of New York City.

The opening sentences of the novel introduce the protagonist and set the playfully ironic tone:

Dimple Dasgupta had set her heart on marrying a neurosurgeon, but her father was looking for engineers in the matrimonial ads. . . . She fantasized about young men with mustaches, dressed in spotless white, peering into opened skulls. Marriage would bring her freedom, cocktail parties on carpeted lawns, fund-raising dinners for noble charities. Marriage would bring her love.

The literary ancestry of this narrative tone is traceable to Austen, particularly to *Pride and Prejudice* (1813). The genre, a comedy of manners about marriage, is also reminiscent of Austen, though Mukherjee chooses to emphasize the woes of marriage rather than its joys (as Austen does). Also unlike Austen, Mukherjee's focus is not upon an intricate character (such as Austen's Elizabeth Bennet), but on a rather simple character.

The name of Mukherjee's protagonist, Dimple, is perhaps a measure of her simplicity (and the author's playfulness with Calcutta chic). In any case, Dimple's mind is portrayed as entirely vacant of ideas other than those associated with securing a husband. To make herself more attractive to prospective husbands, Dimple wants to lighten her wheatish complexion with creams, increase her bust by isometrics, and finish herself with a bachelor of arts degree. She fails on all three fronts. Her father does manage a match for her, however, not with a neurosurgeon but with an engineer intent upon emigrating, preferably to the United States.

Through courtship and early marriage, Mukherjee's comedy of manners continues, with complaining in-laws, unsatisfied romantic expectations, and Dimple's predictable disillusion with her groom and the married state. The comic events, however, take on a darker tinge with two incidents that indicate Dimple's naïve penchant toward violence as a quick solution to problems. One incident involves her chasing and braining a mouse. This image of violence is used as a leitmotif by Mukherjee; it stays with Dimple, and her consciousness flashes back to it several times during the course of the novel. The image also appears to be a teasing reference to the opening scene of Richard Wright's *Native Son* (1940), in which his protagonist smashes a rat with a frying pan. Indeed, Dimple later in the novel asks an American friend to tell her Wright's story (though the scene is transposed from Wright's original Chicago to Harlem).

The other graphic episode occurs when Dimple has an unwanted pregnancy and, thinking of a baby as an impediment to immigration, induces an abortion by (ironically) skipping rope. The abortion episode connects imagistically to the mouse killing, because that animal was smashed in a pile of baby clothes, and its remains are described as looking pregnant. This interweaving of imagery, theme, allusion, and characterization is illustrative of Mukherjee's complex and subtle artistry.

Soon afterward, the immigration papers come through for her husband, Amit Basu, and the couple departs India. Dimple's entry into the New World is occasion for Mukherjee to depict the comedy of errors of émigrés unused to new mores; the clashes of culture are initially slight and amusing, but they accrue to become a considerable shock to Dimple's fragile psychological balance.

Although Indian society had seemed overly structured and authoritarian (especially with parents controlling their children's marriages so absolutely), it had, in actuality, provided Dimple with clear behavioral guidelines. In the United States, by contrast, there appears to be so much freedom that Dimple loses her bearings in a seeming ocean of permissiveness. That there are American structural taboos as fastidious as Hindu ones, but which

are incomprehensible to Dimple, is illustrated by her attempt to buy cheesecake from a kosher butcher.

Migration to the United States also reduces the Indian status of her husband: No longer master of his house, he is suffered as a guest by his host and becomes just another job-seeking immigrant. Amit is consequently reduced in Dimple's eyes. Dimple is also fascinated by liberated and Americanized Indian women such as Ina Mullick, whom she finds rather incomprehensible and repellent. Mainstream American foods, too, are problematic; she forces herself to eat hamburger (beef being taboo and odious for Hindus), then vomits it up privately. Dimple feels so defeated by American life that she likes nothing better than to stay in bed all day watching television—in fact, television becomes her version of life in America.

Meanwhile, the violence of American life bombards Dimple—talk of random shootings, cautionary tales of mugging in the streets, crime statistics in the news, murder on the television soap operas. These elements, many of them amusing in isolation, add up to a substantial cultural trauma for the susceptible Dimple. Furthermore, she begins an affair with a white American, while Amit becomes increasingly obtuse, antipathetic, and unmanly in her eyes. Mukherjee subtly builds up Dimple's predisposition to bloodshed by describing Amit's cutting a finger while changing a lightbulb and Dimple's accidentally wounding his hand with a paring knife when he attempts romance in the kitchen. Finally Dimple goes completely insane, and she decapitates Amit—an act that shows her perversely and grossly taking the power she had desired at the beginning of the novel by wanting marriage to a neurosurgeon.

Wife is an accomplished psychological novel about a young Asian immigrant woman who goes violently insane. Mukherjee creates with insightful deftness the psyche of a weak-minded, unhappy, and perplexed wife undergoing the shock of transition from the highly structured but protective society of India to the apparently freer but infinitely more puzzling society of the United States. The controlling irony of Mukherjee's narrative is the perfect medium for depicting this murderous but naïve woman whom the reader can understand but with whom the reader cannot fully empathize. In this novel, too, Mukherjee has defined a primary sphere of her artistic endeavor—the psychological world of the South Asian woman facing the challenge of immigration to the United States with its attendant traumata of culture shock, its rush of freedom, its responsibility of self-definition, and its access to power.

JASMINE

First published: 1989
Type of work: Novel

While emigrating from India to the United States, a young Asian woman struggles against destiny to create her own identity and resists racial and sexual stereotypes to assert her humanity.

Soon after garnering the 1988 National Book Critics Circle Award for her second collection of short stories, titled *The Middleman, and Other Stories*, Mukherjee published her exciting and accomplished novel *Jasmine*. In fact, the novel grew out of one of the *Middleman* stories, also titled "Jasmine," whose protagonist persisted in the author's imagination, demanding to be reincarnated or born again in a lengthier genre. *Jasmine* is a novel about survival; it is also an account of an immigrant minority woman's metamorphosis, self-invention, and self-empowerment. Inasmuch as the protagonist is a woman, the novel holds great interest for feminists. Insofar as she is an Indian, and much of the book dwells upon her experience in the United States, the novel adds another episode to the epic of the Asian diaspora to America.

In this tightly crafted book, which uses time shifts extensively, all the major themes and motifs are established in the opening chapter. Its first sentence begins with the phrase "Lifetimes ago," which immediately introduces the structuring theme of metamorphosis or reincarnation, and indeed, the protagonist is known by different names (signifying different identities and different lives) at different stages in the novel. The first chapter also introduces the main conflict in the novel by describing an astrologer's prophecy of Jasmine's exile and widowhood and Jasmine's violent resistance to the astrologer: It is the conflict between a

humanistic-existential individualism (Jasmine's) and a cosmic-determinist worldview (the astrologer's).

In resisting the astrologer, Jasmine bites her tongue and scars her own forehead, but instead of succumbing to these wounds (to be born female in her society is already to be wounded), Jasmine resolutely metamorphoses them into advantages. She imagines the wound in her forehead to be a Siva-like sage's third eye to scan invisible worlds, and the bloody tongue is an attribute of the powerful destructor goddess Kali (an image that reappears in the novel when Jasmine kills a rapist). The opening chapter then closes on two unforgettable images: As Jasmine swims wrathfully in the river, she bumps into the carcass of a drowned dog and tastes the stench of the water—both images affect her like curses then, but she is to exorcize them dramatically later in the novel.

Jasmine's native village is in the Punjab, India, where the birth of a girl is an affliction. Her mother, in fact, tries to strangle Jasmine, her fifth daughter; however, Jasmine, who was then named Jyoti, survives and grows into an intelligent girl able to obtain more than the usual amount of education. Jyoti also evinces an enjoyment of power. When electricity comes to the village, she loves the feeling of being "totally in control" as she flicks the light switch. One day she particularly "feels a buzz of power" when she smashes in the skull of a

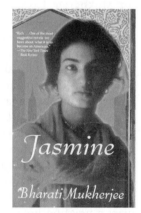

dog who attacks the village women during their morning toilet. This image of her killing the dog recalls, and in some measure indicates an overcoming of, the curse and destiny laid upon her by the astrologer. Another dead dog image will reappear in connection with a would-be lover's suicide in America.

The astrologer's prophecy of widowhood, however, comes true. Contrary to family expectation, when Jyoti is fourteen years old, she marries for love an enlightened engineering student who further educates her and renames her Jasmine. He wishes to emigrate to the United States, but before that can happen, he is blown up by a Sikh terrorist bomb. In India, the protagonist has two names, suggestive of the two conflicting cultures of the subcontinent: Jyoti is a Hindi and Hindu name, whereas Jasmine is a Persian-Arabic and Muslim name; respectively, the names mean "light" and "sweetness," the two elements which English poet Matthew Arnold thought could save culture from anarchy.

Jasmine then sets out for the United States to realize her husband's immigration dream by proxy and also, like a virtuous Hindu widow, to commit *suttee* by cremating his suit (in lieu of his corpse) and immolating herself in the flames. Paradoxically, during her odyssey to achieve this, Jasmine has to sell herself unvirtuously for food and passage. When a Vietnam veteran turned smuggler rapes her and makes fun of her husband's suit, however, she strikes back and kills him instead of stabbing herself. It is noteworthy that when Jasmine kills, she first slits her own tongue; through this image Mukherjee lessens Jasmine's personal responsibility in the killing by ritualizing the act, for Mukherjee has imagistically transformed Jasmine into an aspect of the goddess Kali, whose mouth is iconically filled with blood.

In seeking virtue and death, Jasmine ironically discovers criminality and a desire to live. She is helped by a kind woman who illegally aids refugees and who renames her Jazzy, another reincarnation. Through her, Jasmine becomes an au pair, a "caregiver," to an academic couple at Columbia University. When the couple's marriage breaks up, the husband, Taylor, becomes Jasmine's lover. He nicknames her Jase, yet another reincarnation.

One day Jasmine is terrified when she recognizes a neighborhood hot-dog vendor as her husband's assassin. Leaving Taylor, she flees New York and, by chance, ends up in Iowa. There she becomes the common-law wife of Bud Ripplemeyer, a prominent small-town banker, and becomes known, in still another reincarnation, as Jane Ripplemeyer. Jasmine refuses to marry him for fear of her astrologer's prophecy of widowhood, and indeed Bud is shot by a distraught farmer facing foreclosure soon after he and Jasmine begin living together. Although Bud does not die, he becomes crippled. Thus Jasmine has to take increasing charge of their

relationship; in sex, for example, she becomes the active partner, even deciding whether Bud should ejaculate. (This situation echoes that of Mukherjee's story "The Tenant," in which the woman sleeps with an armless man.) When Jasmine becomes pregnant, it is an event over which she is more in charge than most women, and it is an indicator of how much Jasmine is now in charge of herself and her life, of how much empowerment she has attained. More than electricity is in the hands of this erstwhile village girl.

If Mukherjee had ended her novel at this point, she would have established Jasmine largely within the archetype of woman as a powerful and supportive caregiver, very much where Charlotte Brontë ended *Jane Eyre*. Aside from Jasmine's being renamed Jane, there are at least two allusions to *Jane Eyre* in *Jasmine*, not to mention that *Jane Eyre* has a wife burned to death, a fate Jasmine once contemplated for herself. Clearly Mukherjee's heroine is intended to look back to Brontë's, but she also looks beyond her. Mukherjee, therefore, ends her novel by endowing her protagonist not only with power but also with the freedom to exercise it. Thus Jasmine, who genuinely loves and cares for Bud, refuses to be bound to his wheelchair (as Jane Eyre is to her blinded Rochester). Instead, although she is ripely pregnant, she deserts Bud when her former lover, Taylor, tracks her down and proposes that she flee with him to find happiness in Berkeley, California.

The novel's ending has provoked controversy. Some readers will criticize Jasmine's decision to leave Bud as irresponsible. Others will argue that Mukherjee is realistically pointing out that liberation has a cost, and that, furthermore, when Jasmine moves westward to a greater freedom and self-actualization, she is merely acting in the time-honored American tradition of lighting out for the territory ahead, a tradition hallowed by Horace Greeley and by Mark Twain's *Adventures of Huckleberry Finn* (1884). Mukherjee's Jasmine has indeed come a long way—not only from the Punjab to America but also from believing that a wife's virtue entails self-immolation to believing that a pregnant woman's happiness justifies her deserting the father of her child for the arms of a lover.

THE HOLDER OF THE WORLD

First published: 1993
Type of work: Novel

Seeking a lost seventeenth century diamond, a twentieth century American woman researcher accesses an American woman in seventeenth century India, using virtual reality to accomplish her task.

In "A Four-Hundred-Year-Old Woman" (1991), Mukherjee revealed plans for *The Holder of the World*: a "major work, historical in nature" about the "making of new Americans." In the finished novel, Mukherjee experiments boldly with several elements: science fiction, historical romance, captivity narrative, framed narrative, and miniature Moghul painting. Through it, Mukherjee claims that Asia has always been important in the making of America.

The aesthetic of miniature Moghul painting disregards spatial and temporal chiaroscuro and equalizes framing peripheries and focal centers. The novel's center is the narrative about Hannah Easton, a woman of seventeenth century Salem, Massachusetts (hence an incipient American). The novel's frame is the narrative of Beigh Masters, a twentieth century woman researcher (the latest American) who traces valuable objects for collectors and antique dealers. The object sought is the most prized diamond in history, "The Emperor's Tear" of Aurangzeb (1618-1707), India's last great Moghul emperor. It had disappeared on a seventeenth century battlefield in India; however, a period Moghul painting had depicted it held by a blonde harem-member named Salem Bibi. Beigh's research identifies her as Hannah Easton, and Mukherjee thus links America and Asia. Hannah's story is a historical romance. Orphaned (apparently) during an American Indian raid, Hannah marries an Irish seaman who joins the prototypically colonialist East India Company, and they settle in seventeenth century Fort St. George, India (now Chennai, once Madras). Hannah's husband turns pirate, neglecting her. During a political uprising, Hannah becomes the captive and then passionate paramour of the Hindu king, Raja Jadav Singh. (Noticeably, Hannah's captivity, like her mother's, results in her sexual liberation while also echoing the captivity of Rama's wife recounted from the *Ramayana*, 300 B.C.E.) Subsequently, Hannah is captured by the Raja's sworn enemy, the Muslim emperor Aurangzeb. During the battle between king and emperor, the Raja is killed, and Aurangzeb's diamond lost. Here science fiction merges with historical romance.

Beigh is having a twentieth century romantic affair with Venn Iyer, a brilliant Indian computer scientist at M.I.T. He invents an interactive virtual-reality machine into which all known data about a past time is input. A present human subject is then inserted to interact with that virtual reality and, by extension, events beyond the input data. Beigh thus enters the virtual battlefield in seventeenth century India and confirms her gut feeling about the Emperor's Tear. Noticeably, this interactivity ironically destabilizes history and even the immortality of art, an irony highlighted by repeated quotations from Keats's "On a Grecian Urn" in the novel. This interactivity also links America with Asia, past with present, and Beigh's peripheral narrative with Hannah's central narrative.

Hannah ends by returning to Salem, birthing en route the Raja's and her daughter, Pearl. In Salem, she reunites with her mother, a shunned Indian lover, and they live on the periphery of Puritan society. Several generations afterward, however, Hannah's legend moves into the center of American literary consciousness when it inspires Nathaniel Hawthorne's masterpiece *The Scarlet Letter* (1850). Thus the virtual reality of Mukherjee's fiction has written India into the beginnings of American literary history.

The Holder of the World, then, is a rich, complex narrative that challenges its readers' notions of discrete historical periods, cultures, and ethnicities. Some may find the novel excessively cerebral; others will delight in its dazzling ideas, surprising characterization and plot, and brilliant hybridizing of fictional form.

Bharati Mukherjee

DESIRABLE DAUGHTERS

First published: 2002
Type of work: Novel

A wealthy immigrant Indian American divorcée seeks to define herself amid threats by the international Indian mafia.

Desirable Daughters employs unusual amounts of autobiographical material in an immigrant novel of self-discovery that combines elements of fairy-tale-like myth with a suspenseful mystery-thriller plot.

The daughters are three sisters from Calcutta (Kolkatta), India, brought up like modern princesses within their protective wealthy Hindu Brahmin caste. They live in the exclusive enclave of Ballygunge, are schooled in English at the Loreto convent by Irish nuns, perform in *The Mikado*, and are shown off by doting parents at cocktail parties. They are obviously modeled on Mukherjee and her two siblings.

Consonant with Mukherjee's persistent immigrant theme, two of the sisters migrate to the United States while one remains in India. Tara, the novel's narrator, is the youngest. She made an arranged marriage to Bish Chatterjee, who epitomizes the Asian immigrant's American Dream by excelling at Stanford University, starting up a dot-com company, and becoming a Silicon Valley multimillionaire before age thirty. However, Tara becomes bored by her marriage, so she realizes another version of the Asian immigrant's American Dream by obtaining a California-style, no-fault divorce and celebrating her liberation with moder-

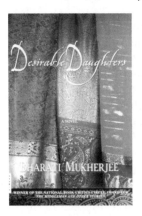

ate promiscuity. She then settles into a pricey home in the Haight-Asbury district of San Francisco with her gay teenage son and her boyfriend, a Hungarian Buddhist handyman biker.

Into Tara's sybaritic American Eden, an old-world serpent intrudes in the shape of a recently arrived Indian youth claiming to be Christopher Dey, the illegitimate son of Tara's eldest sister, Padma; he professes only a wish to find his birth mother. Tara is suspicious of Christopher, especially when his alleged father suddenly dies in a traffic accident in Bombay (Mumbai), where Parvati, the second sister, lives in a moneyed high-rise overlooking a squalid fisher village.

At the first sign of trouble, Tara's boyfriend decamps. Tara visits Padma, now living in New York, hoping to find out the truth. Padma is in deep denial, having married a rather complacent Indian man and having become both a successful purveyor of fashion design in New Jersey and a rising television personality in Queens. When Padma returns to San Francisco, she briefly reunites with former husband Bish for a night of make-up sex, which climaxes with a bomb blowing up her house. Tara is badly burned, and Bish is confined to a wheelchair indefinitely. During their convalescence, the couple are drawn together again, and Tara regains a desire to reconnect with her Indian roots. She therefore visits her parents, now retired to a hilltop village where they await death. There she becomes more aware of her namesake, the fairy-tale-like ancestress who married a tree at age five because her fiancé died of snakebite. Tara regains a sense of connection to things Indian through meditating on this ancestress who died participating in India's liberation from Britain's Empire. *Desirable Daughters*, then, provides a searching, critical picture of the materially successful Indian immigrant community in America. It also entertains as a cross-cultural whodunit, beguiles with a tinge of fairy tale, and provides depth by reaching after Indian spirituality. For its curious readers, there is a sequel: *The Tree Bride* (2004).

"THE WORLD ACCORDING TO HSÜ"

First published: 1983 (collected in *Darkness*, 1985)
Type of work: Short story

A Eurasian woman and her white Canadian husband vacation on an island off Africa while attempting to decide whether to relocate from Montreal to Toronto.

This story is to be found in Mukherjee's first collection of short fiction, titled *Darkness* (1985). Like most of its companion stories in this collection, it records, analyzes, and dramatizes the tribulations of South Asian immigrants in North America. These *Darkness* stories are painful, often violent, and either tragic or ironic; their collective title seems to be an ironic inversion of the way in which the West thinks of itself as a locus of freedom, opportunity, and enlightenment in contrast to benighted developing countries. The irony is especially mordant when one hears in Mukherjee's title echoes of Joseph Conrad's *Heart of Darkness* (1902), condemning nineteenth century European colonialism, and V. S. Naipaul's *An Area of Darkness* (1964), an Asian-denigrating travelogue about India. For Mukherjee, it appears that darkness has overtaken North America, supposedly the leading light of the Western world.

It is racism, a darkness of the mind toward the darkness of another's skin, that most taints North American life. The racism of Canada, especially, receives the brunt of Mukherjee's resentment in "The World According to Hsü." Indeed, in her introduction to these stories, Mukherjee says that during her fourteen-year sojourn in Canada, white Canadians commonly assumed that she was a prostitute, a shoplifter, or a domestic, and that Canadian society routinely made crippling assumptions about the imagined disabilities of immigrants of color.

In "The World According to Hsü," Ratna Clayton, a Eurasian woman of Indian descent, and her husband, Graeme Clayton, a white Canadian professor, are vacationing on an island nation in the Indian Ocean off the African coast. The couple is trying to decide whether to move their home from

French Montreal to Anglo Toronto in order to advance the husband's career. As if in concert with their decision making, a military coup occurs on the island. The dispiriting uncertainty and irritable meanness of being uprooted and homeless, which is a major theme of this and several of Mukherjee's works, is reflected in a backdrop of seedy caravanseries, uneasy politics, and directionless supporting characters that are as expertly evoked as anything in works by Graham Greene or Naipaul.

Ratna is reluctant to move because of her experience of Toronto racists: "In Toronto, she was not a Canadian, not even Indian. She was something called, after the imported idiom of London, a Paki. And for Pakis, Toronto was hell." She also recalls a Punjabi boy's having been struck by a car with a bumper sticker that read: "Keep Canada green. Paint a Paki." Conflict, Mukherjee hints bitterly, seems to be fundamental to the world, not only conflict between races in Canada, between political ideologies in developing nations, or between couples in marriage. The principle of conflict is also embedded in the very structure of the planet.

The metaphor for this lies in the story's title, which derives from an article that Ratna's husband is reading on plate tectonics. The article is written by a scientist named Hsü and describes how continents have been formed by plates of the earth's surface smashing or grating against one another. It is a metaphor of abrasion that sums up Ratna's experience of universal racism through differing times of her life: When she was a child growing up in India, Ratna was jeered as a "white rat," and now that she is an adult in Canada, she is taunted as a "Paki."

Informed by this geological metaphor of fundamental and ubiquitous conflict, the apparently hopeful ending of the story is really ironic: "She poured herself another glass [of wine], feeling for the moment at home in that collection of Indians and Europeans babbling in English and remembered dialects. No matter where she lived, she would never feel so at home again." Initially, this last sentence may seem hopeful and comforting—Ratna feels at home. If being "at home" means feeling at ease, secure, stable, and free from conflict, however, then Ratna is only deluding herself. The fact tenaciously remains that she is an alien on that island, being regarded as a Canadian by the Third World islanders, and that she is a second-class citizen in Canada, being disregarded as a Third World person there. Furthermore, she is surrounded by babbling tourists who are without homes on that island, an island in political turmoil. Therefore, although the final sentence of the story sounds hopeful, it is in fact an ironic and despairing statement implying that Ratna will never really be "at home" anywhere.

"ANGELA"

First published: 1984 (collected in *Darkness*, 1985)
Type of work: Short story

A young refugee girl from Bangladesh tries to adjust to her adoptive home in Iowa.

This story is included in Mukherjee's collection *Darkness* and in *The Best American Short Stories, 1985*, edited by Gail Godwin and Shannon Ravennel.

"Angela" is not a happily ending story of a refugee successfully finding life and liberty, and pursuing happiness, in the United States. Rather, it is a subtle psychological analysis of a survivor, of how survival can entail feelings of guilt and obligation, and of how survivors can be exploited by their rescuers.

The story begins with Angela, a teenage refugee from Bangladesh, at the bedside of her adoptive sister Delia Brandon in Van Buren County Hospital, Iowa. Delia is comatose after an automobile crash, one which Angela survived with hardly a scratch. Naturally, Angela feels guilty that she, not Delia, has survived the accident unscathed—Delia was the one who had instigated Angela's adoption by the Brandons. Besides, Sister Stella at the orphanage had taught Angela a Christian account of salvation, as if it were some institution of savings and loans: "The Lord saved you. Now it's your turn to do him credit."

Indeed, Angela's list of indebtedness to the Almighty for letting her survive is lengthy: Surviving the death of both parents at the age of six, she also survived the political upheaval of Bangladesh, racing through "leechy paddy-fields" to avoid "the rapes, the dogs chewing dead bodies, the soldiers." The only scars she retains are those that occurred when her nipples had been sliced off. Afterward,

Angela had found refuge in a Catholic orphanage, and eventually she was adopted by the Brandons, a farming family in Iowa, where Angela is now a cheerleader in high school.

Angela's survival is little short of a marvel, a miracle, a holy mystery—terms which occur in Angela's first-person narrative. She would even seem to be an angel—or at least to be under the guardianship of one, a manifestation of God's "grace" to fallen and violent humankind. If Angela is an angel, however, she is a dark one, and not by virtue of complexion only. She says that the cook at the orphanage used to "chop wings off crows . . . so I could sew myself a sturdy pair of angel wings," and she continues, "I visualize grace as a black, tropical bat, cutting through dusk on blunt ugly wings." This is not the usual dove of light. Through such imagery, Mukherjee makes the reader approach grace and miracle with circumspection and irony.

The reader is also led to question how unmixed a miracle Angela's apparent good fortune may be and under what a load of obligation and guilt she is placed thereby. Clearly, she is obligated to the Brandons and feels guilty that the Almighty had visited injury on the Brandons' daughter rather than on herself during their accident. Further, it would appear that the Brandons, in turn, are obligated to a Dr. Menezies, an Indian physician who is attending to Delia and who also seems to be helping the Brandons fend off foreclosure on their farm.

Dr. Menezies, who is nearly forty years old, wants to marry Angela, but she is not attracted to him. Angela herself yearns for the self-development of going to college and the freedom of pursuing a career. Such desires would, of course, be dashed if she were to accept Dr. Menezies's marriage proposal, entailing duplexes and babies. Yet marriage to Dr. Menezies would, under the circumstances, be tantamount to a discharging of Angela's indebtedness to the Brandons, as well as an assuagement for the guilt of having somehow undeservedly survived her accident unscathed. Exploiting Angela's sense of obligation, Dr. Menezies tries to dissuade her from going to college: "I don't think you are so selfish."

Mukherjee ends the story with this dilemma exquisitely and excruciatingly imaged by Angela: As Angela falls asleep, she dreams in a sensuously ambiguous image of leeches feeding on her nippleless breasts—a richly ironic conflation of the repulsive and the medicinal, of suffering and nurturing, of the appearance of grace and the reality of exploitation.

SUMMARY

Mukherjee's short stories and novels bring unique insight and profundity to the immigration, expatriation, and assimilation of South Asians, especially South Asian women, in North America. She explores the effects of racism, sexism, violence, and human exploitation with consummate skill, measured realism, and moving drama. There is an implacable resentment of racism in her works, but there is also an implicit hope in the redeeming possibilities of love and in the positive aspects of United States society, in which individuals of color, even women of color, may realize their full humanity and empower themselves. Mukherjee's artistry is characterized by her frequent use of irony, imagistic leitmotifs that grow into meaningful symbols, literary and mythological allusions, a supple and exuberant wielding of multiple American idioms, and acute psychological penetration into a wide assortment of characters.

C. L. Chua

DISCUSSION TOPICS

- How does Bharati Mukherjee depict violent scenes and violent people? How does she make them useful for her thematic purpose?

- What evidence is there in Mukherjee's fiction that its author was a student of Indian mythology and history?

- Discuss how Mukherjee uses literary allusions to enrich the meaning of her narratives. (Some writers to bear in mind would be Matthew Arnold, John Keats, Nathaniel Hawthorne, and Charlotte Brontë.)

- For Mukherjee, what is the impact of American society on the immigrant Indian woman?

- In what ways does racism show up in Mukherjee's work?

- How does Mukherjee use the names of characters (for example, Jasmine, Jyoti, Jane) to develop themes in her fiction?

BIBLIOGRAPHY

By the Author

SHORT FICTION:
Darkness, 1985
"The Management of Grief," 1988
The Middleman, and Other Stories, 1988

LONG FICTION:
The Tiger's Daughter, 1972
Wife, 1975
Jasmine, 1989
The Holder of the World, 1993
Leave It to Me, 1997
Desirable Daughters, 2002
The Tree Bride, 2004

NONFICTION:
Days and Nights in Calcutta, 1977 (with Clark Blaise)
The Sorrow and the Terror: The Haunting Legacy of the Air India Tragedy, 1987 (with Blaise)

About the Author
Alam, Fakrul. *Bharati Mukherjee*. New York: Twayne, 1996.

Desai, Anita. "Outcasts: *Darkness* by Bharati Mukherjee." *London Magazine*, December, 1985/January, 1986, 143-146.

Dhawan, R. K. *The Fiction of Bharati Mukherjee: A Critical Symposium*. New Delhi, India: Prestige, 1996.

Mukherjee, Bharati. "Beyond Multiculturalism: Surviving the Nineties." In *Race: An Anthology in the First Person*, edited by Bart Schneider. New York: Three Rivers, 1997.

_____. "A Four-Hundred-Year-Old Woman." In *The Writer on Her Work: II*, edited by Janet Sternberg. New York: Norton, 1991.

_____. "An Invisible Woman." *Saturday Night* 96 (March, 1981): 36-40.

_____. Interview by Alison B. Carb. *Massachusetts Review* 29 (Winter, 1988): 645-654.

_____. Interview by Geoff Hancock. *Canadian Fiction Magazine* 59 (1987): 30-44.

_____. Interview by Suzanne Ruta. *Women's Review of Books*, July, 2002, 13.

Naipaul, V. S. "A Conversation with V. S. Naipaul." Interview by Bharati Mukherjee and Robert Boyers. *Salmagundi* 54 (Fall, 1981): 4-22.

Nazareth, Peter. "Total Vision." *Canadian Literature* 110 (Fall, 1986): 184-191.

Nelson, Emmanuel, ed. *Bharati Mukherjee: Critical Perspectives*. New York: Garland, 1993.

Courtesy, Vancouver International Writers Festival

ALICE MUNRO

Born: Wingham, Ontario, Canada
July 10, 1931

By focusing almost exclusively on short fiction which explores the intimate experience of ordinary women, Munro has not only mastered the short-story form but has also elevated it to new heights.

BIOGRAPHY

Alice Munro was born Alice Ann Laidlaw, the eldest of three children of Robert Laidlaw and Anne Chamney, on July 10, 1931. The family lived in a nineteenth century brick farmhouse at the edge of Wingham, Ontario, the small town usually disguised in her fiction as Walley, Jubilee, or Hanratty. Munro's father, a descendant of Scottish pioneers, raised silver foxes and, later, mink. For the first two grades, Munro attended the rough Lowertown School modeled in "Privilege" (1978), where she was the only child in her class to pass first grade. At her mother's insistence, she was transferred to the Wingham public schools where, living in imagination and books, she felt even more isolated. She worked on an unfinished gothic novel during high school, influenced by Emily Brontë's *Wuthering Heights* (1847).

After World War II the popular demand for furs lessened, and eventually the fox farm failed; times were so hard that the Laidlaws had to burn sawdust for heat. In 1947 Robert Laidlaw took a job as night watchman at the local iron foundry, raising turkeys as a sideline. Anne Laidlaw, an elementary teacher of Irish descent, had been forced to abandon her career because married women were not allowed to teach. In her mid-forties she developed a devastating form of Parkinson's disease contracted from the encephalitis virus. Munro had to do all the housework from the time she was twelve and as a teenager worked as a maid for a Toronto family.

Her feelings toward her mother were intensely ambivalent, and there were frequent clashes.

Winning a two-year scholarship enabled Munro to attend the University of Western Ontario, where in 1949 she entered the journalism program, switching to English in her second year. At her boardinghouse she received a full breakfast but had a meager food allowance of thirty-five cents for the rest of the day. She held two library jobs and sold her blood for extra income. In the spring of 1950, she published her first story, "The Dimensions of a Shadow," in *Folio*, the campus literary magazine. By then she was engaged to James Munro, a fellow student. When her scholarship expired in 1951, she was forced to leave school, returning home to care for her temporarily bedridden mother. She and James were married at her parents' home in Wingham just after Christmas.

Munro's eldest daughter, Sheila, has noted that her parents' marriage paralleled in many respects the mismatched backgrounds of Patrick and Rose in Munro's story "The Beggar Maid" (1977). While Munro's circumstances were modest, James's father was a well-to-do accountant for the Toronto branch of Eaton's department store. James took a managerial job at Eaton's in Vancouver, British Columbia.

Munro struggled to find a time and place for her writing, torn between her own needs and society's expectations of her as a wife and mother. In 1953 she sold her first commercial story, "A Basket of Strawberries," to *Mayfair*, which unfortunately went out of business. That same year her daughter Sheila was born; Jenny and Andrea would follow in 1957 and 1966. Munro began to publish in other magazines, including *Chatelaine* and *McCall's*, while her stories were featured on the Canadian radio series *Anthology*. She remained an omnivorous reader, especially of American writers Carson McCullers, Flannery O'Connor, and Eudora Welty. Working alone amid the clutter of daily life, she had little contact with other writers until much later. She battled not only the conformity of the 1950's but also a general condescension toward women writers, visible in a 1961 newspaper article about her, headlined "Housewife Finds Time to Write Short Stories."

Publishers warned Munro that they could not sell a short-story collection before she published a novel, considered a more prestigious literary form. Accordingly, she began a novel in 1959, the year her mother died, but her writing was soon blocked when she suffered an ulcer and panic attacks. Eventually she produced several stories for the largely autobiographical *Dance of the Happy Shades* (1968), among them "A Trip to the Coast," with its distinct overtones of Flannery O'Connor, and the remarkable "The Peace of Utrecht." This first collection, dedicated to her father, would win Canada's most prestigious prize, the Governor General's Award.

In 1963 James Munro left Eaton's to open a bookstore in Victoria, British Columbia. There Munro wrote in the mornings and worked at the bookstore. She submitted "Boys and Girls" to a University of Victoria creative writing class, where it was dismissed by the professor as something a typical housewife would write, a comment that effectively paralyzed her for a year. The move to a finer home in 1966 exacerbated difficulties in her marriage. As James became increasingly prosperous and conservative, she grew more rebellious.

Lives of Girls and Women (1971), Munro's second book, was published as a novel, winning the Canadian Booksellers' Award and firmly establishing her reputation as a Canadian writer of note. By 1972 her twenty-year marriage was disintegrating. The following summer, with her two younger daughters in tow, she taught a creative writing class at the University of Notre Dame in British Columbia and then returned to the University of Western Ontario to become writer-in-residence. With her next collection, *Something I've Been Meaning to Tell You: Thirteen Stories* (1974), she broadened her subject matter, thereafter publishing a new book roughly every four years.

Munro married Gerald Fremlin, an urban geographer and former college friend, in 1976. That fall, after issuing twenty years of rejection slips, *The New Yorker* accepted several of her stories. The first, "Royal Beatings," was published the following year and became the lead story for Munro's fourth book, *Who Do You Think You Are?* (1978; published in the United States as *The Beggar Maid: Stories of Flo and Rose*, 1979), which garnered another Governor General's Award.

As the winner of the Canada-Australia Literary Prize (1978), Munro visited Australia and later traveled to China with a group of Canadian writers. *The Moons of Jupiter* appeared in 1982, followed by *The Progress of Love* (1986), for which she earned a third Governor's General's Award, and *Friend of My Youth* (1990), dedicated to her mother. *Open Secrets* (1994) received the W. H. Smith Award for the best book published in the United Kingdom in 1995. *The Love of a Good Woman* (1998) won the National Book Critics Circle Award and the PEN/Malamud Award for short fiction as well as Canada's esteemed Giller Prize of $25,000. *Hateship, Friendship, Courtship, Loveship, Marriage* (2001) was followed by *Runaway* in 2004, which was awarded a second Giller Prize. Munro and her husband divide their time between Clinton, Ontario, and Comox, British Columbia.

ANALYSIS

Munro is one of very few modern writers who have built a reputation solely through the writing of stories, a form that has generally been regarded as of lesser consequence than the novel. Even though the publishers of her second book, *Lives of Girls and Women* (1971), called it a novel, Munro rejected a chronological approach and clustered its chapters around themes, as in a book of linked stories. When her American publisher pressured her to rewrite her fourth book, *Who Do You Think You Are?* (1978), as a novel to improve sales, she turned it into a story sequence, unified by the character of Rose. By the 1980's, what author Joyce Carol Oates calls Munro's "stories that have the density . . . of other writers' novels" cannot accurately be referred to as "short" stories; their length suggests a greater complexity.

Munro's subject is the intricate detail of human experience, viewed almost always from a female perspective and with special attention to the mother-daughter relationship. She traces the lives of women whom the 2004 Giller Prize jury called "locally Canadian, remarkably ordinary, and at the same time startlingly universal." The lives she observes may be stunted or blossoming; her central character may become an actress or waitress. While the earlier work explores the coming of age of a young, lower-middle-class girl who learns hard lessons on her way to maturity, in time these initiation stories begin to address social and political issues like patriarchy or abortion rights. Munro never passes judgment on her characters; they have made their choices, too frequently the wrong ones.

Her style is realistic and without sentimentality, often evoking a strong sense of her native region and its history. (Her settings have expanded over time to include British Columbia, Scotland, Ireland, central Europe, and even Australia.) A prime example is her well-known story "Meneseteung" (1988), titled with the Native American name for the river commonly known as the Maitland (or Peregrine), which flowed near the border of her parents' farm. This story offers a detailed, unembellished view of life on the Ontario frontier, providing an ironic contrast to the delicate verse written by a nineteenth century Canadian poetess.

Munro has remarked that all her writing is essentially autobiographical. Several of the early stories appear to be reminiscences, yet there is always artifice at work. Like Rose's father in the powerful "Royal Beatings" (1977), Munro's father occasionally beat her, and his death after heart surgery inspired another story, "The Moons of Jupiter" (1978); yet the details in these stories go far beyond her personal experience. Her striking ambivalence toward her mother—embarrassment, shame, and later, guilt—surfaces whenever a teenage daughter struggles with a mother who is disfigured, ill, or dying from a degenerative disease. Anne Laidlaw's death in 1959 triggered "The Peace of Utrecht" (1960), and her uncontrollable trembling appears in "The Ottawa Valley" (1974), where Munro writes: "The problem, the only problem, is my mother. And she is the one of course that I am trying to get . . . to describe, to illumine, to celebrate, to *get rid*, of her . . . for she looms too close, just as she always did."

Munro's early penchant for gothic novels sometimes allows her to edge toward the bizarre. In one of her most gothic stories, she manages to create a sense of vulnerability and menace from an experience she shared with Gerald Fremlin. In a rural area stood a wall she remembered, set with colored glass mosaics. There the couple, urged to enter the nearby farmhouse, encountered four drunken men, one naked, playing cards in a windowless room. She included this event, partially transformed, in "Save the Reaper" (1998).

Typically, Munro withholds information from a story, believing that the less one reveals, the better, and many of her characters follow this custom of silence or omission. She prefers that her reader fill in the gaps and often inserts a key word or phrase that will take on new significance with a second reading. Particularly noteworthy is the way she handles the fluidity of time, employing time shifts—skipping, reversing, doubling around to take a second look. She explains, "I don't take up a story and follow it as if it were a road, taking me somewhere . . . I go into it, and move back and forth and settle here and there, and stay in it for a while."

Ambiguity, the shifting perception of truth, is another favorite device. In most cases, there are multiple and conflicting truths, which Munro may reveal through a characteristic double vision of past and present, perhaps by means of someone returning home who sees old haunts, old loves, through different eyes. She may offer the conflicting perceptions of two characters, as she does with Rose and Flo in *Who Do You Think You Are?* Such treatment frequently results in an ironic discrepancy between appearance and reality.

"HOW I MET MY HUSBAND"

First published: 1974 (collected in *Something I've Been Meaning to Tell You*, 1974)

Type of work: Short story

A hired girl has her first encounter with romance and determines what kind of woman she will be.

A typical early story, "How I Met My Husband" introduces a young girl's initiation into adulthood, as narrated by her mature self, and exemplifies the double vision frequently found in Munro's work.

When Edie, a naïve farm girl and high-school dropout, is hired as a maid by the new veterinarian, Dr. Peebles, she is awed by his home's modern conveniences: pink bathroom fixtures, an automatic washer, ice cubes. Edie is keenly aware of society's lofty attitude toward hired help and country people, yet she unconsciously exhibits the same prejudice toward shiftless Loretta Bird, an unwelcome neighbor.

The Peebles family lives across the road from the old fairgrounds where one day a small plane lands, sparking all sorts of conjecture. That afternoon the barnstorming pilot Chris Watters, who offers plane rides for a dollar, seeks permission to use the Peebles's pump and instead finds Edie trying on Mrs. Peebles's long dress and jewelry while the family is gone. Edie is immediately smitten.

When Alice, the pilot's fiancé and a former army nurse, arrives unexpectedly, Dr. Peebles follows local custom by inviting her to stay with them. Tension escalates as Alice tries to convince Chris to marry her, but he is clearly reluctant and soon disappears. Viciously turning on Edie, Alice flounces after him. As Edie waits for Chris's promised letter at the mailbox, she meets a young mail carrier who will soon become her husband. Unlike Alice, Edie decides, "If there were women all through life waiting, and women busy and not waiting, I knew which I had to be."

"ROYAL BEATINGS"

First published: 1977 (collected in *Who Do You Think You Are?*, 1978; in the United States as *The Beggar Maid: Stories of Flo and Rose*, 1979)

Type of work: Short story

A conflict intensifies the already ambivalent relationships between Rose, her stepmother Flo, and her father.

"Royal Beatings," one of Munro's best-known stories, reveals the bonds of love and hate, brutalities great and small, within a family. Nothing is simple in this story, which features a surprisingly intricate plot as well as convoluted time and tense shifts. It begins late in the Depression years in the poorest section of Hanratty, where Rose lives with her father and stepmother, Flo, behind their grocery and furniture repair store. One day Flo relates an account of a previous thrashing, when three young men attacked the father of the grotesque dwarf Becky Tyde, who sometimes visits the store. The child Rose cannot fit Flo's story together with her present life, for they seem unrelated.

Flo's tale foreshadows a second beating, this time suffered by the preteen Rose—a brutal ritual which builds, erupts, and then collapses. When Rose talks back to her stepmother once too often, Flo goads Rose's father into punishing her. The narrative shifts into present tense to render a horrific account of the first "royal beating" that cheeky Rose endures, then switches to future tense to describe the ritual that will follow: a repentant Flo coming to her room to bring a salve for her back, a tray of food, chocolate milk. Years later, the adult Rose sees a television interview with an elderly man from Hanratty, someone from Flo's story, and is finally able to connect the strands of the past to the present.

"PRUE"

First published: 1981 (collected in *The Moons of Jupiter*, 1982)

Type of work: Short story

This character study of a stunted life examines a middle-aged woman who reacts to a failed relationship.

Only five pages long, "Prue" is a brief history of a pleasant, good-humored woman, once a dining room hostess in British Columbia and presently a Toronto clerk. Divorced and with grown children when she met Gordon, a wealthy neurologist, she lived with him off and on before he and his wife finally divorced. One evening Gordon admits he has acquired a jealous young lover with whom he is infatuated, but he wants to return to Prue in a few years and marry her. Prue treats this development as a good joke with which to regale her friends.

What she does not tell them is that the next morning she steals one of Gordon's gold and amber cufflinks, which she stores secretly with other mementos in a tobacco tin which her children once gave her. Such souvenirs, which are neither expensive nor worthless, she simply takes, perhaps as something tangible to hold for herself. Prue reveals herself as a woman familiar with disillusion and empty relationships, which she deflects by anecdotes and humor even as she appears to move on. The unspoken truth of her emotions is withheld, concealed like the objects she keeps in the tin.

"CIRCLE OF PRAYER"

First published: 1986 (collected in *The Progress of Love*, 1986)
Type of work: Short story

A single mother struggles with her teenage daughter and the memory of the husband, of which she is still learning to let go.

In "Circle of Prayer," Munro has raised time shifts to the next level, with a story so completely out of chronological order that it demands a close reading. Trudy, a single mother, works from four to midnight at the Home for Mentally Handicapped Adults. When she hears that her fifteen-year-old daughter's classmate, Tracy Lee, has been killed in an automobile crash, Trudy fears for her daughter Robin, who feigns indifference to the death.

Trudy drinks her morning coffee and thinks of her husband Dan—their first meeting, their courtship and life together. She remembers their arguments when he left her to live with a younger woman, Genevieve. Last summer Robin returned after a month with her father, upset because he seemed happier with Genevieve than at their home.

Rebellious Robin comes home at noon to change clothes so that she can join her classmates for an afternoon visitation at the funeral home. When the girls drop their jewelry into Tracy Lee's open coffin as a symbolic gesture, Robin adds her dead grandmother's jet beads. Trudy confronts her for taking the beads without permission and insists on an explanation, but the real issue for both is Dan, not the necklace: their grief, not their anger. Janet, Trudy's fellow worker, advises her to pray for

the return of the jet beads. Janet belongs to a secret Circle of Prayer and believes that, when everyone in the circle prays together, prayer will be answered. Trudy responds sarcastically that perhaps God will return Dan, the beads, even Tracy Lee.

Trudy recalls her honeymoon, when she watched Dan's mother playing the piano and perceived the older woman's sadness through her own joy. When Dan left her, she was aware of her love for him as well as her own unhappiness, a confused jumble of emotions. Suddenly Robin telephones, implying a reconciliation, and unlike most of Munro's stories, the mother-daughter relationship begins to heal.

"WIGTIME"

First published: 1989 (collected in *Friend of My Youth*, 1990)
Type of work: Short story

Two high-school friends reunite as mature women, regretting little.

The longer, looser structure of "Wigtime" suggests the mounting complexity of Munro's work. When Anita, now divorced, comes home to Walley to care for her dying mother, she reconnects with her friend Margot, whom she has not seen in thirty years. Both were once farm girls near Lake Huron, coming of age in the late 1940's, and they recall high school life, wedding fantasies, and the cups of steaming coffee as they waited at Teresa Gault's grocery for her husband Reuel, the school bus driver. Teresa, a French war bride, spoke to them bluntly, sometimes alarming Anita, who was uncomfortable yet fascinated by details of sex and miscarriage.

The two friends have not confessed the painful truths of their lives before. Margot used to make her life with an abusive father sound like a slapstick comedy, but while Anita was hospitalized with appendicitis, Margot began a relationship with Reuel and eventually married him, abandoning her dream of becoming a nurse. When she was warned that Reuel was unfaithful to her, as he had once been to Teresa, she disguised herself as a hippie to spy on him with their young baby-sitter. From her discovery of this affair, she has negotiated a new house and the comfortable life she presently enjoys. Both Anita and Margot have survived, as has Teresa in her own way, housed in the county home's psychiatric wing. All have settled for their present lives, and Munro points out with characteristic restraint, "They are fairly happy."

"A REAL LIFE"

First published: 1992 (collected in *Open Secrets*, 1994)
Type of work: Short story

Three friends with differing attitudes toward marriage find that they must modify their expectations.

Munro creates sly pockets of humor in "A Real Life" as she introduces Dorrie Beck, the descendant of a pioneer Ontario family who is currently in reduced circumstances. In spite of a brief social education at Whitby Ladies College, where she developed beautiful handwriting, Dorrie has evolved into a strong, competent countrywoman. She does a man's work, can trap and shoot with the best, and is oblivious to the social graces.

Her friend Millicent has settled into a prosaic marriage with a man nearly twenty years older than she, who owns three farms, including the Beck family farm, where Dorrie still lives alone. When Millicent gives an evening supper for the Anglican minister and his visitor Mr. Speirs, she invites Dorrie and Muriel Snow, a single, thirtyish music teacher who is desper-

VINTAGE MUNRO

ately seeking a husband. Even though Muriel instantly sets her cap for Mr. Speirs, he is more impressed by Dorrie, who arrives late because she has to shoot a feral cat that may be rabid. Speirs corresponds with Dorrie from his home in Australia, and they decide to marry, after which she will live there with him.

The two friends sew Dorrie's wedding dress while she stands about miserably in her woolen underwear. While Dorrie has second thoughts about the wedding, Millicent convinces her that she cannot bow out because only marriage can give her "a real life."

Self-reliant Dorrie reluctantly submits to the prison of marriage because it is expected of her, but fortunately it offers her even more freedom. She continues an active outdoor life in Australia, growing fat and rich. Ironically, the flirtatious Muriel willingly marries a widowed minister and loses all of her former independence, while Millicent ends her days alone.

"SAVE THE REAPER"

First published: 1998 (collected in *The Love of a Good Woman*, 1998)
Type of work: Short story

A grandmother comes face to face with evil near her childhood retreat and is forced to reexamine her life.

"Save the Reaper" is one of the most disturbing stories Munro has written. Eve, an actress, is driving in a rural area with her two young grandchildren. In the car, her grandson Philip imagines alien space invaders in other cars, which they then follow. The game is Eve's; she used to play it with her daughter Sophie. Eve has generally fond memories of her daughter and blames their past estrangement on Sophie's husband and mother-in-law. However, her idyllic vacation with Sophie and the grandchildren on the shores of Lake Huron is cut short when her daughter secretly phones her husband, asking him to rescue her. Forced to recognize her real relationship with her child, Eve must constantly reassess what she believes to be true.

As Eve tries to recall places of interest to charm her grandson, her faulty memory of a wall decorated with glass mosaics finds her turning off the road onto private property to ask directions from the driver of a pickup truck which is blocking her way. He leads her into a dilapidated farmhouse where four sinister people sit in a littered, windowless room, drinking and playing poker. One man is naked. Eve suddenly realizes that the situation is out of control; she has put the children in real danger, as well as herself, in what is apparently a drug house. Still, she agrees to give a young woman hitchhiker a ride to town, has even given the girl directions to her cabin, where after this night Eve will be alone. She is terrified, with an impending sense of disaster.

Summary

One of the most impressive things about Munro's fiction is that she is able to write about ordinary people and their problems with "an art that works to conceal itself." Breaking nearly every rule of the traditional short story, she has transformed the genre. Her talent is widely respected, and her contemporaries praise her. Cynthia Ozick has compared her to a classic Russian author ("She is our Chekhov"), while Mona Simpson and Jonathan Franzen, among others, have suggested that Munro is worthy of a Nobel Prize. Munro has broken ground for subsequent generations of women writers by increasing an awareness of the whole of female experience, with clear vision, insight, and compassion.

Joanne McCarthy

Discussion Topics

- What types of initiation do Alice Munro's characters undergo?

- Examine Munro's treatment of the various relationships between women. What kinds of male-female relationships does she explore?

- Munro was one the first women writers to explore frankly all aspects of sexuality from a female perspective. How does her treatment of this subject differ from that of male writers you have read?

- What techniques does Munro use to conceal information in a story, and what are their effects?

- How do her frequent departures from chronological time affect a story?

- How does she employ the device of double vision to enrich a story?

Bibliography

By the Author

SHORT FICTION:
Dance of the Happy Shades, 1968
Something I've Been Meaning to Tell You: Thirteen Stories, 1974
Who Do You Think You Are?, 1978 (pb. in U.S. as *The Beggar Maid: Stories of Flo and Rose,* 1979)
The Moons of Jupiter: Stories, 1982
The Progress of Love, 1986
Friend of My Youth: Stories, 1990
Open Secrets: Stories, 1994
Selected Stories, 1996
The Love of a Good Woman: Stories, 1998
Hateship, Friendship, Courtship, Loveship, Marriage, 2001
No Love Lost, 2003
Vintage Munro, 2004
Runaway: Stories, 2004

LONG FICTION:
Lives of Girls and Women, 1971

About the Author

Franzen, Jonathan. "Alice's Wonderland." *The New York Times Book Review,* November 14, 2004, 1, 14-16.

Howells, Coral Ann. *Alice Munro.* Manchester, England: Manchester University Press, 1998.

McCulloch, Jeanne, and Mona Simpson. "The Art of Fiction CXXXVII." *Paris Review* 131 (Summer, 1994): 226-264.

Moore, Lorrie. "Leave Them and Love Them." *The Atlantic Monthly* 294, no. 5 (December, 2004): 125.

Munro, Sheila. *Lives of Mothers and Daughters: Growing Up with Alice Munro.* Toronto: McClelland & Stewart, 2001.

Ross, Catherine Sheldrick. *Alice Munro: A Double Life.* Toronto: ECW Press, 1992.

Simpson, Mona. "A Quiet Genius." *The Atlantic Monthly* 288, no. 5 (December, 2001): 126.

WALTER DEAN MYERS

Born: Martinsburg, West Virginia
August 12, 1937

Myers writes realistic stories about African American youth coping with complex social and ethical issues and finding values by which to live.

Courtesy, HarperCollins

BIOGRAPHY

Walter Dean Myers was born in West Virginia into a large family. When he was three years old, his mother died. Burdened by poverty, his father sent Myers to live with foster parents in New York City. The foster parents, Herbert and Florence Dean, raised the boy in Harlem, which Myers remembers as teeming with life and excitement. Myers changed his original middle name, Milton, to Dean in honor of his foster parents.

Myers's foster mother read to him every day until he could read for himself. Myers was a good student in the sense that he was literate, but he became known as a discipline problem in school. He had a speech impediment that prevented people from understanding what he was saying. His classmates teased him, and Myers responded with anger. He spent many days in the principal's office or on suspension.

He received some guidance from his fifth-grade teacher, who thought that writing down words would help him with his speech problem. He filled notebooks with poems and stories but did not consider writing as a career. When not in school, Myers hung out with the street gangs and played basketball until it was too dark to see. Later in his life, the game of basketball would be a prominent feature in several of his books.

At age sixteen, Myers dropped out of school, and he joined the Army the next year. After his tour, he returned to Harlem and worked in a series of low-paying jobs. At the same time, he began to write for magazines. He entered a writing contest sponsored by the Council on Interracial Books for Children and won first place. The entry was his first book, *Where Does the Day Go?* (1969), which won in the picture book category. Myers wrote a few more books for preschoolers before directing his efforts toward teenagers. *Fast Sam, Cool Clyde, and Stuff* (1975) was his first young-adult novel.

For twenty years, Myers worked as an editor during the day and wrote fiction at night. When the company he worked for laid him off, he became a full-time writer. As a result, Myers has been prolific, publishing more than five dozen books for young people. *Monster* (1999) won the first Michael O. Printz Award. Two of his other books received Newbery Honor Awards. He is the father of three children and lives with his wife in New Jersey.

ANALYSIS

Myers is best known as an author of children's literature and young-adult fiction. He has also written nonfiction books focusing on African American history. One of his primary goals as a writer is to create novels that intrigue and instruct children and teens. His target audience seems to be young impoverished people of color who have been neglected by mainstream literature. However, any young person struggling with coming-of-age issues can relate to Myers's characters. He realistically portrays contemporary and historical figures with whom his young readers can identify. His plots are action-packed and fast-moving, yet his settings and descriptions are rendered in great detail. His contemporary characters tend to be drawn from the ghetto world that he once knew intimately.

A thread that runs through many of his books for teens is the search for ideals. Myers writes about young people overcoming a harsh environment, senseless violence, and dysfunctional families by developing inner values. His characters face complex ethical choices but usually find an honorable path. As an author, it is Myers's intent to instill values in young people who have been devalued or undervalued themselves.

Myers believes that in order to reach his readers, they must be able to identify with the actions, thoughts, and emotions of his protagonists. The language, settings, and plots must be relevant to young people, especially marginalized African Americans. He often uses the first-person viewpoint, which provides immediate access to the protagonist's mind. In seeking to establish common ground with his adolescent readers, he uses slang frequently. Some readers in the twenty-first century might find some of the language dated; however, the plot lines and themes that inform Myers's work have already endured—and been enjoyed—for decades.

Although his books tend to be written from the perspective of an inner-city, African American male, his coming-of-age theme is universal. The crisis may vary from book to book, but each protagonist endures a rite of passage from childhood into adulthood. In *Hoops* (1981), a gifted high-school basketball player discovers from a has-been pro that the real game of life does not have a scoreboard and that only inner values can guide his next moves. The main character in *Fallen Angels* (1988) goes through a classic rite of passage—war. As a soldier, he learns how to love and retain his own humanity despite the senseless violence of war. In *Monster*, a sixteen-year-old man on trial for his life begins to question his role in a vicious crime. He wonders if he is guilty of perpetuating the ruthless laws of the ghetto, regardless of whether the court acquits him.

Myers uses setting to emphasize the shift from childhood to adulthood. The backdrops for his stories are usually unequivocally adult. His young characters find themselves making decisions in the real world and facing real consequences. For example, in *The Young Landlords* (1979), a group of teens takes on the responsibility of managing a ghetto apartment building and learns a great deal about themselves in the process. A prison and a courtroom become Steve Harmon's entire world in *Monster*, and there are few environments more mortal than the battlefield in *Fallen Angels*.

In essence, Myers writes about young people making choices. This is not unique in young-adult fiction. However, Myers's characters tend to be faced with choices that have life-or-death consequences. When Cal in *Hoops* decides not to go along with the gang controlling a tournament, his decision ends in his death. In *Fallen Angels*, every step that Richie Perry takes "out in the boonies" (the Vietnamese jungle) could cause or prevent another death. The subject matter and language in Myers's books are often raw. Gambling, war, drug use, suicide, teen pregnancy, homicide, adoption, and parental neglect are subjects that have brought three of his books to the edge of censorship by school systems. While these topics may seem dramatically harsh to some readers, they are merely reflections of daily life to others. One of Myers's gifts is showing young people, regardless of age, race, and social status, that they can live up to their ideals in any situation.

HOOPS

First published: 1981
Type of work: Novel

A young basketball player learns from a mentor about the financial and spiritual risks of the game.

In *Hoops*, Myers makes the game of basketball symbolize the game of life. Basketball was one of Myers's passions; it was an escape from the frustrations of school, a time to bond with other kids his age, and just plain fun. He depicts the basketball scenes in his books with astounding clarity and from an insider's perspective. *Hoops* seems at first to be an action-packed sports novel but is soon revealed as a moral tale about choices and integrity.

The main character in *Hoops* is seventeen-year-old Lonnie Jackson, who clings to a dream that he will become a professional basketball player. He is a senior in high school and is feeling tense about what his next steps in life will be. Basketball could be a way out of Harlem, a way to accrue status in the world, and a way to have some self-esteem. Lonnie is one of the best players in Harlem. He believes that there is a real chance that his dream could come true.

Lonnie rarely stays at home with his mother. He has an arrangement with the manager of a hotel called The Grant where he does some cleaning in exchange for a place to sleep. One of the first incidents in the book is a robbery at a liquor store across the street from the hotel. While the criminals are herding staff and customers into the back, Lonnie grabs a case of scotch to sell. This incident paints a picture of Lonnie's environment and of his own cunning adaptation to that environment.

Myers often uses the first-person viewpoint to engage his young-adult readers. Lonnie's thoughts and feelings are skillfully articulated, exposing conflicts and concerns about love, sex, money, family, and honor. Specifically, Lonnie's conflicts in *Hoops* revolve around basketball, his mother, his girlfriend, and Cal.

Cal, a former pro player who was ousted from the league for gambling, coaches Lonnie's team. Cal is now a semi-homeless alcoholic but with enough caring to warn Lonnie about the ugly side of the game. Lonnie starts to look up to Cal, whom

he at first considered a useless wino. As Lonnie grows closer to Cal, he sees a broken man with a broken past who still manages to instill trust in the team members. As the story builds to its climax, the team is playing in a tournament with big gambling money riding on the outcome.

Toward the end of the book, Cal is ordered by mob leaders to keep Lonnie out of the game, which would result in the team's loss. Cal tells Lonnie that basketball is like life: "Everybody plays the game with what they got." At first, Cal does sit Lonnie down, but as the tournament game progresses, he suddenly calls for Lonnie, and the team wins the

game. However, this spells doom for Cal, who is viciously stabbed in the team locker room.

Hoops takes place in a terrifying world where gangs roam the streets in malicious packs and Lonnie's girlfriend is injected with heroin because she learns about a mobster's involvement in the tournament fix. The reader follows Lonnie's growth from a tough, self-centered kid who cares about nothing except basketball to a more mature young man who sees that even a person as fallen as Cal can overcome his weakness and become a moral force in the midst of corruption.

FALLEN ANGELS

First published: 1988
Type of work: Novel

At seventeen years old, Richie Perry enters the Vietnam War and discovers a world of horrors and heroes.

Myers dedicated *Fallen Angels* to his brother who was killed in the Vietnam War. Myers himself joined the Army at age seventeen because it seemed to him that he had few other options. The protagonist of *Fallen Angels*, Richie Perry, is also seventeen when he enlists in the Army. The young man believes at first that he will not see any combat because he has injured his knee stateside. However, he soon discovers that the wheels of paperwork processing grind slowly in the Army, and he finds himself in the muggy jungles of Vietnam.

The story is one of courage, conflict, and deep numbing confusion about a soldier's role in the Vietnam War. Myers tells the story from Richie's point of view and spares the reader no detail of the young man's terror, the firefights and bombing, the killings, and the deaths of his companions, who are the fallen angels referred to in the book's title. Realistic language and settings play an important role in helping contemporary readers relate to the environment of brutal fighting in a Southeast Asian jungle.

Racial tension exists in the novel, but it is overshadowed by the intense fear and confusion generated by the war. The language can be vulgar, yet it seems to fit in with the raw, rugged life that the characters experience out in the jungle. In this book, the environment is overwhelming; death and injury surround Richie and his comrades, dwarfing the concerns of ordinary life (otherwise known as the World).

Initially, Richie yearns to get back to the World, back to his stateside, civilian life. Gradually, he begins to shed his childlike dream of being a hero to his younger brother and focuses on the crucially important issue: staying alive. He realizes that he does not know how to pray and starts to form a spiritual outlook. He begins to love the men that fight alongside him, to think not only of himself, but also of his comrades in arms. Myers makes it clear that the war has changed Richie forever and that the World has become the foreign land.

MONSTER

First published: 1999
Type of work: Novel

In order to cope with his trial for murder, a young man writes a screenplay as though he were in a movie about his own life.

Monster is presented in an unusual format: a screenplay interspersed with facsimiles of a handwritten journal. The book is illustrated with photos, court sketches, even fingerprints. It won Myers the first Michael O. Printz Award for literary excellence in young-adult fiction.

The fictional author of this screenplay-journal is sixteen-year-old Steve Harmon. He has been accused of acting as a lookout during a homicide. If he is convicted, he could spend the rest of his life in prison. The book describes his weeks of incarceration, his trial, and its outcome. Steve writes in the screenplay format because he wants to become a filmmaker, and because it is a way to distance or disassociate himself from the unfolding nightmare of his life. He can see himself and others as simply actors in a movie.

As the book opens, Steve has already learned that the best time to cry in jail is at night. When other prisoners are screaming and yelling, a little sniffle cannot be heard. He realizes that he must not show weakness in jail, just as he could not show weakness on the street. When he looks in the small scratched mirror over the steel sink in his cell, he does not recognize himself. He starts to wonder if he is becoming some kind of evil changeling. Within the first page of the book, Myers characteristically creates a clear picture of Steve and his predicament. Myers grabs the reader's attention immediately by using the first-person viewpoint to express the character's emotions and by describing in sharp physical detail a harsh, disturbing setting.

The prosecutor calls Steve a monster during opening arguments. Steve begins to wonder obsessively if he is a good person or a monster after all. What constitutes a good person? In Steve's milieu, drug use, petty crimes, and running the streets are just a part of life. His alleged presence during the robbery-homicide raises questions about his choices. Just as his survival in prison depends on displaying a hardened exterior, so his survival on the streets depended on doing little jobs for gang leaders.

Steve insists in his journal that "he didn't do nothing." However, his defense lawyer, Ms. O'Brien, has some concerns. She is afraid that the jury will not "see a difference between [him] and all the bad guys taking the stand," that Steve might be tarred with the same brush as his fellow defendants. Steve intuits that Ms. O'Brien thinks he is guilty and is merely doing her job in the courtroom. Myers does not state the facts of the crime in the book, so the reader is left wondering if Steve was or was not a lookout at the crime scene. This question is literally illustrated by two captioned photos in the book. They both appear to be stills from a store's videotape, showing Steve in the store. The captions read: "What was I doing?" and "What was I thinking?" It is not clear if the photos are anxious figments of Steve's imagination or tell-tale hints that he was actually in that store.

Finally, Steve is found not guilty. He spontaneously reaches out to hug Ms. O'Brien, who turns away stiffly, indicating that there is something bad about Steve despite his acquittal. *Monster* is thoroughly ambiguous about Steve's role in the crime. It is ambiguous about Steve's basic nature, his goodness or badness. The book leaves the reader to ponder about whether guilt equals goodness and whether acquittal equals innocence.

SUMMARY

Harsh reality becomes the foundation for growth in Myers's books about young people living in poverty and without hope. His characters struggle to perceive the possibilities of a positive future and to learn values such as integrity, honor, and morality in a world that marginalizes them.

Janet M. Ball

BIBLIOGRAPHY

By the Author

CHILDREN'S LITERATURE:
Where Does the Day Go?, 1969
The Dancers, 1972
The Dragon Takes a Wife, 1972
Fly, Jimmy, Fly!, 1974
Fast Sam, Cool Clyde, and Stuff, 1975
The World of Work: A Guide to Choosing a Career, 1975
Social Welfare, 1976
Brainstorm, 1977
Mojo and the Russians, 1977
Victory for Jamie, 1977
It Ain't All for Nothin', 1978
The Young Landlords, 1979
The Black Pearl and the Ghost: Or, One Mystery After Another, 1980
The Golden Serpent, 1980
Hoops, 1981
The Legend of Tarik, 1981
Won't Know Till I Get There, 1982
The Nicholas Factor, 1983
Tales of a Dead King, 1983
Motown and Didi: A Love Story, 1984
Mr. Monkey and the Gotcha Bird, 1984
The Outside Shot, 1984
Sweet Illusions, 1987
Crystal, 1987
Fallen Angels, 1988
Me, Mop, and the Moondance Kid, 1988
Scorpions, 1988
The Mouse Rap, 1990
Now Is Your Time! The African-American Struggle for Freedom, 1991
Mop, Moondance, and the Nagasaki Knights, 1992
The Righteous Revenge of Artemis Bonner, 1992

DISCUSSION TOPICS

- Walter Dean Myers writes to instill values into young people. What values do his characters develop in his books?

- How does Myers use setting to create conflict in his books?

- What are some of the social, psychological, or economic obstacles that Myers's characters overcome?

- What are some of the controversial subjects explored by Myers? Why do some authorities consider these subjects unsuitable for young adults?

- In what ways do good and evil and guilt and innocence motivate Myers's characters?

- How does Myers indicate the "coming-of-age" theme in his young adult books?

Walter Dean Myers

Somewhere in the Darkness, 1992
Brown Angels: An Album of Pictures and Verse, 1993 (poetry)
Malcolm X: By Any Means Necessary, 1993
A Place Called Heartbreak: A Story of Vietnam, 1993
Young Martin's Promise, 1993
Darnell Rock Reporting, 1994
The Glory Field, 1994
Glorious Angels: A Celebration of Children, 1995 (poetry)
One More River to Cross: An African-American Photograph Album, 1995
Shadow of the Red Moon, 1995
The Story of the Three Kingdoms, 1995
How Mr. Monkey Saw the Whole World, 1996
Slam!, 1996
Smiffy Blue, Ace Crime Detective: The Case of the Missing Ruby, and Other Stories, 1996
Toussaint L'Ouverture: The Fight for Haiti's Freedom, 1996
Harlem, 1997
Amistad: A Long Road of Freedom, 1998
Angel to Angel: A Mother's Gift of Love, 1998
At Her Majesty's Request: An African Princess in Victorian England, 1999
The Journal of Scott Pendleton Collins: A WWII Soldier, 1999
The Journal of Joshua Loper: A Black Cowboy, 1999
Monster, 1999
The Blues of Flat Brown, 2000
145th Street, 2000 (short stories)
Bad Boy: A Memoir, 2001
The Journal of Biddy Owens: The Negro Leagues, 2001
Three Swords for Granada, 2002
The Beast, 2003
Blues Journey, 2003 (Christopher Myers, illustrator)
The Dream Bearer, 2003
Antarctica, 2004
Here in Harlem: Poems in Many Voices, 2004
I've Seen the Promised Land, 2004 (Leonard Jenkins, illustrator)
Shooter, 2004
USS "Constellation": Pride of the American Navy, 2004
Autobiography of My Dead Brother, 2005 (Christopher Myers, illustrator)

About the Author

Bishop, Rudine Sims. *Presenting Walter Dean Myers.* Boston: Twayne, 1990.

Burshtein, Karen. *Walter Dean Myers.* New York: Rosen, 2004.

Jordan, Denise M. *Walter Dean Myers: Writer for Real Teens.* Berkeley Heights, N.J.: Enslow, 1999.

McElmeel, Sharron L. "A Profile: Walter Dean Myers. *Book Report* 20, no. 2 (September/October, 2001): 42-45.

Smith, Amanda. "Walter Dean Myers." *Publishers Weekly* 239, nos. 32/33 (July 20, 1992): 217-218.

VLADIMIR NABOKOV

Born: St. Petersburg, Russia
April 23, 1899
Died: Montreux, Switzerland
July 2, 1977

Nabokov was unique in that he became a major author writing in both Russian and English. He wrote stories, novels, poetry, memoirs, plays, critical essays, reviews, lectures, and translations.

Library of Congress

BIOGRAPHY

Vladimir Vladimirovich Nabokov's life divides neatly into four phases, each lasting approximately twenty years. The oldest of five siblings, he was born April 10 (Old Style), 1899, to an aristocratic and wealthy family in St. Petersburg. Nabokov later insisted on the New Style birth date of April 23, because it coincided with William Shakespeare's.

Nabokov's grandfather, Dmitri Nikolayevich, had been state minister of justice for two czars. His father, Vladimir Dmitrievich, a prominent liberal statesman, was married to Elena Rukavishnikova, a beautiful woman from an extremely rich family. Vladimir's parents adored their firstborn child and raised him with enormous love and care. Nabokov eloquently evoked his childhood in his lyrical memoir, *Conclusive Evidence* (1951), expanded and retitled *Speak, Memory* (1966).

After the 1917 Bolshevik Revolution, life became increasingly dangerous for Nabokov's father. In 1919, the Nabokovs fled Russia. Vladimir, who had learned both French and English from governesses, enrolled in the University of Cambridge's Trinity College. Although he spent much of his time there writing poems and playing tennis, he graduated in 1922 with first-class honors in French and Russian. Meanwhile, the other family members had settled in Berlin. Ten days after Nabokov's arrival from Cambridge, his father was assassinated on March 28 by right-wing extremist Russian expatriates who had intended their bullets for another

target. Vladimir took up residence in Berlin. In 1925, he married Vera Slonim, an attractive, brilliant Jewish émigré, with whom his temperament and interests remained happily matched for the rest of his life.

Vladimir and Vera Nabokov stayed in Berlin until 1937, then moved to Paris for three years. In the 1920's and 1930's, Nabokov wrote nine novels, about forty stories, and considerable poetry. He also gave tennis and boxing lessons, composed chess problems and crossword puzzles for newspapers, and engaged in entomological research. He would become an expert on butterflies' genitalia. His most important novels during this period are commonly considered to be *Zashchita Luzhina* (1929; *The Defense*, 1964) and *Dar* (1937-1938; *The Gift*, 1963).

Nabokov's third phase started in 1940, when he escaped the Nazi menace by emigrating to the United States. After a one-term lectureship at Stanford University, he spent the following seven years as a part-time instructor at Wellesley College, while also working as a lepidopterist at Harvard University's Museum of Comparative Zoology. During those years he published two novels in English, *The Real Life of Sebastian Knight* (1941) and *Bend Sinister* (1947). He also wrote a brilliant as well as eccentric study of Nikolai Gogol (1944), whose absurdist perspective deeply influenced Nabokov's writing.

From 1948 to 1959 he held a professorship at Cornell University, becoming a campus celebrity. Nabokov specialized in a course called Masters of European Fiction (in English), alternately charming and provoking his students with witty lectures, demanding examinations, and, occasionally, unfair treatment: He wanted to expel one student for disagreeing with his dismissal of Fyodor Dostoevski's literary worth.

During his summer vacations in the early 1950's, Nabokov wrote his most notorious and popular novel, *Lolita*. The book was at first refused publication by several American firms. In 1955, a Parisian English-language publisher, Olympia Press, issued the novel. By 1958, Putnam's took a chance and published it in New York, and the novel became the year's sensational seller. In 1962, *Lolita* was made into a film by Stanley Kubrick, starring James Mason as Humbert Humbert.

Nabokov's earnings from *Lolita*, which included film rights and a hefty fee for writing the screenplay, made him financially independent. In 1959, he left Cornell to travel in Europe for two years. In 1961, he established residence at an elegant hotel on the banks of Switzerland's Lake Geneva, where he would enjoy fifteen more productive years. He revised his autobiography; translated his Russian long and short fiction into English, either by himself or in collaboration with his son, Dmitri; produced a four-volume translation of and commentary on Aleksandr Pushkin's novel in verse, *Evgeny Onegin* (1833; Nabokov's version, *Eugene Onegin*, 1964); and wrote several brilliant new novels, including *Pale Fire* (1962) and *Ada or Ardor: A Family Chronicle* (1969). In his last years, he appeared to suffer from some form of cancer, which he declined to identify. He died in a hospital in Switzerland on July 2, 1977.

ANALYSIS

Nabokov's work has received considerable critical acclaim, and a consensus has been reached that he was at least a distinguished and arguably a great writer. He has exerted a major influence on contemporary authors such as Anthony Burgess, John Barth, Thomas Pynchon, William Gass, Tom Stoppard, Philip Roth, John Updike, and Milan Kundera. Nabokov wrote at least three masterful novels: *The Gift*, *Lolita*, and *Pale Fire*. Several of his stories, including "Vesna Fialte" ("Spring in Fialta") and "Signs and Symbols," are among the century's finest; his autobiography rivals Marcel Proust's in the intensity and lyricism of its nostalgia.

Nabokov's work is never intentionally didactic, sociological, ideological, or psychologically oriented; he detested moralistic, message-ridden writing. While his fictive world is filled with aberrant and bizarre characters—pederasts, buffoons, cripples, and obsessives of one sort or another—they are described not as psychological types but as representatives of the overwhelming vulgarity, freakishness, and pathos that corrupt human nature imposes on the sublimity of the natural and aesthetic world. Aestheticism is Nabokov's secular religion, and his grotesques, such *Lolita*'s Humbert Humbert, *Pale Fire*'s Charles Kinbote, and *The Defense*'s Luzhin, are offenses against the sensitivity of the artistic imagination.

Nabokov's antirealism brings him firmly into the fold of impressionism, which was inspired by the Impressionist painters Edouard Manet, Edgar Degas, and Claude Monet. Impressionistic writers employ highly selective details to stress the subjectivity of the moment's fleeting effect upon their consciousness. Neglecting accumulation of verisimilar details, they prefer to focus on memories and moods, seeking to evoke moments of ardent emotion. Nabokov's literary company includes Gustave Flaubert, Ivan Turgenev, Henry James, Joseph Conrad, Virginia Woolf, and, particularly, Proust. Nabokov's art privileges images and impressions as they flash through the limited consciousness of the observer/narrator. The protagonist may be mad or morally eccentric, however; thus, the reader must beware of empathizing too closely with the central character, who may be schizophrenic, manipulative, confused, or otherwise unreliable.

Nabokov was a difficult, enigmatic, and complex writer. He delighted in playing self-consciously with the reader's credibility, considering himself a magician in command of innumerable artifices. He loved to devise absorbing, convoluted games that often baffle the unwary reader. Many of his texts are composed like daunting chess problems, with many levels of perception, structural false bottoms, and illusory plot patterns.

For example, *Pale Fire*, which is apparently an exegesis of a long poem, has a chimerical confusion of identities and realities. Dream fantasies constitute the fictive worlds of *Bend Sinister* and *Priglashenie na kazn'* (1938; *Invitation to a Beheading*, 1959). The Clare Quilty episode of *Lolita* parodies the conventions of melodrama. Several novels, including *Kamera obskura* (1932; *Camera Obscura*, 1936; *Laughter in the Dark*, 1938) and *The Real Life of Sebastian Knight*, mock the mannerisms of the mystery story. Nabokov's love of playing games with the reader has caused some critics to accuse him of preferring brilliantly designed surfaces to serious explorations of significant human experiences.

Nabokov's puzzle-making fun and games, however, often concerns an underlying sadness. Many of the protagonists in his novels and stories face the grim horrors of an uncaring, senseless, sorrowful world. His persistent themes are the anguish of being unloved, the fragility of memory, and the brutishness of willfully inflicted pain. Though Nabokov practiced art for the sake of art, he scorned the sadism of such artists in his fiction as *Laughter in the Dark*'s Axel Rex, *Lolita*'s Humbert Humbert and Clare Quilty, and *Ada or Ardor*'s Van Veen.

Nabokov's art not only affirms a supremely talented author's precision of language, parodistic wit, and sharpness of observation but also celebrates the sanctity of life and the necessity of creative freedom. For example, Lolita is selfish, vulgar, shallow, and materialistic, but Humbert is nevertheless guilty of having deprived her of much of her childhood. While portraying Humbert with dazzling brilliance, Nabokov denies him the moral sympathy he extends to the victim.

THE REAL LIFE OF SEBASTIAN KNIGHT

First published: 1941
Type of work: Novel

A man loses his own identity while trying to write the fictional biography of his lost brother.

The Real Life of Sebastian Knight, Nabokov's first novel in English, anticipates *Pale Fire* and *Look at the Harlequins!* (1974) in being a fictional biography of a brilliant writer who has died recently. As the reader accompanies the narrator, V., on his search for knowledge about the novelist Sebastian Knight, both reader and protagonist learn less and less about their subject, until it becomes apparent that Knight's "real life" is undiscoverable.

Nabokov parodies the formula and apparatus of the detective story. V. rushes about, interviewing people who knew Sebastian, only to amass contradictory and confusing knowledge that is highly colored by his informants' self-interest. V.'s poise disintegrates as he spends many days learning less and less about his subject and following the obscure trails of Knight's correspondence. The women he interviews dupe him, and he quarrels with people whose regard for Knight is less favorable than his.

Many of the novel's stratagems resemble those of a chess game. The aptly named Knight had a mistress named Clare Bishop and a mother named Virginia—a common term for the chess queen is "virgin." V. often believes that he has become the pawn of ambiguous circumstances. Moreover, Knight's given name, Sebastian, alludes to the third century Christian martyr who was killed by arrows.

The novel also alludes to Shakespeare's comedy *Twelfth Night* (1601-1602), which is crowded with mistaken identities and features twin brothers named Sebastian. Knight had a half brother, and the novel strongly implies that V. may be he. Knight's father was Russian, and his mother was English. Thus, V. and Knight may well be divided halves of a single identity: Nabokov.

With its involuted development and inconclusive ending, the novel contrasts the duplicity of reality with the permanence of art. Real life is an infinite maze, whose center is unreachable. The one real life is that of the writer's work. V. is on sure ground only when he analyzes Knight's writings; everything else is quicksand.

LOLITA

First published: 1955
Type of work: Novel

A pedophilic European intellectual falls in tormented love with a teenager.

Lolita, generally considered Nabokov's greatest novel, unites wildly grotesque parody, farce, and pathos with two powerful, shocking subjects: the passionate feelings of a grown man toward a pubescent girl and the complex nature of romantic love, which is not only tender and generous but also ruthless and even totalitarian.

The novel's middle-aged, middle-European narrator "writes" this book as his confession while in a prison cell awaiting trial for murder. His double-talk name, Humbert Humbert, sets the tone of punning parody that pervades the text, as various people address him as Humberg, Herbert, Humbird, Humberger, and Humbug. Humbert Humbert traces his sexual obsession for "nymphets"—girls between the ages of nine and fourteen—to a case of interrupted coitus when he was thirteen years old; he and a certain Annabel Leigh had the beginnings of their first affair, forever aborted by her premature death of typhus. (The allusions to Edgar Allan Poe's poem and life number at least twenty; Nabokov refers to many other writers, including Shakespeare, John Keats, Flaubert, James Joyce, Proust, and T. S. Eliot.) After his marriage to a "life-sized" woman in Paris ends ridiculously, Humbert emigrates to the United States.

Here Humbert discovers Lolita Haze, a twelve-year-old, gum-chewing, Coke-gurgling, comic-book-addicted, blatantly bratty schoolgirl. Humbert agrees to marry Charlotte, her vapid, pretentious, widowed mother, in order to be near the irresistible daughter. When Charlotte learns of his pedophilia through reading his diary, she runs distractedly out of the house and conveniently is killed by a passing car before she can publicize his perversion.

Having laid his wife to rest, the widower undertakes the clumsy comedy of seducing his stepdaughter, who, by no means sexually innocent, volunteers to show her would-be ravisher what intercourse is all about. He registers his shock:

> Suffice it to say that not a trace of modesty did I perceive in this beautiful hardly formed young girl whom modern co-education, juvenile mores, the campfire racket and so forth had utterly and hopelessly depraved. . . . My life was handled by little Lo in an energetic, matter-of-fact manner as if it were an insensate gadget unconnected with me.

"Hum" and "La" engage in a parody of incest—he stands legally *in loco parentis*—as they traverse the continent. They encounter a neon-lit landscape of highways, gas stations, billboards, coffee shops, jukeboxes, and motels. Humbert finds Lolita coolly acquiescent to his caresses at times, peevishly self-centered at others, and capable of quickly shifting from dreamy childishness to trashy vulgarity to whining waywardness.

The couple is shadowed by a playwright, Clare Quilty ("Clearly Guilty"?), who is a peekaboo parody of the psychological double that was made famous by E. T. A. Hoffmann and Dostoevski. Both Humbert and Quilty are authors, love word puzzles, dress similarly, and are addicted to deviant sex. Quilty spirits Lolita away from Humbert, has a brief liaison with her, then discards her when she refuses to serve the boys whom he prefers to her.

Several years later, Humbert is contacted by Lolita, who desperately needs money. She is seventeen, married, plain, pale, and pregnant. In a moving episode, he discovers that he is ardently in love with her, despite her worn looks and sagging flesh. She will not return to him, but she does give him Quilty's address. Humbert then kills Quilty in a farcically protracted scene. The "editor's" preface tells the reader that Lolita died in childbirth, and Humbert succumbed to cardiac arrest.

The novel works on many levels: It is a remorseless satire of middle-class, immature America and a seriocomic commentary on Continental-American cultural relations. More profoundly, it is a moving romance in the medieval tradition of courtly love, with the afflicted Humbert Humbert displaying his derangement by obsessional devotion and self-pitying masochism. He submits himself to his emotionally unattainable mistress as her slavish servant, glorying in her cruelly capricious power over him.

On a deeper level, *Lolita* is a study in the pathology of Romantic yearning for unattainable, immortal bliss. Humbert hungers for an ideal condition of supernatural, bewitching enchantment which nymphets represent—a state beyond finite space and time. His search cannot be satisfied by a flesh-and-blood adolescent: He seeks an immortal being in a never-never land, a divine faunlet. His immortal Lolita can be realized only through Nabokov's marvelous art, which manages to transform perversion into literature.

PNIN

First published: 1957
Type of work: Novel

A Russian émigré professor tries to adapt to the alien planet of the United States.

The title character of *Pnin* is a bald, myopic, middle-aged, spindly-legged professor of Russian at Waindell College, which is somewhere in New England. Timofey Pnin is a meticulous scholar who massages a multitude of details as he researches a long-standing project: A commentary on his native Russia's folklore and literature that will reflect in miniature the major events of Russian history up to the Bolshevik Revolution. In his classes, Pnin wages Pyrrhic warfare against the English language, often digressing from his academic text to undertake mirthful excursions into his past.

Simple existence usually confounds Pnin. He manages to lose the soles of his canvas shoes in a washing machine; he fails his automobile driving test; he takes the wrong train after having carefully consulted an outdated timetable. It is not surprising that a cruel colleague, Jack Cockerell, makes a social career out of mimicking Pnin's words and gestures. Pnin is a comically inept character, whose Chaplinesque, Quixotic qualities render him essentially harmless, gentle, generous, and pathetically vulnerable.

Life has punished him. In 1925, in Paris, Pnin married the melodramatic and severely neurotic Liza Bogolepov, to save her from threatened suicide after an affair with another man. In 1938, Liza deserted him for a German psychiatrist, Eric Wind. When she returned a year later, Pnin forgave her, and they reunited and took the boat together for America—only to have Wind show up on the same ship and depart with Liza after it docked in New York. When Liza reappears in Pnin's life at Waindell, Pnin again forgives her and asks her to return to him; the sole purpose of her visit, however, is to ask him to help support her son by Wind, Victor.

Liza tells Pnin that she intends to forsake Wind for a poet and no longer wishes to be responsible for her son's upbringing. In spite of these humiliations, Pnin still loves Liza. He would be happy "to

hold her, to keep her—just as she was—with her cruelty, with him, her vulgarity, with her blinding blue eyes, with her miserable poetry, with her fat feet, with her impure, dry, sordid, infantile soul." Illogically yet unconditionally, Pnin adores this histrionic, pretentious, destructively evil woman. Here Nabokov establishes one of his absolute, magical premises, akin to Luzhin's madness and Humbert's nympholepsy.

Pnin's life could easily be considered a catalog of losses: his native land and its culture; his parents; his first love, Mira Belochkin, who died in a Nazi concentration camp; his wife; and, at the novel's end, his position at Waindell. Nabokov avoids the temptation of satirizing him as the absentminded, sweet, pathetically unfortunate professor. He treats him warmly, endearingly, and respectfully. More important, he provides Pnin with several shields against defeatism and despair.

Pnin has energy, buoyancy, and a capacity for delighting in life. After Liza leaves him for what the reader hopes is the last time, he accedes to the need of a thirsty squirrel by holding down the lever of a water fountain. He is willing to wrestle with his fate even though he usually loses. After grieving for a few days over the loss of his teeth, Pnin welcomes the miracle of his dentures, which Nabokov describes as a "firm mouthful of efficient, alabastrine, humane America."

The novel's ending is open to varying interpretations. Its narrator replaces Pnin as professor of Russian and reveals that he was responsible for Liza's seduction in Paris in the 1920's. Pnin, driving a sedan overloaded with all of his possessions, spurts out of Waindell into the open road, "where there was simply no saying what miracle might happen." Pnin has no job, little money, and no set destination. Instead of being a portrait of a victim in flight, however, the book seeks to delineate an optimistic adventurer chancing his luck in the hills beyond Waindell. Possibly Nabokov meant to signify that Pnin, like Pavel Chichikov at the end of Gogol's *Myortrye dushi* (1842; *Dead*

Souls), was intent on creating his own fate in existential style. Thus, the most affectionately drawn and moving of Nabokov's characters will insist, as he departs his book, that harm and pain need not be the world's norm, and that the pangs of exile need not defeat a courageous sufferer.

PALE FIRE

First published: 1962
Type of work: Novel

This reader's-trap, cat-and-mouse satire involves a long poem, edited and analyzed by a lunatic scholar who considers himself an exiled monarch.

Pale Fire is Nabokov's most intricate, ingenious, and controversial novel, extravagantly lauded by some of his critics and assailed as coldly concerned with only technique and gamesmanship by others.

The book begins with a brief foreword written by an academician, Dr. Charles Kinbote, who introduces a 999-line poem in heroic couplets, "Pale Fire," composed by the prominent American poet John Francis Shade, who has recently died. After the poem's text, Kinbote engages in more than two hundred pages of line-by-line interpretations. The book ends with the requisite index.

A homely man who resembles Robert Frost, Shade teaches at Wordsmith College in New Wye, Appalachia. Specializing in the poetry of Alexander Pope, Shade creates a masterpiece that is closer to William Wordsworth's pastoral themes. (Wordsmith is a combination of two poets' names: Wordsworth and Oliver Goldsmith.) The card game in Pope's spirited satire *The Rape of the Lock* (1712) is ombre, which is the French word for shade, or shadow. In *Pale Fire*, John Shade turns out to be the trump in Kinbote's bizarre game.

Kinbote describes himself as an émigré scholar who has fled his native country of Zembla. In the index, he defines Zembla as "a distant northern land" near Russia. Pope mentions it in his *Essay on Man* (1733): "At Greenland, Zembla, or the Lord knows where." A group of islands, Novaya Zemlya, exists in the Arctic Ocean, north of Archangel. Kinbote has lived next door to John and Sybil

Shade, in a house he has rented from Judge Goldsworth, of the law faculty, who is away on a sabbatical. At the time Kinbote is writing his commentary, however, he has left Appalachia and is living in a small southwestern town. Shade has been killed by a man named Jack Grey, and Kinbote has gone into hiding to edit, with the widow's permission, the poet's manuscript for publication.

Kinbote, however, is a victim of brilliant delusions. He believes himself to be an intimate friend of Shade, although they met rarely and Sybil Shade detests him for his snooping on the family with his binoculars. In his commentary, Kinbote strongly suggests that it was he who had provided the poet with the inspiration and subject of his final work. He twists Shade's verses to suit his grandiose needs and narrates, in his interpretations, the very saga he had dinned into the bard's tolerant but indifferent ears. The reader is thus thrust into a maze of complexities: he or she must attend to Kinbote's vividly dramatic interpretation of the poem while simultaneously surmising the far more prosaic truth obscured by Kinbote's annotations.

According to Kinbote, the poem deals with Zembla's last king, Charles the Beloved, whose reign was peaceful, progressive, and humane. Forced to flee by a fascist revolution, Charles escaped from Zembla by motorboat and fled to the United States, where an American sympathizer who was also a trustee of Wordsmith College found him a post on the college's language faculty. In short, Kinbote is King Charles. Meanwhile, Zembla's secret police hired a killer, Jakobus Gradus, alias Jacques d'Argus or Jack Grey, to murder the royal exile. The commentary follows Gradus's journey to New Wye, where he fires at the king but mistakenly kills Shade.

The alert reader will perceive that this plot also has a false bottom. Charles the Beloved and his colorful dynastic saga are the chimeras of Kinbote's disordered mind. Kinbote is actually a harmless refugee scholar named Botkin who teaches in Wordsmith's Languages Department. Shade knew of his mania and compassionately indulged it, while the campus at large mocked and ostracized Botkin. The gunman, whose name is Jack Grey, is an escaped madman who had been sent to the state asylum for the insane by Judge Goldsworth. Thus, Goldsworth was Grey's target, not Botkin or Shade. Moreover, the paranoid politics of Zembla are transpositions of the standard academic factional-ism that infests the college, which Botkin has trans-formed into fantasies of persecution.

The poem and novel's title stems from Act IV, Scene 3, of Shakespeare's *Timon of Athens* (1607-1608):

> The sun's a thief, and with his great attraction
> Robs the vast sea; the moon's an arrant thief,
> And her pale fire she snatches from the sun;
> The sea's a thief, whose liquid surge resolves
> The moon into salt tears.

The theme of these lines is a cosmic cycle of univer-sal theft, with everything in nature working at a dis-tance to borrow its light or force from something else, completely transforming what it takes.

Art, suggests Nabokov, is also part of this cycle. All reflection, including poetic representation, can be considered a theft from reality, which in turn is always plagiarizing from itself. Botkin has stolen Shade's poem and imposed his own interpretation. The division of this novel into Shade's poem and Kinbote/Botkin's fanciful commentary, however, offers a unified work of art. *Pale Fire* explores the two opposing poles of aesthetic sensibility. Shade symbolized the honest, modest, and questioning intelligence that seeks patiently to discover a mean-ingful design in the cosmos through art.

Kinbote/Botkin personifies the obsessional side of the creative imagination, which imposes its pri-vate order on the chaos of experience and is pre-pared to distort or ignore any inconvenient facts obstructing its path. Kinbote/Botkin is also a suc-cessful author: His mythical kingdom is a literary achievement that entrances the reader. The visions of the craftsman and the madman thus stand in equipoise, both sharing in the title's implications. On another level, Nabokov's novel circles like a moon, or pale fire, around the bright flames of Shakespeare's and Pope's genius.

ADA OR ARDOR

First published: 1969
Type of work: Novel

An affirmation of art as the enshrinement of love and victory over mortality.

Ada or Ardor is the most luxuriant, playful, diffi-cult, allusive, ambitious, and overblown of Nabo-kov's novels. It is a memoir largely written by Van Veen when he is in his nineties that narrates his love for his sister Ada. As "a family chronicle," it has a hefty nineteenth century range, replete with printed genealogies, thwarted romances, duels, and a happily-ever-after ending in which the vener-able Ada is finally reunited with her childhood swain, Van.

The inattentive reader will, however, tread a tor-tuous path through the text, for Nabokov has laced it with bristling erudition, trilingual puns, ogreish conundrums, and Joycean dislocations of time and space. The work is also insistently self-conscious: Its author frequently comments on the arduous pro-cess of creating his book, sometimes implying that its readers will never understand many of its intrica-cies. He is undoubtedly right.

The central family plot involves two incestuous generations. The two Durmanov sisters, Aqua and Marina, are married to two first cousins, Dementiy (nicknamed Demon) Veen and Daniel (nick-named Red) Veen. Though Demon is married to Aqua, he has an extensive liaison with Marina. He and Aqua apparently have a son, Ivan (nicknamed Van), who is actually the son of Demon and Ma-rina. To hide the scandal, Demon and Marina take advantage of the mentally disturbed Aqua to switch baby Van for Aqua's stillborn baby. The fertile Ma-rina is also the mother of Demon's other bastard child, Ada, as well as of another daughter, Lucinda (nicknamed Lucette), this one of Marina and her husband, Red.

This genealogical maze serves as the prelude to the lifelong love between the ostensible first cous-ins but actual siblings, Van and Ada Veen. The af-fair begins in the Edenic arbors of Ardis, the family estate, when Van is fourteen and Ada is twelve. Ardis is a parody of Eden, and Van and Ada parody Adam and Eve. Ardis Park is located in a half-fantastic nineteenth century United States which includes films, automobiles, and a town called Lolita, Texas. The geographies of Russia and America are combined. For example, Ardis Park lies on the boundary of a Russian village called Gamlet, which is full of "kerchiefed peasant nymphs"; in Utah, a motor court preserves Leo Tolstoy's footprints in clay. Van and Ada inhabit the superior world of Terra, while the rest of the world resides in Demonia or Antiterra, the hell of human limitations.

Van is Nabokov's sort of artist: His favorite trick as a youth is to turn the world upside down by walking on his hands, exactly as his creator composes inverted fictions. The word Ada is a palindrome; moreover, read from the middle out in either direction, it spells *da*, which is the Russian word for yes. The latter may be interpreted as an allusion to Molly Bloom's many yeses in the concluding chapter of Joyce's *Ulysses* (1922). "*Ardis*" may remind some readers of the motto *ars gratia artis* (art for the sake of art), which would be a fitting emblem both for this novel and Nabokov's entire career.

In *Ada or Ardor,* the author offers his private myth of human beginnings, with Van and Ada as his primal humans. Van is *Homo poeticus*: Writing is his particular talent, and poetic awareness is his especial endowment. Ada, who becomes his sometime collaborator in their later life together, has Nabokov's passion for natural history, particularly the love of flowers, trees, and butterflies. Together, Van and Ada form a privileged, imperial couple.

Unfortunately, they spend many years apart. Their parents separate them when they discover the youngsters' affair, thus playing out the Fall. For years, both spend their energetic erotism in numerous amours and are enveloped in the sins of lust, jealousy, and callousness. Van almost murders two of Ada's lovers and arranges to blind a servant who tries to blackmail him and Ada with incriminating photographs. At twenty-one, Ada contracts a marriage of convenience with an American rancher, Andrey Vinelander, who dies twenty-nine years later. Ada's half sister Lucette falls in love with Van, but he refuses to exploit her vulnerability. When Lucette despairingly drowns herself, Van and Ada are jolted into awareness of the misery and tragedy besetting the world beyond the greenness of Ardis.

Van and Ada are finally free to spend their remaining lives together when she is fifty to his fifty-two. They must now contend with the reality of their physical failings in the face of approaching death. He has become the artist-philosopher and she the botanist-biologist—all aspects of Nabokov. They discover that collaborative writing will reconcile them to time's hostility.

In part 4 of the five-part novel, Van summarizes his philosophy in an anti-Einsteinian discourse on time and space which considers past and present as linked by associated, accumulated images captured by memory. This is an arch-Proustian concept, despite Nabokov's caution to "beware . . . of the marcel wave of fashionable art; avoid the Proustian bed." The framing devices of *Ada* parallel those of Proust's *A la recherche du temps perdu* (1913-1927; *Remembrance of Things Past*, 1922-1931). At *Ada*'s end, the reader is informed that Van and Ada have composed the very text that is about to conclude and that most of this work has been a prelude to the very act of creation which the book promises (and summarizes) in its final pages.

On the penultimate page the author gives the assurance that "the story proceeds at a spanking pace." In fact, the work often saunters self-indulgently as Nabokov treats himself to myriad puns, literary asides, and jokes against jokes in a dazzlingly polyglot glitter of words. He has never been a more agile verbal acrobat. Significantly, Van and Ada delight (as did their progenitor) in playing Scrabble, using a set that was given them by Baron Klim Avidov—an anagrammatically camouflaged Vladimir Nabokov.

SPEAK, MEMORY: AN AUTOBIOGRAPHY REVISITED

First published: 1966
Type of work: Autobiography

A lyrically written testament to the meaning that exile has for an acutely sensitive and responsive artist.

Speak, Memory: An Autobiography Revisited covers thirty-seven of Nabokov's first forty-one years, from August, 1903, to May, 1940. It is a considerable revision of his first partial autobiography, *Conclusive Evidence*. Most of the chapters of *Conclusive Evidence* first appeared in *The New Yorker* between 1948 and 1950 and were published as a book in 1951. In the foreword, Nabokov states that the book provides conclusive evidence of his existence. He had planned to title its British edition *Speak, Mnemosyne,* invoking the Greeks' goddess of memory and mother of the Muses, but the publishing firm of Gollancz vetoed that notion. The references to memory, in whatever language, provide an apt link to Proust: Both writers employ memory as a richly sensuous medium that enables their art to vault over the abysses of time; both practice, as their core credo, the pursuit of aesthetic bliss in their treatment of such experiences as love, grief, rejection, desire, tenderness, loss, and ecstasy.

The first paragraph of *Speak, Memory* links the narrator/author to another major writer of nuance and scruple: Samuel Beckett. Nabokov recalls his fears when, as a young boy, he saw homemade motion pictures taken by his parents weeks before his birth. They featured the brand-new carriage awaiting him "with the smug, encroaching air of a coffin"—as if he had died before he had been delivered. It is no wonder that Nabokov begins the book with the somber comment, "The cradle rocks above an abyss, and common sense tells us that our existence is but a brief crack of light between two eternities of darkness." Beckett's *En attendant Godot* (1952; *Waiting for Godot,* 1954) twice uses the same morbid metaphor: "They give birth astride of a grave, the light gleams an instant, then it's night once more."

Most of this work's fifteen chapters, however, portray a lyrically happy—hence Proustian rather than Beckettian—childhood. With his wealthy, gifted, and adoring family, the firstborn Vladimir lived in a townhouse in prerevolutionary St. Petersburg and at Vyra, an idyllic, rambling country estate. For the author and his two brothers and two sisters, their existence as children was a paradisal lesson in love, order, respect, and responsibility—until the 1917 Revolution. Vladimir's mother read aloud to him in three languages, encouraged his attempts at poetry, and nourished his delight in sounds and colors.

In chapter 2, Nabokov describes his earliest aesthetic experiences: mild synesthetic hallucinations, such as hearing in colors and linking the letters of the alphabet with such textures as vulcanized rubber with the hard *g* and weathered wood with *a.*

Such synesthesia has a rich literary heritage, including the work of Symbolist poets and the French novelist Joris-Karl Huysmans. Nabokov regrets that the muse of music never touched his susceptibility: "Music . . . affects me merely as an arbitrary succession of more or less irritating sounds."

In chapter 9, Nabokov magnificently renders his tall, humane, courageous, and imposing father. A former Guards officer, he was a law lecturer at the Imperial School of Jurisprudence. He was an editor for liberal newspapers, held a seat in Russia's first parliament, opposed both anti-Semitism and capital punishment, and served a three-month prison term in 1908 for having written articles assailing the czar's despotism. Vladimir Dmitrievich also knew hundreds of Russian verses, loved Charles Dickens, and "prized highly Stendhal, [Honoré de] Balzac and [Émile] Zola, three detestable mediocrities from *my* point of view."

The author climaxes this chapter with an account of a duel his father almost fought against the editor of a right-wing paper that had printed a scurrilous article about him. The possibility of losing his father shocked young Vladimir into awareness of their deep affection for each other. Writing that the editor ended the affair with an abject apology, Nabokov recalls the assassination of his father which would occur ten years later and is grateful that, back in 1912, "several lines of play in a difficult chess composition were not blended yet on the board." The image is essentially Nabokovian: Exactly as each move on a chessboard affects all subsequent moves, so his father's reprieve from an encounter with death will cause him to make moves which will finally result in his murder. In Nabokov's worldview, all events are somehow organically connected.

Speak, Memory re-creates with superlative skill not only the ethos of an idyllic upbringing but also the social upheaval of exile. Nabokov rhapsodically recounts the first creation of his poems and his first pursuits of butterflies. Best of all, he provides a poignant account of adolescent first love between him and the teenage Tamara in 1915. He pictures "the tender, moist gleam on her lower eyelid" but is discreet about describing their sexual union: "In one particular pine grove . . . I parted the fabric of fancy, I tasted reality." They took to the woods in summer, to museums and cinemas in winter. They parted in 1916—he cannot recall the cause—only to meet by chance on a train in 1917 for a few minutes. When Tamara left him at the station, he recalls, even "today no alien marginalia can dim the purity of the pain."

In chapter 14, Nabokov deals with the spectral world of émigré society in Europe during the 1920's and 1930's. He kept himself too occupied to wallow in self-pity and has only scorn for refugees who chronically lamented their lost wealth and estates. In *Conclusive Evidence*, Nabokov remarked that, among the younger exiled Russian writers, the only one who turned out to be a major achiever was V. Sirin. In *Speak, Memory*, Sirin is no longer called a major figure—only "the loneliest and most arrogant one." The narrator devotes a page to him, citing favorable and unfavorable responses to Sirin's books, and concludes "Across the dark sky of exile, Sirin passed . . . like a meteor, and disappeared, leaving nothing much else behind him than a vague sense of uneasiness."

Readers need to know that "Sirin" was the pen name Nabokov himself assumed during this period, at first to avoid confusion with his famous father, and then as an established habit. Such deadpan self-mockery and misleading of his public is characteristic of the games he would play with increasing relish in his later fiction, particularly in *Pale Fire* and *Ada or Ardor.*

SUMMARY

Nabokov was a prodigiously gifted literary jeweler who sometimes cut deeply into human experience and at other times preferred to play clever games on its surface. At his worst, he sought to trick the reader with exotic wordplay, cultural booby traps, and exhibitionistic displays of stylistic arabesques. In his best work, such as *Lolita; Speak, Memory; Pnin;* and *Pale Fire,* however, he is a poetic fabulist and magician whose aestheticism is at the service of love, tenderness, compassion, kindness, empathy, grief, loneliness, wonder, and, above all, great art.

Gerhard Brand

BIBLIOGRAPHY

By the Author

LONG FICTION:
Mashenka, 1926 (*Mary*, 1970)
Korol', dama, valet, 1928 (*King, Queen, Knave*, 1968)
Zashchita Luzhina, 1929 (serial), 1930 (book; *The Defense*, 1964)
Podvig, 1932 (*Glory*, 1971)
Kamera obskura, 1932 (*Camera Obscura*, 1936; revised as *Laughter in the Dark*, 1938)
Otchayanie, 1934 (serial), 1936 (book; *Despair*, 1937; revised 1966)
Priglashenie na kazn', 1935-1936 (serial), 1938 (book; *Invitation to a Beheading*, 1959)
Dar, 1937-1938 (serial), 1952 (book; *The Gift*, 1963)
The Real Life of Sebastian Knight, 1941
Bend Sinister, 1947
Lolita, 1955
Pnin, 1957
Pale Fire, 1962
Ada or Ardor: A Family Chronicle, 1969
Transparent Things, 1972
Look at the Harlequins!, 1974

SHORT FICTION:
Vozrashchenie Chorba, 1930
Soglyadatay, 1938
Nine Stories, 1947

Vesna v Fialte i drugie rasskazy, 1956
Nabokov's Dozen: A Collection of Thirteen Stories, 1958
Nabokov's Quartet, 1966
A Russian Beauty, and Other Stories, 1973
Tyrants Destroyed, and Other Stories, 1975
Details of a Sunset, and Other Stories, 1976

DRAMA:
Smert', pb. 1923
Dedushka, pb. 1923
Polius, pb. 1924
Tragediya gospodina Morna, pb. 1924
Chelovek iz SSSR, pb. 1927
Sobytiye, pr., pb. 1938
Izobretenie Val'sa, pb. 1938 (*The Waltz Invention,* 1966)

SCREENPLAY:
Lolita, 1962

POETRY:
Stikhi, 1916
Dva puti, 1918
Gorny put, 1923
Grozd', 1923
Stikhotvorenia, 1929-1951, 1952
Poems, 1959
Poems and Problems, 1970

NONFICTION:
Nikolai Gogol, 1944
Conclusive Evidence: A Memoir, 1951
Drugie berega, 1954
Speak, Memory: An Autobiography Revisited, 1966 (revision of *Conclusive Evidence* and *Drugie berega*)
Strong Opinions, 1973
The Nabokov-Wilson Letters, 1940-1971, 1979
Lectures on Literature: British, French, and German, 1980
Lectures on Russian Literature, 1981
Lectures on Don Quixote, 1983
Vladimir Nabokov: Selected Letters, 1940-1977, 1989

TRANSLATIONS:
Anya v strane chudes, 1923 (of Lewis Carroll's novel *Alice's Adventures in Wonderland*)
Three Russian Poets: Translations of Pushkin, Lermontov, and Tiutchev, 1944 (with Dmitri Nabokov)
A Hero of Our Time, 1958 (of Mikhail Lermontov's novel; with Dmitri Nabokov)
The Song of Igor's Campaign, 1960 (of the twelfth century epic *Slovo o polki Igoreve*)
Eugene Onegin, 1964 (of Alexander Pushkin's novel)

DISCUSSION TOPICS

- Has the experience of exile figured significantly in Vladimir Nabokov's work other than in his autobiographical writings?

- Identify some of Nabokov's unreliable narrators and demonstrate their unreliability.

- Does Nabokov's habit of playing games with the reader ever serve a serious purpose?

- What is a "false bottom," and what works of Nabokov's contain them?

- Of the literary allusions in *Lolita,* which seem most effective?

- Discuss *Lolita* as a "remorseless satire of middle-class, immature America."

About the Author

Alexandrov, Vladimir E. *Nabokov's Otherworld.* Princeton, N.J.: Princeton University Press, 1991.
Bloom, Harold, ed. *Vladimir Nabokov.* New York: Chelsea House, 1987.
Boyd, Brian. *Vladimir Nabokov: The Russian Years.* Princeton, N.J.: Princeton University Press, 1990.
_____. *Vladimir Nabokov: The American Years.* Princeton, N.J.: Princeton University Press, 1991.
Field, Andrew. *VN: The Life and Art of Vladimir Nabokov.* New York: Crown, 1986.

Vladimir Nabokov

Foster, John Burt. *Nabokov's Art of Memory and European Modernism.* Princeton, N.J.: Princeton University Press, 1993.

Grayson, Jane. *Vladimir Nabokov.* Woodstock, N.Y.: Overlook Press, 2002.

Grayson, Jane, Arnold B. McMillin, and Priscilla Meyer, eds. *Nabokov's World: Reading Nabokov.* New York: Palgrave Macmillan, 2002.

Larmour, Davbid. H. J., ed. *Discourse and Ideology in Nabokov's Prose.* New York: Routledge, 2002.

Nicol, Charles, and Gennady Barabtarlo, eds. *A Small Alpine Form: Studies in Nabokov's Short Fiction.* New York: Garland, 1993.

Parker, Stephen Jan. *Understanding Vladimir Nabokov.* Columbia: University of South Carolina Press, 1987.

Pifer, Ellen. *Nabokov and the Novel.* Cambridge, Mass.: Harvard University Press, 1980.

_____, ed. *Vladimir Nabokov's "Lolita": A Casebook.* New York: Oxford University Press, 2003.

Schiff, Stacy. *Véra (Mrs. Vladimir Nabokov): Portrait of a Marriage.* New York: Random House, 1999.

Shapiro, Gavriel, ed. *Nabokov at Cornell.* Ithaca, N.Y.: Cornell University Press, 2003.

Shrayer, Maxim D. *The World of Nabokov's Stories.* Austin: University of Texas Press, 1999.

Toker, Leona. *Nabokov: The Mystery of Literary Structures.* Ithaca, N.Y: Cornell University Press, 1989.

GLORIA NAYLOR

Born: New York, New York
January 25, 1950

Naylor is a distinguished novelist best known for representing the experiences and views of black women.

BIOGRAPHY

Gloria Naylor was born on January 25, 1950, in New York City, the daughter of Roosevelt Naylor, a transit worker, and Alberta McAlpin Naylor, a telephone operator. Her parents had moved from Mississippi only a few months before. The oldest of three sisters, Naylor grew up and attended schools in New York. As a young person she was shy but was an avid reader. In high school, she immersed herself in such classic British authors as Charlotte and Emily Brontë, Jane Austen, and Charles Dickens, whose influences can be seen in Naylor's writing.

The young Naylor also felt a strong sense of religious dedication. In 1968, after graduation from high school, she began working as a missionary for the Jehovah's Witnesses, whose headquarters is in Brooklyn. She spent the next seven years as a missionary in New York, North Carolina, and Florida—travels that obviously provided materials for and influenced the settings of her novels. The strongest evidence of her early religious background might be the lingering fundamentalist outlook of her novels, wherein—for other reasons besides religion—characters are often divided into the redeemed or the damned.

In 1975, Naylor left the Jehovah's Witnesses and returned to New York City, where she worked as a hotel telephone operator while attending Brooklyn College of the City University of New York. At Brooklyn College, Naylor studied creative writing and read the book that was most influential in shap-

ing her career, *The Bluest Eye* (1970), by the black woman novelist Toni Morrison. Morrison was a model for the young Naylor, inspiring her to write fiction and to focus on the realities of black women.

In 1981, Naylor received her B.A. in English from Brooklyn College; then, with a fellowship, she moved on to Yale University. While at Yale, she published *The Women of Brewster Place* (1982), which in 1983 won the American Book Award for best first novel. That same year, Naylor won the Distinguished Writer Award of the Mid-Atlantic Writers Association and received her M.A. in Afro-American Studies from Yale.

Thereafter, Naylor found herself much in demand as a visiting writer and lecturer. During the summer of 1983, she was writer-in-residence at Cummington Community of the Arts in Massachusetts; during 1983-1984, she was a visiting lecturer at George Washington University; during the fall of 1985, she was a cultural exchange lecturer for the United States Information Agency in India. Naylor's second novel, *Linden Hills*, also appeared in 1985.

Further awards and invitations followed. Naylor received a National Endowment for the Arts fellowship in 1985, the Candace Award of the National Coalition of 100 Black Women in 1986, and a Guggenheim Fellowship in 1988. She was a scholar-in-residence at the University of Pennsylvania in 1986, a visiting lecturer at Princeton University in 1986-1987, a visiting professor at New York University in 1986 and Boston University in 1987, Fannie Hurst Visiting Professor at Brandeis University in 1988, and a senior fellow at Cornell University's Society for the Humanities in 1988.

In 1988, Naylor published her third novel, *Mama Day*, to even greater applause. Not all of her work was instantly successful, particularly her attempts to write television screenplays. Two screenplays written in 1984 and 1985 remained unproduced for a time, but a television miniseries of *The Women of Brewster Place*, featuring Oprah Winfrey and a host of other stars, was broadcast and was well received.

Meanwhile, Naylor expanded her literary efforts in other directions. In 1984, she became a contributing editor to *Callaloo: An Afro-American and African Journal of Arts and Letters*, and she has contributed articles to a wide range of periodicals including *Essence, People, Life, Ms., Ontario Review,* and *The Southern Review.* In 1986, she also wrote a column for *The New York Times* titled *Hers.*

ANALYSIS

Naylor has stated that, as a young reader, she was impressed by the lack of fiction reflecting the experiences and perspectives of black women. Besides the British classics, she read the works of such American authors as the southern white man William Faulkner. Even established black writers were almost all male and reflected a male perspective. There was a severe shortage of fiction that spoke directly to her, a black woman—the invisible woman of American literature. Naylor set out deliberately to help rectify this situation, or this injustice, by writing fiction that brought black women to the foreground.

Naylor began writing during the heyday of the women's movement, which had articulated a vast body of feminist thought. Although sometimes contradictory, feminist thinking at that time generally stressed the uniqueness of women at the same time that it called for their political equality within society and the family. More doctrinaire thinkers glorified woman as hero—a figure somehow more sensitive, loving, responsible, and courageous than the male of the species. Naylor's views on black women are permeated by these various strains of feminism.

In Naylor's work, however, feminism is layered onto more old-fashioned influences that work in concert with it. One set of influences is literary. From such writers as the Brontës, Dickens, Faulkner, and Morrison, Naylor appears to have developed, underneath her surface realism, a taste for romanticism that sometimes verges on the melodramatic or gothic.

The romantic streak comes out, for example, in many of Naylor's characters. Emotional, obsessive, and unforgiving, they are prone to extreme gestures: A single trait or event can set their whole life course or shatter relationships. As a result, the characters are somewhat one-dimensional, if not stereotypical, but they are nevertheless memorable. Notable examples are Luther Nedeed, who imprisons his wife and child in the basement, and the old conjure woman Mama Day.

Naylor's romanticism is also apparent in her heavy use of symbolism, which can almost make her seem to be a latter-day Nathaniel Hawthorne. As in Hawthorne, the weather usually cooperates with the mood of her story: a week of gloomy rain after the tragic climax of *The Women of Brewster Place*, bone-chilling December cold in *Linden Hills*, and a hurricane in *Mama Day.* Her novels are filled with such obviously symbolic details as an eerie howl that comes floating up the hillside or "the pinks"—imaginary blobs of pink slime—that pursue Norman Anderson in *Linden Hills.* (The influence of horror films can also be noted here.)

Most obvious of all is the symbolism of place: Brewster Place is a dead-end street, Linden Hills is laid out like Dante's Hell, and the barrier island in *Mama Day* recalls the magical isle of William Shakespeare's *The Tempest* (1611). Indeed, Naylor is so intent on the symbolism of her settings that she is occasionally careless about their literal accuracy. In depicting the South, for example, she has crape myrtle blooming in the spring, sugar cane growing in middle Tennessee, and interstate highways heading north years before they were actually built.

Besides literary romanticism, another influence affecting Naylor's feminism is her early religious background. In her fiction, Naylor is no longer a missionary for any religion; on the contrary, as a former insider she portrays religious hypocrites and self-righteous bigots with deadly accuracy. Rather, she seems to have transferred her original missionary fervor into her feminism and, in the process, retained some of the trappings of religious thought. In particular, there is a tendency in her earlier work to demonize men (black and white). In a conversation with Toni Morrison that appeared in *The Southern Review*, Naylor said that she had tried hard to avoid portraying men negatively in *The Women of Brewster Place* and thought she had succeeded. This statement is rather astounding, as practically all the men in the novel are scoundrels, except for a kindly old wino—who is killed for his troubles by a lesbian.

In *Linden Hills*, Naylor relents somewhat. Two easygoing young black men, poets, are the informal heroes, or at least sympathetic observers, of the novel (in the symbolic scheme, they play a modern-day Dante and Vergil). Luther Nedeed is a scoundrel of the old school, however; one of his black ancestors is even rumored to have "financed gunrunners to the Confederacy." Within the symbolic scheme, Luther is the devil himself, ruling over the middle-class hell of Linden Hills from its lowest, richest level.

In *Mama Day*, Naylor relents even more, offering the character George Andrews as her portrait of a good man. A gentle, understanding, hardworking engineer who loves his wife, George even comes across as a better person than most women in the book, including his wife, Cocoa. George is not a woman, however, and hence he has serious limitations deriving from his masculine propensity to approach things in a strictly rational manner—a severe kind of tunnel vision. George's failure to understand the wider worlds of nature and the supernatural inhabited by the women proves to be fatal. Over these worlds reigns old Mama Day, representing the powers that be. She is the antithesis of the demonized Luther Nedeed.

Such is the feminist gospel according to Naylor. Whether it will ultimately be limiting to her work remains to be seen, but as Naylor's varying portrayals of men indicate, her thinking has continued to develop. Naylor's abilities as a writer have progressed, as well: Her style has improved, she has tried new techniques, and with each book she has taken on a more difficult task and succeeded. Naylor's work contains much more than feminism. Her concern with serious themes is relieved by a sense of humor that presents an effective representation of black banter and repartee. She provides an intimate glimpse into black life at all levels and a daring critique of its problems. Her interest in these difficulties, while sometimes related to her feminism, at other times seems to supersede it. Outstanding among the problems that her characters face are discrimination, poverty, family breakups, and, in particular, the question of black identity.

THE WOMEN OF BREWSTER PLACE

First published: 1982
Type of work: Novel

Seven black women struggle to cope with life on a dead-end ghetto street.

Naylor began her celebration of black women's lives with *The Women of Brewster Place: A Novel in Seven Stories*. Exhibiting the varied backgrounds and experiences of seven different women, the seven stories of its subtitle can be read separately, but they are united by their setting and by characters who reappear from one story to the next. The stories also perform a kind of counterpoint to one another, with various parallels and contrasts. However varied the courses of their lives have been, the women now share a common fate: They have all arrived at the dead-end ghetto of Brewster Place, not only a racial and socioeconomic enclave but also a dumping ground for used women.

Mattie Michael, the motherly figure on the block, grew up in Tennessee and arrived on Brewster Place via repeated betrayals by the men in her life. During her youth, one weak moment in a basil patch with the sweet-talking Butch left her pregnant, for which her father brutally beat her and kicked her out. Finding refuge first with her friend Etta Mae Johnson and then in the home of another woman, Eva Turner, Mattie devoted her life to raising and pampering her son, Basil. Basil eventually repaid her by killing a man in a tavern brawl and, after Mattie posted her house for bail, skipping town. Minus son and home, Mattie also left town and headed for Brewster Place, located in a bleak northern city resembling Brooklyn, where she feels a sense of cultural dislocation on top of her other losses.

What brings Mattie to Brewster Place specifically is a remaining personal tie there to Lucielia Louise Turner, or "Ciel," the granddaughter of Eva Thiner, to whom Mattie is a mother in all but name. Mattie's presence and support are needed, because Ciel's life is devastated by her boyfriend Eugene, who is absent for long stretches and abusive when he is around. Eugene makes Ciel terminate her second pregnancy with an abortion and then indirectly causes the death of their first child, Serena. After that, Eugene is no longer welcome.

Mattie also takes in her old friend Etta Mae Johnson, a femme fatale who has lived the high life with various men around the country but whose beauty is now fading. Etta Mae has hopes of marrying a good man and settling down, and she sets her sights on a charismatic preacher. The preacher, however, turns out to be a sleazy womanizer interested only in using her for a one-night stand.

It is somewhat difficult to feel sorry for Etta Mae, as she has been using men all of her life, just as it is somewhat difficult to sympathize with another of the seven women, Cora Lee. Cora Lee has loved babies from the day she was born and started having them as soon as she was able; now the number is up to seven, and assorted anonymous men continue to share her bed.

The other three women have arrived at Brewster Place more or less voluntarily. Kiswana Browne is an ardent but naïve social reformer who grew up amid the affluence of nearby Linden Hills; Brewster Place offers plenty of opportunities for her. Lorraine and Theresa are lesbian lovers who hope to find a private retreat in Brewster Place, but it is not to be. They are spied on by the old prude Sophie, who tries to stir up the street against them. The most brutal scene in the novel occurs when Lorraine is viciously raped by C. C. Baker and his alley-dwelling youth gang.

Naylor saves some of her strongest description for these young men, who "always moved in a pack" because they "needed the others continually near to verify their existence" and who, "with their black skin, ninth-grade diplomas, and fifty-word vocabularies . . . continually surnamed each other Man and clutched at their crotches, readying the equipment they deemed necessary to be summoned at any moment into Superfly heaven." The only halfway decent man in the whole novel is old Ben, the wino janitor who befriends Lorraine and is later killed by her when she becomes crazed.

Thus, the Brewster Place community gains its strength from its women. Despite their clashing backgrounds, the women recognize their common fates and bond with one another. Instead of crushing them, their past and present miseries form the basis for their caring. Although victimized by society generally and by men specifically, they are able, through their black sisterhood, their community,

to feel a positive sense of identity. The women rise up together in anger, love, and hope, forming a block association, throwing a block party, and—at least in Mattie's dream—tearing down the ghetto wall.

LINDEN HILLS

First published: 1985
Type of work: Novel

In suburban Linden Hills, affluent black people make their own middle-class hell.

The other extreme of contemporary black life is shown in *Linden Hills*, set in an affluent black suburb. In contrast to Brewster Place, Linden Hills is dominated by men, most notably by undertaker Luther Nedeed. Luther's ancestors settled and laid out Linden Hills, and now Luther controls it through the Tupelo Realty Corporation and his personal influence. The suburb's name, like its allure, is deceptive: Linden Hills is actually not several hills but only part of one hillside— a large, V-shaped area intersected by eight streets that curve around and down the slope. The further down the hillside one goes, the richer the residents become; in other words, the higher they climb in the socioeconomic hierarchy, the lower they sink in the moral order. Luther Nedeed's home is at the very bottom, conveniently next to the graveyard.

Naylor's symbolism seems to echo D. H. Lawrence's sentiment that America is a death society. The fact that an undertaker presides over Linden Hills throws a certain pall over the suburb, but even more unsettling is the suburb's street plan, which recalls the geography of Dante's Hell. Two young unemployed poets, Lester and Willie (corresponding to Vergil and Dante), are introduced. Under the guise of earning some Christmas money by doing odd jobs in the neighborhood, the young poets lead the reader on a guided tour of Linden Hills. The broad parallels to Dante's Inferno in *La divina commedia* (c. 1320; *The Divine Comedy*, 1802) make it abundantly clear that *Linden Hills* is an allegory of the lost souls of affluent black people.

As the young poets move down the hillside, they come across varied examples of people who have sold out. One is Lester's sister Roxanne, a Wellesley College graduate who feels that black Africans in Zimbabwe are not ready to form their own nation. Other examples include Winston Alcott, a young homosexual lawyer who denies his lover David and gets married to achieve respectability; Xavier Donnell, a junior executive who fears that marrying Roxanne might hurt his chances at General Motors; Maxwell Smyth, a fellow corporate climber who confirms Xavier's decision to dump her; Chester Parker, who can hardly wait to bury his dead wife before he remarries; the Right Reverend Michael T. Hollis, a sleazy, hypocritical moral leader of Linden Hills; and Dr. Daniel Braithwaite, whose authorized twelve-volume history of Linden Hills makes no moral judgments.

The archetypal dead soul is Luther Nedeed. At the wake for Lycentia Parker, Luther voices Linden Hills's opposition to a low-income housing project planned for Putney Wayne, a neighboring black ghetto, and proposes joining forces with the racist Wayne County Citizens Alliance in defense of property values. Luther saves his most soulless behavior for those closest to him. The horror story of how he treats his wife and child runs, in excerpts, throughout the novel. For generations, the Nedeed men have been marrying light-skinned women, but when his own wife bears a light-skinned son, Luther disowns them and locks them away in a disused basement morgue. The child starves to death, but, after reading old letters, journals, and cookbooks that document a long history of abuse heaped on Nedeed wives, Willa Prescott Nedeed makes her way back up the stairs to confront the devil himself.

Linden Hills is a powerful and sweeping indictment of black middle-class life. The broad parallels to Dante's *Inferno*, while effective for satirical and moral purposes, are somewhat forced, not allowing for enough fine-tuning. Naylor probably does not mean to condemn the black middle class as a whole or to imply that affluence is itself a problem; after all, lack of money and of decent surroundings was among the problems facing the women of Brewster Place. Rather, Naylor seems to warn that affluence poses special dangers to black identity. If the price for affluence is the loss of one's soul—compromise of one's moral standards and emotional life, adoption of white values, and denial of other black people and one's own roots—then it is too high.

MAMA DAY

First published: 1988
Type of work: Novel

Mama Day reigns over the natural and spirit world of an indigenous black culture.

If *Linden Hills* strains credulity, then the main setting of *Mama Day* is even more unbelievable, if not downright mythical: Willow Springs, a southern coastal island relatively unwashed by the tides of racism. The island is populated by the descendants of white slaveholder Bascombe Wade and his black wife Sapphira and of other slaves that he freed and deeded land to back in 1823. Since that time, the island has been plagued mainly by malaria, Union soldiers, sandy soil, two big depressions, and hurricanes. The fictitious barrier island lies off the coast of South Carolina and Georgia but is owned by no state. Willow Springs is a backwater of history where the people have been mostly left to themselves, and they have developed a black American culture strongly connected to the land, to their historical beginnings, and even to their African roots.

Willow Springs is a daring concept—an effort to imagine what black life might have been like in America if left free to develop on its own. Naylor acknowledges the concept's utopian aspects by drawing parallels between Willow Springs and the magical island in William Shakespeare's *The Tempest* (1611). Yet the conjuring that goes on in Willow Springs recalls the conjuring in *Sundiata: An Epic of Old Mali* (a translation of the thirteenth century African epic published in 1965) and the good magic and bad magic still practiced in parts of Africa. Also very real are the closeness to the land, the recognized status of individuals within the community, the slow pace of life, and the presence of the past—

things that rural southerners, black and white, miss when they move to northern cities.

In the novel, such a person is Ophelia "Cocoa" Day, who was born on Willow Springs and raised by her grandmother Abigail and great-aunt Miranda  "Mama" Day (descendants of Bascombe and Sapphira Wade). Cocoa left Willow Springs to work in New York City, but she is drawn back to the island for regular August visits. In New York, the novel's other setting, Cocoa meets George Andrews, a black engineer who was raised in an orphanage, and they eventually get married. The contrasts between the two—George gentle and straightforward, Cocoa spoiled and insecure—suggest the novel's underlying cultural clash, but this split does not become critical until George visits Willow Springs with Cocoa.

While George appreciates black life on Willow Springs, it is way beyond his urbanized, rationalistic range, particularly when a hurricane hits and when he becomes involved in a conjuring match between Mama Day and her nemesis, Ruby. Mama Day has a wealth of knowledge about herbs and various natural phenomena that she uses for the purposes of healing and aiding new life. The reader senses that much has been passed down to her from others who no longer live but whose spirits nourish the rich fabric of Willow Springs. In contrast, the evil-spirited Ruby uses the same knowledge, mixed with hoodoo, to kill anyone whom she perceives might take away her man, Junior Lee. Several women have already met terrible fates because they had contact with the philandering Junior Lee.

Unfortunately, at a party given in honor of Cocoa and George, Junior Lee follows Cocoa out to the porch and attempts to rape her, and Ruby catches him. The next day, Ruby sees Cocoa walking down the road and asks her to stop; Ruby apologizes for Junior Lee's behavior and offers to massage and braid Cocoa's hair the way she did when Cocoa was little. Right before the party, Mama Day had felt a big hurricane coming and death in the air. During the hurricane Cocoa becomes disoriented, and huge welts cover her head and face. Mama Day realizes that Ruby has poisoned Cocoa by rubbing nightshade into her head. Mama Day cuts off Cocoa's hair and works a counteracting salve into her scalp, but Cocoa is already badly poisoned.

Meanwhile, the hurricane has wreaked terrible havoc and taken out the wooden bridge between Willow Springs and the mainland. With all the boats destroyed and no telephones, George exhausts himself working to restore the bridge and get Cocoa off the island to a doctor. His efforts do not succeed, however, and, in desperation, he is forced to try Mama Day's solution. She sends him to "the other place," the island's original homeplace, to get whatever he finds behind an old brooding hen. Doubting George finds nothing, is attacked by the old hen, and dies of a weak heart.

George's doubts and weak heart represent the limits of his rationalistic outlook, his inability to participate fully in the island's culture and to comprehend Mama Day's powers. There is no doubt that those powers are real. Before George undertakes his fatal mission, Mama Day deals with Ruby by calling out three warnings, whacking each side of Ruby's house with a stick, and sprinkling a circle of silvery dust around the house. The results are two lightning strikes on Ruby's house, the second one exploding it with Ruby inside.

SUMMARY

In her novels, Naylor surveys contemporary black American life, ranging from an urban ghetto to an affluent suburb to a pristine southern island. While few white characters appear in her work, racism is a constant background factor, affecting the circumstances of black existence and the sense of black identity. Naylor also writes as a dedicated feminist who celebrates the lives and special powers of black women.

The male characters in Naylor's work tend either to be demonized or emasculated. Whether Naylor's doctrinaire feminism and her related tendency to write in grand, sweeping strokes will ultimately limit her development remains to be seen. Yet these same features help to account for a powerful, mythic quality in Naylor's writing.

Harold Branam

BIBLIOGRAPHY

By the Author

LONG FICTION:

The Women of Brewster Place: A Novel in Seven Stories,
1982
Linden Hills, 1985
Mama Day, 1988
Bailey's Café, 1992
The Men of Brewster Place, 1998
1996, 2004

NONFICTION:

Conversations with Gloria Naylor, 2004 (Maxine
Lavon Montgomery, editor)

EDITED TEXT:

*Children of the Night: The Best Short Stories by Black
Writers, 1967 to the Present,* 1995

About the Author

Bell, Bernard W. *The Afro-American Novel and Its Tradition.* Amherst: University of Massachusetts
Press, 1987.

Braxton, Joanne M., and Andrée Nicola McLaughlin, eds. *Wild Women in the Whirlwind: Afra-American Culture
and the Contemporary Literary Renaissance.* New Brunswick, N.J.: Rutgers University Press, 1990.

Carby, Hazel V. *Reconstructing Womanhood: The Emergence of the Afro-American Woman Novelist.* New York: Oxford University Press, 1987.

Felton, Sharon, and Michelle C. Loris, eds. *The Critical Response to Gloria Naylor.* Westport, Conn.: Greenwood
Press, 1997.

Fowler, Virginia C. *Gloria Naylor: In Search of Sanctuary.* New York: Twayne, 1996.

Gates, Henry Louis, Jr. "Significant Others." *Contemporary Literature* 29 (Winter, 1988): 606-623.

Gates, Henry Louis, Jr., and K. A. Appiah, eds. *Gloria Naylor: Critical Perspectives Past and Present.* New York:
Amistad, 1993.

Harris-Lopez, Trudier. *The Power of the Porch: The Storyteller's Craft in Zora Neale Hurston, Gloria Naylor, and
Randall Kenan.* Athens: University of Georgia Press, 1996.

Homans, Margaret. "The Woman in the Cave: Recent Feminist Fictions and the Classical Underworld." *Contemporary Literature* 29 (Fall, 1988): 369-402.

Kelley, Margot Anne, ed. *Gloria Naylor's Early Novels.* Gainesville: University of Florida Press, 1999.

Montgomery, Maxine Lavon, ed. *Conversations with Gloria Naylor.* Jackson: University Press of Mississippi,
2004.

Naylor, Gloria, and Toni Morrison. "A Conversation." *The Southern Review* 21 (Summer, 1985): 567-593.

Stave, Shirley A., ed. *Gloria Naylor: Strategy and Technique, Magic and Myth.* Newark: University of Delaware
Press, 2001.

Whitt, Margaret Earley. *Understanding Gloria Naylor.* Columbia: University of South Carolina Press, 1999.

Wilson, Charles E. *Gloria Naylor: A Critical Companion.* Westport, Conn.: Greenwood Press, 2001.

DISCUSSION TOPICS

- How is Gloria Naylor's religious background evident in her novels?

- How has feminism influenced the characters and themes of Naylor's novels?

- In what senses are Naylor's novels gothic
  or melodramatic?

- Discuss Naylor's use of weather imagery.

- Are Naylor's male characters well rounded
  or stereotypical?

- How are the seven stories in *The Women of
  Brewster Place* unified thematically?

- Compare the characters and themes of
  The Women of Brewster Place and *The Men of
  Brewster Place.*

- How is *Linden Hills* an attack upon middle-
  class African American values?

ANAÏS NIN

Born: Paris, France
February 21, 1903
Died: Los Angeles, California
January 14, 1977

Nin developed a highly imagistic idiom for expressing the creativity and sensuality of the female psyche and created a unique document of personal history.

BIOGRAPHY

Anaïs Nin was born near Paris on February 21, 1903, into an international, aristocratic, and cultured family. Her parents were Joaquin Nin y Castellano, a Spanish composer and pianist, and Rosa Culmell Nin, a classical singer of French and Danish descent. Their marriage was volatile and ended with Joaquin's desertion for a younger woman. In 1914, the young Anaïs, with her mother and brothers Thorvald and Joaquin, sailed from Barcelona to a new life in New York.

On this journey, Nin began keeping a diary, first as an ongoing letter to her estranged father and then as a detailed record of her experiences and feelings, a record she would maintain throughout her life. The move to the United States was not a happy one for her; she struggled to learn English and felt unwelcome in the impersonal metropolis. An introspective, sensitive, critical, and imaginative child, she attended Catholic school in New York without enthusiasm. At the age of sixteen, after a teacher criticized her writing, she dropped out and pursued self-education in public libraries. Meanwhile, she worked as a model for artists and illustrators to augment her family's income.

In the early 1920's Nin studied briefly at Columbia University and spent time with relatives in Havana, Cuba. She fell in love with a New York banker named Hugh Guiler, and the couple was married in Havana in March, 1923. Though the passion of the marriage faded within several years as Nin realized its limitations and developed her identity as a writer, it remained intact and was, in an unconventional way, successful. Guiler, under the name of Ian Hugo, later provided illustrations for his wife's novels. Nin rarely talked about him, however, and all references to him were edited out of her diary before its first publication in 1966.

Shortly after their marriage, Guiler was transferred to Paris. For Nin it was a return home. In 1924, she saw her father for the first time in a decade and confronted their complex relationship. She continued her self-education and writing, pursued a brief career as a Spanish dancer, and developed many lasting and influential friendships. A teacher named Hélène Boussinescq introduced Nin to modern writers; she and her cousin Eduardo Sánchez shared a fascination with psychological pioneers Sigmund Freud and Carl Jung and novelists D. H. Lawrence and Marcel Proust.

Nin's continuous writing led to her first book, *D. H. Lawrence: An Unprofessional Study*, published in Paris in 1932. Financial difficulties she suffered following the stock market crash of 1929 led Nin to relocate to a small house in the Parisian suburb of Louveciennes, where she entertained a steady stream of visiting artists and intellectuals. She became intimate with the emerging American writer Henry Miller and his wife June, and Nin strongly encouraged Miller's first novel, *Tropic of Cancer* (1934).

Miller exposed Nin to his underground milieu of gangsters, addicts, and prostitutes. Her interest in the human psyche led her into psychoanalysis, first with the noted French analyst René Allendy and then with Otto Rank, a controversial disciple of Freud. Her other intimates included French theatrical innovator Antonin Artaud, Peruvian musician and revolutionary Gonzalo More, and the young British author Lawrence Durrell. Throughout her life, both in Paris and in the United States, Nin's social sphere included bright and fascinating figures; these people became like family to her, and she shared their aspirations and struggles.

In 1934, Nin gave birth to a stillborn child, a traumatic experience which led to deeper spiritual and emotional introspection. Later that year, she accepted an invitation to assist Rank in New York and begin a career as a psychoanalyst. She soon became disenchanted with both New York and her promising practice and returned to writing and Paris, where she lived in a houseboat on the Seine and began looking for a publisher for her prose poem *House of Incest*. Finding a publisher proved difficult, however, because her writing was considered too surrealistic and visionary. Nin, Miller, and others in the "Villa Seurat circle" initiated Siana Editions to ensure publication of avant-garde works such as *House of Incest* (1936). In 1939, she published the novella *Winter of Artifice*, which focused on a woman's reunion with her estranged but idolized father.

The imminence of World War II in Europe drove Nin and Guiler back to New York, where publishers were apprehensive about her work, just as European publishers had been. She thus purchased a secondhand, foot-operated printing press and published limited editions of her works from her Greenwich Village apartment. With the publication in 1944 of *Under a Glass Bell*, a volume of short stories, Nin finally received critical attention. Praise from such noted reviewers as Edmund Wilson validated her literary standing in the eyes of both mainstream readers and established publishers. There followed in succession *Ladders to Fire* (1946), *Children of the Albatross* (1947), *The Four-Chambered Heart* (1950), *A Spy in the House of Love* (1954), *Solar Barque* (1958), and *Seduction of the Minotaur* (1961). With the last two titles considered together, the five novels appeared as a "continuous novel" in 1959 under the title *Cities of the Interior.*

During this period, Nin traveled across the United States by car, journeyed throughout Mexico, and settled in Los Angeles. Her diary was now a multivolume compilation reflecting a half-century of living, and many of Nin's friends urged her to publish it. During the 1950's Nin had become determined to destroy it, but she ultimately sat down to the task of its editing. The first volume appeared in 1966, with publication completed in ten more volumes over two decades. *The Diary of Anaïs Nin* was an instant literary sensation and made Nin an international celebrity.

Nin received numerous honors and awards, including her 1974 election to the National Institute of Arts and Letters. She traveled widely—to Asia, North Africa, and the South Pacific—and lectured frequently. She also continued writing, and her publications included *Collages* (1964), *The Novel of the Future* (1968), and *In Favor of the Sensitive Man, and Other Essays* (1976). The threat of cancer led to Nin's effective retirement in 1974, and the disease finally took her life on January 14, 1977, in her home in Los Angeles. According to her wishes, her ashes were scattered over the Pacific Ocean. The publication of *Delta of Venus* (1977) and *Little Birds* (1979), two volumes of short erotic fiction written for a private patron during the 1940's, placed her for the first time on best-seller lists.

ANALYSIS

Nin's life and writings span and reflect a good part of the twentieth century. Her work as a whole is less broad in terms of style and technique than it is deep; she was very concerned with certain themes and issues and explored them with imagination and rigor through her writing.

A central question for Nin was the role of women in modern society and their relationships to men and to one another. Nin wrote from an insistently feminine perspective—not out of a precious or meek femininity but rather from a keen awareness of women's psychic and social dependence on and involvement in a male-dominated culture and their continual struggle for identity and independence as women. Through the heroines appearing and reappearing in her stories and novels—Stella, Djuna, Lillian, and Sabina—Nin applied careful and sensitive introspection to women and their modes of artistic, spiritual, emotional, and sensual expression and their roles as daughters, lovers, and autonomous individuals. These explorations mirrored and expanded upon specific issues in Nin's own life, as an abandoned daughter, an ambivalent wife, and a woman writer putting forth a unique, and uniquely feminine, voice into an overwhelmingly male literary tradition.

She did, however, know that tradition well. Through her personal studies, she had read and appreciated many of its greatest writers, both in French—François Rabelais, Gustave Flaubert, and Victor Hugo—and in English—Ralph Waldo Emerson, Edgar Allan Poe, and Alfred, Lord Tennyson. Her true literary mentors were Marcel Proust and D. H. Lawrence. Though French was Nin's first language, she used it only in her early diaries; upon her arrival in New York, she vigorously applied herself to mastering English and never left it once she had succeeded. Her narrative voice remains truly international; her stories, like her life, are set primarily in New York and Paris milieus of artists, polyglots, and expatriates, where national identities fade and universal human qualities come into focus.

Unlike many writers in the European literary tradition, Nin eschewed conventional notions of plot, language, characterization, and style and responded rather to development in other artistic disciplines. Whereas she basically distrusted words because of their ability to obfuscate or lie, she loved and had an inherent faith in music and art. Her musical family certainly influenced her, and her experiences with commercial art, professional dance, and artists and sculptors such as André Breton, Salvador Dali, and Yanko Varda acquainted her with the principles of surrealism and reinforced her faith in the power of sensually evocative images. Her writing is infused with such images, as well as with the rhythms and suggestions of both jazz and classical music.

An equally strong influence was Nin's involvement with the practice of psychoanalysis. As both a subject and an analyst working with articulate and strong-minded theoreticians in the growing discipline, Nin developed a keen and untiring sensitivity to the details and dynamics of human behavior. The careful scrutiny she attained through introspection applied equally well to observation of others. In terms of her writing, "character" is not a static or fixed entity but a reflection of the constant flux of life. Her characters, while being distinct

individuals, exhibit a multiplicity of personality: They are mutable, they embody contradictions, and they are capable of dramatic transformations which nevertheless sustain their inherent integrity. Nin knew the theater and had performed in both films and dances; she recognized the potential in any individual to act, to become, and to wear costumes and masks, intentionally or not, that create unique patterns of behavior. The sequencing and spontaneous alteration of such patterns ultimately determine personality and character.

In a corresponding manner, Nin was never concerned with linear plot, logical ordering, or precise chronology. Rather than painstakingly structure her stories and novels, she would determine the starting premises of a work—the possibilities of characterization, the themes, the recurring motifs or images—and then improvise, determining many of the plot specifics as she progressed. As a result, readers expecting a conventionally composed story will be disappointed, for the movement that Nin achieves is less from a beginning to an end than from a surface to a center, or from an interior seed to an expansive truth. One of her favorite dicta, taken from the psychoanalyst Carl Jung, was "proceed from the dream outward."

As both analyst and writer, Nin was fascinated with dreams. She often used her own dreams as a source of ideas and images for her writing. Dreams seemed to her a tunnel into the inner world of emotion, which is the world that she sought to portray. Adapting the principles of Emersonian Transcendentalism as well as the stream-of-consciousness and interior monologue techniques of novelists James Joyce and Virginia Woolf to her own sensibility and vision, Nin focused on a psychological reality only tangentially related to appearances and surfaces. In her works, the phenomenological world is little more than dressing on the true reality of emotion and soul. Fact is subjugated to feeling, and sensory experience is less important in itself than for the images and perceptions it suggests in the complex labyrinth of personality.

Nin ultimately left the practice of psychoanalysis to devote her full energies to writing. As the volume of her work attests, writing was a deeply felt need. It helped her to articulate and capture the fleeting past as well as to formulate decisions and attitudes for the future. Through the steady practice of writing, at first spontaneously and intuitively, she naturally arrived at the elements of craft—the criteria by which artistic decisions are made. Her journey as a writer was from first- to third-person narrative, from introspection to outward vision, from obscurity to fame, and from innocence and insecurity to wisdom and courage.

For years, even after her literary stature and widespread recognition were established, Nin's writing was often criticized as murky, meaningless, solipsistic, neurotic, and inaccessible. Readers often lack the patience and imagination—that is, the ability to formulate and respond to images—that her writing requires. Yet millions of readers, especially women and adolescents, have found a personal truth in the psychological reality that Nin depicts. People and relationships were crucial to her, and she strove to create a unique connection with every individual she encountered; "I would like to meet the whole world at once," she wrote. The same individual connection is the goal of her writing.

HOUSE OF INCEST

First published: 1936
Type of work: Novel

In a dreamlike and mutable landscape of haunting images, a struggle occurs to liberate the self from the tyranny of neurosis and narcissism.

House of Incest was Nin's first published work of fiction. Though she was thirty-three years old when it was published and had been writing continuously for two decades, it exhibits the youthfulness of a first work in both its indulgence and its freedom. Nin called *House of Incest* a "prose poem" rather than a novel and, referring to a work by the French poet Arthur Rimbaud, "a woman's *Season in Hell.*" She also took inspiration from Octave Mirbeau's 1898 painting *Le Jardin des supplices* (*The Garden of Tortures*). The seven sections of *House of Incest*, each headed with a figure or glyph of distantly suggested astrological or mythological significance, can be seen as the seven days of creation, seven heavens, or seven hells. Rather than a story, this prose poem is a series of images and parables united by thematic patterns.

Written in the first-person voice in a highly poetic and imagistic idiom, *House of Incest* relates the inner experiences and sensations of a woman, or perhaps several women, in the House of Incest. Given Nin's views of the multiplicity of personality, resolving the single or multiple nature of the protagonist is less relevant than the nature of the various interactions described. The narrative begins with the protagonist's description of her birth, experienced as an emergence from a primordial sea.

It goes on to depict two dramatic situations: an obsessive lesbian relationship involving the dependent narrator, Jeanne, and her dismissive lover, named Sabina, and Jeanne's guilt-ridden incestuous pursuit of and flight from her brother. The narrator then encounters cryptic figures and herself becomes a dancer deprived of her arms even as she achieves, in the closing paragraphs, harmony with her world and hope for freedom.

The house of incest itself is a metaphor for the human body and psyche as they are trapped in self-obsession. In the section dealing with Jeanne and incest, the house is described as worn, static, and rotting. Nin is portraying the meaninglessness of a life without a true regard for or appreciation of others. Just as the lesbian relationship becomes compulsive, draining, and destructive, so the incestuous passion is not a true love of other but a love of self as perceived or manifested in the blood relation. Though the situations portrayed are unconventional, Nin is not making moral judgments on them as such; rather, she uses the homosexual and incestuous passions to express the emptiness of love derived from narcissistic impulses.

The language of *House of Incest* is characterized by unrestrained lyricism and emotional exuberance. The images Nin employs combine natural, material, and corporal elements to striking effect, such as "[f]ishes made of velvet, of organdie with lace fangs." Evocations of violence—acid, scissors, serpents, and storms—are set against those of vitality—the sea, eggs, and orgasms. The text is richly filled with allusions drawn from the fields of metallurgy, alchemy, astronomy, geography, and biology. Nin utilized poetic techniques of sound—alliteration, rhythm, and repetition—to create musical values in the piece:

The steel necklace on her throat flashed like summer lightning and the sound of steel was like the clashing of swords. . . . Le pas d'acier. . . . The steel of New York's skeleton buried in granite, buried standing up. Le pas d'acier . . . notes hammered on the steel-stringed guitars of the gypsies, on the steel arms of chairs dulled with her breath; steel mail curtains falling like the flail of hail, steel bars and steel barrage cracking. Her necklace thrown around the world's neck, unmeltable.

The suggestion of real contexts, places, and languages; the juxtaposition of mineral reality with breath and emotion; and the nervelike tautness of a guitar string all exemplify the many elements that recur and undergo transformations of meaning through the course of the prose poem.

In the preface to the piece and at various points throughout are references to the book itself. Often set apart or emphasized with block letters, these references become an object of meaning within the narrative. The book in the reader's hands is alternately the truth as the narrator can tell it and the narrator's place of refuge from the weight of truth. How the book reflects the characters and how they are reflections of one another become central to the issue of telling the simple truth or evading oneself and others with lies. Thus, when the armless dancer turns "towards daylight" at the end, *House of Incest* concludes with a suggestion that truth is emerging from the darkness within.

A SPY IN THE HOUSE OF LOVE

First published: 1954
Type of work: Novel

A woman explores the multiplicity of her personality through a series of erotic and emotional adventures with a variety of men.

A Spy in the House of Love is the fourth installment in Nin's "continuous novel" titled *Cities of the Interior.* The latter unites six shorter individual works and focuses on three women—Djuna, Lillian, and Sabina—and the men in their lives. The novels are not necessarily sequential but are connected by a network of characters, settings, imagery, and language. Thus, they do not need to be read in any particular order and, though certain information and echoes may be missed, each volume stands as a complete work independent of the others.

A Spy in the House of Love focuses on Sabina, a fiery actress who is only partially content in her marriage to an attentive but dull husband, Alan, and yearns for erotic and spiritual stimulation. While performing in an amateurish production of *Cinderella* in Provincetown, on Massachusetts's Cape Cod, she is seduced by a romantically visualized Austrian singer named Philip. At a jazz club in New York, she indulges in an affair with Mambo, an exotic and sensuous drummer. In a Long Island beach town, a grounded British pilot named John captivates her imagination with his dark, angry intensity. She becomes a nurturing mother figure for Donald, a lively young jester. She also encounters Jay, a perceptive artist and her former lover in Paris. During and between these "multiple peregrinations of love," she returns to the comfort of her marital home and Alan's trusting paternal love.

A controlling image for the novel is taken from Marcel Duchamp's Dadaist painting *Nude Descending a Staircase, No. 2* (1912), which presents a fractured image of a woman's multiple outlines. Nin's portrait of Sabina is equally fractured, for each of the selves that she becomes or discovers with her different lovers is a valid though incomplete expression of her identity. As an actress skilled with vocal, physical, cosmetic, and behavioral transformations, her various identities are accentuated. Nin's portrait is not one of perversity or psychosis, however; Sabina illustrates the multiplicity of personality that Nin perceived in herself and in all individuals who actively respond to their environments.

Sabina's journey through the novel tracks the continuous manifestation and aggravation of the inner tension she feels between her need for peace, stability, and intimacy and her desire for freedom, motion, and anonymity. Such is the mutability of her nature that each interaction or encounter stimulates a pronounced and often opposite response. Sabina is a restless soul; her congress with Philip or John fulfills her fantasies while simultaneously heightening her need to return to Alan. Yet Sabina is repeatedly unable to take the meaningful essence from each encounter; her longing and dissatisfaction are not relieved by passionate, imaginative sexual liaisons. Even as she pursues adventure, she is haunted by guilt and tantalized by the possibility of discovery. As her struggle approaches climactic proportions, it is only in a final chance encounter with her wise and sensitive friend Djuna that Sabina directly confronts the essential turmoil of her life and begins to find remedy and rescue.

Nin gives Sabina's inner turmoil concrete expression through the device of the "lie detector"— a mysterious man who appears to Sabina in the opening paragraph, follows her through her adventures, and ultimately receives her confession and pronounces psychic judgment upon her. The lie detector is not a real or imagined character so much as another manifestation of Sabina's personality, the one which holds the key to achieving a harmonious sense of identity.

A Spy in the House of Love exhibits Nin's characteristic use of imagery to depict psychological reality, including imagery of voyages, excavations, labyrinths, prisons, fire, and bodies of water. In addition, specific objects take on metaphorical significance, such as the black cape that symbolizes Sabina's distrust and hostility. A recurrent motif involving modes of transportation—the grounded aviator and his bicycle, the sailboat in which Philip seduces Sabina, the Parisian elevator in which she and Jay had sex years before—signify Sabina's restlessness and recklessness, as do the descriptions of her random and incessant gesturing. In the various encounters of the novel, Nin has carefully detailed gesture and behavior to convey the precise dynamics of human interaction.

Finally, music is another device used throughout the novel. In addition to the jazz played in Mambo's club, compositions by Richard Wagner, Igor Stravinsky, Ludwig van Beethoven, and Claude Debussy are heard by characters within the narrative. Donald even alludes to Stravinsky when he calls Sabina his "Firebird." The music combines with the evocative language and imagery to give texture and sensuality to this account of a passionate woman's search for freedom and meaning.

THE DIARY OF ANAÏS NIN

First published: 1966-1986
Type of work: Diary

Nin's lifelong diary documents the details of her fascinating life and stands as a unique accomplishment in English and in women's literature.

Nin began keeping a diary on July 25, 1914, as an ongoing letter to her father that she hoped would someday bring him back to her family. Sixty years later, in the summer of 1974, Nin concluded her diary while enjoying the exotic landscape and culture of Bali. During those six decades, her personal journal of daily life and experience grew to 150 volumes, or some fifteen thousand typewritten pages. It is unquestionably her masterpiece, both as a literary work and as a social document of the artistic life of the twentieth century.

The diary reflects Nin's creative attitude toward existence and the connection she perceived between life and literature. She viewed life as an adventure, or as a story that the individual freely and imaginatively creates and narrates to herself. The diary eventually developed a persona, becoming a friend, a confidant, and a place to go for escape or succor, or at times even an enemy, an agent of deceit, and a threatening obsession. Whatever her feelings were at the moment, Nin came to her diary for uninhibited introspection and absolute truthfulness; even when the truth of her feelings or aspirations were not to be reckoned, her earnestness was unflagging.

On one level, the diary is a record of Nin's external life. She faithfully detailed the specifics of her daily movements, including her adjustment to New York, her adolescence, her courtship and marriage, her explorations into sensuality and sexuality, her activities as an aspiring writer and psychoanalyst, her travels between Europe and America, the homes she occupied, the people with whom she associated, the publication of her books, her movements in later life, and the rewards and difficulties of celebrity and wealth. Her skills as a writer are evident in the descriptions of her life's settings and the sketches of her friends and colleagues. Many prominent individuals are sharply drawn, including Henry Miller, his wife June, Lawrence Durrell, Gonzalo More, Eduardo Sanchez, Otto Rank, John Erskine, and others.

On another level, Nin's diary, like her fiction, delves into psychological reality. In her diary, she recorded sensations and emotions, including her ambivalent feelings toward her father, her internal struggles with her conflicting roles as wife and artist, her search for a sense of identity amid frequent relocation and alienation, the frustrations of literary rejection, and her soul-searching deliberations and anxieties over publication of the diary itself.

Multiplicity of personality, a theme prevalent in the fiction, is reflected in the apparent contradictions and reinterpretations found throughout the successive volumes of the diary. Nin's rigorous honesty communicates the constant changeability and unpredictability of her life. "It is my thousand years of womanhood I am recording," she wrote in 1966, "a thousand women."

Through the course of the volumes in which the diary has been published, from *Linotte: The Early Diary of Anaïs Nin, 1914-1920* (1978) to *The Diary of Anaïs Nin: 1966-1974* (1980), several general developments can be seen. Nin began as a shy, sensitive, and uncertain child and grew into an enlightened, wise, and mature woman. The earlier volumes are characterized by deep introspection, while in the later years Nin wrote more about other people and the world she observed. By the 1970's, Nin came to her diary much less regularly, and it took on the qualities of a scrapbook.

Aware from the beginning of the need to make artistic choices, Nin gradually developed her form and craft as she progressed. Her diary was also at times a literary playground, as with her 1928 "diary within a diary" of the imagination-inspired fantasy character "Imagy." She gave names to individual volumes, from "The Childhood Diary," "Diary of a Fiancée," and "Diary of a Wife," to the more expressive "John," "The House," "The Woman Who Died," "Disintegration," and the last books, "The Book of Pain" and "The Book of Music."

The titles, the experiments, and her habits of greeting and signing off each entry give evidence of conscious artistry during the actual composition. In the 1960's, the decision to publish the diary led to a second, more formal editing process. Respect for the privacy of individuals mentioned in the diary and the final shape of the published version—originally it was to be condensed into a single volume—became issues. As a result of those concerns, certain individuals or questionable sections were edited out, decisions were made about how to divide the entirety into volumes, and parts were altered for purposes of consistency and flow. The process of preparing the diary for publication was a natural final stage in the evolution of Nin's artistry, for it further refined her editing skills and made public what was probably the most important private relationship of her life. As she wrote in the spring of 1972, what began as a dialogue with the self had "become a correspondence with the world."

Throughout the transitions of her life and the development of her writing, both so vividly documented in the diary, Nin's generosity and optimism shone. As she approached the end of her life, she chose to end its monumental journal with entries written under the spell of Bali rather than lead her readers through the devastation of cancer. In a brief excerpt from "The Book of Music," included as an epilogue to the diary, Nin meditated on death:

> Yes, music indicates another place, a better place. . . . One should think of this place joyfully. Then if it follows death, it is a beautiful place. A lovely thing to look forward to—a promised land. So I shall die in music, into music, with music.

SUMMARY

"I believe one writes because one has to create a world in which one can live," Nin wrote in 1954, responding by letter to a reader's question. "I had to create a world of my own, like a climate, a country, an atmosphere in which I could breathe, reign, and re-create myself when destroyed by living." More than most writers, Nin's work and life were intricately interwoven; through her novels and diary, she created a world ideally suited to her unique sensibility and filled with imagination and insight that speak to generations of readers.

Barry Mann

BIBLIOGRAPHY

By the Author

LONG FICTION:
House of Incest, 1936
Winter of Artifice, 1939
Winter of Artifice: Three Novelettes, 1945 (contains *Winter of Artifice*, "Stella," and "The Voice")
This Hunger, 1945
Ladders to Fire, 1946
Children of the Albatross, 1947
The Four-Chambered Heart, 1950
A Spy in the House of Love, 1954
Solar Barque, 1958
Cities of the Interior: A Continuous Novel, 1959 (contains *Ladders to Fire*, *Children of the Albatross*, *The Four-Chambered Heart*, *A Spy in the House of Love*, and *Solar Barque*)
Seduction of the Minotaur, 1961
Collages, 1964

SHORT FICTION:
Under a Glass Bell, and Other Stories, 1944
Delta of Venus: Erotica, 1977
Waste of Timelessness, and Other Early Stories, 1977
Little Birds: Erotica, 1979

NONFICTION:
D. H. Lawrence: An Unprofessional Study, 1932
Realism and Reality, 1946
On Writing, 1947
The Diary of Anaïs Nin: 1931-1934, 1966
The Diary of Anaïs Nin: 1934-1939, 1967
The Novel of the Future, 1968
The Diary of Anaïs Nin: 1939-1944, 1969
The Diary of Anaïs Nin: 1944-1947, 1971
Paris Revisited, 1972
The Diary of Anaïs Nin: 1947-1955, 1974
A Photographic Supplement to the Diary of Anaïs Nin, 1974
A Woman Speaks: The Lectures, Seminars, and Interviews of Anaïs Nin, 1975
The Diary of Anaïs Nin: 1955-1966, 1976
In Favor of the Sensitive Man, and Other Essays, 1976
Linotte: The Early Diary of Anaïs Nin, 1914-1920, 1978
The Diary of Anaïs Nin: 1966-1974, 1980
The Early Diary of Anaïs Nin: Volume Two, 1920-1923, 1982
The Early Diary of Anaïs Nin: Volume Three, 1923-1927, 1983
The Early Diary of Anaïs Nin: Volume Four, 1927-1931, 1985
Henry and June: From the Unexpurgated Diary of Anaïs Nin, 1986
A Literate Passion: Letters of Anaïs Nin and Henry Miller, 1932-1953, 1987

DISCUSSION TOPICS

- What is the function of music in Anaïs Nin's *A Spy in the House of Love*?

- To what extent is Nin's fiction accessible to male readers?

- Nin's "literary mentors" are Marcel Proust and D. H. Lawrence. What does she owe to each?

- What literary techniques usually classed as "poetic" serve Nin's prose?

- Nin's diary has had to be edited to protect persons named in it. Can a diary be candid, be sensitive to the privacy of others still alive, and be publishable?

About the Author

Blair, Deirdre. *Anaïs Nin: A Biography.* New York: G. P. Putnam's Sons, 1995.

Fitch, Noel Riley. *Anaïs: The Erotic Life of Anaïs Nin.* Boston: Little, Brown, 1993.

Franklin, Benjamin, and Duane Schneider. *Anaïs Nin: An Introduction.* Athens: Ohio University Press, 1979.

Hinz, Evelyn J., ed. *A Woman Speaks: The Lectures, Seminars, and Interviews of Anaïs Nin.* Chicago: Swallow Press, 1975.

Nin, Anaïs. *A Literate Passion: Letters of Anaïs Nin and Henry Miller.* Edited by Gunther Stuhlmann. New York: Harcourt Brace Jovanovich, 1987.

Pierpont, Claudia Roth. *Passionate Minds: Women Rewriting the World.* New York: Alfred A. Knopf, 2000.

Scholar, Nancy. *Anaïs Nin.* Boston: Twayne, 1984.

Tookey, Helen. *Anaïs Nin, Fictionality and Femininity: Playing a Thousand Roles.* New York: Oxford University Press, 2003.

FRANK NORRIS

Born: Chicago, Illinois
March 5, 1870
Died: San Francisco, California
October 25, 1902

One of America's leading naturalistic writers, Norris was also a Romantic moralist whose acclaimed novels depicted human failings while attesting a belief in nature's ultimate benevolence toward humankind.

Library of Congress

BIOGRAPHY

Benjamin Franklin Norris, Jr., was born in Chicago on March 5, 1870, the first of five children born to Gertrude Doggett Norris and Benjamin Franklin Norris, Sr., the wealthy owner of a wholesale jewelry business. Only two boys besides Frank survived infancy; Lester was born in 1878 (and died in 1887), and Charles was born in 1881. Because of Frank, Sr.'s, health problems, the Norrises moved to Oakland, California, in 1882 and the following year settled in San Francisco.

After attending a preparatory school and Boys' High School, neither of which suited his limited interest in schooling, Frank was enrolled in the San Francisco Art Association, where he studied painting. Although he studied art in London and Paris, his interest in painting soon waned, and after two years he returned home.

During this time, however, he had begun to write. His first article, "Clothes of Steel," was published in the *San Francisco Chronicle* shortly after his return in 1889. The following year, he entered the University of California at Berkeley as a limited-status student. By this time, Norris knew precisely what career would suit him: College was preparatory to becoming a professional writer. It was at Berkeley that Norris first read the naturalistic works of French novelist Émile Zola that greatly influenced his own developing literary philosophy.

While Norris was attending college, his parents filed for divorce. His father soon remarried; Frank, Charles, and their mother moved to Massachusetts, where Frank studied creative writing at Harvard University for one year. It was during this period that he began writing *McTeague* (1899) and *Vandover and the Brute* (1914).

When Norris left Harvard, he traveled and wrote sketches in South Africa, but he was forced to return to San Francisco when his involvement in the political aspects of the Boer War resulted in his expulsion from the country. It was a disheartening event, but it resulted in a unique opportunity: In San Francisco, he became an assistant editor on a weekly publication, *The Wave*. The magazine published several of his short stories and serialized his first novel, a pirate story titled *Moran of the Lady Letty* (1898). In spite of the poor quality of this work, it caught the attention of the editor of *McClure's Magazine* in New York, who offered Norris a position.

As a writer for *McClure's Magazine*, Norris met William Dean Howells, who would become his greatest supporter, and was sent to Cuba to cover the Spanish-American War. It was during this assignment that Norris met Stephen Crane and Richard Harding Davis—who would become his literary competitors—and Frederic Remington, the artist. The trip was a painful experience all around for Norris. Raised in a luxurious and sheltered atmosphere, he found the realities of war horrifying. Moreover, the magazine decided not to publish his stories.

In San Francisco once again, Norris found success both personally and professionally. His relationship with Jeannette Black, who encouraged his work and appreciated the realistic character of his fiction, led to their marriage on January 12, 1900. They returned east and lived first in the elite residential area of New York's Washington Square and then settled into their own home in Roselle, New Jersey. Additionally, both *McTeague* and *Blix* were published in 1899, and Norris began his research in California for his next project, *The Octopus* (1901).

Norris knew that the graphic realism and naturalistic philosophy of *McTeague* would be controversial, but he was able to withstand the ensuing literary scandal in large part because of the publication by the influential Howells of a supportive analytical essay on the novel that compared Norris to Zola and Charles Dickens. Several New York critics praised Norris's novel, but many deemed it repulsive, unhealthy, and sordid, reflecting the genteel attitudes at the end of the nineteenth century. One review is representative of the offense that many readers felt upon reading the novel:

> Mr. Norris has written pages for which there is absolutely no excuse, and his needless sins against good taste and delicacy are fatal spots upon his work. *McTeague* undoubtedly will be widely read . . . but we pray that a kind fate may bring it only to those of vigorous mind and, shall we say it, strong stomach.

Norris, however, was already deeply involved in the research for his next project, a projected trilogy that would follow the growth, production, and distribution of wheat.

As Norris prepared to write the first novel of the trilogy, he moved from *McClure's Magazine* to a position of a reader for Doubleday, Page, and Company, a new publishing company. This position was meant to afford Norris a reasonable income and time for his writing, but he also found himself embroiled in a major literary controversy. For the past several years, Norris had been developing and reshaping a literary philosophy that embraced naturalism but retained the transcendental belief in human potential. When, as a reader, he read a manuscript by Theodore Dreiser titled *Sister Carrie* (1900), he recognized not only a kindred spirit but also an extraordinary novel. Upon his recommendation, Dreiser's novel was accepted for publication.

Although the publisher later sought, unsuccessfully, to negate Dreiser's contract, Norris continued to support the publication of what has come to be known as one of America's major naturalistic works of fiction.

The Octopus (1901) was the most successful novel of Norris's career. When it appeared he was already living in Chicago and collecting materials for the second novel of the trilogy. Although he and his wife were joyful over the birth of a daughter, Jeannette, Jr., on February 9, 1902, he had become dissatisfied with industrialized urban settings while writing *The Pit* (1903) and decided that he and his family would prosper by moving back to San Francisco before they began a world cruise aboard a tramp steamer to gather materials for the final novel in the trilogy, which was to be titled *The Wolf*.

Norris was at the prime of his career: His previous novel had sold more than thirty thousand copies, he was publishing short stories again, and he was drafting ideas for another trilogy, on the Battle of Gettysburg. While Jeannette was recovering from an operation for appendicitis, however, Norris became ill. To his peril, he ignored his discomforts, and he died on October 25, 1902, from peritonitis that developed from a perforated appendix. He was thirty-two years old.

ANALYSIS

Once deemed the "father of American naturalism," Norris is better understood as an author who delved into a variety of literary modes as a means of blending his naturalistic recognition of human failings and the potential emergence of a brute self with his romantic belief in the capacity of love to reform people into becoming their better selves.

What Norris sought to capture in his novels was a record of modern life. While he recognized literature as a marketable item (like any other commodity), he also believed that it had the capacity to express the life of the people. This should not necessarily be taken as a call for democratization of American life, however; Norris's fiction is rife with the elitist and racist attitudes that shaped late nineteenth century American culture. Norris asserted, however, that the people have a right not to be deluded by illusionary views of life that relate only the heroic and self-sacrificing elements of human nature. What he deemed a "right to truth" meant that history, as well as emotions, must be truthfully rendered, depicted as they are and not as people would like them to be. This demands that the writer responsibly and objectively confront the society in which he or she lives.

The purpose behind every novel and the responsibilities that its author embraced in the act of writing were of great interest to Norris. His desire to define the moral responsibilities of an author grew, in large part, out of changes that were occurring in publishing trends at the turn of the twentieth century. Because of a significant increase in the number of Americans who had benefited from some form of education and thus had the capacity to consume a large quantity of printed matter, inexpensive and "easy reading" works were being published in record numbers. The authors of these works, however, often had little concern for the quality of information that they delivered.

Against such an influx of irresponsible publications, Norris suggested certain criteria for writers of novels. In essays such as "The Novel with a Purpose" (1902) and "The Responsibilities of the Novelist" (1902), Norris asserted that while lesser novelists simply told a story, the works by writers with higher artistic yearnings would entail a study of human motivations and representative human characteristics.

This required the novelist to draw fictional characters from his or her observations of actual people and to realize that the purpose of the highest form of the novel was to reform (while maintaining a keen eye for aesthetics and the action of the story), to bring the reader to a moral rather than a popular conclusion. Because readers will believe whatever is rendered with skill, that places upon the author a tremendous responsibility to act with the greatest awareness and sincerity.

There was an ongoing debate at the turn of the twentieth century over the need for someone to produce the "great American novel." In this respect, Norris's belief in evolutionary processes was brought to bear upon the issue. The United States had not yet sufficiently developed a nationalistic spirit, he asserted, and such a spirit was required before any nation could produce a national epic. Like other realistic authors of the period, including Rebecca Harding Davis, Hamlin Garland, and Sarah Orne Jewett, Norris believed that a writer

should present the essential factors of a particular region of the country. Only after the accumulation of these particular studies could the United States hope to develop its own great novel.

Norris's shifting alliance between realism (which he defined as fiction devoted to the subject of typical life) and romanticism (fiction that focused upon the exceptional rather than the normal) suggests his own lifelong struggle to find a literary means of expressing his fears for and beliefs in the capacity of human beings to shape their lives. If he ultimately failed to synthesize these elements, it is a failure representative of that modern life which he sought to record.

Norris's early fiction was often sentimental and romantic. His first long publication was a romantic poem titled *Yvernelle: A Tale of Feudal France* (1892) that reflected his fascination with medieval themes and was highly moralistic in tone. Although the poem was a work of his apprenticeship years, the attention to romantic moralism remained long after the settings of his fiction moved from medieval to modern times. Years later, Norris still asserted that "preparations of effect" were the central feature of "fiction mechanics." The difference between the hack writer and the great writer was the subtlety with which they rendered those preparations.

As Norris matured as a writer, his naturalistic philosophy developed into a belief that human beings are always destined to fail against the indifference and power of natural forces, of nature itself. In *The Octopus*, he expressed these ideas most clearly:

> Men were nothings, mere animalcules, mere ephemerides that fluttered and fell and were forgotten between dawn and dusk. . . . Men were naught, death was naught, life was naught; FORCE only existed—FORCE that brought men into the world, FORCE that crowded them out of it to make way for the succeeding generation, FORCE that made the wheat grow, FORCE that garnered it from the soil to give place to the succeeding crop.

Most prevalent in Norris's large category of forces that controlled human beings were those of heredity and environment. Yet this evolutionary process as it related to human beings was not envisioned by Norris as a debilitating feature of human development but rather as the capacity for humankind to evolve into the perfect species. Thus, if in describing human failings, Norris depicted the force of sexual desire as one of the most overpowering facets of human nature, one that often devolved into a bestial, self-serving lust for gratification, he also acknowledged the regenerative capacity of the human spirit.

A year before his death, Norris published a short essay titled "The True Reward of the Novelist" (1901). The reward could not be defined in terms of popularity or sales; it came from the knowledge that the author had told his or her audience the truth as he or she knew it. Such honesty and realism did not preclude romance, Norris asserted:

> The difficult thing is to get at the life immediately around you, the very life in which you move. No romance in it? No romance in *you*, poor fool. As much romance on Michigan Avenue as there is realism in King Arthur's court. It is as you choose to see it.

That recognition, then, becomes the ultimate responsibility of the novelist.

McTeague

First published: 1899
Type of work: Novel

In late nineteenth century San Francisco, a community is completely disrupted when temptations and greed bring out the brute nature of its inhabitants.

Norris had begun writing *McTeague* while a student at Harvard, but by the time of its publication seven years later, in 1899, the influence of French and Russian naturalism was well recognized in American literary communities. Yet no native novelist had yet created quite so grim and unyielding a representation as Norris did in this, his first major novel. *McTeague* is deeply indebted to the works of Zola, whose naturalistic-romantic vision of the complex nature of human relationships and the compelling forces which led men and women into destructive behavior patterns reflected and encouraged Norris's own beliefs. Although Norris would continue to incorporate the techniques of naturalism into his fiction, *McTeague* stands as his purest experiment in the genre.

As Norris would later counsel in his essays on fiction, he focused in this novel on one area in one region of the United States: Polk Street in San Francisco. More specifically, the novel follows a particular period of time in the life of "Mac" McTeague, a dentist on Polk Street. McTeague's initial mood of melancholy and nostalgia for the country life of his youth reflects the sense of loss that has come with the prosperity of his urban existence.

Like all naturalists, Norris did not assert that environment alone could be blamed for the present condition of humankind's slow evolution, and it is the brute strength of McTeague that is most striking. This beastlike nature, which Norris believed was a hereditary feature of all people, lies beneath the surface of McTeague's lumbering presence. When circumstances threaten to reveal that he had never received proper certification as a dentist, the facade of his personality is ruptured and the uncontrollable brute self emerges.

Although Norris believed that there had been no great American women novelists and that this phenomenon was attributable to the fact that women led sheltered lives which did not allow them to study "real" life, he did not limit his depiction of the brute self to men. If McTeague's base nature is rooted in masculine strength, his wife's innate baseness is depicted in her greed.

When Trina, his wife, wins five thousand dollars in a lottery, her sweet nature gives way to that of one obsessed with the money she receives. It is this greed that comes to pervade the novel, as McTeague, his friend Marcus Schouler, and minor characters Maria Macapa and the Polish Jew, Mr. Zerkow, are changed by the intrusion of money—or the lust for it—into their lives. Norris satirically renders this facet of human nature through the grotesquely enormous gold tooth that McTeague hangs outside his place of business. The day that McTeague removes the gold tooth from its crate, he sets in motion the "trap" (the naturalistic symbol of the forces that propel human beings toward their fate) that will result in his death.

As the various characters become more and more enamored of money, they devolve into violent, animalistic creatures. McTeague, like his father, begins to drink excessively, and his lustful nature soon rages out of control. Trina's affection for her husband is replaced by her own lust—for constant contact with the coins themselves. Marcus, who had unwittingly given the winning lottery ticket to Trina in the hope of luring her away from McTeague, is enraged at his loss. Once simply an inept and untrained dog surgeon, he becomes doglike himself in his brutish anger. In the final scene of the novel, both he and McTeague have devolved to such a stage that they crawl on all fours in the arid landscape.

Norris firmly believed that the naturalist, like any author, was necessarily a moralist. In the violent deaths of McTeague, Trina, Marcus, Maria, and Zerkow, he renders the punishment that he believed such greed demands.

There are two other characters in the novel who are often overlooked but who extend Norris's moralistic depiction of modern life: Old Grannis and Miss Baker. The pathetic romance of the two elderly people, as they carry on a vicarious courtship without speaking or meeting, represents the isolation and fear that dominates modern urbanized society. Unlike the other main characters in the novel, they do survive, but their tragic failure to engage in any meaningful exchange is Norris's ironic prophecy for American life: They are old, they are separated physically and spiritually, and when they die with no offspring, they will take with them any hope for the future of the Polk Street community.

Through such depictions, *McTeague* became more than a classic text in American naturalism. It is also a record of Norris's concern for the future of the novel and for the future of American society.

THE OCTOPUS

First published: 1901
Type of work: Novel

Against the fertile landscape of nineteenth century California's wheat fields, the men who grow the wheat must confront the ruthless railroad barons.

Subtitled *A Story of California, The Octopus* was the first novel in a projected trilogy that Norris envisioned as an epic study of the cultivation, processing, and distribution of wheat; the wheat would move from the Western fields to Chicago's marketplace to the starving peoples of Europe.

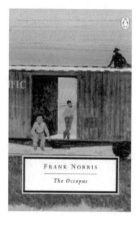

In the United States, the Populist Party had been formed in 1891 as a collective Western movement by farmers and labor against the rise of political "machines" and trust organizations that threatened the farmers' livelihood. The party's demise, which would occur around 1904, was already foreshadowed at the time Norris was completing *The Octopus*. Several American authors, from Rebecca Harding Davis to Thorstein Veblen, had recognized the dangers inherent in contrived economic shifts and made political trusts the center of their literature. Although Norris had no direct involvement in the Populist movement, his novel stands securely among the major social protest novels of the turn of the twentieth century.

No other novel by Norris so clearly combines his naturalistic and romantic philosophies. *The Octopus* is a study in natural versus unnatural forces: the wheat versus the railroad and its representatives, nature's boundaries versus the steel tentacles of the railroad's artificial boundaries, the unnatural "Other" force of rape (literal and metaphoric) that destroys the natural force of love.

Combining his beliefs about the appropriate scope of an American novel (to depict the realities of a particular region) and the sense of alienation in contemporary society, Norris creates as his protagonist an artist, the poet Presley, who spends a summer in California's San Joaquin Valley, where he tries to find a purpose for his poetry. The narrative structure of the novel coincides with Presley's indecisiveness about whether a realistic or romantic vision is the most truthful art form and reflects Norris's own waffling opinions.

Through Presley's eyes, however, the reader discovers the intricate processes of growing wheat and the tenacious hold that the railroad conglomerate has on the fate of the farmers. Without a decent price and reasonable travel schedules, the farmers' crops can be destroyed more readily by the trust's false manipulations of the market than by the indifference of natural weather conditions. The demise of all the farmers in the novel represents Norris's belief that no one can withstand the power of such forces.

In the community of the San Joaquin wheat growers, Norris discovered a setting that allowed him to study human interactions in everyday circumstances and in moments of crisis. If this community represents those who love the land and respect its fertile power, it is also symbolic of the fact that no region is safe from the brutal nature of human beings. This dark side of human nature is openly depicted in the railroad characters, from the corporate leaders to their pawn, Shelgrim. As in *McTeague*, Norris also continues his study of how temptation can lead even the best of people into false actions. Thus Magnus Derrick, the leader of the community, becomes the railroad's dupe, while his son extends this betrayal to open association with the enemy.

The rape of Angèle becomes a metaphor for the exploitation of the entire community by an intrusive "Other." The railroad is a known perpetrator, but its ability to pervade the community before many inhabitants had realized its presence and brute nature is symbolized in the mystery surrounding Angèle's rape and death. Her lover Vanamee's obsession with discovering the truth parallels Presley's obsessive artistic quest. That both remain thwarted in their goals at the novel's end reflects Norris's belief in the dangerously elusive nature of truth itself; however, through the efforts of each character he also reveals the worthiness of that quest.

Vanamee's mystic experiences can hardly be termed naturalistic or realistic, but they embrace Norris's belief in a moral purpose. The shepherd's sense of loss at the death of Angèle is the beginning of a philosophic journey which culminates in his belief that, although individuals cannot withstand irresistible forces, the good will ultimately prevail. This is a dramatic turn toward the romantic for Norris.

This philosophy prevails at the end of the novel through the characters of Presley, Vanamee, and Hilma Tree. Hilma's natural sensuousness represents a human correlation with the fertility of the land, and it is her love that converts Annixter from a vulgar, brutal man into a loving and nurturing human being. If Annixter's slaughter, like Angèle's, depicts the indifferent nature of force, the survival of Hilma Tree embraces Vanamee's—and Norris's—belief in the prevailing nature of good over evil. If the railroad won in California, other forces would prevail on a wider, epic scale because *"the WHEAT remained.* Untouched, unassailable, undefiled, that mighty world force, that nourisher of nations."

As the final line of the novel states, "all things surely, inevitably, resistlessly work together for good." It was as true for philosophic and literary battles as it was for the battle of the wheat fields.

THE PIT

First published: 1903
Type of work: Novel

"Cornering" the supply of wheat in the Chicago futures market, done practically on a whim, leads to the financial and moral decline of a wealthy speculator.

The Pit was the second novel in Norris's proposed trilogy called "The Epic of the Wheat." In this "story of Chicago," Norris moves from the production of wheat to its distribution on world markets, from the natural countryside of California to the artificial terrain of futures speculation. Continuing his portrayal of the effects of temptation and greed, Norris also depicts the decline evident in the space of only one generation—from the moral generation of elders who made their money through honest labor to their degenerate offspring who labor only after money and the power it bestows.

The Pit was Norris's most successful novel in terms of sales and initial reception; this may have been aided in part by its publication so soon after his sudden death, but it was also a novel that spoke directly to the times. Every major American naturalist, from Stephen Crane to Jack London and from Rebecca Harding Davis to Edith Wharton, acknowledged through their fiction that speculation—gambling on the future—had become an ironic indicator not only of economic but also of social "progress" in the United States.

Norris's plot of Curtis Jadwin's fascinating and ruthless efforts to corner the Chicago wheat market was based on an actual event in 1897, when Joseph Leiter attempted such a feat. In fictionalizing the story, Norris reflected upon the cultural implications of such daring maneuvers. He was interested not only in the consequences of illegal market manipulations but also in the facets of human nature that would lead someone to commit such an act. In Curtis Jadwin, one discovers a man whose life is so financially secure (but without direction, without goals for achievement) that, for him, the adventure of such an endeavor becomes its greatest appeal. Norris had predicted in *The Octopus* that the wheat would always prevail as a natural force; in *The Pit*, he demonstrates that power against all calculations of human reason when an unexpected bumper crop thwarts Jadwin's illegal designs.

Against this background, Norris also studied another cultural current of the turn of the century: the rise of the so-called New Woman. Suffragist and women's rights movements had flourished, to greater or lesser degrees, for most of the nineteenth century. At the end of the century, women had finally made several inroads into the public arena. The New Woman—self-liberated, intelligent, and outspoken—was juxtaposed against the True Woman, the domestic and dominated self-sacrificing "angel of the house." These issues had dominated women's writings for decades, and *The Pit* represents Norris's first major engagement with such issues.

His character Laura Dearborn had been raised in New England, the home of the culturally imposed True Womanhood. To escape such oppressive attitudes, she moved to Chicago. Although she had several suitors, Laura was attracted to Jadwin's potential life of wealth and luxury, and she agreed to marry him. Thus she traps herself, in spite of her liberating endeavors. When Jadwin becomes involved in his market schemes, Laura seeks solace in flirtations with the artist Sheldon Corthell. Such a love affair is the stuff from which popular novels were made, and Norris specifically suggests, as he had in his nonfiction, the falseness of such novels' representations of love and romance.

In depicting Laura's affair with Corthell and her attempt at arousing her husband's interest once again with a dance of seduction, Norris acknowledges the reality of women's sexual needs. Ironically, however, Norris cannot complete this depiction of a New Woman. When her husband's business fails, Laura returns to woman's self-sacrificing role and accepts the "duties" of marriage. Norris asserts this is the achievement of love over self-love, but he thereby negates the process of a woman's movement toward liberation by seeing self-love as a negative force that must be overcome.

The Pit seems to conclude with a sentimentalized vision of the poorer, but now happy, couple and of their rejection of the debilitating urban lifestyle. As they almost literally ride off into the sunset, Laura looks back at the city landscape, seeing

> the tall gray office buildings, the murk of rain, the haze of light in the heavens, and raised against it, the pile of the Board of Trade building, black, monolithic, crouching on its foundations like a monstrous sphinx with blind eyes, silent, grave— crouching there without a soul, without a sign of life, under the night and the drifting veil of rain.

Thus Norris seemingly leaves the reader with the demise of evil and the prevailing spirit of goodness—"light in the heavens."

This reading, however, would ignore the irony of Norris's conclusion: Jadwin intends to move west and go into the railroad business. The consequences of this, as depicted in *The Octopus*, are ominous for the entire United States. If Jadwin had been defeated by the natural force of the wheat, he is about to attempt to control his nemesis through manipulation of the steel tentacles of the railroad.

Because Norris died before he could begin the third novel of the series, this conclusion leaves the battle between the wheat and the machine, unintentionally but appropriately, without resolution.

SUMMARY

Norris was not consistent in his literary philosophies, sometimes advocating realism, sometimes romanticism; if he blended literary techniques, however, it was because he recognized that those techniques were vehicles for expression and not truths in themselves. He created graphic and dramatically powerful novels which addressed the issues of his day and have continued to speak to debates on human nature and social progress.

For a young man who died just as he was maturing as a writer, he left a surprisingly large body of work which influenced writers who followed him and has retained its place in American literature's exploration of regional realism.

Sharon M. Harris

BIBLIOGRAPHY

By the Author

LONG FICTION:
Moran of the Lady Letty, 1898
McTeague, 1899
Blix, 1899
A Man's Woman, 1900
The Octopus: A Story of California, 1901
The Pit, 1903
Vandover and the Brute, 1914

SHORT FICTION:
A Deal in Wheat, and Other Stories of the New and Old West, 1903
The Joyous Miracle, 1906
The Third Circle, 1909
Frank Norris of "The Wave," 1931 (Oscar Lewis, editor)

POETRY:
Yvernelle: A Tale of Feudal France, 1892
Two Poems and "Kim" Reviewed, 1930

NONFICTION:
The Responsibilities of the Novelist, 1903
The Surrender of Santiago, 1917
The Letters of Frank Norris, 1956
The Literary Criticism of Frank Norris, 1964 (Donald Pizer, editor)

MISCELLANEOUS:
The Complete Edition of Frank Norris, 1928

About the Author

Boyd, Jennifer. *Frank Norris: Spatial Form and Narrative Time*. New York: Peter Lang, 1993.

Graham, Don, ed. *Critical Essays on Frank Norris*. Boston: G. K. Hall, 1980.

McElrath, Joseph R., Jr. "Beyond San Francisco: Frank Norris's Invention of Northern California." In *San Francisco in Fiction: Essays in a Regional Literature*, edited by David Fine and Paul Skenazy. Albuquerque: University of New Mexico Press, 1995.

_____. *Frank Norris Revisited*. New York: Twayne, 1992.

Marut, David. "Sam Lewiston's Bad Timing: A Note on the Economic Context of 'A Deal in Wheat.'" *American Literary Realism* 27 (Fall, 1994): 74-80.

Pizer, Donald. *The Novels of Frank Norris*. Bloomington: Indiana University Press, 1966.

_____, ed. *The Literary Criticism of Frank Norris*. Austin: University of Texas Press, 1964.

DISCUSSION TOPICS

- In what respects is Frank Norris the most thoroughgoing American exponent of literary naturalism as developed by Emile Zola?

- How appropriate is the San Francisco setting of *McTeague*?

- What is naturalistic in Norris's characterization of McTeague? In what ways is he a romantic character?

- In the two completed volumes of his trilogy, does Norris oversimplify the relationship of "wheat" and "the machine"?

- Does Norris carry out in his novels the responsibilities he outlines in "The Responsibilities of the Novelist"?

JOYCE CAROL OATES

Born: Lockport, New York
June 16, 1938

Recognized as a talented novelist and master of the short story, Oates has prolifically and passionately depicted the personal dislocation and troubled national identity of contemporary America.

© Norman Seeff

BIOGRAPHY

Joyce Carol Oates was born on June 16, 1938, in Lockport, New York, a small city on the Erie Barge Canal near Buffalo, to Fredric James and Caroline (Bush) Oates. Her father was a tool and die designer, and Oates's childhood was spent in a rural town, where she attended a one-room schoolhouse. From earliest memory she wanted to be an author. As a small child she drew pictures to tell stories; later she wrote them out, sometimes producing handwritten books of up to two hundred pages with carefully designed covers.

Oates's childhood was simple and happy, and she developed a closeness to her parents that flourished in her adult years. Her brother, Fredric, Jr., was born in 1943, and her sister, Lynn Ann, in 1956; in that year Oates graduated from Williamsville Central High School, where she had written for the school newspaper, and was entering Syracuse University under a New York State Regents Scholarship, the first in her family to attend college. During her freshman year, a tachycardiac seizure during a basketball game profoundly affected her view of life by bringing her face-to-face with her mortality. She continued writing stories, and in 1959 she was selected cowinner of the *Mademoiselle* college fiction award for "In the Old World." An excellent student, she was elected to Phi Beta Kappa and graduated in 1960 at the top of her class.

She received a Knapp Fellowship to pursue graduate work at the University of Wisconsin, where she met a Ph.D. candidate named Raymond Joseph Smith. She and Smith were married on January 23, 1961, and later that year she received her M.A. in English. Smith and Oates moved to Texas, where he taught in Beaumont and she began doctoral work at Rice University in Houston; however, with one of her stories appearing on the honor roll of Martha Foley's *Best American Short Stories*, Oates soon decided to devote herself to her writing.

Her first collection of stories, *By the North Gate*, appeared in 1963, followed a year later by her first novel, *With Shuddering Fall*, which, like many of her stories, depicted passionate individuals and violent situations. In 1967, *A Garden of Earthly Delights* appeared as the first novel in a thematic trilogy exploring the American obsession with money. It was followed by *Expensive People* (1968) and *them* (1969), the latter earning the 1970 National Book Award.

Oates taught at the University of Detroit from 1961 to 1967, when she and Smith accepted teaching positions at the University of Windsor in Ontario, Canada. A prolific author, Oates continued publishing stories in such periodicals as *Literary Review*, *Prairie Schooner*, and *Cosmopolitan*, and she produced a steady flow of books, including the novels *Wonderland* (1971), *Do with Me What You Will* (1973), *The Assassins: A Book of Hours* (1975), *Childwold* (1976), *Son of the Morning* (1978), and *Angel of Light* (1981); the story collections *Upon the Sweeping Flood* (1966), *The Wheel of Love* (1970), *Where Are You Going, Where Have You Been?* (1974), *The Goddess and Other Women* (1974), *The Seduction*

(1975), *Night-Side* (1977), and *A Sentimental Education: Stories* (1980); and volumes of poetry titled *Anonymous Sins, and Other Poems* (1969), *Angel Fire* (1973) and *Women Whose Lives Are Food, Men Whose Lives Are Money* (1978). Various other writings—essays, plays, and reviews—add to the unusual breadth of her oeuvre.

In 1978, Oates moved to New Jersey to become the Roger S. Berlind Distinguished Professor in the Humanities at Princeton University. From their home, she and Smith edited *The Ontario Review* and ran a small publishing company associated with the literary magazine. As her body of work grew, so did its formal and thematic diversity. *Bellefleur* (1980), *A Bloodsmoor Romance* (1982), and *Mysteries of Winterthurn* (1984) are experimental ventures into the genres, respectively, of the family chronicle, the romance, and the gothic mystery. After the experimental trilogy, her work turned more toward a modern naturalism. In the 1980's, her output included the novels *Solstice* (1985), *You Must Remember This* (1987), and *American Appetites* (1989) and the collections *Raven's Wing* (1986) and *The Assignation* (1988). In the 1990's, her novels included *Because It Is Bitter, and Because It Is My Heart* (1990), *Black Water* (1992), *Foxfire: Confessions of a Girl Gang* (1993), *What I Lived For* (1994), *We Were the Mulvaneys* (1996), and *Broke Heart Blues* (1999), as well as the short-story collections *Haunted: Tales of the Grotesque* (1994) and *The Collector of Hearts* (1998), the poetry collection *Tenderness* (1996), and several collections of plays. She continued her prolific output into the twenty-first century, with novels such as *Blonde* (2000), *I'll Take You There* (2002), and *The Falls* (2004), as well as the short-story collections *Faithless: Tales of Transgression* (2001) and *I Am No One You Know* (2004).

Oates's many honors include several O. Henry Awards for her short stories, Guggenheim and Rosenthal Fellowships, and election to the American Academy and Institute of Arts and Letters. She has had several National Book Award, National Book Critics Circle Award, and Pulitzer Prize nominations for her fiction, and in 2001 she won the National Book Award again for *Blonde*. In 2003, she was the recipient of the Common Wealth Award for Distinguished Service in Literature. She has traveled and lectured widely, and in December, 1987, was among a group of American artists, writers, and intellectuals invited to greet Soviet president Mikhail Gorbachev at the Soviet embassy in Washington, D.C. Over the years, her works have been translated into many other forms, including film, theatre, opera, and sound recordings. She has produced books on subjects as diverse as art and boxing, and has written widely on modern literature, collecting thirty-eight pieces from *The New York Review of Books, The Times Literary Supplement,* and *The New York Times Book Review* into *Uncensored: Views and (Re)views* (2005). Her extensive expression as a writer, thinker, and teacher have ensured Oates's role as a respected and vigorous participant in American intellectual and literary life from the 1960's onward.

ANALYSIS

In a literary tradition populated by many figures known for a single play or a handful of painstakingly wrought novels, Oates is notable first for her consistently prodigious output. Hundreds of stories and poems, printed and anthologized in a wide variety of publications, and dozens of novels, novellas, plays, essays, prefaces, and reviews have come from her pen, with an equally wide variety of settings, themes, genres, and styles. This productivity has even been a source of some criticism, inspiring suspicions that Oates works too fast and carelessly, that she lacks the basic self-censorship necessary to a writer. Oates, unaffected by criticism, has never slowed her pace. While some of her novels seem more felt than planned, and some of her stories inevitably overlap, Oates is a writer whose meanings can be appreciated cumulatively and whose craft and imagination are beyond question.

A more serious criticism is that her writing, especially in the 1960's and 1970's, is too violent, too dark, too obsessed with blood and death. (In 1981, in an essay in *The New York Times Book Review* titled "Why Is Your Writing So Violent?," Oates branded such criticism blatantly sexist and asserted the female novelist's right to depict nature as she sees it.) A typical Oates novel may feature mass murder, rape, suicide, arson, an automobile crash, or an autopsy, portrayed with detachment and graphic detail. Such violence is less a literal portrayal of the author's experience of life (though her great grandfather committed suicide in a rage after trying to kill his wife, Oates's own life has been relatively sedate) than an expression of the violence she sees beneath the surface of American life.

One of Oates's primary concerns is the shape of American identity in the twentieth century. Her novels often trace the lives of prototypical Americans and can be seen as paradigms of their collective history. Very aware of her parents' experiences through the 1930's, Oates often places the Depression at the beginning, chronologically if not narratively, of the stories she tells, for that is the source of much of the history of the 1960's, 1970's, and 1980's. (In *Bellefleur*, she goes further back to trace all of American history through a single family chronicle.) Many of her works are set in an imaginary Eden County, modeled on the Erie and Niagara counties of western New York. As the name suggests, Eden County is a mythical paradise where Oates depicts the American loss of innocence. *Because It Is Bitter, and Because It Is My Heart, What I Lived For, We Were the Mulvaneys*, and *Broke Heart Blues* continued to mine this theme in this setting in the 1990's.

Oates documents, and at times seems to prophesy, this loss of innocence through a pattern reflecting the American national heritage. This historical paradigm involves derivation from a strong familial tradition, be it the migrant workers of *A Garden of Earthly Delights* or the patricians of *The Assassins: A Book of Hours*; dislocation, often violent and senseless, from that home or tradition; the search for parent figures; the lack of fixed identity; acceptance of the American Dream, with all of its materialistic manifestations; emergence from poverty and anonymity; the obsession that arrives with single-minded pursuits; and the vacuity and transparency of contemporary American modes of being and communicating. *Black Water*, in 1992, was a thinly veiled retelling of the 1969 tragedy at Chappaquiddick, Massachusetts, where the young Mary Jo Kopechne drowned in the car of Senator Edward Kennedy, while *Blonde*, which won the National Book Award in 2001, was a fictional reworking of the life of Marilyn Monroe.

This paradigm is not inviolate, nor does it inform all of Oates's work. One of her most noted novels, *them*, is drawn quite faithfully from the life experience of a woman Oates knew while teaching in Detroit, and *Marya: A Life* (1986) is based to an extent on her mother's and her own early lives. Conversely, the stories in *Marriages and Infidelities* (1972) are modeled on (and even named for) earlier stories by acknowledged masters, such as James Joyce's "The Dead" (1914) and Franz Kafka's *Die Verwandlung* (1915; "The Metamorphosis," 1936), and their appreciation can depend on familiarity with—indeed, "marriage" to—their predecessors. A number of her works, including the satirical collection *The Hungry Ghosts: Seven Allusive Comedies* (1974), are set in academic institutions not unlike Oates's own universities of Windsor and Princeton.

Whatever the setting and the model for dramatic movement, certain themes are central. Oates is fascinated with the multiple facets of individual personality, and her characters often undergo dramatic upheavals and transformations (which are larger metaphorical expressions of the violence of modern life). They are constantly questioning who and where they are, constantly feeling detached from their bodies and their immediate experiences of the world. Nothing is certain or fixed. In such a whirlwind, emotion and sensation are all one can really know and trust; having a name; as the fundamental unit of identity, becomes of paramount importance.

Many of Oates's novels and stories, therefore, based in the emotional reality of a character, have a surrealistic quality. Oates is fascinated with dreams; not only do her characters relate theirs, but also the lines between perception, imagination, and dream or nightmare often become hazy. Because objective reality is unavailable, people become trapped within their own personalities, and connections between them are often tenuous and false. Many of the short stories, such as "The Census-Taker" (1963), "Where Are You Going, Where Have You Been?" (1966), "How I Contemplated the World from the Detroit House of Correction and Began My Life Over Again" (1969), "Queen of the Night" (1979), and "The Seasons" (1985), focus on jarring and unsuccessful encounters or relationships between very disparate personalities.

Generally, Oates's style is controlled and detached; her narrative voices do not cater to the reader but demand that the reader make necessary connections and assumptions. Her works are sometimes challenging puzzles that require careful attention. She is a skilled technician who uses precise and explicit language and portrays personality through detailed sketching of both interior and exterior reality. Not surprisingly, the imagery Oates employs is often violent: exposed flesh, broken glass, explosions, floods, fire. All these elements—

the detachment, the ambiguity, the detail, the imagery—combine to create an uncertain world where reality is constantly reconceived and reimagined through the window of perception, and truth—historical, subjective, and psychic—is everchanging.

A GARDEN OF EARTHLY DELIGHTS

First published: 1967, revised 2003
Type of work: Novel

A woman's quest to escape her impoverished past bequeaths to her son a world full of power but empty of meaning and identity.

A Garden of Earthly Delights is a novel that portrays the American economic system and the ills suffered both by those who fail and by those who succeed in it. Oates tells the story of Clara, from the day of her birth among migrant laborers to her waning years watching television in a nursing home, and the men—father, lovers, son—who define her life experience.

The title is taken from a dramatic triptych by the fifteenth century Dutch painter Hieronymus Bosch. The three panels of the original *Garden of Earthly Delights* illustrate Eve's creation in paradise, the debauchery of her descendants, and humankind's punishment in hell. Oates's novel mirrors this structure in its three sections. The first, titled "Carleton," focuses on a bitter migrant laborer named Carleton Walpole as he takes his growing family from state to state, struggling to control his rage and maintain his lost sense of dignity. Clara, the third and favorite of his five children, learns to look beyond the distress and misery of their migrant existence and eventually runs off with a virtual stranger to find a better life.

The second section, "Lowry," follows Clara through adolescence. The stranger, an enigmatic drifter named Lowry, sets her up in a small southern town, but he is involved in shady activities and soon disappears, spurning her obsessive love and unknowingly leaving her pregnant. Clara, a survivor, has attracted the attentions of a wealthy landowner, Curt Revere; she becomes his mistress, leads him to believe he is the father of her child, accepts his boundless generosity, and, with the death of his ailing wife, becomes the second Mrs. Revere.

Now established in comfort and wealth, having achieved a perfect vision of the American Dream, Clara consolidates her power. The third section of the novel, "Swan," focuses on Clara's son Steven (whom she calls Swan) and the pressures he feels growing up an outsider among someone else's wealth, destined to inherit it but unable to make sense of his destiny or to fulfill his mother's exaggerated expectations for him.

Within this structure, the narrative moves chronologically but with a greatly modulated pace. Oates relates individual scenes or periods in the lives of her characters with slow and careful accuracy and feeling, and then shifts the action months or years ahead, establishing the passage of time casually with age or year references. Such shifts highlight the suddenness of the events and changes that have occurred. This irregular flow serves to emphasize, as if microscopically, certain telling moments or encounters. Carleton's rage explodes during an arm-wrestling match, and he kills his best friend, an event that Clara recalls throughout her life. A jaunt into a nearby town where Clara impulsively steals a flag, her first night with Lowry, and her decision to run away are vividly portrayed and establish the fearlessness and pride that will bring tragedy in later life. A pivotal encounter comes at the end of the second section when, after years of silence, Lowry shows up at Clara's house to reclaim her: She does not love Revere, and she feels a flood of emotion at the sight of Lowry, but her resolution to accumulate power at any cost is too firm, and she sends her former lover—and her only hope for true happiness—away forever.

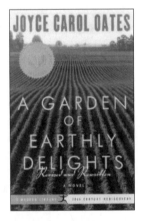

Swan, however, only three years old at the time, is affected by Lowry—by some deep instinct of his own paternity—and the knowledge of that ominous visitor stays with him. Swan is not at home with Revere and his rightful sons, for Swan's true identity has been sacrificed to Clara's lust for power. Though she acts with his future supremacy in mind, she cannot understand his psychic needs, and, in the novel's ultimate violent act, he refuses the power she has achieved for him and renders the struggles of her life meaningless.

Clara's is a very American story, for her ascent and accomplishments reach a point of diminishing returns, but she refuses to relent. Set against a subtly drawn backdrop of national events from the 1920's through the 1960's—the Depression, the renewal of industrial prosperity, the transformation of race relations and erosion of class structures in the South—Clara's story takes on wider repercussions as an American fable, with implicit commentary on the misguided motives and empty values of American political and materialistic ethics.

WONDERLAND

First published: 1971
Type of work: Novel

A young man undergoes a series of transformations as he comes to maturity and strives for identity in a dreamlike American landscape.

Wonderland bears certain rough similarities to *A Garden of Earthly Delights*. It follows three generations of a family through stages of rage, searching, and emptiness. It offers critical comment on the lust for knowledge and power. It spans a particular period of American political and economic history. It moves irregularly, with sudden shifts and changes. It also draws on another work of art as a model. *Wonderland*, is, however, stylistically much less naturalistic, its commentary more satirical, and its concern for the issues of dislocation and identity more fully focused on a single central character, Jesse.

As the title suggests, Oates used Lewis Carroll's *Alice's Adventures in Wonderland* (1865) as a thematic source for her novel. Like Alice, Jesse bursts into new worlds and must deal with characters that verge on caricatures and that parallel the Mad Hatter, Cheshire Cat, and others. Oates has taken Carroll's thematic framework and applied it sharply and imaginatively to the American scene.

The novel begins abruptly: Fourteen-year-old Jesse Harte returns home one day to find his family murdered by his crazed father. Jesse escapes through a window (like Alice's "looking glass") and is orphaned by his father's suicide. Emotionally numbed, Jesse embarks on a passive search for replacements—for a father figure, for a home, for a viable belief system, for a name that is truly his. He lives first with his silent, bitter grandfather (taking the surname Vogel), then with uncomprehending cousins, then in an orphanage.

Book 1 of the novel is titled "Variations on an American Hymn," and most of it details Jesse's life with the Pedersens, his adoptive family of freaks. The father is a dogmatic, morphine-addicted doctor/mystic, the mother an obsequious alcoholic, the son a blithering piano virtuoso, the daughter an angry mathematical genius. The Pedersens are all grotesquely obese, and with them Jesse expands accordingly. He takes their name and their ways but never gives himself completely to the doctor's maniacal egoism. In the end, after helping Mrs. Pedersen in an aborted attempt to escape, Jesse is disowned, dislocated, and, again, nameless.

He goes to college at the University of Michigan to study medicine and, an excellent student, falls under the tutelage of Drs. Cady and Perrault and an errant scientist and poet named T. W. Monk (whose poem "Wonderland" provides the epigraph to Oates's novel). Each of the men expresses a distinct and limited worldview—empiricism, behaviorism, nihilism—which Jesse adopts to a point but is unable to accept fully or embody.

He becomes a brilliant surgeon, marries Cady's daughter Helene, and fathers two daughters, but the marriage is unfulfilling, and Jesse becomes inexplicably obsessed with a woman he encounters at a chance moment in the emergency room—Reva Denk, whose name suggests "think/dream." Book 2, titled "The Finite Passing of an Infinite Passion," ends with Jesse's impulsive decision to begin a new life with Reva, and, once she agrees, his equally impulsive decision to return at once to Helene.

Book 3, "Dreaming America," alternates between Jesse's search for his runaway daughter Shelly and her angry, enigmatic letters home declaring insistently that his pursuits—of knowledge, of love, of wealth, of metaphysical supremacy—have ruined her life. Her letters contain veiled hints, and when Jesse finally locates her among a community of draft dodgers in Toronto, the novel ends on a reservedly optimistic note.

Throughout *Wonderland*, Oates's language and imagery are palpable and graphic. Certain scenes are striking: Hilda Pedersen gluttonously devouring chocolates during a mathematical competition; Helene's obsession with her own reproductive capacities turning to panic during a gynecological examination; a man, who turns out to be Reva's lover, arriving at Jesse's hospital self-mutilated; later, Jesse symbolically mutilating himself with a rusty razor before abandoning Reva. Such scenes reinforce the thematic presence of science and medicine as means of knowing and experiencing life. There are recurrent perceptions of living organisms as reduced to their simplest form, protoplasm, and as beings that emerge from and consume other beings. The concept of "homeostasis"—the natural tendency toward balance—which Dr. Pedersen asks Jesse to explain one evening at the dinner table, provides a standard for the desirable pattern of functioning that Jesse, not to mention the gallery of characters that surround him, cannot achieve.

Wonderland—which is also the name of the new shopping mall where the dissatisfied Helene meets her lover—is an Oatesian world of unnatural proportions where, like the Pedersens' obesity, ideas, emotions, and aspirations are often ridiculously reduced or magnified. The portraits Oates creates are exaggerated, narcissistic, and often very comical.

The only exception is Jesse, who lacks an inherent personality and becomes a reflection or embodiment of the people and ideas around him. Thus, the other characters take on the dimensions of allegory: They become emotional or philosophical options for him to review and try, but his movement through and experience of them, like his movement from name to name and home to home, leaves him at the novel's end only barely less innocent and passive than he was at its start. Ultimately, his search for identity and longing for a sense of solidity in his existence are the only reliable facts of his life.

THE ASSASSINS: A BOOK OF HOURS

First published: 1975
Type of work: Novel

After the supposed assassination of a prominent politician, his brothers and widow struggle to find meaning in their lives.

The Assassins: A Book of Hours is perhaps Oates's darkest and most pessimistic novel. It takes its subtitle from a canonical book that ends with the Office of the Dead, and it is concerned with characters mourning or obsessed with death.

The four characters central to the novel are Andrew Petrie, a former senator from New York and outspoken political observer; his brothers Hugh and Stephen; and his widow, Yvonne. Andrew himself is dead and appears only through memory or flashback; Hugh, Yvonne, and Stephen provide the viewpoints for the three parts of the novel, which are accordingly named for them.

"Hugh" begins enigmatically, and only later does it become evident that his diffuse and convoluted first-person narrative takes place within his conscious mind as he lies inexpressive and paralyzed in a hospital bed. Hugh is a bitter and sardonic political cartoonist who has devoted his life to hating and lampooning all that his successful older brother represents. His character—greedy, impotent, hypochondriac, alcoholic—is expressed through his obsessive rantings as he recounts his experience during the year following Andrew's death. Without Andrew, Hugh's life lacks the pivot on which it had turned. Consumed with a desire to discover his brother's assassins and convinced that Yvonne holds the key, he embarks on a maniacal pursuit of her and ends up a professional and romantic failure—even failing in his dramatically staged but essentially comic attempt at suicide.

Yvonne, the object of Hugh's deluded affections, is left completely isolated by her husband's death. Assisting the police, she draws up a list of Andrew's potential enemies, but the list is really an emblem of her own paranoia, for she views all others as her personal enemies and recedes further into her own private world. Having immersed herself completely in Andrew's intellectual life and their marriage, she strives after his death to continue his work, but soon that also loses meaning. She engages in casual affairs with various men connected with Andrew, but she is both frigid and incapable of bringing her lovers pleasure. Part 2, "Yvonne," ends with a violent scenario of Yvonne's death at the hands of ax-wielding assassins.

"Stephen" focuses on the youngest Petrie brother, who experienced a religious awakening as a teenager, dissociated himself completely from his family and its wealth, and has been living in a religious retreat. His last meeting with Andrew was a fiery one, and Andrew's death now challenges the peace Stephen has found by forcing him to acknowledge himself as a Petrie. In attending the funeral, in meeting with Hugh in New York and Yvonne in Albany, the firmness of his Jesuit foundation begins to disintegrate, and he finds himself deprived of his sense of God, and with it his sense of himself. He becomes an aimless and ever-accommodating drifter.

The three parts of the novel treat the same events, encounters, and revelations through three disparate perceptions; together they suggest an objective account of events and define the limitations of the individual personalities. The novel abounds in carefully wrought detail and corroboration, and it is populated with a world of other characters: the Petries' father, a ruthless judge now in retirement; their sister Doris, a plump suburban busybody; their cousin Pamela, a superficial society woman; their cousin Harvey, Andrew's cutthroat rival; Andrew's sensuous first wife, Willa, and brilliant son Michael; Hugh's psychoanalysts, Drs. Wynand and Swann; and the mysterious Raschke, a political activist from both Yvonne's and Stephen's pasts.

There is an element of mystery throughout *The Assassins*, for Hugh's desire to locate Andrew's assassins renders all the characters suspect and creates expectations that the murder will be solved at the end of the novel. The title and the mystery are misleading, however, for Oates's "assassins" are the characters themselves, who, through their obsessions and limited vision, unwittingly murder themselves and one another. It is even intimated that Andrew's death, on which so much depends, was not an assassination at all but a carefully disguised suicide.

The Assassins is a challenging novel, for Oates demands that the reader join together the disparate elements of the story. Though the three sections are expressed through three different temperaments, they all have a staccato, nearly stream-of-consciousness flow which can blend memory, conjecture, dream, imagination, and physical reality into a single stratum of experience. Thus, certain issues are unclear: Hugh's condition at the outset, the circumstances of Andrew's death, and whether Yvonne's brutal murder is real or imagined.

Such questions fade beneath the psychic weight of the novel. Philosophically, the work shows the influence of the American philosopher William James, whose *The Varieties of Religious Experience* (1902) may have suggested a thematic model. James was concerned with the tyranny of pluralism and the inability of individuals to connect. *The Assassins* portrays three philosophical approaches— Hugh reduces all to two dimensions, ridiculing it; Yvonne reduces all to reason, sterilizing it; and Stephen reduces all to God, subsuming it in mystery— and all the approaches fail, leaving the characters trapped within their own egos. They deny necessary aspects of reality, thereby denying the possibility of love, and effectively assassinate any real life that exists within.

SOLSTICE

First published: 1985
Type of work: Novel

A friendship between two women, a newly divorced young schoolteacher and a flamboyant and somewhat celebrated painter, develops to an intensity that threatens their lives.

During the early part of her career, Oates was viewed as a woman writer on the periphery of the women's movement. In the 1980's, her writing began to focus more frequently on stories and characters with particularly feminine or feminist concerns. *Solstice*, like *Marya: A Life* which followed it, exemplifies this development, portraying a relationship between two women in a small Pennsylvania town.

Monica Jensen, recently divorced and attempting to start a new life in the wake of her failed marriage, has relocated from New York City and accepted a teaching assignment at the local boys' academy. Sheila Trask, older and more worldly, is a successful artist, the widow of a famous sculptor; she lives alone and detached from the community in a fine old country house. The novel, which is told from Monica's viewpoint, is divided into four sections that reflect four stages in her development.

The first, titled, "The Scar," details Monica's adjustment to country life, her first casual encounters with Sheila, and her growing attraction to the other's lively personality. Sheila is the stronger of the two, and Monica, in emotional recovery, is timid, hesitant, and flattered to accept Sheila's friendly attention.

As the two become acquainted, their friendship becomes the foundation of their social lives. "The Mirror-Ghoul," the second section, shows the process by which the women come to know each other's strengths and weaknesses, to provide necessary support, to reflect each other. On Sheila's urging, they begin frequenting local taverns and bowling alleys, pretending to be lively country divorcees; this activity delights Sheila but leads to adventures and moral considerations that discomfort and frighten Monica. Eventually, Sheila becomes demanding and burdensome to Monica; Monica withdraws. Sheila's work suffers, and she drinks and takes pills; by Christmas, mere months after their first meeting, their confrontations crescendo and plummet into silence. Sheila disappears; Monica assumes she has gone globe-trotting to Paris or Morocco.

Part 3 is "Holiday," a period of separation. Monica returns to her family in Indiana for the New Year holiday and mourns the passing of her golden adolescence. Returning from vacation, she is keenly aware of Sheila's absence. She begins dating an attorney but without feeling any passion; she becomes more involved with her work and students; she misses Sheila but tries not to think of her.

Then Sheila returns, and with her the relationship, the obsessive behavior, and the manipulation. Monica can identify the effect that Sheila is having on her, but she cannot stop it. She allows herself to become indispensable to Sheila's life, including the running of the house and the arrangement of an upcoming exhibition. She neglects her own work at school, then her health as well, until she is relieved of her teaching responsibilities. Her friendship with Sheila is now consuming and debilitating: The women lose the ability to console or support each other, move in and out of illness, and behave with veiled malice or open spite. In the end, Monica's health deteriorates so dramatically that Sheila finds her helpless and rushes her to the hospital, where she possibly may die.

The title of this last section, "Labyrinth," is taken from a painting Sheila is doing of the mythical Ariadne and her arduous journey out of the maze of the Minotaur's palace. The novel is itself Monica's account of her similar journey, and the narrative twists and turns with labyrinthine complexity. It is also, as the title suggests, about a sort of solstice—the passing of two distinct and very different bodies in a close, rare, and distorting conjunction.

Solstice is episodic; it creates portraits of Monica, Sheila, and their interaction through occasional moments, diverse comments, and unconnected impressions. It is more straightforward and naturalistic than much of Oates's writing, yet its apparent simplicity is misleading, for beneath the daily texture of the relationship portrayed, even at its most intense moments, is a deeper reality of repressed emotion and personality. Monica, seeking an easy escape from a painful past—including an abortion to which she rarely refers—and Sheila, using sham joy and passion to avoid facing her art, her fear, and her loneliness, both refuse to confront the deeper truths of their lives. Their emotional dishonesty renders their friendship futile and brings them, by the novel's inconclusive end, to the brink of tragedy.

BECAUSE IT IS BITTER, AND BECAUSE IT IS MY HEART

First published: 1990
Type of work: Novel

The violent link between a young white girl and a black schoolmate follows them through their lives, underscoring race relations in mid-twentieth century America.

Because It Is Bitter, and Because It Is My Heart has many of the elements that readers come to expect from

Joyce Carol Oates—violence, drama, mystery—but also the complex social and economic portrait of American life in the 1950's and 1960's that she is so good at drawing. The story of Iris Courtney and Jinx Fairchild is another Oates account of adolescent love and frustration, but it is also a searing portrait of the effects of social class and race in the United States.

The novel is broken into three parts and an epilogue. Part 1 opens with the discovery of the body of "Little Red" Garlock in the Cassadaga River in Hammond, New York, sixty miles south of Lake Ontario. Vicious and deranged, the boy has followed fourteen-year-old Iris one night in April, 1956. When Jinx tries to protect her, the two boys fight, and Jinx kills Little Red with a rock and dumps his body in the river. The murder is neither witnessed nor solved, but its consequences will haunt Iris and Jinx. Drawn by mutual attraction and guilt to each other, they speak of their connection only rarely. Iris is isolated in a downwardly mobile white family, with an alcoholic mother and a gambler father. She avoids her parents through schoolwork, and after their separation, the mother dies of her addiction. Iris wins a scholarship to nearby Syracuse University and loses herself in the study of art history, but she continues her isolated life.

Jinx Fairchild's life seems more promising. A talented basketball player, he focuses on his sport even more after the crime and seems poised for a college scholarship and a way out of Hammond. In a final game, however, Jinx falls awkwardly and breaks his leg, thus destroying any chance of a better future. It is clear that in some way Jinx has punished himself for his crime. A few years later, he is working in a machine shop, married and with children, and finally gets away in 1963 by joining the U.S. Army and heading for death in Vietnam.

Iris at least escapes: Working for a brilliant art historian at Syracuse, she allows herself to be figuratively adopted by Dr. Savage and his wife and in the epilogue is engaged to their son, Alan. On a final visit to Hammond, Iris finds a picture that Jinx has left her and confesses, "I loved him." Connected by the crime, they have been kept apart, not only by their guilt but also by the class and racial lines drawn so clearly in Hammond in the 1950's and early 1960's. At the end of the novel, John F. Kennedy has been assassinated, the Civil Rights movement has started, and those lines are starting to change. Oates captures well the thoughts, feelings, and conversations of young people, but she is equally adroit in drawing the larger socioeconomic portrait of Americans, young and old, fixed in their racial and class positions in the middle of the twentieth century.

"WHERE ARE YOU GOING, WHERE HAVE YOU BEEN?"

First published: 1966 (collected in *Where Are You Going, Where Have You Been?*, 1974)
Type of work: Short story

A teenage girl escapes her family's mundane life, only to fall into a dreamlike journey toward sexuality and death.

Of all Joyce Carol Oates's stories, "Where Are You Going, Where Have You Been?" has generated the most critical commentary and the most discussion. After it was originally published, Oates added the dedication to Bob Dylan for his song "It's All Over Now Baby Blue" (where the title question occurs), a song she called "very beautiful, very disturbing," and which recalled to her the legend of Death and the Maiden. The story itself moves from intense psychological realism to surreal myth.

The story starts innocently enough with a description of the fifteen-year-old Connie, who, like many adolescent girls, sleepwalks through life listening to music only she seems to hear. Connie and her friends frequent the mall, and she has begun some kind of sexual experimentation and has been with boys "the way it was in movies and promised in songs."

The mythic journey begins one hot Sunday afternoon when Connie is home alone—having refused to accompany her family to a barbecue—and two boys in an open jalopy pull into her driveway. She recognizes one of them from the mall the night before, but she knows neither and, as she talks with the driver through her screen door, the scene becomes more and more dreamlike. The driver introduces himself as "Arnold Friend" and his passenger as "Ellie," but something is wrong about both of them. For one thing, Arnold's language—the rambling patter with which he assaults her—is out-of-date. In addition, although he wears the standard 1950's dress of jeans and tight shirt, he has trouble walking in his boots, seems to be wearing a wig, and is older than he appears. He invites her to come riding with them, and Connie is mesmerized, dizzied by his incantatory words. He knows intimate details of her life that no stranger could know and threatens her family, and she feels helpless to resist him. She opens the door to a "land that Connie had never seen before and did not recognize except to know that she was going to it."

On one level, Oates seems to be blaming the shallow Connie for her fate, and there certainly is a hint of criticism here for young people seduced by mass culture, especially music, and the "trashy daydreams" of teenage love. At a deeper level of the story, however, Connie and Arnold are acting out some mythic dance. "Arnold Friend" is a rough approximation of "An Old Friend"—the devil, the Antichrist, Pan, and/or death. He draws an X in the air—a cross turned on its side—and both he and Connie exclaim "Christ!" The theme of Death and the Maiden, of a young girl seduced not toward sex but toward extinction, runs beneath this powerful and disturbing story. Beneath the superficial strains of popular music and adolescent culture, Oates warns, lurks the sexuality that leads, if not to death, then to a violent end of innocence.

"IN THE REGION OF ICE"

First published: 1966 (collected in *The Wheel of Love*, 1970)
Type of work: Short story

A nun's encounter with a brilliant but disturbed young man illustrates her emotional isolation and spiritual sterility.

"In the Region of Ice," first published in *The Atlantic Monthly* and later in the collection *The Wheel of Love*, won the O. Henry first prize in short fiction for 1967. It shares with other early Oates works, including the novel *Son of the Morning* (1978) and the story "Shame" (1968), a religious protagonist and a concern for spiritual issues. Sister Irene teaches the works of William Shakespeare at a small, Catholic university. For all practical purposes, she lives "in the region of ice"—a region void of feeling and passion. She is perfectly comfortable in front of a class lecturing on literature, but otherwise she is timid and essentially incapable of developing meaningful human contact.

Into her insulated existence comes Allen Weinstein, a brilliant but emotionally disturbed Jewish student. Having failed to cope successfully in his own discipline, history, and obsessed with the reality of ideas, he sits in on Irene's class and, unlike the other students, challenges and engages her. Eventually he dominates the class, inspiring the hatred of his classmates but awakening intellectual and emotional life in the professor.

The story is narrated through Irene's viewpoint, and Oates carefully charts the emotional journey she travels in response to Allen's erratic and striking behavior. Inexplicably, Irene finds herself anticipating Allen's presence and feeling hurt at his absence; her emotional life becomes dependent on his behavior, moods, and ideas. Their relationship, through her perception, is like a dance of intellectual passion and spiritual magnetism.

Then Allen stops coming to class. After a prolonged absence, he contacts Irene from a sanatorium with a veiled plea for help: quoting Claudio in Shakespeare's *Measure for Measure* (1604), he begs her to communicate his passion to his father. As Irene goes to the Weinstein home to do Allen's bidding, she feels a religious awakening, a sense of her Christianity and the true meaning of sacrifice, but her heroism quickly fades, and she allows herself to be bullied by Allen's hateful, exasperated, unsympathetic father.

Later, released from the sanatorium and desperate to leave the country, Allen comes to Irene for emotional and financial support, but she painfully and inarticulately denies him. Now, as throughout their unusual relationship, she is equally aware of his desire to establish a meaningful communion and of her own inability to oblige. She is simply terrified of being connected to another human being. While Allen is clearly on the edge of sanity, Irene's situation is more pathetic, for she is knowingly trapped within the trivial limits of her own selfhood. Even the inevitable news of Allen's suicide provokes only a longing for feeling but no true emotional response.

Like "Where Are You Going, Where Have You Been?," "In the Region of Ice" details the effects of a male intruder into the life of a female protagonist. Here, the emotional power of the story lies in the lack of response, in the utter sterility that remains invulnerable against great passion and anguish. Oates depicts in Sister Irene the very human discrepancy between the ideals of the mind and the limits of the individual will in real life. The "ice" of the title goes beyond the cold clarity of academia and the chosen celibacy of the nun's habit to describe the irony of an emotionally frigid human being taking refuge in a frail travesty of spiritual and humanitarian fullness.

"How I Contemplated the World from the Detroit House of Correction and Began My Life Over Again"

First published: 1969 (collected in *The Wheel of Love*, 1970)
Type of work: Short story

The graphic confessions of a teenage runaway reveal the gap between suburban wealth and inner-city poverty.

Like a number of Joyce Carol Oates's titles, both short stories such as "Where Are You Going, Where Have You Been?" and novels such as *Foxfire*, "How I Contemplated the World from the Detroit House of Correction and Began My Life Over Again" describes a troubled teenage girl. Subtitled "Notes for an Essay for an English Class at Baldwin Country Day School; Poking Around in Debris; Disgust and Curiosity; A Revelation of the Meaning of Life; A Happy Ending . . . ," the story nervously straddles this double focus: On one hand, an outline for a composition any teenager might write for English class, the story also unfolds as a vivid descent into a violent world of sex and drugs.

The form of the story seems to contradict its content. Each of the numbered paragraphs in this prose outline comes under one of twelve major sections: "I Events," "II Characters," and so on, but this apparent attempt to order reality quickly breaks down as the content of the essay reveals itself: A sixteen-year-old girl has been caught stealing gloves from an expensive suburban Detroit store, and her shoplifting is only a hint of deeper problems. Later, the girl takes a bus to inner-city Detroit, where for two weeks she lives with a thirty-five-year-old drug addict named Simon and his prostitute girlfriend, Clarita. When Simon tires of the girl, he passes her to friends and finally to the police, where she is savagely beaten by two girls in a lavatory of the Detroit House of Correction. By the last section ("XII Events"), she has been returned home, repeating to herself, almost like a mantra meant to produce happiness, "*I will never leave home, this is my home. . . .*"

In all of its graphic violence, the story is a powerful indictment of contemporary, 1960's American society. As quickly becomes clear, the girl is a member of a dysfunctional family, her troubled brother away at a boarding school, her doctor-father's only advice after her tragedy, "Honey, we're going to forget all about this." The story also dramatizes the gap between rich and poor in the United States, between a life of privilege at an elite private school in a wealthy Detroit suburb and the bleak inner-city world of poverty, drugs, and prostitution just a few miles away.

The structure of the story in fact perfectly frames its content, in the tension between the cold, mechanical outline of the theme and the surreal stream of consciousness from the disturbed girl within. Beneath the apparent calm and privilege of this suburban life—like the rigid outline of the composition itself—lies a world of pain and suffering. The outline, like the girl, however, soon breaks down, and events start to repeat themselves. Like the car "perpetually turning" into the Bloomfield Hills driveway, the story is a cycle that repeats itself. As the girl confesses halfway through her outline, "Would I go back to Simon again? Would I lie down with him in all that filth and craziness? Over and over again." The nightmare appears bound to recur.

"IN THE AUTUMN OF THE YEAR"

First published: 1978 (collected in *A Sentimental Education*, 1980)
Type of work: Short story

A successful poet is forced by her former lover's son to reexamine the only passionate romance of her life.

"In the Autumn of the Year" received an O. Henry Award in 1979, a year after its first publication in *The Bennington Review*. Like many of Oates's stories, it tells of a single but important encounter between a man and a woman from different backgrounds and with different attitudes.

The protagonist, Eleanor Gerhardt, is a Pulitzer Prize-winning poet, an articulate spinster suggestive of the nineteenth century American poet Emily Dickinson, who has come to a small New England college to accept an award. Her host for the visit is Benjamin Höller, a man she knew as a boy in Boston, because at the time she was his father's mistress. Eleanor, now sixty-three years old, lives life with a sense of its near-completion. She lives in the past and no longer considers herself an active, feeling woman. Never married, her passion for Edwin Höller and the dramatic dissolution of their relationship form a memory that she sustains, though she has not seen him in decades and he is now dead. Upon meeting Benjamin and throughout her visit in his midst, her consciousness shifts back and forth from the uneventful present to the tumultuous and deeply felt past.

Then, in a casual meeting after the ceremony, Benjamin and Eleanor start discussing his father. To Eleanor's surprise, Benjamin expresses accumulated anger and hatred. As he openly confronts her with his father's cruelty, her own insensitivity, the cheapness of their affair, and their responsibility for the emotional misery of his childhood, her sentimental vision of the past is shattered. She tries impulsively to protest her innocence, but she is shocked and left essentially speechless. Benjamin offers her the love letters and suicide threats that she sent to Edwin upon their separation, but she cannot face them and denies their authenticity. In the end, alone, she tosses the unopened letters in the fire, as if so doing will alleviate her guilt and folly.

Oates uses balance to create powerful emotional dynamics. The juxtaposition of immediate experience and memory communicates the temporal and emotional dislocation with which Eleanor perceives her existence in the "autumn" of her life. Her detached contemplation of seemingly imminent death and the subsequent disposition of her worldly goods contrasts sharply with the suicidal desperation she recalls enduring when Edwin deserted her. The device of remembering a distant past in which she imagined a distant future—now arrived—reinforces the swirling sense of her life.

The second half of the story comes suddenly and unexpectedly, and Benjamin's brutal honesty plays against the complacent politeness of their earlier encounters. Unbeknown to Eleanor, he provides a missing piece to the puzzle of her life. Without the delusions by which her past drained her present of meaning, she is forced to face the past honestly and, recognizing its mixed qualities, to let go of it. Through this encounter, she can begin to take responsibility for her continued existence and for the long-repressed reality of herself as a woman who is still very much alive and capable of deep feeling.

"RAVEN'S WING"

First published: 1985 (collected in *Raven's Wing*, 1986)
Type of work: Short story

A husband's fascination with a wounded racehorse imperceptibly reinvigorates his marriage with warmth and understanding.

"Raven's Wing," a story in the volume of the same title, first appeared in *Esquire* and was included in *The Best American Short Stories, 1985*. It is a brief story, told with simplicity and subtlety and without the violence and passion of much of Oates's other work, presenting a slice-of-life view of a rather ordinary marriage.

Billy is thirty-two years old and has been married to his twenty-four-year-old second wife, Linda, for barely a year. Though Linda is pregnant, Billy feels little passion for or interest in her, and he treats her with indifference and condescension. Linda, in turn, to stimulate his attention, baits, teases, and spites him. Their conversations are empty and end in noncommittal bickering.

Billy, who likes racing and gambling, becomes fascinated with a two-million-dollar racehorse named Raven's Wing after it is crippled during a race. Linda cannot understand Billy's fascination with the horse's sheer size and value—he tells her that she lacks the adequate "frame of reference." He resourcefully finds a way to visit Raven's Wing in Pennsylvania, where it is recovering from major surgery, and, eye-to-eye with it, feels a sense of connection, an implicit mixture of awe, sympathy, and trust.

The story ends a short time later in two brief scenes. Billy gives Linda a pair of delicate earrings and finds excitement in watching her put them on. Weeks later, as he talks on the telephone, Linda comes to him warmly, holding out a few strands of coarse black hair, and presses close against him.

In "Raven's Wing," rather than stating Billy's true feelings, of which he himself is only hazily aware, Oates suggests them through the details of external reality. Billy's boredom with his home life is contrasted by his unexpected fascination with the racehorse. When he has "the vague idea" that Linda is pregnant with "another man's baby," and when he has sudden violent impulses toward her, he is responding less to her character or behavior than to his own inner discontent. In reality, it is his own "frame of reference" that is inadequate.

Oates's story is about perception—about how things appear differently through the blurring lens of familiarity and routine. At one point, Billy remembers seeing a beautiful woman on the street; only after a moment did he realize that it was Linda, unusually dressed up and looking very sexy.

At another point, Linda, seeking to engage him, says that if men had to have the babies they probably would not do it; Billy barely hears her, just as he does not appreciate how full his own life truly is, if he would only recognize it.

It is the encounter with Raven's Wing that helps him to see. His fascination with the crippled creature betrays an unconscious awareness of the crippled state of his own psyche. Billy's astonishment at the size, beauty, and value of the prize animal implicitly compares with the insensitivity of his attitude toward Linda. Similarly, the millions of dollars spent to save the horse for stud purposes humble Billy and bring home the reality of Linda's pregnancy, of the very human power they share to love, to support, and to create.

The end of the story suggests, through the gift of the earrings, a more comfortable intimacy and Billy's heightened awareness of Linda, indicating that the nature of their relationship has undergone a slight but very important shift. The black hairs that Linda holds, which are never explicitly identified, are a good luck souvenir from the mane of Raven's Wing.

SUMMARY

The novels and stories of Oates offer a plethora of subjects, styles, themes, and philosophical concerns; given their wide publication and anthologizing, they have reached an unusually large audience. Throughout Oates's work is a concern not only to articulate her perception of personal and social conditions but also to delve imaginatively into the depths of meaning she finds there. By dreaming and re-imagining America, she invites her readers to explore the true nature of the world around them.

Barry Mann; updated by David Peck

BIBLIOGRAPHY

By the Author

LONG FICTION:
With Shuddering Fall, 1964
A Garden of Earthly Delights, 1967, revised 2003
Expensive People, 1968
them, 1969
Wonderland, 1971

Do with Me What You Will, 1973
The Assassins: A Book of Hours, 1975
Childwold, 1976
The Triumph of the Spider Monkey, 1976
Son of the Morning, 1978
Unholy Loves, 1979
Cybele, 1979
Bellefleur, 1980
Angel of Light, 1981
A Bloodsmoor Romance, 1982
Mysteries of Winterthurn, 1984
Solstice, 1985
Marya: A Life, 1986
Lives of the Twins, 1987 (as Rosamond Smith)
You Must Remember This, 1987
American Appetites, 1989
Soul/Mate, 1989 (as Smith)
Because It Is Bitter, and Because It Is My Heart, 1990
I Lock My Door upon Myself, 1990
Nemesis, 1990 (as Smith)
The Rise of Life on Earth, 1991
Black Water, 1992
Snake Eyes, 1992 (as Smith)
Foxfire: Confessions of a Girl Gang, 1993
What I Lived For, 1994
You Can't Catch Me, 1995 (as Smith)
Zombie, 1995
We Were the Mulvaneys, 1996
First Love, 1996
Man Crazy, 1997
My Heart Laid Bare, 1998
Broke Heart Blues, 1999
Starr Bright Will Be with You Soon, 1999 (as Smith)
Blonde, 2000
The Barrens, 2001 (as Smith)
Middle Age: A Romance, 2001
Beasts, 2002
I'll Take You There, 2002
The Tattooed Girl, 2003
Rape: A Love Story, 2003
The Falls, 2004

SHORT FICTION:
By the North Gate, 1963
Upon the Sweeping Flood, 1966
The Wheel of Love, 1970
Marriages and Infidelities, 1972
The Goddess and Other Women, 1974
The Hungry Ghosts: Seven Allusive Comedies, 1974
Where Are You Going, Where Have You Been?, 1974

DISCUSSION TOPICS

- Identify the gothic elements in the fiction of Joyce Carol Oates.

- Oates has been accused of excessive violence in her novels and stories. What purpose does it serve in her fiction?

- How does point of view operate in an Oates novel or short story? Is it consistent? Does it shift among different characters?

- What does Oates say about contemporary American society? What are its preoccupations, its limitations?

- How does the American family thrive in Oates's works? What are its strengths, and what are its problems?

- Do Oates's protagonists come to some understanding of their identity?

The Poisoned Kiss, 1975
The Seduction, 1975
Crossing the Border, 1976
Night-Side, 1977
All the Good People I've Left Behind, 1978
The Lamb of Abyssalia, 1979
A Sentimental Education, 1980
Last Days, 1984
Raven's Wing, 1986
The Assignation, 1988
Heat, and Other Stories, 1991
Where Is Here?, 1992
Haunted: Tales of the Grotesque, 1994
Will You Always Love Me?, 1994
The Collector of Hearts, 1998
Faithless: Tales of Transgression, 2001
I Am No One You Know, 2004

POETRY:
Women in Love, 1968
Anonymous Sins, and Other Poems, 1969
Love and Its Derangements, 1970
Angel Fire, 1973
The Fabulous Beasts, 1975
Women Whose Lives Are Food, Men Whose Lives Are Money, 1978
Invisible Woman: New and Selected Poems, 1970-1982, 1982
The Luxury of Sin, 1984
The Time Traveler, 1989
Tenderness, 1996

DRAMA:
Miracle Play, pr. 1974
Three Plays, pb. 1980
In Darkest America: Two Plays, pb. 1991
I Stand Before You Naked, pb. 1991
Twelve Plays, pb. 1991
The Perfectionist, and Other Plays, pb. 1995
New Plays, pb. 1998

NONFICTION:
The Edge of Impossibility: Tragic Forms in Literature, 1972
The Hostile Sun: The Poetry of D. H. Lawrence, 1973
New Heaven, New Earth: The Visionary Experience in Literature, 1974
Contraries: Essays, 1981
The Profane Art: Essays and Reviews, 1983
On Boxing, 1987
(Woman) Writer: Occasions and Opportunities, 1988
George Bellows: American Artist, 1995
Where I've Been, and Where I'm Going: Essays, Reviews, and Prose, 1999
The Faith of a Writer: Life, Craft, Art, 2003
Uncensored: Views and (Re)views, 2005

CHILDREN'S LITERATURE:
Come Meet Muffin, 1998
Big Mouth and Ugly Girl, 2002
Freaky Green Eyes, 2003

EDITED TEXTS:
Scenes from American Life: Contemporary Short Fiction, 1972
The Best American Short Stories 1979, 1979 (with Shannon Ravenel)
Night Walks: A Bedside Companion, 1982
First Person Singular: Writers on Their Craft, 1983
The Best American Essays, 1991
The Oxford Book of American Short Stories, 1992
American Gothic Tales, 1996
Snapshots: Twentieth Century Mother-Daughter Fiction, 2000 (with Janet Berliner)

About the Author

Bender, Eileen Teper. *Joyce Carol Oates: Artist in Residence.* Bloomington: Indiana University Press, 1987.

Bloom, Harold, ed. *Modern Critical Views: Joyce Carol Oates.* New York: Chelsea House, 1987.

Cologne-Brookes, Gavin. *Dark Eyes on America: The Novels of Joyce Carol Oates.* Baton Rouge: Louisiana State University Press, 2005.

Creighton, Joanne V. *Joyce Carol Oates: Novels of the Middle Years.* New York: Twayne, 1992.

Daly, Brenda O. *Lavish Self-Divisions: The Novels of Joyce Carol Oates.* Jackson: University Press of Mississippi, 1996.

Johnson, Greg. *Invisible Writer: A Biography of Joyce Carol Oates.* New York: Dutton, 1998.

_____. *Understanding Joyce Carol Oates.* Columbia: University of South Carolina Press, 1987.

Wagner-Martin, Linda, ed. *Critical Essays on Joyce Carol Oates.* Boston: G. K. Hall, 1979.

TIM O'BRIEN

Born: Austin, Minnesota
October 1, 1946

Long considered to be the most talented writer of the Vietnam War experience, O'Brien explores the ground between courage and cowardice, love and betrayal, and storytelling and truth in his highly regarded short stories and novels.

Marion Ettlinger/Library of Congress

BIOGRAPHY

Tim O'Brien was born as William Timothy O'Brien, Jr., in Austin, Minnesota on October 1, 1946, to William Timothy O'Brien, an insurance agent, and Ave E. Schultz O'Brien, a second-grade teacher. His parents met each other while serving in the Navy during World War II. O'Brien's sister Kathleen was born one year later, and his brother Greg ten years after O'Brien's birth. The family moved to the small town of Worthington, Minnesota, while O'Brien was in elementary school, and they remained there throughout his childhood and adolescence. Growing up in such a small town impacted O'Brien greatly and influenced his decision about going into the military.

The O'Brien family was deeply involved in reading and language. As a member of the Worthington library board, Mr. O'Brien brought home many books for the children to read. Indeed, each member of the O'Brien household seems to have been a dedicated reader.

O'Brien's relationship with his father was a sometimes troubled one. Although O'Brien admired his father's knowledge and intellect, the senior O'Brien's alcoholism damaged what might have otherwise been a close relationship. When he was drinking, William O'Brien was cruel to the youngster. Further, his father was frequently institutionalized for alcoholism, and young O'Brien felt his absence keenly. It was difficult for him to

talk about his home situation with other youngsters, and it left him often feeling awkward and self-conscious. As a result of this, O'Brien began a childhood fascination with magic. He performed in many venues around Worthington. Although his interest faded with time, his early connection to magic surfaces in his novel *In the Lake of the Woods* (1994).

O'Brien graduated from Worthington in 1964 and began studying at Macalester College in St. Paul, Minnesota. During his senior year, he served as student body president. Although Macalester was quiet compared to other colleges and universities where war protests were becoming increasingly violent, O'Brien opposed the war and worked for the nomination of Eugene McCarthy for president.

In 1968, O'Brien graduated from Macalester Phi Beta Kappa and summa cum laude. Within two weeks of graduation, he received his draft notice. O'Brien details this experience in his memoir *If I Die in a Combat Zone, Box Me Up and Ship Me Home* (1973). He soon found himself in Vietnam and in combat.

Some of O'Brien's most difficult experiences occurred while serving in an area known as "Pinkville" in 1969. Both My Lai and My Khe, the sites of American massacres of Vietnamese villagers in 1968, are located in this area. Pinkville was a place of great danger and ambiguity; it was difficult for the soldiers to distinguish friend from foe.

After returning from Vietnam, O'Brien enrolled in the fall of 1970 at Harvard University to begin doctoral work in political science. At the same time, he expanded his own writing. He served summer internships at *The Washington Post* and eventually took a job there in 1973-1974. In 1973, he married Anne Weller, who also worked in the publishing business.

Although O'Brien continued with his graduate work while writing his early novels, he left Harvard about 1976, his dissertation unfinished. He published *If I Die in a Combat Zone, Box Me Up and Ship Me Home* in 1973; *Northern Lights* in 1975; and *Going After Cacciato* in 1978. Not only did two stories from *Going After Cacciato* win O. Henry Awards, but the book itself also captured the 1979 National Book Award. *Going After Cacciato* received both critical and popular acclaim, with many readers judging it to be the finest work to date on the Vietnam War.

O'Brien turned slightly from his Vietnam material with his next novel, *The Nuclear Age* (1981), in that he sets the book in the United States during the Cold War. The book did not receive strong reviews, and few critics have undertaken studies of this volume. Throughout his writing of *The Nuclear Age* and in the years immediately after its publication, O'Brien began publishing in magazines a series of short stories about Vietnam. One of these stories, "The Things They Carried," won the National Magazine Award in Fiction in 1989.

In 1990, O'Brien published a volume of fiction comprising these stories and additional new material called *The Things They Carried*. *The New York Times* selected the book as one of the ten best works of fiction for the year, and the *Chicago Tribune* awarded the novel its Heartland Prize. *The Things They Carried* was also a finalist for the Pulitzer Prize in 1990 and went on to win both the Melcher Award and the Prix du Meilleur Livre Étranger (Prize for the Best Book by a Foreign Writer) in France.

O'Brien's next book, *In the Lake of the Woods*, appeared in 1994, a particularly difficult year for O'Brien, in spite of this novel's success; it was named by *Time* magazine as the best work of fiction for the year and later won the James Fenimore Cooper Prize. He returned to Vietnam for his first visit since the war; he separated from his wife (they divorced in 1995); and he endured the breakup of an important relationship. Some of this is evident in his anguished essay "The Vietnam in Me," which appeared in *The New York Times Magazine* on October 2, 1994.

In 1998, O'Brien published his next novel, *Tomcat in Love*, the story of a not-so-nice linguistics professor. Critics were sharply divided in their response to the book. O'Brien's eighth book, *July, July*, published in 2002, follows the lives of the class of 1969 as they return for their thirty-year class reunion. In 1999, O'Brien moved to Southwest Texas State University where, as of 2005, he continued to teach creative writing.

ANALYSIS

All of O'Brien's books touch on the Vietnam War, if only peripherally. However, *Going After Cacciato*, *The Things They Carried*, and *In the Lake of the Woods*, along with the memoir *If I Die in a Combat Zone, Box Me Up and Ship Me Home*, are deeply concerned with the experience of the war. O'Brien uses the Vietnam War as a means to explore courage, memory, truth, and the art of storytelling in these books.

Courage, and its reverse, cowardice, are important themes throughout O'Brien's work. In both his memoir and his stories such as "On the Rainy River" from *The Things They Carried*, O'Brien reaches the conclusion that he found himself in the infantry not because he was brave but rather because he lacked the courage to go to Canada in order not to have to participate in what he believed was an immoral war. In *Going After Cacciato*, the central event of the book is Paul Berlin's collapse from fear as his unit rushes Cacciato's position. Unable to control his bladder, Berlin finds his response to fear to be both shameful and humiliating. Although he dreams of the Silver Star, he experiences himself as cowardly. The Silver Star figures as a central image in a series of stories in *The Things They Carried* as well: "Speaking of Courage," "Notes," and "In the Field" all relate the events surrounding the death of a particularly beloved character, Kiowa, in a sewage field. For character Norman Bowker, this event is the central one of his life. He believes that a failure of courage causes Kiowa's death and also costs him his chance at a Silver Star. In a particularly metafictional story, "Notes," the narrator (who also is named Tim O'Brien) considers the event, noting that Bowker "did not freeze up or lose the Silver Star for valor. That part of the story is my own." These closing lines reveal some of the most difficult and interesting parts of the novel: Does O'Brien imply here that he was a coward? Does he imply that, as a writer, he created the situation and thus all parts of the story are his own?

O'Brien also uses memory (and most particularly traumatic memory) as an important theme in his work. In *Going After Cacciato*, Paul Berlin's memories and imagination serve to structure the entire novel. Likewise, *The Things They Carried* uses as a device the memories of narrator Tim O'Brien (as distinct from writer Tim O'Brien) some twenty years after the close of the war. In both of these books, O'Brien uses a few central events, generally the death of comrades, and then circles around them, retelling the story with increasing detail. By so doing, he leads the reader on a journey of discovery, one in which the story becomes clearer as it goes along. The journey becomes increasingly circuitous, however, with his later books. In *In the Lake of the Woods*, for example, O'Brien appears to be leading the reader to a resolution of the central mystery of Kathy Wade's disappearance. However, resolution is not to be had in this ambiguous, self-reflexive novel that uses all of the conventions of the mystery story but none of the expected outcomes.

Finally, and perhaps most important, O'Brien explores the way stories are told throughout his work. In *Going After Cacciato*, he demonstrates how the mind sifts through the jetsam and flotsam of past experience and past knowledge to piece together a coherent narrative. In stories such as "How to Tell a True War Story" from *The Things They Carried*, he demonstrates the way truth always seems to be just around the next story, if only the words are right. Finally, in *In the Lake of the Woods* he explores the whole notion of revision, how memories can be erased, rewritten, and revised to produce a narration with which one can live. Tellingly, O'Brien himself revises his stories. There are subtle differences between the early versions of the stories of *The Things They Carried* when they appeared in magazines and the later versions when they were collected in the book. He also has revised *Going After Cacciato* between editions of the book. It is small wonder, then, that the subject of revision itself surfaces in stories such as "Notes," "How to Tell a True War Story," and in his novels, particularly *In the Lake of the Woods*. The chapters called "Hypothesis" in this novel are, after all, revision after revision of what could have happened, what might have happened, what did happen, and what did not happen.

GOING AFTER CACCIATO

First published: 1978; revised, 1989
Type of work: Novel

An army private reflects on and imagines a journey to Paris as he stands sentry duty in Vietnam.

Going After Cacciato, O'Brien's third published book, was a breakthrough for the writer. He returned to his experiences in Vietnam, first developed in his 1973 memoir, *If I Die in a Combat Zone, Box Me Up and Ship Me Home*, for his material; however, *Going After Cacciato* is a very different book from the earlier one in content, style, theme, and organization. Winner of the 1979 National Book Award, the book was widely regarded at its publication as the finest work of the Vietnam War experience.

O'Brien organizes the book into three threads that weave together a fully realized novel. One thread is the story of Spec Four Paul Berlin's experiences over the previous six months during his tour of duty in Vietnam. The sixteen chapters constituting this thread are not arranged chronologically. At the heart of these chapters are the deaths of several of Berlin's companions, the desertion of Cacciato, and Berlin's responses to both. Another strand forms ten chapters of the novel, each titled "The Observation Post." These chapters are set in the present time, as Berlin stands guard duty overnight. The chapters are particularly important to the structure of the novel, because they provide for the reader Berlin's musings and waking dreams of what has happened to him. He imagines both what has really happened and what might have happened. The remaining thread of twenty chapters concerns a journey to Paris as the group of soldiers chase after Cacciato. Readers gradually realize that the journey to Paris is completely imaginary, set off by Berlin's nocturnal meanderings as he tries to make sense of the reality of his past six months in Vietnam. Ulti-

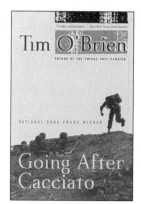

mately, the journey to Paris seems no more or no less fantastic than the "reality" of the Vietnam experience.

The first chapter of the novel, "Going After Cacciato," has been widely anthologized as a stand-alone story. "It was a bad time," the story opens, before listing the boys in the squad who have met death, disease, or disability, before turning to a description of the day that Cacciato goes AWOL, leaving not only his squad but also the Vietnam War behind.

Following the opening chapter is the first "Observation Post" chapter of the book. In this chapter, as others with the same title, Berlin literally observes his external and internal realities. Most of all, Berlin considers courage and cowardice. Berlin's consideration results in an elaborately plotted journey to Paris that includes not only the members of his squad, a member of the Viet Cong, and a beautiful woman, but it also includes allusions to many of the major genres and works of literature and popular culture, including Lewis Carroll, Ernest Hemingway, and the "road" movies of Bing Crosby and Bob Hope. It is as if Berlin concocts the story of the Vietnam War with pieces and parts of American culture floating through his daydreams.

The last chapter of the novel returns to the first, signaled by the repetition of the title, "Going After Cacciato." In this chapter, the reader finally can piece together what has happened in the book: At the moment of the squad's first attempt to capture Cacciato, Berlin collapses in fear and wets his pants. The rest of the novel is Berlin's response to this event as he tries to come to terms with what he views as shameful and visible evidence of his own cowardice.

THE THINGS THEY CARRIED

First published: 1990
Type of work: Short stories

A composite work of intertwining stories narrates the experiences of Alpha Company in Vietnam through the voice of character Tim O'Brien.

When *The Things They Carried* appeared in 1990, critics were overwhelmingly positive in their re-

sponses. Indeed, this work continues to be O'Brien's most studied and applauded. Another Vietnam War book, *The Things They Carried* does not fit neatly into any conventional generic distinction. Scholars are divided over whether to treat the book as a collection of interwoven short stories, as a novel, or as a fictionalized memoir. O'Brien calls the book simply "A Work of Fiction," refusing to corral the book into one genre or another.

Many of the chapters of the book were at one time published as short stories in a variety of periodicals; five of the stories first appeared in *Esquire*. The title story, "The Things They Carried," and "How to Tell a True War Story" are perhaps the most frequently anthologized of O'Brien's short stories. Something happens in this book, however, that seems to push it beyond a simple collection of stories. The juxtaposition of the stories along with the additional material O'Brien wrote for the book work together synchronistically, and the effect of reading *The Things They Carried* as a complete work is very different from reading the stories individually. The characters, events, and memories swirl through the stories, turning back on themselves, self-revising as they go. What the reader learns in one story opens possibilities for the later stories.

The first story is, fittingly enough, "The Things They Carried." On first reading, the story seems to be just a list of the things that Alpha Company carries with them as they trudge through the Vietnamese countryside. However, O'Brien's attention to both the physical and emotional weight of the items demonstrates that this is not just a catalog of things but rather an inventory of trauma, something short-story writer Charles Baxter notes in a 1999 article in the journal *Ploughshares*. The items structure both the story and the book; they introduce a cast of characters, and a list of events that the following stories detail.

Although *The Things They Carry* is not a book that can easily be discussed in terms of plot, it is a book in which a great deal happens. It is essentially the stories of the men (or boys, as they might more appropriately be called) of Alpha Company, generally filtered through the voice of the narrator, a character named Tim O'Brien, who shares with the author not only his name but also his age and his profession. The stories, then, produce a sort of double vision: that of a forty-three-year-old writer, considering the Vietnam War from a distance, and the impressions of a young soldier who finds himself in the middle of war he does not believe in for reasons he does not understand.

IN THE LAKE OF THE WOODS

First published: 1994
Type of work: Novel

The wife of a Vietnam-veteran-turned-politician disappears in the Minnesota north woods after the secret of her husband's participation in a massacre is revealed.

In the Lake of the Woods is also a novel concerning the Vietnam War. Although it shares many similar themes and stylistic choices with *Going After Cacciato* and *The Things They Carried*, it also introduces much more explicitly the American involvement in the massacres at My Lai and surrounding villages.

The book is the story of the disappearance of politician and Vietnam War veteran John Wade's wife Kathy while the couple is vacationing at an isolated cabin in the north woods of Minnesota. Wade has just been soundly defeated in a primary election for the United States Senate. It was fully expected that Wade would easily win the election until the news media discovered that Wade had participated in the My Lai massacre during his tour of duty in 1968.

The book has thirty chapters. Some of the chapters have titles such as "What He Did Next," "What Was Found," and "Where They Looked." The purpose of these chapters is to move the story of Kathy's disappearance and the subsequent investigation forward. These chapters are interspersed with chapters called "Evidence," and others called "Hypothesis." The evidence chapters are excerpts from both real and imaginary texts, including handbooks on magic; transcripts from the court-martial trial of William Calley for the atrocities at My Lai; and interviews with characters about Wade's childhood and his marriage to Kathy. Each of the sources is footnoted at the bottom of the page. This device contributes to the reader expec-

tation that evidence will lead somewhere. Certainly, the accumulation of detail in these chapters is designed to build a case, but the ambiguity of the entire narrative makes it impossible to "read" the evidence convincingly.

In the "Hypothesis" chapters, an unnamed narrator offers suggestions of what might have happened to Kathy. These narratives are so convincing in detail that readers have to remind themselves that these are only hypotheses. That they are so believable is a tribute both to O'Brien's skill and to the reader's need to know what "really" happened.

A fourth set of chapters has titles such as "The Nature of Marriage," "The Nature of the Beast," and "The Nature of Politics." These are the flashback chapters in which the details of Wade's childhood, his courtship of Kathy, his marriage, his political career, and, most important, his military service are revealed. The details are troubling: Wade emerges as a man damaged by his father and his nation, someone who could, quite possibly, pour boiling water on his wife's face while she is sleeping.

By the end of the novel, the reader has learned a great deal about John and Kathy Wade, about the Vietnam War, about the nature of investigation and evidence, and about storytelling. What the reader does not learn, however, is what has happened to Kathy, or, for that matter to John, who disappears on the Lake of the Woods himself in the closing scene.

SUMMARY

Tim O'Brien's fiction has changed the way readers think about the Vietnam War, about truth, and about storytelling itself. Powerfully concrete, subtle in detail, his novels and stories examine deeply what it means to be alive and what it means to make difficult choices in crisis situations.

His shifting narratives and repeated reconstructions force readers to follow where he leads. "The angle shapes reality," the narrator of *In the Lake of the Woods* tells the reader, "Partly window, partly mirror, the angle is where memory dissolves." So it is with O'Brien's work: Each time the reader returns to reread the stories and novels, the angle shifts, and a new set of perspectives opens.

Diane Andrews Henningfeld

BIBLIOGRAPHY

By the Author

LONG FICTION:
Northern Lights, 1975
Going After Cacciato, 1978, revised 1989
The Nuclear Age, 1981 (limited edition), 1985
In the Lake of the Woods, 1994
Tomcat in Love, 1998
July, July, 2002

SHORT FICTION:
The Things They Carried, 1990

NONFICTION:
If I Die in a Combat Zone, Box Me Up and Ship Me Home, 1973, revised 1979
"The Vietnam in Me," 1994

About the Author

Bates, Milton J. *The Wars We Took to Vietnam: Cultural Conflict and Storytelling*. Berkeley: University of California Press, 1996.

Heberle, Mark A. *A Trauma Artist: Tim O'Brien and the Fiction of Vietnam*. Iowa City: University of Iowa Press, 2001.

Herzog, Tobey C. *Tim O'Brien*. New York: Twayne, 1997.

Kaplan, Steven. *Understanding Tim O'Brien*. Columbia: University of South Carolina Press, 1995.

O'Brien, Tim. "The Vietnam in Me." *New York Times Magazine*, October 2, 1994, 48-57.

_____. "You Can't Talk with People You Demonize." In *Patriots: The Vietnam War Remembered from All Sides*, edited by Christian G. Appy. New York: Viking, 2003.

Schroeder, Eric James. *Vietnam, We've All Been There: Interviews with American Writers*. Westport, Conn.: Praeger Press, 1992.

Smith, Patrick. *Tim O'Brien: A Critical Companion*. Westport, Conn.: Greenwood Press, 2005.

Taylor, Mark. "Tim O'Brien's War." *Centennial Review* 29 (Spring, 1995): 213-229.

Vernon, Alex. *Soldiers Once and Still: Ernest Hemingway, James Salter, and Tim O'Brien*. Iowa City: University of Iowa Press, 2004.

DISCUSSION TOPICS

- What is a "true" war story for Tim O'Brien? How does he explore this in his books that concern Vietnam?

- O'Brien spent a year in Vietnam in the general area where the My Lai massacre occurred the year before he arrived in Vietnam. How does My Lai surface in each of his books, particularly in *The Things They Carried* and *In the Lake of the Woods*?

- Many critics have suggested that O'Brien's books are at least as much about the way memory works as they are about the Vietnam War. How does memory become a theme as well as an organizing device in O'Brien's work?

- Fathers and sons figure prominently in several of O'Brien's stories and novels. How does the relationship between the father and son affect the outcomes of these stories?

- "How to Tell a True War Story" and "Lives of the Dead" from *The Things They Carried* are stories about the writing of stories. What does O'Brien reveal about the purposes of stories?

- *In the Lake of the Woods* can be called a detective story in that it is an investigation of a disappearance. What detective story conventions does O'Brien use in the novel and how does his use of them both fulfill, and undermine the reader's expectations?

FLANNERY O'CONNOR

Born: Savannah, Georgia
March 25, 1925
Died: Milledgeville, Georgia
August 3, 1964

In her stories and two short novels, O'Connor combined religious themes from her Roman Catholic vision with comically realistic characters from the rural protestant South to create a fiction that is simultaneously serious and comic.

Courtesy, Georgia College & State University,
Special Collections

BIOGRAPHY

Mary Flannery O'Connor was born in Savannah, Georgia, on March 25, 1925, the only child of Edward Flannery and Regina Cline O'Connor. Both her parents were Roman Catholics from active Catholic families, a religious heritage that had a deep effect on her thinking and writing. As a child, she attended parochial school and early developed an interest in domestic birds and poultry. In her later writings she recalled that, when she was five, a newsreel company came to film her pet bantam chicken, which could walk both forward and backward. Years later, in a high school home economics class, she responded to an assignment to make a child's garment by creating a white piqué coat for a pet chicken. Also during her early years, O'Connor began to develop a talent for drawing and cartooning, an interest which remained with her through her life.

In 1938, her father was diagnosed as having disseminated lupus, a progressive disease in which the body forms antibodies to its own tissues. With that, the family moved from Savannah to Milledgeville, Georgia, where Regina O'Connor's father had been mayor. Edward O'Connor died in February of 1941, and Flannery remained in Milledgeville for most of the rest of her life, with time away only during her brief period of healthy adulthood between 1945 and 1950.

In 1942, O'Connor entered Georgia State College for Women (now Women's College of Georgia) in Milledgeville. She graduated with an A.B. degree in English and social sciences in 1945. During her college years, her interests were divided between fiction writing and cartooning. She did both, along with editing, for college publications. After her graduation, she decided to attend the Writers' Workshop at the University of Iowa, where she had been awarded a fellowship on the basis of some of her stories, which one of her teachers had submitted to the workshop. It was about this time that she began to drop "Mary" and to use "Flannery" alone as a writing name.

The Writers' Workshop, founded by Paul Engle, was the most prestigious program of its kind when O'Connor was a student there, and she learned much from the experience. One biographer, Harold Fickett, records her willingness to accept criticism from the workshop and her willingness to rewrite work in accord with her teachers' suggestions. This sort of docility probably did not come easily to O'Connor, who was a person of strong convictions and a willingness to stand up for them. During her time at Iowa, she began to publish stories; her first publication was "The Geranium" in *Accent* in 1946. That story was one of the six of her thesis collection for the M.F.A. degree, which she received in 1947. She stayed on at Iowa for an additional year, teaching and writing the beginnings of her first novel, *Wise Blood* (1952). Her start on that book earned her the Rinehart-Iowa Prize for a first novel.

O'Connor spent much of 1948 at Yaddo, an artists' colony at Saratoga Springs, New York, where she continued to work on *Wise Blood* and where she formed some literary friendships, particularly with the poet Robert Lowell, who introduced her to editor Robert Giroux, who would later publish her work. Through him she made the lifelong friendship of poet and teacher Robert Fitzgerald and his wife, Sally. They, too, were Catholic, and when O'Connor decided to leave Yaddo, after a short stay in New York, she arranged to board with the Fitzgerald family at their home in Ridgefield, Connecticut. O'Connor found that a happy time during which, as Harold Fickett records, after Mass, she spent her mornings writing, her afternoons writing letters (including a daily letter to her mother), and her evenings with the Fitzgeralds.

At Christmas, 1950, on the train home to Milledgeville, O'Connor suffered her first attack of lupus. The drug ACTH finally brought the disease under control, but hers had been a serious attack, and her recovery was slow. She was very weak and debilitated for months. Her slow recovery led her to give up her plans to return to the North; for the rest of her life she lived with her mother on her dairy farm, Andalusia, near Milledgeville.

O'Connor's relationship with her mother is reflected in many of her letters, which convey the pair's deep affection and her mother's selfless caregiving, as well as the inevitable stresses which accompanied their living together. For the most part, O'Connor's references to those stresses are indirect and offered with ironic humor (sometimes in a mock-backwoods style) which suggests that even when O'Connor was irritated with her mother's occasional insensitivity to her literary work, she was always certain of her mother's devotion to her and always returned that love, while expressing it in her own style. She once gave her mother a donkey for Mother's Day, saying it was the gift for a mother who had everything.

Through much of the rest of her life, O'Connor followed a standard routine of writing in the morning, riding into Milledgeville for lunch, reading, painting, and caring for her large flock of peafowl and other birds in the afternoons and evenings. After about 1955, she had to use aluminum crutches because the ACTH had weakened her bones so that they would not support her weight. Nevertheless, as her literary reputation increased, she ac-

cepted as many lecture invitations as she could. Some of her addresses have been published as *Mystery and Manners* (1969).

Only once did O'Connor travel abroad, in 1958, when her mother persuaded her to travel to Lourdes, France, in the hope of a miraculous cure for her lupus. The trip was an arduous one, and O'Connor undertook it mostly to please her mother. After the trip, she wrote to a friend, "Now for the rest of my life I can forget about going to Europe, having went." Her mother's dreamed-of cure did not occur.

During her years at Andalusia, O'Connor wrote and published a collection of short stories, *A Good Man Is Hard to Find* (1955), and a second novel, *The Violent Bear It Away* (1960). At her death, she had just completed a second collection of stories, published posthumously as *Everything That Rises Must Converge* (1965). She also carried on a voluminous correspondence with other writers, publishers, friends, and readers, some of which is collected in *The Habit of Being: Letters* (1979), edited by her friend Sally Fitzgerald. O'Connor's letters testify to her lively sense of humor (often self-deprecating) and to her interest in the opinions, reading habits, and spiritual states of the people she loved.

In 1964, O'Connor had surgery for the removal of a fibroid tumor. The surgery was successful, but it reactivated her lupus, and her condition deteriorated as she fought to finish her second collection of stories. She died in Milledgeville on August 3, 1964, at the age of thirty-nine.

ANALYSIS

O'Connor always saw herself as writing from an explicitly Christian point of view; indeed, given her convictions, that was the only way she could consider writing. She saw her religion as liberation and considered it a vocation in much the way one might be called to the priesthood. At the same time, she resented the sentimental expectations that people frequently hold toward what they might call "religious" fiction—maudlin stories about deathbed conversions and inspirational saints' lives.

O'Connor undermined those expectations by her use of humor; she avoided pious characters and conventionally "churchy" settings. Instead, she drew her characters and settings from the rural South she knew so well. Those characters were sometimes labeled grotesques by critics and scholars, but she rejected the term, feeling that it originated with writers who understood the South as little as they understood Christianity, a condition of ignorance she intended to remedy. She understood that she was writing to a secular world, and she intended to instruct it in the Christian understanding of grace and redemption as the elements most central to human life. At the same time, O'Connor recognized the dangers of becoming a sermonizer instead of an artist (she talked about that issue in some of her addresses), although the satiric humor in her style, the violence in her plots, and her strange characters made it unlikely that she would fall into that difficulty.

O'Connor's themes return to the issue of grace and redemption again and again. In her first novel, *Wise Blood*, the central character, Hazel Motes, begins as a man who is determined to escape the compelling image of Jesus which haunts him. His death, however, is an affirmation of grace, as O'Connor is careful to make clear in imagery which suggests that in his death Hazel is returning to Bethlehem.

O'Connor's other novel, *The Violent Bear It Away*, has a similar major theme. Its central character is Francis Marion Tarwater, a boy who, like Motes, is attempting to escape a calling. At the end of the novel, however, he is setting out to return to the city in his new role as prophet. What both Motes and Tarwater have experienced is the lacerating effect of God's grace, a grace which, O'Connor implies, is far removed from its syrupy portrayal in popular hymns. Instead, it seems to have more in common with the terrifying experiences of Old Testament prophets, for whom it is manifested as God's relentless insistence on bestowing mercy as he chooses.

O'Connor's short stories reveal similar thematic material. In "A Good Man Is Hard to Find" (1953), one sees a foolish and self-centered old woman who comes to a moment of grace just as she ceases mouthing platitudes to a mass murderer who is going to kill her seconds later. In "Revelation" (1964), smug, self-satisfied Ruby Turpin has a vision that teaches her what she never before understood—that the last shall be first in Heaven and that her material well-being is not necessarily a mark of divine favor. Similarly, in "The River" (1955), the little boy simply accepts the preacher's assertion that baptism in the river leads to the kingdom of Christ. It also leads to his death by drowning, but, as

O'Connor shows from the rest of the characters, he has paradoxically died into life, while people such as his worldly parents are caught in a sort of living death.

Violence is often an element in O'Connor's stories; in fact, she once said that her own faith made her conscious of the constant presence of death in the world, and her illness must have had the same effect. That probably explains the large number of deaths in her stories, and it may also account for the strong sense of danger in many of them. In "Good Country People" (1955), for example, Hulga's wooden leg is stolen by a dishonest Bible salesman. In "Revelation," mentioned above, Mrs. Turpin is attacked in the doctor's office by a girl who has suddenly gone mad.

Events and characters such as these are the source of the charge that O'Connor's characters are grotesques. The word seems to imply that they are too exaggerated to belong in realistic fiction. Early critics, especially, had a difficult time understanding what O'Connor intended, and they often believed that characters such as Tarwater and Hazel Motes were simply insane or too out of touch with modern values (which the critics themselves, O'Connor felt, too often embodied) to be taken seriously. O'Connor's comments about her own work, however, make clear that she was quite serious about them. Her backwoods preachers, she believed, came closer to understanding the human condition in relationship to God than any number of psychologists, teachers, and sociologists, none of whom ever appear very flatteringly in her fiction.

Another way of looking at the issue of the grotesque in O'Connor's work, however, may lend more weight to the charge. Her novels and stories are peopled almost entirely with characters who are the result of O'Connor's satiric view of the world. They are often funny, but they are almost always unpleasant.

Enoch Emery in *Wise Blood* is an excellent example of this kind of characterizing. Almost everything about him is simultaneously funny and terrible. His ignorance is responsible for much of his grotesque response to the world. He hates and fears the zoo animals he guards; he never knows how ludicrous he looks to others, and so he imagines that the ugly cook at the snack shop is in love with him and that no one knows he hides in the bushes to watch the women at the swimming pool.

His only real hero is Gonga the Gorilla from films. It is characteristic of O'Connor's work that even Enoch Emery's father, who never appears in the novel at all, is another example of ugliness and brutality. On his return from the penitentiary, Enoch's father gave him a gag gift: a can that appeared to contain peanut brittle but, when opened, released a steel spring that popped out and broke Enoch's two front teeth.

Again and again O'Connor offers comic but extremely unflattering pictures of the people who inhabit her characters' worlds. In "Revelation," for example, all the people in the doctor's office are grimly funny reminders of the varieties of human ugliness—Mrs. Turpin, who offends the reader with smugness and bigotry; Mary Grace, the mad girl who goes to college but who makes her ugliness even worse by making faces at Mrs. Turpin; the "white trash" family that sits immobile in poverty, ignorance, and dirt. Even Mrs. Turpin's husband, Claud, a man she really loves, is revealed by his racist jokes to be as corrupt as everyone else in the story.

Unremitting human ugliness is a source of much of O'Connor's humor. She is able to present the dirty, the disfigured, and the stupid as also funny and recognizable as inhabitants of the real world. Because they are almost the only inhabitants of O'Connor's fictional world, they probably justify the term grotesque.

Another characteristic of O'Connor's style that concerns her characters is her use of southern dialects, especially those associated with poor white people. In her earlier stories, she often indicated some of their quality with spelling. In *Wise Blood*, for example, the phrase "worse than having them" is spelled "worsen havinum." O'Connor reduced the number of such dialect indicators in her later work, but she always took joy in the sounds and sometimes the flamboyance of southern speech. "THE PROPHET I RAISE UP OUT OF THIS BOY WILL BURN YOUR EYES CLEAN," old Tarwater writes to his worldly nephew. In "A Good Man Is Hard to Find," the Misfit quotes his father speaking about him: "It's some that can live their whole life out without asking about it and it's others has to know why it is, and this boy is one of the latters."

One other issue about O'Connor's characters deserves mention, and that concerns race. O'Connor's stories almost all contain black characters—not surprisingly, as all but one are set in the South. O'Connor wrote much of her work in the period just before the first nationwide attention to civil rights, so it may seem curious that she never addressed that issue directly in her fiction. Some scholars have made an effort to find evidence of her sympathy for the growing Civil Rights movement in her work, but such evidence is very slight, if it exists at all.

O'Connor herself implied that southern black and white people inhabited worlds that were so different that a white writer could never really expect to understand the black world. Still, her black characters seem no less attractive than her white ones (none of them is very sympathetic anyway), and the racist comments in her stories come from characters who are themselves racists and would be likely to say such things (a good example is the doctor's office conversations in "Revelation").

In contrast to her basically satiric view of human characters, O'Connor's physical descriptions of people and landscapes are often serious, dramatic, and weighted with symbolism. References to eyes and their color and to the various colors and qualities of the sky are numerous in almost every story. The sky and particularly the sun often seem intended to evoke images of God and Christ looking down on the world. The sun is an ancient symbol for Christ, and O'Connor's descriptions make clear that the references are intentional. Another frequent symbol in her work is the use of birds to suggest the Holy Spirit or even, in the case of peacocks, Christ himself. Other animals sometimes appear as well, particularly pigs and monkeys, which often seem intended to suggest the bestial nature of fallen humanity, intelligent but debased and corrupt (the pigs in "Revelation" and Gonga in *Wise Blood* are good examples).

Like many writers, O'Connor often gave symbolic or evocative names to her characters, and they are often worth considering in that light. Mary Grace in "Revelation," for example, is certainly an agent of divine grace in that story. Hazel ("Haze") Motes's name seems to draw one's attention to his cloudy or hazy vision, reminding the reader of the biblical injunction not to try to take the mote or speck from another's eye until one has removed the beam from one's own. Tarwater, the protagonist of *The Violent Bear It Away*, simply has the name of an old folk remedy.

O'Connor's literary reputation has risen steadily since her death. Modern readers are increasingly likely to see her serious intentions while relishing her humor. Her debt to Nathaniel Hawthorne has long been noted, but some scholars have begun to notice, too, her debt to Mark Twain—the former for his concern for moral issues, the latter for his comic view. It is on that combination of qualities that O'Connor's reputation rests.

WISE BLOOD

First published: 1952
Type of work: Novel

A backwoods preacher attempts to escape his call but at last gives in to a sort of martyrdom.

Wise Blood was O'Connor's first novel; she began work on it while she was still in the Iowa Writers' Workshop. It embodies most of her major themes, and it contains some of her best comedy. It is flawed, however, by her difficulties in pulling the two parts of the plot together. The Enoch Emery story is never fully integrated into the Hazel Motes story. O'Connor also had difficulties clarifying the issues about Motes's past that have turned him into what she called a "Christian *malgre lui,*" a Christian in spite of himself.

The novel opens on a train as Hazel Motes leaves the Army. He is the grandson of a backwoods preacher, but he finds the image of a Jesus who insists on claiming the human recipients of his mercy to be unbearably disturbing. He has resisted inheriting his grandfather's role, that of preaching from the hood of a car to listeners on a small-town square. Hazel has long decided that he wants to avoid that Jesus, first by trying to avoid sin and later by asserting that Jesus is nothing more than a trick.

Even on the train, however, O'Connor makes clear that Hazel's cheap blue suit—brand-new, with the price tag ($11.98) still attached—and his black hat look exactly like the traditional garb of the preacher he refuses to be. Nevertheless, Hazel startles his worldly fellow passengers by suddenly claiming that if they are saved he would not want to be. Like many such comments in O'Connor's work, this carries an ironic weight, for it is quite clear that

salvation is the last thing the ladies in the dining car desire.

When Hazel arrives in the city of Taulkinham, he heads for the house of a prostitute, Leora Watts, as the next step in asserting that sin is an irrelevant issue in his life. Significantly, however, both the cab driver and Leora herself identify Hazel as a preacher, an identification he violently rejects. Soon Hazel sees a street preacher, Asa Hawks, who claims to have blinded himself as a demonstration of faith, although early in the novel the reader learns that his blindness is a sham. Hazel is both drawn to and repelled by Hawks and his adolescent daughter Sabbath Lily. Gradually it comes to Hazel that seducing Hawks's daughter would make a dramatic assertion of sin's irrelevance.

In the course of seeking Hawks's house, Hazel meets Enoch Emery. Enoch is eager to tell Hazel— or anyone—his story, about how his father gave him to a welfare woman who sent him off to the Rodemill Boys' Bible Academy and from whom he later escaped. Now he works for the city as a zoo guard. Desperately lonely and not very smart, Enoch ignores Hazel's rebuffs and follows him like a puppy, offering to help him find where Hawks lives. Like Hawks, Enoch senses Hazel's intense concern with Jesus. Hawks, in fact, says that some preacher has left his mark on Haze, but Hazel insists that he believes in nothing at all.

To prove his point, Hazel sets about buying a car, an ancient, rat-colored Essex, for which he pays forty dollars. The car seems to be Hazel's vision of American materialism ("Nobody with a good car needs to be justified," he says), but significantly he uses it exactly as his grandfather had used his Ford, as a platform to preach from. His one attempt to use the car in a "traditional" American way, for a date with Sabbath Lily, turns out to be a travesty. It is notable that the first thing Hazel does with his car is to stop in the middle of the highway to read a "Jesus Saves" sign.

Meanwhile, Enoch Emery is acting out his own sort of religion. Enoch claims to have "wise blood," which tells him what to do, and, in fact, he acts mostly from instinct. He insists that Hazel meet him at the park where he works, and after an elaborate set of ritual activities that include going through the zoo to ridicule the animals, Enoch leads Hazel to the city museum. Enoch finds it a place of enormous mystery because its name is carved, Roman-style, on the front, MVSEVM, creating a word that Enoch is unable to pronounce—like Yahweh, the unutterable name of God in the Old Testament. Inside the museum, Enoch shows Hazel the tiny, mummified man which has captured his imagination, but Hazel is unimpressed.

Hazel has rented a room in the house where Hawks and his daughter live, begun his plan to seduce Sabbath Lily (a plan he executes with a remarkable lack of finesse), and started a sort of church, the Church of Christ Without Christ, to dramatize his rejection of faith. Hazel's preaching is met with public indifference; however, after a few nights, he gains a disciple in the form of a former radio preacher, Onnie Jay Holy (his real name is Hoover Shoats), who shows no understanding of Hazel's message but is certain that money can be made from it if they "keep it sweet." He cannot understand why Hazel is unwilling to collect money from his audience. When Hazel runs him off, Holy threatens to run Hazel out of business.

Holy attempts to make good on that threat with a rival preacher whom he calls the True Prophet, a man who preaches the Holy Church of Christ Without Christ directly across the street from Hazel's post. The two are dressed exactly alike. Hazel's only comment is ambiguous: "If you don't hunt it down and kill it, it'll kill you." When Hazel returns to his room, he is met by Sabbath Lily, who tells him that Hawks has abandoned her, presumably because Hazel discovered his fraudulent blindness. She moves in with Hazel.

On the heels of these events, Enoch Emery reenters the plot. Listening to his wise blood, Enoch has undergone what can only be described as purification rituals, cleaning his room and fasting to prepare for stealing what he believes to be the "new jesus" of Hazel's church—the mummy from the city museum. He delivers the mummy to Sabbath Lily, who is supposed to keep it for Hazel. Enoch then disappears from the novel in a dramatic way: He steals Gonga's gorilla suit from the actor who impersonates the monster and travels to the country. The reader last sees him, stripped of his human clothing and identity, standing in his gorilla suit in the countryside, happy at last.

Returning to Sabbath Lily, Hazel finds her holding the mummy. O'Connor takes pains to make the scene look like a parody of a Madonna and Holy Child, an effect which is heightened by Hazel's blurred vision; he is wearing his mother's old reading glasses, the ones she used to read the Bible. Infuriated by the sight, he seizes the mummy and bangs it against the wall, releasing the sawdust inside it. Like Hazel's perception of Jesus, it is empty and worthless. On that note, Sabbath Lily leaves him, saying that she always knew that he wanted nothing but Jesus anyway.

Hazel hunts down the True Prophet, Solace Layfield, follows him home, and prepares to run over him with the Essex. O'Connor's' imagery makes clear that in some sense it is himself that Hazel is killing, perhaps especially his fraudulent self. Unlike the True Prophet, Hazel's deception is his insistence that no redemption exists, that Jesus is nothing but trickery. For that reason it is significant that Layfield dies after making a confession of his sins and calling on Jesus. In an ironic reversal of Hazel, Layfield's preaching was false, but his life finally recognized the truth.

Hazel now has only one thing left—the Essex. In it, he sets out to find new preaching territory, but he is stopped by a policeman who discovers that he has no driver's license. Casually, callously, the policeman pushes the Essex off a cliff. "Them that don't have a car don't need a license," he says, unknowingly echoing Hazel's comments about justification. Hazel has now been stripped of all the trappings of his faithless life—his church, his sexual attachment, and his car. He has come to the dark night that opens his eyes and—with the same sort of irony that Oedipus's life fulfilled—having seen the truth, Hazel blinds himself.

The rest of the novel is told from the point of view of Mrs. Flood, his scheming and dishonest landlady. The idea of self-mortification as a penance is completely foreign to her; she never understands why Hazel has blinded himself or why he cares nothing about his social security check or why he might feel a need to punish himself. Hazel says only that he has done these things "to pay." Gradually Mrs. Flood becomes less interested in stealing from Hazel and more interested in understanding him. She is especially fascinated by his ruined eyes, which somehow remind her of the light of the star on Christmas cards. After Hazel has wandered away from home, sick and blind, he is found in a ditch by two policemen who casually, meaninglessly, beat him to death.

They return the body to Mrs. Flood, who is moved by the sight to think of that retreating point of light which O'Connor has already described. The implications are that Hazel has been reborn in the ditch where he died, that he is moving back to Bethlehem, called by the truly wise blood of Christ, and perhaps that even the venal Mrs. Flood has begun a similar journey.

THE VIOLENT BEAR IT AWAY

First published: 1960
Type of work: Novel

A young man tries to escape his late uncle's directive to baptize his cousin but finds the spiritual legacy unavoidable.

The Violent Bear It Away shares many qualities with *Wise Blood.* Francis Marion Tarwater is much like Hazel Motes in his efforts to escape what seems to be a divine call and, like Hazel, he at last must give in to God's imperative. This novel is more tightly unified than *Wise Blood.* Although it lacks some of *Wise Blood*'s humor, it also lacks its loose ends.

Francis Marion Tarwater (named for the Swamp Fox, the Revolutionary War hero) has been raised in the woods by his great-uncle Mason Tarwater, a bootlegger and prophet. Mason has assured young Francis that he will inherit his great-uncle's call and that after Mason's death, the young man's first task will be to baptize Bishop, his retarded cousin, the son of Tarwater's nephew Rayber. When Rayber was seven, old Tarwater had kidnapped him, taking him to the backwoods and baptizing him, though he kept him only a few days. Years later, old Tarwater had kidnapped Francis Marion, the son of Rayber's promiscuous sister; this time he managed to keep the child. He has raised him to be a prophet who will carry on his own tradition by rescuing young Bishop from his father's godless life.

Young Tarwater has doubts about his calling, however, from the very beginning of the novel, and when his great-uncle dies, he quickly rejects his first task, which is to bury the old man according to his carefully rehearsed plans. Instead, the boy (he is fourteen) gets drunk, and, rather than digging the decent grave his great-uncle expected, Tarwater burns down the cabin with, as he supposes, his great-uncle's body in it. Only much later does he learn that a neighboring black man, shocked at the boy's faithlessness, buried the old man while the boy was unconscious.

In this early section of the novel, O'Connor introduces a character called "the stranger," who is actually a voice in young Tarwater's head. Tarwater and the stranger have a series of dialogues in which it becomes clear that the stranger represents a version of the kind of rationalism that Rayber displays—perhaps an even more cynical kind, as it actually rejects the old man's religion, while Rayber mostly ignores it.

Having disposed of his great-uncle, Tarwater decides to go to the city to see his uncle Rayber, whom he saw once, years before. At Rayber's house, Tarwater discovers that his uncle intends to reverse the kidnapping. Just as the old man once tried to save Rayber, Rayber now intends to save Tarwater from what he can see only as religious mania. In his sterile, academic way, he believes that Tarwater and his uncles are mere relics from a superstitious past. Old Tarwater himself had once stayed for a while at Rayber's house, hoping to get access to his soul, but he gave up in horror and disgust when he realized that Rayber had made him the subject of an article in an academic journal.

Young Tarwater's feelings about Rayber are ambivalent. On one hand, he has nothing but contempt for his passionless uncle, who seems trapped in his own rationalistic view of the world. He also finds his young cousin Bishop (an interesting name for the child of an atheist) to be repellent, even while the child seems drawn to him. On the other hand, despite the whisperings of the stranger, it is clear that Tarwater feels his call as surely as Hazel Motes felt his. Rayber recognizes that nearly every time Tarwater and Bishop are near water, Tarwater considers performing the baptism. In fact, Rayber tries to defuse the issue by offering to allow Tarwater to do the baptism in an attempt to make the sacrament meaningless, but Tarwater will have none of it.

Wandering the city at night in an effort to escape Rayber's constant talk, Tarwater gazes for a long time in a bakery window. Later, he spends a long time at a revival, listening to a child evangelist. Tarwater is wrestling with his great-uncle's promise to turn him into a prophet who will burn Rayber's eyes clean, a calling he wishes to reject as completely as he rejects Bishop. Ironically, Rayber, the rational man, has also tried to reject his son by attempting to drown him, an attempt that failed when he lost his nerve. At Lake Cherokee, on a fishing trip organized by Rayber, Tarwater both baptizes and drowns Bishop.

From this point on in the novel, O'Connor emphasizes Tarwater's hunger; it is a hunger nothing can fill. He vomits up the hot dogs he ate at the lake. Hitchhiking home, he accepts a sandwich from a truck driver but cannot eat it; his mind rejects food even while his body cries for it.

This hunger is part of the novel's central metaphor. Eyes and vision dominated *Wise Blood* (they are important here, too), but in *The Violent Bear It Away* the central image is the "bread of life," to which Tarwater refers again and again. The bread of life is a New Testament metaphor for Jesus and is the central image of the sacrament of Communion. That seems to be the bread Tarwater was gazing at in the bakery; that is the bread he concluded he did not hunger for when his great-uncle preached to him. When Tarwater first sees Bishop, however, he has a sudden vision of "his own stricken image of himself, trudging into the distance in the bleeding stinking mad shadow of Jesus, until at least he received his reward, a broken fish, a multiplied loaf."

Tarwater's hunger is spiritual, and it cannot be filled by the drugged liquor in the satanic stranger's flask that Tarwater drinks on his ride home, even though he exclaims that it tastes better than the bread of life. That evil stranger takes the unconscious Tarwater to the deep woods and rapes him. When he regains consciousness, Tarwater knows what has happened and somehow recognizes that the event is like the biblical Jonah's being swallowed by the fish; it is God's directing him into prophecy. He returns home and has a vision of old Tarwater's feasting on the miraculous loaves and fishes. Suddenly he understands the source of his hunger and starts out for the city to begin his career of prophecy.

Aside from bread, fish fill the other part of the novel's metaphoric structure. They appear not only in Tarwater's vision but also in almost every mention of old Tarwater's eyes. It is even on a fishing trip that Bishop is baptized, a baptism which O'Connor means the reader to take seriously, even though Tarwater has not yet accepted his calling, for the power of the sacrament exists outside the failings of the one celebrating it. The novel's conclusion suggests that now Tarwater will turn his attention to Rayber and the rest of the city.

"A GOOD MAN IS HARD TO FIND"

First published: 1953 (collected in *A Good Man Is Hard to Find*, 1955)
Type of work: Short story

A smug old woman is jolted out of her complacency by a confrontation with a mass murderer.

"A Good Man Is Hard to Find" is one of O'Connor's most frequently anthologized short stories, and it makes an excellent illustration of her ability to combine grotesque humor with serious thematic material.

The story opens as a family prepares to go on vacation in Florida. The story focuses immediately on the grandmother, who wants to visit relatives in east Tennessee and who uses the escape of the Misfit, a murderer, from prison to try to persuade her son, Bailey, to change his mind. He refuses. The two grandchildren, John Wesley and June Star, are quickly characterized as smart alecks who nevertheless understand their grandmother and her motives very well. When the family sets out, the grandmother is resigned to making the best of things. She is first to get into the car and has even, secretly, brought along her cat. As she rides along, her conversation is conventional, self-centered, and shallow.

When the family stops for lunch at a barbeque stand, their conversation again turns to the Misfit, and the adults agree that people are simply not as nice as they used to be. Later, back in the car, the grandmother persuades Bailey to take a road which she imagines (wrongly, as it turns out) will lead by an old mansion. Suddenly the cat escapes its basket and jumps on Bailey's neck, and the car runs into the ditch. As the family assesses its injuries, a man who is obviously the Misfit drives up with his armed henchmen. The grandmother immediately feels that she recognizes him as someone she has known all of her life, and she tells him that she knows who he is.

Methodically, the henchmen lead first Bailey and then the mother and children off to be shot in the woods while the Misfit begins to talk about himself and his life of crime. He blames his career on Jesus, who, he says, threw everything "off balance" by raising the dead. Because the Misfit cannot be sure that the miracle really occurred, he cannot know how to think about it. If Jesus really raised the dead, the Misfit says, the only logical response would be to drop everything and follow him. If he did not, then life is meaningless and only crime makes sense: "No pleasure but in meanness."

The grandmother is terrified; she knows that she, too, will be shot. Yet she knows something more, and suddenly she stops her empty prayers and meaningless assertions that the Misfit is a "good man," to utter perhaps the truest words of her life in telling him that he is one of her own children. At that, the Misfit shoots her, but he says that she would have been a good woman if someone had been there to shoot her every minute of her life. O'Connor intends the reader to take the Misfit's comments seriously (he is the most serious-minded character in the story, after all) and notice that the grandmother, in her moment of receiving grace, has recognized that she and the Misfit (and presumably all the rest of humanity) are related as children of God. She is left in death smiling up at God's sky.

"THE ARTIFICIAL NIGGER"

First published: 1955 (collected in *The Complete Stories*, 1971)
Type of work: Short story

Old Mr. Head and his grandson overcome their estrangement in a reconciliation brought on by a plaster statue.

In "The Artificial Nigger," Old Mr. Head and his ten-year-old grandson, Nelson, live in a state of subdued tension in which each works to outdo the other. Their planned trip to Atlanta (they live in rural Georgia) has made this competition worse. Even though Nelson has never been to the city, he is cheekily sure that he will enjoy it.

Gradually the reader understands that Mr. Head is thoroughly uncertain of his own ability to manage in the city, and he uses the sight of the city's black people (a race Nelson has never seen) as a sort of weapon over Nelson, a threat of something foreign that he may find frightening but with which his grandfather can claim, not quite accurately, to be familiar. Nelson is unimpressed with his grandfather's talk.

When they arrive in the city, Mr. Head is frightened by Nelson's immediate delight in it and by his refusal to be intimidated by the unfamiliar. After walking for a while, they become lost and, at the same time, realize that they have also lost their lunch bag. Nelson takes things into his own hands and asks directions from a black woman to whom he feels drawn, but Mr. Head's resentment grows. At last, while Nelson naps at the curbside, Mr. Head finds a way to retaliate and hides from the boy.

When Nelson wakens, he thinks he has been abandoned and races into the street, knocking down an old woman. That is when Mr. Head commits his worst sin and denies knowing Nelson at all. His grandson is deeply wounded and refuses all of his grandfather's subsequent attempts to make peace. Mr. Head feels certain that this is a divine judgment on him. They walk on in separate misery, getting ever more lost, until Mr. Head cries out to a passing stranger, "Oh Gawd I'm Lost!" The two are rescued with directions to the train station.

It is the sight of a plaster lawn statue of a black man (or child, the statue being too battered to be easily identified) that really reconciles the pair. The statue's pictured misery seems to be a monument to the black man's victory, a portrayal which moves both Mr. Head and his grandson. The notion that, in a city which already has so many black people, someone should feel the necessity to make an artificial one strikes them both as mysterious and somehow powerful. Reunited, they travel home peacefully, having miraculously escaped the consequences of their anger.

"GOOD COUNTRY PEOPLE"

First published: 1955 (collected in *The Complete Stories*, 1971)
Type of work: Short story

Hulga's negative view of the world is challenged by the even greater nihilism of a dishonest Bible salesman.

In "Good Country People," Mrs. Hopewell's perennial optimism is balanced by what seems to be her daughter Joy's self-chosen misery. It is characteristic of Joy's attitude that she has changed her name to Hulga, evidently because it is the ugliest name she can think of. In that way, her name matches her faded sweatshirt, her scowl, and her wooden leg (she lost her leg in a hunting accident long before). While her mother is frustrated by her daughter's bad temper, she is equally frustrated by her daughter's Ph.D. in philosophy, a degree which makes her unable easily to identify her daughter's achievement to others. She worries that Hulga never seems to enjoy anything, not even young men.

That makes her concerned when Hulga, an atheist who refuses to let her mother keep a Bible in the parlor, confronts Manley Pointer, a fresh-faced and earnest-seeming Bible salesman who wins Mrs. Hopewell's trusting heart with his brave stories of childhood hardships and religious devotion. Partly as a joke, Hulga agrees to meet Pointer on a picnic. The falsity of their relationship is marked by the thirty-two-year-old Hulga telling Pointer that she is seventeen, while he calls her both brave and sweet. It has occurred to Hulga that she might be able to seduce Pointer.

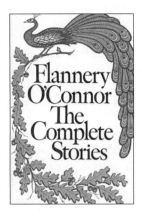

At the picnic it becomes clear that Pointer has similar ideas and that, in fact, he is far more cynical than Hulga. His hollow Bible contains playing cards, whiskey, and condoms. He is hardly one of the "good country people" of the title. Perhaps that cynicism is what wins enough of Hulga's confidence that she lets him see her wooden leg and even remove it from her, although she feels helpless without it. That is when Pointer announces that he collects things such as glass eyes and wooden legs, marks of his own complete nihilism. "I been believing in nothing ever since I was born!" he exclaims. Hulga is left in the hayloft to think about the real meaning of unbelief.

"REVELATION"

First published: 1964 (collected in *The Complete Stories*, 1971)
Type of work: Short story

A smug, self-satisfied woman wakens to new values when she is attacked in a doctor's office and then experiences a vision.

"Revelation" opens in a doctor's waiting room where Ruby Turpin is waiting with her husband, Claud. As she often does, Mrs. Turpin passes the time by categorizing the other waiting-room inhabitants by class—"white trash," middle class (like her), and so forth. This is the segregated South, so there are no black people here, but Mrs. Turpin is happy to judge them, too.

She identifies a pleasant-looking woman as one of her own class, and they begin an idle conversation that centers first on their possessions and eventually on their disapproval of civil rights demonstrators. They conclude that it would be a good idea to send all black people back to Africa. During this conversation, the other woman's daughter, Mary Grace, an obese college student with severe acne, has been making faces directly at Mrs. Turpin. At last Mary Grace cracks entirely, throws her book (*Human Development*) at Mrs. Turpin, and then physically attacks her. When Mary Grace has been subdued, Mrs. Turpin begins to think that the girl has a message for her, and when she moves closer, Mary Grace calls her a warthog and tells her to go back to hell where she came from.

Later, at home, Mrs. Turpin is deeply shaken by the message. At last, while hosing down the hogs, she questions God about why he sent her such a message when there was plenty of "trash" in the room to receive it. His answer comes in the form of a vision of people marching to Heaven, a procession led by all the people she has most held in contempt. The vision fades, and Mrs. Turpin returns to the house in the midst of a cricket chorus of hallelujahs. Critics have disagreed about the meaning of the end of this story, but Mrs. Turpin's serious acceptance of the violent message of grace and the imagery of the ending seem to suggest that her vision was a gift of mercy that has clarified her vision of the world, its people, and her possessions.

SUMMARY

Serious fiction with religious themes has never been common in American literature, and perhaps that explains part of why O'Connor has frequently been misunderstood. When one views her work in the context of her Catholic orthodoxy, however, its focus becomes clear. The fact that most of her characters are evangelical Protestants simply reflects her use of the population around her to inhabit her stories. Her intense concern with divine grace and redemption as the central facts of human life does not preclude her use of humor to communicate her ideas about that concern and her distrust of the secular rationalism that she believed pervades most of American life.

Ann D. Garbett

DISCUSSION TOPICS

- What evidence is there in Flannery O'Connor's fiction that its author was a devout Roman Catholic?

- According to the title of one of O'Connor's stories, "A Good Man Is Hard to Find." Can you find any good men in her work? What makes them "good"?

- How does violence function in O'Connor's work?

- O'Connor's fiction is often said to be characterized by "black humor." How does O'Connor create humor in her work?

- How does O'Connor use the motif of a journey to organize her fictions?

- In what ways does racism show up in O'Connor's work?

- How does O'Connor use the names of characters (for example, Hazel Motes, Francis Marion Tarwater, Mr. Head) to develop themes in her fiction?

- O'Connor's work is often described as "grotesque." In what ways can her characters and plots be considered grotesque?

BIBLIOGRAPHY

By the Author

SHORT FICTION:
A Good Man Is Hard to Find, 1955
"Good Country People," 1955
"Revelation," 1964
Everything That Rises Must Converge, 1965
The Complete Stories, 1971

LONG FICTION:
Wise Blood, 1952
The Violent Bear It Away, 1960

NONFICTION:
Mystery and Manners, 1969
The Habit of Being: Letters, 1979
The Presence of Grace, 1983
The Correspondence of Flannery O'Connor and Brainard Cheneys, 1986

MISCELLANEOUS:
Collected Works, 1988

About the Author
Asals, Frederick. *Flannery O'Connor: The Imagination of Extremity.* Athens: University of Georgia Press, 1982.
_____. *"A Good Man Is Hard to Find": Flannery O'Connor.* New Brunswick, N.J.: Rutgers University Press, 1993.
Caruso, Teresa, ed. *"On the Subject of the Feminist Business": Re-reading Flannery O'Connor.* New York: Peter Lang, 2004.
Lake, Christina Bieber. *The Incarnational Art of Flannery O'Connor.* Macon, Ga.: Mercer University Press, 2005.
O'Gorman, Farrell. *Peculiar Crossroads: Flannery O'Connor, Walker Percy, and Catholic Vision in Postwar Southern Fiction.* Baton Rouge: Louisiana State University Press, 2004.
Orvell, Miles. *Flannery O'Connor: An Introduction.* Jackson: University Press of Mississippi, 1991.
Paulson, Suzanne Morrow. *Flannery O'Connor: A Study of the Short Fiction.* Boston: Twayne, 1988.
Rath, Sura P., and Mary Neff Shaw, eds. *Flannery O'Connor: New Perspectives.* Athens: University of Georgia Press, 1996.
Robillard, Douglas, Jr. *The Critical Response to Flannery O'Connor.* Westport, Conn.: Praeger, 2004.
Spivey, Ted R. *Flannery O'Connor: The Woman, the Thinker, the Visionary.* Macon, Ga.: Mercer University Press, 1995.